Real Estate Principles

Third Edition

Rockwell Publishing Company

By Rockwell Publishing Company
13218 N.E. 20th
Bellevue, WA 98005
(425)747-7272 / 1-800-221-9347

Third Edition

ISBN: 978-1-939259-56-1

PRINTED IN THE UNITED STATES OF AMERICA

Table of Contents

Chapter 1

An Introduction to Real Estate

I. The Real Estate Industry
II. Real Estate Transactions
III. Real Estate Brokerage
  A. Brokers and salespersons
  B. Brokerage services
    1. Services for sellers
    2. Services for buyers
IV. Real Estate as a Career
  A. Working as a real estate agent
  B. Real estate companies
    1. Types of companies
    2. Support for agents
    3. Agents' responsibilities
  C. Compensation of agents
    1. Commission splits
    2. Employment status and tax withholding
  D. Professional associations
V. Real Estate and the Law
  A. Types of laws
  B. Laws regarding real estate agents
  C. Laws concerning transactions
  D. Laws concerning property

Chapter Overview

Real Estate Principles is a textbook for students preparing for a career in real estate. It covers the topics that a student is expected to be familiar with in order to pass a state real estate examination, obtain a real estate license, and begin working as a real estate agent. This includes a wide range of fundamental concepts, legal rules, and industry practices.

Before you begin studying the substantive material, it will be helpful to have an overview of the real estate business. This chapter provides introductory information about the real estate industry, real estate transactions, real estate brokerage, real estate as a career, and the types of laws that affect real estate. Many of the topics in this chapter will also be covered in greater detail in later chapters.

The Real Estate Industry

The real estate industry is a large and influential sector of the U.S. economy, employing millions of people nationwide. It includes not only real estate brokers and agents, but also property managers, relocation specialists, real estate investment counselors, real estate appraisers, home inspectors, title company employees, escrow agents, and real estate developers. The real estate industry is closely allied with the construction industry, and also with the mortgage industry—the financial institutions, private companies, and other investors that provide financing to real estate owners, developers, and buyers.

The real estate industry is divided into two main branches: residential real estate and commercial real estate. The residential branch is concerned with all types of housing: single-family homes, apartment buildings, condominium units, and so on. The commercial branch is concerned with retail property, shopping centers, office buildings, and industrial property such as factories and warehouses. It's a common practice for real estate agents, appraisers, and others in the industry to specialize in either residential or commercial property; many also choose to focus on either sales or rentals. In rural communities, agricultural property and vacant land are additional areas of specialization.

Several million real estate transactions take place in the United States every year, representing billions of dollars in economic activity. Statistics concerning real estate are among the data economists use to evaluate the health of the economy. On a monthly basis, along with statistics about employment, consumer prices, and other economic indicators, the federal government releases national and regional figures for various types of real estate activity, such as existing home sales, construction permits issued, and housing starts (the number of dwelling units on which construction began during the month). An increase in real estate activity is considered a sign that the national economy is improving; a decrease is a sign that the economy may be slowing down. Investors pay attention to these statistics and take them into account in making investment decisions. Thus, real estate activity affects the overall economy both directly and indirectly.

Although real estate activity has a national economic impact, the real estate business is essentially a local business, dealing with property in a particular area or neighborhood. It's carried out one property at a time, one transaction at a time. So let's look at how real estate transactions work.

Real Estate Transactions

A real estate transaction may be a sale, a lease, or an exchange, and it may involve residential, commercial, industrial, or agricultural property. The most basic type of real estate transaction, however, is the sale of a home. In most places, residential sales account for a large share of real estate activity, and new real estate agents often work exclusively on this type of transaction. Because of this, our focus here (and in much of the rest of the book) will be on home sales.

In the sale of a home, someone who owns a home and wants to sell it (a seller) transfers ownership of the property to someone who wants to buy it (a buyer) at an agreed price. Ownership is transferred by means of a deed, a legal document that the seller gives to the buyer (see Chapter 4).

Although this simple transfer of ownership is the central event in a home sale, a typical transaction is considerably more complicated. The details vary from one part of the country to another, but in many places a transaction includes all of the following steps and stages:

- listing the property,
- showing the property,
- submission and consideration of offers to purchase,
- negotiations between seller and buyer,
- execution of a contract,
- property inspection(s),
- financing arrangements,
- appraisal of the property,
- closing preparations,
- the buyer's walk-through, and
- closing.

Listing. Most sellers put their homes on the market by listing them with a real estate agent. When property is listed, the seller signs a contract agreeing to pay compensation (a commission) in exchange for the agent's efforts to find a buyer. In most cases, the real estate agent—referred to as the **listing agent**—will submit information about the property to a **multiple listing service**, an organization of real estate agents that distributes information about listed properties to its members. The listing agent also advertises the property in a variety of other ways in order to attract possible buyers. (We'll discuss the role of the listing agent in greater detail later in this chapter.)

Showing the Property. Once a home has been listed, real estate agents show the property to interested buyers. A buyer may tour the home with his own agent, with the listing agent, or with another agent from the multiple listing service. The agent points out particular features of the property and answers the buyer's questions.

Offers. A buyer who wants to purchase the home submits a written **offer to purchase** for the seller's consideration. An offer to purchase states the price the buyer is willing to pay; it also specifies the **closing date** (the date on which the transfer of title would take place) and other terms of sale that would apply if the seller accepted the offer. If the real estate market is active and the property is desirable, the seller is likely to receive competing offers from several different buyers.

Each offer is usually accompanied by a **deposit**, a sum of money tendered to the seller to show that the offer is serious and made in good faith. If the seller rejects a buyer's offer, the deposit will be returned to the buyer. If the seller accepts an offer, but the transaction later falls through, the buyer may be entitled to have the deposit returned or the seller may be entitled to keep it, depending on the circumstances. (See Chapters 7 and 8.)

Negotiations. After receiving an offer from a buyer, the seller may want to negotiate changes in the terms the buyer has proposed; for example, the seller might want a slightly higher price or a different closing date. In that case, the seller notifies the buyer that the offer will be accepted if the buyer agrees to the specified changes. This is called a **counteroffer**. The buyer may respond to the seller's counteroffer with another counteroffer, and the parties will negotiate until either the seller decides to accept the buyer's terms or the buyer decides to give up on purchasing the home.

Contract. When a buyer's offer is accepted, the seller and the buyer enter into a legally binding contract. Depending on what part of the country you're in, this contract may be called a purchase agreement, purchase contract, sales contract, purchase and sale agreement, contract of purchase and sale, earnest money agreement, offer and acceptance, or deposit receipt. In the contract, the seller agrees to sell the property, and the buyer agrees to buy it, for the price and on the terms that they've agreed to.

In most cases, the contract between the buyer and seller is contingent on the fulfillment of certain conditions specified in the contract. For example, the contract might be contingent on whether the buyer can obtain the necessary financing for the purchase, or whether a home inspector gives the buyer a satisfactory report concerning the condition of the property. If the conditions stated in the contract are not met (if the buyer isn't able to get a loan, or the home inspector's report is unfavorable), the contract terminates; the parties are no longer obligated to proceed with the transaction.

Inspections. The buyer may order a home inspection, to have the construction and the condition of the home evaluated. Professional inspections of other aspects of the property may also be arranged; for example, there might be a pest inspection or a soil stability test. As was just mentioned, the contract between the buyer and the seller may be contingent on inspection results.

Financing. Unless the buyer is able to pay for the property with cash, he must arrange financing for the purchase. This usually means borrowing most of the purchase price from a mortgage lender and coming up with cash for the remainder (the down-

Fig. 1.1 Steps and stages in a typical residential real estate transaction

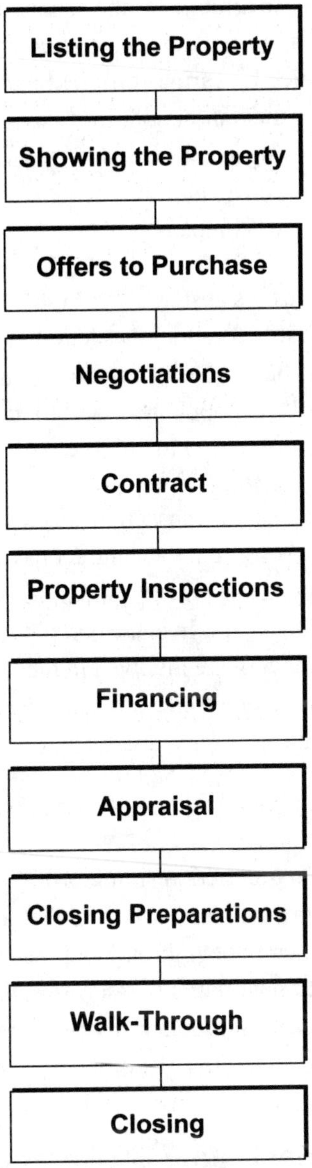

payment). The buyer fills out a loan application with detailed information about his financial situation, and based on that information the lender decides whether or not to make the requested loan.

Appraisal. Before approving the buyer's loan application, the lender requires a formal appraisal of the home, because the property will serve as collateral for the loan. The real estate appraiser evaluates the property and provides an estimate of its market value to the lender. The lender will not approve the buyer's loan unless the appraisal shows that the property meets the lender's standards and is worth approximately what the buyer has agreed to pay for it.

Closing Preparations. Between the time that a buyer and seller enter into a contract and the time the sale is ready to close, many important tasks must be completed. For example, it might be necessary to arrange for the seller's mortgage to be paid off, order a title insurance policy, and have the deed and other documents recorded. These and other details may be handled by various different parties, or by one person who is acting as the **closing agent** for the transaction. In states where escrow is used, the escrow agent is generally the closing agent (see Chapter 14). In other states, the closing agent might be a real estate broker, an attorney, an employee of the buyer's lender, or an employee of the title insurance company.

Walk-Through. In many places it's customary for the buyer to revisit the property and inspect it one final time just before the transaction closes. This is called the buyer's walk-through. It gives the buyer the opportunity to make sure that any required repairs have been done properly, the appliances and fixtures are working, and the property is in the condition it's supposed to be in.

Closing. The final step in a real estate transaction is called **closing** or **settlement**. When all of the requirements set forth in the contract have been fulfilled, the final documents are executed, the purchase price is paid to the seller, the deed is delivered to the buyer, and the transaction closes. In some parts of the country, the closing takes place at a meeting attended by everyone involved in the transaction—the seller, the buyer, their real estate agents and/or attorneys, a representative from the buyer's lender, a representative from the title company, and the closing agent. In other places, the closing agent coordinates the final details and has separate meetings with the seller and the buyer to close the transaction.

To keep this description of a transaction simple, we've mentioned only a few of the ways that real estate agents may be involved. In fact, real estate agents representing the seller and/or buyer typically help throughout the entire process—preparing and presenting offers, handling negotiations, discussing financing options, and so on. In the next section, we'll take a closer look at what real estate agents do.

Real Estate Brokerage

A **broker** is someone who acts as an intermediary in a transaction, helping to arrange the purchase or sale of goods, services, or other commodities on behalf of others. For example, a stockbroker helps an investor buy and sell corporate stocks. Similarly, a real estate broker helps real estate buyers and sellers buy and sell property. This is called real estate brokerage.

Brokers and Salespersons

After obtaining a real estate license, a new agent goes to work for an established broker. This isn't merely an industry custom, but a requirement of the state license laws. The license issued to a new agent—which is called a **real estate salesperson's license** in most states—generally allows the agent to work with members of the public in real estate transactions only if supervised by a real estate broker. Someone who wants to obtain a real estate broker's license is required to have either a certain number of years of experience as a real estate salesperson or additional real estate education, or both. (Licensing requirements are discussed in Chapter 10, which covers the regulation of the real estate profession.)

The distinction between a real estate broker and a real estate salesperson is important in some contexts, but not in others. When the distinction doesn't matter, we'll use "real estate agent" as a generic term for a person who sells real estate, licensed either as a broker or as a salesperson. Note that the term "realtor" should not be used interchangeably with "real estate agent." A REALTOR® is specifically a member of the National Association of REALTORS®, a professional organization that we'll discuss later in the chapter.

Brokerage Services

Some people choose to buy or sell property on their own, without the assistance of a real estate agent. However, the great majority of both buyers and sellers recognize the value of a real estate agent's services. A good agent can save them time and money and help them avoid costly mistakes. Here's a brief catalogue of the main services real estate agents provide.

Services for Sellers. To market a home successfully, it's necessary to price the property competitively, prepare it for showing, advertise it effectively, and show it to prospective buyers (often to dozens of them). Once a buyer is found, terms of sale must be negotiated, a contract must be executed, and other required paperwork must be completed. It's a rare homeowner who has the time, knowledge, and skills needed to accomplish all of these tasks.

Pricing the Property. Deciding how much to ask for a home is a critical step in selling it. If the home is priced too high, it won't sell quickly, and it may not sell at all. Buyers looking for homes in the listed price range will expect "more house" for the money and won't make offers. And those who would be interested in the home at a lower price may not even come to see it, because it's out of their price range. On the other hand, underpricing the property could mean the loss of thousands of dollars.

To help a seller decide on a realistic listing price, a real estate agent uses a technique called competitive market analysis, comparing the seller's home to similar ones in the neighborhood (see Chapter 13). Competitive market analysis draws on the agent's familiarity with the area, knowledge of recent sales and listings, and understanding of what factors matter the most in determining market value. Many sellers feel that a real estate agent's expert advice on pricing is well worth the cost of the agent's services.

Preparing the Home. The nicer a home looks, the easier it is to attract buyers and the more they'll be willing to pay. There are usually many things that could be done to make a home more attractive, but naturally the seller doesn't want to spend any more money or effort on this than necessary. A real estate agent can point out which steps will be worthwhile and which won't.

Example: The Weissmans are getting ready to sell their home. They've been wondering whether they should paint the exterior, since that hasn't been done for several years. Their listing agent tells them that repainting probably won't increase the market value of the property enough to justify the expense. But the agent is able to suggest several inexpensive repairs that will make the home considerably easier to sell.

How much needs to be done to prepare a home for showing depends both on the condition of the home and on conditions in the real estate market. In expensive housing markets, some agents specialize in redecorating homes so that they'll sell for as much as possible. This is called **staging** a home. In some cases, most of the seller's furniture is put into storage and temporarily replaced with modern furniture owned or rented by the agent, so that the house looks like it's straight out of a magazine. It isn't considered necessary or worthwhile to go that far in preparing every home for showing, but the practice is a dramatic illustration of the kind of expertise and services real estate agents can offer sellers.

Effective Advertising. Of course, advertising is a key part of marketing any product, including real estate. Home sellers rely on real estate agents to know what types of advertisements in what types of media will be most effective for their property. Depending on the home and the area in question, a classified ad in the newspaper, a mailed flyer, a display ad in a "Homes For Sale" magazine, or a spot on a particular website might be essential, or might be a waste of time.

One of the most important services that a real estate agent offers a home seller is submitting information about the home to the multiple listing service (MLS) that the agent belongs to. As explained earlier, an MLS is an organization of real estate agents who share information about their listings. The MLS database is the main tool that real estate agents working with buyers use to locate suitable properties for their clients, so a home listed in the database receives much wider exposure than a FSBO that's not. (A FSBO, generally pronounced "fizz-bo," is a home that's "for sale by owner," as opposed to listed with a real estate agent.)

Showing the Property. The listing agent will present the seller's home in the best possible light to prospective buyers and also to other real estate agents who bring buyers to see it. It's against the law to misrepresent the property or hide its flaws, but the listing agent can make sure that none of the positive features are overlooked and may also be able to suggest options for addressing some of the problems.

In many parts of the country, holding an **open house** is considered an important way to show a home. The listing agent announces that the property will be available for viewing on a certain day during specified hours; the agent then spends the scheduled time at the home, greeting buyers and agents and answering their questions. An open house makes it easy for a lot of people to see the property without having to make an appointment.

At other times, agents from the MLS can bring buyers to the house when the seller isn't there by using the **keybox** provided to the seller by the listing agent. A keybox is a device that holds a copy of the house key, which the seller can padlock to a porch railing or in some other appropriate place outside when she isn't going to be home. Visiting agents open the keybox with a combination or electronic device obtained from the MLS, take the house key out to unlock the door, and then return it to the keybox. The keybox arrangement is very convenient for sellers as well as for agents and buyers, and it's only available for listed homes. When a home is for sale by owner, the seller generally has to be there in person to show the property to buyers and agents; that can be a lot of trouble for the seller and may limit the property's exposure.

Negotiations and Paperwork. When a buyer makes an offer to purchase, the listing agent presents the offer to the seller, going over the terms, pointing out anything that the seller should give particular consideration to, and helping the seller decide whether or not to accept the offer. If the seller wants to make a counteroffer, the agent fills out the appropriate form and presents it to the buyer or the buyer's agent. In many cases the listing agent negotiates on the seller's behalf, working out a compromise that's acceptable to both parties.

The legal complexity of real estate transactions has increased considerably in recent decades. A home seller is required by law to disclose certain types of information to the buyer (see Chapter 9), and in many states the disclosure requirements are extensive. The seller typically relies on the listing agent to provide all of the necessary disclosure forms and help fill them out. The agent isn't qualified to give legal or financial advice, but should be able to tell the seller when it would be advisable to consult a lawyer or an accountant.

Monitoring the Closing Process. After the seller has entered into a contract with a buyer, the listing agent continues to help with the transaction. The agent may serve as a liaison between the seller and the buyer and other parties—the home inspector, a contractor hired to make repairs, the title company representative, and so on. If a problem arises, the agent can help the seller resolve it and keep the transaction on track.

Services for Buyers. Real estate agents help home buyers find the right property, enter into a contract to buy it, obtain the necessary financing, and complete the purchase. A buyer might be referred to an agent by a friend, or might find an agent by visiting or calling a brokerage office or searching the Internet. Or, instead of deliberately seeking the assistance of a real estate agent, a buyer might see an attractive home with a "For Sale" sign and call the listing agent directly, or drop by when the listing agent is holding an open house. When a buyer isn't accompanied by another agent, it's the listing agent who shows the buyer the property. If the agent makes a favorable impression, the buyer might ask the agent to show him other houses.

Depending on state law and on contractual arrangements, a real estate agent working with a buyer may or may not be acting as the buyer's representative (see Chapter 9). If the agent is legally representing the seller instead of the buyer, or representing both parties as a dual agent, that will have an impact on the ways in which the agent can help the buyer. However, even a seller's agent can provide many services to a buyer. This issue is discussed in Chapter 9, and so are the reasons why a buyer might prefer to work with an agent who represents only the buyer's interests.

In an initial interview with a buyer, an agent determines the kind of property that the buyer is looking for and the general price range the buyer can afford. The agent may discuss financing options and advise the buyer to apply to a mortgage lender to get preapproved for financing (see Chapter 12).

To find homes that meet the buyer's criteria, the agent will search the MLS database and possibly check some other sources. The next step is to take the buyer to see selected properties. The agent will tour each house with the buyer, pointing things out and answering questions based on the listing information, other information obtained from the seller or the listing agent, and the agent's own expertise. The process of showing the buyer homes may take only a few days or continue over the course of weeks or even months.

Once the buyer decides to make an offer on a home, the agent's role will depend in part on whether the agent is representing the buyer, the seller, or both parties. If acting as the buyer's representative, the agent will advise the buyer on how much to offer for the property and negotiate with the seller or the seller's agent on the buyer's behalf. Whether or not the agent is representing the buyer, the agent will usually help the buyer fill out the purchase agreement form and will present the buyer's offer to the seller or the seller's agent. If there's a counteroffer, the agent will explain it to the buyer and submit the buyer's response. The agent will also explain the purpose of the various disclosure statements that the buyer receives and, if appropriate, recommend that the buyer see a lawyer or get other professional advice about the transaction.

After the purchase agreement has been signed, the agent may help the buyer with the financing arrangements, follow up on any contingencies in the contract, and shepherd the buyer through the closing process.

The services of a real estate agent are especially important for buyers who are relocating to another area, moving out of town or out of state. If the new location is far away and unfamiliar, it's much easier for a buyer to have a local agent look for suitable housing than to go there in person, learn about the different neighborhoods, and find a house on her own.

Real Estate as a Career

Real estate is a flexible, lucrative, and enjoyable career for many people, although it's not for everyone. In this section, we'll discuss what it's like to work as a real estate agent, the different types of real estate companies an agent can work for, how agents are compensated, and the professional associations agents can join.

Working as a Real Estate Agent

For all practical purposes, real estate agents work for themselves. Even though an agent must be affiliated with a broker, most brokers expect their agents to generate their own business. To a great extent, it's up to an agent to get new listings and find prospective buyers. An agent must therefore be self-motivated and disciplined to earn a good living.

Brokers usually don't require their agents to work on a fixed schedule, so agents have a lot of freedom. Established agents can choose how much to work based on their own financial needs, temperament, and ambition. However, a part-time effort generally isn't enough to get a new agent off the ground. It takes a big investment of time and energy to build a clientele. Successful agents work hard.

Also, even though agents don't have a fixed schedule, that doesn't mean their time is their own. Since most home buyers and sellers hold down full-time jobs, a lot of real estate activity takes place outside of ordinary business hours. Agents often have to work evenings, weekends, and holidays, making themselves available when buyers and sellers want them.

In addition, real estate agents have to get along with all kinds of people. It may be necessary to spend a lot of time with certain clients or customers, some of them likable, some of them not. And because a real estate transaction is a very big deal for most people, it's not uncommon for buyers and sellers to be anxious, short-tempered, or demanding. Someone who doesn't honestly enjoy meeting and working closely with people will probably be miserable in a real estate career.

Real estate agents also must be able to tolerate uncertainty and rejection. There are a lot of ups and downs in the real estate business. Sometimes a listed property never sells. Sometimes a transaction falls through because of an unresolvable conflict. Sometimes an agent has to hear "no" dozens of times before getting to hear one "yes." A real estate agent must be able to handle all of this calmly or even cheerfully. An agent with the stamina and determination to keep going in spite of setbacks is likely to be well rewarded in the long run.

Real Estate Companies

Although real estate agents work very independently, an agent's career can be strongly affected by the brokerage he works for. There's a lot of variety among real estate companies, and it's important for an agent to find a good fit.

Types of Companies. Real estate brokerage businesses range from single-broker firms to very large companies with hundreds of agents and dozens of branch offices. They may be independent or part of a local or national franchise. Some companies work with all types of property and offer other real estate services in addition to brokerage, such as property management, escrow, or investment counseling. Other companies are very specialized, handling only certain types of property or certain types of transactions. For example, a commercial real estate firm might do nothing but tax-deferred exchanges (see Chapter 15); a residential brokerage might focus strictly on subdivision sales. There are also companies that specialize in representing home buyers instead of listing properties for sellers; this has been a significant trend in many parts of the country.

The particular type of company an agent should work for depends entirely on the agent's own preferences and interests. Bigger companies and franchises have some advantages, such as greater name recognition, but there are many small, independent companies with good clienteles and high profits.

Support for Agents. Another way in which real estate companies differ is in the services and support they provide for their agents. When deciding where to work, a new real estate agent should take the following considerations into account.

Training. Real estate is a complicated field, and there's a lot to learn about everything from sales techniques to environmental issues. It's also essential to keep up with changes in laws and regulations affecting real estate. So one of the most important services a company can offer an agent—particularly a new agent—is ongoing training. Some companies have a formal training program; others simply provide the opportunity to work closely with a more experienced agent. The sink-or-swim approach, where new agents are given little or no guidance, can work out very badly for the agents and for their clients.

Facilities and Expenses. Most companies provide an agent with a telephone, a desk, and access to a computer, a fax machine, and a copier. It's very useful to have a pleasant office for meeting with clients and customers, where there's a receptionist, secretarial support, and other help, but an agent may have to pay for those advantages either directly (with a monthly fee) or indirectly. As we'll discuss shortly, a company that offers a lot of amenities typically takes a larger bite out of an agent's commission than a company with more basic facilities.

Almost all companies require agents to pay for the expenses they incur in the course of their business activities, such as the cost of their business cards, car maintenance and gas, and cell phone service. In many cases, agents also bear the cost of advertising their listings and their services, including the cost of "For Sale" signs. An agent should ask about a company's policy in regard to all of these outlays.

Memberships. In most areas, membership in the local multiple listing service is essential, and it's a rare real estate company that doesn't provide MLS membership to its agents. Some companies also offer their agents membership in one or more professional trade associations. These associations typically give their members valuable information and training, and they're a good way to network with others in the real estate business. Professional associations are discussed later in the chapter.

Agents' Responsibilities. As we said earlier, real estate agents have a lot of freedom and generally don't have to work on a fixed schedule. However, many companies have some minimal requirements for their agents. For example, an agent might be expected to spend some time on **floor duty** each week. During the hours that an agent is assigned to floor duty, she must be at the office and handle all of the telephone calls and drop-in visits from prospective buyers or sellers. (This isn't just drudgery; if the callers or visitors don't ask to speak with a particular agent, the agent on floor duty can help them and, hopefully, retain them as clients or customers.)

Real estate companies differ in the extent to which they monitor their agents' level of activity and productivity. Some brokers set specific sales goals for their agents to meet and encourage competition among the agents. If an agent doesn't seem to be working hard enough or getting results, he may be let go. Other brokers allow even new agents to set their own pace, with the understanding that those who aren't getting listings or making sales will eventually drop out on their own. In choosing a company, an agent has to judge whether she will thrive in a high-pressure office or do better in a low-key atmosphere.

Compensation of Real Estate Agents

Most real estate agents are compensated entirely by commission, without any base salary. An agent's commission is usually a share of the brokerage commission paid by the seller when a listed home is sold.

Commission Splits. In a typical listing agreement, the seller agrees to pay a specified percentage of the sales price as a brokerage commission when the transaction closes. (See Chapter 8.) The commission paid by the seller is shared between the real estate brokers and agents involved in the transaction. This ordinarily includes the listing broker, the listing agent, the selling broker, and the selling agent. The listing agent, as you know, is the real estate agent who got the listing and helped the seller sell the home. The listing broker is the company that the listing agent works for. The **selling agent** is the real estate agent who found the buyer for the home. The selling broker is the company that the selling agent works for. (For more information about the roles of the listing agent and the selling agent, see Chapter 9.)

The sharing of a brokerage commission among the real estate agents involved in a transaction is called the **commission split**. The seller pays the commission to the listing broker, and then the listing broker divides the commission amount with the selling broker. Then the listing broker pays the listing agent a share, and the selling broker pays the selling agent a share.

Example: A seller lists her home with an agent who works for ABC Realty. The seller agrees to pay a brokerage commission of 6% of the price the home sells for. Eventually the seller accepts a $200,000 offer from a buyer who's been working with an agent from XYZ Realty.

At closing, the seller pays ABC Realty a commission of $12,000 (6% of $200,000). ABC Realty pays half of that amount, $6,000, to XYZ Realty, the selling broker. Out of its $6,000 share, ABC pays $3,000 to the listing agent, the agent who actually got the listing and marketed the property. Out of its $6,000 share, XYZ pays $3,000 to the selling agent, the one who found the buyer.

The commission shares are paid in this way because in most states, by law, a real estate agent can only receive payment from his own broker, not directly from a seller or buyer or from another broker. (See Chapter 10.)

The percentage of the commission that the selling broker is entitled to receive from the listing broker is usually set by the multiple listing service that both brokers belong to. In most cases, each broker gets 50%, as in the example.

In the example, each of the agents received 50% of his or her broker's share, but that isn't necessarily the case. For instance, instead of 50%, an agent might be paid 40%, 45%, or 60% of the broker's share. The specific percentage of the commission split depends on the agent's employment agreement with the broker. When an agent is hired, the broker tells the agent what the commission split will be. (An agent who does well may be able to negotiate a larger percentage later on.)

As a general rule, the commission split is related to the support services and facilities that the broker provides for agents. A broker that offers extensive support services and plush offices will typically keep a larger share of the commission than a broker with limited facilities and services.

Some companies let their agents have 100% of the commissions they earn. Instead of taking a portion of an agent's commission, the broker charges a **desk fee**. That means the agent must pay the broker a monthly fee for working in the office, in addition to paying for all of her own expenses. For the most part, only established agents can afford this arrangement.

Fig. 1.2 Employee vs. independent contractor

Employee	Independent Contractor
• Works under direct control of employer • Taxes withheld from compensation by employer	• Works without employer's direct control • Responsible for paying own taxes

Employment Status and Tax Withholding. For certain purposes, a real estate agent is classified either as an employee of his broker or as an independent contractor. An **independent contractor** is someone who's hired to perform a particular job and uses her own judgment to decide how the job should be completed. By contrast, an **employee** is hired to perform whatever tasks the employer requires, and is given instructions on how to accomplish each task. An employee is supervised and controlled much more closely than an independent contractor. Various employment and tax laws apply only when someone is hired as an employee, and not when someone is hired as an independent contractor.

Whether a real estate agent is his broker's employee or an independent contractor depends on the degree of control the broker exercises over the agent. If the broker closely directs the activities of the agent and controls how the agent carries out her work, the agent may be considered an employee. For example, if a broker required an agent to work on a set schedule, told the agent when to go where, and decided what steps the agent should take in marketing each property, the agent would be considered the broker's employee for tax purposes.

As we've discussed, most brokers exercise much less control over a real estate agent's work than that. They generally focus on the end results—listings, closings, and satisfied clients—and not on the details of how the agent accomplishes those results. A broker usually isn't concerned with where the agent is or what she is doing at any given time. The agent is paid on the basis of results (by commission) rather than hours spent on the job. Thus, in most cases, a real estate agent is an independent contractor, not the broker's employee.

If a real estate agent were an employee, the broker would be required to withhold money from the agent's compensation to pay certain federal and state taxes (income tax, social security, and, in most states, unemployment insurance and workers' compensation). An independent contractor, on the other hand, is responsible for paying his own social security and income taxes. Depending on state law, he may not be eligible for unemployment payments or workers' compensation.

The Internal Revenue Service provides that a real estate agent will be considered an independent contractor for federal income tax purposes if three conditions are met:

1. the individual is a licensed real estate salesperson;
2. substantially all of her compensation is based on commission rather than hours worked; and
3. the services are performed under a written contract providing that the individual will not be treated as an employee for federal tax purposes.

Note than even when a real estate agent is considered an independent contractor for tax purposes, he may be treated as an employee under other laws. For example, classification of agents as independent contractors for tax purposes doesn't affect a broker's supervisory responsibilities under state license laws (see Chapter 10).

Professional Associations

There are numerous professional associations in the real estate industry. They provide their members with information, training, and opportunities for networking. In some cases, they also offer professional designations based on education and experience in particular areas of specialization. The general public often sees membership in a professional association as an indication of competence and trustworthiness.

Some professional associations have adopted codes of ethics for their members. A professional code of ethics sets standards of conduct for the members of a profession to meet in their dealings with the public and with other members of the profession. It provides guidance on how to handle ethical dilemmas with integrity and fairness. Failure to comply with an association's code of ethics can lead to expulsion.

For real estate agents, the code of ethics adopted by the National Association of REALTORS® (NAR) has been especially influential. NAR is the largest and best-known real estate professional association in the United States; there are also affiliated state organizations. Only brokers and agents who belong to NAR can refer to themselves as REALTORS®.

Among the many other professional associations in the real estate industry are the National Association of Real Estate Brokers (NAREB®), the National Association of Exclusive Buyer Agents (NAEBA), the Real Estate Buyer's Agent Council (REBAC), the Appraisal Institute, the American Society of Appraisers (ASA), the Building and Office Managers Association (BOMA), the Institute of Real Estate Management (IREM®), the American Society of Real Estate Counselors (ASREC), and the Real Estate Educators Association (REEA). There's also an organization for real estate regulators, the National Association of Real Estate License Law Officials (NARELLO).

Real Estate and the Law

The law has a greater impact on real estate than on most other fields; the real estate business itself is heavily regulated for the protection of the public, and legal issues play a substantial role in real estate transactions. We'll end the chapter with an overview of the ways in which the law affects real estate agents, real estate transactions, and real estate ownership.

Types of Laws

To understand the laws that affect real estate and real estate agents, it's helpful to have a general understanding of the different types of laws. In the United States, there are federal, state, and local laws. Federal laws apply to everyone in the country; state laws apply to everyone in a particular state; and local laws apply only to those in a particular city, county, or other local jurisdiction. The laws that affect real estate tend to be state laws, but there are quite a few exceptions, such as federal environmental laws and civil rights laws, and local zoning ordinances and subdivision regulations.

Laws can also be classified as statutory laws, administrative regulations, or judicial rulings. **Statutory laws** have been enacted by a legislative body (such as the U.S. Congress, a state legislature, or a city council) to govern a particular issue or a whole field of activity. **Administrative regulations** have been adopted by the officials in charge of a federal, state, or local administrative agency, such as the federal Department of Housing and Urban Development, the state real estate licensing agency, or the county building department.

Judicial rulings, also called **case law**, are the decisions made by federal, state, or local judges. To decide court cases, judges interpret how statutory laws and administrative regulations should be applied to specific circumstances. They also apply rules established in **precedents**, which are earlier court cases in the same jurisdiction. In some contexts, long-established judicial rulings are referred to as **common law** rules.

In addition to statutes, administrative regulations, and judicial rulings, there is **constitutional law**. The country as a whole is governed by the U.S. Constitution, and each state has its own constitution as well. Constitutional law is largely concerned with the structure and the powers of the government. A judge may rule that a particular statute or administrative regulation violates the constitution, either because the legislative or administrative body that passed the law exceeded constitutional limitations on its powers or because the law violated constitutional provisions. A law that has been declared unconstitutional cannot be enforced.

Laws Regarding Real Estate Agents

The laws that govern the business activities of real estate agents fall into two main groups: license laws and laws concerning agency.

Each state has its own real estate license law, which sets the requirements that must be met in order to become licensed as a real estate broker or salesperson in that state. In addition, the license law has rules for brokerages and other real estate businesses, and rules concerning the conduct of real estate agents in transactions and other interactions with the public. It also lists the grounds for disciplinary action against a real estate agent—the violations that can lead to the suspension or revocation of an agent's license. Real estate license laws are covered in Chapter 10.

The other body of law that has the greatest impact on a real estate agent's work is agency law. This refers to the rules that govern the relationship between an agent—a person who's acting as the legal representative of another—and the person she is representing. General agency law (which is typically a combination of state statutory law and judicial rulings) applies to agency relationships in any context, including real estate transactions. Some states have specific statutes concerning real estate agency relationships; these statutes may either take the place of or supplement general agency law. Agency is discussed in Chapter 9.

Laws Concerning Transactions

In addition to knowing about the laws that directly govern their own work, real estate agents need to know about the laws that govern real estate transactions.

Like other types of business transactions, real estate transactions are largely governed by the body of rules known as contract law. These rules determine how and when a legally binding contract between two or more people is formed, and how a court will enforce a contract if one of the parties fails to do what he promised to do. In addition to general contract law, there are laws concerning the specific types of contracts that are used in real estate transactions, such as listing agreements and purchase agreements. General contract law is covered in Chapter 7, and the various types of real estate contracts are covered in Chapter 8. Real estate transactions are also affected by federal and state civil rights laws, which are covered in Chapter 16.

Laws Concerning Property

Real estate agents are also expected to have a general knowledge of property law. This is the body of laws governing ownership of property—both personal property and real property (real estate). It includes rules concerning:

- what constitutes real property,
- a property owner's rights, and the limitations on those rights,
- the different forms ownership can take,
- interests other than ownership that can be held in real estate, and
- how ownership and other property interests can be transferred from one person to another.

For the most part, real estate agents don't deal directly with the legal issues involved in property ownership. Issues such as the best way for a buyer to take title or the validity of a deed are the province of real estate lawyers, and a real estate agent who tries to advise clients about these matters could be charged with the unauthorized practice of law. However, since property is at the center of a real estate agent's work, it is useful for an agent to have an understanding of property law. The various aspects of property law are covered in Chapters 2 through 6.

Chapter Summary

1. The real estate industry includes real estate brokers and agents, property managers, relocation specialists, real estate investment counselors, real estate appraisers, home inspectors, title company employees, escrow agents, and real estate developers. It is closely allied with the construction industry and the mortgage industry.

2. The steps and stages in a typical home sale include listing the property, showing the property to buyers, offers to purchase, negotiations between buyer and seller, execution of the purchase agreement, property inspections, financing arrangements, appraisal of the property, closing preparations, the buyer's walk-through, and closing.

3. Among the services that real estate agents provide to home sellers are helping to price the home, preparing the home for showing, submitting property information to the multiple listing service, advertising the home, showing the home to buyers, negotiating with buyers, filling out the purchase agreement, assisting with disclosure forms and other paperwork, and keeping the closing process on track.

4. Among the services that real estate agents provide to home buyers are finding suitable properties for them to consider, showing them homes, preparing offers for them, helping them obtain financing, and monitoring the closing process.

5. A real estate agent deciding whether to go to work for a particular company should consider the company's size and atmosphere; the responsibilities agents are required to fulfill; the training, facilities, and other support services available for agents; and the commission split.

6. A real estate salesperson generally sets his own schedule and is not closely controlled by the broker. A salesperson is usually considered an independent contractor for tax purposes, so the broker isn't required to withhold taxes and social security from the salesperson's compensation.

7. Our legal system has federal, state, and local laws. They include statutory laws, administrative regulations, and judicial rulings (case law), all of which must be constitutional. A real estate agent's work is governed by the state real estate license law and the state laws concerning agency representation. Real estate transactions are governed by state laws concerning contracts in general and real estate contracts in particular, and also by federal and state civil rights laws. Real estate ownership is governed by property law, a state's laws concerning property rights.

Key Terms

Listing—A written contract between a seller and a broker, in which the seller hires the broker to find a buyer for the property. Also called a listing agreement.

Listing agent—A real estate agent who assists a seller in finding a buyer for a property.

Multiple listing service—An organization of real estate agents that share information about listed properties with each other.

Offer to purchase—A seller's offer to purchase states the offered price as well as the closing date and other terms of sale.

Closing—The final step in a real estate transaction, in which the purchase price and deed are exchanged and title is transferred. Also called settlement.

Closing date—The date on which closing takes place and title is transferred.

Purchase agreement—The sales contract between the buyer and seller. Also called a purchase and sale agreement or deposit receipt.

Real estate salesperson—A real estate agent licensed to work under the supervision of a real estate broker.

Real estate broker—A real estate agent licensed to assist and represent buyers and sellers in real estate transactions, in exchange for compensation.

Staging—Cleaning and redecorating a listed home in order to make it as attractive as possible.

FSBO—A property that is "for sale by owner," not listed with a real estate agent.

Open house—A scheduled period of time when the listing agent is available at a listed home to greet drop-in buyers and clients and answer questions about the property.

Keybox—A box holding a key for visiting agents to use to gain access to the house. Agents use a combination or electronic device obtained from the MLS to open the keybox.

Floor duty—Assigned time during which an agent must be present at the office to handle incoming phone calls and prospective buyers and sellers who drop in.

Selling agent—A real estate agent that assists a buyer in finding a property to purchase.

Commission split—An arrangement in which the listing broker and selling broker share the commission paid to the listing broker by the seller.

Independent contractor—A person hired to perform a particular job and to carry out those duties without extensive supervision or instruction.

Statutory law—Laws enacted by a federal, state, or local legislative body.

Administrative regulations—Rules adopted by a federal, state, or local administrative agency.

Case law—Judicial rulings that form a body of law, setting precedents to be followed in later court cases.

Common law—Long-established judicial rules.

Chapter Quiz

1. The last step in a real estate transaction is:
   a) property inspections
   b) closing
   c) appraisal
   d) walk-through

2. A real estate agent can help a seller by:
   a) giving advice on pricing the property
   b) holding an open house
   c) advertising the property on the MLS and in the newspaper
   d) All of the above

3. A real estate agent can help a buyer by:
   a) staging the home for showing
   b) providing financing
   c) negotiating the purchase and sale agreement
   d) All of the above

4. Most real estate brokerages pay for an agent's:
   a) training
   b) gas and car upkeep
   c) cell phone
   d) MLS membership correct Answer

5. A home sells for $375,000. The parties are represented by Listing Salesperson and Selling Salesperson. The seller pays a commission of 6% to Listing Broker, who has agreed to a 50-50 commission split with Selling Broker. If both brokers split their shares equally with their salespersons, how much does each salesperson receive?
   a) $22,500
   b) $11,250
   c) $5,625
   d) $2,812.50

6. A desk fee is:
   a) used to pay for office facilities and expenses
   b) usually charged in lieu of taking part of the agent's commission
   c) collected by a brokerage on a monthly basis
   d) All of the above

7. If a salesperson is an independent contractor, which of the following is true?
   a) The broker will still be responsible for supervising the salesperson's work
   b) The broker will withhold taxes and social security
   c) The salesperson must be paid a regular salary
   d) The broker will give the salesperson detailed instructions for marketing each property

8. A real estate salesperson's status as independent contractor or employee is important because it determines:
   a) the number of hours the salesperson must work
   b) the broker's responsibility for the salesperson's actions
   c) whether the broker withholds social security and income taxes
   d) whether the broker carries workers' compensation insurance

9. Laws enacted by a legislative body are known as:
   a) case law
   b) administrative law
   c) constitutional law
   d) statutory law correct Answer

10. Real estate agents need at least a basic understanding of:
    a) agency law
    b) contract law
    c) property law
    d) All of the above

Answer Key

1. b) The last step is a real estate transaction is the closing, or settlement.

2. d) A listing agent typically helps a seller decide on an asking price, hold an open house, and advertise the property.

3. c) A selling agent assists the buyer with negotiations, but does not usually act as the lender. Staging a home for sale is something a listing agent helps a seller with.

4. d) A brokerage usually pays for an agent's membership in the multiple listing service, but may not cover the agent's training costs. Agents are typically responsible for their own transportation, advertising, and cell phone expenses.

5. c) The commission shared between Listing Broker and Selling Broker is 6% of $375,000, or $22,500. Each broker thus gets $11,250, which they then split with their respective salespersons. Therefore, each salesperson receives $5,625.

6. d) A brokerage that does not collect part of the salesperson's commission may instead charge a monthly desk fee to cover office operating costs.

7. a) A salesperson who is treated as an independent contractor for tax purposes must still be supervised by the broker.

8. c) If a salesperson is an independent contractor, the broker is not required to withhold social security and income taxes from the salesperson's paycheck.

9. d) Statutory laws are enacted by federal, state, and local legislatures.

10. d) It's important that a real estate agent be familiar with the basic rules of agency, contract, and property law.

Chapter 2

The Nature of Real Property

I. Types of Property
   A. Tangible vs. intangible property
   B. Real property vs. personal property
II. Elements of Real Property
   A. Land and the inverted pyramid
   B. Improvements
III. Appurtenances
   A. Air rights
   B. Water rights
   C. Solid mineral rights
   D. Oil and gas rights
   E. Other appurtenant rights
IV. Attachments
   A. Natural attachments
   B. Man-made attachments (fixtures)
   C. Annexation vs. severance
   D. Distinguishing fixtures from personal property
      1. Written agreement
      2. Method of attachment
      3. Adaptation of the item to the realty
      4. Intention of the annexor
      5. Relationship of the parties
   E. Mobile homes as fixtures
V. Characteristics of Real Property
   A. Physical characteristics
   B. Economic characteristics
VI. Land Description
   A. Surveys
   B. Methods of description
      1. Metes and bounds descriptions
      2. Government survey descriptions
      3. Lot and block descriptions
      4. Other methods of description
      5. Elevations and air lots

Chapter Overview

Real estate agents are concerned not just with the sale of land and houses, but with the sale of real property. Real property includes the land and improvements, and it also encompasses the rights that go along with ownership of land. The first part of this chapter explains those rights, which are known as appurtenances. It also explains natural attachments and fixtures, which are sold as part of the land, and the distinction between fixtures and personal property, which ordinarily isn't transferred with the land. The second part of this chapter explains methods of legal description—the different ways in which a parcel of land may be identified in legal documents to prevent confusion about its boundaries or ownership.

Types of Property

Property is a fundamental and familiar concept. For the purposes of our discussion, this simple definition will be sufficient: Property is something that can be owned or possessed.

Property may be tangible or intangible. **Tangible property** (sometimes called corporeal property) has a physical presence; it can be felt or touched, as in the case of a shoe or a table or a house. **Intangible property** (incorporeal property) is non-physical and abstract. For example, ownership rights such as an author's copyrights or an inventor's patent rights are intangible property. Also, items that represent value, such as bank accounts, stocks, and currency, are considered to be intangible property. Whether an item of property is tangible or intangible may determine how it will be treated under some state tax laws.

All property, whether tangible or intangible, is classified either as **real property** (also called realty) or as **personal property** (also called personalty or chattels). Real property is commonly defined as land, anything affixed or attached to the land, and anything incidental or appurtenant to the land. Sometimes real property is described as "immovable." Personal property, by contrast, is usually movable. A car, a sofa, and jewelry are simple examples of personal property. Anything that is not real property is personal property.

The distinction between real and personal property is very important in real estate transactions. When a piece of land is sold, anything that is considered part of the real property is transferred to the buyers along with the land, unless otherwise agreed. But if an item is considered personal property, the sellers can take it with them when they move away.

Elements of Real Property

The principal component of real property is land. But land is more than just the surface of the earth. It also includes the **subsurface**—everything beneath the surface down to the center of the earth—and the **airspace**—everything above the surface, to the upper reaches of the sky.

A parcel of real property can be imagined as an inverted pyramid, with its tip at the center of the globe and its base above the earth's surface. The landowner owns not only the earth's surface within the boundaries of the parcel, but also everything under or over the surface.

Fig. 2.1 The inverted pyramid

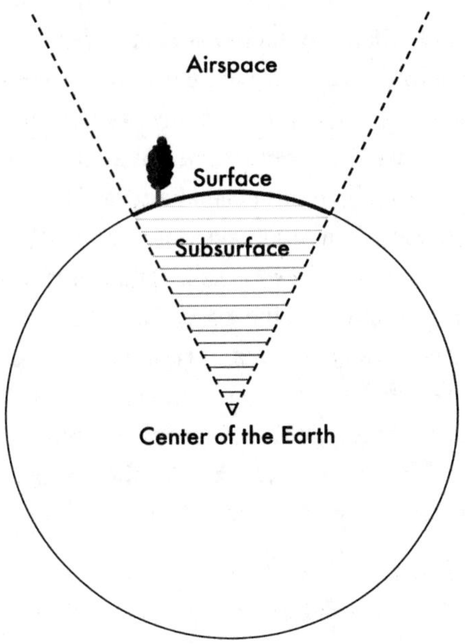

In addition to the land itself, **improvements** to the land are also part of the landowner's real property. Improvements are things that have been added to, built on, or done to the land to improve or develop it. A house, a driveway, a fence, and landscaping are all examples of improvements.

The intangible rights, privileges, and interests associated with land ownership are also considered part of the real property. Think of real property as the land and improvements plus a bundle of rights. The owner's bundle of rights includes the right to possess, use, enjoy, encumber, will, sell, or do nothing at all with the land. Of course, these rights aren't absolute; they're subject to government regulation. (See Chapter 6.)

Appurtenances

In addition to the basic bundle of ownership rights, a landowner has appurtenant rights. An appurtenance is a right or interest that goes along with or pertains to a piece of land. A landowner's property may include any or all of these appurtenances:

- air rights,
- water rights,
- solid mineral rights,
- oil and gas rights, and
- support rights.

Appurtenances are ordinarily transferred along with the land, but the landowner can sell certain appurtenant rights separately from the land. For example, the owner may keep the land but sell his mineral rights to a mining company.

Air Rights

The term **air rights** refers to a landowner's appurtenant right to use the airspace above her land. In theory, a landowner's air rights extend to the upper limits of the sky. In practice, however, this is no longer true. Congress gave the federal government complete control over the nation's airspace. A landowner still has the exclusive right to use the lower reaches of airspace over his property, but may do nothing that would interfere with normal air traffic.

On the other hand, sometimes air traffic interferes with a property owner's right to the normal use of her land. If aircraft overflights cause substantial harm to a landowner, he may sue the government for some form of reimbursement. The classic example is an airport built right next to a chicken farm. The noise and vibrations from overflights are so severe that the chickens no longer lay eggs. If the land cannot be used for any other reasonable purpose, the value of the land is significantly diminished. The landowners may be able to force the government to condemn the property and compensate them for its fair market value. (See the discussion of inverse condemnation in Chapter 4.)

Water Rights

The right to use water can be—but is not necessarily—an appurtenant right, tied to land ownership. Because water is vital for agriculture, industry, and day-to-day living, water rights are an important issue in many areas.

Water is found both on the surface of the earth and beneath the surface. Surface water may be confined to a channel or basin, or it may be unconfined water, such as runoff or flood water.

In regard to confined surface waters, there are two basic types of property rights:

1. riparian rights, and
2. appropriative rights.

In the U.S., the laws concerning water rights vary from state to state. In the eastern part of the country, where water is generally plentiful, most states use the riparian rights system, in which water rights are tied to land ownership. States in the western part of the country, where water is often scarce, generally use some version of the appropriative rights system. Some states combine the two systems.

Riparian Rights. Riparian rights are the water rights of a landowner with respect to water that flows through or adjacent to his property. Such a landowner, called a riparian landowner, has a right to make reasonable use of a stream's natural flow. A riparian landowner also has the right to use stream water for domestic uses, such as drinking, bathing, and watering a personal-use produce garden. Upstream landowners aren't allowed to use the water in ways that could deprive downstream owners of its use; they must not substantially diminish the stream's flow in quantity, quality, or velocity.

Whether a riparian owner also owns the land under the stream depends on whether the stream is **navigable** or not. A waterway is generally considered navigable if it is large enough to be used in commerce. If a stream is not navigable, the riparian owner owns the land under the water. (If the stream is the boundary between two parcels of land, each owner owns the land under the water to the midpoint of the streambed.) If a stream is navigable, the government owns the land under the water and the riparian landowner owns the land only to the mean high water mark of the streambed. The general public has the right to use navigable waterways for transportation and recreation.

Property located beside a lake, as opposed to a river or stream, is called **littoral** property. Owners of littoral property are entitled to have the lake maintained at its natural level, and to use the lake for fishing or recreation. The owners are also entitled to have the natural purity of the lake's waters maintained. If the lake is not navigable, each littoral owner owns a portion of the lake bed adjacent to her property.

There's an important restriction on a riparian or littoral owner's water rights. A riparian or littoral owner is not permitted to divert water from a stream or lake for use on non-riparian land—that is, land that does not adjoin the stream or lake from which the water is taken.

> **Example:** Brown is a riparian landowner. She owns Parcel A, property that borders the Swiftwater River. She also owns Parcel B, property that is about 300 feet inland. She cannot divert water from the Swiftwater River to irrigate the crops on her non-riparian property.

In addition, riparian owners do not have the right to limitless water; however, they are entitled to a reasonable amount of water for beneficial uses, leaving the remaining supplies for non-riparian appropriative users.

Appropriative Rights. Riparian and littoral rights are tied to ownership of land beside a body of water. The other major type of water rights, appropriative rights, do not depend on land ownership. Instead, appropriative rights depend on priority of use ("first in time, first in right").

Historically, appropriative rights were based on the legal doctrine of **prior appropriation**, which held that the first person to take (appropriate) water from a stream or lake and put it to use had the right to continue that use. Other users might also appropriate available water from the stream or lake, but during periods when there wasn't enough water to meet the needs of all users, earlier users had priority over later users. The first user could take as much water as needed for his established use, even if that meant there wouldn't be any left over for the other users.

The doctrine of prior appropriation, in modified form, has been incorporated into the statutory laws of most western states. In these states, water resources are now held by the government in trust for the public and allocated through a permit system. To establish an appropriative right, someone who wants to use water from a particular lake or stream applies to the state government for a permit. It is not necessary for the applicant to own land beside the body of water, and the water taken does not have to be used on property adjacent to the water source. The applicant must demonstrate that the water will be put to a beneficial use, such as irrigation or power generation.

If someone with an appropriative right fails to use the water for a certain period of time, she is likely to lose the appropriative right. Another person can then apply for a permit to use the water.

Ground Water. Subsurface water, commonly called ground water, may flow in underground channels or collect in porous underground layers called aquifers. Ground water that isn't confined in an underground channel is called **percolating water**.

Landowners can bring ground water to the surface by drilling a well. The natural level below which percolating water can be located in a piece of land is called the **water table**. Depending on the properties of the soil and other geological conditions, the water table may be near the surface or quite deep.

The use of ground water is governed in a variety of different ways, depending on state law. In some cases, the prior appropriation system applies to ground water as well as surface water. Alternatively, landowners may have **overlying rights** in regard to the water in aquifers under their land. Overlying rights are similar to riparian rights; a landowner is allowed to make reasonable use of the ground water, but may not transport it for use on other land.

Solid Mineral Rights

Land may contain a wide range of solid minerals, such as coal, copper, gemstones, or gold. As a general rule, a landowner owns all of the solid minerals within the "inverted pyramid" under the surface of her property. These minerals are considered to be real property until they are extracted from the earth, at which point they become personal property.

As we mentioned earlier, a landowner can sell his mineral rights separately from the rest of the property. When rights to a particular mineral are sold, the purchaser automatically acquires an implied easement—the right to enter the land in order to extract the minerals.

Oil and Gas Rights

In their natural state, oil and gas lie trapped beneath the surface in porous layers of earth. However, unlike solid minerals, oil and gas are not stationary. When an oil or gas reservoir is tapped, the oil or gas begins to flow toward the point where the reservoir has been pierced by the well. A well on one parcel of land can attract all of the oil or gas from the surrounding properties. Because of this, oil and gas are sometimes called "fugitive substances" (a term that also may be applied to water). Their fugitive nature makes ownership of oil and gas more complicated than ownership of solid minerals.

Until a reservoir is tapped, ownership of the oil or gas is governed by one of two theories. In states that follow the **ownership theory**, oil and gas are owned as real property, in the same way that unextracted solid minerals are owned. A landowner can transfer oil and gas ownership by deed; the person acquiring the interest receives the bundle of rights associated with real property.

In contrast, in states that follow the **nonownership theory**, a landowner doesn't own the oil and gas beneath the surface. Instead, the landowner has an exclusive right to drill and gains ownership of the oil or gas when it is brought to the surface. The right to drill can be sold or leased, but it is not considered an interest in real property.

In all states, oil or gas that is pumped to the surface is governed by the "rule of capture." A landowner owns all of the oil or gas produced from wells on her property, even if it has migrated from neighboring land. The oil or gas becomes the personal property of the landowner once it is brought to the surface and "captured."

The rule of capture has the effect of stimulating oil and gas production, since the only way for a landowner to protect his interest in the underlying oil or gas is to drill an offset well to keep the oil or gas from migrating to the neighbor's well.

Oil and Gas Leases. An oil and gas lease grants the lessee the right to use the surface of the land in order to remove oil and gas from the ground. Landowners who lack the necessary equipment or capital for drilling often grant this type of lease to an oil company in exchange for a royalty or a share of the profits.

Other Appurtenant Rights

In addition to rights concerning air, water, minerals, and oil and gas, there are some other important appurtenant rights.

A piece of land is supported by the other land that surrounds it. A landowner has **support rights**—the right to the natural support provided by the land beside and beneath her property. **Lateral support** is support from adjacent land; it may be disturbed by construction or excavations on neighboring property. **Subjacent support**—support from the underlying earth—may become an issue when a landowner sells his mineral rights.

Easements and restrictive covenants also create appurtenant rights. These are discussed in detail in Chapter 5.

Attachments

After land and appurtenances, attachments—things that are affixed or attached to land—are the third component of real property. There are two types of attachments:

1. natural, and
2. man-made.

Natural Attachments

Plants attached to the earth by roots, such as trees, shrubs, garden plants, or agricultural crops, are called natural attachments. They are divided into two main categories: *fructus naturales* ("fruits of nature"), plants that grow without cultivation, and *fructus industriales* ("fruits of industry"), plants cultivated by people. While both categories of natural attachments are considered to be real property, the annual crops from *fructus industriales* are generally treated as personal property. Thus, the trees in a cultivated apple orchard would be realty, but the apples themselves would be personalty.

Another term for annually cultivated crops is "emblements." A special rule called the **doctrine of emblements** applies to crops planted by a tenant farmer. If the tenancy is for an indefinite period of time and it is terminated through no fault of the tenant before the crops are ready for harvest, the tenant has the right to re-enter the land and harvest the first crop that matures after the tenancy is terminated.

Man-made Attachments: Fixtures

Things that are attached to the land by people are called **fixtures**. Houses, fences, and cement patios are all examples of fixtures. Like natural attachments, fixtures are considered to be part of the real property.

Fixtures always start out as personal property. For example, lumber is personal property, but it becomes a fixture when it's used to build a fence. It is sometimes difficult to determine whether a particular item has become a fixture or is still personal property. If the item is personal property, the owner can remove it from the property when the land is sold. But if the item is a fixture, it's transferred to the buyer along with the land unless otherwise agreed.

Annexation and Severance

Personal property becomes a fixture through **annexation**, which is the act of adding something on to real property. There are two types of annexation: physical and constructive. An item is **physically annexed** to real property when it has been affixed to, embedded in, or otherwise permanently attached to the land or improvements. An item is **constructively annexed** to real property if it is a necessary or working part of the realty. (We'll discuss this concept in more detail in the next section.)

Natural attachments and fixtures may also be converted into personal property. **Severance** is the separation of something from real property (the opposite of annexation). For example, a tree is severed from the land when the landowner cuts it down. Similarly, crops such as apples or wheat are severed from the realty when they are harvested.

Distinguishing Fixtures from Personal Property

Buyers and sellers sometimes disagree as to exactly what has been purchased and sold. For instance, is an heirloom chandelier installed by the seller real property that's transferred to the buyer, or can the seller remove it when he moves out?

The easiest way to avoid such a controversy is to put the intentions of the parties in writing. If there is a written agreement between a buyer and a seller (or between a landlord and a tenant) stipulating how a particular item will be treated—as part of the real estate or as personal property—then a court will enforce that agreement. The stipulation between a buyer and seller would ordinarily be found in their purchase agreement. For example, if a seller plans to take certain shrubs from the property before the transaction closes, a statement to that effect should be included in the purchase agreement, since shrubs are usually considered part of the real property.

Similarly, if the seller intends to transfer personal property, such as a couch, to the buyer, that should also be stated in the purchase agreement. In addition to the deed conveying title to the real property, a separate document called a **bill of sale** should be provided to the buyer. A bill of sale conveys title to personal property.

In the absence of a written agreement, courts apply a series of tests to classify the item in dispute. These tests include:

- the method of attachment,
- adaptation of the item to the realty,
- the intention of the annexor, and
- the relationship of the parties.

Method of Attachment. As a general rule, any item a person permanently attaches to the land becomes a part of the real estate. A permanent attachment occurs when the item is:

- attached to the land by roots, like a tree or shrub;
- embedded in the earth, like sewer lines or a septic tank;
- permanently resting on the land, like a storage shed; or
- affixed by any other enduring method, such as cement, plaster, or nails.

It isn't absolutely necessary for an item to be physically attached to the real property in order to be considered a fixture. There may be physical annexation even without actual attachment. The force of gravity alone may be sufficient, as in the case of a building with no foundation. Also, an article enclosed within a building may be considered annexed to the real property if it cannot be removed without dismantling it or tearing down part of the building.

In addition, even easily movable articles may be considered constructively attached to the real property, if they are essential parts of other fixtures. For example, the key to the front door of a house is a fixture. Also, fixtures that have been temporarily removed for servicing or repair remain legally attached to the real property. For example, a built-in dishwasher that has been sent to the repair shop is still considered to be a part of the house in which it is ordinarily installed.

Adaptation of the Item to the Realty. If an unattached article was designed or adapted specifically for use on a particular property, it is probably a fixture. Examples include the pews in a church, and storm windows made for a particular building.

Fig. 2.2 Fixture tests

- **M**ethod of attachment
- **A**daptation to the realty
- **R**elationship of the parties
- **I**ntention of the annexor
- **A**greement in writing

The acronym MARIA is often used as a memory aid for the fixture tests.

Intention of the Annexor. The method of attachment was once regarded as the most important test in determining whether an item was a fixture, but over time the courts decided that test was too rigid. It did not allow for special situations where something permanently affixed would be more justly classified as personal property. Now the intention of the annexor is considered a more important test. Courts try to determine what the person who annexed the item to the property intended. Did she intend the item to become part of the realty or to remain personal property? Each of the other tests, including method of attachment, is viewed as objective evidence of this intention. For instance, permanently embedding a birdbath in concrete indicates an intention to make the item a permanent fixture, while just setting a birdbath out in the yard does not.

Relationship of the Parties. Intent is also indicated by the relationship of the parties to the property. Was the item installed by the property owner or by a tenant? It's generally assumed that a tenant who installs new lighting, for example, probably does so with the intention of removing the lighting when the lease expires. But it's assumed that a property owner making the same alteration is trying to improve the property and doesn't intend to remove the lighting when the property is sold. So an item that would be considered personal property if installed by a tenant might be considered a fixture if installed by an owner.

Items that tenants install in order to carry on a trade or business are called **trade fixtures**. Trade fixtures generally remain personal property and may be removed by the tenant unless there is a contrary provision in the lease, or unless the fixtures have become an integral part of the land or improvements. In the latter case, if the tenant still wants to remove the fixtures, it is her responsibility to either restore the property to its original condition, or else compensate the landlord for any physical damage resulting from the removal. Trade fixtures that are not removed by the tenant become the property of the landlord.

Mobile Homes as Fixtures

The distinction between fixtures and personal property has special significance in connection with mobile homes. Mobile homes have developed from house-trailers in trailer parks to modern manufactured homes: large factory-built structures that can be set permanently on a full-sized lot.

In many states, a manufactured home is considered personal property until it is permanently attached to land by removing the wheels or unloading it from the truck and mounting it on a concrete pad or other foundation. Once the manufactured home has been permanently attached to land, it's considered part of the real property.

The classification of a manufactured home as real or personal property can determine how it is taxed and what rules govern its sale. For example, depending on state law, the sale of a manufactured home without land might be treated as the sale of a motor vehicle, subject to sales tax and vehicle licensing requirements. On the other hand, the sale of an identical manufactured home along with the subdivision lot it's been placed on would be treated just like the sale of a site-built home on such a lot.

A real estate agent should be aware of local laws and regulations regarding the sale and lease of manufactured homes. In some states, it's illegal to sell manufactured housing without a special dealer license; in others, no special license is necessary.

Characteristics of Real Property

Real property is a commodity, sold on the open market like other products. But the fundamental component of real property—land—has special characteristics that distinguish it from other commodities and affect how it is used, valued, and bought and sold. These characteristics can be divided into two general categories: physical characteristics and economic characteristics.

Physical Characteristics

The distinguishing physical characteristics of land are immobility, indestructibility, and uniqueness.

Immobility. Land cannot be moved; it is fixed in place. Soil, sand, and minerals can be removed from a parcel of land, and the topography can be reshaped by natural forces or human action. The parcel's geographic location on the earth cannot be changed, however.

Indestructibility. A parcel of land is essentially indestructible. The durability and permanence of land are among the reasons that real property is regarded as an especially secure investment.

Of course, physical durability isn't the same thing as economic durability, and many different factors may reduce the value of a parcel of land. For example, a population shift, a zoning change, or an economic slowdown might lower property values. Yet even when the value of a parcel of land drops sharply, the land itself isn't destroyed.

Uniqueness. There are no identical parcels of land. While it's possible for one parcel to be substantially similar to another, each parcel has a different geographic location, so each one is unique. The characteristic of uniqueness is also referred to as non-homogeneity.

Economic Characteristics

The distinguishing economic characteristics of land are scarcity, improvements, permanence of investment, and area preference.

Scarcity. Scarcity is a characteristic of land because the supply of usable land in a given area is finite; there's only so much of it. The scarcity of land in a particular area depends on the demand for land there. In a place where demand for land is high (a big city, for example), land is economically scarce, even though plenty of land is available elsewhere (in nearby rural areas, for example).

Improvements. A parcel of land can be improved in ways that will have a substantial impact on its use and value, and certain types of improvements will also affect the use and value of neighboring land. For example, construction of an apartment building or a gas station on one parcel may affect how the neighboring parcels are developed or how much they're worth (or both). This economic characteristic is sometimes called modification.

Permanence of Investment. Capital and labor invested in land and improvements generally represent a substantial investment that will provide stable returns over the long term. Also, once the investment has been made, the land and improvements can't be moved to another place where demand for them would be greater. These aspects of real estate investment are referred to as **permanence of investment** or **fixity**. Because of this characteristic, investing in real estate requires greater deliberation and more careful long-term planning than many other types of investments.

Area Preference. The effect that preference for a particular location (or situs) can have on land is referred to as **area preference**. The importance of area preference is the basis of this old joke: "What are the three most important factors to consider in evaluating real estate? Location, location, and location."

As a result of area preference, the value of two parcels of land may be very different even though the parcels are the same in nearly every respect other than location.

> **Example:** Lot A and Lot B are the same size and shape and equally suitable for the construction of a home. The only real difference between them is that Lot A is right beside a lake and Lot B is four blocks away from the lake. Because of area preference, Lot A sells for almost twice as much as Lot B.

For residential properties, a wide variety of factors (including climate, views, neighborhood prestige, availability of employment, and access to shopping and schools) may influence area preference. Other factors come into play for commercial and industrial properties.

Land Description

When ownership of real property is transferred from one person to another, the legal documents used in the transaction must specify what piece of land is being conveyed. The section of a document that identifies the land is called the **property description** or **legal description**. It's essential for the description to be clear and accurate; an ambiguous or uncertain description could make a contract or a deed invalid, and confusion over exactly what land was transferred could cause problems not only for the parties involved in the current transaction, but also for the parties in future transactions. To ensure the necessary accuracy, land is described using one of the three main methods of legal description, which we'll discuss shortly.

When filling in a property description on a contract form, a real estate agent copies the established description from the seller's deed, or from another reliable source such as a title report. If the description is at all complicated, it's best to photocopy it and attach the copy to the contract, instead of copying the description by hand. All of the parties to the contract must initial and date the attachment.

Surveys

In most cases a property's legal description is based on a **survey** of the property. When a parcel of property is surveyed, land surveyors go to the site and locate the exact boundaries of the parcel, using extremely precise compasses and other surveying equipment. They typically place metal pipes, stakes, or other markers at the corners of the parcel. After completing a survey, the surveyors prepare a legal description and a **survey sketch**. The survey sketch is a drawing that shows the location, boundaries, and dimensions of the parcel. It may also show the size and location of buildings on the property.

Land surveys have a variety of uses. When property is subdivided, a survey is used to establish lot boundaries. Surveys are also used to prevent or settle boundary disputes between neighbors. When a parcel of land is being sold, potential buyers may have the land surveyed in order to determine the exact boundaries and discover any encroachments (see Chapter 6). Sometimes mortgage lenders and title companies require a survey in connection with a loan or title insurance.

In most states, surveyors are required to be licensed by the state. Surveys are generally prepared according to standards developed by the American Land Title Association and the American Congress on Surveying and Mapping. These are known as the ALTA/ACSM standards.

Methods of Description

There are three major methods used to describe land in legal documents:

- the metes and bounds method,
- the government survey method, and
- the recorded map method.

Metes and Bounds Descriptions. The metes and bounds method is the oldest of the three methods of land description. In a metes and bounds description, a parcel of land is described by specifying the location of its boundaries. The boundaries are described by reference to three things:

- **monuments**, which may be natural objects such as boulders, trees, or rivers, or man-made objects such as roads or survey markers;

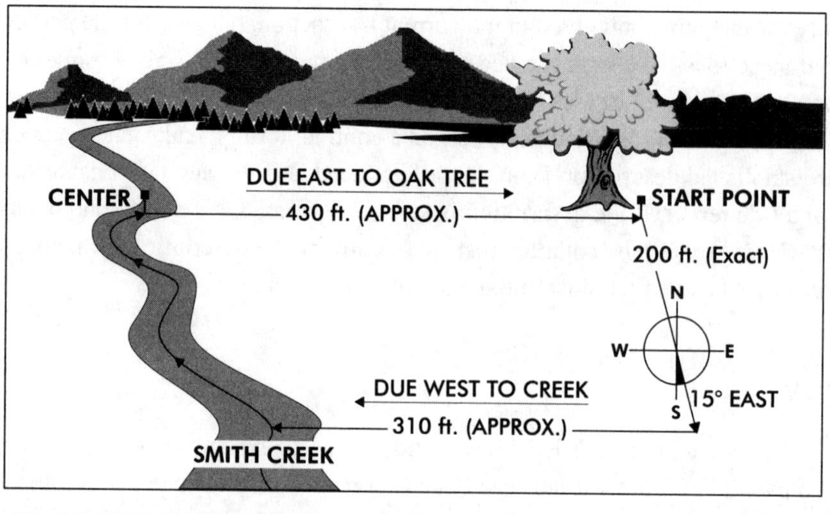

Fig. 2.3 Metes and bounds description

A tract of land, located in Smith County and described as follows: "Beginning at the old oak tree, thence south 15° east, 200 feet, thence north 90° west, 310 feet more or less to the centerline of Smith Creek, thence northwesterly along the centerline of Smith Creek to a point directly west of the old oak tree, thence north 90° east, 430 feet more or less to the point of beginning."

- **courses** (directions), in the form of compass readings; and
- **distances**, measured in any convenient units of length.

Reading a Metes and Bounds Description. A metes and bounds description first specifies a **point of beginning**, which is a convenient and well-defined point on one of the parcel's boundary lines. A monument may be used as the point of beginning ("Beginning at the old oak tree," for example), or the point of beginning may be described by reference to a monument ("Beginning at a point 200 feet north of the old oak tree," for example).

After establishing the point of beginning, the description then specifies a series of courses and distances. For example, "north, 100 feet" is a course and distance; so is "south 30 degrees east, 263.5 feet." By starting at the point of beginning and following the courses and distances given, a surveyor could walk along the parcel's boundary lines, all the way around and back to the point of beginning. A metes and bounds description must end up back at the point of beginning; otherwise, it wouldn't describe a totally enclosed tract of land.

Types of Monuments. Early metes and bounds descriptions often used natural objects such as "the old oak tree" as monuments, but those aren't very reliable reference points; they don't necessarily maintain their exact locations over time, and they may also be destroyed. Modern descriptions use monuments that are more firmly fixed and durable, such as survey markers or bench marks (discussed later in the chapter).

Compass Bearings. Directions or courses in metes and bounds descriptions are given in a peculiar fashion. A direction is described by reference to its deviation from either north or south, whichever is closer. Thus, northwest is written as north 45° west, since it is a deviation of 45 degrees to the west of north. Similarly, south-southeast is written south 22½° east, since it is a deviation of 22½ degrees to the east of south. East and west are both written relative to north: north 90° east and north 90° west, respectively. (There are 360 degrees in a circle.)

Fig. 2.4 Compass bearings

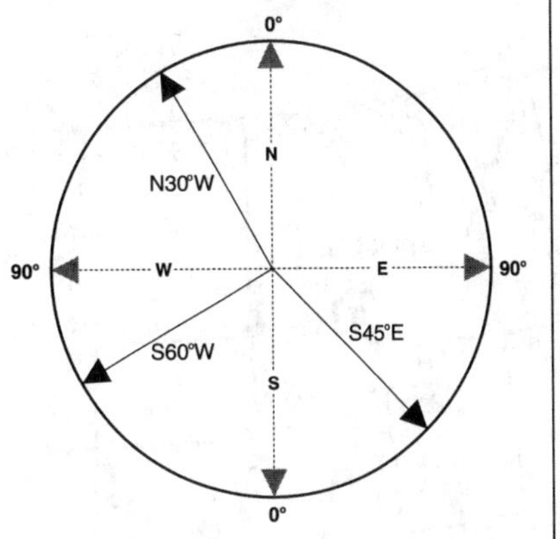

Resolving Discrepancies. To specify the direction or length of a boundary, monuments are sometimes used in conjunction with courses and distances, as in "northerly along the eastern edge of Front Street 100 feet" or "north, 100 feet more or less, to the centerline of Smith Creek." If there's a discrepancy between a monument and a course or distance, the monument takes precedence. In the examples just given, the first boundary would be along the edge of Front Street, even if that edge does not run due north, and the second boundary would extend to the center of Smith Creek, even if the actual distance to that point is not exactly 100 feet.

Discrepancies may also occur between other elements of a metes and bounds description. To resolve them, the following order of priority is used:

1. natural monuments,
2. man-made monuments,
3. courses,
4. distances,
5. names (e.g., "Smith Farm"),
6. areas (e.g., "40 acres").

In case of a conflict between any two of these elements in a description, the one with higher priority prevails.

A discrepancy in a metes and bounds description may be the result of imprecise measurement when the description was originally written. Also, as we mentioned, some monuments don't stay in exactly the same position over the years, and that can give rise to discrepancies.

Government Survey Descriptions. In the government survey system, also called the rectangular survey or public land survey system, land is described by reference to a grid of lines established by a survey. (These are imaginary lines, like the longitude and latitude lines on a globe.) This system of land description was created by the federal Land Ordinance of 1785, after most of the land in the eastern states already had been settled and described using the metes and bounds method. Thus, government survey descriptions are mainly used west of the Mississippi River.

The terminology used in the government survey system may seem confusing at first, and we recommend that you study the accompanying diagrams closely.

Fig. 2.5 Principal meridians and base lines

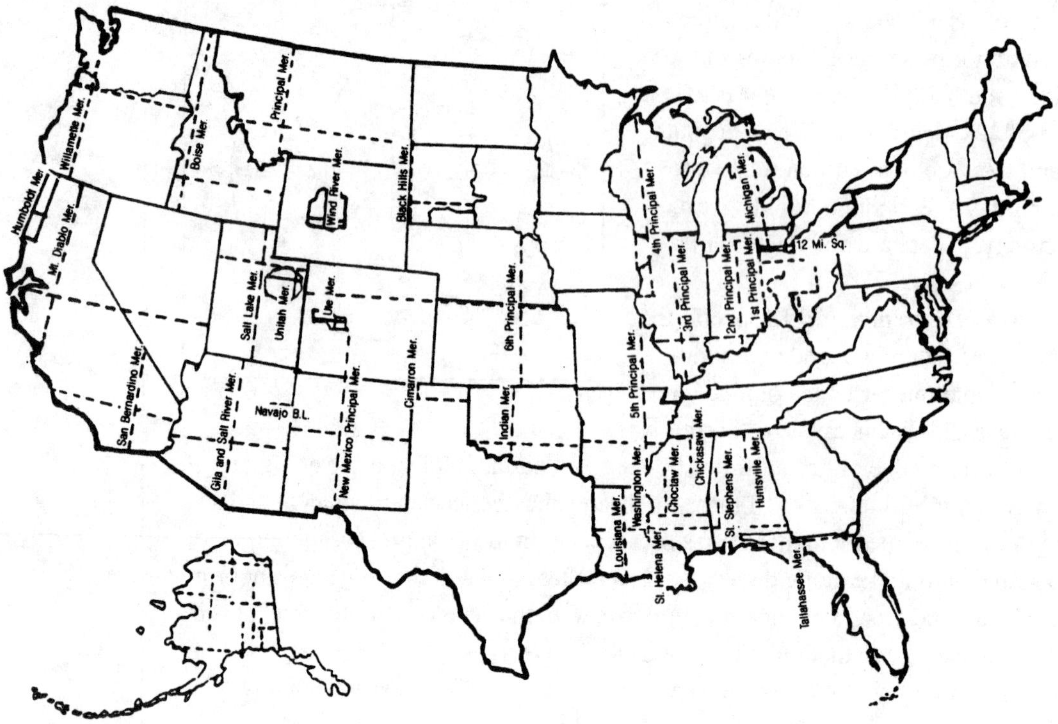

Fig. 2.6 Units of land measurement

UNITS OF MEASUREMENT FOR LAND	
UNITS OF AREA	1 Tract = 24 mi. x 24 mi. (576 sq. mi) = 16 townships 1 Township = 6 mi. x 6 mi. (36 sq. mi) = 36 sections 1 Section* = 1 mi. x 1 mi. (1 sq. mi) = 640 acres 1 Acre = 43,560 sq. ft. = 160 sq. rods 1 Square Acre = 208.71 ft. x 208.71 ft.
UNITS OF LENGTH	1 Mile = 5,280 ft. = 320 rods = 80 chains 1 Rod = 16½ ft. 1 Chain = 66 ft. = 4 rods

* Note: To determine the area of partial sections, simply multiply the fraction of the section by 640. For example,

1 half-section = ½ x 640 = 320 acres
1 quarter-section = ¼ x 640 = 160 acres
1 quarter-quarter section = ¼ x ¼ x 640 = 40 acres

Fig. 2.7 East/west lines are township lines; north/south lines are range lines.

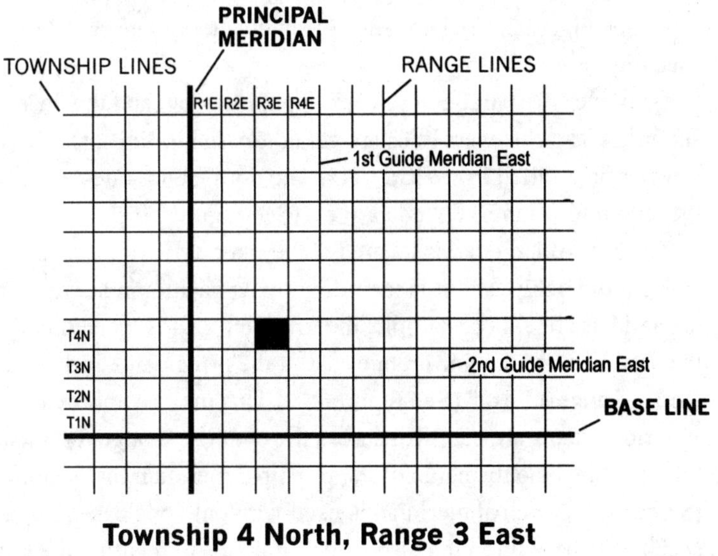

Fig. 2.8
A township contains 36 sections.

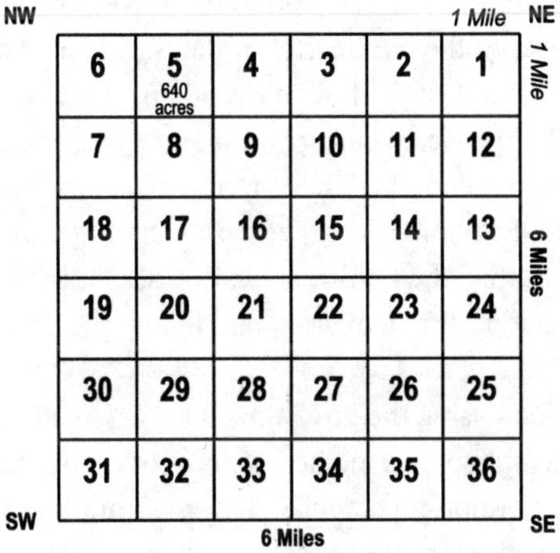

Fig. 2.9
A section can be divided up into smaller parcels.

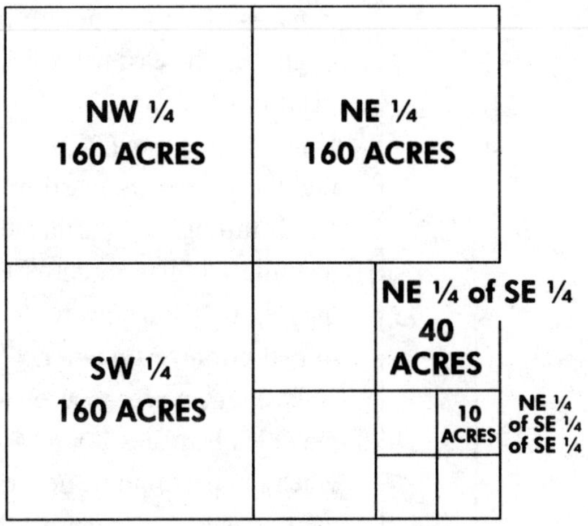

The system is made up of a series of large grids covering the United States. Each of these grids is composed of two sets of lines, one set running north/south, the other east/west. Each grid is identified by a **principal meridian**, which is the original north/south line established in that grid, and by a **base line**, which is the original east/west line. (See Figure 2.7.) There are 35 principal meridians and 32 baselines in the system. (See Figure 2.5.)

Grid lines run parallel to the principal meridian and the base line at intervals of six miles. The east/west lines are called **township lines**, and they divide the land into rows or tiers called **township tiers**. The north/south lines, called **range lines**, divide the land into columns called **ranges**. (See Figure 2.7.)

The area of land that is located at the intersection of a range and a township tier is called a **township**, and it is identified by its position relative to the principal meridian and base line. For example, the township that is located in the fourth tier north of the base line and the third range east of the principal meridian is called "Township 4 North, Range 3 East." (See Figure 2.7.) This may be abbreviated "T4N, R3E."

Grid systems are identical across the country, so a government survey description must include the name of the principal meridian that's being used as a reference. (Since each principal meridian is used with only one base line, it isn't necessary to specify the base line.) It's also a good practice to mention the county and state where the land is situated, to avoid any possible confusion. So, for example, a complete description of a township might be T4N, R3E of the Mt. Diablo Meridian, Sacramento County, State of California.

Each township measures 36 square miles and contains 36 sections. Each section is one square mile, or 640 acres. The sections are numbered in a special way, starting with the northeast corner and moving west, then down a row and eastward, snaking back and forth and ending with the southeast corner. (See Figure 2.8.)

Smaller parcels of land can be identified by reference to sections and partial sections, as illustrated in Figure 2.9. For example, the description for a five-acre parcel might be "the east half of the NW quarter of the NE quarter of the SW quarter of Section 12, Township 6 South, Range 10 East of the Indian Meridian, Bryan County, State of Oklahoma." To locate a parcel of property on a government survey map, first find the section in question, then start at the end of the description and work backwards through the partial sections to the beginning. In other words, find Section 12, then the southwest quarter of section 12, then the northeast quarter of that southwest quarter, then the northwest quarter of that northeast quarter, and finally the east half of that northwest quarter.

Even in an area where land is described using the government survey method, it may also be necessary to use the metes and bounds method. This is true, for example, when the parcel to be described is small or non-rectangular. The government survey method is used to identify the general location of the parcel, but then the metes and bounds method is used to specify the parcel's precise location and boundaries.

Correction Lines. Because of the curvature of the earth, range lines are not exactly parallel; they converge very gradually as they go north. (If they were extended all the way north, range lines would meet at the North Pole.) To compensate for this, there is a **correction line** every 24 miles north and south of a base line. There is also a **guide meridian** every 24 miles to the east and west of the principal meridian.

Every fourth range line is a guide meridian and every fourth township line is a correction line. Each guide meridian runs only as far north or south as the next correction line (24 miles); correction lines run as far as the next guide meridian. The 24-by-24-mile area created by a guide meridian and a correction line is called a **government check** or **quadrangle**.

Government Lots. Partial sections that have an irregular shape or aren't the standard size are called **government lots**. Each government lot is assigned a lot number and referred to by that number.

Government lots arise in a variety of situations. Some occur because a body of water or other obstacle makes it impossible to survey a section that's exactly one mile square. Other government lots are necessary because certain sections have an excess or shortage of land as a result of the system of correction lines explained above. The government lots created for this reason are usually along the north and west boundaries of a township.

Lot and Block Descriptions. The lot and block method of land description is also referred to as the recorded map or recorded plat method. It was developed to make legal descriptions of subdivided land more convenient, and it's now the method of description used for most property in urban areas.

When land is subdivided, a surveyor uses the metes and bound method or the government survey method to map out lots and blocks (groups of lots surrounded by streets) on a subdivision map called a **plat** or **plat map**. The plat is then recorded in the county where the land is located. (See Chapter 4 for a discussion of the recording system.)

Once a plat has been recorded, a reference to one of the lot numbers on the specified plat is a sufficient legal description of the lot. Since a precise description of the lot's location and boundaries is already on file in the county recorder's office, that description may be incorporated into any legal document simply by stating the lot number and the block number (if any) and the name of the subdivision.

Fig. 2.10 Plat map

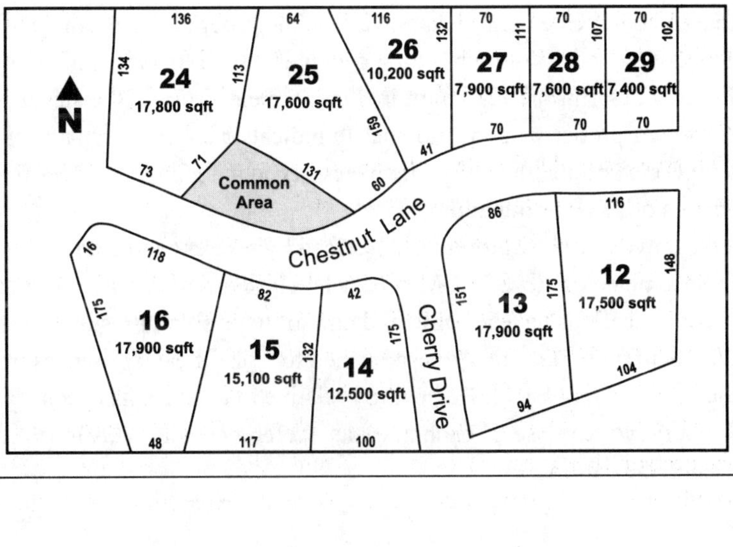

Example: The lot and block description for a particular single-family property is Lot 59, Block 48, Highland Creek Subdivision, in the City of Charlotte, County of Mecklenburg, State of North Carolina, as shown in map book 29, page 341, in the Register of Deeds Office of said county. By looking up the plat for this subdivision in the county map book, you could find the precise location and dimensions of this parcel.

Plat maps frequently contain a considerable amount of useful information beyond a detailed description of lot boundaries. For example, they may include area measurements, the location and dimensions of any easements, the location of survey markers, and a list of use restrictions applying to the land. (Note, however, that studying a plat map is not a substitute for a title search. See Chapter 4.)

Other Methods of Description. There are other ways of describing land besides the three major methods of description we've discussed. When an adequate description of property is already a matter of public record—contained in a recorded document—then a simple reference to that earlier document serves as an adequate property description in a new document. (For example, "All that land described in the deed recorded under recording number 92122401503 in Arapahoe County, Colorado.") References to records of survey may be used, if they have been recorded in the county where the property is located.

Also, generalized descriptions such as "all my lands" or "Smith Farm" can be adequate, as long as they make it possible to determine the precise boundaries of the property being described. But it's always best to use the least ambiguous description possible, to prevent future problems. This is especially true if the property owner has several properties in one area.

In most states, a property's street address or common name is not considered an adequate legal description. Also, as a general rule, neither a tax assessor's parcel number nor the land description given on a property tax bill should be used as a legal description for the property.

Elevations and Air Lots. Not every parcel of real property can be described simply in terms of its position on the face of the earth. Descriptions of some forms of real property must also indicate their elevation above the ground. For example, a unit on an upper story of a condominium building occupies a specific parcel of airspace—an **air lot**. The legal description of the unit includes the elevation of the air lot.

In other cases, a property description has to indicate a specific distance or position underground. For example, that might be necessary in a document concerning subsurface rights in oil, gas, or minerals.

A position above or below ground is described by reference to a **datum**, which is an established plane of elevation. Mean sea level is commonly used as a datum, although most large cities have an official datum of their own. Subsidiary reference points, called **bench marks**, are also established to make it easier to measure elevation. A bench mark is a point whose position relative to a datum has been accurately measured. A surveyor can use a bench mark as a reference when it is more convenient than using the datum.

Chapter Summary

1. Property may be either tangible or intangible. There are two main types of property: real property and personal property. Real property is the land, anything affixed to the land, and anything appurtenant to the land. Movable items, such as furniture, are usually personal property.

2. Appurtenances to land include air rights, water rights, mineral rights, oil and gas rights, and support rights.

3. Attachments may be natural (growing plants) or man-made (fixtures). In the absence of a written agreement, the tests used to distinguish fixtures from personal property are: the method of attachment, the adaptation of the item to the realty, the intention of the annexor, and the relationship of the parties.

4. Land has certain distinguishing physical and economic characteristics. The physical characteristics of land include immobility, indestructibility, and uniqueness. The economic characteristics of land include scarcity, improvements, permanence of investment, and area preference or situs.

5. Legal documents concerning real property must include an adequate description of the land, preferably the legal description. There are three major methods of legal description: metes and bounds, government survey, and lot and block.

Key Terms

Real property—Land, anything affixed to land (attachments), and anything incidental or appurtenant to land (appurtenances).

Personal property—Anything that is not real property. Its main characteristic is movability.

Appurtenance—A right incidental to the land that is transferred with it.

Annexation—The process or act of attaching or adding personal property to real property, so that it becomes part of the real property. Annexation may be actual or constructive.

Severance—The separation of fixtures or other attachments from real property, so that the items become personal property.

Emblements—Crops, such as wheat, produced annually through the labor of the cultivator.

Trade fixtures—Personal property attached to real property by a tenant for use in his trade or business. The tenant is allowed to remove trade fixtures when the tenancy ends.

Riparian rights—The water rights of a landowner whose land borders on a stream or other surface water. Riparian rights allow only reasonable use of the water.

Littoral land—Land bordered by a stationary body of water, such as a lake or pond.

Appropriative rights—Water rights established by obtaining a government permit, and not based on ownership of land beside a body of water.

Lateral support—The support that a piece of land receives from the surrounding land.

Subjacent support—The support that a piece of land receives from the underlying earth.

Area preference—The effect that preference for a particular location can have on the value of a piece of land.

Survey—The technical process by which the precise boundaries of a parcel of land are located and identified.

Metes and bounds—A system of land description in which the boundaries of a parcel of land are described by reference to monuments, courses, and distances.

Monument—A visible marker (natural or artificial) used in a survey or a metes and bounds description to establish the boundaries of a piece of property.

Point of beginning—The starting point in a metes and bounds description; a monument or a point described by reference to a monument.

Course—In a metes and bounds description, a direction, stated in terms of a compass bearing.

Distance—In a metes and bounds description, the length of a boundary, measured in any convenient unit of length.

Government survey—A system of land description in which the land is divided into squares called townships, and each township is, in turn, divided up into 36 sections, each one square mile.

Principal meridian—In the government survey system, the main north-south line in a particular grid, used as the starting point in numbering the ranges and township tiers.

Range—In the government survey system, a strip of land six miles wide, running north and south.

Section—One square mile of land, containing 640 acres. There are 36 sections in a township.

Township—The intersection of a range and a township tier in the government survey system. It is a parcel of land that is six miles square and contains 36 sections.

Government lot—In the government survey system, a partial section that is assigned a government lot number because it has an irregular shape or isn't the standard size.

Lot and block—The system of description used for subdivided land. The properties within a subdivision are assigned lot numbers on a survey map called a plat, which is then recorded. The location and dimensions of a particular lot can be determined by consulting the recorded plat.

Air lot—A parcel of property above the surface of the earth, not containing any land: for example, a condominium unit on the third floor.

Chapter Quiz

1. Real property is equivalent to:
   a) land
   b) personal property
   c) land, attachments, and appurtenances
   d) land and water

2. The most important consideration in determining whether an article is a fixture is:
   a) physical attachment
   b) the annexor's intention
   c) adaptation of the article to the realty
   d) the intended use of the article

3. Articles installed in or on realty by tenants for use in a business are called:
   a) personalty
   b) trade fixtures
   c) emblements
   d) easements

4. A right that goes with or pertains to real property is called:
   a) an attachment
   b) an appurtenance
   c) personal property
   d) a fixture

5. A landowner's rights regarding water in a stream flowing through her land are called:
   a) riparian rights
   b) littoral rights
   c) appropriative rights
   d) easement rights

6. Minerals become personal property when they are:
   a) surveyed
   b) extracted from the land
   c) taken to a refinery
   d) claimed

7. Rights to oil and gas are determined by:
   a) the rule of capture
   b) offset wells
   c) the Bureau of Land Management
   d) the Department of the Interior

8. Whether land borders on a lake or stream is irrelevant under the system of:
   a) riparian rights
   b) capture rights
   c) littoral rights
   d) appropriative rights

9. Ted's property is damaged by sinkholes caused by old coal mining tunnels beneath his land. The rights implicated in this situation are:
   a) riparian rights
   b) subjacent support rights
   c) lateral support rights
   d) appropriative rights

10. Which of the following is most likely to be considered part of the real property?
    a) Piano
    b) Dining room table
    c) Living room drapes
    d) Kitchen sink

11. Which of the following is a distinguishing physical characteristic of land?
    a) Immobility
    b) Intangibility
    c) Incorporeality
    d) Impermanence

12. A section of a township contains the following number of acres:
    a) 360
    b) 580
    c) 640
    d) 760

13. A parcel that measures one-quarter of a mile by one-quarter of a mile is:
    a) $^1/_4$ of a section
    b) $^1/_8$ of a section
    c) $^1/_{16}$ of a section
    d) $^1/_{36}$ of a section

14. The distance between the east and west boundary lines of a township is:
    a) one mile
    b) two miles
    c) six miles
    d) ten miles

15. A township contains 36 sections that are numbered consecutively 1 through 36. The last section in the township is located in the:
    a) southeast corner
    b) southwest corner
    c) northeast corner
    d) northwest corner

Answer Key

1. c) Real property is made up of land, everything that is attached to the land (e.g., fixtures), and everything that is appurtenant to the land (e.g., water rights).

2. b) The intention of the party who attached the item is the primary consideration in determining whether it is a fixture. The other tests provide evidence of the party's intention.

3. b) An article installed by a tenant for use in a business is called a trade fixture, and it remains the tenant's personal property.

4. b) An appurtenance is a right or interest that goes with land. Riparian rights are an example.

5. a) A landowner's rights concerning the use of the water that flows through his land are called riparian rights.

6. b) Minerals become personal property when they are extracted from the land.

7. a) The rule of capture determines ownership of oil and gas. A landowner owns all of the oil or gas removed from a well on her property, even if the oil or gas was originally beneath someone else's property.

8. d) To obtain a water appropriation permit, it is not necessary to own riparian or littoral land.

9. b) Subjacent support rights involve support from the underlying earth.

10. d) Unlike the other items listed, the kitchen sink is a fixture, and therefore it is part of the real property.

11. a) The distinguishing physical characteristics of land are immobility, indestructibility, and uniqueness.

12. c) In the government survey system of land description, one section contains 640 acres.

13. c) A section is one mile on each side, a quarter section is ½ mile on each side, and a quarter of a quarter section is ¼ mile on each side.

14. c) A township measures six miles by six miles.

15. a) Section 36 is always in the southeast corner of a township.

Chapter 3

Real Property Ownership

I. Systems of Land Ownership
II. Estates in Land
    A. Freehold estates
        1. Fee simple absolute estate
        2. Fee simple defeasible estate
        3. Life estate
    B. Leasehold estates
        1. Estate for years
        2. Periodic tenancy
        3. Tenancy at will
        4. Tenancy at sufferance
III. Methods of Holding Title
    A. In severalty
    B. Concurrently
        1. Tenancy in common
        2. Joint tenancy
        3. Community property
        4. Tenancy by the entirety
        5. Dower and curtesy
    C. Forms of business ownership
        1. Partnerships
        2. Corporations
        3. Limited liability companies
        4. Joint ventures
        5. Trusts
IV. Common Interest Developments
    A. Condominiums
    B. Townhouses
    C. Planned unit developments
    D. Cooperatives
    E. Timeshares

Chapter Overview

Real property ownership can take many different forms. An owner typically has full title to the property and full possession of it, but that isn't necessarily the case. An owner may have a more limited interest instead of full title, or may allow someone else (a tenant) to take possession of the property without taking title. In addition, a property may be owned by more than one person at the same time, which is called concurrent ownership. The first part of this chapter explains the various types of ownership interests, and also the types of interests that tenants may have. The second part of this chapter explains concurrent ownership and the different ways co-owners may hold title.

Systems of Land Ownership

In the United States, we take the ownership of land by private individuals for granted, but it hasn't been a part of every social system. For example, some tribal societies didn't recognize any form of property ownership; others didn't view land as something that could be owned. Under the communist governments established during the twentieth century in Eastern Europe, China, and other parts of the world, private property was generally abolished, and all land became state-owned.

A system of land ownership that's historically important for real property law is the **feudal system**, which prevailed in England and other parts of Europe during the Middle Ages. Under the feudal system, all land belonged to the sovereign or king. In exchange for pledges of loyalty and military support, the king granted large land holdings to the most important noblemen. Those noblemen, in turn, granted portions of their holdings to a hierarchy of minor noblemen. Most people were peasants or serfs, who farmed the land as tenants of their lords and could not hold title to it.

Over the course of centuries, the feudal system gradually gave way to the system we're familiar with, sometimes called the **allodial system**. In the allodial system, ordinary citizens are allowed to own land, and they can own it absolutely, rather than at the will of a lord or sovereign. As you'll see in this chapter, however, some of the terminology still used in property law has its roots in the feudal system.

Estates in Land

In real property law, the word **estate** refers to an interest in land that is or may become **possessory**. In other words, someone now has, or may have in the future, the right to possess the property—the right to exclusively occupy and use it. An estate may also be called a tenancy.

The different types of estates are distinguished by two features: the duration (how long the estate holder has the right of possession); and the time of possession (whether the estate holder has the right to possess the property right now, or not until sometime in the future).

It is important to note that while all estates are interests in land, not every interest in land is an estate. Interests that are not estates are called nonpossessory interests. For example, a mortgage gives a lender a financial interest in the property (a lien), but this interest is not an estate, because it is not a possessory interest. Nonpossessory interests are covered in Chapter 5.

Estates fall into two categories:

1. freehold estates, and
2. leasehold (less-than-freehold) estates.

A **freehold** estate is an interest in real property that has an indeterminable (not fixed or certain) duration. The holder of such an estate is usually referred to as an owner. All other possessory interests are leasehold (less-than-freehold) estates. A leasehold estate has a limited duration (a one-year lease is an example). The holder of a leasehold estate is referred to as a tenant; a tenant has possession of the property but not title.

Both types of estates can exist in the same piece of property at the same time. For instance, the owner of a freehold estate may lease the property to a tenant, who then has a leasehold estate in the same property. (When two or more parties have interests in the same property, their mutual relationship is referred to as "privity.")

Freehold Estates

The freehold estate got its name back in the Middle Ages—it originally referred to the holdings of a freeman under the English feudal system.

Freehold estates can be subdivided into fee simple estates and life estates. There are two basic types of fee simple estates: the fee simple absolute and the fee simple defeasible.

Fee Simple Absolute. The fee simple absolute estate is usually just called the fee simple. (The term "absolute" is used only to distinguish it from a fee simple defeasible, discussed below.) The fee simple absolute is the greatest estate that can exist in land, the highest and most complete form of ownership. It is of potentially infinite duration and represents the whole "bundle of rights."

A fee simple estate is freely transferable from one owner to another. It is also inheritable (it can be inherited by the owner's heirs when he dies), so it is sometimes referred to as the **estate of inheritance**. A fee simple estate has no set termination point, and theoretically can be owned forever by the titleholder and her heirs. When a fee simple owner transfers title by deed, it is presumed that the grantee (the new owner) receives a fee simple absolute estate, unless the deed includes language that indicates an intent to confer a lesser estate (such as a life estate, which will be described shortly).

Fee Simple Defeasible. A fee simple estate may be qualified when it is transferred from one owner to another. For example, in a deed, the grantor may specify that the grantee's estate will continue only as long as a certain condition is met, or until a certain event occurs.

Example: Able conveys a parcel of land to "Barney and his heirs so long as it is used for church purposes, and if it is no longer used for church purposes it shall revert back to Able or his heirs."

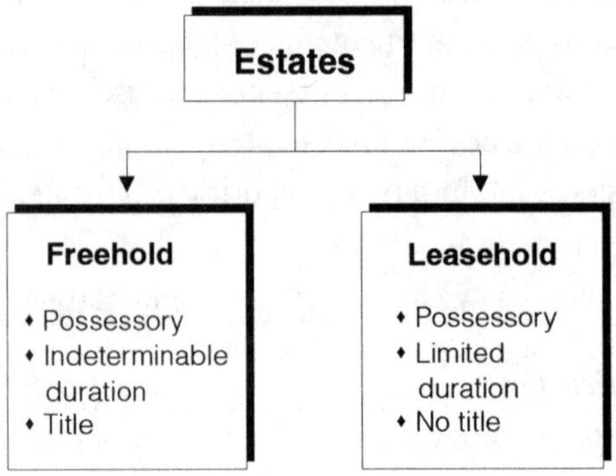

Fig. 3.1 Characteristics of estates

This type of qualification or condition creates a fee simple defeasible estate, also known as a defeasible fee, qualified fee, base fee, or conditional fee. The owner of a fee simple defeasible holds the same interest as the owner of a fee simple absolute, except that the defeasible owner's interest is subject to termination.

There are two types of defeasible or qualified fees: the fee simple determinable, and the fee simple subject to a condition subsequent. The distinction between them is quite technical and depends on the specific language used in the deed in which the estate is created. A **fee simple determinable** ends automatically if the condition is violated; the property reverts back to the grantor without legal action by the grantor. Language in a deed that would create a fee simple determinable includes phrases such as "so long as," "during," or "until." A **fee simple subject to a condition subsequent** doesn't end automatically when the condition is breached. The grantor must take legal action to terminate the estate. This type of estate may be created by the words "if" or "on the condition that."

Defeasible fee estates of either type are uncommon nowadays. Many real estate agents will never encounter a fee simple defeasible in the course of their careers. The overwhelming majority of fee ownership interests are fee simple absolute estates.

Life Estates. An estate for life is a freehold estate whose duration is limited to the lifetime of a specified person or persons.

Example: Noel gives a parcel of property to Beatrice for her lifetime, calling for a reversion of title to Noel upon Beatrice's death. Beatrice is the life tenant (holder of the life estate), and the duration of the life estate is measured by her lifetime.

The measuring life may be that of the life tenant (as in the example above, where Beatrice's life is the measuring life) or it may be the life of another person. Suppose, for example, Veronica gives a parcel of property to Howard for the life of Charlie. Howard has a life estate which will end when Charlie dies. This type of estate, known as a life estate **pur autre vie** ("for another's life"), is sometimes used to create security for ailing parents or disabled children who are unable to provide for themselves.

While the fee simple estate is a perpetual estate, the life estate is a lesser estate because it is limited in duration. In granting a life estate, a fee simple owner transfers only part of what she owns, so there must be something left over after the life estate terminates. What remains is either an estate in reversion or an estate in remainder. These are known as future interests.

Estate in Reversion. If the grantor stipulates that the property will revert back to the grantor at the end of the measuring life, the grantor holds an estate in reversion. The grantor has a future possessory interest in the property. Upon the death of the person whose life the estate is measured by, the property will revert to the **reversioner**—the grantor or his heirs.

Estate in Remainder. If the grantor stipulates that the property should go to a person other than the grantor at the end of the measuring life, that other person has an estate in remainder and is called the **remainderman**. The only difference between reversion and remainder estates is that the former is held by the grantor and the latter by a third party. (If the grantor doesn't name a remainderman, an estate in reversion is created.) The interest that will pass to the designated party on the death of the life tenant is a fee simple estate.

Example: Ann deeds her property "to Barbara for life, and then to Colin." Colin is the remainderman, and he will own the property in fee simple when Barbara dies and the life estate ends.

If Ann had simply deeded the property "to Barbara for life," without naming a remainderman, then fee simple ownership of the property would revert to Ann (or, if Ann has died in the meantime, to Ann's heirs) upon Barbara's death.

Rights and Duties of Life Tenants. A life tenant has the same rights as a fee simple owner, including the right to profits or rents, and the right to lease or mortgage the property. A life tenant also has the same duties as a fee simple owner: to pay taxes, assessments, and liens.

Because someone else has a future interest in the property, a life tenant must not commit **waste**, which means that the life tenant must not engage in acts that will permanently damage the property and harm the interests of the reversionary or remainder estate. The holder of the future interest (the reversioner or remainderman) generally has the right to inspect the property periodically.

A life tenant may transfer or lease her interest in the property. But it should be noted that the life tenant can give, sell, or lease only that which he has. In other words, a lease given by a life tenant will terminate upon the death of the person designated as the measuring life. The lease need not be honored by a remainderman. Similarly, a mortgage on a life estate loses its status as a valid lien upon the death of the person named as the measuring life. However, if a life tenant leases or mortgages the property and later dies, but the life estate continues because the person who is the measuring life is still alive, the lease or mortgage will continue according to its terms.

Leasehold Estates

Less-than-freehold estates are more commonly called **leasehold estates**. (In certain legal contexts, they're sometimes called "chattels real.") The holder of a leasehold estate is the tenant, who does not own the property, but rather has a right to exclusive possession of the property for a specified period.

The leasehold is created with a **lease**. The parties to a lease are the **landlord** (or **lessor**), who is the owner of the property, and the **tenant (lessee)**, the party with the right of possession. The lease creates the relationship of landlord and tenant. It grants the tenant the right of exclusive possession, with a reversion of the possessory rights to the landlord at the end of the rental period. During the term of the lease, the landlord's interest may be referred to as a **leased fee**.

The lease is a contract and its provisions are interpreted under contract law. We'll discuss lease contracts in more detail in Chapter 17, Property Management. For now, we'll simply describe the four types of leasehold estates. They are:

1. estate for years,
2. periodic tenancy,
3. tenancy at will, and
4. tenancy at sufferance.

Estate for Years. The estate for years (also called a term tenancy), is a tenancy for a fixed term. Note that the name "estate for years" is slightly misleading, in the sense that the duration need not be for a year or a period of years; it simply must be for some fixed term.

Example: Bob rents a cabin in the mountains from Clark for a period from June 1 through September 15. Bob has an estate for years because the rental term is fixed.

An estate for years can be created only by express agreement. It terminates automatically when the agreed term expires; neither party has to give notice of termination. If either the landlord or the tenant wants to terminate an estate for years before the end of the lease period, she may do so only if the other party consents. Termination of a lease by mutual consent is called **surrender**.

Fig. 3.2 Types of estates

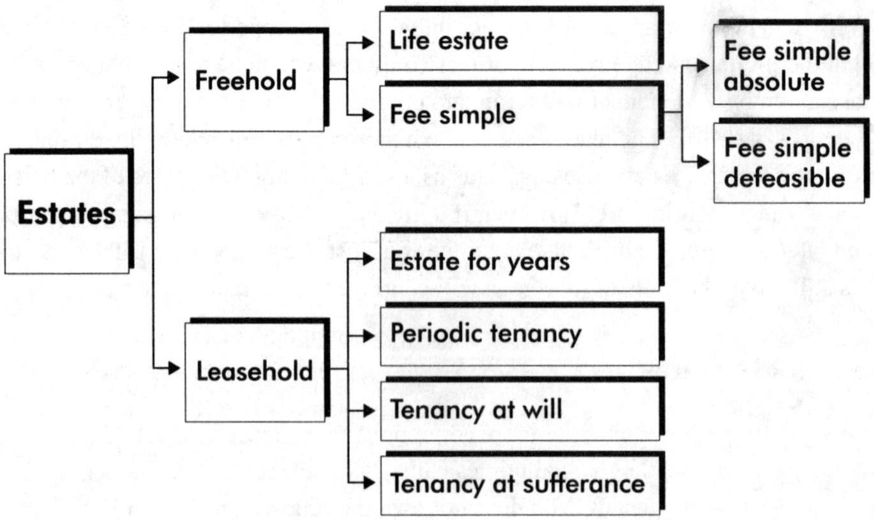

Unless the lease includes a no-assignment clause, an estate for years is assignable—that is, the tenant can assign his interest to another person.

Periodic Tenancy. A periodic tenancy, also called a periodic estate or an estate from period to period, has no fixed termination date. It lasts for a specific period (for example, one year, one month, or one week) and continues for successive similar periods (another year, month, or week) until either party gives the other proper notice of termination. Unlike an estate for years, which terminates automatically, a periodic tenancy automatically renews itself at the end of each period, unless one of the parties gives notice. Failure to give proper notice of termination results in the automatic extension of the lease for an additional period. The amount of notice required depends on state law.

Like an estate for years, a periodic tenancy is assignable unless assignment is prohibited by the terms of the lease agreement.

Tenancy at Will. In a tenancy at will (sometimes called an estate at will), the tenant has possession of the property with the landlord's consent for an indefinite period. A tenancy at will may arise when a periodic tenancy or an estate for years has terminated and the parties have not yet negotiated the terms of a new lease.

A tenancy at will is based on the mutual consent of the landlord and tenant, and it can be terminated at the will of either party at any time. Note, however, that most states require the terminating party to give the other party reasonable notice of termination; how much notice will be considered reasonable depends on state law.

Unlike an estate for years or a periodic tenancy, which are not affected by the death of the landlord or tenant, a tenancy at will automatically expires upon the death of either the landlord or the tenant. Also, a tenancy at will is not assignable.

Tenancy at Sufferance. The tenancy at sufferance is the lowest type of estate; in fact, though it's sometimes called an "estate at sufferance," technically it isn't an estate at all. A tenancy at sufferance arises when a tenant who came into possession of the property lawfully, under a valid lease, holds over after the lease has expired. The tenant (referred to as a **holdover tenant**) continues in possession of the premises, but without the consent of the landlord.

> **Example:** Tenant Joe has a one-year lease with Landlord Sam. At the end of the term, Joe refuses to move out. Joe initially obtained possession of the property legally (under a valid lease), but he is remaining on the property without Sam's consent. Joe is a holdover tenant, or tenant at sufferance.

Tenancy at sufferance is essentially a way of distinguishing between someone who entered into possession of the property legally, but no longer has a right to possession, and a trespasser, who never had permission to enter the land in the first place. Because a tenant at sufferance does not hold an estate (a possessory interest in the property), the landlord is not required to give the tenant notice of termination. Even so, in most places a tenant at sufferance cannot simply be forced off the property; the landlord is required to follow the proper legal procedures for eviction.

Methods of Holding Title

Title to real property may be held by one person, which is called ownership in severalty, or it may be held by two or more persons at the same time, which is called concurrent ownership.

Ownership in Severalty

When one person holds title to property individually, the property is owned **in severalty**. The term is derived from the word "sever," which means to keep separate or apart. A sole owner is free to dispose of the property at will. Real property may be owned in severalty by a natural person (a human being) or an artificial person (such as a corporation, a city, or a state).

Concurrent Ownership

Concurrent ownership (or **co-ownership**) exists when two or more people share title to a piece of property simultaneously. Concurrent ownership can take a number of different forms, depending on state law, and each form has distinctive legal characteristics. The forms of concurrent ownership include:

- tenancy in common,
- joint tenancy,
- community property, and
- tenancy by the entirety.

In addition, a few states recognize dower and curtesy rights, which give married people ownership interests in their spouse's property.

Tenancy in Common. Tenancy in common is the most basic form of concurrent ownership. In a tenancy in common, two or more individuals each have an **undivided interest** in a single piece of property. This means that each tenant in common has a right to share possession of the whole property, not just a specified part of it. One tenant in common can't be excluded from any portion of the property by the co-tenants. This is referred to as **unity of possession**.

Tenants in common may have equal or unequal interests. For example, if three people own property as tenants in common, they might each have a one-third interest in the property, or one of them might have a one-half interest in the property and each of the other two a one-quarter interest. But no matter how small a tenant in common's ownership interest is, he is still entitled to share possession of the whole property.

A tenant in common may deed her interest to someone else, without obtaining the consent of the other co-tenants. A tenant in common may also mortgage her interest without the others' consent. At death, a tenant in common's interest is transferred according to the terms of her will, or to the legal heirs.

Creating a Tenancy in Common. If a deed transferring land to two or more unmarried individuals doesn't specify how they are taking title, they take title as tenants in common. Co-owners may also choose tenancy in common by specifying this in the deed, adding "as tenants in common" after their names. If a deed does not state each tenant in common's fractional interest, the law presumes that the interests are equal.

Termination of Tenancy in Common. A tenancy in common may be terminated by a **partition suit**, a legal action that divides the ownership interests in the property and destroys the unity of possession. If possible, the court will actually divide the land into separate parcels and assign a parcel to each of the former co-tenants. If the property cannot be divided fairly, the court will order the property to be sold and the proceeds divided among the co-tenants in accordance with their fractional interests.

Joint Tenancy. The second form of concurrent ownership is joint tenancy. In a joint tenancy, two or more individuals are joint and equal owners of the property. The key feature that distinguishes joint tenancy from tenancy in common is the **right of survivorship**: on the death of one of the joint tenants, his interest automatically passes by operation of law to the other joint tenant(s). (See Figure 3.3.)

Creating a Joint Tenancy. To create a joint tenancy, the "four unities of title" must exist. These unities are:

- unity of interest,
- unity of title,
- unity of time, and
- unity of possession.

These four unities signify that each joint tenant has an equal interest in the property (unity of interest), that each received title through the same deed or will (unity of title), which was executed and delivered at a single time (unity of time), and that each is entitled to undivided possession of the property (unity of possession). If any one of these unities does not exist when the tenancy is created, a joint tenancy is not established.

Since title passes directly to the other joint tenant(s) upon the death of one joint tenant (because of the right of survivorship), property held in joint tenancy can't be willed. The heirs of a deceased joint tenant receive no interest in the joint tenancy property.

> **Example:** Jim, Sue, and Bill own property as joint tenants. Jim dies. Sue and Bill now own the entire property fifty-fifty. Jim's heirs cannot make any legal claim to the property. On his death, it ceased to be a part of his estate. Accordingly, the property is not subject to probate and could not have been willed by Jim.

Avoiding the delay and cost of probate proceedings (see Chapter 4) is one of the primary advantages of joint tenancy. Also, the survivors hold the property free from the claims of the deceased tenant's creditors and from any liens against her interest. The cost of avoiding probate is that a joint tenant gives up the right to dispose of his interest in the property by will.

Termination of Joint Tenancy. Like a tenancy in common, a joint tenancy can be terminated through a partition suit. But a joint tenancy also terminates automatically if any one of the four unities is destroyed. A joint tenant is free to convey his interest

Fig. 3.3 Tenancy in common vs. joint tenancy: death of a co-owner

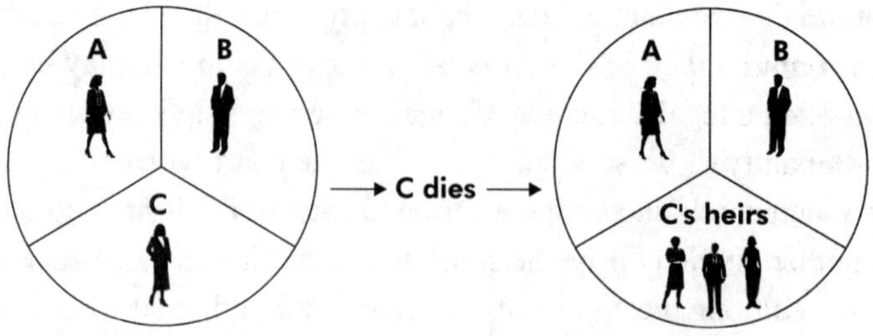

A, B, and C owned property as tenants in common. Then C died, and her heirs inherited her share of the property. Now the property is owned by A, B, and C's heirs as tenants in common.

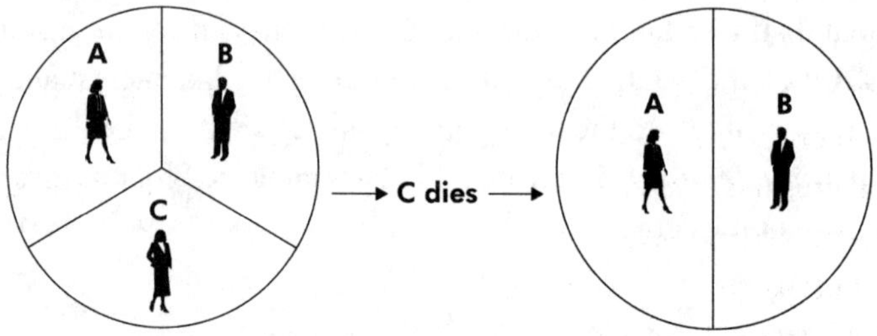

A, B, and C owned property as joint tenants, each with a 1/3 interest. Then C died. Now, by the right of survivorship A and B own the property as joint tenants, each with a 1/2 interest.

in the property to someone else. However, a conveyance destroys the unities of time and title. This terminates the joint tenancy with respect to the ownership of the conveying joint tenant.

> **Example:** Aaron, Bob, and Carrie own a piece of property as joint tenants. If Aaron conveys his interest to Alice, that terminates the joint tenancy with respect to that one-third interest. Since Alice didn't receive title through the same deed or at the same time as Bob and Carrie, Alice can't be a joint tenant. Bob and Carrie are still joint tenants in relation to one another, but Alice holds title as a tenant in common.

However, if a joint tenant executes a mortgage against her interest, that doesn't break the unity of title. The joint tenancy remains intact and valid.

Joint Tenancy and State Law. For the most part, the rules concerning joint tenancy that we've given here are the traditional common law rules. In many states, these rules have been modified by statute in various ways.

Note that in some states, a joint tenancy will not include the right of survivorship unless the intent to create this right is clearly stated in the deed or other document of conveyance. Also, several states do not recognize joint tenancy at all, although their laws do provide alternative means for creating rights of survivorship between unmarried parties.

Community Property. In certain states, ownership of property by married couples is governed by the community property system. This system is used in Arizona,

California, Idaho, Louisiana, Nevada, New Mexico, Texas, Washington, and Wisconsin. In addition, Alaska allows married couples to elect into the community property system by written agreement.

Under the community property system, all of the property owned by a married couple is classified either as the separate property of one spouse or as the community property of husband and wife.

A spouse's **separate property** is the property he or she owned before the marriage, together with any property he or she acquires during the marriage by inheritance, will, gift, or purchase with separate funds. All other property the husband or wife acquires during the marriage is **community property**. For example, property purchased with wages earned by either spouse during the marriage is community property. Each spouse has an undivided one-half interest in the community property.

The separate property of either spouse is free from the interests and claims of the other spouse; it may be transferred or encumbered without the approval or interference of the other spouse. A conveyance or encumbrance of community real property, however, requires the approval of both spouses. (The rules concerning transfer of community personal property vary from state to state.)

A married person is free to will his or her separate property to anyone. In addition, a married person has the right to will his or her undivided one-half interest in all community property to someone other than his or her spouse. If a married person dies intestate (without a will), his or her half interest in the community property may go to the surviving spouse or to the deceased spouse's descendants, depending on state law.

Tenancy by the Entirety. In most states that do not have a community property system, married couples may hold title to property as tenants by the entirety. A tenancy by the entirety (sometimes called tenancy by the entireties) involves the right of survivorship and is quite similar to a joint tenancy, but there are some differences. For one thing, a tenancy by the entirety can only be created by a married couple. Also, a tenant by the entirety cannot convey his interest without the consent of the other tenant (the spouse).

In some states, the intent to create a tenancy by the entirety must be specifically stated in the deed by which the property is acquired. In other states, the tenancy is created automatically when a married couple acquires real property.

A tenancy by the entirety may be terminated in any of the following ways:

- The spouses may agree to terminate the tenancy and execute a new deed.
- The spouses may divorce, in which case they become tenants in common.
- One spouse may die, in which case the surviving spouse becomes the sole owner of the property.
- A court may order the tenancy dissolved and the property sold, in order to pay a judgment against the spouses as joint debtors.

Tenancy by the entirety is not recognized in the states that use a community property system. It has been abolished in a number of other states as well.

Dower and Curtesy. In a few states, dower and curtesy laws still exist. Dower rights give a wife an interest in her husband's real property; curtesy rights give a husband an interest in his wife's real property. Upon the death of a husband or wife, the surviving spouse is entitled to a share of the deceased spouse's real property, even if the property has been willed to someone else. (The share is a one-half or one-third interest in the property, depending on state law.) The surviving spouse's interest lasts for the rest of his or her life.

Dower and curtesy laws generally permit a wife to dispose of her property without the husband's consent or signature; a husband, on the other hand, must have the wife's signature to dispose of his property. For this reason, dower rights are considered much stronger than curtesy rights. In states that still recognize dower and curtesy, when a married man transfers title to real property, it's important to have the wife also sign the deed. By signing the deed, the wife relinquishes her dower rights. Without this relinquishment, the wife might be able to claim an interest in the property after the death of the husband.

The majority of states have eliminated dower and curtesy laws and replaced them with probate laws that give a surviving spouse an elective share of a deceased spouse's real property. States with community property regimes have never recognized dower and curtesy rights.

Forms of Business Ownership

The discussion so far has focused on real property ownership by individuals, whether in severalty or concurrently. Real property can also be owned by business entities.

A business association may be organized as a:

- partnership,
- corporation,
- limited liability company,
- joint venture, or
- trust.

The parties who create a business entity usually decide which form of organization to use based on tax consequences and other considerations, such as the owners' personal liability for the business's debts. The form of organization affects how a business entity holds title to real property.

Partnerships. A partnership is generally defined as an association of two or more persons to carry on a business for profit, as co-owners. There are two types of partnerships: general and limited. In every state except Louisiana, partnerships are governed by the Uniform Partnership Act and the Uniform Limited Partnership Act.

General Partnerships. A general partnership is formed by contract. Although the contract isn't legally required to be in writing, it's advisable to spell out all the terms in a written agreement.

The partners in a general partnership all share in the profits and management of the partnership. Unless otherwise agreed, each one has an equal share of the profits and losses, and each has an equal voice in management and control of the business.

Each general partner has **unlimited liability**, which means that a partner can be held personally liable for the debts of the partnership. In other words, if the business is unable to pay its debts, its creditors can collect the money owed from an individual partner's personal assets.

Each partner is both a principal for and an agent of the general partnership for business purposes. Thus, the authorized acts of one partner (including the execution of legal documents) are binding on the partnership. A partnership is a fiduciary relationship; all the partners have a duty to act with utmost good faith toward one another. (See Chapter 9 for a discussion of agency and fiduciary relationships.)

In general, property acquired for the partnership's business is **partnership property**. Title to partnership property may be held in the names of one or more of the partners, or it may be held in the name of the partnership itself.

Unless otherwise agreed, each partner has an equal right to possess and use all partnership property for partnership purposes. However, a partner is not a co-owner of the partnership property and has no transferable interest in it. Partnership property is not subject to the claims of creditors of individual partners; it can be reached only by creditors of the partnership.

When title to partnership property is held in the partnership's name, it must also be conveyed in the partnership's name. Since each partner is an agent for the partnership, any authorized partner can sign the deed. When a partner dies, her rights in the partnership property pass to the surviving partners, and not to the deceased partner's heirs.

Limited Partnerships. A limited partnership is a partnership with one or more general partners and one or more limited partners. The general partners have unlimited liability for the limited partnership's debts and obligations. By contrast, the limited partners have limited liability (that is, they cannot be held personally liable for the partnership's debts and obligations).

The Uniform Limited Partnership Act originally allowed only general partners to manage or control the partnership's business; limited partners would lose their limited liability if they participated in management or control. The act now allows limited partners full participation without affecting their limited liability.

Corporations. A corporation is owned by its shareholders, individuals who purchase shares of stock in the company as an investment. But the corporation is legally a separate entity from its shareholders. In the eyes of the law, a corporation is an "artificial person." It can enter into contracts, own property, and incur debts and liabilities, just like a natural person (a human individual).

Shares in a corporation are **securities**. A security is an ownership interest that represents only an investment in an enterprise, without managerial control over it. Securities are regulated by the federal government through the Securities and Exchange Commission (SEC), and also by some state governments. Before a business can sell securities to the general public, the business must register the securities with the SEC and disclose specified information to investors. Laws concerning the sale of securities are sometimes called **blue sky laws**. (Note that shares of corporate stock aren't the only type of business interest classified as securities. For example, interests in a limited partnership are often securities.)

Every state provides for the establishment of corporations under state law, requiring articles of incorporation and other documents to be filed with the state government. A corporation is called a **domestic corporation** in the state where it was established. A **foreign corporation** is a corporation organized in a different state.

A corporation is capable of perpetual existence; the death of a shareholder does not affect its operation. Corporate property is owned by the corporation in severalty, not by the shareholders. The shareholders own only a right to share in the profits of the business. Their liability is limited.

The main drawback to the corporate form of organization is double taxation. First, the corporation must pay corporate income taxes on any profits it generates. Then, if the profits are distributed to the shareholders as dividends, the same money is taxed again as the personal income of the shareholders. Business investors can avoid double taxation by choosing a different form of organization, such as a partnership or a trust.

Note that a corporation cannot co-own property in joint tenancy. Since a corporation has a potentially perpetual existence, the other joint tenant could not really have a right of survivorship. Thus, when a corporation co-owns real property with another entity or person, they hold title as tenants in common.

Limited Liability Companies. In many states, business owners can organize their business as a limited liability company (LLC), which combines the advantages of the corporate and partnership forms.

To create an LLC, two or more business owners draw up an LLC operating agreement and file articles of organization with the state. LLC agreements can be quite flexible; the owners (referred to as members) can choose virtually any manner of allocating income, losses, or appreciation among themselves.

LLC members have the flexibility of a general partnership when it comes to managing the business. Certain members may be appointed to manage the company, or all of the members may manage the company. All managing members can bind the LLC with their actions. However, unlike general partners, an LLC's managing members are not personally liable for the company's liabilities. LLC members have the same type of limited liability enjoyed by corporate stockholders or limited partners. Regardless of their level of participation in the company, LLC members risk only their initial investment in the company.

As we noted, a major disadvantage of the corporate form of ownership is the double taxation imposed on corporations and their stockholders. Income earned by an LLC, on the other hand, is taxed only as the personal income of each member, in the same manner as partnership income.

Joint Ventures. A joint venture is similar to a partnership, except that it is created for a single business transaction or for a series of individual transactions. It is not intended to be an ongoing business of indefinite duration. Joint ventures are generally governed by the same rules as partnerships. An example of a joint venture would be a property owner, an architect, and a building contractor joining together to design and construct a particular building.

Trusts. In a trust, one or more **trustees** manage property for the benefit of others (the **beneficiaries**). A trust instrument vests title to the property in the trustees, who have only the powers expressly granted in the instrument. Trusts are sometimes used as a form of business ownership.

The person who creates a trust (by executing the trust instrument that appoints the trustees and establishes the rules they must follow) is called the **trustor**. A **living trust** or **inter vivos trust** is one that is established while the trustor is still alive. A **testamentary trust** is one established under the terms of the trustor's will.

Real Estate Investment Trusts. A real estate investment trust (REIT) is an entity created by investors to finance large real estate projects. The Internal Revenue Code offers tax benefits to real estate investors who organize their business as an REIT. An REIT must have at least 100 investors and at least 75% of its investment assets must be in real estate. Shares in an REIT are securities, subject to federal regulation.

An REIT isn't subject to double taxation. As long as at least 90% of its income is distributed to the shareholders, the trust pays taxes only on the earnings it retains. Yet the investors, like corporate shareholders, are shielded from liability for the REIT's debts.

Syndication. Some businesses are referred to as syndicates. A syndicate is simply a business association in which investors pool their money together to establish and carry on an enterprise. A real estate syndicate is one in which the investors' money is used to purchase, manage, and/or develop a piece of real estate.

Note that a syndicate is not a specific type of legal entity. It may be organized as a partnership, corporation, limited liability company, or trust. Real estate investment trusts and real estate limited partnerships are both examples of real estate syndicates.

Common Interest Developments

Condominiums, planned unit developments, and other common interest developments provide alternatives to ownership of a traditional single-family home. In a sense, they combine aspects of individual ownership with aspects of concurrent ownership. They have become popular because of their efficient use of increasingly valuable land. State laws usually have very specific requirements concerning the creation and management of common interest developments.

Condominiums

Someone who buys a unit in a condominium owns the unit itself in severalty, but shares ownership of the common elements with other unit owners as tenants in common. **Common elements** (also called common areas) are aspects of the condominium property that all of the unit owners have the right to use, such as the driveway, lobby, courtyard, or elevator. The land itself, the roof, and any recreational facilities such as a swimming pool are also considered common elements.

Some features may be designated as **limited common elements**, which are reserved for the owners of certain units. For example, an assigned parking space would be a limited common element. A feature such as a balcony, which is designed for use with a particular unit but is outside of the unit itself, would also be a limited common element.

Each unit owner obtains separate financing to buy his unit, receives an individual property tax bill, and may acquire a title insurance policy for the unit. A lien can attach to a single unit, so that the unit can be foreclosed on separately, without affecting the other units in the condominium.

The condominium is managed by the **unit owners association**, which collects regular and special assessments from each owner for the maintenance, repair, and insurance of the common elements. (The regular assessments, often collected on a monthly basis, are sometimes called condo fees or dues.) Management decisions are typically made by an elected board of directors. Certain aspects of the way in which a unit owners association is governed may be dictated by state law.

The sale of an individual unit in a condominium ordinarily doesn't require the approval of the other unit owners, although some owners associations retain a right of first refusal on the sale of any unit. This means that if a unit owner decides to sell her unit, the association has the right to purchase it. If the association declines, the owner can sell the unit to a third party, but the price can't be lower than the price that was offered to the association. In most states, the seller is required to give prospective buyers a copy of the bylaws, the latest financial statement, and the CC&Rs (covenants, conditions, and restrictions) of the condominium project, including notice of any prior restrictions on renting the unit. When the sale of the unit is completed, the seller's interest in the common elements passes to the buyer.

A condominium usually involves one or more multi-family residential buildings, but commercial and industrial properties can also be developed as condominiums. To establish a condominium, the developer must record a condominium plan and declaration. Condominium projects are generally regulated as subdivisions.

Sometimes the owner of an apartment complex will find it profitable to change the complex into a condominium. This process, called **conversion**, may be regulated to protect renters who will be displaced. For instance, when an apartment building is converted to a condominium project, the owner may be required to give tenants six months' advance written notice of the conversion.

Townhouses

A townhouse development consists of multi-story, single-family homes built on small parcels of land. Townhouses may or may not share walls with neighboring units, and the developments sometimes have owners associations similar to those in condominium developments.

Townhouse ownership is similar to condominium ownership in that the owner holds an individual ownership interest in his unit and an undivided shared interest in the townhouse development's common areas. However, the townhouse owner also owns the land underneath the townhouse unit, and townhouses cannot be stacked on top of each other.

Planned Unit Developments

In a planned unit development (PUD), a buyer purchases a single-family home and the parcel of land on which it is located, along with a shared interest in the development's common areas. These parcels may be relatively small, in order to maximize the space available for common areas; in fact, housing density may be twice that of a typical subdivision.

A PUD's common areas might include a park or other open areas, a swimming pool or other recreational facilities, and even a retail shopping area. As in condominium developments, owners in a PUD belong to a homeowners association and are typically subject to numerous restrictions in the form of CC&Rs.

Cooperatives

In a cooperative, ownership of the property is vested in a single entity—usually a nonprofit corporation. The residents of the cooperative building own shares in the corporation, rather than owning the property itself. They are tenants with long-term **proprietary leases** on their units; they do not hold title to their units. In other words, they have leasehold estates in the property.

To establish a cooperative, the corporation gets a mortgage loan to buy or construct the building, and other funds are raised by selling shares in the corporation to prospective tenants. The rent that each tenant pays to the corporation is a pro rata share of the mortgage, taxes, operating expenses, and other debts for the whole property. The cooperative corporation is managed by an elected board of directors. If one tenant defaults on her share of the mortgage payments, the other tenants must make up the difference or risk having the mortgage on the entire project foreclosed. This is also true for tax assessments and other liens.

In some cooperatives, a tenant cannot transfer stock or assign his proprietary lease to a new tenant without the consent of the governing board or a majority of the members. This approval process is used to screen out undesirable tenants; however, discrimination in violation of fair housing laws is not allowed (see Chapter 16).

Most cooperatives were created in large eastern cities during the first half of the twentieth century, before the condominium form of ownership had been developed. Nowadays, when a multi-family building is constructed as or converted to a common interest development, it's much more likely to be a condominium than a cooperative.

Timeshares

In a timeshare arrangement, multiple owners purchase interests in a property, typically a vacation home or resort. Instead of purchasing all of the rights to an individual unit, a buyer purchases a "time slot," or the right to use the facilities for a specified amount of time each year. Timesharing has become popular in many vacation areas of the United States, where ownership of a unit for the entire year is, for most people, both expensive and unnecessary. Each state has its own laws governing the sale and ownership of timeshares.

Timeshare ownership can take two forms: a timeshare estate, or a timeshare use. With a **timeshare estate**, also called interval ownership, the buyer receives a fee simple interest in the property for a specific time period. As an owner, the buyer shares responsibility for maintenance, taxes, and common area expenses (these are prorated according to the number of ownership periods in the property). In turn, the buyer also shares in any appreciation or equity increase in the property.

With a **timeshare use**, the buyer only purchases the right to use the property for a certain time period each year for a specified number of years (20 years, for example). The buyer does not actually become an owner and thus is not responsible for property expenses, nor does she benefit from an increase in the property's value.

Chapter Summary

1. An estate is a possessory interest in real property. Someone who has a freehold estate has title to the property and is considered an owner. Someone who has a leasehold (less-than-freehold) estate has possession of the property, but does not have title.

2. Freehold estates include the fee simple absolute, the fee simple defeasible, and the life estate. A life estate lasts only as long as a specified person is alive; then the property either reverts to the grantor or else passes to the remainderman. Leasehold estates include the estate for years, the periodic tenancy, and the tenancy at will. (The tenancy at sufferance, which arises when a tenant holds over without the landlord's permission, is not really an estate.)

3. Title to real property can be held in severalty or concurrently. The methods of concurrent ownership are tenancy in common, joint tenancy, community property, and tenancy by the entirety. Tenancy in common is recognized in all states; each of the others is recognized only in certain states. The distinguishing feature of a joint tenancy is the right of survivorship. Community property and tenancy by the entirety are forms of ownership available only to married couples. In some states, married couples have dower and curtesy rights.

4. Real property can be owned by a business, which may be organized as a general or limited partnership, a corporation, a limited liability company, a joint venture, or a real estate investment trust.

5. Common interest developments include condominiums, townhouses, planned unit developments, cooperatives, and timeshares. In condominiums, townhouses, and planned unit developments, each unit is separately owned, and all the unit owners share ownership of the common elements as tenants in common. A cooperative is owned by a corporation; a resident owns shares in the corporation, and has a proprietary lease for a particular unit. In a timeshare arrangement, multiple owners share a vacation property, with each one's right of possession limited to a specified period each year.

Key Terms

Estate—An interest in land that is or may become possessory.

Freehold estate—A possessory interest that has an indeterminable duration and includes title.

Less-than-freehold (leasehold) estate—A possessory interest that has a limited duration and does not include title.

Fee simple absolute—The highest and most complete form of ownership, which is of potentially infinite duration.

Fee simple defeasible—A fee simple estate that carries a qualification, so that ownership may revert to the grantor if a specified event occurs or a condition is not met. Also called a defeasible fee or qualified fee.

Life estate—A freehold estate whose duration is measured by the lifetime of one or more persons.

Waste—Permanent damage to real property caused by the party in possession, harming the interests of other estate holders.

Estate for years—A leasehold estate with a fixed term. Also called a term tenancy.

Periodic tenancy—A leasehold estate that is renewed at the end of each period unless one party gives notice of termination. Also called a periodic estate.

Tenancy at will—A leasehold estate that may arise after a periodic tenancy or an estate for years terminates; the tenant occupies the property with the landlord's consent, but the duration of the tenancy is uncertain. Also called an estate at will.

Ownership in severalty—Sole ownership of property.

Tenancy in common—Joint ownership where there is no right of survivorship.

Joint tenancy—Joint ownership with right of survivorship.

Right of survivorship—The right by which the surviving joint tenant(s) acquire a joint tenant's interest in the property upon her death.

Community property—Property owned jointly by husband and wife (in states that use a community property system).

Tenancy by the entirety—A form of joint ownership of property by a married couple; recognized in most states that do not use a community property system.

Dower and curtesy rights—Dower rights give a wife an interest in her husband's real property; curtesy rights give a husband an interest in his wife's real property.

Partnership—An association of two or more persons to carry on a business for profit, as co-owners. In a general partnership, all of the partners have unlimited liability for the debts of the business. In a limited partnership, the limited partners are shielded from personal liability for the debts of the business, but the general partners are not.

Corporation—An artificial person; a legal entity separate from its shareholders.

Limited liability company—A form of business organization that is an alternative to a partnership or corporation.

Real estate investment trust—An entity that invests primarily in real estate and that can qualify for tax advantages if certain requirements are met.

Condominium—A property that has been developed so that individual unit owners have separate title to their own units, but share ownership of the common elements as tenants in common.

Cooperative—A property that is owned by a corporation and tenanted by shareholders in the corporation who have proprietary leases for their units.

Planned unit development—A development with smaller lots placed close together, in order to leave more land available for open space and other common areas.

Timeshare—An ownership interest or use right that gives a holder a right to possession of the property for a specific limited period of time each year.

Chapter Quiz

1. A fee simple title in real estate is of indefinite duration, and can be:
   a) freely transferred
   b) encumbered
   c) inherited
   d) All of the above

2. A conveyance of title with the condition that the land shall not be used for the sale of intoxicating beverages creates a:
   a) less-than-freehold estate
   b) fee simple defeasible
   c) life estate
   d) reservation

3. Lewis was given real property for the term of his natural life. Which of the following statements is incorrect?
   a) Lewis has a freehold estate
   b) Lewis has a fee simple estate
   c) Lewis is the life tenant
   d) If Lewis leases the property to someone else, the lease will terminate if Lewis dies during its term

4. Baker sold a property to Lane, but reserved a life estate for himself and remained in possession. Later Baker sells his life estate to Clark and surrenders possession to Clark. Lane then demands immediate possession as fee owner. Which of the following is true?
   a) Lane is entitled to possession
   b) Clark should sue Baker for return of the purchase price
   c) Baker is liable for damages
   d) Clark can retain possession during Baker's lifetime

5. Cobb owns a property in fee simple; he deeds it to Smith for the life of Jones. Which of the following is true?
   a) Jones holds a life estate; Smith holds an estate in reversion
   b) Smith holds a life estate; Cobb holds an estate in remainder
   c) Smith holds a fee simple estate; Jones holds a life estate
   d) Smith holds a life estate; Cobb holds an estate in reversion

6. Johnston, a life tenant, decides to cut down all the trees on the ten-acre property and sell them as timber. Mendez, the remainderman, can stop Johnston's actions because:
   a) a life tenant is never permitted to cut down any trees on the property for any reason
   b) a life tenant cannot commit waste
   c) Mendez's interest is superior to Johnston's, since it is a possessory estate
   d) None of the above; Mendez has no legal grounds for stopping Johnston

7. Jones and Adams signed an agreement for the use and possession of real estate, for a period of 120 days. This is a/an:
   a) estate for years
   b) tenancy at sufferance
   c) periodic tenancy
   d) tenancy at will

8. The four unities of title, time, interest, and possession are necessary for a:
   a) tenancy in common
   b) partnership
   c) mortgage
   d) joint tenancy

9. Which of the following is incorrect? Joint tenants always have:
   a) equal rights to possession of the property
   b) the right to will good title to heirs
   c) the right of survivorship
   d) equal interests in the property

10. A, B, and C own property as joint tenants. C dies and B sells her interest in the property to D. The property is now owned:
    a) as joint tenants by A, D, and C's widow E, his sole heir
    b) by A and D as joint tenants
    c) by A and D as tenants in common
    d) None of the above

11. Asher and Blake own real property together. Asher has a one-third interest and Blake has a two-thirds interest. How do they hold title?
    a) Community property
    b) Tenancy at will
    c) Joint tenancy
    d) Tenancy in common

12. All of the following statements about a corporation are true, except:
    a) a corporation has a potentially perpetual existence
    b) each shareholder is individually liable for the corporation's acts
    c) corporations are subject to double taxation
    d) a corporation can enter into contracts in essentially the same way as an individual person

13. A real estate investment trust is required to:
    a) invest primarily in real estate
    b) have at least 150 participating investors
    c) have investors accept liability for the trust's acts
    d) be incorporated in the state in which it does business

14. In a condominium:
    a) individual units are owned in severalty, while common elements are owned in joint tenancy
    b) individual units are owned in joint tenancy, while common elements are owned in severalty
    c) individual units are owned in severalty, while common elements are owned in tenancy in common
    d) the entire building is owned in tenancy in common, with residents owning shares

15. A unit in a cooperative is owned:
    a) in severalty by its resident
    b) by the corporation that owns the building, in which the resident owns shares
    c) in tenancy in common among all residents of the building
    d) in partnership among all residents of the building

Answer Key

1. d) A fee simple owner has the full bundle of rights.

2. b) A fee simple defeasible is an estate that will fail if a certain event occurs.

3. b) Although a life estate is a freehold estate, it is not a fee simple estate.

4. d) Baker was entitled to sell his life estate to Clark. Clark can retain possession during Baker's lifetime.

5. d) Smith has possession of the property for the duration of Jones's life, so Smith has a life estate. Cobb has an estate in reversion, because the property will revert to Cobb after Jones's death.

6. b) A life tenant cannot commit waste, which means that the life tenant cannot damage the property or harm the interests of the remainderman.

7. a) An estate for years (or term tenancy) has a set termination date.

8. d) A valid joint tenancy requires all four unities: title, time, interest, possession.

9. b) A joint tenant cannot will his interest in the property. The right of survivorship means the surviving joint tenants acquire the deceased tenant's title.

10. c) When C dies, his interest in the property goes to the other joint tenants, A and B. When B sells her interest to D, the joint tenancy is terminated and a tenancy in common is created between A and D.

11. d) Because their interests in the property are unequal, Asher and Blake must be tenants in common.

12. b) A corporation's shareholders have limited liability for the corporation's actions.

13. a) A real estate investment trust must invest primarily in real estate. The minimum number of investors is 100, not 150.

14. c) In a condominium, residents own their individual units in severalty, but own the common elements as tenants in common.

15. b) A cooperative is owned by a business entity, usually a corporation. Residents purchase shares in the corporation and receive long-term leases, rather than title to their units.

Chapter 4

Transferring Ownership

I. Title and Alienation
II. Voluntary Alienation
  A. Patents
  B. Deeds
    1. Types of deeds
    2. Requirements for a valid deed
    3. Acknowledgment, delivery, and acceptance
  C. Wills
III. Involuntary Alienation
  A. Dedication
  B. Intestate succession
  C. Escheat
  D. Condemnation
  E. Court decisions
  F. Adverse possession
  G. Accession
IV. Recording
  A. Recording procedures
  B. Legal effects of recording
    1. Notice
    2. Priority
V. Title Protection
  A. Title searches
  B. Types of title protection
    1. Abstracts of title
    2. Opinions and certificates of title
    3. Title insurance
    4. Torrens system
VI. Security Interests in Fixtures

Chapter Overview

A real property owner may transfer ownership of the property to someone else by choice, as when an owner deeds property to a buyer or wills it to a friend. Ownership of real property may also be transferred involuntarily, as in a foreclosure sale or a condemnation. This chapter explains the various ways (voluntary and involuntary) in which title to real property may change hands. It also discusses how and why deeds and other documents are recorded, and how title insurance and other forms of title protection work.

Title and Alienation

We'll begin by clarifying some terminology. A person who owns property is said to have **title** to it. Title is an abstract concept that refers to the rights of ownership. In connection with certain types of property, "title" is also used to refer to an actual document that serves as proof of ownership. For example, the owner of an automobile has a certificate of ownership that's generally called the title. That isn't the way the term is used in the real estate field, however. A real property owner doesn't have a document called the title to the property; instead, the document that provides proof of ownership is called a deed. You may hear a deed informally referred to as the title, but that's not considered strictly correct.

Problems with a real property owner's title are called **title defects** or **clouds** on title. For example, if someone other than the current owner claims an interest in the property based on a transaction that took place long ago, that claim is a title defect or cloud on the owner's title. The owner might have to take legal action to resolve the claim and remove the defect or clear away the cloud. Title that is free from serious defects is called **marketable title**.

The process of transferring ownership of (title to) real property from one party to another is called **alienation**. Alienation may be either voluntary or involuntary. Voluntary alienation occurs when an owner deliberately transfers title to someone else. Involuntary alienation, a transfer of title without any action by the owner, can be the result of rule of law, accession, or occupancy (adverse possession). We'll examine the different methods of voluntary alienation, then discuss involuntary alienation.

Voluntary Alienation

Voluntary alienation of real property includes the transfer of title by patent, by deed, or by will.

Patents

Title to real property originates with the sovereign government. The government holds title to all of the land within its borders, except the land that it has granted to various other entities or persons. Title to land is transferred from the government to a private party with a document known as a **land patent**. The patent is the ultimate source of title for all land under private ownership. A transfer of title from the government to a private party by means of a patent is referred to as a **public grant**.

Deeds

The most common method of voluntary alienation is transfer by deed. With a deed, the owner of real property, called the **grantor**, transfers all or part of his interest in the property to another party, called the **grantee**. The process of transferring real property by deed is known as **conveyance**. A grantor conveys real property to a grantee by means of a deed.

Types of Deeds. There are many different types of deeds, including warranty deeds (general and special), grant deeds, bargain and sale deeds, quitclaim deeds, and deeds executed under court order. However, not every type of deed is recognized in every state.

General Warranty Deed. The general warranty deed (also known simply as the warranty deed) is the most widely used type of deed, the one that's considered standard in a majority of the states. This type of deed gives the greatest protection to the grantee.

With a general warranty deed, the grantor makes certain basic promises to the grantee concerning the title to the property. These promises, called **covenants**, are guarantees against title defects. If the covenants are breached, the grantee has a right to sue the grantor for financial compensation. The covenants apply not only to defects that may have arisen during the grantor's tenure (period of ownership), but also to any defects that arose before the grantor owned the property.

The first covenant is called the **covenant of seisin**. Seisin (also spelled seizin) means possession of property under a claim of ownership. The covenant of seisin is a promise that the grantor actually owns the property interest that's being transferred to the grantee.

The **covenant of right to convey** is a promise that the grantor has the power (the legal capacity) to make the conveyance. Note that this covenant is fulfilled if the person executing the deed is an agent of the owner and has the authority to transfer the interest in question. (The right to convey is sometimes considered part of the covenant of seisin, rather than a separate covenant.)

The **covenant against encumbrances** warrants that the property is not burdened by any undisclosed easements, mortgages, liens, or other rights of third parties. If there are encumbrances, they must be disclosed in the deed.

The **covenant of quiet enjoyment** is a guarantee that the grantee will be able to possess the property in peace, undisturbed by any lawful claim made by a third party. (It does not protect the grantee from claims that have no legal basis, which are called spurious claims.)

The **covenant of further assurance** warrants that the grantor will provide the grantee with any additional instruments (legal documents) that are needed, or take any other steps required, to make the grantee's title good.

Fig. 4.1 Example of a warranty deed

Warranty Deed

THIS INDENTURE, Made the 21st day of December, in the year two thousand fourteen, between Alan S. Matsumoto of the County of Middleton and the State of Anystate, hereinafter called the GRANTOR, and Joseph R. Shapiro and Helen L. Shapiro, residing at 3406 N.W. 66th St., Anytown, Anystate, hereinafter called the GRANTEE.

WITNESSETH that in consideration of the sum of ten dollars ($10.00) and other valuable consideration in hand paid by the Grantee to the Grantor, the Grantor conveys and warrants unto the Grantee, the Grantee's heirs, successors and assigns forever, the following described land, situated in the County of Middleton, State of Anystate:

LOT 12, BLOCK 8, JASPERSON ADDITION TO THE CITY OF ANYTOWN, ACCORDING TO THE PLAT THEREOF RECORDED IN VOLUME 10 OF PLATS, PAGE 94,RECORDS OF MIDDLETON COUNTY, ANYSTATE.

Subject to: [list encumbrances the property will be subject to, e.g. mortgages, easements, etc.].

Utility easement over western 20 feet of property in favor of Megapower Company, recording number 920923016098.

The Grantor is lawfully seized in fee simple of the above property, and has good right to convey the same.

The Grantee shall peaceably and quietly enjoy the above property.

The Grantor will forever warrant and defend the title to the above property against the lawful claims and demands of all persons.

TO HAVE AND TO HOLD the same, together with all the buildings, improvements and appurtenances belonging thereto, if any, to the Grantee and Grantee's heirs, successors and assigns forever.

IN WITNESS WHEREOF, Grantor has signed and sealed this deed, the day and year above written. Signed, sealed, and delivered in the presence of:

Gary Martinez
Witness

Alan S. Matsumoto
Grantor

Claire M. Vincent
Notary Public

Notary Public in and for the State of Anystate

[Notary Seal]

Residing at Anytown

My appointment expires 01-16-16

The final covenant in the warranty deed is the **covenant of warranty forever**. This is a promise that the grantor will defend the grantee's title against any claims superior to the grantee's that existed when the conveyance was made.

In most states these covenants are implied when certain words are included in the language of the deed or when a statutory warranty deed form is used; they do not have to be expressly stated in the deed. Other states require the covenants to be set forth in the deed.

At one time, the covenants in a deed were the grantee's only protection against title defects. Today, however, most grantees rely on title insurance or some other form of title protection instead of the covenants in their deed. (Title protection is discussed at the end of this chapter.)

One important characteristic that distinguishes warranty deeds from some other types of deeds is that warranty deeds convey **after-acquired title**. This means that if the grantor's title was defective at the time the deed was executed, but the grantor later acquires a more perfect title, the additional interest passes automatically to the grantee under the original deed.

> **Example:** Warner conveyed her property to Meyers on June 1, using a general warranty deed. However, because of a problem with an earlier deed, Warner did not have valid title to the property on June 1. On August 12, Warner received good title to the property under a properly executed deed. On that same day, Meyers automatically acquired good title to the property.

Special Warranty Deed. A special (or limited) warranty deed contains the same covenants found in a general warranty deed, but the scope of the covenants is limited to defects that arose during the grantor's tenure. The grantor makes no assurances regarding defects that already may have existed before the grantor acquired the property.

Special warranty deeds are most often used by entities that don't have the authority to make more extensive warranties, such as a corporation or a fiduciary. (A fiduciary is someone who has been empowered to act on behalf of another person; examples include a trustee, a court-appointed guardian, or the executor of a deceased person's estate.) Someone who acquired title at a tax sale or foreclosure sale might also use a special warranty deed to convey the property.

Special warranty deeds convey after-acquired title, in exactly the same way that general warranty deeds do.

Grant Deed. In a few states, grant deeds are used instead of warranty deeds. A grant deed generally includes the term "grant" in its words of conveyance and carries two warranties:

1. the grantor has not previously conveyed title to anyone else, and
2. the grantor has not caused any encumbrances to attach to the property other than those already disclosed.

Depending on state law, these two basic warranties may apply even if they are not expressly stated in the grant deed. Additional covenants may be added to the deed if the parties wish to do so.

Like a warranty deed, a grant deed conveys after-acquired title to the grantee.

Bargain and Sale Deed. Unlike the types of deeds we've discussed so far, a bargain and sale deed offers the grantee no warranties or covenants. A grantor who executes a bargain and sale deed implies that he owns the property, but doesn't guarantee even that much. Also, this type of deed won't convey after-acquired title to the grantee.

Because of these limitations, in many states bargain and sale deeds are never or rarely used. In other states, their use tends to be restricted to special circumstances.

Quitclaim Deed. A quitclaim deed contains no warranties of any sort, and it will not convey after-acquired title. In fact, unlike a bargain and sale deed, a quitclaim deed does not even imply that the grantor owns the property. It conveys only whatever interest the grantor has when the deed is delivered to the grantee. If the grantor has no interest at that time, the deed conveys nothing. But if the grantor does have an interest in the property, a quitclaim deed will convey it just as well as any other type of deed.

One common reason for using a quitclaim deed is to correct a technical flaw in an earlier conveyance. A quitclaim deed used in this fashion is sometimes called a correction deed, a reformation deed, or a deed of confirmation.

Example: Henderson conveys property to Schilling using a general warranty deed. Later Schilling notices that his name is spelled "Shilling" on the deed. Since it could cause confusion about who owns the property or cause the deed to be overlooked in a title search, the misspelling creates a cloud on Schilling's title. To correct this problem, Schilling asks Henderson to execute a quitclaim deed with his name spelled correctly that includes a statement indicating that this is a correction of the earlier deed.

A quitclaim deed can also be used to prevent or clear away clouds caused by the possibility that someone other than the current owner might be able to claim an interest in the property.

Example: Williams, a married woman, owns some land separately from her husband. She conveys it to Goldstein using a general warranty deed, but her husband doesn't sign the deed. Although this was a valid conveyance without the husband's signature, it's possible that he could later claim an interest in the property. (This might be true in a community property state or a state that recognizes dower and curtesy. See Chapter 3.) To clear away the cloud this possibility creates, Goldstein (or a later owner) could ask Mr. Williams to execute a quitclaim deed releasing any interest he might have.

A transfer of real property between family members is often made with a quitclaim deed. This type of deed is also used when the grantor is unsure of the validity of her title and wishes to avoid giving any warranties.

Example: Alvarez holds title by virtue of an inheritance that is being challenged in probate court. If Alvarez wants to transfer the property, she will probably use a quitclaim deed, because she is not sure that her title is valid.

In a quitclaim deed, words such as "grant" or "convey" should be avoided. The use of these words may imply that the grantor is warranting the title. A quitclaim deed should use only terms such as "release," "remise," or "quitclaim" to describe the transfer.

Deeds Executed by Court Order. A deed executed by court order is used to convey title after a court-ordered sale of property. A common example is the **sheriff's deed** used to transfer property to the highest bidder at a court-ordered foreclosure sale (see Chapter 11). Court-ordered deeds usually state the exact amount of the purchase price approved by the court and carry no warranties.

Other Deeds. You may hear reference to various other deeds, such as a tax deed, a trustee's deed, an executor's deed, or a gift deed. For the most part, these aren't actually special types of deeds, but one of the types we've already described (such as a special warranty deed or a quitclaim deed) that's being used in a particular situation or for a particular purpose. For example, a **gift deed** is simply a deed that conveys property as a gift to the grantee; the grantor may choose whether to use a warranty deed or a quitclaim deed for that purpose. (As we'll discuss shortly, in a gift deed the recital of consideration says that the consideration for the transfer was "love and affection," instead of specifying monetary consideration.)

A deed of trust (or trust deed) is a security instrument similar to a mortgage, not a deed that is used to transfer title. Deeds of trust are discussed in Chapter 11.

Requirements for a Valid Deed. A deed will transfer title only if it meets the requirements for validity set by state law. To be valid in most states, a deed must:

- be in writing,
- identify the parties,
- have a legally competent grantor,
- have a living grantee,
- be signed by the grantor,
- include an adequate description of the property,
- recite the consideration exchanged,
- contain words of conveyance (the granting clause),
- define the interest conveyed (the habendum clause), and
- state any exclusions or reservations.

In Writing. Each state has a law called the **statute of frauds**, which requires certain contracts and other legal transactions to be in writing. With only a few minor exceptions, the statute of frauds applies to any transfer of an interest in real property. An unwritten deed cannot transfer title; it has no legal effect.

Identification of the Parties. Both the grantor and the grantee must be identified in the deed. The name of the grantor must be spelled correctly and consistently. The grantee's name is not strictly required, as long as there is a description that makes identification possible, such as "John T. Smith's only sister."

At one time, when property was conveyed by or to a husband and wife, the deed would commonly say (for example), "John T. Smith, et ux." "Et ux." is a Latin abbreviation that means "and wife." Now the standard practice is to give the name of each spouse in full.

You may also encounter the Latin abbreviation "et al.," which means "and others." For example, if several co-owners are conveying property, the deed might list one or two of them by name and then use "et al." to refer to the other grantors. However, although the abbreviation is useful in other contexts, it shouldn't be used on a deed except in unusual circumstances.

Legally Competent Grantor. A deed is valid only if the grantor is legally competent when she executes the deed. This generally means that the grantor must have reached the age of majority (18 years old in most states) and must be of sound mind.

A grantor is generally considered to be of sound mind if he understands the nature and effect of the deed at the time of conveyance. If the grantor is not of sound mind, the deed may be either void or voidable, depending on state law. (The distinction between void and voidable is discussed in Chapter 7.)

Living Grantee. The grantee does not have to be legally competent in order for the deed to be valid. It is only necessary for the grantee to be alive (or, if the grantee is a corporation, legally in existence) and identifiable when the deed is executed.

Signed by the Grantor. In addition to requiring a deed to be in writing, the statute of frauds also requires it to be signed by the party who is to be bound by the transfer—the grantor. (Note that the grantee does not ordinarily sign the deed.) A deed is considered to be executed when the grantor signs it. If the grantor's signature is a forgery, the deed is void.

If the grantor can't sign her full name (due to disability or illiteracy), she may sign by making a mark, such as an X. But a signature by mark must be accompanied by the signatures of witnesses who can attest to the grantor's execution of the deed.

A deed may also be signed by the grantor's **attorney in fact**. The attorney in fact (not necessarily a lawyer) is someone the grantor has appointed to act on his behalf in a document called a **power of attorney**. The power of attorney must specifically authorize the attorney in fact to convey the property, and in many states it must be recorded along with the deed.

If there is more than one grantor, each grantor must sign the deed. If the previous deed named several grantees, all of them must sign as grantors on the new deed when they convey the property to someone else.

When a married person conveys title to real property, his or her spouse may also be required to sign the deed, in order to waive any marital rights provided by state law. (See Chapter 3.)

In some states, the grantor's signature must be witnessed, and the witnesses (generally two) must also sign the deed in order for it to be valid. In addition, a number of eastern states require a seal after the grantor's signature.

Most states now allow legal documents such as deeds to be signed electronically using a special mark or encoded symbol. As long as they meet certain requirements, these electronic signatures satisfy the statute of frauds.

The law regarding conveyances of real property made by corporations varies significantly from one state to another. As a general rule, a deed from a corporation must be signed by an authorized officer of the corporation, and the signature must be accompanied by the corporate seal. The authority to convey real property may be derived from the bylaws of the corporation or from a resolution passed by the board of directors.

Description of the Property. A valid deed must contain an adequate description of the property to be conveyed. Although the property's full legal description should always be used, a deed may be valid without it, as long as it includes a description that would enable the property to be identified. (Land description is discussed in Chapter 2.)

Recital of Consideration. In most states, a deed must include a statement concerning the consideration given to the grantor by the grantee in exchange for the property. **Consideration** is something of value, such as money or property, exchanged by the parties to a contract or other transaction. As a general rule, a contract or conveyance is valid only if the parties exchange consideration; in other words, each party must give the other something of value (see Chapter 7).

The recital of consideration in a deed usually states a nominal dollar amount rather than the actual purchase price. For example, many deeds say "in consideration of $1.00 and other valuable consideration," or just "for valuable consideration." This type of nominal recital serves to indicate that the grantee purchased the property instead of receiving it as a gift, without disclosing how much was actually paid for the property. As mentioned earlier, if the grantee received the property as a gift, the recital of consideration usually says "love and affection." The distinction matters because in some situations property transferred as a gift could be reached by the grantor's creditors.

A recital of nominal consideration is not used in court-ordered deeds, such as a sheriff's deed or a tax deed. In those, the actual purchase price approved by the court is specified.

Words of Conveyance. A deed must include words of conveyance, also called a **granting clause**. This means that there must be a word or a phrase that expresses the grantor's intention of transferring an interest in real property. In most states, the single word "grant," or something similar, is sufficient.

Habendum Clause. Many states require a deed to contain a habendum clause, which may be part of, or directly after, the granting clause. A habendum clause begins with the words "to have and to hold" and describes the interest being conveyed to the grantee. A grantor may convey her fee simple interest or only a portion of that interest, such as a life estate (see Chapter 3). Unless otherwise specified in the deed, the grantor's entire interest is presumed to pass to the grantee.

If there is more than one grantee, the deed should also specify how the grantees are taking title. For example, it might state that they will hold title as tenants in common, or as joint tenants.

Exclusions and Reservations. An **exclusions and reservations clause** lists encumbrances on the property (such as easements, private restrictions, or liens) that the grantee will be taking title subject to. Keep in mind, however, that valid encumbrances may remain in force even if they aren't listed in the deed (see Chapter 5).

Date of Execution. A deed usually states the date on which it was executed, but that isn't legally required. As we'll discuss in the next section, title actually passes not when the deed is executed but when the deed is delivered to the grantee.

Acknowledgment, Delivery, and Acceptance. To convey real property, more than a valid deed is necessary; a proper conveyance also requires acknowledgment, delivery, and acceptance.

Acknowledgment occurs when the grantor swears before a notary public or other official witness authorized by state law (such as a judge, court clerk, or recording office clerk) that his signature is genuine and voluntary. This is a way of protecting against forgery.

The witness cannot be a person who has an interest in the transfer. For example, if a grandmother deeds her property to her granddaughter, who is a notary public, the granddaughter should not be the one to notarize the deed.

Technically, a deed may be considered valid even if the grantor's signature is not acknowledged. However, in most states an unacknowledged deed cannot be recorded.

A valid deed becomes effective, so that title is transferred, when the deed is **delivered** to the grantee. (One exception: under the Torrens system, which is discussed later in this chapter, title does not pass until the deed has been examined and registered.) Delivery must occur while the grantor is alive.

Example: When Sam Wiggins died, a deed was found in his safe deposit box. The deed was a conveyance of Sam's house to his nephew, Frank Wiggins. But the deed was void, because it was not delivered to Frank during Sam's lifetime.

Delivery is more than the mere physical transfer of the document; the grantor's intent is a key element of delivery. The grantor must have the intention of immediately transferring title to the grantee. The conveyance is completed when the grantee **accepts** delivery of the deed. The grantee may accept delivery of the deed through a third party who is acting as her representative, such as an escrow agent or attorney.

Example: Clark deeds his property to Martinez. Clark hands the deed to Martinez's attorney, with the intention of immediately transferring ownership to Martinez. This is considered delivery to an agent of the grantee, and the title transfer is effective.

Because delivery of a deed involves some complicated legal issues, a real estate lawyer should be consulted when there is a question concerning delivery.

A grantee's **acceptance** of a deed is rarely challenged. Courts often presume that a deed has been accepted if the transfer is beneficial to the grantee or the grantee is in possession of the deed.

Wills

Transfer by will is another method of voluntary alienation. A will (or testament) is a legal document in which a person specifies how his property is to be distributed after he dies. The person who makes a will is referred to as the **testator**. Someone who dies with a valid will is said to have died **testate**; someone who dies without a valid will is said to have died **intestate**. (Intestacy is discussed later in this chapter.)

Those who receive property through a will are generally called the **beneficiaries** of the will. A gift of personal property in a will is called a **bequest** or **legacy**; a testator **bequeaths** personal property to **legatees**. A gift of real property in a will is called a **devise**; a testator **devises** real property to **devisees**. An amendment to a will is called a **codicil**. A codicil may contain additional instructions or change the terms of the will.

Legal Requirements. In most states, a **formal will** is valid if it is:

1. in writing,
2. signed by a testator with legal capacity, and
3. attested to by competent witnesses.

Two witnesses are usually required, although some states require more than two. The testator must sign the will in the presence of the witnesses, and the witnesses must sign an acknowledgment that the testator declared the document to be his will. The witnesses should not be beneficiaries of the will.

At the time the will is made, the testator must have **testamentary capacity**. This means that the testator must be of legal age (in most states, 18 years old) and of sound mind. To be considered of sound mind for the purpose of making a will, the testator must understand the nature and extent of her property, the identity of her natural heirs, and how the property will be distributed under the will.

Other Types of Wills. In addition to formal wills, some states also recognize a type of unwitnessed will called a **holographic will**. A holographic will is written entirely in the testator's own handwriting. The will must be signed and dated by the testator, but witnesses to the signature aren't required. If a portion of a holographic will is typewritten or pre-printed, those provisions are usually disregarded by the probate court.

Another type of will recognized in some states is a **nuncupative will**. This is an oral (spoken) will, made when the testator is near death, and declared before one or more witnesses. The witnesses are usually required to write out what the testator says and sign the document as witnesses. If the testator recovers, the will is not valid. Since a conveyance of real property must be in writing, states that recognize nuncupative wills generally allow only personal property to be willed in this way. Some states restrict the use of nuncupative wills to persons serving in the military.

Just like formal wills, holographic wills and nuncupative wills are valid only if the testator has testamentary capacity at the time the will is made.

Probate. Probate is the procedure by which a will is proved valid and the testator's directions are carried out. Upon the death of the testator, the will is submitted to the probate court (sometimes called the surrogate court). Under the court's supervision, the estate property is managed and distributed to the beneficiaries by an **executor** appointed in the will. If the testator did not name an executor, the court will appoint an **administrator** to perform those

Fig. 4.2 Will terminology

Will Terminology

Testator: One who makes a will.

Bequeath: To transfer personal property by will.

Devise: To transfer real property by will.

Executor: Appointed by the testator to carry out the instructions in the will.

Administrator: Appointed by the court if no executor named.

Probate: Procedure to prove a will's validity.

functions. In some states, either an executor or an administrator is referred to as a **personal representative**.

Before the estate property is distributed, the validity of the will may be contested in the probate court. The court will rule on the validity and terms of the will, then order the distribution of the estate. The executor or administrator is responsible for paying off the testator's debts and paying any applicable federal or state estate taxes out of the estate assets.

If the estate includes real property, the executor or administrator conveys it (either to the devisees or, if the property is being sold, to the purchaser) with an executor's deed. Depending on state law, the conveyance may have to be approved by the probate court. (And if a real estate broker handles the sale, the listing agreement and commission rate may also be subject to court approval.)

Note that a will does not create any interest in property until the testator has died and the will has been probated. While the testator is still alive, she can modify or revoke the will at any time.

Involuntary Alienation

The patent, the deed, and the will are the three most common methods of transferring property voluntarily. We will now look at the different ways interests in real property can be conveyed without any voluntary action on the part of the owner.

Involuntary alienation of real property can be the result of rule of law, adverse possession, or accession. Alienation by rule of law includes dedication, intestate succession and escheat, condemnation, and court decisions regarding real property.

Dedication

When a private owner donates real property to the public, it is called dedication. While dedication may be voluntary (for example, a philanthropist might deed land to the city for a park, as a gift), most often it is required in exchange for a benefit from a public entity.

Example: The county requires a land developer to dedicate land within a new subdivision for public streets. Otherwise, the county will deny permission to subdivide.

This type of dedication is called **statutory dedication** because it involves compliance with relevant statutory procedures. In the example above, a statute or ordinance requires that land for streets and utilities must be dedicated before a parcel can be subdivided.

A second type of dedication is called **common law dedication**. The usual requirement for common law dedication is the owner's acquiescence in the public's use of his property for a prolonged period of time. If property has been used by the public long enough, a government entity can pass an ordinance accepting a common law dedication. The dedication may be treated as a transfer of ownership, or it may establish only a public easement, depending on the circumstances. (Easements are discussed in Chapter 5.)

Example: Barker owns some lakefront property. For many years, people from town have walked across a corner of his lot to gain access to the lake, and Barker has done nothing to prevent this. Barker's acquiescence to this public use would probably be considered a common law dedication of an easement.

Intestate Succession

A person who dies without leaving a valid will is said to have died intestate. The law provides for the distribution of an intestate person's property by a process called **intestate succession**. The rules of intestate succession vary from state to state. Typically the property passes to the surviving spouse, if any; next in line are any surviving children; and if there's no surviving spouse or child, the property goes to the nearest surviving relatives (the next of kin).

Persons who take property by intestate succession are called **heirs** or **distributees**. They are said to have received property by **descent**, rather than by devise or bequest. Intestate succession is supervised by the probate court. The court appoints an administrator or personal representative who distributes the property in the manner required by statute.

Escheat

If a person dies intestate and the probate court is unable to locate any heirs, then the intestate person's property **escheats**. That means title to the property passes to the state or county government. Since the government is the ultimate source of title to property, it is also the ultimate heir when there are no intervening interested parties. To obtain title to the property, the government must follow the appropriate legal procedures. The government may also take ownership of abandoned property through escheat.

Condemnation

The government has the constitutional power to take private property for public use, as long as it pays just compensation to the owner of the condemned property. The government's power to condemn (take) property is called the power of **eminent domain**. Before the power of eminent domain can be exercised, the following requirements must be met:

- The use must be a **public use**—that is, it must benefit the public.
- The condemning entity must pay **just compensation** to the owner.

Taking property for a public park would qualify as a public use. In cases of mixed public and private benefit the question is more difficult, but generally there is no authority for the government to take one person's land for the sole purpose of turning it over to another person. A 2005 Supreme Court decision held that condemnation pursuant to a carefully formulated plan to promote economic development is a valid public use.

As a general rule, just compensation is the fair market value of the property. The power of eminent domain may be exercised by any government entity, and also by some semi-public entities, such as utility companies.

Inverse Condemnation. If a property owner feels that her property has been taken or damaged by a public entity, she may file a lawsuit called an inverse condemnation action to force the government to pay the fair market value of the property.

Court Decisions

Title to property can be conveyed by court order in accordance with state statutes and the common law precedents. The most common forms of court action affecting title to property are quiet title actions, suits for partition, foreclosures, and bankruptcies.

Quiet Title. A quiet title action is used to remove a cloud on the title when the title cannot be cleared by the more peaceful means of an agreement and a quitclaim deed. In a quiet title action, the court decides questions of property ownership. The result is a binding determination of the various parties' interests in a particular piece of real estate.

> **Example:** A seller has found a potential buyer for his property. However, a title search uncovers a gap in the title: the public records don't indicate who owned the property for a certain time period.
>
> The seller files a quiet title action in the county court. The defendants in the action are all persons who have a potential interest in the seller's property. This includes the mystery person who held title during the gap, even though his name is unknown.
>
> The seller asks the court to declare his title valid, thereby "quieting title" to the land. If no defendants appear to challenge the seller's title, the court will grant the seller's request. The buyer can then safely rely on the court's decision and consummate the sale.

Suit for Partition. A suit for partition is a means of dividing property held by more than one person when the co-owners cannot agree on how to divide it. For example, joint tenants may wish to end their joint tenancy but be unable to decide among themselves who gets what portion of the property. The court divides the property for them, and the owners are then bound by the court's decision. In many cases, the court will order the property sold and the proceeds divided among the co-owners.

> **Example:** Green and Black are joint tenants. The joint tenancy property is a vacation home in the mountains. After a serious argument, Green and Black decide they want to terminate their joint tenancy. However, they can't agree on how to divide the property. Green wants to put the property up for sale and divide the proceeds. Black wants to buy out Green's interest and keep the vacation home for himself, but Green says Black isn't offering him enough money.

Finally, Green files a suit for partition. The court orders the vacation home sold and divides the proceeds equally between Green and Black. Black must abide by this decision, even though it isn't what he wanted.

Foreclosure Actions. Someone who holds a lien against real property may force the sale of the property if the debt secured by the lien is not paid. Foreclosure is available for any type of lien that attaches to real property, including mortgages, deeds of trust, construction liens, and judgment liens. (See Chapter 11 for further discussion of foreclosure.)

Bankruptcy. Property may also be conveyed by order of a bankruptcy court. Once a bankruptcy petition is filed, the court has the authority to distribute the eligible property of the debtor in order to satisfy creditors' claims. The debtor's real property may be sold to satisfy the claims of mortgage lenders or other creditors.

Adverse Possession

Adverse possession, another form of involuntary alienation, is the process by which the possession and use of property can mature into title. The law of adverse possession encourages the fullest and most productive use of land. Also called **title by prescription**, it provides that someone who actually uses property may eventually attain a greater interest in that property than the owner who does not use it. The precise requirements for obtaining title by adverse possession vary from state to state. These requirements are often highly technical, and they must be followed exactly in order to obtain title. Legal counsel should be obtained in transactions where title may be affected by adverse possession.

Requirements. Most states have five basic requirements for adverse possession. Possession of the land must be:

1. actual,
2. open and notorious,
3. hostile to the owner's interest,
4. exclusive, and
5. continuous and uninterrupted for a specific period of time.

Actual. Actual possession means occupation and use of the property in a manner appropriate to the type of property. Residence on the property is not required unless residence is the appropriate use. Thus, actual possession of farmland may be achieved by fencing the land and planting crops, while actual possession of urban property would require a residential or commercial use of the property.

Open and Notorious. The requirement of "open and notorious" possession means that the possession must put the true owner on notice that her interest in the property is being threatened. Open and notorious possession and actual possession overlap. Actual possession generally constitutes reasonable notice to the world that the adverse possessor is occupying the property.

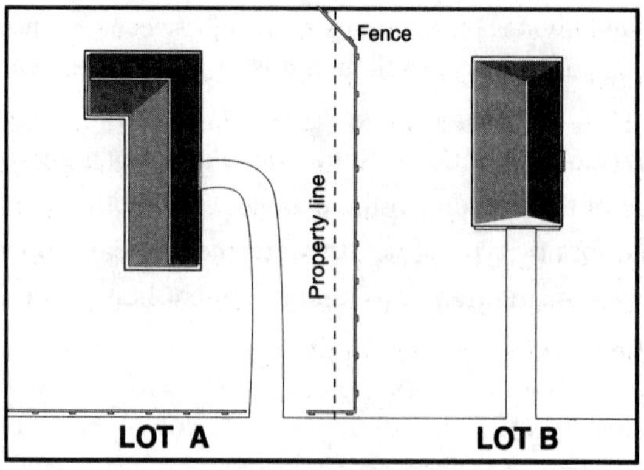

Fig. 4.3 Adverse possession
Use of property (here, the strip between Lot A's fence and the true property line) can mature into title by the process of adverse possession.

Hostile. The adverse possessor's use of the property must be "hostile" to the true owner's interest. This is generally understood to mean that the property is being used without the owner's permission and in a manner that is inconsistent with the owner's rights. Ordinarily, if the adverse possessor uses the property (without permission) in the same way that an owner would use it, then the hostility requirement is satisfied.

Exclusive. An adverse possessor must have exclusive possession of the property; in other words, the true owner must be excluded from possession. Someone who is sharing use of the property with the true owner (even without the owner's knowledge) cannot acquire title by adverse possession.

Continuous and Uninterrupted. An adverse possessor must have continuous and uninterrupted possession of the property for the length of time prescribed by state statute. The statutory periods required in different states vary widely, ranging from five to thirty years. Some states also require an adverse possessor to pay taxes on the property during the period of possession.

In some cases, intermittent use of the property may be enough to fulfill the continuity requirement. This is true if the property is a type that an owner would ordinarily use only at certain times of year, such as seasonal farmland or summer resort property. However, the continuity requirement is not met if the adverse possessor fails to use the property for a significant period when it would ordinarily be used, or if the true owner interrupts the period of exclusive possession.

Successive adverse possessors can add together their periods of possession to equal the statutory time period; this is called **tacking**.

> **Example:** Tanaka adversely possesses property for four years, and then transfers possession to White, who possesses the property for three years. White can claim title because the total period of adverse possession is more than five years.

Claim of Right or Color of Title. Some states draw a distinction between possession under a claim of right and possession under color of title. It's called **color of title** when the adverse possessor has a good faith but mistaken belief that he's the true owner of the property, based on an invalid deed (or some other defective instrument).

By contrast, an adverse possessor under a **claim of right** doesn't necessarily believe that she owns the property; she has no deed and often knows that she isn't the true owner. However, her actions demonstrate that, nevertheless, she intends to claim ownership of the property. For example, someone who moves onto apparently abandoned property, constructs a building, and begins using it, would be occupying the property under a claim of right.

How the distinction between claim of right and color of title affects adverse possession depends on state law. One common rule is that an adverse possessor with color of title may acquire title to all of the property described in his invalid deed, even if he occupies only part of the property. And in some states, the required period of possession is shorter if the adverse possessor has color of title. For example, a state might generally require ten years of continuous and uninterrupted possession, but cut that requirement to only seven years if the adverse possessor has color of title.

Perfecting Title. Since the adverse possessor's interest is not recorded, he must take additional steps to acquire marketable title. Unless the true owner is willing to provide a quitclaim deed, the adverse possessor must file a quiet title action.

Government Property. Note that title to government-owned land cannot be acquired by adverse possession.

Accession

Accession refers to any addition to real property from natural or man-made causes. An addition to one person's property sometimes involves the involuntary alienation of another person's property. In some cases, this type of involuntary alienation occurs as a result of one of these natural processes:

- accretion,
- reliction,
- erosion, and
- avulsion.

Accretion. Waterborne soil may be deposited on land beside a body of water. The deposited soil is called **alluvion** or **alluvium**, and the process is called **accretion**. When alluvion is gradually added to a parcel of property adjoining a stream or lake, the landowner acquires title to the additional land. A key feature of accretion is that the buildup of soil must be so gradual that the process is virtually imperceptible.

Reliction. The water in a stream or lake may gradually recede; this retreat from the land is called **reliction**, or sometimes **dereliction**. When a parcel of property is enlarged by reliction, the landowner acquires title to the newly exposed land. Like accretion, reliction must be very gradual.

Erosion. A property owner's land may be lost through the process of **erosion**, which is the wearing away of land by natural processes. Erosion may be caused by wind, rain, or flowing water, and (like accretion or reliction) it is a very gradual process. Soil that moves from one parcel of property onto another as a result of erosion ordinarily becomes part of the parcel where it settles.

Avulsion. Accretion, reliction, and erosion are all gradual processes that only become evident over the course of many years. By contrast, **avulsion** happens suddenly. It occurs when land is violently torn away by heavy rain, flowing water, or waves, and then is deposited somewhere else (as in a mudslide), or when land is exposed by a sudden change in a watercourse. Avulsion does not necessarily result in involuntary alienation of the land that has been moved or exposed. The original owner still has title to it, if there is some way to claim it. If unclaimed, it eventually becomes part of the property it is now attached to.

Recording

Once an interest in real property has been transferred (voluntarily or involuntarily), the new owner protects that interest by submitting the deed or other document of conveyance to a county official for recording. When a document is recorded, it is placed in the public record and anyone who's interested can look it up and read it. The recording system provides convenient access to information regarding ownership of real property.

Recording Procedures

Every state has a recording act, a statute that specifies the procedures for placing deeds and other documents pertaining to real property in the public record. Documents usually must be recorded in the county where the land is located. Each county has a recording office, which may be called the county recorder's office, county clerk's office, county registrar's office, or the office of the recorder of deeds. Depending on the requirements of state law, records may be kept on microfilm, in a computer database, or in some other form. When a document is filed for recording, the recording office copies or scans it and then returns the original to the person who submitted it.

Recording Requirements. Almost any document affecting title to real property may be recorded: a deed, a mortgage, a grant of easement, an abstract of judgment, an option, a lis pendens (a notice of pending legal proceedings that may affect property), and so on. As a general rule, leases are recorded only if they have a term longer than one year. Purchase agreements between buyers and sellers are ordinarily not recorded. Also note that the recording of a deed or other document that contains a racially restrictive covenant is prohibited by federal law. (See Chapter 16.)

The recording office is likely to have specific rules concerning the physical format of documents to be recorded. For example, there may be rules concerning the size or type of paper or the width of the margins.

As we discussed earlier, to protect against forgery, a deed generally must be acknowledged by the grantor and notarized before it can be recorded. This requirement may also apply to other types of documents.

Sometimes certain taxes have to be paid before a deed can be recorded. For example, in some places a deed won't be accepted for recording unless the property taxes are current. Many states charge a tax on real estate transfers, called a conveyance tax, transfer tax, or real property excise tax (see Chapter 6). In these states, a deed will be recorded only if it bears a special stamp or other evidence indicating that the conveyance tax has been paid or that the transaction is exempt from the tax. The conveyance tax is often collected at the recording office when a deed is filed for recording.

Organization of Records. Documents are recorded chronologically, in the order in which they were filed for recording at the recording office. Each recorded document is assigned a recording number.

To make it possible to locate particular documents, recorded documents have traditionally been indexed. Most recording offices maintain a **grantor index**, in which deeds and other documents are listed alphabetically by the last name of each grantor, and a **grantee index**, in which they're listed alphabetically by the last name of each grantee. To examine or obtain a copy of a particular document, it's typically necessary to look it up in the index under either the grantor's name or the grantee's name to find the recording number, and then use the recording number to locate the document.

Using the grantee index, it's possible to follow a property's **chain of title** backward in time, to verify the validity of the current owner's title. The chain of title is the series of deeds that transferred ownership of the property from one owner to the next.

Example: The parcel of land known locally as the Abbott property first came into private ownership in 1890, when the government transferred title to Charles Abbott by means of a land patent. It's currently supposed to be owned by Eileen Fleming.

To verify Fleming's claim of ownership, you need to trace the chain of title backward to make sure it's unbroken. The first step is to look up Fleming's name in the grantee index. The index lists a deed recorded in 1990 which shows that title to the property was conveyed to Fleming by someone named Emerson. Next, you look up Emerson's name in the same index and find a 1976 deed to Emerson from Downing. Next you find a 1952 deed to Downing from Cleaver, a 1938 deed to Cleaver from Benson, and a 1915 deed to Benson from Abbott. Thus, there is an unbroken chain of title from Abbott to Fleming.

The last step in verifying Fleming's ownership is to look up her name in the grantor index to make sure she hasn't deeded the property to anyone else. You don't find her name there, so it's safe to conclude that she is indeed the current owner.

Mortgages as well as deeds may be listed in the grantor and grantee indexes, or there may be separate mortgagor and mortgagee indexes. Some recorder's offices also maintain a **tract index**. In a tract index, all documents affecting a particular tract (parcel of property) are listed together, which is very convenient. Documents are located by looking up a property's tract number or legal description in the tract index.

Today, computerization has made indexing less important. Depending on the state and county, often computer searches can be used to locate documents in the public record.

The Legal Effects of Recording

Having a document recorded has two extremely important legal consequences. It provides notice of the interest conveyed in the document, and it establishes the priority of that interest.

Notice. Many legal issues depend on whether a person had **notice** of certain information. If someone had notice of a particular fact, that means she *knew it or should have known it*, and that may affect her legal rights in a situation. There are three types of notice: actual notice, constructive notice, and inquiry notice. Our immediate focus will be on the distinction between actual notice and constructive notice; inquiry notice will be explained later.

Actual notice is straightforward. A person has actual notice of a fact if he actually knows about it. He personally observed it, read about it, or was told about it. By contrast, a person has **constructive notice** of a fact if, in the eyes of the law, she should have known about it, whether or not she actually did.

Recording a document gives constructive notice to "the world" (the public at large) of the property interest set forth in the document. Anyone who acquires an interest in a particular property is legally held to know about all earlier recorded interests in that property, whether or not he has actually checked the public record.

Example: Jones owns Haystack Farm. She sells the farm to Chen, who immediately records his deed in the county where the farm is located. One week later, Jones sells Haystack Farm to Brown. Jones pretends she still owns the farm, and Brown just takes her word for it, instead of checking the county's public record. But since Jones no longer holds title, her deed to Brown conveys no interest in the property. Brown discovers this sometime later, when he and Chen both try to assert ownership of the property.

Although Brown didn't actually know about the conveyance from Jones to Chen, he had constructive notice of it; he could have found out about it by checking the public record. As a result, Brown has no legal claim to the property. Chen owns Haystack Farm. Brown could sue Jones to get his money back, but she may be difficult to find.

A deed may be valid even though it isn't recorded. But a grantee who fails to record his deed can lose title to a **subsequent good faith purchaser without notice**: someone who later buys the property in good faith and without actual or constructive notice of the earlier conveyance. In a conflict between two purchasers, the one who records her deed first generally has good title to the property—even if the other purchaser's deed was executed first.

Example: Jones sells Haystack Farm to Chen, but Chen does not record his deed. One week later, Jones sells the same property to Brown. No one tells Brown about the previous conveyance to Chen.

Since Chen's deed hasn't been recorded, Brown doesn't have constructive notice of Chen's interest in the property. Even if Brown does a title search, there's nothing in the public record to indicate that Jones no longer owns the property.

Brown qualifies as a subsequent good faith purchaser without notice. If he records his deed before Chen records his, Brown has good title to the property.

Priority. As the example above illustrates, in addition to providing constructive notice, recording a document concerning a property interest establishes the priority of that interest. Priority refers to the precedence of certain rights over others; the general rule is "first to record, first in right." Once a deed or other document is recorded, the interest set forth in that document has priority over subsequent claims. That's why recorded documents are numbered chronologically in the order in which they're received at the recording office, and a record is kept not only of the date but the time of day a document is filed. The issue of priority is especially important in regard to liens; this is discussed in greater detail in Chapter 5.

Wild Deeds. In some situations, even though a document has been recorded, it won't be discovered in a properly conducted title search.

> **Example:** Suppose Smith sells property to Montgomery, who fails to record her deed. Not long thereafter, Montgomery conveys the property to Klein, who promptly records his deed.
>
> If Smith then makes another conveyance of the same property to Walker, Walker will not be able to discover Klein's interest because Klein is not in Smith's chain of title. There is a break in the chain of title between Smith and Klein because the connecting deed was not recorded.

A deed that's outside of a chain of title is called a **wild deed**. A subsequent purchaser (such as Walker in the example) usually is not charged with constructive notice of a wild deed.

Inquiry Notice. As we mentioned earlier, there's a third type of notice in addition to actual notice and constructive notice: inquiry notice, sometimes called implied notice. Inquiry notice arises in situations where there are "red flags"—signs of a possible problem that a prudent person would not overlook. Someone who has inquiry notice concerning an issue is expected to make further inquiry into it, to follow up by asking someone or consulting some other source of information. Failure to do so may affect his right to sue later on. As a general rule, the law requires someone with inquiry notice to make a reasonably diligent effort to obtain more information.

One situation in which inquiry notice comes up is when a piece of property is for sale and someone other than the seller is in possession of the property. Possession of property suggests a possible interest in it; for example, the person in possession might be a tenant or an adverse possessor. Potential buyers will generally be held to have inquiry notice of the interest, if any, of the person in possession.

Title Protection

Under the terms of most purchase agreements, the seller is required to deliver marketable title to the buyer at closing. Title is considered marketable if it is free from serious defects and the seller's ability to convey it is unrestricted. In this section, we'll look at the steps buyers can take to determine whether a seller has marketable title and to protect themselves against title problems.

Title Searches

Title protection for a buyer is based on a **title search**. In a title search, someone examines the public records in the county where the property is located to find all recorded documents and other records that may affect the property's title. Buyers could do a title search on their own, but nearly everyone takes the wiser course and has an expert conduct the search. This may be a real estate attorney, an employee of a title company, or an abstractor (see below).

Chain of Title. One essential step in a title search is tracing the chain of title, the series of deeds that link the current owner of the property (the seller) to all of the previous owners, to make sure that the chain is unbroken. (See the example concerning this process in our earlier discussion of grantor and grantee indexes.) If there's a missing link—a gap in the chain—the seller's title may not be valid. A gap might result from an unrecorded deed, a conveyance of the property under a different name than the one used on the previous deed, or various other circumstances in the property's history. To resolve this and establish marketable title, the seller may have to file a quiet title action, a type of lawsuit that was discussed earlier in the chapter.

Encumbrances. In addition to tracing the chain of title, a title searcher looks for documents concerning encumbrances. Encumbrances are interests in property held by parties other than the owner, such as liens, easements, and private restrictions (see Chapter 5). A prospective buyer needs to know about any encumbrances that are still in effect.

Scope of Search. Keep in mind that title searching isn't limited to recorded documents such as deeds and mortgages. A complete title search also involves checking other public records, such as tax records, probate records, and court records of judgments, divorce decrees, and other actions that may affect title to real property.

Note that there are certain types of title problems, such as encroachments and adverse possession, that won't be revealed by a title search, because there are no public records regarding them. To discover or rule out those problems, it's necessary to visit and inspect the property itself.

Marketable Title Act. To make title searches easier, some states have a law called the Marketable Title Act. Under such a statute, claims against property that have been inactive for decades (the specific length of time differs from state to state) are invalidated. As a result, it isn't necessary to go back beyond that limit when performing a title search.

In a state that doesn't have this type of law, it is often customary to limit title searches in a similar way, at least for certain types of property. Even though a claim based on something that happened several decades ago could still be valid, the likelihood that someone would pursue such a claim now is so slim that it's considered safe to ignore it.

Types of Title Protection

Although some form of title protection is available in every state, different types are used in different parts of the country. We'll look at abstracts of title, title opinions and certificates of title, title insurance, and Torrens registration.

Abstracts of Title. The parties to a real estate transaction, or anyone else who's concerned with the condition of a property's title, may hire an attorney or a licensed specialist called an abstractor to perform a title search and prepare an **abstract of title**. An abstract of title is a chronological summary of all of the documents that may affect the title to the property. It includes the source and location of each document, along with a list of all public records that were searched.

Opinions and Certificates of Title. An abstract of title only provides information, without any interpretation of that information. In many places, the parties to a real estate transaction hire an attorney or abstractor to prepare not only an abstract but also an **opinion of title**, also called a **certificate of title**. The opinion or certificate of title presents a formal opinion as to who the true owner of the property is and who else holds legitimate interests in the property.

In states where title abstracts and opinions or certificates are used, it is often customary for them to be passed on from one owner to the next. Each time the property changes hands, the seller pays to have the abstract and the opinion or certificate updated for the buyer.

If the person who prepares an opinion or certificate of title overlooks something in the public records or renders an incorrect opinion, she can be sued for negligence and held liable for the mistake. However, that doesn't give the parties any protection against latent title defects—hidden problems with the title. For example, there's usually no way for an attorney or abstractor (or any title searcher) to tell if a deed in the chain of title was a forgery. If that turned out to be the case, the attorney or abstractor couldn't be held liable, because there wasn't any negligence on his part.

Title Insurance. Title insurance was developed to protect the policy holder against latent title defects, while also providing a summary of all of the documents that may affect the title to the property. Title insurance is now considered essential in many states, but there are still a number of states where it is not used.

In a title insurance policy, the title insurance company agrees to indemnify the policy holder against (reimburse him for) losses caused by defects in the title, except for any defects specifically excluded from coverage. The title company will also handle the legal defense of any claims covered by the policy.

Before issuing a policy, the title insurance company performs a title search and prepares a **title report** (also called a preliminary commitment) describing the condition of the title. The report lists all defects and encumbrances of record; these items will be excluded from the policy coverage. After receiving the report, the parties to a transaction may arrange to have certain liens paid off or other encumbrances removed before closing.

The insurance policy is issued when the transaction closes. The premium for the policy is paid at closing; a single premium covers the entire life of the policy. Which party pays the premium is determined by agreement or local custom; in some parts of the country, the seller pays for the policy; in others, the seller pays a fee for the title search and the buyer pays the insurance premium.

Interests Insured. In states where title insurance is used, most transactions involve two policies; each insures the particular interest that the policy holder has in the property.

An **owner's policy** insures the title of the buyer (the new owner). The amount of coverage provided by an owner's policy is usually the purchase price of the property, and the coverage lasts as long as the owner or the owner's heirs have an interest in the property. As a general rule, an owner's policy cannot be assigned—that is, transferred from one party to another. However, the buyer may be able to obtain an updated version of the seller's policy at a lower reissue rate through the seller's title insurance company.

A **lender's policy** protects the lien priority of the mortgage lender that is financing the purchase of the property. A lender's policy differs from an owner's policy in several ways. First, the coverage of a lender's policy declines as the loan balance decreases and terminates once the loan is paid off. Also, if the lender sells the loan to another lender, the title policy may be assigned to the other lender.

Lenders generally require the buyer to purchase a lender's policy as a condition of making the loan. In most cases, the lender's policy must be an extended coverage policy (see below).

Extent of Coverage. The extent of coverage provided by a title insurance policy varies according to the terms of the policy. Traditionally, the two most common types of policies have been the standard coverage policy and the extended coverage policy.

A **standard coverage policy** was traditionally used to insure the property owner (the buyer) against defects in title, including hidden risks such as forgery. It does not insure against the interests of a person in actual possession of the property (such as an adverse possessor), against title defects known by the owner but not disclosed to the title insurer, nor against interests that would be discovered through an inspection of the premises (such as an encroachment).

If a buyer wants coverage for a specific item not included in the standard policy, it may be possible to purchase an **endorsement** to cover that item.

An **extended coverage policy** (sometimes called an ALTA policy, after the American Land Title Association) insures against all matters covered by the standard policy, plus matters not of public record, such as the rights of parties in possession of the property, unrecorded mechanic's liens, and encroachments. The title company often sends an inspector or surveyor to look over the property before issuing an extended coverage policy.

In addition to standard and extended coverage, in some states title companies offer a third commonly used type of policy, **homeowner's coverage,** for transactions that involve residential property with up to four units. This policy provides the buyer with much more extensive coverage than a traditional standard coverage policy. In fact, a homeowner's title policy covers most of the same title problems that an extended coverage policy does, plus some additional ones, such as violations of restrictive covenants.

Limitations on Coverage. Title insurance policies may be limited in a number of ways. As mentioned above, all defects and encumbrances of record are listed in the policy and excluded from coverage. In addition, the liability of the title company cannot exceed the face value of the policy.

Fig. 4.4 Comparison of standard, extended, and homeowner's title insurance

	Standard Coverage	Extended Coverage	Homeowner's Coverage
Unmarketable title	X	X	X
Latent defects in title (forged deed, incompetent grantor)	X	X	X
Incorrect legal descriptions or clerical errors in recorded documents	X	X	X
Undisclosed heirs in improperly probated wills	X	X	X
Nondelivery of deeds or delivery of deeds after grantors' death	X	X	X
Unrecorded liens		X	X
Claims of parties in possession (tenants, adverse possessors)		X	X
Matters discovered by survey (incorrect boundary lines, easements, incorrect area)		X	X
Subdivision regulation violations			X
Zoning or building code violations			X
Claims that arise post-closing			X

Title insurance never protects a landowner from losses due to governmental action such as condemnation or zoning changes. Restrictive covenants, certain water rights, and special assessments are also generally excluded from coverage.

Torrens System. In several states, the Torrens system of land title registration is available (although some of those states are phasing it out). When title to property is registered in the Torrens system, the **Torrens certificate of title** provides definitive evidence of valid ownership and the condition of the title. For registered property, it isn't necessary to perform a standard title search of recorded documents to determine who owns the property and who holds other interests in it; consulting the Torrens certificate is sufficient.

To register property in the Torrens system, the owner submits an application. An abstract of title is prepared, and there is a quiet title action, giving anyone who may hold an interest in the property an opportunity to assert her claim in court. If the court determines that the applicant for registration has valid title, the state registrar of titles issues a Torrens certificate. The Torrens certificate lists the owner's name and the liens and other encumbrances on the title. (Certain types of encumbrances, such as federal and state tax liens, are not listed.) A Torrens certificate should not be confused with the certificate of title we discussed earlier, which is an attorney or abstractor's opinion of a property's title.

Once title is registered, any subsequent liens or transfers of interests must be noted on the Torrens certificate to provide constructive notice. Liens and transfers that aren't listed generally won't be binding on subsequent purchasers of the property.

Under the Torrens system, a grantee does not receive title when the grantor executes the deed. The grantee must take the deed to the registrar, who issues a new certificate of title in the grantee's name, effectively transferring title.

Security Interests in Fixtures

As we discussed in Chapter 2, a fixture is an item of personal property (a chattel) that has been attached to real property and is now considered part of the real property, for most purposes. When the real property is sold, the fixtures are sold along with it, unless otherwise agreed.

However, when a property owner purchases an item that's going to become a fixture, such as a built-in appliance, it's quite common for the purchase to be financed—paid for in installments over time. In that case, the fixture itself usually serves as security for the financing, in much the same way that a home is security for the mortgage financing that was used to purchase it. If the creditor that sold the fixture to the owner isn't paid, the fixture can be repossessed.

When real estate is transferred, it's necessary to determine whether anyone holds a security interest in any of the fixtures (because the financing hasn't been paid off yet). Security interests in fixtures are governed by the **Uniform Commercial Code** (UCC), which has been adopted in some form by all 50 states.

Under the UCC, to create a security interest in personal property (whether or not it will become a fixture on real property), the buyer must sign a security agreement that describes the property purchased. Then the creditor who financed the purchase must record a **financing statement** (sometimes called a **chattel mortgage**). The recording gives the public constructive notice of the security interest.

Once a security interest in a fixture has been established in this way, the security interest will survive even when the ownership of the real property changes hands. If the previous owner (the seller) defaults on the financing, the creditor has the right to enter the property and remove the fixture. On the other hand, if the creditor didn't record a financing statement, the purchaser of the real property is protected against removal of the fixture.

Chapter Summary

1. A transfer of ownership of property from one person to another is called alienation. Alienation may be either voluntary or involuntary.

2. Property may be transferred voluntarily by patent, deed, or will. The deed is the most common way of voluntarily transferring property. To be valid, a deed typically must be in writing, identify the parties, be signed by a competent grantor, have a living grantee, contain words of conveyance, and include an adequate description of the property and a recital of consideration. A successful conveyance requires delivery and acceptance as well as a valid deed.

3. When a person dies, his real property is transferred to devisees under a will, or to heirs by the rules of intestate succession. A person who dies without a valid will is said to have died intestate. Property from a deceased person's estate is distributed under the jurisdiction of the probate court. If a person dies without a valid will and without heirs, the property escheats to the government.

4. In addition to intestate succession and escheat, there are several other methods of involuntary alienation, including dedication, condemnation, court decisions, and adverse possession. When someone uses property openly and continuously without the owner's permission for the statutory period, she may acquire title by adverse possession.

5. Ownership of real property is sometimes involuntarily transferred by accession. This may be the result of natural forces, such as accretion, reliction, erosion, or avulsion.

6. Documents affecting real property are recorded to provide constructive notice of their contents to the world. Recording also establishes the priority of an interest in property.

7. Before purchasing real property, a buyer should have a title search performed and obtain some form of title protection. This may be an abstract and opinion of title or certificate of title, or it may be a title insurance policy.

8. A security interest in personal property or a fixture is established by recording a financing statement. As with personal property, a fixture can be repossessed by a secured creditor who isn't paid.

Key Terms

Title—In regard to real property, the owner's rights in the property. (The document used to transfer ownership of real property is called the deed, not the title.)

Marketable title—Title to real property that is free from serious defects, and which the seller has an unrestricted right to convey.

Alienation—The transfer of title or an interest in property from one person to another. Alienation may be voluntary or involuntary.

Deed—A written instrument that, when properly executed, delivered, and accepted, conveys title or ownership of real property from the grantor to the grantee.

Warranty deed—The type of deed that provides the greatest protection to a buyer. Its covenants cover title defects and claims that may have arisen during or before the grantor's period of ownership. Also called a general warranty deed.

Grant deed—A deed that has fewer covenants than a general warranty deed, which is used instead of a general warranty deed in certain states.

Special warranty deed—A deed with the same covenants as a general warranty deed, except that the covenants only cover title defects and claims that arose while the grantor held title to the property.

Bargain and sale deed—A deed that contains no warranties or covenants, but does carry the implication that the grantor owns the property described in the deed.

Quitclaim deed—A deed that conveys and releases whatever interest in a piece of real property that the grantor may have. It carries no warranties of any kind.

Acknowledgment—A formal declaration made before an authorized official, such as a notary public or county clerk, by a person who has signed a document; he states that the signature is genuine and voluntary.

Will—The written declaration of an individual that designates how her estate will be disposed of after death.

Intestate—When a person dies without leaving a valid will, she dies intestate.

Escheat—The reversion of property to the government when a person dies without leaving a valid will and without heirs entitled to the property.

Adverse possession—A means by which a person may acquire title to property by using it openly and continuously without the owner's permission for the period required by state statute.

Dedication—When a private owner voluntarily or involuntarily gives real property to the public.

Eminent domain—The power of the government to take (condemn) private property for public use, upon payment of just compensation to the owner.

Condemnation—The act of taking private property for public use under the power of eminent domain.

Accession—Any addition to real property from natural or artificial causes.

Chain of title—The series of deeds by which title to a piece of property was transferred from one owner to the next, over the course of the property's history.

Constructive notice—When the law charges a person with knowledge of a fact because he should have known it, whether or not he actually did.

Wild deed—A recorded deed that is outside the chain of title and cannot be located through the grantor-grantee system of indexing.

Recording—Filing a document with the appropriate county officials so that it will be placed in the public record.

Title search—An examination of public records to determine all rights and interests in a piece of real property.

Abstract of title—A condensed history of the recorded interests in a piece of real property.

Opinion of title—An opinion concerning the ownership of and other interests in a piece of real property, often prepared by an attorney based on an abstract of title. Also called a certificate of title.

Title insurance—An insurance policy that indemnifies a buyer or a lender against losses resulting from title defects that have not been excepted from coverage.

Title report—A report issued after a title search by a title insurance company, listing all defects and encumbrances of record.

Financing statement—A document filed for recording by a creditor to establish a security interest in personal property or a fixture.

Chapter Quiz

1. The process of transferring real property is called:
   a) avulsion
   b) quitclaim
   c) alienation
   d) dereliction

2. The government transfers title to private parties by means of a/an:
   a) patent
   b) deed
   c) quitclaim
   d) escheat

3. A warranty deed warrants that:
   a) there are absolutely no encumbrances against the property
   b) the grantor owns the property and has the right to convey it
   c) the purchase price was fair and equitable
   d) title has been duly recorded

4. Clouds on title can be cleared by:
   a) a suit for partition
   b) title insurance
   c) adverse possession
   d) a quitclaim deed

5. A valid deed must refer to a grantee who is:
   a) mentally competent
   b) over 21 years old
   c) identifiable
   d) intestate

6. Conveyance requires a valid deed, plus:
   a) recording
   b) delivery
   c) acceptance
   d) Both b) and c)

7. A person who makes a will is called a/an:
   a) grantor
   b) executor
   c) testator
   d) escheat

8. An unwitnessed, handwritten will is called a:
   a) formal will
   b) holographic will
   c) nuncupative will
   d) None of the above

9. The process through which possession of property can result in ownership of the property is called:
   a) fee simple
   b) succession
   c) adverse possession
   d) reliction

10. A quitclaim deed conveys:
    a) whatever interest the grantor has
    b) an interest in personal property
    c) only property acquired by adverse possession
    d) only marital rights

11. The main reason why a grantee should make sure the deed gets recorded is to:
    a) give constructive notice of his interest in the property
    b) show acceptance of the conveyance
    c) make the transfer of title effective
    d) prevent adverse possession

12. To be valid, a deed must:
    a) be in writing
    b) be signed by the grantor
    c) include a property description
    d) All of the above

13. When a cloud on the title cannot be cleared in some other way, this judicial proceeding is used to decide ownership:
    a) quiet title action
    b) suit for partition
    c) interpleader action
    d) reformation action

14. All of the following are requirements for adverse possession, except:
    a) actual, open, and notorious possession
    b) continuous and uninterrupted possession
    c) hostile possession
    d) tacking

15. A standard title insurance policy would protect against:
    a) adverse possession
    b) encroachments
    c) a forged deed
    d) condemnation

Answer Key

1. c) The general term for a transfer of ownership of real property from one party to another is alienation.

2. a) The government transfers title to property with a patent.

3. b) A warranty deed warrants that the grantor owns the property and has the right to convey it.

4. d) A quitclaim deed can be used to clear clouds on title.

5. c) The grantee is only required to be identifiable. She need not be mentally competent or over 21.

6. d) To convey title successfully, a deed must be delivered and accepted.

7. c) The person who makes a will is called the testator.

8. b) A will that is handwritten by the testator and not witnessed is a holographic will.

9. c) Adverse possession encourages the full use of land by providing a means by which a user may acquire ownership rights.

10. a) A quitclaim deed transfers whatever interest the grantor has. If the grantor has good title, it conveys good title. If the grantor has no interest in the property, it conveys nothing at all.

11. a) Recording a deed gives constructive notice of the grantee's interest.

12. d) Under the statute of frauds, a deed must be in writing and signed by a competent grantor to be valid. A deed must also contain an adequate description of the property conveyed.

13. a) A quiet title action provides a binding judicial determination of the parties' interests in a piece of real estate.

14. d) All of these are among the requirements for adverse possession, except tacking. Although an adverse possessor may use tacking to fulfill the statutory time requirement, tacking is not itself a requirement.

15. c) Standard title insurance coverage insures only against title defects (such as a forged deed), not against matters that are not part of the public record (such as encroachments and adverse possession). Also, title insurance does not insure against government actions such as condemnation.

Chapter 5

Encumbrances

- I. Financial Encumbrances (Liens)
  - A. Types of liens
    1. Mortgages
    2. Deeds of trust
    3. Mechanic's liens
    4. Judgment liens
    5. Attachment liens
    6. Property tax liens
    7. Special assessments
    8. Other tax liens
    9. Miscellaneous liens
  - B. Lien priority
  - C. Homestead laws
- II. Nonfinancial Encumbrances
  - A. Easements
    1. Types of easements
    2. Creating an easement
    3. Terminating an easement
  - B. Profits
  - C. Related concepts
    1. Licenses
    2. Encroachments
    3. Nuisances
  - D. Private restrictions

Chapter Overview

An interest in real property may be held by someone other than the property owner or a tenant; such an interest is called an encumbrance. Nearly every property has encumbrances against it. Some encumbrances represent another person's financial interest in the property. Other encumbrances involve another person's right to make use of the property or to restrict how the owner uses it.

The first part of this chapter explains financial encumbrances, including mortgages and other types of liens. The second part of this chapter covers the non-financial encumbrances, including easements and private restrictions, and some related concepts.

Encumbrances

An encumbrance is a nonpossessory right or interest in real property held by someone other than the property owner. The interest can be financial or nonfinancial in nature. A financial encumbrance affects title only; a nonfinancial encumbrance also affects the use or physical condition of the property.

Financial Encumbrances (Liens)

Financial encumbrances are more commonly called **liens**. A lien is a security interest in property; it is held by a creditor of the property owner. If the owner doesn't pay off the debt owed to the creditor, the security interest allows the creditor to force the property to be sold, so that the creditor can collect the debt out of the sale proceeds. This is called **foreclosure**. The most familiar example of a lien is a mortgage.

A creditor who has a lien against (a security interest in) a debtor's property is called a **secured creditor**, a **lienholder**, or a **lienor**. (The debtor may also be called the **lienee**.) The lien does not prevent the debtor from transferring the property, but the new owner takes title subject to the lien. The creditor can still foreclose if the debt is not repaid, even though the debtor no longer owns the property.

When a lien becomes legally effective, it is said to **attach** to the property. The date of attachment can be very important, since it may affect the lien's priority in relation to other liens. (Lien priority will be discussed shortly.)

Liens may be voluntary or involuntary. A **voluntary lien** is one the debtor voluntarily gives to the creditor, usually as security for a loan. The two types of voluntary liens are mortgages and deeds of trust. **Involuntary liens** (sometimes called statutory liens) are given to creditors without the property owner's consent, by operation of law. Examples of involuntary liens are property tax liens and judgment liens.

Example: Dunn sues Bronson for injuries sustained in a car crash and wins a $125,000 judgment. The judgment can become a lien against Bronson's property.

Liens may also be classified as general or specific. A **general lien** attaches to all of the debtor's property. For instance, the judgment lien in the example is a general lien. Any property owned by Bronson (in the example above) could be encumbered by the judgment lien. On the other hand, a **specific lien** attaches only to a particular piece of property. A mortgage is an example of a specific lien. It is a lien against only the particular piece of property offered as security for the loan.

Types of Liens

The most common types of liens against real property include mortgages, deeds of trust, mechanic's liens, judgment liens, attachment liens, and tax and assessment liens.

Mortgages. A mortgage is a specific, voluntary lien created by a contract between the property owner (the **mortgagor**) and the creditor (the **mortgagee**). The mortgagee is usually a lender, who will not loan money unless the borrower gives a lien as security for repayment. With the lien in place, the property serves as collateral for the loan.

Deeds of Trust. A deed of trust (also called a trust deed) is used for the same purpose as a mortgage. However, there are three parties to a trust deed rather than the two found in a mortgage transaction. The borrower is called the **trustor**; the lender or creditor is called the **beneficiary**; and there is an independent third party (often an attorney or title insurance company) called the **trustee**. The most significant difference between mortgages and deeds of trust is in the foreclosure process. Mortgages and deeds of trust are discussed in more detail in Chapter 11.

Mechanic's Liens. A person who provides labor, materials, or professional services for the improvement of real property may be entitled to claim a **mechanic's lien** against the property. For example, if a plumber who is involved in remodeling a bathroom isn't paid, he can claim a lien against the property for the amount owed. Eventually, if necessary, the plumber could foreclose on the lien, forcing the property to be sold to pay the debt.

A mechanic's lien is a specific, involuntary lien, attaching only to the property where work was performed or materials were supplied. In some places, mechanic's liens are called **construction liens**. A mechanic's lien claimed by someone who provides materials (as opposed to labor) is sometimes called a **materialman's lien**.

Many improvement projects involve a complex hierarchy of contractors, subcontractors, laborers, and materials suppliers, all of whom may be entitled to claim liens. In some states, even if the property owner already has paid the general contractor, subcontractors who haven't been paid by the general contractor can still file mechanic's liens. As a result, the owner could end up having to pay twice for the same labor or materials.

A mechanic's lien claimant must comply with certain deadlines and other requirements set by state statute; these vary considerably from state to state. As a general rule, a claim of lien must be filed for recording in the county where the property is located within a certain period, such as 30, 60, or 90 days. The claim period might start on the date the contract for the work is signed, on the date the work begins, on the date the work is completed, or on some other date specified in the statute. Filing a claim of lien is called **perfecting** the lien.

Mechanic's lien statutes also set a deadline for foreclosure, usually requiring the lien claimant to file a court action within a specified period after the lien was recorded. The time period allowed is often short, so that the claim (which creates a cloud on the property owner's title) will be resolved quickly.

> **Example:** Allworthy is having her house remodeled. The general contractor and subcontractors who work on the project have a right to claim mechanic's liens if they aren't paid. Under the mechanic's lien statute in Allworthy's state, a claim of lien must be filed for recording within 60 days after the claimant stops working on the property. To foreclose, the claimant must file a lawsuit within 120 days after the claim is recorded.

Note that a mechanic's lien may attach to the property (become legally effective) even before the claim of lien is recorded. For instance, a state statute might specify that the lien attaches as of the date on which the first materials or services are provided for the project.

Thus, there are generally three key dates concerning a mechanic's lien: the date on which the lien attaches, the deadline for recording the claim, and the deadline for foreclosure.

Judgment Liens. When a lawsuit is decided by a court, the judge issues a decree called a **judgment**. If the decree orders the losing party to pay a certain sum of money to the winning party, it's called a money judgment. The party who wins a money judgment (the judgment creditor) is entitled to a lien against the property of the losing party (the judgment debtor). As we mentioned earlier, judgment liens are involuntary, general liens.

A judgment lien ordinarily attaches only to property owned by the debtor in the county where the judgment was issued. If the debtor owns property in other counties in the same state, the creditor can file a notice of the judgment lien in the public record in those counties as well. The lien may also attach to any property acquired by the debtor during the lien period (the length of time the creditor has to take action on the lien).

Once a judgment lien has attached, the debtor must pay the judgment to free the property from the lien. If it's not paid, the creditor can foreclose, and the property will be sold by a designated official (often the county sheriff) to satisfy the judgment. To order the sale, the court issues a **writ of execution**.

Fig. 5.1 Lien classifications

	Voluntary	Involuntary
Specific	Mortgages Deeds of trust	Property taxes Special assessments Mechanic's liens
General		Judgment liens IRS liens

Attachment Liens. When someone files a lawsuit, there is a danger that by the time a judgment is entered, the **defendant** (the party sued) will have sold his property and disappeared, leaving the other party with little more than a piece of paper. To prevent this, the **plaintiff** (the person who started the lawsuit) can ask the court to issue a writ of attachment. A **writ of attachment** directs the sheriff to place a lien on the defendant's property that will satisfy the judgment the plaintiff is seeking. The writ of attachment is recorded and creates a lien on the defendant's real property.

Also, when a lawsuit that may affect title to real property is pending, the plaintiff may record a document giving notice of the lawsuit. This document is called a **lis pendens**, which is Latin for "action pending," and it serves to give notice of a pending legal action that may affect title. While a lis pendens is not a lien, anyone who purchases the property identified in the lis pendens has constructive notice of the pending lawsuit and therefore is bound by any judgment that results from the suit, even though that person is not a party to the lawsuit.

Property Tax Liens. Property is assessed (appraised for tax purposes) and taxed according to its value. When property taxes are levied, a lien attaches to the property until they are paid. Property tax liens are involuntary, specific liens. (Property taxation is discussed in more detail in Chapter 6.)

Special Assessments. Special assessments result from local improvements, such as road paving or sewer lines, that benefit some, but not all, property owners within the county. The properties that have benefited from the improvement are assessed for their share of the cost of the improvement. The assessment creates an involuntary, specific lien against the property. (Special assessments are also discussed in Chapter 6.)

Other Tax Liens. Many other taxes, such as federal income taxes, estate or inheritance taxes, and gift taxes, can result in involuntary liens against property. Unlike property tax liens and special assessment liens, these other tax liens are usually general liens that attach to all of the debtor's property.

Miscellaneous Liens. Depending on state law, it may be possible to create a lien against real property for child support or spousal maintenance (alimony), bail bonds, or various other special types of debts. In addition, condominium and homeowners' associations usually have the power to impose liens for unpaid assessments.

Lien Priority

It's very common for a piece of property to have more than one lien against it. (For example, most homes are encumbered with at least a property tax lien and a mortgage or deed of trust lien.) In some cases, the dollar amounts of all the liens against a property add up to more than the property sells for at a foreclosure sale. When this happens, the sale proceeds are not allocated among all of the lienholders in a pro rata fashion (proportionate distribution). Instead, the liens are paid off according to their priority. This means that the lien with the highest priority is paid off first. If any money is left over, the lien with the second highest priority is paid off, and so forth. A particular lienholder might receive only partial payment, or even no payment at all.

As a general rule, lien priority is determined by the date a lien was recorded. The lien that was recorded first will be paid off first, even though another lien may have been created first.

Example: Suppose Baker borrows money from two banks—$5,000 from National Bank on March 17, and $5,000 from State Bank on May 5 of the same year. Baker gives mortgages to both banks when the loan funds are received. If National Bank does not record its mortgage until July 14, but State Bank records its mortgage promptly on May 5, State Bank's lien will be paid before National Bank's in the event of foreclosure.

While "first in time, first in right" is the general rule in regard to liens, there are some important exceptions. Certain types of liens are given special priority. This is true of property tax and special assessment liens; they have priority over all other liens, regardless of when those other liens attached to the property.

Example: The Cullens bought their house on August 12, 2001, and their mortgage was recorded on the same date. It has priority over later liens against the property, which include a home equity loan recorded on June 6, 2007, and a judgment lien based on a judgment entered on November 16, 2008. However, none of these liens, not even the 2001 mortgage, has priority over the lien for the annual property taxes, which only attached to the Cullens' house on January 1 of this year. In the event of a foreclosure, the property tax lien would be paid off first.

Mechanic's liens are another exception to the general rule. Their priority is determined not by the date the claim of lien is recorded, but by the date that the lien attached to the property. As explained earlier, the time when a mechanic's lien attaches depends on statutory rules that vary from state to state; in most cases, attachment happens before the claim of lien is actually recorded.

Lien priority can be changed. A creditor who holds a lien with higher priority can agree to **subordinate** the claim to another lien, allowing the second creditor to take priority. Subordination agreements are discussed in more detail in Chapter 11.

Homestead Laws

Many states have laws that give homeowners limited protection against lien foreclosure; these are called homestead laws. A **homestead** is generally defined as an owner-occupied dwelling, together with any appurtenant buildings and land. The purpose of homestead laws is to help homeowners avoid losing their home to creditors.

Homestead laws typically offer protection only against judgment liens and attachment liens. They do not apply to specific liens against the homestead property, such as mortgages, deeds of trust, or mechanic's liens. Also, homestead protection usually doesn't apply to certain other types of liens, such as liens for child support or spousal maintenance.

In some states, homestead protection is automatic, and the only requirement is for the owner to occupy the property as a principal residence. Other states require the owner to record a notice called a **declaration of homestead.**

Fig. 5.2 Types of encumbrances

Financial Encumbrances	Nonfinancial Encumbrances
• Mortgages • Deeds of trust • Mechanic's liens • Judgment liens • Attachment liens • Property tax liens • Other tax liens	• Easements • Profits • Private restrictions

Exemption. A few states protect homestead property from judgment liens altogether, but in most states judgment creditors are allowed to foreclose on a homestead. In these states, the property is protected by a **homestead exemption,** which means that a certain amount of the property's value is exempt from creditors' claims. The amount of the exemption is specified in the homestead law.

> **Example:** In the state where Norris lives, the homestead exemption is $40,000. If a judgment creditor were to foreclose on Norris's home, $40,000 of the foreclosure sale proceeds would be set aside for Norris.

When a judgment lien against homestead property is foreclosed on, liens that are not subject to the exemption (such as the homeowner's mortgage) are paid first. Next, the homeowner receives the exemption amount. After that, the judgment creditor and any remaining lienholders are paid in order of priority, and any surplus goes to the homeowner. (If the proceeds of a foreclosure sale would not be more than enough to pay off the liens that the homestead law doesn't apply to and also cover the exemption amount, then the judgment creditor won't be allowed to foreclose—there would be no point.)

Homestead protection may continue for a certain period after the foreclosure, shielding a portion of the sale proceeds (the exemption amount) from creditors. This gives the former owner a chance to buy a new home, reinvesting the money in another homestead property.

Termination. Homestead protection may terminate when the property is sold, when the homesteader files a declaration of abandonment, or when the homesteader files a declaration of homestead on another property. (Once again, this depends on state law.) Funds from the voluntary sale of homestead property, up to the amount of the homestead exemption, may be protected from judgment creditors in the same way that the proceeds of a forced sale are protected, to allow the homesteader to purchase another home.

Nonfinancial Encumbrances

While financial encumbrances affect only title to property, nonfinancial encumbrances affect the physical use or condition of the property itself. Thus, a property owner can find the use of her land limited by a right or interest held by someone else.

Nonfinancial encumbrances include easements, profits, and private restrictions. We'll also cover licenses, encroachments, and nuisances in this section; they too involve someone using another's property or affecting the owner's use of it, although they aren't actually interests in real property.

Easements

An easement is a right to use another person's land for a particular purpose. It is a nonpossessory interest in land; the easement holder has a right to use the land, but has no title or right of possession. An easement is not an estate.

> **Example:** Keller and Drummel own neighboring lots. Keller has an easement across a portion of Drummel's property that gives her access to the public road. Keller has the right to make reasonable use of the easement to get to and from her property. However, she doesn't have the right to build a shed on the easement, plant a garden on it, or use it in any way other than as a driveway. On the other hand, Drummel doesn't have the right to use the portion of his property that's subject to the easement in any way that would prevent Keller from using it as a driveway.

Types of Easements. There are two main types of easements: easements appurtenant and easements in gross.

Easements Appurtenant. An easement appurtenant burdens one parcel of land for the benefit of another parcel of land. The parcel with the benefit is called the **dominant tenement**; the one with the burden is called the **servient tenement**. The owner of the dominant tenement is called the **dominant tenant**; the owner of the servient tenement is the **servient tenant**. Do not confuse the term "tenement," which is the land, with "tenant," which is the landowner.

The most common type of easement appurtenant is one that gives a property owner the right to cross a neighbor's land to reach his own land, like the driveway easement in our earlier example. This type of easement is sometimes called a **right of way** or an **easement for ingress and egress** (entering and exiting). In Figure 5.3, Lot B has an easement appurtenant across Lot A. The easement provides access to Lot B from the public road. Lot B is the dominant tenement. Lot A is the servient tenement.

An easement appurtenant "runs with the land." This phrase means that if either the dominant tenement or the servient tenement is transferred to a new owner, the new owner also acquires the benefit or the burden of the easement. Refer to Figure 5.3 again. If Lot B were sold, the new owner would still have an easement across Lot A. If Lot A were sold, the new owner would still bear the burden of allowing the owner of Lot B to use the easement.

Fig. 5.3 Easement appurtenant

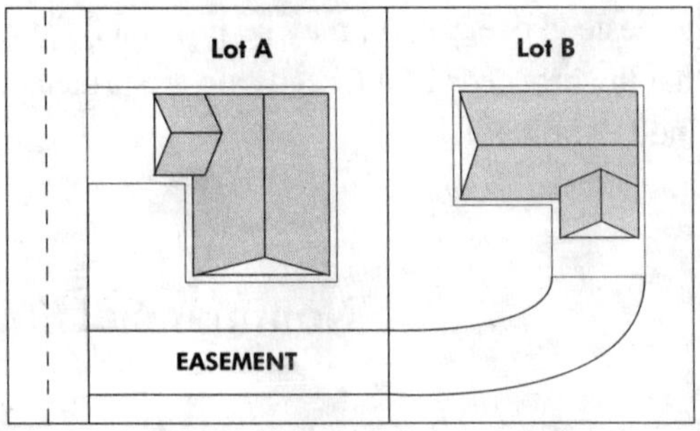

That's true even if the new owner was unaware of the easement at the time of purchase. Once an easement is established, it doesn't have to be mentioned in the deed in order to be binding on future owners.

An easement that benefits a parcel of land is called an easement appurtenant because it goes along with ownership of the land like other appurtenances (air rights, for example). The easement is appurtenant to the dominant tenement.

There's a special type of easement appurtenant known as a party wall easement. A **party wall** is a wall or fence that sits on the boundary line between two lots and whose ownership is shared by the owners of the lots. Each lot owner owns the half of the wall or fence that sits on her side of the boundary, and has an easement appurtenant for the other half. For a party wall easement, the parties should have a detailed written agreement to establish their rights and obligations.

Easements in Gross. An easement in gross benefits a person (a dominant tenant) rather than a parcel of land. When someone has an easement in gross, there is no dominant tenement, only a servient tenement.

> **Example:** Wilson has the right to enter Able's land and swim in Able's pond. Wilson is a dominant tenant with an easement in gross over Able's land (the servient tenement). The easement serves Wilson, not a parcel of land.

An easement in gross runs with the servient tenement. Referring back to the example above, if Able sells his land, the new owner will have to allow Wilson to swim in the pond.

Most easements in gross are commercial easements. The most common example is an easement held by a utility company that allows company employees to enter property to install and service the utility lines.

Commercial easements can be assigned—transferred from one utility company to another. With a personal easement in gross, whether or not the dominant tenant can transfer or assign the easement rights depends on state law.

Creating an Easement. Easements (whether appurtenant or in gross) can be created in any of the following ways:

- express grant,
- express reservation,
- necessity,
- implication,
- prescription,
- dedication, or
- condemnation.

Express Grant. An easement is created by express grant when a property owner grants someone else the right to use the property. The grant must be put into writing and comply with all of the other requirements for conveyance of an interest in land (see Chapter 4).

When granting an easement, the grantor does not have to specify the location of the easement. For example, a grant of an easement "across Lot A for purposes of ingress and egress" would be valid (assuming that all of the other requirements for a proper conveyance are met).

A person can grant an easement only in the interest that she holds. For instance, if a tenant grants an easement in the leased property, the easement will exist only for the term of the lease.

A fee simple owner may grant an easement that will last in perpetuity (indefinitely), or for the life of the grantor, or only for a specified term.

Express Reservation. A landowner who is conveying a portion of his property may reserve an easement in that parcel to benefit the parcel of land that is retained. Like an express grant, an express reservation must be put into writing.

Example: Carmichael owns 100 acres beside a state highway. She sells 40 acres, including all the highway frontage. In the deed, she reserves to herself an easement across the conveyed land so that she will have access to her remaining 60 acres.

Necessity. An easement by necessity arises when a property cannot be accessed by its owner. For example, if a property is landlocked (entirely surrounded by other privately owned land) and has no access to a public street, the owner is entitled to an easement running from the property to the nearest street. In some states, an easement by necessity is created automatically; other states require the property owner to go to court to obtain the easement.

Implication. An easement by implication is created when a property is divided and part of it is transferred to another owner. The easement can be either an implied grant or an implied reservation. This type of easement can arise only when a property is divided into more than one lot, and the grantor neglects to grant or reserve an easement on one lot for the benefit of the other. The easement is implied by law instead.

There are usually two requirements for an easement to be created by implication:

1. it must be reasonably necessary for the enjoyment of the property, and
2. there must have been apparent prior use.

The second requirement is fulfilled if the use was established before the property was divided, and would have been apparent to prospective purchasers in an inspection of the property.

An easement by implication is similar to an easement by necessity. In some states, the laws concerning easements by necessity and easements by implication have developed so that there is no significant difference between the two.

Prescription. An easement by prescription (also called a prescriptive easement) is created through long-term use of land without the permission of the landowner. Acquiring a prescriptive easement is similar to acquiring ownership through adverse possession (see Chapter 4). Here are the requirements for a prescriptive easement:

- the use is **open and notorious** (apparent to the landowner);
- the use is **hostile** (without the landowner's permission); and
- the use is **reasonably continuous** for the period of time specified by state law (anywhere from five to twenty years).

Unlike adverse possession, a prescriptive easement usually doesn't require exclusive use of the property. In other words, a prescriptive easement may be created even if the landowner is also using the property.

Landowners can protect against prescriptive easements by recording a **notice of consent**, giving express permission for a certain use of their property. Since prescription requires use without the owner's permission, this prevents the creation of a prescriptive easement. The permission can later be revoked by recording a notice of revocation.

Dedication. A private landowner may grant an easement to the public to use some portion of her property for a public purpose, such as a sidewalk. The dedication may be expressly stated, or it may be implied.

Condemnation. The government may exercise its power of eminent domain and condemn private property to gain an easement for a public purpose, such as a road. This power may also be exercised by private companies that serve the public, such as railroad and utility companies.

Terminating an Easement. An easement can be terminated in any of the following ways:

- release,
- merger,
- failure of purpose (or necessity no longer exists),
- abandonment, or
- prescription.

Release. The holder of an easement may release his rights in the servient tenement. This would be accomplished with a written document, usually a quitclaim deed from the easement holder to the owner of the servient tenement.

Merger. Since an easement is, by definition, the right to make a certain use of another person's land, if the dominant and servient tenements come to be owned by the same person, the easement is no longer necessary and therefore is terminated. This is called merger; ownership of the dominant tenement has merged with ownership of the servient tenement.

Failure of Purpose. If the purpose for which an easement was created ceases, then the easement terminates. Similarly, an easement by necessity will terminate once the need no longer exists. For example, if a landlocked owner holds an easement by necessity and then buys an adjoining parcel that provides access to the first property, the easement is terminated.

Abandonment. An easement is also terminated if the easement holder abandons it. This usually requires acts by the holder indicating an intent to abandon the easement. Mere non-use is generally not considered to be abandonment.

Example: The dominant tenant builds a fence that blocks any further use of an easement that had been used for ingress and egress. Under the circumstances, it would be reasonable for the servient tenant to conclude that the easement has been abandoned.

Some states make an exception to this rule for prescriptive easements. If a prescriptive easement is not used for a specified period of time (for example, five years), the servient tenant may ask a court to rule that the easement has terminated, even though the dominant tenant has done nothing that indicates an intent to abandon it.

Prescription. Easements can be created by prescription, and they can also be extinguished by prescription. This happens if the servient tenant prevents the dominant tenant from using the easement for the period required by state law for prescription.

Example: The servient tenant builds a brick wall around his property. The dominant tenant can no longer use her easement for ingress and egress. If the wall remains undisturbed for the period required by state law, then the easement will be terminated by prescription.

Profits

A profit is the right to take something away from land that belongs to someone else. For example, it might be the right to take timber, peat, or gravel from someone else's land. The difference between a profit and an easement is that the easement is just a right to use another's land, but a profit allows the removal of something from the land. As a general rule, a profit must be created in writing or by prescription.

Licenses

Like an easement, a license gives someone the right to make some use of another person's land. However, easements and licenses are different in many ways. An easement is created in writing or through action of law. Ordinarily, a license is just spoken permission to cross, hunt or fish on, or make some other use of a landowner's property. An easement is irrevocable, but a license can be revoked at the will of the landowner. In general, easements are permanent and licenses are temporary. A license is a personal right that does not run with or pass with the land. It cannot be assigned. Since the license is revocable at the will of the landowner, it is not actually considered an encumbrance or an interest in the property.

Encroachments

An encroachment is something that intrudes from one person's land onto another's without authorization, such as a fence or garage built partially over the property line onto the neighbor's land (see Figure 5.4). Most encroachments are unintentional, resulting from a mistake concerning the exact location of the property line.

An encroachment may be considered a **trespass** if it violates a property owner's rights of possession. A court can order the removal of an encroachment through a judicial action called an **ejectment**. Alternatively, if the cost of the removal would be too great, the court could order the encroacher to pay damages to the property owner.

Technically, an encroachment is not an encumbrance because it is not a right or interest held by the encroacher. However, a property owner who ignores an encroachment for too long might lose the right to have the encroachment removed. The encroachment could ripen into a prescriptive easement if allowed to remain for the period required for prescription under state law.

Nuisances

A nuisance is an activity or a condition on neighboring property that interferes with a property owner's reasonable use or enjoyment of her own property. Common

Fig. 5.4 Encroachments

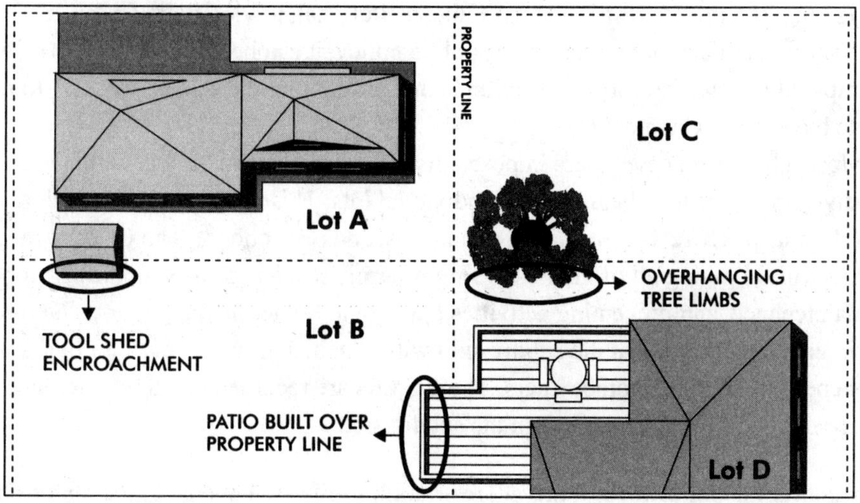

examples include odors, noises, and interference with communication signals. Like an encroachment, a nuisance isn't truly an encumbrance, but rather a violation of an owner's possessory rights.

A private nuisance affects only a few surrounding people. For example, rotting garbage in a neighbor's backyard would be a private nuisance. A public nuisance affects a larger community's health or welfare; jet noise and industrial emissions are examples. A property owner may ask a court for an injunction against a private or public nuisance, or may sue for damages.

A related concept is the **attractive nuisance** doctrine. The owner of a property with a feature that is dangerous and attractive to children, such as an unfenced swimming pool or construction site, may be held liable for any harm resulting from failure to keep out trespassing children.

Private Restrictions

Private restrictions, also called **deed restrictions** or **restrictive covenants**, are restrictions on a property's use that were imposed by a previous owner, or perhaps by the current owner. Like easements, private restrictions can "run with the land," binding all subsequent owners of the property.

> **Example:** When the Graysons sold their property in 1940, they included a restriction in the deed stating that the poplar trees in the front yard must not be cut down. Everyone who's owned the property since then, including the current owner, has had to comply with the Graysons' wishes regarding the trees.

While restrictions are often imposed in a deed, as in the example, they can also be created by written agreement between the current property owner and a neighbor or some other party. This type of restriction could also run with the land and be binding on all future owners.

As long as a private restriction isn't unconstitutional, in violation of a law, or contrary to a judicial determination of public policy, it can be enforced in court. (An example of an unenforceable restriction is one prohibiting the sale of property to non-white buyers; see Chapter 16.)

Most subdivision developers impose a list of restrictions on all lots within the subdivision before they begin selling individual lots. This is called a **declaration of restrictions** or **CC&Rs** (covenants, conditions, and restrictions). The CC&Rs might include rules limiting all of the lots to single-family residential use, requiring property maintenance, and preventing activities that would bother the neighbors. The rules are intended to ensure that the subdivision will remain a desirable place to live, for the benefit of all of the homeowners. The CC&Rs are recorded and then referenced in the deeds used to convey the lots in the subdivision.

Covenants vs. Conditions. A private restriction is either a covenant or a condition. A **covenant** is a promise to do or not do something, as in a contract. A property owner who violates a covenant may be sued, leading to an injunction (a court order directing the owner to comply with the covenant) or, less often, payment of damages for failure to comply. Violation of a **condition** can have more serious consequences. A condition in a deed makes the grantee's title conditional, so that he owns a fee simple defeasible rather than a fee simple absolute (see Chapter 3). Breach of the condition could result in forfeiture of title.

Whether a particular restriction is a covenant or a condition depends on the wording in the deed. Courts try to avoid forfeiture, which is considered a harsh remedy, so they will usually interpret a restriction as a covenant rather than a condition if there is any ambiguity. (Note that CC&Rs are virtually always covenants, even though the term includes the word "conditions.")

Termination of Restrictions. It's up to the property owners within a subdivision to enforce the CC&Rs. If the residents have failed to enforce a particular restriction in the past, they may no longer be able to enforce it.

> **Example:** The subdivision's CC&Rs state that recreational vehicles may not be parked within view of the street. Over the years, however, many homeowners have broken this rule and their neighbors haven't complained. If someone tries to start enforcing the parking restriction now, a court might rule that it has been abandoned and is no longer enforceable.

A private restriction will also terminate if its purpose can no longer be achieved. For example, this might occur because zoning changes and other factors have dramatically altered the character of the neighborhood. If there's a private restriction limiting a property to single-family residential use, but most of the surrounding properties are now used for light industry, the restriction may no longer be enforceable.

Chapter Summary

1. An encumbrance is a nonpossessory right or interest in real property held by someone other than the property owner. Encumbrances may be financial or nonfinancial.

2. A financial encumbrance (a lien) affects title to property. It gives a creditor the right to foreclose and use the sale proceeds to pay off the debt. A lien is either voluntary or involuntary, and either general or specific. Some of the most common types of liens are mortgages, deeds of trust, mechanic's liens, judgment liens, attachment liens, and tax liens.

3. A nonfinancial encumbrance affects the use or condition of the property. Nonfinancial encumbrances include easements, profits, and private restrictions.

4. An easement gives the easement holder the right to use someone else's property (or a portion of the property) for a specified purpose. An easement runs with the land, affecting the title of subsequent owners of the property or properties in question.

5. An easement appurtenant burdens one parcel of land (the servient tenement) for the benefit of another parcel (the dominant tenement). An easement in gross burdens a parcel of land for the benefit of a person, not another parcel of land.

6. Licenses, encroachments, and nuisances also may affect the use or condition of property. They are not classified as encumbrances, however, because they are not interests in real property.

7. Private restrictions affect how an owner may use his own property. Like easements, private restrictions run with the land. A declaration of CC&Rs recorded by a subdivision developer is binding on the future owners of the subdivision lots.

Key Terms

Encumbrance—An interest in real property held by someone other than the property owner.

Voluntary lien—A security interest given to a creditor voluntarily.

Involuntary lien—A security interest given to a creditor by operation of law.

General lien—A lien that attaches to all of a debtor's property.

Specific lien—A lien that attaches only to one particular piece of property.

Mechanic's lien—A lien on property in favor of someone who provided labor or materials to improve it. Also called a construction lien or materialman's lien.

Judgment lien—A lien held by someone who has won a judgment in a lawsuit, attaching to property owned by the person who lost the lawsuit.

Easement—A property interest that gives the holder the right to use another's land for a particular purpose.

Easement appurtenant—An easement that burdens one parcel of land (the servient tenement) for the benefit of another parcel (the dominant tenement).

Easement in gross—An easement that benefits a person rather than a parcel of land.

Easement by prescription—An easement created by continuous use for a period determined by state law, without the landowner's permission. Also called a prescriptive easement.

Party wall easement—An easement where ownership of a boundary wall or fence is shared by adjacent landowners.

Merger—When both the dominant tenement and the servient tenement are acquired by one owner, resulting in termination of the easement.

Abandonment—One of the ways in which an easement may terminate; it generally requires action by the easement holder indicating an intent to abandon the easement.

Profit—The right to take something (such as timber) from another's land.

License—Revocable permission to enter another's land, which does not create an interest in the property.

Encroachment—Something that intrudes onto neighboring property, such as a tree branch or a fence.

Nuisance—An activity or condition on nearby property that interferes with a property owner's reasonable use and enjoyment of her property.

Attractive nuisance— A property feature that is dangerous and attractive to children, such as an unfenced swimming pool or construction site.

CC&Rs—Covenants, conditions, and restrictions; private restrictions imposed by a subdivision developer.

Condition—A restriction on a property owner's use of his land that may result in forfeiture of title if violated.

Restrictive covenant—A property owner's promise to refrain from using her land in a specified way, which may be enforced by an injunction or damages, but cannot lead to forfeiture of title.

Chapter Quiz

1. Real estate property tax liens are:
   a) general, involuntary liens
   b) general, voluntary liens
   c) specific, voluntary liens
   d) specific, involuntary liens

2. A lawsuit against Thatcher is pending. The court rules that a lien should be placed on his farm, holding it as security in case of a negative judgment. This is:
   a) adverse possession
   b) prescription
   c) an attachment
   d) an easement

3. A recorded document that informs potential buyers that the property may become subject to a judgment in a lawsuit is a:
   a) lis pendens
   b) writ of execution
   c) writ of attachment
   d) habendum clause

4. Which of the following has priority over a mortgage, no matter how long ago the mortgage was recorded?
   a) Deed of trust
   b) Judgment lien
   c) Property tax lien
   d) None of the above

5. If there were two deeds of trust against the same property and you needed to know which one had higher priority, you could find this information at the county recorder's office. The priority is usually established by:
   a) the printed trust deed forms, which have the words "first deed of trust" and "second deed of trust" on their face
   b) the date and time of recording
   c) the county auditor's stamp, which says "first trust deed" or "second trust deed"
   d) the execution date of each document

6. When there's an easement appurtenant, the dominant tenement:
   a) can be used only for purposes of ingress and egress
   b) is burdened by the easement
   c) receives the benefit of the easement
   d) cannot be sold

7. You have the right to cross another's land to get to your house. You probably own a:
   a) dominant tenement
   b) servient tenement
   c) Both of the above
   d) Neither of the above

8. An easement in gross benefits a:
   a) dominant tenement
   b) servient tenement
   c) Both of the above
   d) Neither of the above

9. Unlike a license, an easement appurtenant:
   a) is not an encumbrance
   b) is considered a possessory interest in real property
   c) runs with the land
   d) can be revoked by the owner of the servient tenement

10. Which of the following is not a method of creating an easement?
    a) Implication
    b) Express grant in a deed
    c) Dedication
    d) Spoken grant

11. The creation of an easement by prescription is similar to acquiring ownership of property by:
    a) adverse possession
    b) escheat
    c) alluvium
    d) intestate succession

12. A has an easement over B's property. If A buys B's property, the easement is:
    a) abandoned
    b) terminated by merger
    c) unaffected
    d) None of the above

13. A porch or balcony that hangs over the established boundary line of a parcel of land is called a/an:
    a) easement in gross
    b) encroachment
    c) easement appurtenant
    d) license

14. All of the following would be considered nuisances, except:
    a) fumes from a paper mill
    b) a house with regular drug-dealing activity
    c) radiation from a microwave tower
    d) a garage built on top of the property line

15. The private restrictions in a subdivision's CC&Rs:
    a) do not run with the land
    b) were most likely imposed by the developer
    c) can terminate only with the approval of a majority of the lot owners
    d) create a lien against the property

Answer Key

1. d) Property tax liens are specific (they attach only to the taxed property) and involuntary.

2. c) In an attachment, a lien is created against the defendant's property, pending the outcome of the lawsuit.

3. a) A lis pendens provides constructive notice of a pending lawsuit that may affect the property described in the document.

4. c) Property tax liens always have priority over other liens.

5. b) The date of recording governs lien priority, rather than the date of execution of the documents.

6. c) The dominant tenement is benefited by the easement; the servient tenement is burdened by the easement. An easement appurtenant is not necessarily an easement for ingress and egress.

7. a) Since you have the right to use another's property to reach your own, you probably own a dominant tenement.

8. d) An easement in gross benefits an individual (the dominant tenant) rather than any parcel of land.

9. c) An easement appurtenant runs with the land, which means that future owners of the servient tenement will have to allow the easement to be used. A license does not run with the land.

10. d) Like any other interest in land, an easement must be granted in writing, unless it is created by operation of law.

11. a) An easement by prescription is obtained in much the same way as ownership by adverse possession: the use must be open and notorious, hostile, and continuous for the length of time required by state law.

12. b) Merger occurs when one person acquires ownership of both the dominant tenement and the servient tenement. Merger terminates the easement.

13. b) An overhanging porch or balcony is an encroachment.

14. d) A structure built on the property line is an encroachment, not a nuisance. A nuisance is an activity or condition on neighboring property that negatively affects an owner's use and enjoyment of his property.

15. b) CC&Rs are usually imposed by the developer. They run with the land, which means that subsequent owners of the subdivision lots must abide by them.

Chapter 6

Public Restrictions on Land

I. Land Use Controls
   A. Comprehensive planning
   B. Zoning
      1. Enforcement
      2. Zoning exceptions and amendments
         a. nonconforming uses
         b. variances
         c. conditional uses
         d. rezones
         e. spot zoning
      3. Zoning vs. private restrictions
   C. Building codes
   D. Subdivision regulations
   E. Floodplain restrictions
   F. Environmental laws
      1. NEPA
      2. CERCLA
      3. Pollution control laws
      4. Other environmental laws

II. Eminent Domain

III. Taxation
   A. General real estate taxes
   B. Special assessments
   C. Conveyance taxes

Chapter Overview

Although a property owner has many rights in regard to his property, those rights are limited by certain powers of the federal, state, and local governments. This chapter examines the ways in which governmental powers affect property ownership most directly. The first part of the chapter explains planning, zoning, and other public restrictions on land use. The second part discusses the government's power to tax property.

Land Use Controls

In the United States, the powers of government are determined by the federal and state constitutions. Thus, efforts by the federal, state, and local governments to control the use of private property raise constitutional issues. When a property owner objects to a land use law, the central question is often whether the law is constitutional—whether the federal or state constitution gives the government the power to interfere with private property rights in this way.

The basis for land use control laws is the **police power**. This is a state's power to adopt and enforce laws and regulations necessary for the protection of the public's health, safety, morals, and general welfare. A state may delegate its police power to local governmental bodies, such as city councils, through legislation known as an enabling act.

It is the police power that allows state and local governments to regulate the use of private property. The federal Constitution does not give the federal government a general power to regulate for the public health, safety, morals, and welfare. But the federal government does have authority to use its other powers (such as the power to regulate interstate commerce) to advance police power objectives.

Exercises of the police power must meet constitutional limitations. As a general rule, a land use law or regulation will be considered constitutional if it meets these four criteria:

1. It is reasonably related to the protection of the public health, safety, morals, or general welfare.
2. It applies in the same manner to all property owners who are similarly situated (it is not discriminatory).
3. It does not reduce a property's value so much that the regulation amounts to a confiscation.
4. It benefits the public by preventing harm that would be caused by the prohibited use of the property.

If a law or regulation does not meet these criteria, it may be challenged as an unconstitutional regulatory taking. Regulatory takings will be discussed later in this chapter.

Government land use controls take a variety of forms: comprehensive plans, zoning ordinances, building codes, subdivision regulations, and environmental laws. All of these are intended to protect the public from problems that unrestricted use of private property can cause.

If two different governmental entities have passed conflicting laws or ordinances based on the police power, the one with the stricter standards of health and safety will apply.

Comprehensive Planning

It's easy to see how unrestricted and unplanned development can have undesirable results. Incompatible uses, such as a dairy farm and a retail shopping center, could end up right next to each other. And even when neighboring uses are compatible, development may be too dense, causing traffic gridlock, pollution, and other problems; or not dense enough, leading to urban and suburban sprawl.

To alleviate problems caused by haphazard, unplanned growth, states typically require their local governments (cities and counties) to have planning agencies, usually referred to as **planning commissions**.

A local government's planning commission is responsible for designing and adopting a long-term plan for all development within the city or county. This may be referred to as the "master plan," "comprehensive plan," or "general plan." The purpose of the plan is to outline the community's development goals and design an overall physical layout to achieve those goals.

In creating a general plan, the planning commission should consider the developed and undeveloped land in the area and evaluate the region's anticipated economic and population growth. The general plan should address housing and transportation needs; community resources, such as utilities, schools, and hospitals; and recreational facilities and open spaces. The plan should build upon existing land use patterns and transportation systems, yet be flexible enough to accommodate future shifts in the economy and population.

Once a general plan has been adopted, all development and all land use regulations for the area must conform to it. To implement the plan, the local government uses its police power to pass zoning ordinances and other laws, and may also use its power of eminent domain to acquire property for public use. (Eminent domain will be discussed later in the chapter.)

Zoning

Zoning ordinances divide a community into areas (zones) that are set aside for specific types of uses, such as residential, commercial, agricultural, or industrial. Each of these basic categories may have subcategories. For instance, an industrial district could be divided into a light industrial zone and a heavy industrial zone; while a residential district could be divided into single-family zones and multi-family zones. The different types of zones are frequently identified by abbreviations—R for Residential, C for Commercial, and so on—but the specific designations vary from one municipality to another.

Example: In Ellington, a medium-sized city, there are three different types of residential zones. In R-1 zones, only single-family homes are permitted. In R-2 zones, dwellings with up to four units are allowed. Larger multi-family buildings (condominiums and rental apartments) can be built in R-3 zones.

Keeping different types of uses in separate zones helps ensure that only compatible uses are located in the same area. Areas zoned for incompatible uses may be separated by **buffer zones**: parks, playgrounds, or undeveloped open space. Some places have **overlay zoning**, which permits a mixture of different uses in a specific area. For example, a planned unit development might contain single-family and multifamily homes, retail businesses, and open space.

Fig. 6.1 Setbacks and side yards

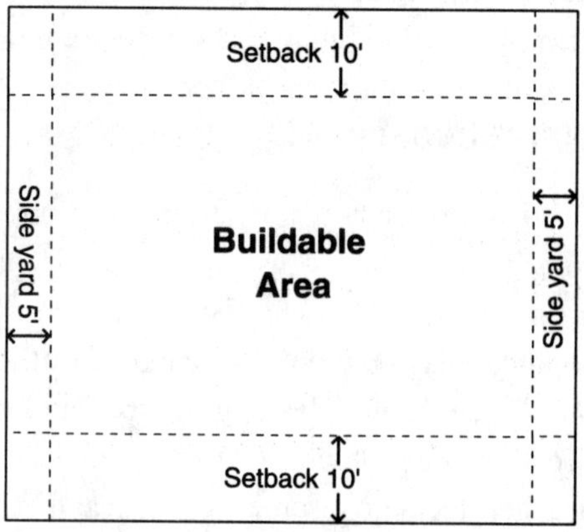

Zoning ordinances typically regulate the height, size, and shape of buildings, as well as their use. The laws also usually include setback and side yard requirements, which prescribe the minimum distance between a building and the property lines (see Figure 6.1). These regulations control population density, provide aesthetic guidelines, and help preserve adequate open space and access to air and daylight.

Enforcement. Zoning is enforced mainly through the use of building permits. Before constructing a building or altering an existing structure, the property owner must apply for a permit. If the proposed construction or alterations do not conform to the zoning laws, the permit will not be issued. Fines or other penalties may be imposed on builders or owners who don't comply with the zoning and permit requirements.

Zoning Exceptions and Amendments. Complications inevitably arise when zoning regulations are administered and enforced. So zoning ordinances provide for certain exceptions and changes to their rules, including:

- nonconforming uses,
- variances,
- conditional uses, and
- rezones.

A zoning exception or revision can be requested by an individual property owner, a developer, or a city or county government. Such requests, along with appeals of zoning decisions, are heard by the local zoning authority, typically referred to as a zoning hearings board or board of adjustment.

Nonconforming Uses. A **nonconforming use** can arise when an area is zoned for the first time, or when a zoning ordinance is amended. Certain established uses that were previously lawful may not conform to the rules laid down in the new ordinance. These nonconforming uses will be permitted to continue.

Example: Smith has been lawfully operating a bakery for seven months when his property is rezoned for single-family residential use. Smith's bakery will be allowed to continue as a nonconforming use. He is not required to apply for a permit.

A nonconforming use provision in a zoning ordinance is sometimes referred to as a grandfather clause. However, even though nonconforming uses are "grandfathered in" and allowed to remain, the local government usually prefers to have all properties in a zone conform to the current rules. So an ordinance might require nonconforming uses to be phased out by a certain deadline (for example, ten years after the ordinance was passed). Even in the absence of such a deadline, the owners of a nonconforming use property are often prohibited from enlarging the use, rebuilding if the property is destroyed, or resuming the use after abandoning it.

Example: Smith's bakery burns to the ground in a terrible fire. The zoning authority will not allow him to rebuild the bakery in this residential zone. He will have to sell the property and use the insurance proceeds to buy a suitable property located in a commercial zone.

Variances. In some cases, if a zoning law were strictly enforced, the property owner's injury would far outweigh the benefit of enforcing the zoning requirement. Under these circumstances, a **variance** may be available. A variance is authorization to build or maintain a structure or use that is prohibited by the zoning ordinance. For example, a variance might authorize construction of a house even though the topography of the lot makes it virtually impossible to comply with normal setback requirements. In most communities, the property owner applies to the local zoning authority for a variance.

A variance usually will not be granted unless the property owner faces severe practical difficulties or undue hardship (not created by the property owner herself) as a result of the zoning. The owner is generally required to prove that the zoning prevents a reasonable use of the land, not merely the most profitable use.

Example: Martinez owns a piece of property that would make a perfect site for a convenience store, but it is in a single-family residential zone. Martinez would not be able to get a variance by claiming that a convenience store would be much more profitable than a single-family home.

Most variances authorize only minor deviations from the zoning law. A variance should not change the essential character of the neighborhood or conflict with the community's general plan.

Conditional Uses. Various special uses, such as schools, hospitals, and churches, don't fit into the ordinary zoning categories. These uses are necessary to the community, yet they may have adverse effects on neighboring properties. In most communities, the zoning authority can issue **conditional use permits** (also called **special exception permits**), allowing a limited number of these uses to operate in compliance with specified conditions. For example, a property owner might be given a conditional use permit to build a private school in a residential neighborhood, as long as the school meets certain requirements for parking, security, and so on.

Rezones. A property owner who believes that her property has been zoned improperly may petition the local zoning authority for a **rezone** (sometimes called a zoning amendment). Before a decision is made on a petition, notice must be given to surrounding landowners and a hearing must be held.

When an area is rezoned to a more restrictive use (for example, a change from multifamily dwellings to single-family dwellings), it's referred to as **downzoning**. An **upzone** is the opposite; the zoning becomes less restrictive. An example of an upzone would be raising the height limits in an urban area to help meet the housing density goals of a comprehensive plan.

Spot Zoning. Spot zoning refers to zoning or rezoning an individual parcel of property differently than the surrounding properties. For example, it would be spot zoning if a city rezoned a single parcel in a residential neighborhood to allow the owner of that parcel to open a business. In many jurisdictions, spot zoning is illegal if it favors a particular property owner without benefiting the neighborhood as a whole or otherwise furthering the city's planning goals.

Zoning vs. Private Restrictions. Sometimes private restrictions impose stricter limits on property than the local zoning ordinance. For example, suppose a property is in a zone that requires lots to have a minimum of 15,000 square feet, while a private restriction on the property prevents it from being subdivided into lots smaller than half an acre (21,780 square feet). The general rule is that the more restrictive requirement must be met. In our example, the private restriction would take precedence over the zoning ordinance, because it is the more restrictive of the two. On the other hand, in cases where the zoning is more restrictive than a private restriction, the zoning will take precedence.

Building Codes

The enactment of building codes is another exercise of the police power that is carried out by local governments. Building codes protect the public from unsafe or unworkmanlike construction. They are often divided into specialized codes, such as a fire code, an electrical code, and a plumbing code. The codes set standards for construction methods and materials. A structure that was built before a new, stricter standard was enacted may still be required to meet the new standard.

Enforcement of building codes is usually accomplished through the building permit system. A property owner must obtain a permit from the city or county before constructing a new building or repairing, improving, or altering an existing building. For example, it is usually necessary to have a building permit in order to add on to a home, to convert a carport into a garage, or even to build a fence. The permit requirement allows officials to examine the building plans to make sure that building codes and zoning ordinances have been satisfied. In some cases, an official will make periodic inspections of the property during construction. Once the completed construction has been inspected and found satisfactory, a **certificate of occupancy** (sometimes called an occupancy permit) is issued.

Subdivision Regulations

Another way in which state and local governments control land use is by regulating subdivisions. A **subdivision** is a division of one parcel of land into two or more parcels or lots. Most subdivisions are residential, although there are also commercial, industrial, and recreational subdivisions. In a traditional residential subdivision, each lot is owned separately and has a single-family home built on it, but common interest developments such as condominiums and PUDs are also subdivisions (see Chapter 3).

Procedural Laws. In most cities and counties detailed procedures have to be followed when land is subdivided. This usually includes submitting a preliminary plat map for approval by local officials before the actual development work is carried out. There are also likely to be specific requirements for utilities, streets, sidewalks, and other physical aspects of the subdivision that the developer must comply with.

Consumer Protection Laws. Some states have consumer protection laws concerning subdivisions. These regulate how subdivided property is advertised to prospective buyers, require certain disclosures, and impose other rules on the sale of lots. For example, purchasers might be given a right of rescission, allowing them to change their minds after signing a contract. This type of state subdivision law shares some of the features of the federal law we'll discuss next, but applies to any sale of subdivided land within the state, not just to interstate sales.

ILSA. The **Interstate Land Sales Full Disclosure Act** (commonly referred to as ILSA) is a federal consumer protection law concerning subdivisions offered for sale or lease in interstate commerce. For example, when a subdivision in a particular state is advertised in a national magazine, the developer may have to comply with ILSA. The interstate commerce element also generally exists when a loan is involved, since loan funds typically come from sources crossing state lines. ILSA generally applies to subdivisions containing 25 or more vacant lots, although numerous exemptions apply.

Under ILSA, developers of subdivisions with 25 or more vacant lots must disclose information to buyers in the form of a property report. The required disclosures include information regarding title to the property, payment and conveyance terms, proximity to schools and recreational areas, availability of utilities, soil conditions, easements or restrictive covenants, and so on. The property report must be given to a prospective buyer before a purchase agreement is signed. Once the report is received, the buyer has a seven-day **right of rescission**. During this "cooling-off period," the buyer is entitled to cancel the sales contract for any reason and have any deposit returned to her.

In addition, ILSA requires developers of subdivisions with 100 or more vacant lots to register their projects with the appropriate federal agency. The statute was originally administered and enforced by the Department of Housing and Urban Development (HUD), but that role has been assumed by the Consumer Financial Protection Bureau.

Floodplain Restrictions

A floodplain is a low-lying area of land located near a waterway or body of water that is prone to flooding during severe weather. When floodplains are populated, periodic flooding can result in injury and loss of life, as well as destruction of property. Frequently, the public bears a large share of the resulting financial costs, through government funding for disaster relief.

Some local governments are now taking steps to discourage new or additional development in floodplains. For example, in some places certain areas are designated as **floodplain districts** or **flood hazard zones** in which residential use and new construction is prohibited.

The federal government helps make flood insurance available to owners of property located in floodplains; this is discussed in Chapter 18.

Environmental Laws

The federal and state governments have enacted a number of laws aimed at preserving and protecting the physical environment, and many local governments have additional environmental regulations. These laws can have a substantial impact on the ways in which a property owner is allowed to use his land.

National Environmental Policy Act (NEPA). NEPA is a federal law that requires federal agencies to prepare an **environmental impact statement** (EIS) for governmental actions that would have a significant impact. NEPA also applies to private uses or developments that require the approval of a federal agency.

An EIS summarizes a proposed project's background information and its probable environmental effects (both positive and negative), along with a list of alternatives to the proposed project. The EIS is typically used by a planning or zoning commission to help assess the potential environmental effects of a project.

Many states have enacted their own versions of NEPA. These laws, known as "little NEPAs," function as state equivalents of the federal law, requiring environmental impact reports for public or private projects with a significant impact on the environment when state or local approval is involved. The state laws are often more restrictive than the federal version.

CERCLA. The Comprehensive Environmental Response, Compensation, and Liability Act, a federal law, concerns liability for environmental cleanup costs. In some cases, the current owners of contaminated property may be required to pay for cleanup, even if they did not cause the contamination.

Pollution Control Laws. Federal legislation sets national standards for air and water quality and requires the states to implement these objectives. Permits are required for the discharge of pollutants into the air or water.

Other Environmental Laws. A variety of other federal, state, and local environmental laws may also affect the development or use of a particular property. In some cases, land that serves as a habitat for endangered species or that has a special ecological value (such as a wetland area) can't be developed at all. It's essential for property buyers to find out about these restrictions before they commit themselves to a purchase. It may be necessary to hire a lawyer who specializes in environmental and land use issues in the local area.

Eminent Domain

As you've seen, the government can regulate the use of private property with different kinds of laws—zoning ordinances, building codes, and so on. All of these laws are based on the police power, the government's power to regulate for the public health, safety, morals, and general welfare. Another governmental power that can be used to control land use is the power of **eminent domain**.

The power of eminent domain is the federal or state government's power to take private property for a public purpose. The Constitution requires payment of **just compensation** to an owner or tenant whose property is taken. A state government may delegate the power of eminent domain to local governments, and to private entities that serve the public, such as utility companies and railroads.

Condemnation is the process by which the government exercises its power of eminent domain. When a particular property is needed for a public purpose, the government first offers to buy it from the owner. If the owner refuses to sell for the price offered, the government files a condemnation lawsuit. The court will order title to the property to be transferred to the government. The owner's only grounds for objection are that the intended use of the property is not a public use, or that the price offered is not just compensation. (Just compensation is usually defined as the fair market value of the property.)

A local government can use the power of eminent domain to implement its general plan. For example, to fulfill the plan's open space goals, several pieces of private property might be condemned for use as a public park.

It is important to understand the distinction between eminent domain and the police power. Eminent domain involves taking property away from the private owner, and the Constitution requires the government to pay the owner compensation. In an exercise of the police power, private property is regulated, but not taken away from the owner. The government is not required to compensate the owner for a proper exercise of the police power, even though the action (such as a zoning change) may significantly reduce the value of the property.

Confusingly, you may also hear the term "condemnation" used to refer to an order by local authorities to temporarily vacate a building for health or safety reasons. This is an exercise of the police power, not the power of eminent domain, and does not entitle persons to just compensation.

It is possible for a municipality to regulate a property so restrictively that it crosses the line between the police power and eminent domain. This is known as a **regulatory taking**, or simply a taking. Although the property remains in the possession of the owner, her use of it has been limited to such an extent that the property might as well have been taken away. If a court finds that a taking has occurred, the government will be required to either remove the regulation or pay the owner just compensation.

Taxation

Real property taxes affect property ownership and may have an impact on how property is developed. The taxes create liens (see Chapter 5), and if the property owner fails to pay, the government can sell the property to collect the money owed. Real property taxation has always been a popular method of raising revenue because land has a fixed location, is basically indestructible, and is impossible to conceal. While collection of other types of taxes can be difficult, collection of taxes on real property generally isn't a problem. Sooner or later, the taxes will almost certainly be collected, with or without the cooperation of the property owner.

In this section, we will discuss these three types of taxes on real property:

- general real estate taxes (also called ad valorem taxes),
- special assessments (also called improvement taxes), and
- conveyance taxes (also called excise taxes).

General Real Estate Taxes

General real estate taxes, often simply called property taxes, are levied to support the general operation and services of government. Public schools and police and fire protection are examples of government services paid for with general real estate tax revenues. These taxes are levied by a number of governmental bodies, such as cities, counties, school districts, fire districts, sanitation districts, and water districts. A single property can be situated in five or six taxing districts.

General real estate taxes must be levied fairly. They must be collected and used for a legal purpose, and properties must be assessed and taxed in a consistent manner.

Assessment. General real estate taxes are **ad valorem** taxes. That means the amount of tax owed depends on the value of the property. The more a property is worth, the more the owner will be required to pay in taxes. The valuation of property for purposes of taxation is called **assessment**. Assessments are carried out by a county or city assessor. Property may be periodically reassessed at intervals set by state law.

Property owners who are dissatisfied with the assessment of their property may appeal, typically to a county board of appeal or board of review. Often, an appeal is based on the property owner's claim that the property tax burden has been applied inconsistently, because similar properties in the neighborhood have been assessed differently.

Since some taxes collected by a county are shared with other counties or with the state, it may be necessary to adjust assessments in a particular county in order to bring it into line with the other counties. This is called **equalization**.

Tax Rates. Taxing bodies set tax rates annually. The tax rate is often expressed in mills: one **mill** equals one-tenth of one cent, that is, $0.001. Ten mills equals one cent, 50 mills equals 5 cents, and 100 mills equals 10 cents.

Tax rates are also expressed in dollars per hundred or dollars per thousand. For example, a tax rate of 50 mills is the same as a rate of $5 per $100 of assessed value, or $50 per $1,000 of assessed value.

Tax rates are applied to each property based on its assessed value. So if the tax rate is 50 mills and the property is assessed at $100,000, the property tax will be $5,000 (.05 × $100,000 = $5,000).

Collection of Taxes. General real estate taxes are levied annually. A property owner may receive one overall tax bill that includes the taxes imposed by all of the taxing bodies that have jurisdiction over the property, or separate bills may be prepared. Taxes may be payable in two semi-annual installments, or in more frequent installments, depending on the jurisdiction.

In some states, taxes are paid during the year for which they are levied; in other states, the taxes are due in advance, at the beginning of the tax year. Note that a tax year is not necessarily the same as a calendar year; for example, in a particular state the tax year might begin on July 1 and run through June 30 of the following calendar year.

Tax Foreclosure. In most places, a lien for general real estate taxes attaches to the property automatically when the taxes are levied and remains in force until they have been paid. If the taxes aren't paid, penalties may be imposed. If the taxes remain delinquent for a certain length of time prescribed by state law, the owner will be given a notice of impending default; after another specified interval, a tax sale will be held. Before the sale, the delinquent taxpayer usually has the right to redeem the property and prevent the sale by paying the taxes owed along with penalties and court costs. If the property isn't redeemed, the sale is held and the purchaser receives a **certificate of sale** (also known as a tax certificate). In some states, the delinquent taxpayer still has the opportunity to redeem the property for a certain period after the sale; this is called the post-sale redemption period. At this stage, the taxpayer generally must pay the amount that was raised at the tax sale, plus interest and costs, in order to redeem the property. If the property isn't redeemed before the redemption period expires, the holder of the certificate of sale is given a **tax deed** and becomes the owner of the property.

Alternatively, in some states, when property taxes become delinquent, title to the property is transferred to the taxing body and a redemption period follows. If the property is not redeemed, the taxing body may keep the property for its own use, or sell it at an auction.

Tax Exemptions. Property tax laws often have numerous total or partial exemptions. Property owned by the federal, state, or local government is totally exempt from taxation; so is most property that is used for religious, educational, charitable, or welfare purposes. In some states, there are also partial exemptions for owner-occupied homes and homes owned by veterans, senior citizens, and the disabled. In addition, local governments may offer property tax reductions to attract industries and sport franchises. Tax exemptions may also be used to create other types of incentives. For example, in areas where open space is scarce, partial exemptions are sometimes used to encourage property owners to keep their land undeveloped or in agricultural use. This is an example of how land use can be controlled through taxation.

Special Assessments

Special assessments, also called local improvement taxes, are levied to pay for improvements that benefit particular properties, such as the installation of street lights or the widening of a street. Only the properties that benefit from the improvement are taxed, on the theory that the value of those properties is increased by the improvement. For instance, the cost of street improvements might be assessed against each lot that benefits from the improvements on the basis of the front footage of the lot. Or the cost might be assessed on a fractional basis, with each benefiting lot required to pay an equal share.

A special assessment is usually a one-time tax, although the property owners may be allowed to pay the assessment off in installments.

Like general real estate taxes, special assessments create liens against the taxed properties. If an owner fails to pay the assessment, the government can foreclose on the property.

Sometimes a city or county will create a special district to be in charge of a particular improvement, such as a sewer installation project or an irrigation system. The district issues bonds to pay for the improvements. To pay off the bonds, the district taxes all of the property within the district.

Here is a summary of the distinctions between general real estate taxes and special assessments:

1. General real estate taxes are levied to pay for ongoing government services, such as police protection. A special assessment is levied to pay for a specific improvement, such as adding sidewalks to a section of street.
2. General real estate taxes are levied against all taxable real property within a taxing district, for the benefit of the entire community. A special assessment, on the other hand, is levied against only those properties that benefit from the improvement in question.
3. General real estate taxes are levied every year. A special assessment is a one-time tax, levied only when a property is benefited by a public improvement.

Conveyance Taxes

In a majority of states, a tax is levied on every sale of real property, unless the property is exempt. This may be called a conveyance tax, transfer tax, deed tax, or excise tax.

Example: In the state where the Carlisles live, there's an excise tax on real estate sales. The tax is based on the sales price of the transferred property, and the tax rate is fifty-five cents per $500 of value (or fraction thereof). When the Carlisles sold their house for $202,200, they were required to pay $222.75 for the excise tax.

$$\$202,200 \div \$500 = 404.40$$
$$405 \times \$0.55 = \$222.75$$

In some places that have a conveyance tax, it doesn't apply to the amount of any loan the buyer is assuming or taking title subject to. In the example above, if the buyer had assumed the sellers' $125,200 mortgage, the tax would have been due only on the $77,000 difference between the sales price and the assumed loan. The tax would then have been only $84.70.

Payment of the conveyance tax is generally the seller's legal responsibility, but if the tax isn't paid it can create a lien against the property, even though the seller no longer owns it. However, payment of the tax is required before the buyer's deed can be recorded. Thus, as a practical matter, the buyer will pay the tax if the seller fails to do so.

The federal government collected a conveyance tax on real property sales until 1968. This was called the documentary transfer tax. It was after the federal tax was repealed that individual states began imposing their own conveyance taxes. Conveyance tax rates vary widely around the country. In some places the tax on a typical home sale is only a few hundred dollars, as in the previous example; in others it may come to thousands of dollars.

Under the federal law, the documentary transfer tax was paid by purchasing documentary tax stamps at the recorder's office. These stamps, which looked essentially like postage stamps, were affixed to the buyer's deed before recording, as proof that the tax had been paid. You may still see the tax stamps on older deeds.

Chapter Summary

1. The police power—the government's power to adopt and enforce laws for the protection of the public health, safety, morals, and general welfare—is the basis for land use control laws.

2. A general plan is a county or city's comprehensive, long-term plan for development. A local government implements its general plan with zoning ordinances and other laws.

3. Zoning ordinances provide for certain exceptions to their rules: nonconforming uses, variances, and conditional uses. They also have procedures for rezones.

4. Building codes set standards for construction materials and practices, to protect the public. The codes are enforced through the building permit system.

5. Floodplains are low-lying areas prone to flooding in severe weather. Some local governments have created floodplain districts in which residential use and new construction is prohibited.

6. A number of federal and state environmental laws affect land use, including NEPA, CERCLA, and pollution control laws.

7. A government entity can use the power of eminent domain to implement its general plan. When property is taken under the power of eminent domain, the government must pay just compensation to the owner. In contrast, compensation is not required when property is merely regulated under the police power. However, a property may be regulated so restrictively that it constitutes a taking, and the government is required to compensate the owner.

8. The government's power to tax also affects property ownership. General real estate taxes are levied each year to pay for ongoing government services. Special assessments are levied to pay for improvements that benefit specific properties. Many states impose a conveyance tax on the sale of real property.

Key Terms

Police power—The power of state governments to regulate for the protection of the public health, safety, morals, and general welfare.

General plan—A comprehensive, long-term plan of development for a community, which is implemented by zoning and other laws. Also called a comprehensive plan or master plan.

Zoning—A method of controlling land use by dividing a community into zones for different types of uses.

Nonconforming use—A formerly legal use that does not conform to a new zoning ordinance, but is nonetheless allowed to continue.

Variance—An authorization to deviate from the rules in a zoning ordinance, granted because strict enforcement would cause undue hardship for the property owner.

Conditional use permit—A permit that allows a special use, such as a school or hospital, to operate in a neighborhood where it would otherwise be prohibited by the zoning.

Rezone—An amendment to a zoning ordinance; a property owner who feels his property has been zoned improperly may apply for a rezone.

Spot zoning—The zoning or rezone of a specific parcel of land, which may be illegal if it benefits only the property's owner and not the community as a whole.

Building codes—Regulations that set minimum standards for construction methods and materials.

Subdivision—The division of one parcel of land into two or more parcels.

Eminent domain—The government's power to take private property for public use, upon payment of just compensation to the owner.

Condemnation—The process of taking property pursuant to the power of eminent domain.

Regulatory taking—When regulations restrict the use of property so severely that a court regards it as the equivalent of a confiscation of property and orders the government to pay the owner just compensation.

General real estate taxes—Taxes levied against real property annually to pay for general government services. They are based on the value of the property taxed (ad valorem). Often simply called property taxes.

Special assessment—A tax levied against property that benefits from a local improvement project, to pay for the project. Also called an improvement tax.

Conveyance tax—A tax levied when a piece of real property is sold. It is based on the selling price of the property. Also called an excise tax, transfer tax, or deed tax.

Chapter Quiz

1. The police power is the government's power to:
   a) take private property for public use
   b) enact laws for the protection of the public health, safety, morals, and general welfare
   c) tax property to pay for police protection
   d) None of the above

2. Which of the following is likely to be controlled by a zoning ordinance?
   a) Use of the property
   b) Building height
   c) Placement of a building on a lot
   d) All of the above

3. Which of the following is NOT likely to be one of the goals of a land use control law?
   a) Ensuring that properties are put to their most profitable use
   b) Controlling growth and population density
   c) Ensuring that neighboring uses are compatible
   d) Preserving access to light and air

4. As a general rule, when a new zoning ordinance goes into effect, nonconforming uses:
   a) must comply with the new law within 90 days
   b) must shut down within 90 days
   c) will be granted conditional use permits
   d) are allowed to continue, but not to expand

5. An owner who feels that his property was improperly zoned should apply for a:
   a) conditional use permit
   b) variance
   c) rezone
   d) nonconforming use permit

6. A property owner is generally required to show undue hardship in order to obtain a:
   a) nonconforming use permit
   b) special exception permit
   c) rezone
   d) variance

7. Which of these is an example of a variance?
   a) Authorizing a hospital to be built in a residential zone
   b) Authorizing a structure to be built only 12 feet from the lot's boundary, although the zoning ordinance requires 15-foot setbacks
   c) Allowing a grocery store to continue in operation after the neighborhood is zoned residential
   d) Approving the subdivision of a parcel of land into two or more lots

8. Which of these is NOT an exercise of the police power?
   a) Condemnation
   b) Building code
   c) Zoning ordinance
   d) Subdivision regulations

9. Eminent domain differs from the police power in that:
   a) the government is required to compensate the property owner
   b) it can be exercised only by the state government, not a city or county government
   c) it affects only the use of the property, not the title
   d) the property must be unimproved

10. The Hancocks are planning to add a room onto their house. Before construction begins, they are probably required to:
    a) request a zoning inspection
    b) submit a proposal to the planning commission
    c) obtain a building permit
    d) All of the above

11. A special assessment is the same thing as a/an:
    a) general real estate tax
    b) improvement tax
    c) real estate excise tax
    d) transfer tax

12. General real estate taxes are:
    a) used to support the general operation and services of government
    b) levied annually
    c) based on the value of the taxed property
    d) All of the above

13. Which of these is a law that requires an environmental impact statement to be prepared in certain circumstances?
    a) ILSA
    b) CERCLA
    c) NEPA
    d) None of the above

14. A conveyance tax is based on the property's:
    a) selling price
    b) fair market value
    c) current use
    d) highest and best use

15. Areas with incompatible uses may be separated by:
    a) buffer zones
    b) rezones
    c) side yards
    d) setbacks

Answer Key

1. b) The police power is the government's power to pass laws (such as zoning ordinances) for the protection of the public health, safety, morals, and general welfare.

2. d) Zoning ordinances typically control the height and placement of buildings as well as type of use.

3. a) Land use controls are not aimed at encouraging the most profitable use of particular properties. In some cases they prohibit more profitable uses that would be detrimental to the public health, safety, morals, or welfare.

4. d) A nonconforming use (a use established before new zoning rules go into effect, which does not comply with those rules) is ordinarily allowed to continue, but the use cannot be expanded, rebuilt after destruction, or resumed after abandonment.

5. c) A rezone is an amendment to the zoning ordinance, giving a particular area a new zoning designation.

6. d) A variance is granted when the property owner shows that strict enforcement of the zoning law would result in undue hardship.

7. b) A variance authorizes the improvement of property in a manner not ordinarily allowed by the zoning ordinance. Most variances permit only minor deviations from the rules.

8. a) Condemnation is an exercise of the power of eminent domain, not the police power.

9. a) When a government body takes property under the power of eminent domain, it is required to pay compensation to the owner. Compensation is ordinarily not required if a property merely loses value due to regulation under the police power.

10. c) A building permit is generally required before an addition or remodeling project is begun, to ensure that the structure will comply with the building codes and zoning.

11. b) A special assessment is also called an improvement tax; it is levied to pay for a particular public improvement.

12. d) All of these statements concerning general real estate taxes are true.

13. c) NEPA is the National Environmental Policy Act. It requires an environmental impact statement to be prepared whenever an action to be taken by (or approved by) the federal government will have a significant effect on the environment.

14. a) A conveyance tax may be levied by the state when title to property is transferred.

15. a) Buffer zones are usually used to separate areas zoned for incompatible uses.

Chapter 7

Contract Law

I. Legal Classifications of Contracts
   A. Express vs. implied
   B. Unilateral vs. bilateral
   C. Executory vs. executed
II. Elements of a Valid Contract
   A. Capacity
   B. Mutual consent
   C. Lawful objective
   D. Consideration
   E. Writing requirement
III. Legal Status of Contracts
   A. Void
   B. Voidable
   C. Unenforceable
   D. Valid
IV. Discharging a Contract
   A. Full performance
   B. Agreement between the parties
   C. Termination
V. Breach of Contract
   A. Rescission
   B. Compensatory damages
   C. Liquidated damages
   D. Specific performance
VI. Tender

Chapter Overview

Contracts are a significant part of the real estate business. Almost everyone has a basic understanding of what a contract is, but real estate agents need more than that. This chapter explains the requirements that must be met in order for a contract to be valid and binding; how a contract can be terminated; what is considered a breach of contract; and what remedies are available when a breach occurs.

Introduction

Real estate licensees deal with contracts on a daily basis: listing agreements, purchase and sale agreements, option agreements, and leases are all contracts. Thus, it is essential for a licensee to understand the basic legal requirements and effects of contracts.

Keep in mind, however, that a real estate licensee may not draft the original language for a contract. Anyone other than a lawyer who drafts a contract for someone else may be charged with the unauthorized practice of law.

Here is a general definition of a **contract**: an agreement between two or more competent persons to do or not do certain things in exchange for consideration. An agreement to sell a car, deliver lumber, or rent an apartment is a contract. And if it meets minimum legal requirements, it can be enforced in court.

Legal Classifications of Contracts

There are certain basic classifications that apply to any contract, no matter what type it is. Every contract is either express or implied, either unilateral or bilateral, and either executory or executed.

Express vs. Implied

An **express** contract is one that has been put into words. It may be written or oral. Each party to the contract has stated what he is willing to do and has been told what to expect from the other party. Most contracts are express. On the other hand, an **implied** contract, or contract by implication, is created by the actions of the parties, not by express agreement.

Example: A written lease agreement expires, but the tenant continues to make payments and the landlord continues to accept them. Both parties have implied their consent to a new lease contract.

Unilateral vs. Bilateral

A contract is **unilateral** if only one of the contracting parties is legally obligated to perform. That party has promised to do a particular thing if the other party does

Fig. 7.1 Contract classifications

Express *Written or oral*	OR	**Implied** *Actions of the parties*
Unilateral *One promise*	OR	**Bilateral** *Two promises*
Executory *Not yet fully performed*	OR	**Executed** *Fully performed*

something else. The other party has not promised to do anything and is not legally obligated to do anything.

> **Example:** In an open listing agreement, a seller promises to pay a real estate broker a commission if the broker finds a buyer for the property. The broker does not promise to try to find a buyer, but if she does, the seller is obligated to pay. An open listing agreement is a unilateral contract.

A **bilateral** contract is formed when each party promises to do something, so that both parties are legally obligated to perform. Most contracts are bilateral.

> **Example:** In a purchase agreement, the seller promises to transfer title to the buyer, and the buyer promises to pay the agreed price to the seller. This is a bilateral contract. Each party has made a promise, and both are obligated to perform.

Executory vs. Executed

An **executory** contract is one that has not yet been performed, or is in the process of being performed. An **executed** contract has been fully performed; the parties have fulfilled the terms of their agreement. With respect to contracts, the terms "executed" and "performed" mean the same thing. (Note that sometimes "executed" can mean "signed": when a contract is executed by the parties, it is signed by the parties. The context surrounding the term will indicate which meaning is intended.)

Elements of a Valid Contract

Four elements are needed for a valid and binding contract that will be enforced by a court:

1. legal capacity to contract,
2. mutual consent,
3. a lawful objective, and
4. consideration.

Capacity

The first requirement for a valid contract is that the parties have the legal capacity to enter into a contract. A person must be the age of majority or legally emancipated to enter into a valid contract, and he must also be competent.

Age of Majority. In most states, eighteen years of age is considered the age of majority. Minors (those under the age of majority) do not have capacity to appoint agents or to enter into contracts. If a minor signs a contract, it is voidable by the minor; that is, it cannot be enforced against him.

> **Example:** A 16-year-old signs a contract to purchase a car. The car dealer cannot enforce the contract against the minor, although the minor could compel the dealer to honor the terms of the agreement.

The purpose of this rule is to prevent people from entering into legally binding agreements when they may be too young to understand the consequences.

In some states, real estate contracts entered into by minors are void. This means a purchase agreement signed by a minor cannot be enforced by either party.

A minor who has been legally emancipated may enter into any type of contract. For example, a 17-year-old who is married is usually considered emancipated and thus may enter into a contract to buy a home. A minor can be emancipated in three ways: by marrying, by serving in the military, or by court order. When a minor who has been emancipated by court order enters into a sales transaction, copies of the emancipation documents should be given to the escrow company so it will know that the minor has the capacity to carry out the transaction.

Competent. A person must also be mentally competent to have capacity to contract. If a person has been declared incompetent by a court, any contract she signs is void. If the party was probably incompetent when the contract was signed, but a court declares her incompetent only after the signing of the contract, the contract may be voidable at the discretion of the court-appointed guardian.

A contract entered into by a person who is temporarily incompetent (for example, under the influence of alcohol or drugs) may be voidable if he takes legal action within a reasonable time after regaining mental competency. Similarly, a court will usually find that a contract entered into by a mentally ill person is voidable at any point during the mental illness and for a reasonable period after the illness ends. Note that the fact that a person is receiving psychiatric treatment does not necessarily mean that she is incompetent.

Necessities Exception. There's an exception to these capacity rules. If a minor or an incompetent person contracts to buy necessities (such as food or medicine), he is required to pay the reasonable value of those items. Housing is not generally considered a necessity for a minor, unless the minor is legally emancipated.

Representing Another. Often, one person has the capacity to represent another person or entity in a contract negotiation. For instance, the affairs of minors and incompetent persons are handled by parents or court-appointed guardians; corporations are represented by properly authorized officers; partnerships are represented by individual partners; deceased persons are represented by executors or administrators; and a competent adult (but not a minor) can appoint another competent adult to act on his behalf through a power of attorney. In each of these cases, the authorized representative can enter into a contract on behalf of the person represented.

Corporations and Partnerships. A corporation may enter into contracts through an individual authorized by the board of directors. In some states, a contract must also have a corporate seal to be valid.

A general partner of a partnership has legal capacity to contract on behalf of the partnership in her name, or in the name of the partnership.

Aliens. An alien has essentially the same property rights as a citizen and may acquire and convey property freely. However, aliens are subject to certain property transfer reporting requirements.

Convicts. Those convicted of crimes and serving time in prison are not automatically deprived of all of their civil rights. Generally, they do not forfeit their property, nor are they prevented from obtaining or transferring real property. In some states, however, an imprisoned felon may not be legally competent to enter into a contract.

Mutual Consent

Mutual consent is the second requirement for a valid contract. Each party must consent to the agreement. Once someone has signed a contract, consent is presumed, so no contract should be signed until its contents are fully understood. A person can't use failure or inability to read an agreement as an excuse for nonperformance. An illiterate person should have a contract explained thoroughly by someone who is concerned with his welfare.

Mutual consent is sometimes called mutual assent, mutuality, or "a meeting of the minds." It is achieved through the process of **offer and acceptance**.

Offer. A contract offer shows the willingness of the person making it (the **offeror**) to enter into a contract under the stated terms. To be valid, an offer must meet two requirements.

1. It must express a willingness to contract. Whatever words make up the offer, they must clearly indicate that the offeror intends to enter into a contract.
2. It must be definite and certain in its terms. A vague offer that does not clearly state what the offeror is proposing is unenforceable.

Note that an advertisement that lists a property's price is not considered a contract offer; it is merely an invitation to negotiate.

Terminating an Offer. Sometimes circumstances change after an offer has been made, or perhaps the offeror has had a change of heart. If an offer terminates before it is accepted, no contract is formed. There are many things that can terminate an offer before it is accepted, including:

- revocation by the offeror,
- lapse of time,
- death or incompetence of the offeror,
- rejection of the offer, or
- a counteroffer.

The offeror can **revoke** the offer at any time until she is notified that the offer has been accepted. To effect a proper "offer and acceptance," the accepting party must not only accept the offer, but must also communicate that acceptance to the offeror before the offer is revoked. (See the discussion of acceptance, below.)

Many offers include a deadline for acceptance. If a deadline is set and acceptance is not communicated within the time allotted, the offer terminates automatically. If a time limit is not stated in the offer, a reasonable amount of time is allowed. What is reasonable is determined by the court if a dispute arises.

If the offeror dies or is declared incompetent before the offer is accepted, it is terminated.

A **rejection** also terminates an offer. Once the **offeree** (the person to whom the offer was made) rejects the offer, he cannot go back later and create a contract by accepting the offer.

Example: Valdez offers to purchase Carter's house for $385,000. Carter rejects the offer the next day. The following week, Carter changes her mind and decides to accept Valdez's offer. But her acceptance at this point does not create a contract, because the offer terminated with her rejection.

A **counteroffer** is sometimes called a qualified acceptance. It is actually a rejection of the offer and a tender of a new offer. Instead of either accepting or rejecting

Fig. 7.2 Mutual consent is achieved through the process of offer and acceptance.

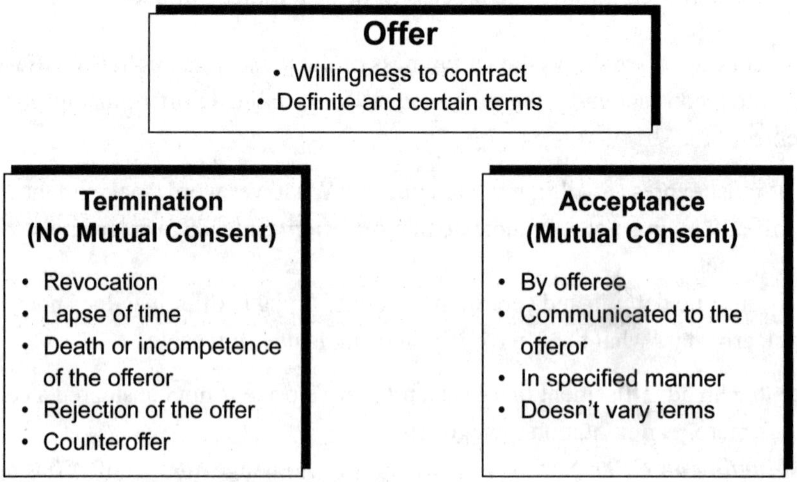

the offer outright, the offeree "accepts" with certain modifications. This happens when some, but not all, of the original terms are unacceptable to the offeree. When there is a counteroffer, the roles of the parties are reversed: the original offeror becomes the offeree and can accept or reject the revised offer. If she chooses to accept the counteroffer, there is a binding contract. If the counteroffer is rejected, the party making the counteroffer cannot go back and accept the original offer. The original offer was terminated by the counteroffer.

Example: Palmer offers to buy Harrison's property under the following conditions: the purchase price is $250,000, the closing date is January 15, and the downpayment is $25,000. Harrison agrees to all the terms but the closing date, which he wants to be February 15. By changing one of the terms, Harrison has rejected Palmer's initial offer and made a counteroffer. Now it is up to Palmer to either accept or reject Harrison's counteroffer.

Acceptance. An offer can be revoked at any time until acceptance has been communicated to the offeror. To create a binding contract, the offeree must communicate acceptance to the offeror in the manner and within the time limit stated in the offer (or before the offer is revoked). If no time or manner of acceptance is stated in the offer, a reasonable time and manner is implied.

Negative Influences. The offeree's acceptance must also be free of any negative influences, such as fraud, mistake, undue influence, or duress. If an offer or acceptance is influenced by any of these negative forces, the contract is voidable by the injured party.

Fraud is misrepresentation of a material fact to another person who relies on the misrepresentation as the truth in deciding to enter into a transaction.

- **Actual fraud** occurs when the person making the statement either knows the statement is false and makes it with an intent to deceive, or doesn't know whether or not the statement is true but makes it anyway. For example, a seller who conceals cracks in the basement and then tells the buyer that the foundation is completely sound is committing actual fraud. A promise that is made without any intent to keep it can also be considered actual fraud.
- **Constructive fraud** occurs when a person who occupies a position of confidence and trust, or who has superior knowledge of the subject matter, makes a false statement with no intent to deceive. For example, if a seller innocently points out incorrect lot boundaries, it may be constructive fraud. Constructive fraud is also called **innocent misrepresentation**.

A **mistake** occurs when the parties are mistaken as to a material fact or the terms of the contract. If there is an ambiguity in negotiations, any contract that is signed may be void for lack of mutual agreement.

Example: Beth offers to buy a barren cow from Carl for $400. The day before Carl is to deliver the cow to Beth, he discovers that the cow is pregnant. This is an example of a mistake of fact. Both Carl and Beth mistakenly believed the cow to be barren. Thus, the contract is voidable.

Mistake does not include failing to read the terms of the contract, bad judgment, or entering into a disadvantageous contract.

Fig. 7.3 Real estate contract requirements

A Valid Real Estate Contract
• Capacity • Mutual consent • Lawful objective • Consideration • In writing

Undue influence is using one's influence to pressure a person into making a contract, or taking advantage of another's distress or weakness of mind to induce him to enter into a contract.

Duress is compelling someone to do something—such as enter into a contract—against her will, with the use of force or constraint or the threat of force or constraint.

Lawful Objective

The third requirement for a valid contract is a lawful objective. Both the purpose of the contract and the consideration for the contract (discussed below) must be lawful. Examples of contracts with unlawful objectives are a contract requiring payment of an interest rate in excess of the state's usury limit, or a contract relating to unlawful gambling. If a contract does not have a lawful objective, it is void.

Sometimes contracts contain some lawful provisions and some unlawful provisions. In these situations, it may be possible to sever the unlawful portions of the contract and enforce the lawful portions.

> **Example:** Callahan and Baker enter into a contract for the sale of an apartment house. A clause in the contract prohibits the buyer from renting the apartments to persons of a certain race. The contract concerning the sale of the property would probably be enforceable, but the racially restrictive clause would be void because it is unlawful.

Consideration

The fourth element of a valid contract is **consideration**. Consideration is something of value exchanged by the contracting parties. It might be money, goods, or services, or a promise to provide money, goods, or services. Whatever form it takes, the consideration must be either a benefit to the party receiving it or a detriment to the party offering it. The typical real estate purchase agreement involves a promise by the purchaser to pay a certain amount of money to the seller at a certain time, and a promise by the seller to convey title to the purchaser when the price has been paid. Both parties have given and received consideration.

While consideration is usually the promise to do a particular act, it can also be a promise to not do a particular act; this is called **forbearance**. For example, Aunt Martha might promise to pay her nephew Charles $1,000 if he promises to stop smoking.

As a general rule, a contract is enforceable as long as the consideration has value, even though the value of the consideration exchanged is unequal. A contract to sell a piece of property worth $220,000 for $190,000 is enforceable. However, in cases where the disparity in value is quite large (for example, a contract to sell a piece of property worth $300,000 for $95,000), a court may refuse to enforce the contract. This is particularly likely to happen if the parties have unequal bargaining power (for example, if the buyer is a real estate developer and the seller is elderly, uneducated, and inexperienced in business).

The Writing Requirement

The requirements we've covered so far—capacity, mutual consent, lawful objective, and consideration—apply to any kind of contract. For most contracts used in real estate transactions, there is a fifth requirement: they must be put into writing, as required by the statute of frauds.

The **statute of frauds** is a state law that requires certain types of contracts to be in writing and signed. Only the types of contracts covered by the statute of frauds have to be in writing; other contracts may be oral.

Each state has its own statute of frauds, and the requirements vary slightly from state to state. As a general rule, however, almost all of the contracts typically used in a real estate transaction are covered by the statute of frauds. In many states, the statute of frauds applies to:

1. an agreement that is not to be performed within a year of its making;
2. any agreement for the sale or exchange of real property or an interest in real property;
3. a lease of real property that will expire more than one year after it was agreed to;
4. an agency agreement authorizing an agent to purchase or sell real property, or lease it for more than one year;
5. an agency agreement authorizing an agent to find a buyer or seller for real property, if the agent will receive compensation (a listing agreement); and
6. an assumption of a mortgage or deed of trust.

The "writing" required by the statute of frauds does not have to be in any particular form, nor does it have to be contained entirely in one document. A note or memorandum about the agreement or a series of letters will suffice, as long as the writing:

1. identifies the subject matter of the contract,
2. indicates an agreement between the parties and its essential terms, and
3. is signed by the parties to be bound.

If the parties fail to put a contract that falls under the statute of frauds in writing, the contract is usually unenforceable. However, occasionally a court will enforce an unwritten agreement. This might occur if there is both evidence that the contract exists and evidence of its terms, and if the party trying to enforce it has completely or substantially performed his contractual obligations. This is rare; the safest course is to put a contract in writing.

If a contract is partly printed and partly handwritten (like a filled-out contract form) and there's a conflict between the handwritten and printed portions, the handwritten portion takes precedence. It's presumed to be a more reliable indication of the parties' intent than the printed portion.

Parol Evidence Rule. In the event of a dispute between parties to a contract, a written agreement provides the best evidence of the terms agreed upon. When a written agreement is considered complete and unambiguous, the parol evidence rule prevents the parties from introducing oral statements or other extraneous evidence (**parol evidence**) to prove the contents of the contract.

Example: McKinney and Francisco signed a listing agreement in which McKinney promised to pay Francisco a 6% commission upon the sale of McKinney's home. After the home sold, McKinney paid Francisco a commission amount equal to 5% of the sale price. Francisco sued McKinney for breach of contract. Because the listing agreement is clear and complete, McKinney cannot introduce evidence that the parties had orally agreed to lower Francisco's commission to 5%.

However, parol evidence will be allowed where the contents of the contract are incomplete or ambiguous, or where it is necessary to prove that the writing was induced by undue influence, duress, or some other negative influence.

Legal Status of Contracts

Four terms are used to describe the legal status of a contract: a contract is void, voidable, unenforceable, or valid. These terms have already been used in our discussion, and now we'll look more closely at what each one means.

Void

A void contract is no contract at all; it has no legal effect. This most often occurs because one of the essential elements, such as mutual consent or consideration, is completely lacking.

Example: Talbot signed a contract promising to deed some property to Worth, but Worth did not offer any consideration in exchange for Talbot's promise. Since the contract is not supported by consideration, it is void.

A void contract may be disregarded. Neither party is required to take legal action to withdraw from the agreement.

Voidable

A voidable contract appears to be valid, but has some defect giving one or both of the parties the power to withdraw from the agreement. For instance, a contract entered into as a result of fraud is voidable by the defrauded party.

Unlike a contract that is void from the outset, a voidable contract can't simply be ignored. Failure to take legal action within a reasonable time may result in a court declaring that the contract was ratified. (If the injured party decides to continue with the agreement, he may expressly ratify it.)

Unenforceable

An unenforceable contract is one that can't be enforced in court for one of the following reasons:

1. its contents cannot be proved,
2. it is voidable by the other party, or
3. the statute of limitations has expired.

Contents Cannot Be Proved. This is most often a problem associated with oral agreements. Even if the law does not require a certain kind of contract to be written, it is a good idea to put it in writing because it avoids confusion and misunderstanding.

Contract Voidable by Other Party. If a contract is voidable by one of the parties, it is unenforceable by the other party. (Note that the party who has the option of voiding the contract can choose instead to enforce the contract against the other party.)

Statute of Limitations Expired. A statute of limitations is a law that sets a deadline for filing a lawsuit. Unless an injured party files suit before the deadline set by the applicable statute of limitations, her legal claim is lost forever. The purpose of a statute of limitations is to prevent lawsuits long after an event, when memories have faded and evidence has been lost.

Every state has a statute of limitations for contracts. If one of the parties to a contract fails to perform his obligations (breaches the contract), the other party must sue within a certain number of years after the breach. Otherwise, the limitations period will run out and the contract will become unenforceable.

The doctrine of **laches** is related to the concept of statutes of limitations. Laches is an equitable principle that courts can use to prevent someone from asserting a

Fig. 7.4 Legal status of contracts

Type of Contract	Legal Effect	Example
Void	No contract at all	An agreement for which there is no consideration
Voidable	Valid until rescinded by one party	A contract entered into as a result of fraud
Unenforceable	One or both parties cannot sue to enforce	A contract after the limitations period expires
Valid	Binding and enforceable	An agreement that meets all the legal requirements

claim after an unreasonable delay. For instance, suppose a property owner knowingly stands by while a neighbor builds a house that encroaches a few feet onto his property. He then sues, demanding that it be torn down. Because the property owner's unreasonable delay caused the neighbor harm, the court may use the doctrine of laches to deny the requested remedy.

Valid

If an agreement has all the essential elements, can be proved in court, and is free of negative influences, it's a valid contract and a judge will enforce it.

Discharging a Contract

Once there is a valid, enforceable contract, it may be discharged by:

1. full performance,
2. agreement between the parties, or
3. termination of the contract.

Full Performance

Full performance means that the parties have performed all of their obligations; the contract has been executed. For example, once the deed to the property has been transferred to the buyer, and the seller has received the purchase price, the purchase and sale agreement has been discharged by full performance.

Agreement Between the Parties

The parties to a contract can agree to discharge the contract in any of the following ways:

- rescission,
- cancellation,
- assignment,
- novation, or
- partial performance.

Rescission. Sometimes the parties to a contract agree that they would be better off if the contract had never been signed. In such a case, they may decide to rescind the contract.

The buyer and seller sign an agreement that terminates their previous agreement and puts them as nearly as possible back in the positions they were in before entering into the initial agreement. If any money or other consideration has changed hands, it will be returned.

In certain circumstances, a contract can be rescinded by court order (rather than by agreement between the parties). Court-ordered rescission is discussed later in this chapter.

Cancellation. A cancellation does not go as far as a rescission. The parties agree to terminate the contract, but previous acts are unaffected. For example, money that was paid prior to the cancellation is not returned.

When contracting to purchase real property, a buyer generally gives the seller a deposit to show that she is acting in good faith and intends to fulfill the terms of their agreement. This is called a **good faith deposit** (or earnest money deposit), and the seller is entitled to keep it if the buyer defaults on the contract. If the buyer and seller agree to terminate the contract and the seller refunds the good faith deposit to the buyer, the contract has been rescinded. If the seller keeps the deposit, the contract has been canceled.

Assignment. Sometimes one of the parties to a contract wants to withdraw by assigning her interest in the contract to another person. As a general rule, a contract can be assigned to another unless a clause in the contract prohibits assignment. Technically, assignment does not discharge the contract. The new party (the assignee) assumes primary liability for the contractual obligations, but the withdrawing party (the assignor) is still secondarily liable.

> **Example:** A buyer is purchasing a home on a land contract over a 15-year period. In the absence of any prohibitive language, she can sell the home, accept a cash downpayment, and assign her contract rights and liabilities to the new buyer. The new buyer would assume primary liability for the contract debt, but the original buyer would retain secondary liability.

One exception to the rule that a contract can be assigned unless otherwise agreed: a personal services contract can't be assigned without the other party's consent.

> **Example:** A nightclub has a contract with a singer for several performances. The singer cannot assign her contract to another singer, because it is a personal services contract. The nightclub management has a right to choose who will be singing in their establishment.

Novation. The term "novation" has two generally accepted meanings. One type of novation is the substitution of a new party into an existing obligation. If a buyer under a real estate contract is released by the seller in favor of a new buyer under the same contract, there has been a novation. The first buyer is relieved of all liability connected with the contract.

Novation may also be the substitution of a new obligation for an old one. If a landlord and tenant agree to tear up a three-year lease in favor of a new ten-year lease, it is a novation.

Assignment vs. Novation. The difference between assignment and novation concerns the withdrawing party's liability. When a contract is assigned, there is continuing liability for the assignor. In a novation, on the other hand, the withdrawing party is released from liability, because he was replaced with an individual who was approved by the other party. Novation, unlike assignment, always requires the other party's consent.

Partial Performance. In some instances, the parties to a contract may agree to discharge a contract after one of the parties has partially performed under the terms of the contract. The parties execute a written agreement stating that the work performed is sufficient to discharge the contract. Partial performance should not be confused with substantial performance, which is discussed below.

Termination

Not all contract disputes can be resolved by the parties. A court may terminate a contract on the basis of substantial performance, impossibility of performance, and through operation of law.

Substantial Performance. The doctrine of **substantial performance** is most often applied to construction contracts. Where one party has performed under the contract, but did not precisely follow the terms, a court may find that the performance is sufficient to discharge the contract.

> **Example:** The Michaelsons contract with Happy Day Construction to build their dream house. After construction is completed, the Michaelsons notice that Happy Day installed kitchen cabinets that are a shade darker than they had originally selected. Under the doctrine of substantial performance, the Michaelsons will be required to pay the contractor for the work performed, less any damage suffered as a result of the contractor's error.

Impossibility. A contract may be terminated when an unforeseen event prevents a party from performing under the contract; in other words, performance becomes legally impossible. For example, you sign an agreement to have Acme Painters paint your house. The day before they are to begin work, the house burns down. The contract is terminated due to impossibility of performance.

Operation of Law. A court may terminate a contract through operation of law, as in voiding a contract signed by a mentally incompetent person. A contract may also be terminated for fraud, undue influence, mistake, or duress.

Breach of Contract

A breach of contract occurs when one of the parties fails, without legal excuse, to perform any of the promises contained in the agreement. The injured party can seek a remedy in court only if the breach is a **material breach**. A breach is material when the promise that has not been fulfilled is an important part of the contract.

Many standard contract forms state that "**time is of the essence**." That phrase is used to warn the parties that timely performance is crucial and failure to meet a deadline would be a material breach. If one party misses a deadline, the other party may choose whether to proceed with the contract or use the time is of the essence clause as the basis for ending it.

When a breach occurs, there are four possible remedies available to the injured party:

- rescission,
- compensatory damages,
- liquidated damages, or
- specific performance.

Rescission

As previously explained, a rescission is a termination of the contract in which the parties are returned to their original positions. In the case of a purchase agreement, the seller refunds the buyer's good faith deposit and the buyer gives up his equitable interest in the property. The rescission can be by agreement, or it can be ordered by a court at the request of one party when the other party has breached the contract.

Compensatory Damages

Financial losses that a party suffers as a result of a breach of contract are referred to as **damages**.

> **Example:** Able, a manufacturer, contracts to buy 50,000 hinges from Baker for $12,000, and Baker promises to deliver the hinges by April 22.
>
> As it turns out, Baker fails to deliver the hinges on time, and Able (in order to fulfill commitments to her customers) must quickly purchase the hinges from another supplier. This other supplier charges Able $17,000—$5,000 more than Baker was charging. Able has suffered $5,000 in damages as a result of Baker's breach of contract.

The most common remedy for a breach of contract is an award of **compensatory damages**. This is a sum of money that a court orders the breaching party to pay to the other party, to compensate the other party for losses suffered as a result of the breach of contract. Compensatory damages are generally intended to put the nonbreaching party in the financial position she would have been in if the breaching party had fulfilled the terms of the contract.

> **Example:** Continuing with the previous example, suppose Able sues Baker for breach of contract. The court orders Baker to pay Able $5,000 in damages. When Baker pays Able the $5,000, that puts Able in the financial position she would have been in if Baker had delivered the hinges on time.

Liquidated Damages

The parties to a contract sometimes agree in advance to an amount that will serve as full compensation to be paid in the event that one of the parties defaults. This sum is called **liquidated damages**.

Fig. 7.5 When a contract is breached

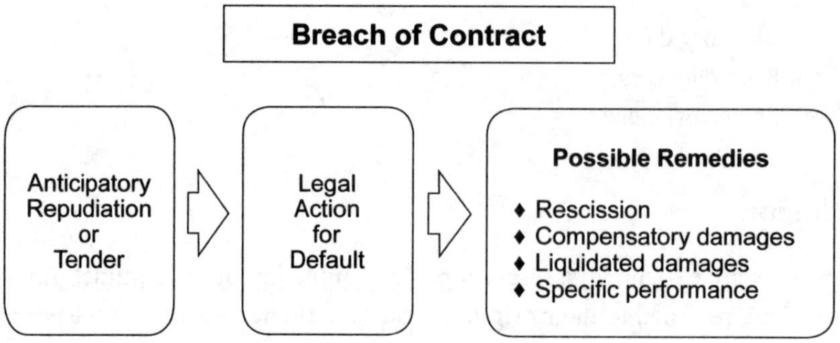

Example: Let's return to the previous example. Now suppose that Able and Baker included a liquidated damages provision in their contract. The provision states that if Baker breaches the agreement, he will pay Able $3,000, and that will serve as full compensation for the breach.

Baker fails to deliver the hinges to Able on time, Able must purchase them from another supplier, and that costs her an extra $5,000. But because of the liquidated damages provision in the contract, Able is only entitled to receive $3,000 from Baker. She can't sue for any additional amount, even though her actual damages were greater than $3,000.

Although a liquidated damages provision limits the amount of compensation the nonbreaching party will receive, it benefits both parties by making it easier to settle their dispute without going to court. It's sometimes difficult for the nonbreaching party to prove the extent of the actual damages she suffered; a liquidated damages provision makes that unnecessary.

In a real estate transaction, the buyer's good faith deposit is often treated as liquidated damages. If the buyer breaches the purchase and sale agreement, the seller is entitled to keep the deposit as liquidated damages. The seller usually can't sue the buyer for an additional amount.

On the other hand, a typical purchase and sale agreement doesn't have a liquidated damages provision that applies if it's the seller who breaches instead of the buyer. If the seller breaches the contract, the buyer can sue for compensatory damages.

Specific Performance

Specific performance is a legal action designed to compel a defaulting party to perform under the terms of the contract. For example, a court can order a seller to sign and deliver a deed to a buyer to complete a purchase.

Specific performance is usually available as a remedy only when monetary damages are not sufficient compensation. For example, when the purchase of real property is involved, the court might order specific performance because there is no other property that is just like the one the seller agreed to sell. Payment of damages would not enable the buyer to purchase another property exactly like it.

Note that if the consideration promised for the property is unreasonable, a court may refuse to order specific performance in the event of a breach.

Tender

A tender is an unconditional offer by one of the contract parties to perform her part of the agreement. It is sometimes referred to as "an offer to make an offer good." A tender is usually made when it appears that the other party is going to default; it is necessary before legal action can be taken to remedy the breach of contract.

Example: A seller suspects that the buyer does not plan to complete the purchase, and he intends to sue the buyer if this happens. The seller must attempt to deliver the deed to the buyer as promised in the purchase and sale agreement. When the tender is made, if the buyer refuses to pay the agreed price and accept the deed, the buyer is placed in default and the seller may then file a lawsuit.

If a buyer has reason to believe the seller does not plan to complete the sale, the buyer tenders by attempting to deliver the full amount promised in the purchase agreement to the seller. When the seller refuses to accept the money and deliver the deed, she is in default.

Sometimes there is an **anticipatory repudiation** by one of the parties. An anticipatory repudiation is a positive statement by the defaulting party indicating that he will not or cannot perform according to the terms of the agreement. When this happens, no tender is necessary as a basis for a legal action.

Chapter Summary

1. A contract is an agreement between two or more competent persons to do or not do certain things in exchange for consideration. Every contract is either express or implied, either unilateral or bilateral, and either executory or executed.

2. For a contract to be valid and binding, the parties must have the legal capacity to contract, and there must be mutual consent (offer and acceptance), a lawful objective, and consideration. The statute of frauds requires real estate contracts to be in writing.

3. A contract may be void, voidable, unenforceable, or valid.

4. An existing contract can be discharged by full performance, by agreement between the parties, or by termination. The parties can agree to terminate the contract by rescission or cancellation, or there can be an assignment or a novation. The parties may agree that partial performance is sufficient to discharge the contract. A contract may be terminated by a court on the basis of substantial performance, impossibility of performance, or by operation of law.

5. A breach of contract occurs when a party fails, without legal excuse, to perform any material promise contained in the agreement. When a breach occurs, the four possible remedies are rescission, compensatory damages, liquidated damages, or specific performance.

Key Terms

Contract—An agreement between two or more competent persons to do or not do certain things in exchange for consideration.

Capacity—A person must be mentally competent and at least 18 years of age to have the capacity to contract.

Mutual consent—The agreement of both parties to the terms of the contract, effected by offer and acceptance.

Offer—A communication that shows the willingness of the person making it (the offeror) to enter into a contract, and that has definite and certain terms.

Acceptance—A communication showing the willingness of the offeree to be bound by the terms of the offer.

Counteroffer—A qualified acceptance. Technically, it is a rejection of the offer, with a new offer made on slightly different terms.

Fraud—The misrepresentation of a material fact to someone who relies on the misrepresentation as the truth in deciding whether to enter into a contract.

Undue influence—Pressuring someone or taking advantage of his distress to induce him to enter into a contract.

Duress—Compelling someone to enter into a contract with the use or threat of force or constraint.

Consideration—Something of value exchanged by the parties to a contract; either a benefit to the party receiving it or a detriment to the party offering it.

Statute of frauds—A state law that requires certain types of contracts (including most contracts related to real estate transactions) to be in writing and signed.

Parol evidence rule—If a written agreement appears complete and unambiguous, parties can't introduce oral statements or other extraneous evidence to prove the contract's contents.

Valid—When a contract contains all of the required elements and is enforceable in court.

Void—When a contract lacks an essential element, so that it has no legal force or effect.

Voidable—When one of the parties can choose to rescind the contract, because of lack of capacity, fraud, etc.

Unenforceable—When a contract cannot be enforced in a court of law because its contents cannot be proved, or it is voidable by the other party, or the statute of limitations has expired.

Rescission—When a contract is terminated and any consideration given is returned, putting the parties as nearly as possible back into the position they were in prior to entering into the contract.

Cancellation—When a contract is terminated but previous contractual acts are unaffected.

Assignment—When one party transfers her rights and obligations under the contract to another party, but remains secondarily liable.

Novation—When one party is completely replaced with another, or one contract is completely replaced with another, and all liability under the original contract ends.

Compensatory damages—An amount that a court orders one party in a lawsuit to pay to the other party as compensation for a breach of contract or other injury.

Liquidated damages—An amount that the parties agree in advance will serve as full compensation if one of them defaults.

Specific performance—A remedy for breach of contract in which the court orders the defaulting party to perform as agreed in the contract.

Tender—An unconditional offer by one of the parties to perform his part of the agreement, made when it appears that the other party is going to default.

Chapter Quiz

1. A contract can be valid and binding even though:
   a) it is not supported by consideration
   b) it does not have a lawful objective
   c) it is not put into writing
   d) there was no offer and acceptance

2. To have legal capacity to contract, a person must have:
   a) reached the age of majority or have been legally emancipated
   b) been declared competent by a court
   c) a high school diploma or general equivalency certificate
   d) All of the above

3. An offer to purchase property would be terminated by any of the following, except:
   a) failure to communicate acceptance of the offer within the prescribed period
   b) revocation after acceptance has been communicated
   c) a qualified acceptance by the offeree
   d) death or insanity of the offeror

4. A counteroffer:
   a) terminates the original offer
   b) will result in a valid contract if accepted by the other party
   c) Both of the above
   d) None of the above

5. Tucker sends Johnson a letter offering to buy property for $400,000 in cash, with the transaction to close in 60 days. Johnson sends Tucker a letter that says, "I accept your offer; however, the closing will take place in 90 days." Which of the following is true?
   a) Johnson's statement is not a valid acceptance
   b) Johnson's statement is a counteroffer
   c) There is no contract unless Tucker accepts the counteroffer
   d) All of the above

6. Which of these could be consideration for a contract?
   a) $163,000
   b) A promise to convey title
   c) A promise to not sell the property during the next 30 days
   d) All of the above

7. An executory contract is one that:
   a) is made by the executor of an estate for the sale of probate property
   b) has not yet been performed
   c) has been completely performed
   d) has been proposed but not accepted by either party

8. A void contract is one that:
   a) lacks an essential contract element
   b) needs to be rescinded by the injured party
   c) can be rescinded by agreement
   d) can no longer be enforced because the deadline set by the statute of limitations has passed

his

r party
ed party
en to rescind it

The statute of frauds is a law that requires:

a) all contracts to be supported by consideration
b) unlawful provisions to be severed from a contract
c) certain contracts to be unilateral
d) certain contracts to be in writing and signed

11. A contract can be discharged by all of the following except:

a) novation
b) performance
c) cancellation
d) breach

12. Brown and Murdock have a five-year contract. After two years, they agree to tear up that contract and replace it with a new ten-year contract. This is an example of:

a) novation
b) rescission
c) duress
d) specific performance

13. Graves and Chung are parties to a contract that doesn't prohibit assignment. If Chung assigns his interest in the contract to Stewart:

a) Graves is not required to fulfill the contract
b) Graves can sue for anticipatory repudiation
c) Chung remains secondarily liable to Graves
d) Chung is relieved of all further liability under the contract

14. A clause in the contract provides that if one party breaches, the other party will be entitled to $3,500 and cannot sue for more than that. This is a:

a) just compensation provision
b) compensation cap
c) satisfaction clause
d) liquidated damages provision

15. The McClures agreed to sell their house to Jacobsen, but then they breached the contract by refusing to go through with the sale. If Jacobsen wants a court order requiring the McClures to convey the house to her as agreed, she should sue for:

a) damages
b) specific performance
c) liquidated damages
d) rescission

Answer Key

1. c) Only certain types of contracts are required to be in writing, but all contracts require consideration, a lawful objective, and offer and acceptance.

2. a) A person has capacity to contract if she has reached the age of majority (or has been legally emancipated) and is mentally competent. It isn't necessary to be declared competent by a court, however.

3. b) If the offeree accepts the offer before the offeror revokes it, a binding contract is formed.

4. c) A counteroffer terminates the original offer (operating as a rejection), but if the counteroffer is then accepted, a valid contract is formed.

5. d) All of the options are true statements.

6. d) Consideration is almost anything of value: money, goods, services, or a promise to do or not do something.

7. b) An executory contract has not yet been performed; an executed contract is one that has been fully performed.

8. a) A contract that lacks an essential element (such as consideration) is void. It has no legal force or effect, so there is nothing to rescind.

9. b) A voidable contract can be rescinded by the injured party.

10. d) The statute of frauds requires certain contracts to be in writing and signed by the party or parties to be bound.

11. d) Performance, cancellation, and novation are all ways of discharging a contract. Breach does not discharge the contract; the breaching party is liable to the other party.

12. a) Novation is the replacement of an existing contract with a new contract, or the replacement of a party to a contract with a new party.

13. c) A contract can be assigned unless otherwise agreed, but the assignor remains secondarily liable to the other party.

14. d) Liquidated damages is an amount the contracting parties agree in advance will be paid as full compensation if one of them breaches the contract.

15. b) If the court granted Jacobsen specific performance, the McClures would be ordered to convey the house as agreed in the contract (not merely to pay Jacobsen damages as compensation).

Chapter 8

Types of Real Estate Contracts

I. Listing Agreements
    A. Earning a commission
        1. Ready, willing, and able buyer
        2. Types of listing agreements
    B. Elements of a listing agreement
II. Purchase Agreements
    A. Typical provisions
    B. Binder
    C. Amendments
    D. Escrow agreements
III. Land Contracts
    A. Rights and responsibilities of the parties
    B. Remedies for default
    C. Reasons for using a land contract
IV. Leases
    A. Requirements for a valid lease
    B. Lease renewal
    C. Transferring leased property
    D. Termination of a lease
V. Option Agreements
    A. Requirements for a valid option
    B. Option rights
    C. Recording an option
    D. Right of first refusal

Chapter Overview

In addition to understanding the basic principles of contract law, real estate agents must be familiar with the specific types of real estate contracts. This chapter describes several types of contracts related to real estate, including listing agreements, purchase agreements, land contracts, leases, and options.

Listing Agreements

A **listing agreement** is a written employment contract between a property seller and a real estate broker. (A copy of the Pennsylvania Association of REALTORS® residential listing agreement form is shown in Figure 8.1.) The seller hires the broker to find a buyer who is ready, willing, and able to buy the property on the seller's terms. A listing agreement does not give the broker the authority to accept offers on behalf of the seller, or to transfer title to the seller's property.

Even though the listing agreement form is frequently filled out and signed by a salesperson working for the listing broker, the contract is between the seller and the broker (not the salesperson). Some states require the broker to sign the contract as well.

Typically, a real estate broker is paid by commission, also called a **brokerage fee.** The commission is usually computed as a percentage of the sales price (the price that the property is sold for), as opposed to the listing price.

In most states, a broker cannot sue a seller to collect a commission unless there was a written listing agreement. There will be conditions set forth in the listing agreement that also must be met before the seller is obligated to pay the broker a commission.

Some states have a specific rule that listing agreements must always be in writing. In other states, an oral listing agreement can exist in theory, but it won't be enforceable in court because of the statute of frauds. A few states recognize oral listing agreements if they are for a period of less than one year. Note that an oral agreement between brokers to split a commission may be enforceable, even when an oral listing agreement is not.

Earning a Commission

A listing agreement can make payment of the broker's commission dependent on any lawful conditions that are mutually acceptable to the broker and the seller. For example, the seller might ask to include a "no sale, no commission" provision in the agreement. This would make the broker's commission payable only if the transaction actually closes and the seller receives full payment from the buyer. If this condition is not met due to circumstances beyond the seller's control (for example, because the buyer couldn't obtain financing), the commission need not be paid. On the other hand, if the condition is not met because of the seller's bad faith or fraud, the broker is still entitled to the commission.

Fig. 8.1 Residential listing agreement

LISTING CONTRACT (SELLER AGENCY CONTRACT) EXCLUSIVE RIGHT TO SELL REAL ESTATE

XLS

This form recommended and approved for, but not restricted to use by, the members of the Pennsylvania Association of Realtors® (PAR).

Broker (Company) ____________________ | Licensee(s) (Name) ____________________

Company Address ____________________ | Direct Phone(s) ____________________

Cell Phone(s) ____________________

Company Phone ____________________ | Fax ____________________

Company Fax ____________________ | Email ____________________

SELLER ____________________

SELLER'S MAILING ADDRESS ____________________

PHONE ____________________ **FAX** ____________________

E-MAIL ____________________

Seller understands that this Listing Contract is between Broker and Seller.

Does Seller have a listing contract for this Property with another broker? ☐ **Yes** ☐ **No**

If yes, explain: ____________________

1. PROPERTY **LISTED PRICE $** ____________________

Address ____________________ ZIP ____________

Municipality (city, borough, township) ____________________

County ____________________ School District ____________________

Zoning ____________________

Present Use ____________________

Identification (For example, Tax ID #; Parcel #; Lot, Block; Deed Book, Page, Recording Date) ____________________

2. STARTING & ENDING DATES OF LISTING CONTRACT (ALSO CALLED "TERM")

(A) No Association of REALTORS® has set or recommended the term of this contract. Broker/Licensee and Seller have discussed and agreed upon the term of this Contract.

(B) **Starting Date:** This Contract starts when signed by Broker and Seller, unless otherwise stated here: ____________

(C) **Ending Date:** This Contract ends at 11:59 PM on ____________. By law, the term of a listing contract may not exceed one year. If the Ending Date written in this Contract creates a term that is longer than one year, the Ending Date is automatically 364 days from the Starting Date of this Contract.

3. DUAL AGENCY

Seller agrees that Broker and Broker's Licensees may also represent the buyer(s) of the Property. A Broker is a Dual Agent when a Broker represents both a buyer and Seller in the same transaction. A Licensee is a Dual Agent when a Licensee represents a buyer and Seller in the same transaction. All of Broker's licensees are also Dual Agents UNLESS there are separate Designated Agents for a buyer and Seller. If the same Licensee is designated for a buyer and Seller, the Licensee is a Dual Agent. Seller understands that Broker is a Dual Agent when a buyer who is represented by Broker is viewing properties listed by Broker.

4. DESIGNATED AGENCY

Designated Agency is applicable, unless checked below. Broker designates the Licensee(s) above to exclusively represent the interests of Seller. If Licensee is also the buyer's agent, then Licensee is a DUAL AGENT.

☐ **Designated Agency is not applicable.**

5. BROKER'S FEE

(A) No Association of REALTORS® has set or recommended the Broker's Fee. Broker and Seller have negotiated the fee that Seller will pay Broker.

(B) Broker's Fee is ______ % of the sale price OR $____________, whichever is greater, AND $____________, paid to Broker by Seller as follows:

1. $____________ of Broker's Fee is earned and due **(non-refundable)** at signing of this Listing Contract, payable to Broker.

Broker/Licensee Initials: ________ **XLS Page 1 of 6** **Seller Initials:** ________

2. **Seller will pay** the balance of **Broker's Fee if:**

a. **Property, or any ownership interest in it, is sold or exchanged during the term of this Contract by Broker, Broker's Licensee(s), Seller, or by any other person or broker, at the listed price or any price acceptable to Seller,** OR

b. A ready, willing, and able buyer is found, during the term of this contract, by Broker or by anyone, including Seller. A willing buyer is one who will pay the listed price or more for the Property, or one who has submitted an offer accepted by Seller, OR

c. Negotiations that are pending at the Ending Date of this Contract result in a sale, OR

d. A Seller signs an agreement of sale then refuses to sell the Property, or if a Seller is unable to Sell the Property because of failing to do all the things required of the Seller in the agreement of sale (Seller default), OR

e. The Property or any part of it is taken by any government for public use (Eminent Domain), in which case Seller will pay from any money paid by the government, OR

f. A sale occurs after the Ending Date of this Contract IF:
(1) The sale occurs within ______________________________ of the Ending Date, AND
(2) The buyer was shown or negotiated to buy the Property during the term of this contract, AND
(3) The Property is not listed under an "exclusive right to sell contract" with another broker at the time of the sale.

(C) If a sale occurs, balance of Broker's Fee will be paid upon delivery of the deed or other evidence of transfer of title or interest. If the Property is transferred by an installment contract, balance of Broker's Fee will be paid upon the execution of the installment contract.

6. BROKER'S FEE IF SETTLEMENT DOES NOT OCCUR

If an agreement of sale is signed and settlement does not occur, and deposit monies are released to Seller, Seller will pay Broker ________________________ of/from deposit monies.

7. COOPERATION WITH OTHER BROKERS

Licensee(s) has explained Broker's company policies about cooperating with other brokers. Broker and Seller agree that Broker will pay **from Broker's Fee** a fee to another broker who procures the buyer, is a member of a Multiple Listing Service (MLS), and who:

(A) ☐ **Represents Seller (SUBAGENT)**. Broker will pay ______________________________ of/from the sale price.

(B) ☐ **Represents the buyer (BUYER'S AGENT)**. Broker will pay ______________________________ of/from the sale price.
A buyer's Agent, even if compensated by Broker for Seller, will represent the interests of the buyer.

(C) ☐ **Does not represent either Seller or a buyer (TRANSACTION LICENSEE).**
Broker will pay ______________________________ of/from the sale price.

8. DUTIES OF BROKER AND SELLER

(A) Broker is acting as a Seller Agent, as described in the Consumer Notice, to market the Property and to negotiate with potential buyers. Broker will use reasonable efforts to find a buyer for the Property.

(B) Seller will cooperate with Broker and assist in the sale of the Property as asked by Broker.

(C) All showings, negotiations and discussions about the sale of the Property, written or oral, will be communicated by Broker on Seller's behalf. All written or oral inquiries that Seller receives or learns about regarding the Property, regardless of the source, will be referred to Broker.

(D) If the Property, or any part of it, is rented, Seller will give any leases to Broker before signing this Contract. If any leases are oral, Seller will provide a written summary of the terms, including amount of rent, ending date, and Tenant's responsibilities.

(E) Seller will not enter into, renew, or modify any leases, or enter into any option to sell, during the term of this Contract without Broker's written consent.

9. BROKER'S SERVICE TO BUYER

Broker may provide services to a buyer for which Broker may accept a fee. Such services may include, but are not limited to: document preparation; ordering certifications required for closing; financial services; title transfer and preparation services; ordering insurance, construction, repair, or inspection services.

10. BROKER NOT RESPONSIBLE FOR DAMAGES

Seller agrees that Broker and Broker's Licensee(s) are not responsible for any damage to the Property or any loss or theft of personal goods from the Property unless such damage, loss or theft is solely and directly caused by Broker or Broker's Licensee(s).

11. DEPOSIT MONEY

(A) Broker, if named in an agreement of sale, will keep all deposit monies paid by or for the buyer in an escrow account until the sale is completed, the agreement of sale is terminated, or the terms of a prior written agreement between the buyer and Seller have been met. This escrow account will be held as required by real estate licensing laws and regulations. Buyer and Seller may name a non-licensee as the escrow holder, in which case the escrow holder will be bound by the terms of the escrow agreement, if any, not by the Real Estate Licensing and Registration Act. Seller agrees that the person keeping the deposit monies may wait to deposit any uncashed check that is received as deposit money until Seller has accepted an offer.

(B) Regardless of the apparent entitlement to deposit monies, Pennsylvania law does not allow a Broker holding deposit monies to determine who is entitled to the deposit monies when settlement does not occur. Broker can only release the deposit monies:

1. If an agreement of sale is terminated prior to settlement and there is no dispute over entitlement to the deposit monies. A written agreement signed by both parties is evidence that there is no dispute regarding deposit monies.

Broker/Licensee Initials: ________ **XLS Page 2 of 6** **Seller Initials:** ________

2. If, after Broker has received deposit monies, Broker receives a written agreement that is signed by Buyer and Seller, directing Broker how to distribute some or all of the deposit monies.
3. According to the terms of a final order of court.
4. According to the terms of a prior written agreement between Buyer and Seller that directs the Broker how to distribute the deposit monies if there is a dispute between the parties that is not resolved.

(C) Seller agrees that if Seller names Broker or Broker's licensee(s) in litigation regarding deposit monies, the attorneys' fees and costs of the Broker(s) and licensee(s) will be paid by Seller.

12. OTHER PROPERTIES

Seller agrees that Broker may list other properties for sale and that Broker may show and sell other properties to prospective buyers.

13. ADDITIONAL OFFERS

Unless prohibited by Seller, if Broker is asked by a buyer or another licensee(s) about the existence of other offers on the Property, Broker will reveal the existence of other offers and whether they were obtained by the Licensee(s) identified in this Contract, by another Licensee(s) working with Broker, or by a by a licensee(s) working for a different Broker. ONCE SELLER ENTERS INTO AN AGREEMENT OF SALE, BROKER IS NOT REQUIRED TO PRESENT OTHER OFFERS.

14. SELLER WILL REVEAL DEFECTS & ENVIRONMENTAL HAZARDS

(A) Seller (including Sellers exempt from the Real Estate Seller Disclosure Law) will disclose all known material defects and/or environmental hazards on a separate disclosure statement. A material defect is a problem or condition that:
1. is a possible danger to those living on the Property, or
2. has a significant, adverse effect on the value of the Property.

The fact that a structural element, system or subsystem is near, at or beyond the end of the normal useful life of such a structural element, system or subsystem is not by itself a material defect.

B. Seller will update the Seller's Property Disclosure Statement as necessary throughout the term of this Listing Contract.

C. If Seller fails to disclose known material defects and/or environmental hazards:
1. Seller will not hold Broker or Licensee(s) responsible in any way;
2. Seller will protect Broker and Licensee(s) from any claims, lawsuits, and actions that result;
3. Seller will pay all of Broker's and Licensee's costs that result. This includes attorneys' fees and court-ordered payments or settlements (money Broker or Licensee pays to end a lawsuit or claim).

15. IF PROPERTY WAS BUILT BEFORE 1978

The Residential Lead-Based Paint Hazard Reduction Act says that any seller of property built before 1978 must give the buyer an EPA pamphlet titled *Protect Your Family From Lead in Your Home*. The seller also must tell the buyer and the broker what the seller knows about lead-based paint and lead-based paint hazards that are in or on the property being sold. Seller must tell the buyer how the seller knows that lead-based paint and lead-based paint hazards are on the property, where the lead-based paint and lead-based paint hazards are, the condition of the painted surfaces, and any other information seller knows about lead-based paint and lead-based paint hazards on the property. Any seller of a pre-1978 structure must also give the buyer any records and reports that the seller has or can get about lead-based paint or lead-based paint hazards in or around the property being sold, the common areas, or other dwellings in multi-family housing. According to the Act, a seller must give a buyer 10 days (unless seller and the buyer agree to a different period of time) from the time an agreement of sale is signed to have a "risk assessment" or inspection for possible lead-based paint hazards done on the property. Buyers may choose not to have the risk assessment or inspection for lead paint hazards done. If the buyer chooses not to have the assessment or inspection, the buyer must inform the seller in writing of the choice. The Act does not require the seller to inspect for lead paint hazards or to correct lead paint hazards on the property. The Act does not apply to housing built in 1978 or later.

16. HOME WARRANTIES

At or before settlement, Seller may purchase a home warranty for the Property from a third-party vendor. Seller understands that a home warranty for the Property does not alter any disclosure requirements of Seller, may not cover or warrant any pre-existing defects of the Property, and will not alter, waive or extend any provisions of the Agreement regarding inspections or certifications that Buyer may elect or waive as part of the Agreement. Seller understands that Broker who recommends a home warranty may have a business relationship with the home warranty company that provides a financial benefit to Broker.

17. RECOVERY FUND

Pennsylvania has a Real Estate Recovery Fund (the Fund) to repay any person who has received a final court ruling (civil judgment) against a Pennsylvania real estate licensee because of fraud, misrepresentation, or deceit in a real estate transaction. The Fund repays persons who have not been able to collect the judgment after trying all lawful ways to do so. For complete details about the Fund, call (717) 783-3658, or (800) 822-2113 (within Pennsylvania) and (717) 783-4854 (outside Pennsylvania).

18. NOTICE TO PERSONS OFFERING TO SELL OR RENT HOUSING IN PENNSYLVANIA

Federal and state laws make it illegal for a seller, a broker, or anyone to use RACE, COLOR, RELIGION or RELIGIOUS CREED, SEX, DISABILITY (physical or mental), FAMILIAL STATUS (children under 18 years of age), AGE (40 or older), NATIONAL ORIGIN, USE OR HANDLING/TRAINING OF SUPPORT OR GUIDE ANIMALS, or the FACT OF RELATIONSHIP OR ASSOCIATION TO AN INDIVIDUAL KNOWN TO HAVE A DISABILITY as reasons for refusing to sell, show, or rent properties, loan money, or set deposit amounts, or as reasons for any decision relating to the sale of property.

Broker/Licensee Initials: ________ **XLS Page 3 of 6** **Seller Initials: ________**

19. TRANSFER OF THIS CONTRACT

(A) Seller agrees that Broker may transfer this Contract to another broker when:
1. Broker stops doing business, OR
2. Broker forms a new real estate business, OR
3. Broker joins his business with another.

(B) Broker will notify Seller immediately in writing if Broker transfers this Contract to another broker. Seller will follow all requirements of this Contract with the new broker.

20. NO OTHER CONTRACTS

Seller will not enter into another listing contract for the property(s) identified in Paragraph 1 with another broker that begins before the Ending Date of this Contract.

21. CONFLICT OF INTEREST

It is a conflict of interest when Broker or Licensee has a financial or personal interest in the property and/or cannot put Seller's interests before any other. If Broker, or any of Broker's licensees, has a conflict of interest, Broker will notify Seller in a timely manner.

22. ENTIRE CONTRACT

This Contract is the entire agreement between Broker and Seller. Any verbal or written agreements that were made before are not a part of this Contract.

23. CHANGES TO THIS CONTRACT

All changes to this Contract must be in writing and signed by Broker and Seller.

24. MARKETING OF PROPERTY

(A) Where permitted, Broker, at Broker's option, may use: for sale sign, lock box, key in office, open houses and advertising in all media, including print and electronic, photographs and videos, unless otherwise stated here: ______________________
____

1. ☐ Seller does not want the listed Property to be displayed on the Internet.
   ☐ Seller does not want the address of the listed Property to be displayed on the Internet.
2. Seller understands and acknowledges that, if the listed Property is not displayed on the Internet, consumers who conduct searches for listings on the Internet will not see information about the listed Property in response to their search.

(B) Seller understands and acknowledges that, if an open house is scheduled, the property address may be published on the Internet in connection to the open house.

(C) There are many ways of marketing properties electronically. Some brokers may use a virtual office website (also known as "VOW") or Internet data exchange (also known as "IDX"), which are governed by specific rules and policies. Sellers have the right to control some elements of how their property is displayed on a VOW and/or IDX websites.
Seller elects to have the following features disabled or discontinued for VOW and IDX websites (check all that apply):
☐ Comments or reviews about Seller's listings, or a hyperlink to such comments or reviews, in immediate conjunction with Seller's listing.
☐ Automated estimates of the market value of Seller's listing, or a hyperlink to such estimates, in immediate conjunction with the Seller's listing.

(D) Multiple Listing Services (MLS)
☐ Broker will not use a Multiple Listing Service (MLS) to advertise the Property.
☐ Broker will use a Multiple Listing Service (MLS) to advertise the Property to other real estate brokers and salespersons. Listing broker shall communicate to the MLS all of Seller's elections made above.

(E) Seller agrees that Broker and Licensee, and the MLS are not responsible for mistakes in the MLS or advertising of the Property.

(F) Other ____

25. PUBLICATION OF SALE PRICE

Seller is aware that the Multiple Listing Service (MLS), newspapers, Web Sites, and other media may publish the final sale price of the Property.

26. COPYRIGHT

In consideration of Broker's efforts to market Seller's Property as stated in this Contract, Seller grants Broker a non-exclusive, world-wide license (the "License") to use any potentially copyrightable materials (the "Materials") which are related to the Property and provided by Seller to Broker or Broker's representative(s). The Materials may include, but are not limited to: photographs, images, video recordings, virtual tours, drawings, written descriptions, remarks, and pricing information related to Seller's Property. This License permits Broker to submit the Materials to one or more multiple listing services, to include the Materials in compilations of property listings, and to otherwise distribute, publicly display, reproduce, publish and produce derivative works from the Materials for any purpose that does not conflict with the express terms of this Contract. The License may not be revoked by Seller and shall survive the ending of this Contract. Seller also grants Broker the right to sublicense to others any of these rights granted to Broker by Seller. Seller represents and warrants to Broker that the License granted to Broker for the Materials does not violate or infringe upon the rights, including any copyrights, of any person or entity. Seller understands that the terms of the License do not grant Seller any legal right to any works that Broker may produce using the Materials.

27. FIXTURES AND PERSONAL PROPERTY

(A) INCLUDED in this sale are all existing items permanently installed in the Property, free of liens, and other items including plumbing; heating; radiator covers; lighting fixtures (including chandeliers and ceiling fans); pool and spa equipment (including covers and cleaning equipment); electric animal fencing systems (excluding collars); garage door openers and transmitters; television antennas; unpotted shrubbery, plantings and trees; any remaining heating and cooking fuels stored on the Property at the time of settlement; smoke detectors and carbon monoxide detectors; sump pumps; storage sheds; fences; mailboxes; wall to wall carpeting; existing window screens, storm windows and screen/storm doors; window covering hardware, shades and blinds; awnings; built-in air conditioners; built-in appliances; the range/oven, unless otherwise stated; and, if owned, water treatment systems, propane tanks, satellite dishes and security systems. Also included: ______________________________

(B) The following items are LEASED (not owned by Seller). Contact the provider/vendor for more information (e.g., water treatment systems, propane tanks, satellite dishes and security systems): ______________________________

(C) EXCLUDED fixtures and items: ______________________________

28. TAXES & SPECIAL ASSESSMENTS

(A) At settlement, Seller will pay one-half of the total Real Estate Transfer Taxes, unless otherwise stated here: ______________________________

(B) Yearly Property Taxes $ ______________ Property Assessed Value $ ______________

(C) Is the property preferentially assessed (including a tax abatement)? ☐ Yes ☐ No
If applicable, how many years remain? ______________

(D) COA/HOA Name ______________ COA/HOA Phone ______________
COA/HOA special assessments $ ______________ Buyer's required capital contribution $ ______________
Please explain: ______________________________

(E) Municipality Assessments $ ______________

(F) COA/HOA Fees $ ______________ ☐ Quarterly ☐ Monthly ☐ Yearly

29. TITLE & POSSESSION

(A) Seller will give possession of Property to a buyer at settlement, or on ______________

(B) At settlement, Seller will give full rights of ownership (fee simple) to a buyer except as follows:
☐ Oil ☐ Gas ☐ Mineral ☐ Other
If checked, please explain: ______________________________

(C) Seller has:
☐ First mortgage with ______________ Amount of balance $ ______________
Address ______________________________
Phone ______________ Acct. # ______________
☐ Second mortgage with ______________ Amount of balance $ ______________
Address ______________________________
Phone ______________ Acct. # ______________
☐ Home Equity line of credit with ______________ Amount of balance $ ______________
Address ______________________________
Phone ______________ Acct. # ______________
☐ Seller authorizes Broker to receive mortgage payoff and/or equity loan payoff information from lender(s).

(D) Seller has:
☐ Judgments $ ______________ ☐ Past Due Municipal Assessment $ ______________
☐ Past Due Property Taxes $ ______________ ☐ Past Due COA/HOA Fees $ ______________
☐ Federal Tax Liens $ ______________ ☐ Past Due COA/HOA Assessments $ ______________
☐ State Tax Liens $ ______________
☐ Other: ______________ $ ______________

(E) If Seller, at any time on or since January 1, 1998, has been obligated to pay support under an order on record in any Pennsylvania county, list the county and the Domestic Relations Number or Docket Number: ______________

30. BUYER FINANCING Seller will accept the following arrangements for buyer to pay for the Property:
☐ Cash ☐ Conventional mortgage ☐ FHA mortgage ☐ VA mortgage
☐ Seller's Assist to buyer (if any) $ ______________, or ______________%

31. SPECIAL INSTRUCTIONS

The Office of the Attorney General has not pre-approved any special conditions or additional terms added by any parties. Any special conditions or additional terms in this Contract must comply with the Pennsylvania Plain Language Consumer Contract Act.

Broker/Licensee Initials: ________ **XLS Page 5 of 6** **Seller Initials:** ________

32. SPECIAL CLAUSES

(A) The following are part of this Listing Contract if checked:

- ☐ Property Description Addendum to Listing Contract (PAR Form XLS-A)
- ☐ Single Agency Addendum (PAR FormSA)
- ☐ Consumer Services Fee Addendum (PAR Form CSF)
- ☐ Vacant Land Addendum to Listing Contract (PAR Form VLA)
- ☐ Short Sale Addendum (PAR Form SSL)
- ☐ ____
- ☐ ____

(B) Additional Terms:

______/______ Seller has read the Consumer Notice as adopted by the State Real Estate Commission at 49 Pa. Code §35.336.

______/______ Seller has received the Seller's Property Disclosure form and agrees to complete and return to Listing Broker in a timely manner, if required.

______/______ Seller has received the Lead-Based Hazards Disclosure form and agrees to complete and return to Listing Broker in a timely manner, if required.

Seller has read the entire Contract before signing. Seller must sign this Contract.

Seller gives permission for Broker to send information about this transaction to the fax number(s) and/or e-mail address(es) listed.

Return of this Agreement, and any addenda and amendments, including return by electronic transmission, bearing the signatures of all parties, constitutes acceptance by the parties.

This Contract may be executed in one or more counterparts, each of which shall be deemed to be an original and which counterparts together shall constitute one and the same Agreement of the Parties.

NOTICE BEFORE SIGNING: IF SELLER HAS LEGAL QUESTIONS, SELLER IS ADVISED TO CONSULT A PENNSYLVANIA REAL ESTATE ATTORNEY.

SELLER ____ **DATE** ____________________

SELLER ____ **DATE** ____________________

SELLER ____ **DATE** ____________________

BROKER (Company Name) ____

ACCEPTED ON BEHALF OF BROKER BY ______________________________ **DATE** ______________

Unless otherwise agreed, however, certain standard rules are followed regarding payment of the broker's commission. These include the rules concerning a ready, willing, and able buyer; and those concerning the three types of listings.

Ready, Willing, and Able Buyer. As a general rule, a listing agreement obligates the seller to pay the listing broker a commission only if a **ready, willing, and able** buyer is found during the listing period.

Acceptable Offer. A buyer is considered "ready and willing" if he makes an offer that meets the seller's stated terms. In the listing agreement, the seller sets forth the terms on which she wants to sell the property: price, closing date, financing arrangements, etc. If a buyer makes an offer that matches those terms, the broker is usually entitled to the commission—even if the seller decides not to accept that offer after all.

When a buyer makes an offer on terms other than those set forth in the listing agreement, the seller can turn down the offer without becoming liable for the broker's commission. But if the seller accepts an offer, he generally is required to pay the broker's commission even if the offer did not match the terms set forth in the listing agreement.

Able to Buy. A ready and willing buyer is considered "able" if she has the capacity to contract and the financial ability to complete the purchase. The buyer must have enough cash to buy the property on the agreed terms, or else be eligible for the necessary financing.

Commission Without Closing. In most states, once a ready, willing, and able buyer has been found, the broker has earned the commission, whether or not the sale is ever completed. When failure to close is the seller's fault, the broker is still entitled to the commission (although the broker might decide not to demand payment). For example, once the seller accepts an offer, he still owes the broker a commission if the sale fails to close for any of these reasons:

- the seller has a change of heart and decides not to sell;
- the seller does not have marketable title;
- the seller is unable to deliver possession of the property to the buyer; or
- the seller and the buyer mutually agree to terminate their contract.

Unless specifically required by the listing agreement, it may not even be necessary for the buyer and seller to execute a written purchase agreement in order for the broker to be entitled to a commission. It can be enough if the buyer and seller have reached an agreement as to the essential terms of the sale: the price, downpayment, loan term, interest rate, and amortization. If the seller backs out before the agreement is put into writing, the broker could still claim the commission.

Sometimes the seller and the broker disagree as to whether the buyer located by the broker was in fact ready, willing, and able. A court will normally presume that the buyer was ready, willing, and able if a written purchase agreement was signed. On the other hand, if no contract has been signed and the agreement between the buyer and the seller is still at the unwritten stage when it falls through, the broker is not entitled to a commission unless he can prove that the buyer was financially able to perform the contract.

A few states follow a rule that the sale of the property must actually close before the broker is entitled to a commission.

Types of Listing Agreements. The circumstances under which a seller is required to pay a broker's commission also depend on the type of listing agreement they have. The three basic types of listing agreements currently used are:

- the open listing,
- the exclusive agency listing, and
- the exclusive right to sell listing.

Open Listing. Under an open listing agreement, the seller is obligated to pay the broker a commission only if the broker was the **procuring cause** of the sale. The procuring cause is the person who was primarily responsible for bringing about the agreement between the parties. To be the procuring cause, a broker (or one of his salespersons) must have personally negotiated the offer from the ready, willing, and able buyer and communicated the offer to the seller.

An open listing is also called a nonexclusive listing, because a seller is free to give open listings to any number of brokers. If a seller signs two open listing agreements with two different brokers, and one of the brokers sells the property, only the broker who made the sale is entitled to a commission. The other broker is not compensated for his efforts. Or if the seller sells the property directly, without the help of either broker, then the seller does not have to pay any commission at all. The sale of the property terminates all outstanding listings.

The open listing arrangement has obvious disadvantages. If two competing brokers both negotiate with the person who ends up buying the property, there may be a dispute over which broker was the procuring cause of the sale. Also, because a broker with an open listing agreement is not assured of a commission when the property sells, he may not put as much effort into marketing the property, so it may take longer to sell. For the most part, open listing agreements are used only when a seller is unwilling to execute an exclusive listing agreement. Multiple listing services generally do not accept open listings.

Exclusive Agency Listing. In an exclusive agency listing, the seller agrees to list with only one broker, but retains the right to sell the property himself without being obligated to pay the broker a commission. The broker is entitled to a commission if anyone other than the seller finds a buyer for the property, but not if the seller finds the buyer without the help of an agent.

Exclusive Right to Sell Listing. Under an exclusive right to sell listing, the seller agrees to list with only one broker, and that broker is entitled to a commission if the property sells during the listing term, regardless of who finds the buyer. Even if the seller makes the sale directly, the broker is still entitled to the commission.

In spite of the designation "exclusive right to sell," remember that this type of listing agreement does not actually authorize the broker to sell the property. As with the other types of listings, the broker is authorized only to submit offers to purchase to the seller.

The exclusive right to sell listing is preferred by most brokers, because it provides the most protection for the broker. It's the type of listing that is most commonly used.

Exclusive vs. Open Listings. Exclusive listings have some important differences from open listings. Because an exclusive listing agreement prevents the seller from working with other brokers, it is important to know how long the agreement will last. Many states require listing agreements to include a specific termination date. In states that do not require this, if the listing agreement does not have a termination date, the law may allow the seller to terminate the agreement at any time, or the agreement may expire after a reasonable time has passed. To avoid this uncertainty, an exclusive listing should always include a date on which the listing agreement will terminate.

There is also a distinction between open and exclusive listings concerning the broker's contractual obligations. An open listing is considered a unilateral contract: the seller promises to pay the broker a commission if the broker finds a buyer, but the broker does not promise to make any effort to do so. If the broker does nothing at all, it is not a breach of contract.

On the other hand, an exclusive listing is considered a bilateral contract. In most exclusive listings, in exchange for the seller's promise to pay a commission no matter who finds a buyer (or if any agent finds a buyer), the broker promises to exercise due diligence and make a reasonable effort to find a buyer.

Buyer Representation Agreements. On the other side of a real estate transaction, buyers are often represented by their own real estate agents. A buyer representation agreement between a broker and a prospective buyer is essentially the counterpart to a listing agreement between the seller and the seller's broker. Unlike a listing agreement with the seller, however, the contract usually does not relate to a specific piece of property. The important elements of a buyer representation agreement primarily involve general agency law and will be discussed in Chapter 9.

Elements of a Listing Agreement

A listing agreement must have all of the essential elements of a valid contract that were discussed in the previous chapter, including competent parties, offer and acceptance, consideration, and a lawful purpose. Also, a listing agreement usually must be in writing and must be signed by the seller. The broker may also sign the listing agreement (although her signature is not required in many states). The broker gives implied consent to the terms of the agreement by starting to market the property.

If there is no written listing agreement, the broker will have difficulty suing the seller for a commission, even though an oral agreement may have established an agency relationship between the broker and the seller (see Chapter 9).

At a minimum, a listing agreement should include provisions that:

- identify the property,
- set acceptable terms of sale,
- grant the broker authority, and
- determine the broker's compensation.

As mentioned earlier, some states also require the listing agreement to include a termination date. In general, it is always a good idea to indicate when the listing will terminate.

Property Description. A listing agreement must identify the seller's property. The street address is useful, but it may not be enough to identify the property with certainty. It's a good idea to attach a legal description of the property to the listing agreement as an exhibit. Any pages attached to a contract should be dated and initialed by the parties, to show that the attachments are intended to be part of the agreement.

Terms of Sale. A listing agreement should specify what the seller wants in the way of an offer. This includes how much money the seller wants for the property (the listing price) and any other terms of sale that matter to the seller. Any items that the seller wants to exclude from or include in the sale that would not otherwise be excluded or included should also be noted in the listing agreement.

As we explained earlier, the seller can reject any offer that doesn't meet the terms of sale described in the listing agreement, without becoming liable for a commission. However, if an offer is made that does meet those terms, and the seller rejects the offer, the broker may be entitled to a commission. Thus, it is very important for all of the essential terms of sale to be set forth clearly and fully in the listing agreement.

Broker's Authority. The listing agreement sets forth the broker's authority to find a buyer for the property. The broker is usually also given the authority to accept and hold good faith deposits on the seller's behalf. In the rare case where a broker is not given authority to accept deposits for the seller and the prospective buyer gives the broker a deposit, then the broker is acting as an agent for the buyer in regard to the deposit. In this case, the seller would not be liable to the buyer if the broker were to lose or misappropriate the deposit.

Commission. A provision stating the rate or amount of the broker's commission is another key part of every listing agreement. The commission is usually computed as a percentage of the sales price. The commission rate or amount must be negotiable between the seller and the broker. In fact, it is a violation of state and federal antitrust laws for brokers to set uniform commission rates. Any discussion of commission rates among members of competing firms could give rise to a charge of price fixing (see Chapter 10).

Some states have additional regulations to prevent price fixing. For example, they may require that the listing agreement contain a statement informing the seller that commission rates must be negotiable. In general, the commission rate or amount should never be pre-printed on the listing agreement form. Instead, the commission should be filled in separately for each transaction.

Sometimes the amount of the broker's commission is not based on a percentage of the sales price. Instead, the seller stipulates the net amount of money she requires from the sale of the property. The broker then tries to sell the property for more than that net amount. When the property is sold, the seller receives the required net and the broker keeps any money in excess of that amount as the commission. This is referred to as a **net listing**.

Example: The seller insists on getting $345,000 from the sale of her property. The broker sells the property for $378,000. $378,000 less the required $345,000 net equals $33,000. Thus, the broker's commission is $33,000. If the broker had sold the property for more, his commission would have been more. Likewise, if the broker had sold the property for less, his commission would have been less.

Net listings are illegal in many states. Even in those states where net listings are legal, they are generally frowned upon; an unscrupulous broker could easily use a net listing to take advantage of a seller. States that allow net listings may have additional restrictions on them to guard against the potential for abuse.

Payment. A broker's commission is typically paid with a check (usually from the proceeds of the sale at closing), but if the seller and the broker agree, the commission payment can take other forms. For instance, it may be in the form of a promissory note, an assignment of an existing promissory note, or an assignment of funds from the buyer to the seller.

Ordinarily, the commission is the only compensation the broker receives. The broker does not present the seller with a bill for expenses incurred in selling the property, unless the seller specifically agreed to this arrangement in the listing agreement.

Safety Clauses. A safety clause (also called an extender clause, protection clause, or protection period clause) is found in most listing agreements. Under this type of provision, the broker is entitled to a commission if the seller sells the property after the listing term expires to any person the broker negotiated with during the listing term. This protects the broker from parties who conspire to deprive the broker of a commission by waiting until the listing has expired before they sign a purchase agreement.

The broker usually has to provide the seller with a list of the parties she negotiated with. That way, the seller will know to whom he can sell the property without becoming liable for a commission. Some states require the broker to provide this list to the seller within a certain timeframe. For example, the broker might be required to provide the list before the listing terminates, or within 72 hours after the termination date. This deadline should be included in the safety clause.

Termination Date. A listing agreement should include a termination date—the date on which the listing will expire and the broker's authority to act on the seller's behalf will end. This is especially important for an exclusive listing, because the seller is not free to work with a different broker until after the listing expires. As was mentioned earlier, the law in many states requires listing agreements to have a definite termination date. This may apply to all listing agreements, or specifically to exclusive listings. Some states also impose a maximum limit on the length of the listing period, such as 90 days.

Distressed Property Listings. As a result of the recent mortgage foreclosure crisis, a number of states have passed distressed property laws that are intended to protect homeowners from foreclosure scams. Under these laws, someone who participates in a transaction with a distressed property owner (the owner of a home in foreclosure or in imminent danger of foreclosure) may be required to use special forms, make certain disclosures, and follow other rules. In some states that have distressed property laws, real estate licensees are subject to these additional requirements.

Purchase Agreements

When a seller accepts a buyer's offer to purchase the property, they enter into a purchase agreement. This agreement is a written contract between the buyer and seller that establishes all of the terms of the sale.

The contract between the buyer and the seller is known by different names in various parts of the country. It may be called a purchase agreement, a contract of purchase and sale, an earnest money agreement, a deposit receipt, or an offer to purchase.

In most transactions, the buyer presents a written, signed offer to the seller along with a good faith deposit. If the seller chooses to accept the offer, he signs the form, and the form then becomes the binding contract of sale.

The statute of frauds requires an agreement to buy and sell real property to be in writing. A copy of the Arizona Association of REALTORS® residential purchase agreement form is shown in Figure 8.2.

The basic provisions of a purchase agreement are fairly simple. The purchase agreement:

- identifies the parties,
- describes the property,
- sets forth the price and method of payment, and
- sets the date for closing the transaction (when title and possession are transferred).

However, most purchase agreements are quite detailed. It's important for the purchase agreement to state all of the terms of the transaction clearly and accurately. Who is required to do what and when depends on the terms of the purchase agreement.

Typical Provisions

A purchase agreement form typically includes the following types of provisions.

Identification of the Parties. The buyer(s) and seller(s) must be properly identified in the agreement. Everyone who has an ownership interest in the property must sign the contract, and each party must have the capacity to enter into a contract. Note that if the seller is married, laws regarding marital property may require that the seller's spouse sign the purchase agreement for it to be enforceable. It is always best to have both spouses sign the contract, to secure the buyer's title to the property.

Description of the Property. The purchase agreement must describe the property with certainty. As with the listing agreement, a full legal description of the property is not always required. Even so, it is still a good practice to include the legal description. If it is too long to fit in the blanks on the form, a copy of the legal description should be initialed by the parties and attached to the purchase agreement as an exhibit.

Fig. 8.2 Residential purchase agreement

BUYER ATTACHMENT

Document updated:
February 2011

ARIZONA association of REALTORS®
REAL SOLUTIONS. REALTOR® SUCCESS.

This attachment should be given to the Buyer prior to the submission of any offer and is not part of the Residential Resale Real Estate Purchase Contract's terms.

ATTENTION BUYER!

You are entering into a legally binding agreement.

☐ **1. Read the entire contract *before* you sign it.**

☐ **2. Review the Residential Seller's Property Disclosure Statement (See Section 4a).**

- This information comes directly from the Seller.
- Investigate any blank spaces, unclear answers or any other information that is important to you.

☐ **3. Review the Inspection Paragraph (see Section 6a).**

If important to you, hire a qualified:

- Mold inspector
- Roof inspector
- Pest inspector
- Pool inspector
- Heating/cooling inspector

Verify square footage (see Section 6b)
Verify the property is on sewer or septic (see Section 6f)

☐ **4. Confirm your ability to obtain insurance and insurability of the property during the inspection period with your insurance agent (see Sections 6a and 6e).**

☐ **5. Apply for your home loan now, if you have not done so already, and provide your lender with all requested information (see Section 2f).**

It is your responsibility to make sure that you and your lender deliver the necessary funds to escrow in sufficient time to allow escrow to close on the agreed upon date. Otherwise, the Seller may cancel the contract.

☐ **6. Read the title commitment within five days of receipt (see Section 3c).**

☐ **7. Read the CC&R's and all other governing documents within five days of receipt (see Section 3c), especially if the home is in a homeowner's association.**

☐ **8. Conduct a thorough final walkthrough (see Section 6m). If the property is unacceptable, speak up. After the closing may be too late.**

You can obtain information through the Buyer's Advisory at http://www.aaronline.com.

Remember, you are urged to consult with an attorney, inspectors, and experts of your choice in any area of interest or concern in the transaction. Be cautious about verbal representations, advertising claims, and information contained in a listing. *Verify anything important to you.*

☑ ***Buyer's Check List***

Buyer Attachment • Updated: February 2011

RESIDENTIAL RESALE REAL ESTATE PURCHASE CONTRACT

Document updated: **February 2011**

ARIZONA association of REALTORS® REAL SOLUTIONS. REALTOR® SUCCESS.

The pre-printed portion of this form has been drafted by the Arizona Association of REALTORS®. Any change in the pre-printed language of this form must be made in a prominent manner. No representations are made as to the legal validity, adequacy and/or effects of any provision, including tax consequences thereof. If you desire legal, tax or other professional advice, please consult your attorney, tax advisor or professional consultant.

1. PROPERTY

1a. **BUYER:** ____
BUYER'S NAME(S)

SELLER: ____ or ☐ as identified in section 9c.
SELLER'S NAME(S)

Buyer agrees to buy and Seller agrees to sell the real property with all improvements, fixtures, and appurtenances thereon or incidental thereto, plus the personal property described herein (collectively the "Premises").

1b. Premises Address: ______________________ Assessor's #: ____________

City: ______________________ County: ______________________ AZ, Zip Code: ____________

Legal Description: ____

1c. $ ____________ Full Purchase Price, paid as outlined below

$ ____________ Earnest money

$ ____________ ______________________

$ ____________ ______________________

____

____

____

1d. **Close of Escrow:** Close of Escrow ("COE") shall occur when the deed is recorded at the appropriate county recorder's office. Buyer and Seller shall comply with all terms and conditions of this Contract, execute and deliver to Escrow Company all closing documents, and perform all other acts necessary in sufficient time to allow COE to occur on ____________ (MONTH) ______ (DAY), 20____ (YEAR) ("COE Date"). If Escrow Company or recorder's office is closed on COE Date, COE shall occur on the next day that both are open for business.

Buyer shall deliver to Escrow Company a cashier's check, wired funds or other immediately available funds to pay any down payment, additional deposits or Buyer's closing costs, and instruct the lender, if applicable, to deliver immediately available funds to Escrow Company, in a sufficient amount and in sufficient time to allow COE to occur on COE Date.

1e. **Possession:** Seller shall deliver possession, occupancy, existing keys and/or means to operate all locks, mailbox, security system/alarms, and all common area facilities to Buyer at COE or ☐ ______________________. Broker(s) recommend that the parties seek appropriate counsel from insurance, legal, tax, and accounting professionals regarding the risks of pre-possession or post-possession of the Premises.

1f. **Addenda Incorporated:** ☐ AS IS ☐ Additional Clause ☐ Assumption and Carryback ☐ Buyer Contingency ☐ Domestic Water Well ☐ H.O.A. ☐ Lead-Based Paint Disclosure ☐ On-site Wastewater Treatment Facility ☐ Short Sale ☐ Other: ______________________

1g. **Fixtures and Personal Property:** Seller agrees that all existing fixtures on the Premises, and any existing personal property specified herein, shall be included in this sale, including the following:

- free-standing range/oven
- ceiling fans
- attached floor coverings
- window and door screens, sun screens
- garage door openers and controls
- outdoor landscaping, fountains, and lighting
- pellet, wood-burning or gas-log stoves
- storage sheds
- light fixtures
- towel, curtain and drapery rods
- flush-mounted speakers
- storm windows and doors
- attached media antennas/ satellite dishes
- attached fireplace equipment
- timers
- draperies and other window coverings
- shutters and awnings
- water-misting systems
- solar systems
- mailbox
- central vacuum, hose, and attachments
- built-in appliances

>>

SELLER | SELLER <Initials   Initials> BUYER | BUYER

If owned by the Seller, the following items also are included in this sale:
- pool and spa equipment (including any mechanical or other cleaning systems)
- security and/or fire systems and/or alarms
- water softeners
- water purification systems

Additional existing personal property included in this sale (if checked): ☐ refrigerator ☐ washer ☐ dryer as described:

____

____

☐ Other: ____

____

Additional existing personal property included shall not be considered part of the Premises and shall be transferred with no monetary value, and free and clear of all liens or encumbrances.

Fixtures and leased items NOT included: ____

IF THIS IS AN ALL CASH SALE, GO TO SECTION 3.

2. FINANCING

2a. **Pre-Qualification:** A completed AAR Pre-Qualification Form ☐ is ☐ is not attached hereto and incorporated herein by reference.

2b. **Loan Contingency:** Buyer's obligation to complete this sale is contingent upon Buyer obtaining loan approval for the loan described in the AAR Loan Status Update ("LSU") form without Prior to Document ("PTD") conditions no later than three (3) days prior to the COE Date. If Buyer is unable to obtain loan approval without PTD conditions, Buyer shall deliver a notice of the inability to obtain loan approval without PTD conditions to Seller or Escrow Company no later than three (3) days prior to the COE Date.

2c. **Unfulfilled Loan Contingency**: This Contract shall be cancelled and Buyer shall be entitled to a return of the Earnest Money if after diligent and good faith effort, Buyer is unable to obtain loan approval without PTD conditions no later than three (3) days prior to the COE Date. Buyer acknowledges that prepaid items paid separately from earnest money are not refundable.

2d. **Interest Rate / Necessary Funds:** Buyer agrees that (i) the inability to obtain loan approval due to the failure to lock the interest rate and "points" by separate written agreement with the lender during the Inspection Period or (ii) the failure to have the down payment or other funds due from Buyer necessary to obtain the loan approval without conditions and close this transaction is not an unfulfilled loan contingency.

2e. **Loan Status Update**: Buyer shall deliver to Seller the LSU with at a minimum lines 1-40 completed describing the current status of the Buyer's proposed loan within five (5) days after Contract acceptance and instruct lender to provide an updated LSU to Broker(s) and Seller upon request.

2f. **Loan Application:** Unless previously completed, during the Inspection Period, Buyer shall (i) complete, sign and deliver to the lender a loan application and grant lender permission to access Buyer's Trimerged Residential Credit Report; and (ii) provide to lender all initial requested signed disclosures and **Initial Requested Documentation** listed in the LSU on lines 32-35.

2g. **Loan Processing During Escrow**: Buyer agrees to diligently work to obtain the loan and will promptly provide the lender with all additional documentation required. **Buyer shall sign all loan documents no later than three (3) days prior to the COE Date.**

2h. **Type of Financing**: ☐ Conventional ☐ FHA ☐ VA ☐ USDA ☐ Assumption ☐ Seller Carryback ☐ ________________
(If financing is to be other than new financing, see attached addendum.)

2i. **Loan Costs**: All costs of obtaining the loan shall be paid by the Buyer, unless otherwise provided for herein.

2j. **Seller Concessions (If Any)**: In addition to the other costs Seller has agreed to pay herein, Seller agrees to pay up to __________% of the Purchase Price or $ ___________ for Buyer's loan costs including pre-paids, impounds and Buyer's title / escrow closing costs.

2k. **VA Loan Costs**: In the event of a VA loan, Seller agrees to pay the escrow fee and up to $ _________________ of loan costs not permitted to be paid by the Buyer, in addition to the other costs Seller has agreed to pay herein, including Seller's Concessions.

2l. **Changes:** Buyer shall immediately notify Seller of any changes in the loan program, financing terms, or lender described in the Pre-Qualification Form if attached hereto or LSU provided within five (5) days after Contract acceptance and shall only make any such changes without the prior written consent of Seller if such changes do not adversely affect Buyer's ability to obtain loan approval without PTD conditions, increase Seller's closing costs, or delay COE.

2m. **Appraisal Contingency:** Buyer's obligation to complete this sale is contingent upon an appraisal of the Premises acceptable to lender for at least the purchase price. If the Premises fail to appraise for the purchase price in any appraisal required by lender, Buyer has five (5) days after notice of the appraised value to cancel this Contract and receive a refund of the Earnest Money or the appraisal contingency shall be waived.

2n. **Appraisal Fee(s):** Appraisal Fee(s), when required by lender, shall be paid by ☐ Buyer ☐ Seller ☐ Other ________________
Appraisal Fee(s) ☐ are ☐ are not included in Seller Concessions, if applicable.

>>

SELLER	SELLER	<Initials	Initials>	BUYER	BUYER

3. TITLE AND ESCROW

3a. **Escrow:** This Contract shall be used as escrow instructions. The Escrow Company employed by the parties to carry out the terms of this Contract shall be:

____
"ESCROW/TITLE COMPANY"

______________________ ______________ ________ ________
ADDRESS CITY STATE ZIP

______________________ ______________ ______________
EMAIL PHONE FAX

3b. **Title and Vesting**: Buyer will take title as determined before COE. Taking title may have significant legal, estate planning and tax consequences. Buyer should obtain legal and tax advice.

3c. **Title Commitment and Title Insurance**: Escrow Company is hereby instructed to obtain and deliver to Buyer and Seller directly, addressed pursuant to 8t and 9c or as otherwise provided, a Commitment for Title Insurance together with complete and legible copies of all documents that will remain as exceptions to Buyer's policy of Title Insurance ("Title Commitment"), including but not limited to Conditions, Covenants and Restrictions ("CC&Rs"); deed restrictions; and easements. Buyer shall have five (5) days after receipt of the Title Commitment and after receipt of notice of any subsequent exceptions to provide notice to Seller of any items disapproved. Seller shall convey title by warranty deed, subject to existing taxes, assessments, covenants, conditions, restrictions, rights of way, easements and all other matters of record. Buyer shall be provided at Seller's expense an American Land Title Association ("ALTA") Homeowner's Title Insurance Policy, or if not available, an ALTA Residential Title Insurance Policy ("Plain Language"/"1-4 units") or, if not available, a Standard Owner's Title Insurance Policy, showing title vested in Buyer. Buyer may acquire extended coverage at Buyer's own additional expense. If applicable, Buyer shall pay the cost of obtaining the ALTA Lender Title Insurance Policy.

3d. **Additional Instructions**: (i) Escrow Company shall promptly furnish notice of pending sale that contains the name and address of the Buyer to any homeowner's association in which the Premises is located. (ii) If the Escrow Company is also acting as the title agency but is not the title insurer issuing the title insurance policy, Escrow Company shall deliver to the Buyer and Seller, upon deposit of funds, a closing protection letter from the title insurer indemnifying the Buyer and Seller for any losses due to fraudulent acts or breach of escrow instructions by the Escrow Company. (iii) All documents necessary to close this transaction shall be executed promptly by Seller and Buyer in the standard form used by Escrow Company. Escrow Company shall modify such documents to the extent necessary to be consistent with this Contract. (iv) Escrow Company fees, unless otherwise stated herein, shall be allocated equally between Seller and Buyer. (v) Escrow Company shall send to all parties and Broker(s) copies of all notices and communications directed to Seller, Buyer and Broker(s). (vi) Escrow Company shall provide Broker(s) access to escrowed materials and information regarding the escrow. (vii) If an Affidavit of Disclosure is provided, Escrow Company shall record the Affidavit at COE.

3e. **Tax Prorations**: Real property taxes payable by the Seller shall be prorated to COE based upon the latest tax information available.

3f. **Release of Earnest Money**: In the event of a dispute between Buyer and Seller regarding any Earnest Money deposited with Escrow Company, Buyer and Seller authorize Escrow Company to release Earnest Money pursuant to the terms and conditions of this Contract in its sole and absolute discretion. Buyer and Seller agree to hold harmless and indemnify Escrow Company against any claim, action or lawsuit of any kind, and from any loss, judgment, or expense, including costs and attorney fees, arising from or relating in any way to the release of Earnest Money.

3g. **Prorations of Assessments and Fees**: All assessments and fees that are not a lien as of the COE, including homeowner's association fees, rents, irrigation fees, and, if assumed, insurance premiums, interest on assessments, interest on encumbrances, and service contracts, shall be prorated as of COE or ☐ Other: ______________________

3h. **Assessment Liens**: The amount of any assessment, other than homeowner's association assessments, that is a lien as of the COE, shall be ☐ paid in full by Seller ☐ prorated and assumed by Buyer. Any assessment that becomes a lien after COE is the Buyer's responsibility.

3i. **IRS and FIRPTA Reporting**: Seller agrees to comply with IRS reporting requirements. If applicable, Seller agrees to complete, sign, and deliver to Escrow Company a certificate indicating whether Seller is a foreign person or a non-resident alien pursuant to the Foreign Investment in Real Property Tax Act ("FIRPTA"). Buyer and Seller acknowledge that if the Seller is a foreign person, the Buyer must withhold a tax equal to 10% of the purchase price, unless an exemption applies.

>>

SELLER	SELLER	<Initials	Initials>	BUYER	BUYER

4. DISCLOSURE

4a. **Seller Property Disclosure Statement ("SPDS")**: Seller shall deliver a completed AAR Residential SPDS form to the Buyer within five (5) days after Contract acceptance. Buyer shall provide notice of any SPDS items disapproved within the Inspection Period or five (5) days after receipt of the SPDS, whichever is later.

4b. **Insurance Claims History**: Seller shall deliver to Buyer a written five-year insurance claims history regarding Premises (or a claims history for the length of time Seller has owned the Premises if less than five years) from Seller's insurance company or an insurance support organization or consumer reporting agency, or if unavailable from these sources, from Seller, within five (5) days after Contract acceptance. (Seller may obscure any reference to date of birth or social security number from the document). Buyer shall provide notice of any items disapproved within the Inspection Period or five (5) days after receipt of the claims history, whichever is later.

4c. **Lead-Based Paint Disclosure**: If the Premises were built prior to 1978, the Seller shall: (i) notify the Buyer of any known lead-based paint ("LBP") or LBP hazards in the Premises; (ii) provide the Buyer with any LBP risk assessments or inspections of the Premises in the Seller's possession; (iii) provide the Buyer with the Disclosure of Information on Lead-based Paint and Lead-based Paint Hazards, and any report, records, pamphlets, and/or other materials referenced therein, including the pamphlet "Protect Your Family from Lead in Your Home" (collectively "LBP Information"). Buyer shall return a signed copy of the Disclosure of Information on Lead-Based Paint and Lead-Based Paint Hazards to Seller prior to COE.

☐ LBP Information was provided prior to Contract acceptance and Buyer acknowledges the opportunity to conduct LBP risk assessments or inspections during Inspection Period.

☐ Seller shall provide LBP Information within five (5) days after Contract acceptance. Buyer may within ten (10) days or __________ days after receipt of the LBP Information conduct or obtain a risk assessment or inspection of the Premises for the presence of LBP or LBP hazards ("Assessment Period"). Buyer may within five (5) days after receipt of the LBP Information or five (5) days after expiration of the Assessment Period cancel this Contract.

Buyer is further advised to use certified contractors to perform renovation, repair or painting projects that disturb lead-based paint in residential properties built before 1978 and to follow specific work practices to prevent lead contamination.

If Premises were constructed prior to 1978, **(BUYER'S INITIALS REQUIRED)** ________ BUYER ________ BUYER

If Premises were constructed in 1978 or later, **(BUYER'S INITIALS REQUIRED)** ________ BUYER ________ BUYER

4d. **Affidavit of Disclosure**: If the Premises is located in an unincorporated area of the county, and five or fewer parcels of property other than subdivided property are being transferred, the Seller shall deliver a completed Affidavit of Disclosure in the form required by law to the Buyer within five (5) days after Contract acceptance. Buyer shall provide notice of any Affidavit of Disclosure items disapproved within the Inspection Period or five (5) days after receipt of the Affidavit of Disclosure, whichever is later.

4e. **Changes During Escrow**: Seller shall immediately notify Buyer of any changes in the Premises or disclosures made herein, in the SPDS, or otherwise. Such notice shall be considered an update of the SPDS. Unless Seller is already obligated by Section 5a or otherwise by this Contract or any amendments hereto, to correct or repair the changed item disclosed, Buyer shall be allowed five (5) days after delivery of such notice to provide notice of disapproval to Seller.

5. WARRANTIES

5a. **Seller Warranties**: Seller warrants and shall maintain and repair the Premises so that at the earlier of possession or COE: (i) all heating, cooling, mechanical, plumbing, and electrical systems (including swimming pool and/or spa, motors, filter systems, cleaning systems, and heaters, if any), free-standing range/oven, and built-in appliances will be in working condition; (ii) all other agreed upon repairs and corrections will be completed pursuant to Section 6j; (iii) the Premises, including all additional existing personal property included in the sale, will be in substantially the same condition as on the date of Contract acceptance; and (iv) all personal property not included in the sale and all debris will be removed from the Premises.

5b. **Warranties that Survive Closing**: Seller warrants that Seller has disclosed to Buyer and Broker(s) all material latent defects and any information concerning the Premises known to Seller, excluding opinions of value, which materially and adversely affect the consideration to be paid by Buyer. Prior to the COE, Seller warrants that payment in full will have been made for all labor, professional services, materials, machinery, fixtures, or tools furnished within the 150 days immediately preceding the COE in connection with the construction, alteration, or repair of any structure on or improvement to the Premises. Seller warrants that the information regarding connection to a sewer system or on-site wastewater treatment facility (conventional septic or alternative) is correct to the best of Seller's knowledge.

5c. **Buyer Warranties**: Buyer warrants that Buyer has disclosed to Seller any information that may materially and adversely affect the Buyer's ability to close escrow or complete the obligations of this Contract. At the earlier of possession of the Premises or COE, Buyer warrants to Seller that Buyer has conducted all desired independent inspections and investigations and accepts the Premises. **Buyer warrants that Buyer is not relying on any verbal representations concerning the Premises except disclosed as follows:**

____

____

>>

SELLER	SELLER	<Initials	Initials>	BUYER	BUYER

6. DUE DILIGENCE

6a. **Inspection Period**: Buyer's Inspection Period shall be ten (10) days or ________ days after Contract acceptance. During the Inspection Period Buyer, at Buyer's expense, shall: (i) conduct all desired physical, environmental, and other types of inspections and investigations to determine the value and condition of the Premises; (ii) make inquiries and consult government agencies, lenders, insurance agents, architects, and other appropriate persons and entities concerning the suitability of the Premises and the surrounding area; (iii) investigate applicable building, zoning, fire, health, and safety codes to determine any potential hazards, violations or defects in the Premises; and (iv) verify any material multiple listing service ("MLS") information. If the presence of sex offenders in the vicinity or the occurrence of a disease, natural death, suicide, homicide or other crime on or in the vicinity is a material matter to the Buyer, it must be investigated by the Buyer during the Inspection Period. Buyer shall keep the Premises free and clear of liens, shall indemnify and hold Seller harmless from all liability, claims, demands, damages, and costs, and shall repair all damages arising from the inspections. Buyer shall provide Seller and Broker(s) upon receipt, at no cost, copies of all inspection reports concerning the Premises obtained by Buyer. Buyer is advised to consult the Arizona Department of Real Estate *Buyer Advisory* provided by AAR to assist in Buyer's due diligence inspections and investigations.

6b. **Square Footage: BUYER IS AWARE THAT ANY REFERENCE TO THE SQUARE FOOTAGE OF THE PREMISES, BOTH THE REAL PROPERTY (LAND) AND IMPROVEMENTS THEREON, IS APPROXIMATE. IF SQUARE FOOTAGE IS A MATERIAL MATTER TO THE BUYER, IT MUST BE INVESTIGATED DURING THE INSPECTION PERIOD.**

6c. **Wood-Destroying Organism or Insect Inspection: IF CURRENT OR PAST WOOD-DESTROYING ORGANISMS OR INSECTS (SUCH AS TERMITES) ARE A MATERIAL MATTER TO THE BUYER, THESE ISSUES MUST BE INVESTIGATED DURING THE INSPECTION PERIOD.** The Buyer shall order and pay for all wood-destroying organism or insect inspections performed during the Inspection Period. If the lender requires an updated Wood-Destroying Organism or Insect Inspection Report prior to COE, it will be performed at Buyer's expense.

6d. **Flood Hazard**: Flood hazard designations or the cost of flood hazard insurance shall be determined by Buyer during the Inspection Period. If the Premises are situated in an area identified as having any special flood hazards by any governmental entity, the lender may require the purchase of flood hazard insurance. Special flood hazards may also affect the ability to encumber or improve the Premises.

6e. **Insurance: IF HOMEOWNER'S INSURANCE IS A MATERIAL MATTER TO THE BUYER, BUYER SHALL APPLY FOR AND OBTAIN WRITTEN CONFIRMATION OF THE AVAILABILITY AND COST OF HOMEOWNER'S INSURANCE FOR THE PREMISES FROM BUYER'S INSURANCE COMPANY DURING THE INSPECTION PERIOD.** Buyer understands that any homeowner's, fire, casualty, or other insurance desired by Buyer or required by lender should be in place at COE.

6f. **Sewer or On-site Wastewater Treatment System**: The Premises are connected to a:

☐ sewer system ☐ septic system ☐ alternative system

IF A SEWER CONNECTION IS A MATERIAL MATTER TO THE BUYER, IT MUST BE INVESTIGATED DURING THE INSPECTION PERIOD. If the Premises are served by a septic or alternative system, the AAR On-site Wastewater Treatment Facility Addendum is incorporated herein by reference.

(BUYER'S INITIALS REQUIRED) ________ BUYER ________ BUYER

6g. **Swimming Pool Barrier Regulations**: During the Inspection Period, Buyer agrees to investigate all applicable state, county, and municipal Swimming Pool barrier regulations and agrees to comply with and pay all costs of compliance with said regulations prior to occupying the Premises, unless otherwise agreed in writing. If the Premises contains a Swimming Pool, Buyer acknowledges receipt of the Arizona Department of Health Services approved private pool safety notice.

(BUYER'S INITIALS REQUIRED) ________ BUYER ________ BUYER

6h. **BUYER ACKNOWLEDGMENT: BUYER RECOGNIZES, ACKNOWLEDGES, AND AGREES THAT BROKER(S) ARE NOT QUALIFIED, NOR LICENSED, TO CONDUCT DUE DILIGENCE WITH RESPECT TO THE PREMISES OR THE SURROUNDING AREA. BUYER IS INSTRUCTED TO CONSULT WITH QUALIFIED LICENSED PROFESSIONALS TO ASSIST IN BUYER'S DUE DILIGENCE EFFORTS. BECAUSE CONDUCTING DUE DILIGENCE WITH RESPECT TO THE PREMISES AND THE SURROUNDING AREA IS BEYOND THE SCOPE OF THE BROKER'S EXPERTISE AND LICENSING, BUYER EXPRESSLY RELEASES AND HOLDS HARMLESS BROKER(S) FROM LIABILITY FOR ANY DEFECTS OR CONDITIONS THAT COULD HAVE BEEN DISCOVERED BY INSPECTION OR INVESTIGATION.**

(BUYER'S INITIALS REQUIRED) ________ BUYER ________ BUYER

6i. **Inspection Period Notice**: Prior to expiration of the Inspection Period, Buyer shall deliver to Seller a signed notice of any items disapproved. AAR's Buyer's Inspection Notice and Seller's Response form is available for this purpose. Buyer shall conduct all desired inspections and investigations prior to delivering such notice to Seller and all Inspection Period items disapproved shall be provided in a single notice.

>>

SELLER	SELLER	<Initials	Initials>	BUYER	BUYER

Residential Resale Real Estate Purchase Contract >>

6j. **Buyer Disapproval**: If Buyer, in Buyer's sole discretion, disapproves of items as allowed herein, Buyer shall deliver to Seller notice of the items disapproved and state in the notice that Buyer elects to either:

(1) immediately cancel this Contract and all Earnest Money shall be released to Buyer, or

(2) provide the Seller an opportunity to correct the items disapproved, in which case:

(a) Seller shall respond in writing within five (5) days or __________ days after delivery to Seller of Buyer's notice of items disapproved. Seller's failure to respond to Buyer in writing within the specified time period shall conclusively be deemed Seller's refusal to correct any of the items disapproved.

(b) **If Seller agrees in writing to correct items disapproved, Seller shall correct the items, complete any repairs in a workmanlike manner and deliver any paid receipts evidencing the corrections and repairs to Buyer three (3) days or ________ days prior to COE Date.**

(c) If Seller is unwilling or unable to correct any of the items disapproved, Buyer may cancel this Contract within five (5) days after delivery of Seller's response or after expiration of the time for Seller's response, whichever occurs first, and all Earnest Money shall be released to Buyer. If Buyer does not cancel this Contract within the five (5) days as provided, Buyer shall close escrow without correction of those items that Seller has not agreed in writing to correct.

VERBAL DISCUSSIONS WILL NOT EXTEND THESE TIME PERIODS. Only a written agreement signed by both parties will extend response times or cancellation rights.

BUYER'S FAILURE TO GIVE NOTICE OF DISAPPROVAL OF ITEMS OR CANCELLATION OF THIS CONTRACT WITHIN THE SPECIFIED TIME PERIOD SHALL CONCLUSIVELY BE DEEMED BUYER'S ELECTION TO PROCEED WITH THE TRANSACTION WITHOUT CORRECTION OF ANY DISAPPROVED ITEMS.

6k. **Notice of Non-Working Warranted Items**: Buyer shall provide Seller with notice of any non-working warranted item(s) of which Buyer becomes aware during the Inspection Period or the Seller warranty for that item(s) shall be waived. Delivery of such notice shall not affect Seller's obligation to maintain or repair the warranted item(s).

6l. **Home Warranty Plan**: Buyer and Seller are advised to investigate the various home warranty plans available for purchase. The parties acknowledge that different home warranty plans have different coverage options, exclusions, limitations, service fees and most plans exclude pre-existing conditions.

☐ A Home Warranty Plan will be ordered by ☐ Buyer or ☐ Seller with the following optional coverage ______________________________, to be issued by ______________________________ at a cost not to exceed $ ______________, to be paid for by ☐ Buyer ☐ Seller

☐ Buyer declines the purchase of a Home Warranty Plan.

6m. **Walkthrough(s):** Seller grants Buyer and Buyer's inspector(s) reasonable access to conduct walkthrough(s) of the Premises for the purpose of satisfying Buyer that any corrections or repairs agreed to by the Seller have been completed, warranted items are in working condition and that the Premises is in substantially the same condition as of the date of Contract acceptance. If Buyer does not conduct such walkthrough(s), Buyer releases Seller and Broker(s) from liability for any defects that could have been discovered.

6n. **Seller's Responsibility Regarding Inspections and Walkthrough(s):** Seller shall make the Premises available for all inspections and walkthrough(s) upon reasonable notice by Buyer. Seller shall, at Seller's expense, have all utilities on, including any propane, until COE to enable Buyer to conduct these inspections and walkthrough(s).

7. REMEDIES

7a. **Cure Period**: A party shall have an opportunity to cure a potential breach of this Contract. If a party fails to comply with any provision of this Contract, the other party shall deliver a notice to the non-complying party specifying the non-compliance. If the non-compliance is not cured within three (3) days after delivery of such notice ("Cure Period"), the failure to comply shall become a breach of Contract.

7b. **Breach**: In the event of a breach of Contract, the non-breaching party may cancel this Contract and/or proceed against the breaching party in any claim or remedy that the non-breaching party may have in law or equity, subject to the Alternative Dispute Resolution obligations set forth herein. In the case of the Seller, because it would be difficult to fix actual damages in the event of Buyer's breach, the Earnest Money may be deemed a reasonable estimate of damages and Seller may, at Seller's option, accept the Earnest Money as Seller's sole right to damages; and in the event of Buyer's breach arising from Buyer's failure to deliver the notice required by Section 2b, or Buyer's inability to obtain loan approval due to the waiver of the appraisal contingency pursuant to Section 2m, Seller shall exercise this option and accept the Earnest Money as Seller's sole right to damages. An unfulfilled contingency is not a breach of Contract. The parties expressly agree that the failure of any party to comply with the terms and conditions of Section 1d to allow COE to occur on the COE Date, if not cured after a cure notice is delivered pursuant to Section 7a, will constitute a material breach of this Contract, rendering the Contract subject to cancellation.

>>

SELLER	SELLER	<Initials	Initials>	BUYER	BUYER

7c. **Alternative Dispute Resolution ("ADR"):** Buyer and Seller agree to mediate any dispute or claim arising out of or relating to this Contract in accordance with the REALTORS® Dispute Resolution System, or as otherwise agreed. All mediation costs shall be paid equally by the parties. In the event that mediation does not resolve all disputes or claims, the unresolved disputes or claims shall be submitted for binding arbitration. In such event, the parties shall agree upon an arbitrator and cooperate in the scheduling of an arbitration hearing. If the parties are unable to agree on an arbitrator, the dispute shall be submitted to the American Arbitration Association ("AAA") in accordance with the AAA Arbitration Rules for the Real Estate Industry. The decision of the arbitrator shall be final and nonappealable. Judgment on the award rendered by the arbitrator may be entered in any court of competent jurisdiction. Notwithstanding the foregoing, either party may opt out of binding arbitration within thirty (30) days after the conclusion of the mediation conference by notice to the other and in such event either party shall have the right to resort to court action.

7d. **Exclusions from ADR**: The following matters are excluded from the requirement for ADR hereunder: (i) any action brought in the Small Claims Division of an Arizona Justice Court (up to $2,500) so long as the matter is not thereafter transferred or removed from the small claims division; (ii) judicial or nonjudicial foreclosure or other action or proceeding to enforce a deed of trust, mortgage, or agreement for sale; (iii) an unlawful entry or detainer action; (iv) the filing or enforcement of a mechanic's lien; or (v) any matter that is within the jurisdiction of a probate court. Further, the filing of a judicial action to enable the recording of a notice of pending action ("lis pendens"), or order of attachment, receivership, injunction, or other provisional remedies shall not constitute a waiver of the obligation to submit the claim to ADR, nor shall such action constitute a breach of the duty to mediate or arbitrate.

7e. **Attorney Fees and Costs**: The prevailing party in any dispute or claim between Buyer and Seller arising out of or relating to this Contract shall be awarded their reasonable attorney fees and costs. Costs shall include, without limitation, attorney fees, expert witness fees, fees paid to investigators, and arbitration costs.

8. ADDITIONAL TERMS AND CONDITIONS

8a. ______________________________

>>

SELLER | SELLER <Initials Initials> BUYER | BUYER

8b. **Risk of Loss**: If there is any loss or damage to the Premises between the date of Contract acceptance and COE or possession, whichever is earlier, by reason of fire, vandalism, flood, earthquake, or act of God, the risk of loss shall be on the Seller, provided, however, that if the cost of repairing such loss or damage would exceed ten percent (10%) of the purchase price, either Seller or Buyer may elect to cancel the Contract.

8c. **Permission**: Buyer and Seller grant Broker(s) permission to advise the public of this Contract.

8d. **Arizona Law**: This Contract shall be governed by Arizona law and jurisdiction is exclusively conferred on the State of Arizona.

8e. **Time is of the Essence**: The parties acknowledge that time is of the essence in the performance of the obligations described herein.

8f. **Compensation**: Seller and Buyer acknowledge that Broker(s) shall be compensated for services rendered as previously agreed by separate written agreement(s), which shall be delivered by Broker(s) to Escrow Company for payment at COE, if not previously paid. If Seller is obligated to pay Broker(s), this Contract shall constitute an irrevocable assignment of Seller's proceeds at COE. If Buyer is obligated to pay Broker(s), payment shall be collected from Buyer as a condition of COE. COMMISSIONS PAYABLE FOR THE SALE, LEASING, OR MANAGEMENT OF PROPERTY ARE NOT SET BY ANY BOARD OR ASSOCIATION OF REALTORS®, OR MULTIPLE LISTING SERVICE, OR IN ANY MANNER OTHER THAN BETWEEN THE BROKER AND CLIENT.

8g. **Copies and Counterparts**: A fully executed facsimile or electronic copy of the Contract shall be treated as an original Contract. This Contract and any other documents required by this Contract may be executed by facsimile or other electronic means and in any number of counterparts, which shall become effective upon delivery as provided for herein, except that the Lead-Based Paint Disclosure Statement may not be signed in counterpart. All counterparts shall be deemed to constitute one instrument, and each counterpart shall be deemed an original.

8h. **Days**: All references to days in this Contract shall be construed as calendar days and a day shall begin at 12:00 a.m. and end at 11:59 p.m.

8i. **Calculating Time Periods**: In computing any time period prescribed or allowed by this Contract, the day of the act or event from which the time period begins to run is not included and the last day of the time period is included. Contract acceptance occurs on the date that the signed Contract (and any incorporated counter offer) is delivered to and received by the appropriate Broker. Acts that must be performed three days prior to the COE Date must be performed three full days prior (i.e., if COE Date is Friday the act must be performed by 11:59 p.m. on Monday).

8j. **Entire Agreement**: This Contract, and any addenda and attachments, shall constitute the entire agreement between Seller and Buyer, shall supersede any other written or oral agreements between Seller and Buyer and can be modified only by a writing signed by Seller and Buyer. The failure to initial any page of this Contract shall not affect the validity or terms of this Contract.

8k. **Subsequent Offers**: Buyer acknowledges that Seller has the right to accept subsequent offers until COE. Seller understands that any subsequent offer accepted by the Seller must be a backup offer contingent on the cancellation of this Contract.

8l. **Cancellation**: A party who wishes to exercise the right of cancellation as allowed herein may cancel this Contract by delivering notice stating the reason for cancellation to the other party or to the Escrow Company. Cancellation shall become effective immediately upon delivery of the cancellation notice.

8m. **Notice**: Unless otherwise provided, delivery of all notices and documentation required or permitted hereunder shall be in writing and deemed delivered and received when: (i) hand-delivered; (ii) sent via facsimile transmission; (iii) sent via electronic mail, if email addresses are provided herein; or (iv) sent by recognized overnight courier service, and addressed to Buyer as indicated in Section 8r, to Seller as indicated in Section 9a and to the Escrow Company indicated in Section 3a.

8n. **Earnest Money**: Earnest Money is in the form of: ☐ Personal Check ☐ Other ______________________
If applicable, Earnest Money has been received by Broker named in Section 8r and upon acceptance of this offer will be deposited with: ☐ Escrow Company ☐ Broker's Trust Account. Buyer acknowledges that failure to pay the required closing funds by the scheduled COE, if not cured after a cure notice is delivered pursuant to Section 7a, shall be construed as a material breach of this contract and all earnest money shall be subject to forfeiture.

8o. **Release of Broker(s): Seller and Buyer hereby expressly release, hold harmless and indemnify Broker(s) in this transaction from any and all liability and responsibility regarding financing, the condition, square footage, lot lines, boundaries, value, rent rolls, environmental problems, sanitation systems, roof, wood infestation, building codes, governmental regulations, insurance, price and terms of sale, return on investment or any other matter relating to the value or condition of the Premises. The parties understand and agree that the Broker(s) do not provide advice on property as an investment and are not qualified to provide financial, legal, or tax advice regarding this real estate transaction.**

(SELLER'S INITIALS REQUIRED) ________ SELLER ________ SELLER **(BUYER'S INITIALS REQUIRED)** ________ BUYER ________ BUYER

8p. **Terms of Acceptance**: This offer will become a binding Contract when acceptance is signed by Seller and a signed copy delivered in person, by mail, facsimile or electronically, and received by Broker named in Section 8r
by ______________________, __________ at __________ a.m./p.m., Mountain Standard Time.
Buyer may withdraw this offer at any time prior to receipt of Seller's signed acceptance. If no signed acceptance is received by this date and time, this offer shall be deemed withdrawn and the Buyer's Earnest Money shall be returned.

>>

SELLER	SELLER	<Initials	Initials>	BUYER	BUYER

Residential Resale Real Estate Purchase Contract >>

8q. THIS CONTRACT CONTAINS NINE PAGES EXCLUSIVE OF ANY ADDENDA AND ATTACHMENTS. PLEASE ENSURE THAT YOU HAVE RECEIVED AND READ ALL NINE PAGES OF THIS OFFER AS WELL AS ANY ADDENDA AND ATTACHMENTS.

8r. **Broker on behalf of Buyer:**

PRINT SALESPERSON'S NAME ______ AGENT CODE ______ PRINT FIRM NAME ______ FIRM CODE ______

FIRM ADDRESS ______ STATE ______ ZIP CODE ______

PREFERRED TELEPHONE ______ FAX ______ EMAIL ______

8s. **Agency Confirmation:** The Broker named in Section 8r above is the agent of (check one):
☐ the Buyer; ☐ the Seller; or ☐ both the Buyer and Seller

8t. **The undersigned agree to purchase the Premises on the terms and conditions herein stated and acknowledge receipt of a copy hereof including the Buyer Attachment.**

^ BUYER'S SIGNATURE ______ MO/DA/YR ______ ^ BUYER'S SIGNATURE ______ MO/DA/YR ______

ADDRESS ______ ADDRESS ______

CITY, STATE, ZIP CODE ______ CITY, STATE, ZIP CODE ______

9. SELLER ACCEPTANCE

9a. **Broker on behalf of Seller:**

PRINT SALESPERSON'S NAME ______ AGENT CODE ______ PRINT FIRM NAME ______ FIRM CODE ______

FIRM ADDRESS ______ STATE ______ ZIP CODE ______

PREFERRED TELEPHONE ______ FAX ______ EMAIL ______

9b. **Agency Confirmation:** The Broker named in Section 9a above is the agent of (check one):
☐ the Seller; or ☐ both the Buyer and Seller

9c. **The undersigned agree to sell the Premises on the terms and conditions herein stated, acknowledge receipt of a copy hereof and grant permission to Broker named on Section 9a to deliver a copy to Buyer.**

☐ Counter Offer is attached, and is incorporated herein by reference. Seller should sign both this offer and the Counter Offer. If there is a conflict between this offer and the Counter Offer, the provisions of the Counter Offer shall be controlling.

^ SELLER'S SIGNATURE ______ MO/DA/YR ______ ^ SELLER'S SIGNATURE ______ MO/DA/YR ______

SELLER'S NAME PRINTED ______ SELLER'S NAME PRINTED ______

ADDRESS ______ ADDRESS ______

CITY, STATE, ZIP CODE ______ CITY, STATE, ZIP CODE ______

☐ **OFFER REJECTED BY SELLER:** ______ MONTH ______ DAY, 20____ YEAR ______ (SELLER'S INITIALS)

For Broker Use Only:
Brokerage File/Log No.______ Manager's Initials______ Broker's Initials______ Date______ MO/DA/YR

Terms of Sale. The purchase agreement should set forth as clearly as possible all of the terms of the sale, such as the total sales price, the amount of the downpayment, the method of payment, and what items are included in or excluded from the sale.

The method of payment should be set forth in detail; the purchase agreement form may include a pre-printed checklist of the most common types of financing arrangements. But regardless of the form used, all of the financing arrangements should be fully described, including the type of loan, the principal amount, the interest rate, how the loan is amortized, the term of the loan, and the monthly payments. (Types of financing programs are discussed in Chapter 12.)

Conditions of Sale. Most purchase agreements are conditional. For example, it is common to condition a sale on the buyer's ability to obtain the necessary financing. If the buyer is unable to obtain the financing after making a good faith effort to do so, she does not have to go through with the purchase, and does not have to forfeit the deposit.

Any and all conditions must be clearly stated in the purchase agreement. A provision that sets forth a condition is called a **contingency clause**. A contingency clause should state exactly what must occur to fulfill the condition, and it should explain how one party is to notify the other when the condition has been fulfilled or waived. There should also be a time limit placed on the condition (for example, if the condition is not fulfilled by January 15, the contract is void). Finally, the contingency clause should explain the parties' rights if the condition is not met or waived.

Condition of the Property. A purchase agreement may include a variety of provisions concerning the condition of the property. The seller may warrant the condition of certain elements (such as the roof, plumbing, or appliances) or else may sell the property "as is." Note that in most states, even if the property is sold "as is," the seller is still subject to state laws that require disclosure of material facts concerning the condition of the property. Some of these disclosures may be included in the purchase agreement, or they may be part of a separate document.

Conveyance and Title. The purchase agreement should specify the type of deed that will be used to convey title to the buyer. Furthermore, title is required to be marketable, meaning that the property is free from undisclosed liens and encumbrances. In addition to the seller's assurances, most buyers will want the additional protection of a title insurance policy. Which party pays for title insurance normally depends on local custom, and this should also be specified in the purchase agreement.

Escrow and Closing. It's a good idea for a purchase agreement to include the arrangements for escrow and closing. At the very least, the agreement should set the closing date for the transaction. Both parties must agree to the identity of the escrow agent; one party can't choose the escrow agent without the other's consent.

Date of Possession. Possession of the property is usually transferred to the buyer on the closing date, but other arrangements can be made in the purchase agreement. If possession will be transferred either before or after closing, the parties should execute a separate rental agreement, sometimes called an **interim occupancy agreement**.

The Uniform Vendor and Purchaser Risk Act, a law that has been adopted in many states, determines who suffers the loss when property subject to a sales contract is damaged or destroyed. This law provides that until possession of the property is transferred to the buyer, the risk of loss is the seller's. For instance, if a house is destroyed by an earthquake the day before possession is transferred to the buyer, the seller bears the loss. Once possession is transferred to the buyer, however, the risk of loss is the buyer's.

The parties may choose to apportion the risk of loss differently by including a **risk clause** in the purchase agreement.

Time is of the Essence. Many purchase agreements contain a clause stating that "time is of the essence" (see Chapter 7). This clause indicates that failure to meet any of the deadlines set in the agreement constitutes a breach of contract.

Good Faith Deposit. A purchase agreement normally requires the buyer to make a good faith deposit (sometimes called an earnest money deposit) at the time of the agreement, to show that the buyer is serious about going through with the transaction. Although the deposit is not required for a valid contract (the seller's promise to sell and the buyer's promise to buy are sufficient consideration), a good faith deposit is almost always part of a real estate transaction. If the agent holds the good faith deposit on the seller's behalf instead of passing the deposit directly to an escrow agent, the purchase agreement serves as the buyer's receipt for the good faith deposit; this is why you may hear the purchase agreement also referred to as a deposit receipt.

The appropriate amount for a good faith deposit varies according to local custom; it can be any amount that both parties agree on. If the buyer goes through with the transaction, the deposit is ordinarily applied to the purchase price.

The purchase agreement should explain the circumstances in which the deposit will be refunded to the buyer or forfeited to the seller. In many cases, the deposit is treated as liquidated damages (see Chapter 7). Some states have laws establishing additional conditions that must be met before the deposit can serve as liquidated damages. For example, the parties may need to initial a liquidated damages provision in the contract, and the amount of the deposit that can be treated as liquidated damages may be limited to a certain percentage of the purchase price.

The form of the deposit should be stated in the contract. A personal check is the most common, but another form of payment—such as a promissory note—may be used. The form of the deposit should be disclosed to the seller before he accepts the offer.

Broker's Compensation. Many purchase agreements also provide for the payment of the broker's commission. In most cases, this provision is merely a reaffirmation of the commission agreement set forth in the listing agreement. But if the broker has risked working under an oral or implied listing agreement, such a provision in the purchase agreement will qualify as a "written agreement," in case the broker needs to sue the seller for the commission.

Binder

In some areas of the United States, the agent or broker does not prepare the purchase agreement. Instead, a shorter document known as a binder is used as the basis for the offer and acceptance. A **binder** states the essential terms of the agreement, such as the purchase price and the amount of the downpayment. Binders are common in the northeastern United States.

The binder is designed to function as a contract between the parties for only a short time. The full purchase agreement is normally drafted by an attorney after the binder has been signed. This agreement replaces the binder as the contract for the sale of the property.

Amendments

After the buyer and seller have signed the purchase agreement, the terms of the contract can be modified only in writing. Oral changes are not legally binding. Sometimes, changes are just written into the original contract and signed by the parties. However, it's much safer to use an amendment form to make changes. All the parties who signed the original agreement must also sign the amendment, or it will be unenforceable.

Don't confuse an amendment with an addendum. An **amendment** is a written modification that occurs after the parties have signed the purchase agreement. An addendum, on the other hand, is an attachment added to the agreement prior to signature. The addendum contains terms that are not contained in the basic purchase agreement; the agreement will refer to and incorporate the contents of the addendum at some point.

A **rider** is another term for a document that is added to a contract. Depending on how it is used, a rider may be either an amendment or an addendum. It is important to be clear as to whether the original agreement incorporates the additional document by reference, or whether the document is supposed to modify an already existing agreement.

Escrow Agreements

After the buyer and seller have agreed on the sale of a property, the transaction needs to close. This will usually involve an additional contract known as an **escrow agreement** or escrow instructions. The escrow agent may have separate contracts with the buyer and the seller or a single contract with both of them, depending on local custom. The escrow agreement is based on the purchase agreement; the purpose of the escrow agreement is to provide instructions so that the terms of the purchase agreement are properly carried out. Escrow and the closing process are discussed in Chapter 14.

Land Contracts

What we'll refer to as a **land contract** is also known by a number of other names: real estate contract, real property sales contract, conditional sales contract, installment sales contract, or contract for deed. Under a land contract, a buyer purchases property on an installment basis, rather than paying the seller the full purchase price all at once. The buyer takes possession of the property immediately, but the seller does not convey title to the buyer until the full price has been paid.

The parties to a land contract are usually referred to as the **vendor** (seller) and the **vendee** (buyer). The following example illustrates how a land contract works.

> **Example:** Bender agrees to buy Jones's farm for $500,000, to be paid at the rate of $50,000 per year, plus 9% interest, for ten years. Jones (the vendor) allows Bender (the vendee) to take possession of the farm, and she promises to convey title to Bender when he has paid the full purchase price. Bender and Jones have entered into a land contract.

During the period in which the vendee is making payments on the contract, the vendor retains **legal title** to the property. The vendor does not deliver the deed to the vendee until the full purchase price has been paid. In the meantime, the vendee is said to have **equitable title** to the property. Equitable title is essentially the right to possess and enjoy the property while paying off the purchase price.

Rights and Responsibilities of the Parties

Both the vendor and the vendee have various rights and responsibilities under a land contract. The vendor retains legal title to the property and has the right to transfer or encumber the property without the vendee's consent. If legal title is transferred, the new owner takes title subject to the rights of the vendee under the land contract.

If the vendor allows liens to be placed on the property, the vendee may end up paying the full contract price only to find that the property is totally encumbered. Usually, the vendee avoids this problem by having the contract recorded, which places prospective lienholders on notice of the land contract. In many states, this will protect the vendee's interest in the property against future encumbrances. The vendee could also insist on a provision in the contract that requires the vendor to maintain marketable title to the property.

The vendee is entitled to possession and use of the property; his main responsibility is to make the required installment payments to the vendor. The vendee is generally also responsible for keeping the property insured and paying the property taxes.

Like the vendor, the vendee has the ability to encumber the property, but few lenders are willing to make loans with a vendee's equitable interest as the only security. The vendee may sell her interest in the property by assigning the right to receive the deed when the contract price has been paid in full. (However, the vendee will remain responsible for making the contract payments unless the vendor releases the vendee from liability.) The vendee also has the right to devise (will) her interest.

Historically, land contracts tended to favor the vendor, and often had provisions restricting the vendee's rights. For example, the contract might prohibit the vendee from recording the contract, or assigning his interest in the property. These provisions are usually discouraged today; many states do not allow the contract to prohibit recording, and some actually require that land contracts be recorded. State laws may also impose other restrictions on land contracts for the protection of the vendee.

Remedies for Default

If the vendee pays the purchase price in full, but the vendor fails to transfer legal title to the property, the vendee can sue for specific performance of the contract (see Chapter 7).

If the vendee defaults (for example, by failing to make the installment payments), the vendor can terminate the contract. The consequences of termination depend on the terms of the contract, as well as on state laws. Traditionally, land contracts contained a forfeiture clause that allowed the vendor to retake possession of the property. The vendor was also allowed to keep any money the vendee had already paid on the contract. Today, however, most states have imposed restrictions on forfeiture as a remedy for default. For example, the vendor may be allowed to retake possession of the property, but would be required to reimburse the vendee for the amount paid to the vendor under the contract. The vendee's reimbursement could be reduced by any damages that the vendor incurred, and by the fair market rental value of the property for the period the vendee was in possession.

> **Example:** Under a land contract, Porter paid Rollins $12,800 over a ten-month period. The rental value of the property for that period was $1,100 per month, or $11,000. Porter stops making installment payments after the tenth month, and Rollins reclaims the property under a forfeiture clause. State law requires Rollins to reimburse the amount paid under the contract, minus the rental value of the property. Porter would be entitled to a reimbursement of only $1,800. ($12,800 – $11,000 = $1,800).

Some states do not allow the vendor to demand forfeiture immediately upon the vendee's default. Instead, the vendor is required to give notice of default to the vendee. The vendee then has a specified period of time in which to cure the default and reinstate the contract. Furthermore, courts in some jurisdictions have held that once the vendee has paid a substantial portion of the contract price, she gains a right of redemption (the right to keep the property by paying off the entire amount of the debt). The right of redemption is a concept normally applied to mortgages, and will be explained in more detail in that context (see Chapter 11).

If the vendee does not cure the default or redeem the property, then the vendor is entitled to retake possession. However, a recorded land contract is a cloud on the property's title; the vendor may need to obtain a quitclaim deed from the vendee or file a quiet title action to make the title marketable again.

A few states do not allow forfeiture as a remedy for default on a land contract at all. Instead, the vendor is required to foreclose on the property like any other lienholder.

Reasons for Using a Land Contract

A land contract is a security instrument that is sometimes used in conjunction with seller financing. The seller extends credit to the buyer and holds title to the property as security for the repayment of the debt. (See Chapter 11 for a detailed discussion of security instruments.) However, because of the vendee's rights of reinstatement, reimbursement, and redemption under a land contract, most people prefer to use mortgages or deeds of trust in seller-financed transactions (see Chapter 11).

Leases

A lease is both a method of conveyance and a contract. A lease conveys a less-than-freehold (leasehold) estate from the owner (the **landlord**) to the **tenant**. As we discussed in Chapter 3, the holder of a leasehold estate does not own the property, but rather has a right to exclusive possession of the property for a specified period of time. Sometimes the landlord and the tenant are said to be "in privity," which means they have a mutual interest in one property.

A lease (also called a **rental agreement**) sets out the rights and responsibilities of the two parties, the landlord and the tenant. In addition, certain covenants and obligations are implied by law in all leases, whether or not they are part of the agreement.

Requirements for a Valid Lease

As with any contract, the parties to a lease must be competent and must both agree to its terms. Consideration (typically, the rental payment) is also required. The amount of the rent and when it is due should be specified.

Under the statute of frauds, a lease must be in writing if the lease term is longer than the statutory period (one year in most states). A lease for a fixed term that should be in writing but is not may be treated as a periodic tenancy instead.

A written lease must be signed by the landlord. The tenant usually signs the lease as well, but the tenant's signature isn't always required. A tenant who takes possession of the property and pays rent is considered to have accepted the terms of the lease. Even so, it's wise to have both parties sign the lease. Also, since a lease is a contract pertaining to real property, a complete and accurate description of the property should be included.

Lease Renewal

A lease may contain a provision that gives the tenant an option to renew the lease at the end of the term. Most renewal options require the tenant to give notice of her intention to exercise the option on or before a specific date.

To renew a lease, the parties often sign a renewal agreement. But a lease may be renewed by implication rather than express agreement. When the tenant makes a lease payment after the lease has expired, and the landlord accepts the payment, that can be considered an implied renewal of the lease.

Transferring Leased Property

A landlord can sell the leased property during the term of the lease, but the buyer takes title subject to the lease. This means the buyer must honor the lease for the remainder of its term. (There's an exception if the property is sold involuntarily. A foreclosure sale purchaser doesn't necessarily have to honor an existing lease.)

The tenant can also transfer his leasehold estate to another party, through assignment, subleasing, or novation. The tenant has the right to assign or sublease without the landlord's consent, unless the lease provides otherwise. A novation always requires the landlord's consent.

In an **assignment**, the tenant transfers the entire unexpired term of the lease.

> **Example:** Landlord leases the premises to Tenant for a period starting January 1, 2013 and ending June 30, 2016. On July 1, 2013, Tenant leases the premises to XYZ Corporation for a term starting July 1, 2013 and ending June 30, 2016. The agreement between Tenant and XYZ is an assignment, because the transfer is for the balance of the unexpired term.

The assignee becomes liable for paying the rent to the landlord (the original lessor) and the assignor (the original tenant) becomes secondarily liable for the rent. This means that the assignee has the primary responsibility for paying the rent, but the original tenant is not fully released from the duty to pay.

In a **sublease**, the original tenant transfers only part of his remaining interest. He may be giving the subtenant (the new tenant) the right to share possession with him, or the right to possess only part of the leased property. Or he may be giving the subtenant the right to possess the whole property, but for only part of the unexpired term.

> **Example:** Landlord leases the premises to Tenant for a period starting January 1, 2013 and ending June 30, 2016. On July 1, 2013, Tenant leases the premises to a subtenant for a period starting July 1, 2013, through June 30, 2015, reserving the last year for himself. This agreement is a sublease because the tenant has transferred less than the balance of the lease term.

The subtenant is liable for the rent to the original tenant, rather than to the landlord, and the original tenant is still liable to the landlord. This situation is sometimes referred to as a **sandwich lease**, because the original tenant is in the middle, sandwiched between the landlord and the subtenant.

A **novation** occurs when a new contract is created and the old contract is extinguished. When an existing lease is

Fig. 8.3 Transferring leased property

Assignment	Tenant transfers the entire unexpired term of the lease
Sublease	Tenant transfers less than the unexpired term of the lease
Novation	Lease is replaced with a new agreement, or one party is replaced by another party

replaced either with a new lease between the same parties, or with a new lease between different parties, it has been novated. The purpose of a novation is to terminate the liability of the tenant under the original lease.

Termination of a Lease

Most leases terminate when the lease term expires and the lease is not renewed. A lease may also be terminated before the end of its term in a variety of ways.

Surrender. A landlord and tenant may mutually agree to terminate a lease before the scheduled end of the lease term. This is called **surrender**. Note that the tenant cannot simply abandon the property in order to get out of the lease. A surrender requires the agreement of both parties.

Actual Eviction. When the landlord expels the tenant from the property, this is called **actual eviction**. However, the landlord cannot simply force the tenant to leave the property. To protect residential tenants, state laws impose a number of requirements on a landlord that wants to terminate a tenant's lease rights. (State landlord/tenant laws are covered in Chapter 17.)

A landlord trying to evict a tenant must take the tenant to court and give the tenant notice of the eviction proceeding. In the court hearing, the landlord must show evidence of the tenant's violation of the lease agreement. The most common reason for eviction is failure to pay rent.

If the tenant refuses to leave when requested, the landlord must go through the legal process. Landlords should never take matters into their own hands. A landlord who tries a "self-help" eviction (forcing the tenant out with threats, or by cutting off the utilities) instead of the legal process may end up defending a costly lawsuit.

Constructive Eviction. Every lease has an implied promise from the landlord to the tenant that he will refrain from unlawfully interfering with the tenant's possession of the leased property. This is known as the **covenant of quiet enjoyment**. Constructive eviction occurs when the landlord causes or permits a substantial interference with the tenant's possession of the property. In these circumstances, the tenant may be justified in abandoning the property and terminating the lease. Other remedies, such as suing for damages or withholding rent payments, may also be available.

Most states require a residential landlord to maintain the property in a habitable condition and make necessary repairs. For example, failure to provide heat to a residential unit in the wintertime has been found to result in constructive eviction. The specific obligations of landlords and tenants will be discussed more specifically in Chapter 17.

Illegal or Unauthorized Use. If the tenant uses the premises in an illegal manner (in violation of the zoning code, for example) or in a manner not authorized by the lease, the tenant has violated the agreement. Depending on the provisions of the agreement, the landlord may be able to terminate the lease.

Even though the lease is terminated, if the tenant remains on the property, she is still a tenant at sufferance (see Chapter 3). The landlord will need to go to court in order to evict the tenant and recover possession of the property.

Foreclosure. If a lien against leased property is foreclosed on because the landlord has defaulted on a loan or other obligation, the foreclosure may terminate the lease. Generally, a foreclosure sale purchaser must honor an existing lease only if it has higher priority than the foreclosed lien.

A federal law passed in 2009 provides tenants of foreclosed properties with some additional protections. Under this law, someone who buys leased residential property at a foreclosure sale is required to honor the lease for the remainder of its term, unless the buyer herself intends to occupy the property as a personal residence. In that case, the buyer must give the tenant 90 days' notice before terminating the tenancy. A residential tenant who doesn't have a lease for a specific term (for example, if it's a month-to-month tenancy) is also entitled to 90 days' notice, whether or not the buyer is planning to move into the home herself. Although this federal law is scheduled to expire at the end of 2014, it's possible that Congress will extend it temporarily or permanently.

Destruction of the Premises. In most states, if a lease is for the use of an entire building, it is presumed to include the land as well. Unless the agreement provides otherwise, the destruction of the building does not terminate the lease. The tenant is not prevented from use and enjoyment of the land, and therefore the purpose of the lease is not frustrated. The tenant will not be relieved from the duty to pay the rent to the end of the rental period. If, however, the lease is only for a part of a building, such as an office, apartment, or commercial space, the destruction of the building frustrates the entire purpose of the lease, so the tenant will be released from the duty to pay rent.

Condemnation. Condemnation of property can also result in premature termination of a lease. (See Chapter 6 for a discussion of condemnation and the power of eminent domain.)

Option Agreements

An **option agreement** is essentially a contract to make a contract. It is sometimes called a contract to keep an offer open. An option agreement creates a right to buy or lease a specified property for a fixed price within a set period of time. The parties to an option agreement are called the **optionor** (the one who grants the option right) and the **optionee** (the one who is granted the option right). In an option to purchase, the optionor is the seller and the optionee is the buyer.

> **Example:** Alvarez is offering to sell his property for $620,000. Conners isn't yet sure that he wants to buy the property, but he doesn't want to lose the opportunity to do so. He asks Alvarez to give him a three-week option to purchase, and Alvarez agrees.

They execute a written option agreement, and Conners pays Alvarez $750 as consideration for the option. The option gives Conners the right to buy the property at the stated price ($620,000) during the next three weeks, but does not obligate him to buy it at all.

The optionor is bound to keep the offer open for the period specified in the option agreement. He is not allowed to sell or lease the property to anyone other than the optionee until the option expires.

If the optionee decides to exercise the option (that is, to buy or lease the property on the stated terms), she must give written notice of acceptance to the optionor. If the optionee fails to exercise the option within the specified time, the option expires automatically.

Requirements for a Valid Option

Because an option is a contract, it must have all of the necessary elements of a contract, including consideration. The consideration may be a nominal amount—there's no set minimum. But some consideration must, in fact, pass from the optionee to the optionor; a mere statement of consideration in the agreement is not sufficient. (There is an exception to this rule for lease/option agreements, where the provisions of the lease are treated as sufficient consideration to support the option.)

An option agreement must be in writing; oral options are unenforceable. Furthermore, since an option to purchase anticipates that a sale may take place, the underlying terms of the sale (price, financing, etc.) should be spelled out in the option agreement.

Option Rights

The executed option gives the optionee a contract right, but does not create an interest in real property. An option is not a lien, and also cannot be used as security for a mortgage or a deed of trust.

The optionee can assign his rights to another party, unless the agreement includes a provision prohibiting assignment. If the optionor dies during the option period, that will not affect the rights of the optionee, who may still exercise the right to purchase or lease. The option contract is binding on the heirs and assignees of the optionor.

Recording an Option

An option agreement may be recorded to give third parties constructive notice of the option. In that case, if the optionee exercises the option, her interest in the property will relate back to the date the option was recorded, taking priority over the rights of intervening third parties.

A recorded option that is not exercised creates a cloud on the optionor's title. The optionor should obtain a release from the optionee and record the release to remove the cloud.

Right of First Refusal

An option should not be confused with a **right of first refusal**, which gives a person the first opportunity to purchase or lease real property if and when it becomes available. For instance, a lease might give the tenant a right of first refusal to purchase the property if the landlord decides to sell it.

Once the property owner offers the property for sale or receives an offer to buy from a third party, the holder of the right of first refusal must be given a chance to match the offer. If he does not want the property or is unwilling to match the offer, the property may be sold to someone else.

Chapter Summary

1. A property owner uses a listing agreement to hire a broker to find a buyer who is ready, willing, and able to buy the owner's property on the owner's terms. There are three different types of listing agreements: open listings, exclusive agency listings, and exclusive right to sell listings. The exclusive right to sell listing is the type most commonly used.

2. Listing agreements must include a property description, the terms of sale the property owner is willing to accept, the amount or rate of the commission, and the conditions under which the commission is earned. Most listing agreements also include a safety clause, which entitles the broker to a commission if the property is sold after the listing expires to anyone the broker negotiated with during the listing term.

3. A purchase agreement form serves as the buyer's offer to purchase, as the receipt for the buyer's earnest money deposit, and, when it is signed by the seller, as the binding purchase and sale contract between the buyer and the seller. The purchase agreement must identify the parties, describe the property, and set forth the price, the method of payment, and the closing date.

4. Under a land contract, the buyer (vendee) purchases the property on an installment basis. The seller (vendor) retains legal title to the property while the contract is being paid off, but the vendee has the right to possess the property during that period. When the vendee has paid the full purchase price, the vendor delivers the deed to the vendee.

5. A landlord-tenant relationship is created with a lease. A lease must be in writing if it will not be fully performed within the required statutory period (one year in most states). A valid lease also requires consideration (usually the rental payment), the signature of the landlord, and a description of the property. Leases can be terminated by mutual agreement or by eviction of the tenant. Eviction may be either actual or constructive.

6. In an option to purchase, the optionee has a right to buy the property at a specified price (but is under no obligation to buy), and the optionor is not allowed to sell the property to anyone other than the optionee during the option period.

Key Terms

Listing agreement—A written employment agreement between a property owner and a real estate broker, in which the owner hires the broker to find a buyer who is ready, willing, and able to buy the owner's property on the owner's terms.

Open listing—A type of listing that requires the property owner to pay a broker's commission only if the broker is the procuring cause of the sale.

Procuring cause—The real estate agent who is primarily responsible for bringing about a sale; the one who actually negotiates an agreement with the ready, willing, and able buyer.

Exclusive agency listing—A type of listing that requires the property owner to pay the broker a commission when the property is sold during the listing term by anyone other than the seller. If the seller finds the buyer, the broker is not entitled to a commission.

Exclusive right to sell listing—A type of listing that requires the property owner to pay the broker a commission if the property is sold during the listing term, no matter who sells the property.

Net listing—A type of listing in which the commission is any amount received from the sale over and above the "net" required by the seller.

Safety clause—A provision in a listing agreement that obligates the seller to pay a commission if the property is sold within a certain period after the listing expires to someone the broker negotiated with during the listing period. Also called a protection clause or protection period clause.

Purchase agreement—A binding contract between a buyer and a seller of real property, and also the receipt for the buyer's earnest money deposit. Also called a deposit receipt or contract of sale.

Contingency clause—A contract clause which provides that unless some specified event occurs, the contract is null and void.

Land contract—A contract for the sale of real property in which the buyer (vendee) pays the purchase price in installments. The vendee takes possession of the property immediately, but the seller (vendor) retains legal title until the full price has been paid.

Lease—A contract in which one party (the tenant or lessee) pays the other (the landlord or lessor) rent in exchange for the possession of real estate. Also called a rental agreement.

Option agreement—An agreement that gives one party the right to buy or lease the other party's property at a set price for a certain period of time.

Chapter Quiz

1. The type of listing that provides for payment of a commission to the listing broker regardless of who sells the property is a/an:
   a) open listing
   b) exclusive agency listing
   c) exclusive right to sell listing
   d) net listing

2. The type of listing that provides for the payment of a commission to the listing broker only if he was the procuring cause of the sale is a/an:
   a) open listing
   b) exclusive agency listing
   c) exclusive right to sell listing
   d) net listing

3. The type of listing that provides for the payment of a commission that consists of any proceeds from the sale over a specified amount is a/an:
   a) open listing
   b) exclusive agency listing
   c) exclusive right to sell listing
   d) net listing

4. The type of listing that provides for the payment of a commission to the listing broker if anyone other than the seller finds the buyer is a/an:
   a) open listing
   b) exclusive agency listing
   c) exclusive right to sell listing
   d) net listing

5. The listing broker has negotiated an offer from a ready, willing, and able buyer that matches the seller's terms of sale set forth in the listing agreement. Which of the following is true?
   a) The seller is required to accept the offer and pay the listing broker a commission
   b) The seller is required to accept the offer, but not required to pay the listing broker a commission
   c) The listing broker has earned the commission, whether or not the seller accepts the offer
   d) The listing broker has not earned the commission unless this is an exclusive agency listing

6. A safety clause provides that:
   a) the broker is entitled to a commission whether or not she is the procuring cause
   b) the buyer must share the cost of the broker's commission
   c) the seller warrants the safety of the premises
   d) the broker is entitled to a commission if the property is sold after the listing expires to someone the broker previously showed the property to

7. A purchase agreement serves as:
   a) the buyer's receipt for the earnest money deposit
   b) the buyer's offer to purchase
   c) a binding contract between the buyer and the seller
   d) All of the above

8. A purchase agreement should state:
   a) only the purchase price, leaving the other terms to be worked out in the final contract
   b) the listing price as well as the purchase price
   c) the total purchase price, the method of payment, and the basic financing terms
   d) the seller's reasons for selling the property

9. A provision in the purchase agreement states that it will not be a binding contract unless the buyer can obtain financing. This provision is called:
   a) a contingency clause
   b) a defeasibility clause
   c) a bump clause
   d) an escrow clause

10. Under a land contract, the vendee initially gets:
    a) possession but not title
    b) title but not possession
    c) possession and title, but not the right to transfer ownership
    d) the right to novate the contract without the vendor's permission

11. To be binding, a lease must be signed by the:
    a) broker
    b) beneficiary
    c) landlord
    d) tenant

12. When leased property is sold, the lease:
    a) automatically terminates
    b) is breached by constructive eviction
    c) must be renegotiated by the tenant and the new owner
    d) is binding on the new owner

13. An oral lease may be valid if it is for less than:
    a) one year
    b) two years
    c) three years
    d) four years

14. When a tenant assigns a lease, the assignee (new tenant) becomes:
    a) secondarily responsible for payment of the rent
    b) the subtenant
    c) primarily responsible for payment of the rent
    d) None of the above

15. If an option is recorded but not exercised, it can:
    a) turn into a right of first refusal
    b) create a cloud on title
    c) be used as security for a loan
    d) create an interest in property

Answer Key

1. c) The exclusive right to sell listing obligates the seller to pay the listing broker a commission if the property sells during the listing period, regardless of who brings about the sale.

2. a) An open listing obligates the seller to pay a commission to the listing broker only if the broker was the procuring cause of the sale.

3. d) A net listing is a way of determining the amount of the commission, rather than the circumstances under which a commission is owed.

4. b) An exclusive agency listing obligates the seller to pay the listing broker a commission if any agent (anyone other than the seller) sells the property.

5. c) When the broker presents an offer from a ready, willing, and able buyer that matches the seller's terms of sale, the broker has earned the commission, whether or not the seller accepts the offer. The seller is under no obligation to accept the offer.

6. d) A safety clause entitles the broker to a commission if the property is sold within a certain time after the listing expires to someone the broker introduced to the property or negotiated with during the listing period.

7. d) The purchase agreement is used to set forth the buyer's offer, and it also serves as the receipt for the earnest money deposit. If the seller signs the form, it becomes a binding contract.

8. c) A purchase agreement should state all of the terms of sale, including the total purchase price, the method of payment, and the terms on which the buyer will finance the purchase. It is the parties' final contract, not a preliminary agreement.

9. a) A provision that makes a purchase agreement contingent on the occurrence of a certain event is called a contingency clause.

10. a) Under a land contract, the vendee (buyer) gets possession of the land right away, but does not acquire title until the purchase price is paid in full.

11. c) Though it is wise to have both the landlord and the tenant sign the lease, only the landlord needs to sign in order for it to be valid. By taking possession of the leased property and paying the rent, a tenant is presumed to have accepted the lease terms.

12. d) The buyer takes title to the leased property subject to the existing lease, and must abide by its terms.

13. a) Leases need not be in writing if they will be fully performed within the statutory period, which in most states is one year after the agreement is made.

14. c) An assignee has primary liability for paying the rent to the landlord. The original tenant retains secondary liability for the rent.

15. b) An option that is recorded but not exercised creates a cloud on the title, which should be cleared by recording a release from the optionee.

Chapter 9

Real Estate Agency Law

I. Introduction to Agency
   A. The agency relationship
   B. Agency law
II. Creating an Agency Relationship
   A. Express agreement
   B. Ratification
   C. Estoppel
   D. Implication
III. Legal Effects of Agency
   A. Scope of authority
   B. Actual vs. apparent authority
   C. Vicarious liability
   D. Imputed knowledge
IV. Duties in an Agency Relationship
   A. Agent's duties to the principal
   B. Agent's duties to third parties
   C. Breach of duty
V. Terminating an Agency
   A. Termination by acts of the parties
   B. Termination by operation of law
VI. Real Estate Agency Relationships
   A. Historical background
   B. Types of agency relationships
      1. Seller agency
      2. Buyer agency
      3. Dual agency
      4. Non-agency
VII. Agency Disclosure Requirements

Chapter Overview

Agency is a special legal relationship that involves certain duties and liabilities. The law of agency governs many aspects of a real estate agent's relationships with clients and customers. The first part of this chapter explains what an agency relationship is and how one is created, and then discusses agency duties and liabilities. The second part of this chapter describes the various types of agency relationships that are possible in real estate transactions; it also discusses agency disclosure requirements.

Introduction to Agency

We'll begin our discussion of real estate agency with some basic definitions and some information about the framework of agency law.

The Agency Relationship

An agency relationship arises when one person authorizes another to represent him, subject to his control, in dealings with third parties. The parties in an agency relationship are the **agent**, the person authorized to represent another; and the **principal**, the party who authorizes and controls the actions of the agent. Persons outside the agency relationship who seek to deal with the principal through the agent are called **third parties**.

There is usually an agency relationship between a property seller and the real estate broker with whom the seller has listed the property. The seller is the principal, who employs the broker to act as her agent. The broker/agent represents the seller/principal's interests in negotiations with potential buyers/third parties. The seller/principal is referred to as the broker's client.

A real estate broker may also have an agency relationship with a buyer. The buyer hires the broker to locate a particular kind of property and negotiate its purchase. The broker is the buyer's agent, and the buyer is that broker's principal (or client).

There is also an agency relationship between a broker and the salespersons who work for the broker. In other words, a real estate salesperson is his broker's agent.

A real estate salesperson is not licensed to represent sellers or buyers directly, without a broker. (See Chapter 10.) So, strictly speaking, in the eyes of the law it's the broker, not the salesperson, who has an agency relationship with a seller or buyer. Of course, in common parlance, salespersons as well as brokers are called real estate agents. Also, as agents of their brokers, salespersons owe essentially the same duties to clients and third parties as their brokers do.

Agency Law

An agency relationship has significant legal implications. For a third party, dealing with the agent can be the legal equivalent of dealing with the principal. For instance, when an agent who is authorized to do so signs a document, it's as if the principal signed the document. And, in some cases, if the agent does something wrong, the principal may be held liable to third parties for harm resulting from the agent's actions.

Those rules are part of general agency law, a body of law that applies to agency relationships in nearly any context. For example, it governs the relationship between lawyer and client, or between trustee and beneficiary. It traditionally has also applied to the relationship between a real estate agent and a buyer or seller. That is still true in some states, but not in others.

In recent years, more and more states have adopted statutes that specifically define and regulate the agency relationships between real estate brokers, salespersons, and clients. Depending on the terms of a particular state's statute, it may either supplement or replace general agency law in regard to real estate agency relationships in that state.

Whether the rules that govern real estate agency relationships in a particular state come from general agency law, a specific state statute, or both, it's extremely important for real estate agents to know them and follow them.

In the first part of the chapter, we'll discuss basic agency concepts. Even if your state has replaced general agency law with a specific statute concerning real estate agency, this discussion should be useful. Real estate agency statutes are based on general agency law and often use many of the same concepts.

Creating an Agency Relationship

No particular formalities are required to create an agency relationship; the only requirement is the consent of both parties. Under general agency law, an agency relationship may be formed in four ways: by express agreement, by ratification, by estoppel, or by implication.

Express Agreement

Most agencies are created by **express agreement**: the principal appoints someone to act as her agent, and the agent accepts the appointment. A written agreement is generally preferable; however, in some states an oral agreement is sufficient to create a valid agency relationship.

The agency agreement does not have to be supported by consideration. Agency rights, responsibilities, and liabilities may arise even when the principal has no contractual obligation to compensate the agent for the services rendered. For example, in most states, a broker cannot sue a seller for compensation unless a written listing agreement exists. Yet even without a written agreement, the broker still may be the seller's agent, with all of the duties and liabilities that agency entails.

Ratification

An agency is created by **ratification** when the principal gives approval after the fact to acts performed by:

- a person who is without authority to act for the principal, or
- an agent whose actions exceed the authority granted by the principal.

The principal may ratify unauthorized acts expressly, or by accepting the benefits of the acts. For example, if the principal accepts a contract offer negotiated by someone who wasn't authorized to negotiate on his behalf, the principal has ratified the agency.

Estoppel

Under the legal doctrine of **estoppel**, a person is not allowed to take a position that contradicts her previous conduct, if someone else has relied on the previous conduct. An agency can be created by estoppel when it would be unfair to a third party to deny the agent's authority, because the principal has allowed the third party to believe there was an agency relationship.

Implication

An agency may be created by **implication** when one person behaves toward another in a way that suggests or implies that he is acting as that other person's agent. If the other person reasonably believes that there is an agency relationship, and the supposed agent fails to correct that impression, he may owe the other person agency duties.

Although agency by implication resembles agency by estoppel, there's a significant difference between them. An agency by estoppel requires the principal to acknowledge that an agency relationship exists, to protect the interests of a third party. An agency by implication requires the agent to acknowledge that an agency relationship exists, to protect the principal's interests.

The Legal Effects of Agency

Once an agency relationship has been established, the principal is bound by acts of the agent that are within the scope of the agent's actual or apparent authority. Under general agency law, the principal may be held liable for harm caused by the agent's negligent or wrongful acts. In addition, the principal may be held to know information that is known to the agent. We will examine each of these legal effects of agency in turn.

Scope of Authority

The extent to which the principal can be bound by the agent's actions depends first of all on the scope of authority granted to the agent. There are three basic types of agents:

- universal agents,
- general agents, and
- special agents.

A **universal agent** is authorized to do anything that can be lawfully delegated to a representative. This type of agent has the greatest degree of authority. Universal agency is much less common than the other two types.

A **general agent** is authorized to handle all of the principal's affairs in one or more specified areas. She has the authority to conduct a wide range of activities on an ongoing basis on behalf of the principal. For example, a business manager who has the authority to handle personnel matters, enter into contracts, and manage the day-to-day operations of the business is considered to be a general agent.

A **special agent** has limited authority to do a specific thing or conduct a specific transaction. For instance, an attorney who is hired to litigate a specific legal matter, such as a person's divorce, is a special agent.

In most cases, a real estate broker is a special agent, because the broker has only limited authority. A seller hires a broker to find a buyer for a particular piece of property, and the broker is authorized only to negotiate with third parties, not to sign a contract on the seller's behalf. A real estate broker can be granted broader powers, but usually is not.

Actual vs. Apparent Authority

An agent may have actual authority to perform an action on the principal's behalf, or else may have only apparent authority.

Actual authority is authority granted to the agent by the principal, either expressly or by implication. Express actual authority is communicated to the agent in express terms, either orally or in writing. Implied actual authority is the authority to do what is necessary to carry out actions that were expressly authorized.

> **Example:** When a seller lists property with a broker, the broker is given express actual authority to find a buyer for the property. Based on custom in the real estate industry, the broker also has the implied actual authority to delegate certain tasks to a licensed salesperson. In contrast, the authority granted to the broker does not imply the power to enter into a contract or execute a deed on the seller's behalf.

Fig. 9.1 Types of agency authority

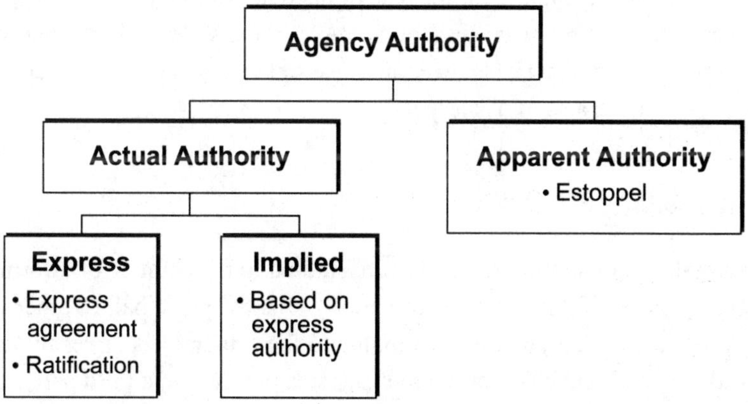

A person has **apparent authority** (or **ostensible authority**) when he has no actual authority to act, but the principal negligently or deliberately allows it to appear that the person's actions are authorized. In other words, the principal's words or conduct lead a third party to believe that this person (the **apparent agent** or **ostensible agent**) has authority to act on behalf of the principal. This type of authority corresponds to an agency created by estoppel, which was explained earlier.

A principal is bound by acts performed within the scope of an ostensible agent's apparent authority. However, declarations of the agent alone cannot establish apparent authority; the principal must be aware of the declarations or acts and make no effort to deny that they are authorized.

A third party has a duty, when dealing with an agent, to make a reasonable effort to discover the scope of the agent's authority. The third party will not be able to hold the principal liable when an agent acts beyond the scope of his actual authority and the principal's conduct does not indicate approval of those acts. When a contract between the principal and a third party limits the agent's authority to make representations, the third party is on notice that any representations made by the agent beyond the written terms of the agreement are unauthorized and not binding on the principal.

Vicarious Liability

A **tort** is a negligent or intentional wrongful act involving breach of a duty imposed by law (as opposed to breach of a contractual duty). It is a mistake, accident, or misconduct that results in an injury or financial harm to another person. For example, negligent driving that results in an accident and injures another driver is a tort. Someone who commits a tort may be sued by the injured party and required to compensate him.

Under general agency law, a principal may be held liable for her agent's negligent or wrongful acts. This is referred to as **vicarious liability**. Thus, a real estate broker can be vicariously liable for the acts of a salesperson who works for the broker.

Under general agency law, it is also possible for a buyer or a seller to be vicariously liable for the acts of his real estate broker, and by extension, for the acts of a salesperson who is working for the broker. However, some state statutes have modified or even eliminated vicarious liability in real estate agency. In those states, a seller or buyer may be held liable for the acts of his real estate broker or salesperson only under very limited circumstances (for example, if the seller or buyer participated in or authorized a wrongful act). But even in those states, a real estate broker is still vicariously liable for the acts of a salesperson.

Imputed Knowledge

Under general agency law, a principal is considered to have notice of information that the agent has, even if the agent never actually tells the principal. In other words, the agent's knowledge is automatically imputed to the principal. As a result, the principal could be held liable for failing to disclose a problem to a third party, even if the agent never informed the principal of the problem. This is referred to as the **imputed knowledge rule**.

In some states, the imputed knowledge rule no longer applies to real estate sellers and buyers. Like vicarious liability, the imputed knowledge rule has been eliminated by real estate agency statutes. In those states, if a broker or salesperson fails to pass information on to a client, the client will not be held to have had notice of that information.

Duties in an Agency Relationship

An agent owes certain duties to her principal, and both the agent and the principal have certain responsibilities to third parties.

The Agent's Duties to the Principal

An agency relationship is a **fiduciary** relationship. A fiduciary is a person who stands in a special position of trust and confidence in relation to someone else. The other party has a legal right to rely on the fiduciary, and the law holds the fiduciary to high standards of conduct.

As a fiduciary, an agent must serve the best interests of the principal. The agent owes the principal these fiduciary duties:

- reasonable care and skill,
- obedience and good faith,
- accounting,
- loyalty, and
- disclosure of material facts.

The agent owes these fiduciary duties to the principal from the time the agency relationship begins until the relationship terminates.

Reasonable Care and Skill. An agent has a duty to use reasonable care and skill in the performance of his duties. If an agent claims to possess certain skills or abilities, the agent must act as a competent person having those skills and abilities would act. For example, a person who holds herself out as a real estate broker must exercise the care and skill that a competent broker would bring to the agency. If the broker (or the broker's salesperson) causes the principal harm due to carelessness or incompetence, the broker will be liable to the principal.

Obedience and Utmost Good Faith. An agent must obey the instructions of the principal and carry them out in utmost good faith. The agent's acts must be in conformity with the purpose and intent of the instructions. A broker can be held liable for any loss caused by failure to obey the principal's instructions.

It is important to note that the duty of obedience and utmost good faith never requires an agent to follow instructions that are unlawful or unethical. If the principal asks the agent to act unlawfully or unethically, the agent should refuse to do so, and terminate the agency relationship.

Accounting. An agent must account for any funds or other valuable items she receives on behalf of the principal. The agent is required to report to the principal on the status of those funds (called **trust funds**) and avoid mixing (**commingling**) them with his own money. Most states require a real estate broker to deposit all trust funds in a special trust or escrow account to prevent improper use of the funds. Trust funds are discussed in more detail in Chapter 10.

Loyalty. The agency relationship is based on confidence, so loyalty is essential. The agent must place the principal's interests above the interests of a third party by refusing to reveal **confidential information**.

> **Example:** In negotiations with a prospective buyer, a seller's real estate agent should not reveal the seller's financial condition or willingness to accept less than the listing price, unless the seller has authorized such a disclosure.

Note that this aspect of the duty of loyalty extends beyond the end of the agency relationship. An agent must not reveal confidential information learned in the course of the agency even after the agency relationship has terminated.

Loyalty to the principal also dictates that the agent must place the principal's interests above her own personal interests. For example, it would be a breach of the duty of loyalty if a buyer's agent encouraged the principal to pay more for a property than it's worth, in order to get a larger commission.

Another rule based on the duty of loyalty is that an agent must not make a **secret profit** from the agency. Any financial gain must be disclosed to the principal.

Disclosure of Material Facts. The agent must inform the principal of any material facts that come to the agent's attention. A **material fact** is any fact that could reasonably be expected to influence the principal's judgment in the transaction. For instance, if a seller's real estate agent discovers that a potential buyer is in a shaky financial situation, the agent must inform the seller, even if it means losing a sale and the subsequent commission.

A real estate agent must be especially careful to avoid these disclosure problems:

- failure to present all offers,
- failure to inform the principal of the property's true value,
- failure to disclose any relationship between the agent and the other party in a transaction, and
- failure to reveal a dual agency.

A real estate agent representing the seller must **present all offers** to the seller, regardless of how unacceptable a particular offer may appear to be. The principal, not the agent, decides whether or not to accept a particular offer. The agent should never hesitate to inform the principal of an offer, even if its acceptance would mean a smaller commission for the agent; the agent's first loyalty must be to the principal. Furthermore, a seller's agent should present an offer even if the prospective buyer did not submit a good faith deposit along with the offer.

An agent is also required to inform the principal of the **property's true value**. It is not improper for a seller's agent to buy the principal's property with the principal's knowledge and consent, and then resell the property for a profit. But the agent must provide the principal with his estimate of the real value of the property before the property is sold. (Note that an ordinary buyer—an unlicensed person who is not acting as the seller's agent—is under no obligation to tell the seller that he plans to resell at a profit.)

The seller's agent must inform the principal if the agent has any **relationship with a buyer**—before the principal decides whether to accept the buyer's offer. If the buyer is a friend, relative, or business associate of the agent, or a company in which the agent has an interest, there may be a conflict of interest. The principal has a right to have this information when making her decision. The agent must also inform the principal if the agent plans to split the commission payment with the buyer.

In addition, the agent is required to reveal a **dual agency**. A dual agency exists when a real estate broker is employed by both the seller and the buyer in the same transaction. In most states, dual agency is legal as long as the broker has fully informed both parties and obtained their consent. However, a conflict of interest is inherent in a dual agency. A seller wants to get the highest possible price for the property, while a buyer wants to pay the lowest possible price. It is difficult, if not impossible, to adequately represent these two opposing interests simultaneously. We'll discuss dual agency and agency disclosure in more detail later in the chapter.

The Agent's Duties to Third Parties

While agents owe obedience and loyalty to their principals, this doesn't mean they can treat third parties with reckless disregard. In fact, in most states courts are holding real estate agents to increasingly higher standards in their interactions with third parties.

As a general rule, a real estate agent owes a third party two basic duties: a duty of reasonable care and skill and a duty of good faith and fair dealing.

Reasonable Care and Skill. An agent must use reasonable care and skill in providing services to third parties as well as to the principal. If the agent's negligence or incompetence harms a third party, the agent may be liable.

Good Faith and Fair Dealing. When representing a seller, real estate agents must disclose all material facts about the property to prospective buyers. They also must avoid inaccuracies in their statements to prospective buyers. Any intentional material misrepresentation may constitute **actual fraud**, and even an unintentional or negligent misrepresentation may be considered **constructive fraud**. In either case, the buyer may have the right to rescind the transaction and/or sue for damages. (Note that these requirements generally apply to sellers as well as their real estate agents; sellers also have a duty to disclose material facts and avoid misrepresentation.)

A distinction is generally drawn between misrepresentations, on the one hand, and opinions, predictions, or "puffing," on the other. These are nonfactual or exaggerated statements that a buyer should realize she can't rely on. Since it isn't reasonable to rely on them, opinions, predictions, and puffing generally aren't actionable—they can't be the basis of a lawsuit.

Examples:

Opinion: *"I think this is the best buy on the market."*
Prediction: *"The properties in this neighborhood could easily double in value over the next ten years."*
Puffing: *"This is a dream house; it has a fabulous view."*

Although statements such as these may not be actionable, it's unethical for a real estate agent to make any statement to a buyer concerning the property or the transaction that the agent doesn't actually believe. Also, something that an agent regards as harmless "sales talk" could be construed as a statement of fact by an unsophisticated buyer. An agent who made the prediction about a dramatic increase in property values given in our example might be on dangerous ground.

Aside from avoiding misrepresentation, both a seller and a seller's agent generally have a duty to disclose any known **latent defects** in the property to buyers. A latent defect is a hidden defect, one that is not discoverable by ordinary inspection.

Example: The seller tells his real estate agent that the roof leaks in heavy rains. This is a latent defect that buyers who are shown the property in ordinary weather won't be able to see for themselves. The seller and the agent are legally required to disclose this problem.

Certain conditions or defects are red flags that may signify more serious underlying problems. For example, cracks in the garage floor or windows and doors that don't close properly may be signs that the foundation is shifting. Or a rotting fence or sagging retaining wall may be evidence that the ground is not draining properly. Sellers and their agents are generally required to disclose problems like these to prospective buyers. An agent doesn't need to be able to determine whether an underlying problem exists; it's usually appropriate, however, to recommend hiring a specialist to take a closer look.

Sometimes property is sold "as is," which means that the seller will not pay for repairs needed to correct property defects. In most states, however, stating that property is for sale "as is" doesn't negate the duty to disclose material facts about the property. The seller and the seller's agent are still required to make the appropriate disclosures.

Duty to Inspect. Traditionally, agents representing the seller were required only to pass on the seller's information about the property to prospective buyers; the law didn't require them to look for problems with the property themselves. Today, however, some states specifically impose a duty of inspection on the agent. In those states, a seller's agent must conduct a reasonably competent and diligent visual inspection of the property and disclose to prospective buyers any material information the inspection reveals.

Stigmatized Properties. There are certain types of information that don't necessarily have to be disclosed to prospective buyers. For example, suppose the property was (or may have been) the site of a crime, a suicide, gang-related activity, or political or religious activity. Such an event may **stigmatize** a property, making it seem undesirable even though its physical condition and title have not been adversely affected.

To protect sellers and property values, many states have passed laws specifying that certain facts that might stigmatize a property are not material and thus need not be disclosed. (Of course, if a prospective buyer asks whether the property was the site of a stigmatizing event or activity, the agent must answer honestly.) On the other hand, some states specifically mandate disclosing the fact that a property was the site of a drug manufacturing lab, since hazardous residues may be left on the property.

When dealing with property that was the site of a potentially stigmatizing event or activity, an agent should carefully check the disclosure requirements that apply in his state. It may be a good idea to seek legal advice.

Note that a real estate agent (or a seller) does not have to disclose that property was occupied by someone with AIDS or HIV. In fact, if a prospective buyer asks an agent whether anyone with AIDS or HIV lived in a house, the agent should not answer the question. To do so could violate fair housing laws that prohibit discrimination based on disability. (See Chapter 16.)

Megan's Law. Since 1996, a federal law has required every state to have a registration program for sex offenders convicted of crimes against children. The federal law and the state laws based on it are commonly called Megan's Law, after a child who was murdered. Upon release from prison, sex offenders must register with a law enforcement agency, and they must also notify the agency whenever they move. Although the specific rules vary from state to state, information concerning registered offenders, including their addresses, must be made available to the public. In some cases, when a registered offender moves into a residential neighborhood, authorities are required to notify the community.

As a general rule, if a home buyer asks a real estate agent whether there are any registered sex offenders in the area, the agent should refer the buyer to the law enforcement agency that makes that information available. If an agent actually knows there is a registered sex offender living in the vicinity of a listed home, the agent may be required to disclose that to prospective buyers. Agents need to know their state's rules concerning this type of disclosure. Some states have passed legislation that protects real estate agents from liability for failure to disclose information about sex offenders, since buyers can obtain the information from other sources.

Seller Disclosure Statement. Many states now require a seller to provide the buyer with a written statement disclosing any known defects in the property. (In some states, this requirement applies only to residential transactions.) Even in states where written disclosures aren't required, real estate agents often encourage their sellers to provide them.

Typically, seller disclosures are made on a standardized form. In states where the seller's agent has a duty to inspect the property, there may be a section on the form for the agent to fill out, disclosing defects revealed by the inspection.

Lead-based Paint Disclosures. Transactions that involve housing built before 1978 are subject to a federal law concerning lead-based paint, which is a health hazard to children. This law requires a seller or a landlord to do all of the following:

- disclose the location of any lead-based paint that he is aware of in the home (in both the dwelling unit and the common areas, if any);
- provide a copy of any report concerning lead-based paint in the home, if it has been inspected; and
- give buyers or tenants a copy of a pamphlet on lead-based paint prepared by the U.S. Environmental Protection Agency.

In addition, buyers (though not tenants) must be offered at least a ten-day period in which to have the home tested for lead-based paint.

Specific warnings must be attached to the purchase agreement or lease, along with signed statements from the parties acknowledging that the requirements of this law have been fulfilled. The signed acknowledgments must be kept for at least three years as proof of compliance.

Other Disclosures. Depending on state law, a seller may be required to provide buyers with a variety of other disclosure statements. For example, if the property is in a flood zone, an earthquake zone, or some other type of hazardous area, it might be necessary to give buyers a separate form disclosing that information.

Breach of Duty

If a real estate broker or salesperson breaches any duties owed to either a principal or a third party, it is considered a tort. (A tort, as we explained earlier, is a wrongful act resulting from a breach of a duty imposed by law.) The party injured by the tort, whether it is the principal or a third party, is then entitled to sue for redress.

The most common remedy in a tort suit is compensatory damages. A court will order the real estate agent to compensate the injured party for the financial loss that the injured party suffered. This might include repaying any commission collected in a transaction. The injured party may also be allowed to rescind the transaction altogether.

If a seller's real estate agent makes misrepresentations to a buyer, the buyer can sue the agent's broker in a tort action. In states where a principal can be held vicariously liable for a real estate agent's torts, the buyer could also sue the broker's principal, the seller. As you'll recall, vicarious liability means that a principal is liable for torts committed by an agent within the scope of the agency. So the seller could be held liable to the buyer even if the seller was not aware of the broker's misrepresentations. An innocent seller who has been held liable for the broker's misconduct could, in turn, sue the broker.

Most real estate brokers now carry **errors and omissions** (E&O) insurance; in some states, they're required to have it. Similar to malpractice insurance, E&O insurance provides coverage for liability resulting from mistakes or negligent acts. If a principal or a third party sues a broker who has E&O insurance for something that the broker or a salesperson did (or failed to do), the broker's insurance company will settle the lawsuit or pay the judgment, up to the policy amount.

Often, a breach of duty by a real estate agent is also a violation of the state's real estate license law. If this is the case, the state licensing agency may take disciplinary action against the agent (and possibly the agent's broker) even if the injured party does not pursue a lawsuit. Disciplinary action may include fines as well as license suspension or revocation (see Chapter 10).

Terminating an Agency

Once an agency relationship has terminated, the agent is no longer authorized to represent the principal. Under general agency law, an agency may be terminated either by acts of the parties or by operation of law.

Termination by Acts of the Parties

The ways in which the parties can terminate an agency relationship include:

- mutual agreement,
- revocation by the principal, and
- renunciation by the agent.

Mutual Agreement. The parties may terminate the agency by mutual agreement at any time. If the original agreement was in writing, the termination agreement should also be in writing.

Principal Revokes. The principal may revoke the agency by firing the agent whenever she wishes. (Remember that an agency relationship requires the consent of both parties.) However, in some cases, revoking an agency breaches a contractual agreement, and the principal may be liable for any damages suffered by the agent because of the breach.

An **agency coupled with an interest** cannot be revoked. An agency is coupled with an interest if the agent has a financial interest in the subject matter of the agency. For instance, if a real estate licensee co-owns a property with other people, and they've authorized him to represent them in selling the property, it's an agency coupled with an interest. The co-owners can't revoke it.

Agent Renounces. An agent can renounce the agency at any time. Like revocation, renunciation may be a breach of contract, in which case the agent could be liable for the principal's damages resulting from the breach. But since an agency contract is a personal services contract (the agent has agreed to provide personal services to the

Fig. 9.2 Termination of agency relationships

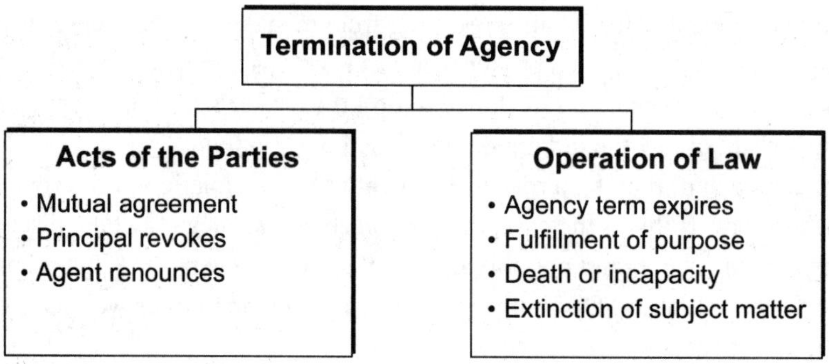

principal), the principal could not demand specific performance as a remedy. The courts will not force a person to perform personal services, because that would violate the constitutional prohibition against involuntary servitude.

Termination by Operation of Law

Several events terminate an agency relationship automatically, without action by either party. These events include:

- expiration of the agency term,
- fulfillment of the purpose of the agency,
- the death or incapacity of either party, and
- extinction of the subject matter.

Expiration of Agency Term. An agency terminates automatically when its term expires. If the agency agreement did not include an expiration date, it is deemed to expire within a reasonable time (which would vary, depending on the type of agency in question). If there is no expiration date, either party may terminate the agency without liability for damages, although the other party might be able to demand reimbursement for expenses incurred before the termination.

Fulfillment of Purpose. An agency relationship terminates when its purpose has been fulfilled. For example, if a broker is hired to sell the principal's property and the broker does so, the agency is terminated by fulfillment.

Death or Incapacity. An agency is terminated before it expires if either the agent or the principal dies. Most states provide that the agency also terminates if either party becomes mentally incompetent. Generally, the agent has no authority to act after the death or incapacity of the principal, even if the agent is unaware of the principal's death or incapacity.

Extinction of Subject Matter. The subject matter of a real estate agency is the property in question. If the property is in any way extinguished (for example, sold or destroyed), the agency automatically terminates.

Real Estate Agency Relationships

A typical residential real estate transaction is likely to involve more than one real estate agent. Someone who wants to find a home in a particular area contacts a real estate broker's office in that area. One of the salespersons who works for that broker will interview the prospective buyer to find out what kind of a home he wants and can afford, and then will show the buyer various suitable properties. Most brokers belong to a multiple listing service, so the salesperson will show the buyer not only homes that are listed directly with her own broker, but also homes that are listed with other MLS members. If the buyer becomes interested in a particular home, negotiations for the purchase of that home will involve the listing agent as well as the salesperson who has been showing properties to the buyer.

Meanwhile, other real estate agents may be showing the same house to other prospective buyers. By the time the transaction closes, it may involve a listing broker, a listing salesperson, a selling broker, and a selling salesperson, in addition to other cooperating agents who showed the home to buyers who didn't want it or didn't offer enough for it.

Understanding the agency relationships in this transaction means understanding which party each of these real estate licensees is representing. As a first step, you should be familiar with all of the following terms.

- **Real estate agent:** Real estate agent is the generic term used to refer to real estate licensees. Real estate brokers are the only real estate agents who are authorized to represent a buyer or a seller directly; real estate salespersons act on behalf of their real estate brokers.
- **Client:** A client is a person who has engaged the services of an agent. A client may be a real estate seller, buyer, landlord, or tenant.
- **Customer:** In transactions where the agent is representing a seller or a landlord, third parties are sometimes referred to as customers. A customer may be a buyer or a tenant.
- **Listing agent:** Either the listing salesperson or the listing broker may be referred to as the listing agent. The listing salesperson is the salesperson who takes the listing on a home. (She may or may not be the one who eventually procures a buyer for the listed home.) The listing broker is the broker that the listing salesperson works for.
- **Selling agent:** Either the selling salesperson or the selling broker may be referred to as the selling agent. The selling salesperson is the salesperson who procures a buyer for a property. (He may or may not have taken the listing for the property sold.) The selling broker is the broker that the selling salesperson works for.
- **Cooperating agent:** A cooperating agent is a licensee who did not take the listing on the property and who attempts to find a buyer. (The cooperating agent who succeeds in procuring a buyer is then the selling agent.)

- **In-house sale:** A sale in which the buyer and the seller are brought together by salespersons working for the same broker.
- **Cooperative sale:** A sale in which the listing agent and the selling agent work for different brokers.

Agency Relationships: A Historical Perspective

In the 1980s, various organizations, including the Federal Trade Commission, the National Association of REALTORS®, and the Association of Real Estate License Law Officials, conducted studies of agency representation in real estate transactions. Those organizations concluded that many real estate buyers and sellers were confused about which party the real estate agent represented. Buyers, in particular, appeared bewildered by the rules of real estate agency. They often thought the real estate agent that they were working with was representing them, when in fact the agent was almost always representing the seller.

Unilateral Offer of Subagency. This confusion was based on a standard provision found in most listing agreements. This provision stated that any member of the multiple listing service who found a buyer for a listed property automatically represented the seller. In other words, the selling broker was considered to be a subagent of the seller. (A **subagent** is an agent of an agent.) This listing provision was referred to as a "unilateral offer of subagency."

As long as this provision remained in listing agreements, it was difficult to enter into a buyer agency relationship. In order to represent a buyer in a particular MLS transaction, a licensee had to reject the offer of subagency in a timely fashion and then enter into a separate written agreement with the buyer. Thus, nearly all licensees represented the seller.

Inadvertent Dual Agency. Under these circumstances, it was easy for a buyer to mistakenly believe that the selling agent was acting as the buyer's agent, not the seller's. After all, the selling agent was working with the buyer on a continuous and usually friendly basis. The agent would often encourage the buyer's loyalty by going out of his way to meet the buyer's needs. As a result, the buyer often told the selling agent confidential information. Yet because the selling agent was representing the seller, she had a duty to pass along that confidential information to the seller. If the agent fulfilled that responsibility, the buyer might well be surprised and dismayed. But in many cases, the selling agent would let her natural desire to help the buyer interfere with the fiduciary duties owed to the seller. This confusion caused trouble for everyone, and sometimes resulted in the creation of an inadvertent dual agency.

Example: Martinez was a salesperson working for Baker Realty. Over the course of several weeks, she showed the Greens many homes. Martinez liked the Greens and worked very hard to find them a good house. She gave them advice about purchasing a home and discussed their financial situation with them. Understandably, the Greens believed that Martinez was their agent. But Martinez did not have an agency agreement with the Greens, and that meant (under the traditional presumption) that she was acting as a seller's agent.

The Greens decided to make an offer on a house listed by Broker Rush. They were very excited about the house, and they told Martinez that they were willing to pay full price for it. Nevertheless, they wanted to start out with an offer that was $5,000 less than the listing price.

If Martinez failed to disclose to the seller that the Greens were willing to pay the full listing price, it would be a breach of her duty of loyalty to the seller. However, her conduct had caused the Greens to believe that she was representing them. Thus, if Martinez did disclose this information to the seller, the Greens could claim that she had breached her duty of loyalty to them. And because she was inadvertently acting as agent for both parties, both could claim that she acted as a dual agent without their consent.

Cooperation and Compensation. In the 1990s, as new legal requirements and various other considerations made real estate transactions more complex, buyers became more interested in having their own agents to represent them. In response to the growing popularity of buyer agency, many multiple listing services replaced the unilateral offer of subagency in their listing agreements with a "cooperation and compensation" provision. Under the terms of this provision, other members of the MLS act only as cooperating agents, not as subagents. A **cooperating agent** is simply any member of the MLS who attempts to find a buyer; the listing agreement does not set any type of agency relationship for a cooperating agent. It becomes up to each individual cooperating agent to decide whether he will represent the seller or the buyer in a given transaction.

Disclosure Laws. In an effort to reduce confusion over agency representation, many states have passed agency disclosure laws—laws that require real estate agents to disclose to both the buyer and the seller which party they are representing in a transaction. But even agency disclosures do not always prevent problems. Real estate agents must understand the consequences of the different types of agency relationships and learn to avoid the pitfalls that certain situations present.

Types of Agency Relationships

There are few restrictions on which party a real estate agent may represent. Generally, the types of agency relationships can be divided into the following categories:

- seller agency,
- buyer agency, and
- dual agency.

In some states, real estate licensees also have the option of establishing non-agency relationships with sellers and buyers.

Seller Agency. As we have seen, traditionally, real estate agents nearly always represented the seller. While buyer agency is now also common, seller agency is still the most prevalent type of real estate agency relationship.

Fig. 9.3 Types of real estate agency relationships

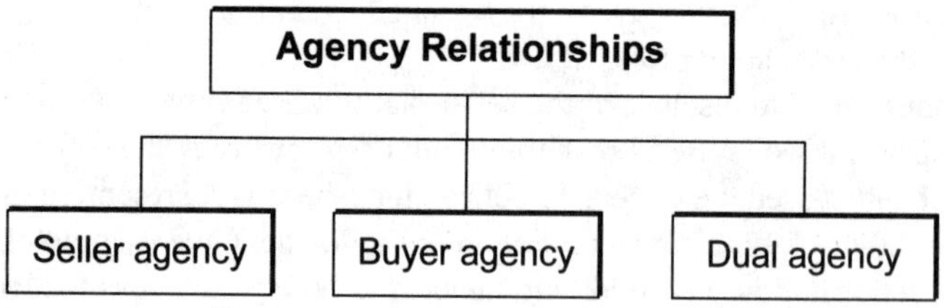

Seller agency relationships are typically created with a listing agreement (discussed in Chapter 8). Under the terms of the listing agreement, the primary task of a seller's agent is to find a buyer for the seller's property at a price that is acceptable to the seller. To accomplish this, the seller's agent advises the seller about preparing the property for sale, helps the seller decide on the listing price, markets the property to advantage, and negotiates on the seller's behalf with selling agents and buyers.

A seller agency relationship can also be created by the words or conduct of the parties, although the broker may be prevented from suing for a commission if there is no written listing agreement. (See the discussion of implied agency earlier in this chapter.)

Seller's Agents and Buyers. Throughout a transaction, a seller's agent must use her best efforts to promote the interests of the seller. Yet the seller's agent may also provide some services to a prospective buyer. For example, the seller's agent may help a buyer who doesn't have his own agent fill out a purchase offer form and apply for financing. These services are considered to be in the best interests of the seller, and thus do not violate the agent's duties to the seller. Of course, the seller's agent must disclose to the buyer that she is acting as the seller's agent.

A seller's agent must be very careful to treat the buyer fairly, but the agent must not act as if he is representing the buyer. In other words, the agent must fully disclose all known material facts and answer the buyer's questions honestly. However, the agent should not give the buyer advice, such as suggesting how much to offer for the listed property.

Example: Harrison, who works for Broker Yates, recently listed Taylor's house. The listing price is $315,000, but Harrison has reason to believe that Taylor would accept an offer of $305,000. Harrison shows the listed house to Markham, who asks Harrison, "How low do you think the seller will go?" Harrison should make it clear to Markham that he is representing Taylor and cannot divulge confidential information to Markham. If he were to divulge confidential information, Taylor could sue Harrison's broker for breach of agency duties.

The situation in which the problem of inadvertent dual agency is most likely to come up is when the listing agent (who always represents the seller) is the one who finds a buyer for the property. This is especially true if the listing agent has had a previous agency relationship with the buyer. It may be difficult for the agent to represent the seller's interests without feeling some loyalty to the buyer as well.

Example: After Harrison finds a buyer for Taylor's house, Taylor asks Harrison to help him find another home. Harrison shows Taylor one of his own listings, a house owned by a seller named Woods.

Under these circumstances, it would be easy for Taylor to think that Harrison is acting as his agent. However, because of the listing agreement with Woods, Harrison is the seller's agent, and he should emphasize this fact to Taylor. Harrison should remind Taylor that he, Harrison, is obligated to disclose material information that Taylor tells him to the seller, and that in all negotiations he will be representing the seller's best interests.

Remember that a real estate agent is not permitted to disclose confidential information about a principal even after the termination of the agency relationship. So Harrison cannot disclose to the seller any confidential information about Taylor that he learned during his agency relationship with Taylor.

Buyer Agency. Many buyers are content with the traditional seller agency relationship, as long as it is fully disclosed. They use the services of a real estate agent because they want access to multiple listing inventory, complete and honest information about properties, and someone to present their offers to sellers. The seller agency relationship often satisfies those requirements nicely, and buyers do not have to commit to a buyer agency relationship to get the help they need. Quite often, however, buyers want more than the services a seller's real estate agent can provide to a customer. Some buyers want advice on property values and help in determining how much to offer for a particular house. They want someone to help them negotiate the terms of the sale and give them advice on confidential matters. For those buyers, a buyer agency relationship is usually the answer.

Advantages of Buyer Agency. The advantages of buyer agency include confidentiality and loyalty, objective advice, help with negotiations, and access to more homes.

A buyer's agent owes agency duties to the buyer, including the duties of confidentiality and loyalty. For many buyers, these two duties are the most important advantages of buyer agency.

Example: Broker Mendez is helping Buyer Jackson find a home. He shows Jackson many houses, and there are two that interest her. One is a large fixer-upper selling for $345,000. The other is a small, newer house in mint condition selling for $330,000. Because Mendez must put Jackson's interests before his own, he advises her to purchase the smaller house because it better suits her needs. He does so even though he would earn a bigger commission if she bought the more expensive house.

Mendez advises Jackson to offer $324,900 for the $330,000 house. Jackson agrees, although she tells Mendez that she is willing to pay the full listing price. Because Mendez is Jackson's agent, he is obligated to keep that confidential. If he were the seller's agent, he would be required to disclose that information to the seller.

A buyer's agent can be relied upon to give the buyer objective advice about the pros and cons of purchasing a particular home. She will point out various issues the buyer should be aware of, such as energy costs, the need for future repairs, and property value trends. By contrast, a seller's agent will present the property in the most positive light and may use expert sales techniques to convince the buyer to sign on the dotted line.

Buyers often feel uncomfortable negotiating for a property, especially one they really want to buy. They may be afraid to make a mistake through ignorance, or they may feel pressured to make a high offer quickly before someone else snaps up the property. A buyer's agent can use his negotiating skills and intimate knowledge of the real estate market to help the buyer get the property on the best possible terms.

A buyer's agent may arrange to be compensated if the buyer purchases any home, even one that isn't listed with a broker. So a buyer's agent may pursue less traditional means of searching for properties, and show the buyer properties that are for sale by owner, properties with open listings, and properties in foreclosure or probate proceedings.

Creation of Buyer Agency. A buyer and a broker usually enter into a buyer agency relationship by executing a written **buyer agency agreement**, also called a buyer representation agreement. (An example is shown in Figure 9.4.) While the terms of buyer agency agreements vary, they generally include provisions addressing the following issues:

- the duration of the agency,
- the general characteristics of the property the buyer wants,
- the price range,
- the conditions under which a fee will be earned,
- who will pay the fee, and
- a description of the broker's duties.

Types of Buyer Agencies. Depending on the buyer agency agreement form used, the buyer and broker may enter into either an exclusive buyer agency or a nonexclusive (open) buyer agency.

Under a nonexclusive or open agreement, the buyer's agent is legally entitled to compensation only if the agent locates a home that the buyer purchases. Since it is nonexclusive, the buyer can enter into this type of agency agreement with as many brokers as he likes. Only the agent who actually finds the property purchased will receive compensation.

If the parties enter into an exclusive buyer agency agreement, the buyer is not allowed to enter into any other agency agreements, and the buyer's agent will be entitled to compensation as long as the buyer purchases the type of home described in the agreement. Even if the buyer found the property without anyone else's help, the buyer's agent will still be compensated. An exclusive buyer agency agreement is sometimes called an exclusive right to represent agreement, or an exclusive authority to purchase agreement.

Buyer's Agent's Compensation. A buyer's agent may be compensated in a number of ways. The three most common are:

- a retainer,
- a seller-paid fee, and/or
- a buyer-paid fee.

A **retainer** is a fee paid up front before services are provided. Some buyer's agents collect a retainer when they enter into a buyer agency relationship, to ensure that their

Figure 9.4 Buyer representation agreement

Page 1 of 2

BUYER-BROKER EXCLUSIVE EMPLOYMENT AGREEMENT

Document updated: **February 2010**

ARIZONA association of REALTORS® REAL SOLUTIONS. REALTOR® SUCCESS.

The pre-printed portion of this form has been drafted by the Arizona Association of REALTORS®. Any change in the pre-printed language of this form must be made in a prominent manner. No representations are made as to the legal validity, adequacy and/or effects of any provision, including tax consequences thereof. If you desire legal, tax or other professional advice, please consult your attorney, tax advisor or professional consultant.

Buyer/Tenant: ______________________________ ("Buyer")

Firm: ______________ (FIRM NAME) **Salesperson:** ______________ (SALESPERSON'S NAME) ("Broker")

Term: This Agreement shall commence on ______________ and expire at 11:59 p.m. on ______________.

Employment: Broker agrees to:

a. locate Property meeting the following general description:
☐ Residential ☐ Land ☐ Commercial ☐ Other: ______________ ("Property");

b. negotiate at Buyer's direction to obtain acceptable terms and conditions for the purchase, exchange, option or lease of the Property;

c. assist Buyer during the transaction within the scope of Broker's expertise and licensing.

Agency Relationship: The agency relationship between Buyer and Broker shall be:

☐ as set forth in the Real Estate Agency Disclosure and Election form.

☐ Other: ______________

Retainer Fee: Buyer agrees to pay Broker a non-refundable fee in the amount of $ ________, which is earned when paid, for initial consultation and research. This fee ☐ **shall; or** ☐ **shall not** be credited against any other compensation owed by Buyer to Broker as pursuant to Lines 27 – 29.

Property Viewings: Buyer agrees to work exclusively with Broker and be accompanied by Broker on Buyer's first visit to any Property. **If Broker does not accompany Buyer on the first visit to any Property, including a model home, new home/lot or "open house" held by a builder, seller or other real estate broker, Buyer acknowledges that the builder, seller or seller's broker may refuse to compensate Broker, which will eliminate any credit against the compensation owed by Buyer to Broker.**

Due Diligence: Once an acceptable Property is located, Buyer agrees to act in good faith to acquire the Property and conduct any inspections/investigations of the Property that Buyer deems material and/or important.

Note: Buyer acknowledges that pursuant to Arizona law, Sellers, Lessors and Brokers are not obligated to disclose that a Property is or has been: (1) the site of a natural death, suicide, homicide, or any crime classified as a felony; (2) owned or occupied by a person exposed to HIV, or diagnosed as having AIDS or any other disease not known to be transmitted through common occupancy of real estate; or (3) located in the vicinity of a sex offender.

Buyer agrees to consult the Arizona Department of Real Estate Buyer Advisory provided by the Arizona Association of REALTORS® at www.aaronline.com to assist in Buyer's inspections and investigations.

Compensation: Buyer agrees to compensate Broker as follows:

The amount of compensation shall be: ______________________________ or the compensation Broker receives from seller or seller's broker, whichever is greater. In either event, Buyer authorizes Broker to accept compensation from seller or seller's broker, which shall be credited against any compensation owed by Buyer to Broker pursuant to this Agreement. Broker's compensation shall be paid at the time of and as a condition of closing or as otherwise agreed upon in writing.

Buyer agrees to pay such compensation if within _______ calendar days after the termination of this Agreement, Buyer enters into an agreement to purchase, exchange, option or lease any Property shown to Buyer or negotiated by Broker on behalf of the Buyer during the term of this Agreement, unless Buyer has entered into a subsequent buyer-broker exclusive employment agreement with another broker.

If completion of any transaction is prevented by Buyer's breach or with the consent of Buyer other than as provided in the purchase contract, the total compensation shall be due and payable by Buyer.

COMMISSIONS PAYABLE ARE NOT SET BY ANY BOARD OR ASSOCIATION OF REALTORS® OR MULTIPLE LISTING SERVICE OR IN ANY MANNER OTHER THAN AS NEGOTIATED BETWEEN BROKER AND BUYER.

>>

Buyer-Broker Exclusive Employment Agreement • Updated: February 2010

Page 1 of 2

Buyer-Broker Exclusive Employment Agreement >>

Additional Terms:

____

____

____

____

____

____

____

____

Equal Housing Opportunity: Broker's policy is to abide by all local, state, and federal laws prohibiting discrimination against any individual or group of individuals. Broker has no duty to disclose the racial, ethnic, or religious composition of any neighborhood, community, or building, nor whether persons with disabilities are housed in any home or facility, except that the Broker may identify housing facilities meeting the needs of a disabled buyer.

Other Potential Buyers: Buyer consents and acknowledges that other potential buyers represented by Broker may consider, make offers on, or acquire an interest in the same or similar properties as Buyer is seeking.

Alternative Dispute Resolution ("ADR"): Buyer and Broker agree to mediate any dispute or claim arising out of or relating to this Agreement in accordance with the mediation procedures of the applicable state or local REALTOR® association or as otherwise agreed. All mediation costs shall be paid equally by the parties. In the event that mediation does not resolve all disputes or claims, the unresolved disputes or claims shall be submitted for binding arbitration. In such event, the parties shall agree upon an arbitrator and cooperate in the scheduling of an arbitration hearing. If the parties are unable to agree on an arbitrator, the dispute shall be submitted to the American Arbitration Association ("AAA") in accordance with the AAA Arbitration Rules for the Real Estate Industry. The decision of the arbitrator shall be final and nonappealable. Judgment on the award rendered by the arbitrator may be entered in any court of competent jurisdiction.

Attorney Fees and Costs: In any non-REALTOR® association proceeding to enforce the compensation due to Broker pursuant to this Agreement, the prevailing party shall be awarded their reasonable attorney fees and arbitration costs.

Arizona Law: This Agreement shall be governed by Arizona law and jurisdiction is exclusively conferred on the State of Arizona.

Copies and Counterparts: This Agreement may be executed by facsimile or other electronic means and in any number of counterparts. A fully executed facsimile or electronic copy of the Agreement shall be treated as an original Agreement.

Entire Agreement: This Agreement, and any addenda and attachments, shall constitute the entire agreement between Buyer and Broker, shall supersede any other written or oral agreements between Buyer and Broker and can be modified only by a writing signed by Buyer and Broker.

Capacity: Buyer warrants that Buyer has the legal capacity, full power and authority to enter into this Agreement and consummate the transaction contemplated hereby on Buyer's own behalf or on behalf of the party Buyer represents, as appropriate.

Acceptance: Buyer hereby agrees to all of the terms and conditions herein and acknowledges receipt of a copy of this Agreement.

^ BUYER'S SIGNATURE	MO/DA/YR	^ BUYER'S SIGNATURE	MO/DA/YR
STREET	CITY	STATE	ZIP CODE
TELEPHONE		FAX	
FIRM NAME		^ SALES PERSON SIGNATURE	MO/DA/YR

For Broker Use Only:

Brokerage File/Log No.__________ Manager's Initials________ Broker's Initials________ Date__________ MO/DA/YR

Buyer-Broker Exclusive Employment Agreement • Updated: February 2010 services won't go entirely uncompensated. The retainer is usually nonrefundable, but it will be credited against any fee or commission that the agent becomes entitled to.

In many cases, a buyer's agent is paid by the seller through a **commission split**. The commission split is based on a provision found in many MLS listing agreements, whereby any cooperating broker who procures a buyer is entitled to the selling broker's portion of the commission, regardless of which party that cooperating broker represents. Note that the source of the agent's commission does not determine the identity of her principal; accepting a seller-paid fee does not create agency duties owed to the seller.

Example: Helman lists his property with Broker Thurston and agrees to pay him a commission of 6% of the sales price. The listing agreement includes a clause that entitles any cooperating broker who procures a buyer to the selling broker's portion of the commission.

Broker Adams has a buyer agency agreement with Gray. Gray offers $450,000 for Helman's house and Helman accepts the offer.

When the transaction closes, Helman pays a $27,000 commission; $13,500 goes to Broker Thurston and $13,500 goes to Broker Adams.

Most buyer representation agreements provide for payment by means of a commission split when the buyer purchases a home that is listed through a multiple listing service. However, a buyer representation agreement may provide for a **buyer-paid fee** instead. The buyer-paid fee might be based on an hourly rate, in which case the agent is essentially a consultant. Alternatively, a buyer's agent may charge a percentage fee, so that the commission is a percentage of the purchase price. A third possibility is a flat fee—a specified sum that is payable if the buyer purchases a property found by the agent.

Some buyer agency agreements provide that the buyer's agent will accept a commission split if one is available, but the buyer will pay the agent a fee if the purchased property was unlisted (for example, if the property was for sale by owner).

Dual Agency. As we explained earlier, a dual agency relationship exists when an agent represents both the seller and the buyer in the same transaction. (By contrast, if an agent is representing only one of the parties, it may be called single agency.) A dual agent owes fiduciary duties to both principals. Because the interests of the buyer and the seller usually conflict, it can be very difficult to represent both without being disloyal to one or both of them.

Example: Broker Kogawa represents both the buyer and the seller in a transaction. The seller informs Kogawa that she is in a big hurry to sell and will accept any reasonable offer. The buyer tells Kogawa that he is very interested in the house and is willing to pay the full listing price. Should Kogawa tell the buyer of the seller's eagerness to sell? Should Kogawa tell the seller about the buyer's willingness to pay the full price?

In fact, it is impossible to fully represent the interests of both parties at the same time, so dual agency is sometimes referred to as **limited agency**.

Dual agency is generally allowed as long as it is disclosed to both parties and they both give their consent to the arrangement in writing. If a real estate agent acts as a dual agent without disclosure and written consent, the agent may not be able to collect a commission. Furthermore, it might be possible for either party to rescind the sales transaction.

It's essential for a real estate agent who is going to act as a dual agent to give the parties a clear and complete explanation of dual agency. A buyer and seller, eager to get on with the business of buying and selling a home, may agree to a dual agency without really understanding what it means. Later, one party might feel that his interests weren't protected and that the agent favored the other party. This often leads to legal action.

Each party to a dual agency should be informed that she will not receive full representation. Certain facts must necessarily be withheld from each party; the dual agent cannot divulge confidential information about one party to the other party. Returning to our previous example, the dual agent must not tell the buyer that the seller is in a hurry, nor tell the seller that the buyer is willing to pay anything other than the amount the buyer has formally offered.

Designated Agency. Dual agency is most likely to occur in an **in-house transaction**, where the listing agent and the selling agent both work for the same broker. Under the laws of some states, in-house transactions are handled in the following way: the listing agent represents the seller only, the selling agent represents the buyer only, and the broker acts as a dual agent, representing both parties.

> **Example:** Salesperson Winston, who works for Broker Roberts, has shown Buyer King several houses over the course of a few weeks. Finally, Winston shows King a house listed by Salesperson Vincent, who also works for Broker Roberts. King decides to make an offer on the house. In this transaction, Winston, the selling salesperson, is the buyer's agent; Vincent, the listing salesperson, is the seller's agent; and Roberts, the broker, is a dual agent. These agency relationships must be disclosed to and agreed to in writing by both the seller and the buyer.

This arrangement is sometimes referred to as a **designated agency**; in effect, the broker is designating one agent to represent the seller and one agent to represent the buyer. Designated agency is not legal in all states.

Inadvertent Dual Agency. As we discussed earlier, a dual agency may be created unintentionally. In fact, many lawsuits involve an accidental or unintended dual agency in which the conduct of the seller's agent, or the personal relationship between the agent and the buyer, is such that an implied agency is created with the buyer. To prevent inadvertent dual agency, a seller's agent must make certain that the buyer understands that the agent is representing the seller, and then act accordingly, never forgetting that he is the seller's agent.

Non-Agency. A number of states now permit an agent to act as a non-agent in a transaction. A non-agent (also referred to as a **transaction broker**, an **intermediary**, or a **facilitator**) does not represent either party in the transaction, but simply assists them with the paperwork and closing. The non-agent does not owe either party fiduciary duties; instead, she owes both of them the duties of reasonable care and skill and good faith and fair dealing. The non-agent cannot disclose confidential information to either party or negotiate on behalf of either party.

Agency Disclosure Requirements

To avoid some of the confusion about who is representing whom, all states now require real estate agents in residential transactions to provide their clients and customers with certain information about agency relationships. The specific requirements vary from state to state.

In many states, real estate agents are required to give any member of the public they work with a pamphlet that describes the different types of real estate agency relationships and the duties that each type of relationship entails.

Some states also require an agent to disclose to each of the parties involved in a transaction which party (or parties) the agent is representing in that transaction. When and how this must be done depends on state law. For example, an agent might be required to make an oral disclosure "as soon as practicable" after meeting a client or customer, and then follow up with a written disclosure before the client or customer signs any written contract. Once again, agents need to be thoroughly familiar with the disclosure requirements in their state.

Chapter Summary

1. In an agency relationship, the agent represents the principal in dealings with third parties. An agent may be a universal agent, a general agent, or a special agent, depending on the scope of authority granted.

2. Most agency relationships are created by express agreement (oral or written), but they can also be created by ratification, estoppel, or implication. Acts performed by an agent or an ostensible agent are binding on the principal if they fall within the scope of the agent's actual or apparent authority.

3. An agent owes fiduciary duties to the principal, including the duties of reasonable care and skill, obedience and utmost good faith, accounting, loyalty, and disclosure of material facts. A seller's agent must inform the principal of all offers, the property's true value, and any relationship between the agent and the buyer.

4. An agent owes third parties the duties of reasonable care and skill, and good faith and fair dealing. Neither the seller nor the seller's agent may misrepresent the property, and they must reveal any known latent defects to prospective buyers.

5. An agency relationship may be terminated by mutual agreement, revocation, renunciation, expiration, fulfillment of purpose, the death or incapacity of either party, or extinction of the subject matter.

6. A seller agency is usually created with a listing agreement. A seller's agent must be careful to avoid conduct that might give rise to an inadvertent agency relationship with the buyer.

7. Buyer's agents can provide special services to buyers, including access to more properties, expert advice, help with negotiating, and loyalty. Buyer agency relationships are generally created with a written buyer agency agreement. A buyer's agent may be paid by the buyer or the seller.

8. Dual agency occurs when an agent represents both the seller and the buyer in the same transaction. Generally, dual agency is legal with the informed written consent of both parties.

9. In a non-agency arrangement, a real estate agent assists a buyer and seller in a transaction but does not represent either party.

10. Real estate agents must provide information about agency relationships to their clients and customers. In many states, disclosures concerning the agency relationships in specific transactions are required.

Key Terms

Principal—The person who authorizes an agent to act on his behalf.

Agent—A person authorized to represent another in dealings with third parties.

Third party—A person seeking to deal with the principal through the agent.

Fiduciary—Someone who holds a special position of trust and confidence in relation to another.

Ratification—When the principal gives approval to unauthorized actions after they are performed, creating an agency relationship after the fact.

Estoppel—When the principal allows a third party to believe an agency relationship exists, so that the principal is estopped (legally precluded) from denying the agency.

Universal agent—An agent authorized to do anything that can lawfully be delegated to another person.

General agent—An agent with authority to handle the principal's affairs in a specific area.

Special agent—An agent with limited authority to do a specific thing or handle a specific transaction.

Actual authority—Authority the principal grants to the agent either expressly or by implication.

Apparent authority—Where no actual authority has been granted, but the principal allows it to appear that the agent is authorized, and therefore is estopped from denying the agency. Also called ostensible authority.

Material fact—Information that could reasonably be expected to affect someone's decision in a transaction.

Latent defect—A property defect that would not necessarily be discovered in an ordinary inspection of the property.

Secret profit—Any financial gain an agent receives as a result of the agency relationship and does not disclose to the principal.

Listing agent—The agent who takes the listing on a property, and who may or may not be the agent who procures a buyer.

Selling agent—The agent who procures a buyer for a property, and who may or may not have taken the listing.

Cooperating agent—Any agent other than the listing agent who attempts to find a buyer for a property.

In-house transaction—A sale in which the buyer and the seller are brought together by salespersons working for the same broker.

Designated agent—A salesperson who has been assigned by her broker to act as the agent of either the seller or the buyer in an in-house transaction.

Cooperative transaction—A sale in which the buyer and the seller are brought together by salespersons who work for two different brokers.

Non-agent—A real estate licensee who assists the buyer and seller in a transaction but does not represent either party. Also referred to as a transaction broker or a facilitator.

Chapter Quiz

1. An agency relationship can be created in any of the following ways, except:
   a) written agreement
   b) oral agreement
   c) ratification
   d) verification

2. An agency relationship requires:
   a) consideration
   b) the consent of both parties
   c) an enforceable contract
   d) None of the above

3. Garcia acted on behalf of Hilton without her authorization. At a later date, Hilton gave her approval to Garcia's actions. This is an example of:
   a) express agreement
   b) ratification
   c) estoppel
   d) assumption of authority

4. A seller lists his home with a broker at $290,000; he asks for a quick sale. When the listing broker shows the home to a buyer, he says the seller is financially insolvent and will take $275,000. The buyer offers $275,000 and the seller accepts. The broker:
   a) did not violate his duties to the seller, because the seller accepted the offer
   b) did not violate his duties to the seller, since he fulfilled the purpose of his agency
   c) violated his duties to the seller by disclosing confidential information to the buyer
   d) was unethical, but did not violate his duties to the seller, since he did not receive a secret profit

5. Stark lists his property with Bell, a licensed broker. Bell shows the property to her cousin, who decides he would like to buy it. Which of the following is true?
   a) Bell can present her cousin's offer to Stark, as long as she tells Stark that the prospective buyer is one of her relatives
   b) Bell violated her fiduciary duties to Stark by showing the property to one of her relatives
   c) It was not unethical for Bell to show the property to a relative, but it would be a violation of her duties if she presented her cousin's offer to Stark
   d) It is not necessary for Bell to tell Stark that the buyer is related to her, as long as he is offering the full listing price for the property

6. An agency relationship can be terminated by:
   a) renunciation without the principal's consent
   b) incapacity of either party
   c) extinction of the subject matter
   d) All of the above

7. A real estate agent tells potential buyers: "This is a really great old house. They just don't make them like this anymore." This statement would be considered:
   a) a misrepresentation
   b) actual fraud
   c) constructive fraud
   d) puffing

8. In most cases, a listing broker:
   a) is authorized to enter into contracts on behalf of the seller
   b) is considered a special agent
   c) Both of the above
   d) Neither of the above

9. Dual agency is:
   a) no longer legal in any state
   b) legal in most states as long as both principals consent to the arrangement in writing
   c) legal in most states as long as the agent receives equal compensation from both principals
   d) encouraged by many professional associations as the best way of representing a client's interests

10. Able listed Glover's property. Able:
    a) cannot give a buyer any information about Glover's property without being considered a dual agent
    b) may give a buyer information about Glover's property without owing agency duties to the buyer
    c) must sign a disclaimer of liability if he presents a buyer's offer to purchase to Glover
    d) is a dual agent

11. An agent owes third parties the duty of:
    a) obedience
    b) accounting
    c) loyalty
    d) reasonable care and skill

12. Which one of the following is not a benefit of buyer agency?
    a) The buyer has access to more properties
    b) The buyer gets the benefit of objective advice
    c) Since the agent represents both parties, the buyer has access to information about the seller's bottom-line sales price
    d) The buyer gets help with negotiating the sales price

13. A buyer's agent:
    a) may not accept compensation paid by the seller
    b) must have a written listing agreement in order to be compensated
    c) may be paid through a commission split
    d) may not receive compensation that is based on the property's sales price

14. A latent defect:
    a) is a material fact
    b) is hidden or not easily observed
    c) must always be disclosed to the buyer
    d) All of the above

15. As a general rule, a dual agent must:
    a) keep each party's negotiating position confidential
    b) disclose all information to both parties, no matter how confidential
    c) act only as a facilitator, with no agency duties to either party
    d) not accept compensation from either party

Answer Key

1. d) An agency relationship may be created by express agreement (written or oral), ratification, estoppel, or implication.

2. b) The consent of both parties is necessary to the creation of an agency relationship, but consideration is not. There does not have to be an enforceable contract between the principal and the agent.

3. b) An agency relationship is created by ratification when the principal gives approval to unauthorized actions after the fact.

4. c) The broker violated the fiduciary duty of loyalty to the principal by disclosing confidential information to a third party.

5. a) A seller's real estate agent is required to tell the seller if the prospective buyer is related to the agent.

6. d) Any of the events listed would terminate an agency relationship.

7. d) This is an example of puffing, an exaggerated statement that the buyers should realize they can't depend on.

8. b) A listing broker is usually a special agent, with limited authority to represent the principal in a particular transaction. A listing broker is ordinarily not authorized to sign contracts on behalf of the principal.

9. b) Dual agency is legal in most states as long as both the seller and the buyer are informed that the agent is representing both of them, and they both give their written consent to the arrangement.

10. b) A seller's agent can give a buyer information about the seller's property without becoming a dual agent.

11. d) An agent owes the principal the duties of obedience and utmost good faith, accounting, and loyalty. An agent owes both the principal and third parties the duty of reasonable care and skill.

12. c) A buyer who retains her own agent does not get information about the seller's negotiating position.

13. c) Buyer's agents often accept a share of the commission that the listing broker receives from the seller. This arrangement does not create an agency relationship between the buyer's agent and the seller.

14. d) A latent defect is one that is hidden or not easily observable. A latent defect is always a material fact and must be disclosed to any prospective buyers by the seller or the seller's agent.

15. a) A dual agent must not disclose confidential information about one party to the other party. This includes information on each party's negotiating position.

Chapter 10

Regulation of the Real Estate Profession

I. Real Estate Licensing
   A. Purpose of licensing
   B. Administration of license laws
   C. When a license is required
   D. Types of licenses
      1. Broker's license
      2. Salesperson's license
      3. Special licenses or permits
   E. Qualifications for a license
   F. License renewal
      1. Late renewal
      2. Inactive status
      3. Continuing education requirements
   G. Disciplinary action
      1. Disciplinary procedures
      2. Grounds for disciplinary action
      3. Real estate recovery funds

II. Broker/Salesperson Relationship
   A. Affiliation with a broker
   B. Broker's supervisory responsibilities
   C. Termination of affiliation

III. Regulation of Business Practices
   A. Brokerage offices
   B. Handling transactions
   C. Recordkeeping
   D. Trust funds
   E. Advertising and promotions

IV. Antitrust Laws and Real Estate Licensees

Chapter Overview

Throughout the United States, the real estate profession is rigorously regulated. Each state has a real estate license law that sets forth not only licensing requirements but also the legal responsibilities that real estate agents must fulfill in their day-to-day work. This chapter discusses typical requirements of real estate license laws and how the laws are administered and enforced. It also explains how antitrust laws affect real estate agents.

Real Estate Licensing

We'll begin by looking at the licensing of real estate agents, including the purpose of licensing, the administration of license laws, the circumstances in which a license is required, the various types of licenses, and the qualifications required for a license.

The Purpose of Licensing

A common way of regulating an industry or profession is to require its members to be licensed. The government can use educational requirements and testing to ensure that license applicants meet a basic standard of competence in their field. And because a license can be suspended or revoked, licensing makes it easier for the government to exercise control over how professional activities are conducted.

Real estate transactions are legally complex and involve large sums of money, and it generally isn't possible to discern the true condition or value of real estate simply by looking at it. As a result, real estate agents are in a position to do considerable harm if they don't know what they're doing, or if they act dishonestly. Requiring real estate agents to be licensed helps protect the public from incompetent and unethical agents.

Administration of Real Estate License Laws

In each state, the legislature has enacted a statute that provides for the licensing of real estate agents and the regulation of their activities. This statute, commonly referred to as the real estate license law, authorizes the creation of a state agency to issue licenses and implement the other provisions of the law. Depending on the state, the agency may be called the Department of Real Estate, the Real Estate Commission, the Real Estate Division of the Department of Licensing, or something similar.

The real estate licensing agency is headed by an official who may be called the Real Estate Commissioner or the Executive Director. For simplicity's sake, we'll refer to this official as the director. In most states, the director is appointed by the state governor. The director's qualifications typically must include a certain number of years as a real estate broker, or equivalent experience in the real estate industry.

Essentially, the director's job is to implement and enforce the provisions of the real estate license law in such a way as to provide the greatest possible protection to members of the public who deal with real estate licensees. The director is given broad powers to accomplish this end, including the authority to:

- adopt and amend administrative regulations necessary for the implementation of the real estate license law statute;
- investigate non-licensees alleged to be performing activities for which a license is required;
- screen and qualify applicants for a license;
- investigate complaints against licensees; and
- hold formal hearings to decide issues involving licensees or license applicants, and, after such a hearing, suspend, revoke, or deny a license.

There is usually a commission (called the Real Estate Commission, the Advisory Commission, or the Real Estate Board) that advises the director on the policies and functions of the real estate licensing agency. The members of the commission may be appointed by the director or by the state governor. In some states, a certain number of positions on the commission are reserved for members of the general public, and the rest are held by real estate brokers.

In most states, every year the commission is required to hold a specified number of meetings that are open to the public. At these meetings, real estate agents and members of the public are given the opportunity to comment on the topics under discussion and raise other issues concerning the real estate profession.

When a Real Estate License is Required

A real estate license law must establish the types of activities for which a real estate license is required. These activities typically include:

- selling, buying, or exchanging real estate;
- negotiating for the sale, purchase, or exchange of real estate; and
- listing or advertising real estate for sale or exchange.

In some states, a real estate license is also required for the negotiation, sale, or purchase of loans secured by real estate; the sale or purchase of real estate securities (such as timeshare interests); and/or property management activities, such as leasing and collecting rents from real estate. In addition, some states require a real estate license for the sale of business opportunities, since the sale of a business sometimes involves a transfer of real estate or the assignment of a lease.

Whatever activities are covered by the license law, a real estate license is generally required only when someone engages in those activities:

1. on behalf of another person, and
2. for compensation or in the expectation of compensation.

Someone who's selling or leasing her own property, or buying property on her own behalf, does not need a license to do so.

Exemptions. A license law typically has a number of specific exemptions from its requirements. For example, it may not be necessary to have a real estate license if you're:

- an attorney engaged in the practice of law;
- a partner or corporate officer acting on behalf of a business organization, with respect to property owned, leased, or to be purchased or leased by the organization;
- acting under a recorded power of attorney from the owner of the property;
- acting under court order (as in the case of an executor, a receiver in bankruptcy, or a trustee); or
- merely performing clerical functions.

In some states, real estate agents may hire an unlicensed **real estate assistant** to help them with their work. This is generally allowed under the clerical exemption, the last one listed above. The license law determines what kinds of tasks may be delegated to an unlicensed assistant. For example, an unlicensed assistant might be allowed to give certain objective information about property (such as the property's address) to members of the public, but not allowed to discuss terms of sale or the condition of the property.

In states where property managers are required to have real estate licenses, an exemption is typically made for resident managers, who live in the apartment complexes where they lease units and collect rents.

Also, for certain types of transactions, it may not be necessary to have a real estate license if you're licensed by another agency. For example, in most states, a licensed securities dealer would not be required to have a real estate license in addition to a securities license in order to handle a transaction involving real estate securities.

Types of Licenses

Most states issue two types of real estate licenses: a broker's license and a salesperson's license. Some states also offer an associate broker's license.

Broker's License. A broker's license authorizes the licensee to engage in any of the activities for which a real estate license is required.

A broker's license may be issued to an individual or to a corporation. For a corporate license, it's usually necessary for at least one corporate officer to be appointed to act as the **designated broker** for the corporation. The designated broker may have to be individually licensed as a broker.

Someone who is licensed as a broker may choose to work for another broker instead of operating his own brokerage. Such a broker is often called an **associate broker**. Some states issue a separate type of license for associate brokers; in other states, associate brokers have an ordinary broker's license. In either case, an associate broker may be authorized to do certain things that a salesperson cannot, such as managing a branch office of a brokerage.

Salesperson's License. A salesperson's license authorizes the licensee to engage in any of the activities for which a real estate license is required, but only under the supervision and control of a licensed broker.

This means that a real estate salesperson cannot act directly for a principal (a seller or buyer) in a real estate transaction. A listing agreement or buyer agency agreement is not a contract between the principal and the salesperson who works with the principal; it's a contract between the principal and the salesperson's employing broker.

Furthermore, a salesperson may receive compensation only from her own employing broker. Principals and cooperating brokers are not allowed to pay a salesperson directly. Instead, they pay the salesperson's employing broker, who then pays the salesperson (see Chapter 1).

In some states, all of the licensees who work for a broker may be referred to as that broker's **affiliated licensees**. The term encompasses licensees who have their own broker's license or an associate broker's license, as well as those who have a salesperson's license.

Special Licenses or Permits. For certain types of activities, a state may require a special license or permit in addition to a real estate license. For example, a licensed real estate broker might be required to obtain a special permit in order to broker a sale of oil or mineral rights separate from land, or in order to sell timeshare interests.

Qualifications for a License

Although the qualifications for a real estate license vary from state to state, there are certain requirements that apply in nearly every state. An applicant for a salesperson's license typically must be at least 18 or 19 years old, have completed one or more basic real estate courses (such as real estate principles), and have passed a written examination. A high school diploma or the equivalent is required in some states, but not in others.

For a broker's license, the applicant generally must have taken additional real estate courses and passed another exam. In addition, a broker's license applicant is commonly required to have a certain number of years of experience as a real estate salesperson, and this may have to be recent experience (for example, within the past five years). In some states, other work experience that is deemed to be equivalent can be substituted for experience as a real estate salesperson. A college degree in real estate may also be considered an acceptable substitute.

Fig. 10.1 Real estate licensees

Broker

- Individual or corporation
- Authorized to operate brokerage and represent clients

Salesperson

- Must be affiliated with a broker
- Cannot represent principal directly

For either a broker's license or a salesperson's license, there are usually some additional requirements concerning honesty. An applicant may be required to provide references from acquaintances who are willing to attest to his honesty and truthfulness. An applicant will be asked about criminal convictions, and the state may perform a background check; a license might not be issued if the applicant was convicted of a felony within a certain number of years prior to the application.

In a growing number of states, a license applicant is required to be fingerprinted. An applicant may also have to submit proof that he is in the United States legally.

Licensees from Other States. When a person who is already licensed as a real estate salesperson or broker in one state applies for a license in another state, she may not have to fulfill all of the usual requirements for licensing. For example, in states that have a two-part real estate examination, divided into a national or general section and a state section, the out-of-state licensee may have to take only the state section.

Moreover, some states have reciprocity agreements with certain other states. For instance, if State A and State B have a reciprocity agreement, someone who has a real estate license in State A may be eligible for a license in State B without taking the licensing exam. (And, of course, the same rule applies to someone licensed in State B who wants to become licensed in State A.) Taking this principle even further, some states will issue a license to a person who is licensed in any other state, without requiring him to take the exam.

License Renewal

A real estate license will expire if it is not renewed periodically. Depending on the state, renewal may be required every year, or every two, three, or four years. The licensee must pay a renewal fee and, in most states, must also submit proof that he has fulfilled a continuing education requirement (see below).

In at least a few states, a real estate license cannot be renewed if the licensee's name appears on a list of people who are delinquent on their child support payments.

Late Renewal. Someone whose license has expired can no longer legally engage in real estate activities. States generally allow for late renewal upon payment of a penalty in addition to the renewal fee. If an expired license is not renewed within a specified period, however, the former licensee may no longer be allowed to renew it. To become licensed again, she may be required to fulfill all of the standard requirements for licensing, including passing the current examination.

Inactive Status. A licensee who plans to take a break from real estate activities but does not want her license to lapse may have the option of applying for inactive status. State law determines the length of time a licensee can remain on inactive status and the requirements for reactivating a license.

Continuing Education. A large majority of states have a continuing education requirement for real estate licensees. In those states, a license cannot be renewed unless the licensee has fulfilled the continuing education requirement. Continuing education is intended to help real estate licensees become more knowledgeable and keep up with changes in the law and other developments in their field.

The number of required course hours varies from state to state, as do the courses that can be accredited for continuing education. Common examples include real estate practices, appraisal, finance, fair housing, agency, and ethics.

Disciplinary Action

Any law designed to regulate a profession will fail if its provisions are ignored by members of the profession. So the director of a state's real estate licensing agency is empowered to enforce the real estate license law by investigating and disciplining licensees who violate its provisions.

Disciplinary Procedures. Generally, the director of the real estate licensing agency is required to investigate the actions of a licensee when someone submits a complaint. The director also has the power to investigate a licensee even when no formal complaint has been made. If the investigation shows that a violation of the license law may have occurred, the director must prepare a statement of charges against the licensee and schedule an administrative hearing to look into the matter. The licensee must be given a certain amount of advance notice of the charges and the hearing date.

There is usually a statute of limitations for violations of the license law, so that an accusation must be filed within a certain number of years after an allegedly unlawful act was committed. If the act involved fraud or misrepresentation, the limitations period typically does not begin until the injured party discovers the problem.

At the hearing, an administrative law judge hears the testimony of witnesses under oath. The accused licensee may appear at the hearing with or without an attorney. The administrative law judge decides whether a violation of law occurred.

If the evidence presented at the hearing substantiates the charges against the licensee, the director has the power to suspend or revoke his license. In some cases, the director also has the power to impose a fine instead of, or in addition to, suspending or revoking the license. The licensee generally has the right to appeal the formal decision to a trial-level state court.

Imposition of a fine or other disciplinary penalty by the director does not protect a licensee from criminal prosecution or from liability in a civil suit based on the same incident.

In a situation that involves an ongoing violation of the license law, the director typically is empowered to request a court to issue a **cease and desist order**, which orders the licensee to stop the illegal conduct in question.

Grounds for Disciplinary Action. A state's real estate license law includes a list of the grounds for suspending, revoking, or denying a license. It is this list of acts or omissions that sets the minimum standards for a licensee's conduct.

The grounds for disciplinary action may range from extremely serious to relatively minor matters. The following list is a sampling of actions and conduct that are typically grounds for disciplinary action against a real estate licensee.

1. Making a substantial misrepresentation (deliberately or negligently making a false statement of fact, or failing to disclose a material fact to a principal).
2. Acting in any way that constitutes fraud or dishonest dealing.
3. Acquiring or renewing a license by fraud, misrepresentation, or deceit.
4. Being convicted of a felony or a misdemeanor involving moral turpitude.
5. Commingling your own money or property with money or property you received or are holding on behalf of a client or customer. (See the discussion of trust funds later in this chapter.)
6. Performing licensed activities negligently or incompetently.
7. As a broker, failing to exercise reasonable supervision over the activities of your affiliated licensees.
8. Employing or compensating an unlicensed person for any act that requires a license.
9. Acting as a dual agent without the knowledge or consent of all of the parties involved. (See Chapter 9.)
10. When selling property in which you have a direct or indirect ownership interest, failing to disclose the nature and extent of that interest to a buyer.
11. Making a secret profit—profiting on a transaction without disclosing the profit to your principal.
12. As a seller's agent, failing to disclose to the seller the nature and extent of any direct or indirect interest in the property that you expect to acquire as a result of the sale.
13. As a seller's agent, willfully failing to present a written offer to purchase to the seller.
14. As a buyer's agent, failing to disclose to the buyer the nature and extent of any direct or indirect ownership interest you have in property that the buyer is considering purchasing.
15. As a buyer's agent, failing to disclose to the buyer any familial, business, or other relationship you have with the owner of property that the buyer is considering purchasing.
16. Violating any state or federal fair housing or civil rights law.
17. Willfully disregarding or violating any provision of the real estate license law.

Keep in mind that in a particular state, a few of the actions we've listed may not violate the license law, and many other actions may be violations even though they aren't listed here.

Real Estate Recovery Funds. A state uses the threat of license suspension or revocation to prevent unscrupulous conduct by real estate licensees. However, suspending a real estate license after the fact does not help someone who lost money because of a licensee's unlawful actions. Of course, the injured party has a right to sue the licensee in a civil court, but what if the licensee has no money or other assets? In that case, a civil judgment would be worthless.

In some states, an injured party in a situation like this can turn to the state real estate recovery fund. This is a fund maintained specifically for reimbursing members of the public who have been injured by a licensee's actions or omissions in a real estate transaction, and who have no other recourse against the licensee. A recovery fund is usually funded with a portion of the license application and renewal fees collected by the state's real estate licensing agency.

Here's how a recovery fund typically works. When someone obtains a civil judgment or arbitration award against a licensee based on the licensee's intentional fraud, misrepresentation, misappropriation of trust funds, or other serious misconduct, the injured party can apply to the recovery fund for payment of the judgment. He usually must be able to show that the licensee has no money or assets that could be seized to pay the judgment.

There may be limits on how much money can be paid out of the recovery fund to a single applicant, for losses in a single transaction, and for losses caused by one licensee. In most cases, when payment is made from the fund, the license of the licensee involved is automatically suspended or revoked (if it hasn't been already) and can't be reinstated unless the licensee repays the fund in full.

The Broker/Salesperson Relationship

In every state, the real estate license law includes provisions concerning the employment relationship between brokers and their affiliated licensees.

Affiliation with a Broker

A real estate salesperson must be affiliated with a broker in order to engage in activities for which a real estate license is required. In some states, a salesperson must submit proof of affiliation before her license will be issued.

Some states require a broker to have a written employment agreement with each affiliated licensee. Even if a written contract is not required by state law, it's usually to the advantage of both parties to have one. Also, a written contract is necessary to establish an affiliated licensee's status as an independent contractor for tax purposes (see Chapter 1).

Brokers are typically required to keep the license certificates of affiliated licensees in their custody. There may also be a requirement for each license certificate to be displayed in the office where the licensee works.

Supervisory Responsibilities

Brokers are responsible for supervising their affiliated licensees, and failure to do so is grounds for disciplinary action. The license law may specify certain supervisory responsibilities, such as reviewing contracts and other documents prepared by an affiliated licensee.

In some states, when an affiliated licensee is fined or has his license suspended or revoked, the broker will also be subject to disciplinary action, unless the broker is able to show that she was not directly involved in the unlawful conduct and handled the matter properly. For example, the broker may be required to show that she reported the matter to the real estate licensing agency immediately upon learning of it.

Of course, in addition to disciplinary action, a broker may face civil liability for losses caused by the misconduct of an affiliated licensee. In other words, a broker may be sued by a client or customer based on an affiliated licensee's actions. (See Chapter 9.)

Termination of Affiliation

The relationship between a broker and an affiliated licensee can be terminated at any time by either party. If an affiliated licensee quits or is discharged, the broker is generally expected to notify the real estate licensing agency that the affiliation has terminated. The broker may also be required to report the circumstances that led to the termination.

In some states, the broker is required to return a terminated licensee's license certificate to the real estate licensing agency. The agency will issue a new certificate when the licensee becomes affiliated with another broker. In other states, the license certificate can be transferred directly from the old broker to the new broker.

In addition to providing for situations in which affiliation is intentionally terminated, each state's license law addresses what will happen to the licenses of affiliated licensees if their broker's license expires or is suspended or revoked, or if the broker dies.

Regulation of Business Practices

A state's real estate license law governs many of the day-to-day business practices of brokers and their affiliated licensees. There are usually provisions concerning brokerage offices, the handling of transactions, recordkeeping, trust funds, and advertising.

Brokerage Offices

A real estate broker is generally required to maintain an office in the state where she is licensed. The real estate licensing agency must be informed of the location of the office and immediately notified of a change of address. In some states, the license law specifically requires a broker's office to be open to the public.

Location and Signage. Many states allow a broker's office to be located in the broker's home, as long as that doesn't violate applicable zoning laws or restrictive covenants. Wherever an office is located, there may have to be a conspicuously placed sign identifying it as a real estate brokerage office.

Business Names. There are often rules about the names that brokers can give their businesses. For example, a real estate broker might be allowed to obtain a license under a fictitious business name, if the business name is properly registered in accordance with state law. However, the real estate licensing agency generally has the power to reject a name that could be misleading or confusing to the public.

> **Example:** John Clement is the sole proprietor of a brokerage business. He decides to call the business Acme Home Sales. He registers the business name as required by state law. After determining that no other broker is using a similar name, the real estate licensing agency issues a license to "John Clement, d.b.a. Acme Home Sales." (The "d.b.a." stands for "doing business as.")
>
> If Clement wanted to call his business the Realty Institute, the licensing agency might not allow him to do so, on the grounds that the name creates the misleading impression that the business is an academic or research institution.

Branch Offices. License laws specify the procedures for establishing and managing branch offices of a brokerage. In most states, there is no limit on the number of branch offices a broker can have, as long as every branch office is licensed or registered with the real estate licensing agency. As a general rule, each office must have a branch manager, who must be licensed as a broker or an associate broker.

Two Businesses in the Same Office. It's not unusual for a real estate broker to be involved in other business activities that are related to, or at least not in conflict with, real estate brokerage. The license law may have rules concerning what types of businesses can be run out of the same office as a brokerage business, and the broker may be required to implement various measures to keep the businesses separate. For example, the broker might have to maintain a separate filing system for each business, instead of combining their records.

Dual-State Brokers. There may be an exception to the general rules regarding brokerage offices for dual-state brokers—brokers who are also actively licensed in another state. If such a broker has an office that's open to the public in State A, then State B won't necessarily require the broker to have an office in State B as well. However, the broker will usually be required to keep all records of a real estate transaction in the state where the property is located.

Handling Transactions

A real estate license law typically includes rules that govern how licensees serve their clients and customers in a real estate transaction, from the negotiation of the purchase agreement through the closing. Here are some examples.

Negotiations. When involved in negotiations between a seller and a buyer, a licensee must present all written communications (including offers and counteroffers) from one party to the other.

Document Copies. In most states, a licensee is responsible for giving the parties to a transaction a copy of every document they sign. The copy usually must be provided at the time the signature is obtained.

Expeditious Performance. When a licensee agrees to undertake certain tasks on behalf of the parties to a transaction (for example, ordering inspections), he is generally obligated to perform those tasks expeditiously—that is, in a timely and efficient manner. An intentional or negligent delay may be grounds for disciplinary action.

Closings. The license law may specify the circumstances in which a real estate broker can serve as the closing agent in a transaction. For example, in some states a broker can handle closing only for a transaction in which she is already providing brokerage services, and may not charge a fee (separate from an ordinary brokerage commission) for closing services.

Recordkeeping

A broker is generally required to keep a copy of all documents connected with a real estate transaction. Depending on the type of transaction, this might include a listing agreement, a purchase agreement, escrow instructions, agency disclosure statements, a seller disclosure statement, settlement statements, a lease, and/or a property management agreement. It might also include trust fund records, which we will discuss shortly.

The documents must be kept for a period of time specified in the license law, such as three years from the closing date. They generally must be available for inspection by the real estate licensing agency. If there is sufficient cause, the agency may audit the records of one or more transactions.

Trust Funds

Throughout the country, the most common reason for disciplinary action against real estate licensees is the mishandling of **trust funds**, money temporarily entrusted to a broker by clients or customers. A state's license law is typically very specific about how trust funds are to be handled, and it's imperative for licensees to be thoroughly acquainted with those rules.

Avoiding Commingling. The purpose of the rules concerning trust funds is to help prevent a broker from making improper use of the funds. To accomplish this, the rules prohibit a broker from **commingling**—mixing trust funds together with the broker's own money.

In most states, a broker is required to maintain one or more **trust accounts** (sometimes called escrow accounts) for funds held on behalf of clients and customers. Trust funds must always be deposited into a trust account, and not into one of the broker's general business accounts or personal accounts. Conversely, the broker's own money must not be placed in a trust account maintained for clients or customers.

The prohibition against commingling makes it more difficult for a broker to "borrow" trust funds, intentionally or accidentally. It also protects trust funds from legal action against a broker. If trust funds were placed in a broker's general account, a judgment creditor might be able to seize those funds along with the broker's own funds.

Trust Account Requirements. The license law typically includes detailed requirements for brokers' trust accounts. For instance, the law might require a trust account to be opened in the broker's name as it appears on the broker's license, in a recognized financial institution in the state where the broker is doing business. The account may have to be specifically designated as a trust account, with the broker as trustee.

If the license law allows trust accounts to be interest-bearing accounts, there are usually rules concerning the disposition of the interest earned. For example, in many states the accruing interest must belong to the client or customer, not to the broker, unless otherwise agreed.

The license law typically also has rules concerning payment of the bank's service charges for a trust account. In some states, a broker is allowed to keep a limited amount of her own money in a trust account to cover the service charges. In other states, that is prohibited; the broker must arrange for trust account service charges to be withdrawn from his general account.

Identifying Trust Funds. Sometimes a licensee mishandles trust funds simply because he doesn't realize that they are trust funds. The most common example of trust funds in a real estate transaction is the good faith deposit (earnest money) that a buyer tenders to a seller with an offer to purchase. (See Chapter 8.) Tenant security deposits held by a property manager on behalf of a property owner are trust funds, as are rents collected by the property manager. So are any other funds belonging to a client or customer that are temporarily in a broker's custody pending delivery to a principal or payment to a third party.

> **Example:** A seller gives money to a broker in advance to cover the cost of advertising the property. In most states, the broker must treat this money in accordance with the rules for trust funds until the broker actually uses it to pay for the advertising.

Handling Trust Funds. In most states, after accepting trust funds from a client or customer, a broker is generally supposed to do one of three things with the funds:

1. deliver them directly to a principal,
2. turn them over to an attorney or an escrow agent to hold in trust (in escrow), or
3. deposit them into a trust account maintained by the broker.

Which of these three actions is appropriate depends on the situation and on any specific instructions given by the client or customer. For example, if a property manager collects a rental payment from a tenant, the management agreement might direct the property manager to give the payment directly to the property owner. A buyer's deposit, on the other hand, is usually held in trust by an attorney, an escrow agent, or a broker and not delivered to the seller until the transaction closes. This is generally governed by the terms of the purchase agreement.

Whichever of the three actions is appropriate, it usually must be done within a short time after the funds come into the broker's possession. The specific deadline is set in the license law. For example, some states require trust funds to be given to a principal, placed in escrow, or deposited into a broker's trust account on the next business day after receipt; other states allow 48 or 72 hours after receipt.

Fig. 10.2 Rules for handling trust funds

Trust Funds

- May not be commingled with broker's own funds.
- Generally must be given to principal, placed in escrow, or deposited into broker's trust account.
- In some states, check for buyer's deposit can be held uncashed until buyer's offer is accepted or rejected.

If a client or customer gives trust funds to an affiliated licensee instead of directly to a broker, the licensee is usually required to turn the funds over to her broker as soon as possible. Alternatively, if so directed by the broker, the licensee may deliver them to a principal, have them placed in escrow, or deposit them into the broker's trust account by the applicable deadline.

Buyers' Deposits. Some states have special rules for handling a buyer's deposit. When a broker receives a deposit check from a buyer, the broker may be allowed to hold the check without depositing it until the seller accepts or rejects the buyer's offer. If the offer is rejected, the check can be returned to the buyer. If the offer is accepted, the broker must deposit the check into the trust account (or give it to an escrow agent) by the applicable deadline, unless the seller gives written instructions to keep holding it uncashed.

Disbursing Trust Funds. In general, trust funds deposited in a broker's trust account must remain there until they are withdrawn and disbursed pursuant to instructions from the owner of the funds. While the owner of trust funds is usually easy to identify, it should be noted that the ownership may change as the real estate transaction progresses. For example, the ownership of a buyer's deposit varies depending on whether or not the buyer's offer has been accepted. Before acceptance, the deposit belongs to the buyer and must be handled according to his instructions. After acceptance, however, ownership is not so clear-cut. The deposit can't be delivered to the seller until the transaction closes or the seller otherwise becomes entitled to it (because the buyer has defaulted); in the meantime, however, it usually can't be returned to the buyer without the seller's express written permission.

If a transaction falls through after the buyer's deposit has been placed in escrow or a broker's trust account, there may be a dispute over the money; the buyer and the seller may each feel entitled to it. In this situation, the escrow agent or broker who holds the funds in trust may file an **interpleader** action, turning the matter over to a court. The court will decide which party is the rightful owner of the funds.

Personal Property. In the unusual event that a client or customer entrusts a broker with an item of personal property, the item generally must be treated in accordance with the rules for trust funds. For example, depending on the property in question, it might be appropriate for the broker to keep it in a safe deposit box at a bank; in that case, the broker might be required to place it in a separate safe deposit box, not in the one that the broker uses for her own papers and belongings.

Trust Fund Records. It's very important to keep proper records of all trust funds, including trust fund checks that are held uncashed, trust funds that are sent directly to escrow, and trust funds that have been released to the owner. Thorough trust fund records enable a broker to prevent overdrafts and prepare accurate accountings for clients. A state's license law often includes detailed requirements for trust account records.

Conversion. Of course, in spite of all of the rules concerning trust accounts, it's still possible for a broker to misappropriate trust funds. This may be referred to as **conversion**; the broker has converted the funds to his own use. Conversion can be the basis for a civil suit by the owner of the trust funds; the broker may be required to make restitution (return the funds), and also pay damages to compensate for losses that resulted from the conversion. Conversion can also be the basis for criminal charges against the broker. It is an extremely serious violation of the license law, of fiduciary duties, and of professional ethics.

Advertising and Promotions

In most states, the real estate license law includes some provisions concerning advertising. Real estate licensees also need to be aware of other laws that regulate advertising, not just those that pertain specifically to real estate.

False Advertising. False advertising is usually a violation of the license law. In some states, it is explicitly listed as grounds for disciplinary action; in other states, it falls within the prohibition against fraud or misrepresentation. False advertising may also be a violation of other state and federal laws.

Blind Ads. Some license laws prohibit real estate licensees from placing blind ads. A **blind ad** is one that fails to include the name of the broker that the licensee who placed the ad works for, and/or fails to indicate that the ad was placed by a licensee. The rule against blind ads may or may not apply when a licensee advertises her own property for sale.

Internet Advertising. In some states, real estate licensees who advertise or provide information about real estate services on the Internet are required to comply with a rule concerning contact with individual customers. There may have to be procedures in place to ensure that only a real estate licensee (or someone exempt from the licensing requirement) responds to inquiries from customers or otherwise communicates directly with individual customers online.

Inducements. Sometimes a real estate licensee offers a gift, prize, or rebate to encourage the recipient to attend a sales presentation. This is sometimes called an **inducement**. In some states, if attendance at a sales presentation is required to obtain a gift, that must be disclosed in the advertisement or solicitation. Any other conditions for receiving inducements must also be disclosed. Also, if an inducement is given to one of the parties in a transaction, that may be considered a material fact that must be disclosed to all of the parties.

Do Not Call Registry. Real estate licensees who solicit business by making "cold calls" to strangers must comply with the Federal Trade Commission's telemarketing rules. It's against the law to make this type of call to someone whose name appears on the National "Do Not Call" Registry, so licensees must check the registry before placing calls (persons who engage in ongoing telemarketing must check the registry at least once every 31 days). There are also "Do Not Email" and "Do Not Fax" registries.

Antitrust Laws and Real Estate Licensees

In addition to the state real estate license law, federal antitrust laws impose certain restrictions on a real estate agent's behavior towards clients, customers, and other agents. Some states also have state antitrust laws.

The main federal antitrust law is the **Sherman Act**. The Sherman Act prohibits any agreement that has the effect of unreasonably restraining trade, including conspiracies. Under the Sherman Act, a **conspiracy** occurs when two or more business entities participate in a common scheme, the effect of which is the unreasonable restraint of trade.

The foundation of antitrust laws is the idea that competition is good for both the economy and society as a whole. While antitrust laws are usually associated with big steel mills, oil companies, and telephone companies, in 1950 antitrust laws were held to apply to the real estate industry. In a landmark case, the United States Supreme Court held that mandatory fee schedules, established and enforced by a real estate board, violated the Sherman Act (*United States v. National Association of Real Estate Boards*).

If a real estate licensee violates antitrust laws, she may be subject to both civil and criminal actions. If an individual is found guilty of violating the Sherman Act, he can be fined up to one million dollars and/or sentenced to ten years' imprisonment. If a corporation is found guilty of violating the Sherman Act, it can be fined up to one hundred million dollars.

The activities that are prohibited by antitrust laws can be grouped into four main categories:

- price fixing (fixing commission rates),
- group boycotts,
- tie-in arrangements, and
- market allocation.

Price Fixing

Price fixing is defined as the cooperative setting of prices or price ranges by competing firms. To avoid the appearance of price fixing, two real estate agents from different brokerages should never discuss their commission rates. (It is a discussion between competing agents that is dangerous; brokers and affiliated licensees that work for the same company can discuss commission rates.) One exception to this general prohibition is that two competing brokers may discuss a commission split—the division of the commission between the listing broker and the selling broker—in a cooperative sale.

Even a casual announcement that a broker is planning on raising his commission rates could lead to antitrust problems.

Example: Broker Wood goes to a dinner given by his local multiple listing service. He is called on to discuss current market conditions and, in the middle of his speech, he announces that he is going to raise his commission rate, no matter what anyone else does. This statement could be viewed as an invitation to conspire to fix prices. If any other MLS members raise their rates in response to his announcement, they could be held to have accepted Wood's invitation to conspire.

Brokers need to understand that they do not have to actually consult with each other to be charged with conspiring to fix commission rates. The kind of scenario described in the previous example is enough to lead to an antitrust lawsuit.

Publications that appear to fix prices are prohibited as well. An MLS or other association that published "recommended" or "going" rates for commissions could be sued for antitrust violations.

Group Boycotts

A group boycott is an agreement between two or more people engaged in a business to exclude another from fair participation in that field. The purpose of a group boycott is to hurt or destroy a competitor, and it is a violation of antitrust laws.

Example: Becker and Jordan are both brokers. Over lunch together, they discuss the business practices of a third broker, Harley. Becker says she thinks Harley is dishonest. Jordan agrees. He says that he's decided not to do business with Harley. He avoids Harley whenever possible, and just doesn't call back if Harley calls to ask about a listed property. He suggests that Becker should do this too. This conversation could be considered an agreement to boycott Harley.

If a broker feels another broker is dishonest or unethical, he may choose not to do business with that other broker. But encouraging other brokers to do the same thing could be considered a group boycott.

Tie-in Arrangements

A tie-in arrangement is defined as "an agreement to sell one product, only on the condition that the buyer also purchases a different (or tied) product..."

Example: Brown is a subdivision developer. Tyson, a builder, wants to buy a lot from Brown and build a house on it. Brown tells Tyson that he will sell him a lot only if Tyson enters into a list-back agreement. In other words, Tyson must sign a contract promising that after he builds a house on the lot, he will list the improved property with Brown. Requiring Tyson to do this as a condition of selling the lot is an illegal tie-in arrangement; Brown is violating antitrust laws.

In the example, note that it's the tie-in arrangement that is the antitrust violation, not the list-back agreement itself. If Tyson wanted to enter into a list-back agreement with Brown, the agreement wouldn't be illegal.

Market Allocation

Market allocation occurs when competing brokerage firms agree not to sell certain products or services in specified areas or to certain customers in specified areas. Market allocation between competing real estate firms is illegal, because it limits competition.

As with group boycotts, it's the collective action that makes market allocation illegal. An individual brokerage firm is free to determine the market areas in which it wants to specialize (if any); similarly, the firm can allocate territory to particular licensees affiliated with the firm. Allocation of territory between competing firms, however, is a violation of antitrust law.

Example: ABC Realty assigns Agent Ava to handle all new customers in the luxury home market, and assigns Agent Paxton to all new customers in the vacant land market. This practice does not violate antitrust law.

However, if ABC Realty and XYZ Realty agreed to allocate customers so that ABC Realty will handle all luxury homes and XYZ Realty will handle all vacant land, this would violate antitrust law.

Avoiding Antitrust Violations

To prevent possible antitrust violations, brokers should:

- always establish their fees and other listing policies independently, without consulting competing firms;
- never use listing forms that contain pre-printed commission rates;
- never imply to a client that the commission rate is fixed or non-negotiable, or refer to a competitor's commission policies when discussing commission rates;
- never discuss their business plans with competitors;
- never tell clients or competitors that they won't do business with a competing firm, or tell them not to work with that firm because of doubts about its competence or integrity; and
- train their licensees to be aware of the types of actions that could be considered antitrust law violations.

Chapter Summary

1. Real estate license laws require those engaging in real estate activities to be licensed; they also regulate the actions of licensees. The purpose of real estate license laws is to protect members of the public who deal with real estate agents.

2. Each state has a real estate licensing agency. The director of the agency implements the provisions of the state's real estate license law by issuing licenses, imposing regulations, investigating the activities of licensees, and taking disciplinary action against those who violate the license law.

3. The real estate license law determines who is required to have a real estate license and sets forth the licensing requirements for brokers and salespersons.

4. The license law also establishes standards of lawful conduct and specifies the grounds for disciplinary action. Disciplinary action may include license suspension or revocation and/or a fine.

5. A real estate salesperson is licensed to engage in real estate activities only when affiliated with a broker and subject to the broker's supervision and control. A broker who fails to supervise a salesperson properly may be subject to disciplinary action.

6. A state's license law typically includes rules concerning brokerage offices, how transactions must be handled, recordkeeping, trust funds, and advertising.

7. Trust funds generally must be deposited into a broker's trust account or a neutral escrow, or else delivered to the principal, soon after they are received. The amount of time allowed is specified in the license law.

8. Antitrust laws prohibit price fixing, group boycotts, tie-in arrangements, and market allocation. Real estate licensees must be especially careful to avoid discussing commission rates with licensees who work for other companies.

Key Terms

Real estate license law—A state statute that governs the licensing and business practices of real estate agents.

Real estate broker—A person who is licensed to represent others for compensation in real estate transactions.

Associate broker—A broker who works for another broker. Some states issue an associate broker's license; in other states, an associate broker has a broker's license.

Real estate salesperson—A person who is licensed to work for and represent a broker in real estate transactions.

Affiliated licensee—Any real estate licensee who works for a broker, whether licensed as a broker, associate broker, or salesperson.

Disciplinary action—Legal action taken by the director of the real estate licensing agency against a licensee for violations of the license law, which may lead to license suspension or revocation.

Recovery fund—In some states, an account funded by license fees that is used to compensate members of the public injured by the unlawful acts of a real estate licensee, when they can't collect a judgment from the licensee.

Trust funds—Funds held by a broker on behalf of clients or customers.

Commingling—Mixing trust funds together with a broker's personal funds or general business funds.

Trust account—A bank account used to keep trust funds segregated from the broker's personal funds and general business funds.

Conversion—When a real estate licensee takes trust funds and uses them for her own purposes.

Blind ad—An advertisement placed by a licensee that fails to disclose the name of the licensee's broker and/or fails to indicate that the ad was placed by a real estate agent.

Inducement—A prize, gift, or rebate used to encourage a member of the public to attend a sales presentation.

Price fixing—The cooperative setting of prices by competing firms.

Group boycott—An agreement between two or more real estate brokers to exclude other brokers from fair participation in real estate activities.

Tie-in arrangement—An agreement to sell one product only on the condition that the buyer also purchases a different product.

Market allocation—An agreement between brokers not to compete with each other in certain areas or markets.

Chapter Quiz

1. The primary purpose of real estate licensing is to:
   a) raise revenue for the state
   b) protect real estate agents from unfair competitive practices
   c) protect the public from incompetent and unethical real estate agents
   d) promote uniform practices in the real estate industry

2. The director of a state's real estate licensing agency typically has all of the following powers, except the power to:
   a) impose regulations that have the force of law
   b) require a hearing into charges against a licensee
   c) suspend or revoke a real estate license
   d) set commission rates for real estate brokers

3. Commingling is:
   a) embezzlement
   b) mixing trust funds with personal funds or general business funds
   c) misappropriation of trust funds
   d) paying a commission to a non-licensed person

4. In most states, a licensed real estate salesperson:
   a) may enter into a contract with a property seller, but not with a prospective buyer
   b) may fill out a listing agreement or purchase agreement form
   c) must be affiliated with a broker, but is not subject to the broker's supervision
   d) may manage a branch office of a brokerage

5. As a general rule, a licensee who has made misrepresentations concerning the condition of a property:
   a) may have his license suspended or revoked only after a formal hearing
   b) is subject to disciplinary action or civil liability, but not both
   c) is required to pay any commission earned from the transaction to the director of the real estate licensing agency
   d) All of the above

6. In most states, all of the following are grounds for disciplinary action against a real estate licensee, except:
   a) violation of a fair housing law
   b) violation of a provision of the license law
   c) failure to renew a real estate license
   d) collecting a secret profit

7. If a real estate licensee used a client's trust funds to make her own mortgage payment, that would be:
   a) reversion
   b) conversion
   c) a secret profit
   d) None of the above

8. In many states, a buyer's deposit check:
   a) must be placed in the broker's general business account, not in his personal account
   b) must be given to the seller as soon as the buyer's offer is accepted
   c) must be held by the seller until the transaction closes
   d) can be held uncashed by the broker until the seller accepts or rejects the buyer's offer

9. While in the possession of a real estate broker, all of the following would be trust funds, except:
   a) a salesperson's share of a commission
   b) a buyer's good faith deposit
   c) a tenant's security deposit
   d) money given to the broker by a buyer to pay for a home inspection

10. The commission rate a listing broker can charge on a sale is determined by:
    a) the director of the real estate licensing agency
    b) the seller and the broker
    c) the multiple listing service
    d) the buyer and the seller

Answer Key

1. c) The primary purpose of real estate licensing is to protect the public from incompetent and unethical real estate agents.

2. d) The director of a state's real estate licensing agency does not set commission rates.

3. b) Mixing trust funds with personal funds or general business funds is called commingling.

4. b) In most states, a salesperson can fill out a contract form, but cannot enter into a contract with a buyer or seller directly, and also cannot manage a branch office of a brokerage. A salesperson must be affiliated with a broker and must be supervised by the broker.

5. a) A licensee is ordinarily entitled to a hearing before her license is suspended or revoked. A licensee could face both disciplinary action and civil liability for misrepresentation.

6. c) Failure to renew one's real estate license is not a violation of the license law (although engaging in real estate activities after one's license has expired would be a violation).

7. b) When a licensee takes a client's money for his own use, he is guilty of conversion.

8. d) In many states, a broker can hold a buyer's deposit check uncashed until the buyer's offer has been accepted or rejected.

9. a) The broker is not holding the salesperson's share of a commission in trust on behalf of a client or customer.

10. b) The listing broker's commission rate is decided by the seller and the broker when they negotiate the terms of their listing agreement.

Chapter 11

Principles of Real Estate Financing

I. Economics of Real Estate Finance
   - A. Real estate cycles
   - B. Interest rates and federal policy

II. Real Estate Finance Markets
   - A. Primary market
   - B. Secondary market
     1. Buying and selling loans
     2. Secondary market entities

III. Real Estate Finance Documents
   - A. Promissory notes
     1. Basic provisions
     2. Types of notes
     3. Signing and endorsing the note
   - B. Security instruments
     1. Relationship between note and security instrument
     2. Title theory vs. lien theory
     3. Mortgage vs. deed of trust
     4. Recording
     5. Instruments as personal property
     6. Assignment
     7. Personal property as collateral
   - C. Finance document provisions
   - D. Foreclosure procedures
     1. Judicial foreclosure
     2. Nonjudicial foreclosure
     3. Comparison of judicial and nonjudicial foreclosure
     4. Junior lienholders
     5. Strict foreclosure
     6. Alternatives to foreclosure
     7. Foreclosure vs. bankruptcy

IV. Seller Financing

V. Types of Mortgage Loans

Market Value
Income Analyses

Chapter Overview

Financing—lending and borrowing money—is essential to the real estate industry. If financing weren't available, buyers would have to pay cash for their property, and very few people could afford to do so. Whether they're working with buyers or sellers, real estate agents need a thorough understanding of the financing process. This chapter starts with background information about real estate cycles, how the government influences real estate finance, and the secondary market. The chapter then goes on to explain how mortgages and other financing instruments work, the foreclosure process, and the various types of mortgage loans. The process of applying for a mortgage loan is covered in Chapter 12.

The Economics of Real Estate Finance

Nearly every buyer needs to borrow money in order to purchase real estate. Whether a particular buyer will be able to obtain a loan depends in part on his personal financial circumstances, and in part on national and local economic conditions. We're going to discuss real estate cycles and the government's role in the economy, to help you understand the economic factors that affect real estate lending.

From a lender's point of view, a loan is an investment. A lender loans money in the expectation of a return on the investment. The borrower will repay the money borrowed, plus interest; the interest is the lender's return.

As a general rule, investors demand a higher return on risky investments than they do on comparatively safe ones. That holds true for loan transactions; the greater the risk that the borrower won't repay the loan, the higher the interest rate charged. But the interest rate a lender charges on a particular loan also depends on market forces and real estate cycles.

Real Estate Cycles

The real estate market is cyclical: it goes through active periods followed by slumps. These periodic shifts in the level of activity in the real estate market are called **real estate cycles**. Residential real estate cycles can be dramatic or moderate, and they can be local or regional. At any given time and place, there may be a buyer's market, where few people are buying and homes sit on the market for a long time, or there may be a seller's market, where many people are buying and homes sell rapidly.

These cycles obey the law of supply and demand. When demand for a product exceeds the supply (a seller's market), the price charged for the product tends to rise, and the price increase stimulates more production. As production increases, more of the demand is satisfied, until eventually the supply outstrips demand and a buyer's market is created. At that point, prices fall and production tapers off until demand catches up with supply, and the cycle begins again.

Real estate cycles are caused by changes in the supply of and demand for mortgage loan funds. The supply of mortgage funds depends on how much money investors have available and choose to invest in real estate loans. The demand for mortgage funds depends on how many people want to purchase real estate and can afford to borrow enough money to do so.

Interest rates represent the price of mortgage funds. They affect supply and demand, and they also fluctuate in response to changes in supply and demand. Interest is sometimes called the cost of money.

Generally, when mortgage funds are plentiful, interest rates are low. When funds are scarce, interest rates are high; this is called a **tight money market**. While interest rates do not usually have an immediate impact on property values, in a tight market, sellers may have to resort to offering to finance part of the purchase price in order to close a sale.

In a healthy economy, supply and demand are more or less in balance. This is the ideal; in reality, the forces affecting supply and demand are constantly changing, and so is the balance between them. But as long as supply and demand are reasonably close, the economy functions well. When supply far exceeds demand, or vice versa, the economy suffers.

Real estate cycles can be moderated, though not eliminated, by factors that either help keep interest rates under control or directly affect the supply of mortgage funds. Federal economic policy plays a key role in moderating real estate cycles.

Interest Rates and Federal Policy

Economic stability is directly tied to the supply of and demand for money. If money is plentiful and can be borrowed cheaply (that is, interest rates are low), increased economic activity is usually the result. On the other hand, if funds are scarce and/or expensive to borrow, an economic slowdown will result.

Thus, manipulation of the availability and cost of money can do much to achieve economic balance. The federal government influences real estate finance, as well as the rest of the U.S. economy, through its **fiscal policy** and its **monetary policy**.

Fiscal Policy. Fiscal policy refers to the way in which the federal government manages its money. Congress and the President determine fiscal policy through tax legislation and the federal budget. The U.S. Treasury implements fiscal policy by managing tax revenues, expenditures, and the national debt.

When the federal government spends more money than it takes in, a shortfall called the **federal deficit** results. It is the Treasury's responsibility to borrow enough money to cover the deficit. It does this by issuing interest-bearing securities that are backed by the U.S. government and purchased by private investors. The securities include Treasury bills, notes, and bonds. Investors often prefer to invest in these government securities instead of other investments, because they are comparatively low-risk.

When the government borrows money, it competes with private industry for available investment funds. Economists and politicians debate what impact this has on the economy. According to some, by draining the number of dollars in circulation, heavy government borrowing may lead to an economic slowdown. The greater the federal deficit, the more money the government has to borrow, and the greater the effect on the economy. Other economists argue that the federal deficit has little effect on interest rates.

The government's taxation policies also affect the supply of and demand for money. As with the deficit, the effect of taxation on the economy is controversial. Basically, when taxes are low, taxpayers have more money to lend and invest. When taxes are high, taxpayers not only have less money to lend or invest, they also may be more likely to invest what money they do have in tax-exempt securities instead of taxable investments. Since real estate and real estate mortgages are taxable investments, this may have a significant impact on the real estate finance industry.

Monetary Policy. Monetary policy refers to the direct control the federal government exerts over the money supply and interest rates. The main goal of monetary policy is to keep the U.S. economy healthy.

Monetary policy is determined by the **Federal Reserve**, commonly called "the Fed." The Federal Reserve System, established in 1913, is the nation's central banking system. It is governed by the Federal Reserve Board and the board's chairman. It has twelve districts nationwide, with a Federal Reserve Bank in each district. Thousands of commercial banks across the country are members of the Federal Reserve.

The Fed is responsible for regulating commercial banks, and it also oversees implementation of the Truth in Lending Act (discussed in Chapter 12). But setting and implementing the government's monetary policy is perhaps the Fed's most important function.

The major objectives of the government's monetary policy are high employment, economic growth, price stability, interest rate stability, and stability in financial and foreign exchange markets. Although these goals are interrelated, we are most concerned with the Federal Reserve policies that affect the availability and cost of borrowed money (interest rates), since those have the most direct impact on the real estate industry.

Fig. 11.1 Federal Reserve districts

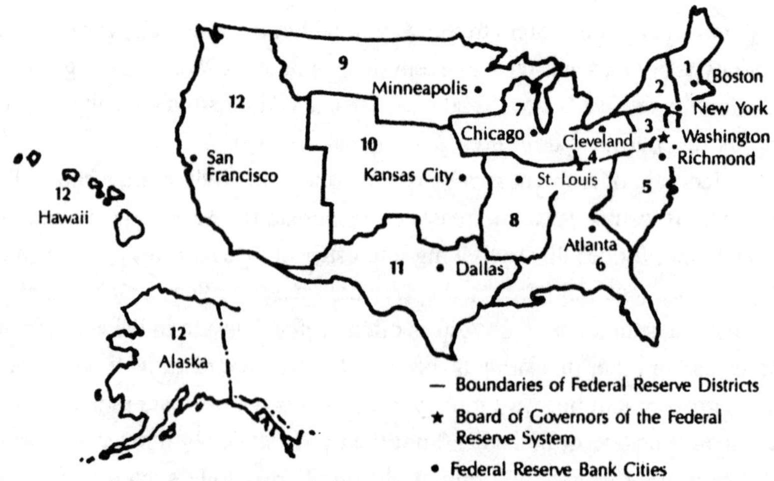

One of the Fed's main goals is to limit **inflation**. Inflation is a general rise in prices of goods and services over time, meaning that each dollar's purchasing power is reduced. Consumer price indexes, which track changes in the price of certain commodities, can be used to track inflation rates.

Inflation tends to occur in periods of rapid economic growth. While economic growth is ideal, too much growth too fast can push prices too high, suddenly causing reduced demand and an economic contraction. By raising interest rates, the Fed can put a brake on inflation.

The Fed uses three tools to implement its monetary policy and influence the economy:

- key interest rates,
- reserve requirements, and
- open market operations.

Key Interest Rates. The Fed has control over two interest rates, the federal funds rate and the discount rate. These are the interest rates charged when a bank borrows money, either from another bank or from a Federal Reserve Bank. When the Fed takes action to raise or lower the interest rates that its member banks have to pay, the banks will typically raise or lower the interest rates they charge their customers. Lower interest rates tend to stimulate the economy, and higher rates tend to slow it down. The Fed may increase rates if it decides that a slower pace is desirable to keep price inflation in check.

Reserve Requirements. Commercial banks are required to keep certain percentages of their customers' funds on deposit at the Federal Reserve Bank. These reserve requirements help prevent financial panics (a "run on the bank") by assuring depositors that their funds are safe and accessible; their bank will always have enough money available to meet unusual customer demand.

Reserve requirements also give the Fed some control over the growth of credit. By increasing reserve requirements, the Fed can reduce the amount of money banks have available to lend. On the other hand, a reduction in reserve requirements frees more money for investment or lending. So an increase in reserve requirements tends to decrease available loan funds and increase interest rates. Conversely, a decrease in reserve requirements tends to increase available loan funds and decrease interest rates.

Open Market Operations. The Fed also buys and sells government securities; these transactions are called open market operations. They are the Fed's chief method of controlling the money supply, and with the money supply, inflation and interest rates. Only money in circulation is considered part of the money supply, so actions by the Fed that put money into circulation increase the money supply, and actions that take money out of circulation decrease it.

When the Fed buys government securities from an investor, it increases the money supply, because the money that the Fed uses to pay for the securities goes into circulation. When the Fed sells government securities, the money the buyer uses to pay for the securities is taken out of circulation, decreasing the money supply. Interest rates tend to fall with increases in the money supply, and to rise with decreases in the money supply.

Other Federal Influences on Finance. Aside from the Federal Reserve, there are a number of other federal agencies, programs, and regulatory systems that have an impact on real estate finance.

Federal Home Loan Bank System. The Federal Home Loan Bank System (FHLB) is made up of twelve regional, privately owned wholesale banks. The banks loan funds to FHLB members—local community lenders—and accept their mortgages and other loans as collateral. The FHLB, which is overseen by the Federal Housing Finance Board, is active in promoting affordable housing.

Federal Deposit Insurance Corporation. The FDIC was created in 1933 to insure bank deposits against bank insolvency. If a bank or savings and loan fails, the FDIC will step in to protect the institution's customers against the loss of their deposited funds, up to specified limits.

HUD. The Department of Housing and Urban Development (HUD) is a federal cabinet department. Among many other things, HUD's responsibilities include urban renewal projects, public housing, FHA-insured loan programs, and enforcement of the Federal Fair Housing Act (see Chapter 16). Ginnie Mae (discussed later in this chapter) and the Federal Housing Administration (discussed in Chapter 12) are both part of HUD.

Rural Housing Service. Formerly known as the Farmers Home Administration or FmHA, the Rural Housing Service is an agency within the Department of Agriculture. To help people living in rural areas purchase and improve their homes, the Rural Housing Service makes loans and grants and also guarantees loans made by lending institutions. In addition, it finances the construction of affordable housing in rural areas. (These loan programs are discussed in Chapter 12.)

Farm Credit System. Originally developed by the federal government, the Farm Credit System is now a privately owned cooperative. It provides financial assistance to farmers, ranchers, and others in rural areas.

Community Reinvestment Act. Congress passed the Community Reinvestment Act (CRA) in 1977 to help ensure that federally supervised financial institutions meet the credit needs of their local communities, including the need for affordable home loans. The federal agencies that oversee financial institutions (the Federal Reserve, the FDIC, the Office of the Comptroller of the Currency, and the Office of Thrift Supervision) periodically evaluate their community lending activities.

Real Estate Finance Markets

There are two "markets" that supply the funds available for real estate loans: the primary market and the secondary market. In addition to using monetary policy to control the money supply and interest rates, another way in which the federal government has helped moderate the severity and duration of real estate cycles is by establishing a strong, nationwide secondary market. The secondary market limits the adverse effects of local economic circumstances on real estate lending. We'll look first at the primary market, then at the secondary market.

Primary Market

The primary market is the market in which mortgage lenders make loans to home buyers. When buyers apply for a loan to finance their purchase, they're seeking a loan in the primary market.

Originally, the primary market was entirely local. It was made up of the various lending institutions in a community—the local banks and savings and loan associations. (Today the primary market is considerably more complicated, since there are interstate lenders, online lenders, nationwide mortgage companies, and so on.) The traditional source of funds for the primary market was the savings of individuals and businesses in the local area. A bank or savings and loan would use the savings deposits of members of the local community to make mortgage loans to members of that same community.

The local economy has a significant effect on the amount of deposited funds available to a lender, and on the local demand for them. When employment is high, consumers are more likely to borrow money for cars, vacations, or homes. Businesses expand and borrow to finance their growth. At the same time, fewer people are saving. This decrease in deposits means that less local money is available for lending, making it difficult to meet the increased demand for loans. On the other hand, when an area is in an economic slump, consumers are more inclined to save than to borrow. Businesses suspend plans for growth. The result is a drop in the demand for money, and the local lending institutions' deposits grow.

Disintermediation is another phenomenon that affects the amount of deposited funds available to lenders. It occurs when depositors withdraw funds from savings accounts and put them into competing investments that offer higher returns, such as stocks and bonds. Changes in interest rates and investment yields can lead to disintermediation.

From a lender's point of view, either too little or too much money on deposit is cause for concern. In the first case, with little money to lend, a lender's primary source of income is affected. In the second case, the lender is paying interest to its depositors, and if it is unable to reinvest the deposited funds quickly, it will lose money.

The solution to these problems has been for lenders to look beyond their local area. When local savings deposits are low, a lender needs to get funds from other parts of the country to lend locally. When local demand for loans is low, a lender needs to send funds to other parts of the country where demand is higher. This is where the secondary market comes in. The secondary market makes it easy for lenders to obtain funds from around the country.

Secondary Market

The secondary market is a national market. In the secondary market, private investors, government agencies, and government-sponsored enterprises buy and sell mortgages secured by real estate in all parts of the United States.

Fig. 11.2 By selling mortgages on the secondary market, lenders obtain funds to make more loans.

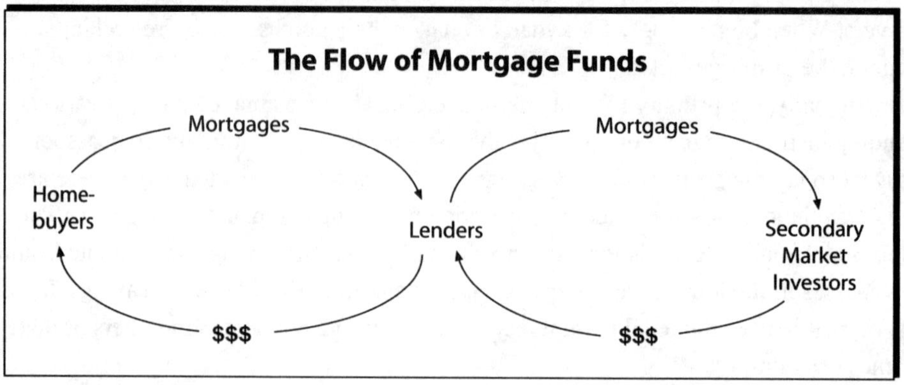

Buying and Selling Loans. Mortgage loans can be bought and sold just like other investments—stocks or bonds, for example. The value of a loan is influenced by the rate of return on the loan compared to the market rate of return, as well as the degree of risk associated with the loan (the likelihood of default). For instance, a **seasoned loan**—one with a history of several years of timely payments by the borrower—is less risky than a new, untested loan. As a result, a seasoned loan is worth more to an investor than a new loan for the same amount.

Investors generally buy mortgage loans at a discount, for less than their face value. However, if a borrower defaults on a loan purchased at a discount, the investor can still foreclose (force the sale of the property to recoup the amount of the debt) for the full face amount of the mortgage. For example, if an investor bought a $100,000 mortgage for $80,000 and the borrower immediately defaulted on the loan, the investor could foreclose for the full $100,000.

The availability of funds in the primary market now depends a great deal on the existence of the national secondary market. As explained above, a particular lender may have either too much or too little money to lend, depending on conditions in the local economy. It is the secondary market that provides balance by transferring funds from areas where there is an excess to areas where there is a shortage. When local demand for loan funds is high, lenders can sell loans they've already made on the secondary market and use the proceeds of those sales to make more loans. When local demand for loan funds is low, lenders can use their excess funds to purchase loans on the secondary market.

The secondary market has a stabilizing effect on local mortgage markets. Lenders are willing to commit themselves to long-term real estate loans even when local funds are scarce, because they can raise more funds by liquidating their loans on the secondary market.

Secondary Market Entities. The federal government has played a central role in developing the secondary market for mortgage loans. It's done this by establishing four secondary market entities: Fannie Mae, Freddie Mac, Ginnie Mae, and Farmer Mac. We'll describe each of these entities shortly, after a general description of what they do.

A secondary market entity buys large numbers of mortgage loans from primary market lenders, and then issues securities using the loans as collateral ("securitizes" the loans). The entity sells these **mortgage-backed securities** to private investors. As the underlying loans are repaid by the borrowers, the secondary market entity passes the payments through to the investors; that's the return on their investment. The securities are guaranteed by the secondary market entity, so the investors will receive their payments from the entity even if borrowers default on some of the underlying loans.

Of course, the secondary market entities don't want to buy loans that carry a high risk of default. To prevent that, the entities have established their own **underwriting standards**. Underwriting standards are the criteria used to evaluate a loan applicant and the property offered as security, to determine if the loan would be a good investment or would involve too much risk. Lenders may apply their own underwriting standards when they make loans, but they generally cannot sell the loans to a secondary market entity unless the loans conform to the entity's underwriting standards. Because most lenders want to have the option of selling their loans on the secondary market, the majority of conventional mortgage loans in the U.S. are now made in accordance with entities' standards. (Underwriting standards are discussed in more detail in Chapter 12.)

Fannie Mae. The most prominent of the secondary market entities is the Federal National Mortgage Association (FNMA), often referred to as "Fannie Mae." Fannie Mae started out as a federal agency in 1938. Its original purpose was to provide a secondary market for FHA-insured loans.

Fannie Mae was eventually reorganized as a private corporation, but it is still chartered by the federal government. It is sometimes referred to as a **government-sponsored enterprise**, or GSE. Fannie Mae purchases conventional, FHA, and VA loans to use as the collateral for its mortgage-backed securities. (These different types of loans are discussed in Chapter 12.)

Freddie Mac. Congress created the Federal Home Loan Mortgage Corporation (FHLMC), nicknamed "Freddie Mac," in 1970. Its original purpose was to assist savings and loan associations (which had been hit particularly hard by a recession) by buying their conventional loans. Freddie Mac is now authorized to purchase and securitize conventional, FHA, and VA loans from any type of lender. Like Fannie Mae, Freddie Mac is a government-sponsored enterprise.

Ginnie Mae. The Government National Mortgage Association (GNMA) is one of the federal agencies that make up HUD. Among many other things, Ginnie Mae guarantees securities backed by loans made through the FHA and VA loan programs. It also provides assistance to urban renewal and housing programs. Note that unlike the other secondary market entities, Ginnie Mae is a government agency, not a government-sponsored enterprise.

Farmer Mac. Like Fannie Mae and Freddie Mac, Farmer Mac (the Federal Agricultural Mortgage Corporation, or FAMC) is a government-sponsored enterprise. It was created by Congress in 1988 to establish a secondary market for agricultural real estate loans and rural housing mortgage loans. Farmer Mac is regulated and supervised by the Farm Credit Administration.

Current Status of Secondary Market Entities. Because of severe financial problems brought on by the recession that began in 2007, the federal government was forced to place both Fannie Mae and Freddie Mac into conservatorship in late 2008. This was essentially a government takeover of both entities, and it will continue until their solvency is restored.

As part of the takeover, Congress also created a new government regulator for the two entities, the Federal Housing Finance Agency (FHFA). Previously, Fannie Mae and Freddie Mac had been supervised by HUD; now Ginnie Mae is the only secondary market entity that HUD has authority over.

Real Estate Finance Documents

Now let's turn to the legal aspects of a real estate finance transaction. Once a buyer has found a lender willing to finance his purchase on acceptable terms, the buyer is required to sign the finance documents. The legal documents used in conjunction with most real estate loans are the promissory note and a security instrument, which is either a mortgage or a deed of trust.

We'll look first at promissory notes, and then at security instruments and foreclosure procedures.

Promissory Notes

A promissory note is a written promise to repay a debt. One person loans another money, and the other signs a promissory note, promising to repay the loan (plus inter-

Fig. 11.3 Promissory note

Promissory Note

FOR VALUE RECEIVED, Maker promises to pay to the order of
____, or to Bearer,

THE SUM OF $__________________________, paid as follows:
$_________ OR MORE per month starting _________________,
including interest at ______% per annum.

ACCELERATION: In the event of default, Payee or Bearer can declare all sums due and payable at once.

____
Maker/Borrower
Date: ________________________

est, in most cases). The borrower who signs the note is called the **maker**, and the lender is called the **payee**. In some states, a bond is used in the place of a promissory note. The basic provisions and rules we will discuss below apply to both notes and bonds.

Basic Provisions. A promissory note states the loan amount (the **principal**), the amount of the payments, when and how the payments are to be made, and the maturity date—when the loan is to be repaid in full.

The note also specifies the interest rate, and whether it is fixed or variable. In many states, the interest rate must not violate the **usury law**. Usury refers to charging an unfairly high interest rate on a loan. To protect consumers, a usury law places a limit on the interest rate lenders may charge on certain types of loans. The maximum rate may be a fixed percentage, or it may be a floating rate, adjusted in response to changes in an economic index.

Naturally, the names of the borrowers will be listed on the promissory note. If each of the borrowers is to be individually liable for the entire loan amount, then the note will state that the borrowers are "jointly and severally" liable for the debt.

A promissory note in a real estate loan transaction does not need to contain a legal description of the property, because the note concerns only the debt, not the property. The legal description is instead included in the security instrument. Because the promissory note does not concern the property, it is ordinarily not recorded.

The note usually explains the consequences of a failure to repay the loan as agreed. Real estate lenders often protect themselves with late charges, acceleration clauses, and similar provisions; these will be discussed later in this chapter.

Types of Notes. There are various types of promissory notes, classified according to the way the principal and interest are paid off. With a **straight note** (also called a **term note**), the periodic payments are interest only payments: they cover the interest that's accruing, but pay back none of the principal. The full amount of the principal is due in a lump sum (called a **balloon payment**) when the loan term ends. With an **installment note**, the periodic payments include part of the principal as well as interest. If the installment note is **fully amortized**, the periodic payments are enough to pay off the entire loan, both principal and interest, by the end of the term. (Amortization is discussed in Chapter 12.)

Whether the payments are interest-only or amortized, the interest paid on a real estate loan is **simple interest**. That means it is computed annually on the remaining principal balance. (This is in contrast to compound interest, which is computed on the principal amount plus the accrued interest.) Since each installment payment on an amortized loan reduces the principal balance, the borrower pays less and less interest over the course of the loan term.

Signing and Endorsing the Note. Though many copies of the note may be prepared, the maker (the borrower) signs only one copy. This is for the maker's protection. A promissory note is usually a **negotiable instrument**, which means the payee (the lender) has the option of assigning the debt to someone else by endorsing the note. (A note is endorsed to transfer the right to payment to another party in the same way that a check is endorsed. A check is another example of a negotiable instrument.) Having only one copy of the note signed by the maker ensures that the payee can assign the note to only one other party. If there were two or three signed copies, it would be possible to assign the note to two or three different parties, so that more than one could demand payment of the same debt from the maker. When the debt is paid off, the signed copy is returned to the maker marked "Paid."

To be negotiable, the note must state that it is payable either "to the order of" someone or "to bearer." To sell the note (at the secondary market level), the payee endorses it to a third party purchaser. If the purchaser buys the note for value, in good faith, and without notice of defenses against it, the purchaser is called a **holder in due course**. If the holder in due course later sues the maker for nonpayment, certain defenses that the maker might have been able to raise against the payee can't be raised against the holder in due course.

If a note is endorsed to a specified person, it is called a special endorsement. Otherwise, the endorsement is said to be "in blank." The payee may also state that the endorsement is **without recourse** (or without warranty). This means that the matter of future payments is strictly between the maker and the third party purchaser; the original payee will not be liable to the holder in due course if the maker fails to pay as agreed. An endorsement without recourse is sometimes called a qualified endorsement.

Security Instruments

When someone borrows money to buy real estate, in addition to signing a promissory note in favor of the lender, he is also required to sign a security instrument. As we said earlier, the security instrument is either a mortgage or a deed of trust.

Relationship between Note and Security Instrument. It's important to understand the relationship between the promissory note and the security instrument. The promissory note is the borrower's binding promise to repay the loan. The security instrument is a contract that makes the real property collateral for the loan; it secures the loan by creating a lien on the property. If the borrower doesn't repay the loan as agreed, the security instrument gives the lender the right to foreclose on the property.

A promissory note can be enforced even if it is not accompanied by a security instrument. If the borrower does not repay as agreed, then the lender can file a lawsuit and obtain a judgment against the defaulting borrower. But without a security instrument, the lender might have no way of collecting the judgment. For example, the borrower may have already sold all of her property, leaving nothing for the lender (now the judgment creditor) to obtain a lien against.

Title Theory vs. Lien Theory. To understand how security instruments work, it's useful to know how they developed. Historically, to protect the lender against default, a real estate borrower was required to transfer title to the property to the lender for the term of the loan. The borrower remained in possession of the property and had the full use of it, but the lender held title until the loan was paid off. If it wasn't paid off as agreed, the lender could take possession of the property.

Fig. 11.4 Purpose of a security instrument

Security Instrument
Mortgage or Deed of Trust

- Makes the borrower's property collateral for the loan
- Gives the lender the power to foreclose if the debt is not paid

This arrangement—in which title to property is given as collateral, but the borrower retains possession—is called **hypothecation**. When title is transferred only as collateral, unaccompanied by possessory rights, it is called legal title, bare title, or naked title. The property rights the borrower retains (without legal title) are referred to as equitable rights or equitable title.

In the United States today, a handful of states still regard the execution of a mortgage or a deed of trust as a transfer of legal title. Those states are called "title theory" states. However, most states now follow "lien theory." According to lien theory, execution of a mortgage or a deed of trust only creates a lien against the property; it does not transfer title. The borrower retains full title to the property throughout the term of the loan, and the lender simply has the right to foreclose the lien if the borrower defaults.

Some states follow "intermediate theory," which mixes title theory and lien theory together. In these states, a mortgage or deed of trust is simply a lien until the borrower defaults. Upon default, the mortgage or deed of trust is governed by title theory.

Today it doesn't make much difference whether a state follows title theory, lien theory, or intermediate theory, in terms of lending and foreclosure procedures; the distinction is more theoretical than practical. Under any of the theories, the borrower will lose the property if the loan is not repaid.

Mortgage vs. Deed of Trust. Now let's consider the two types of real property security instruments: mortgages and deeds of trust. Both are contracts in which a real property owner gives someone else a security interest in the property, usually as collateral for a loan. The most important difference between a mortgage and a deed of trust concerns the procedures for foreclosure if the borrower defaults. We will discuss the foreclosure process later in this chapter.

There are two parties to a mortgage: the **mortgagor** and the **mortgagee**. The mortgagor is the property owner and borrower. The mortgagee is the lender.

A deed of trust (sometimes called a trust deed) has three parties: the **trustor** or **grantor** (the borrower), the **beneficiary** (the lender), and the **trustee**. The trustee is a neutral third party who will handle the foreclosure process, if that proves necessary.

The terminology used in a deed of trust has its roots in title theory. The document itself is called a "deed," and it purports to convey legal title to the trustee. The trustee holds the deed "in trust" pending repayment of the debt. When the loan has been repaid, the trustee "reconveys" legal title to the trustor. Even so, deeds of trust are used in lien theory and intermediate theory states as well as title theory states.

Note that the terms "mortgage" and "mortgage loan" are often used to refer to any type of loan secured by real property, whether the security instrument actually used in the transaction is a mortgage or deed of trust.

Recording. Whether it's a mortgage or a deed of trust, the lender should always record the security instrument immediately after the loan is made. The security instrument does not have to be recorded to create a valid lien on the property, but without recording only the lender and borrower would know the lien exists. Other parties who acquired an interest in the property without notice of the lender's security interest would not be subject to it, and subsequent liens would have priority over the lender's.

Instruments as Personal Property. Note that even though it creates a lien against real property, a mortgage or deed of trust is itself classified as personal property. A promissory note is also personal property.

Assignment. When a lender sells a loan secured by a mortgage or deed of trust to an investor, in addition to endorsing the promissory note, the lender executes a document called an **assignment of mortgage** (or deed of trust).

The investor may request an **offset statement** from the borrower. In an offset statement, the borrower confirms the status of the loan (the interest rate, principal balance, etc.) and describes any claims that could affect the investor's interest. The investor may also obtain a similar statement concerning the loan's status from the lender; this is called a **beneficiary's statement**. In some states, either an offset statement or a beneficiary's statement may be referred to as an **estoppel certificate**.

Personal Property as Collateral. Of course, personal property as well as real property may be used as collateral for a loan. When a borrower transfers possession of an item of personal property to a lender pending repayment of the loan, it is called a **pledge**. Alternatively, the borrower may retain possession of the personal property and give the lender a security interest in it. In that case, the borrower signs a document called a **security agreement**. A security agreement is the equivalent of a mortgage or deed of trust for personal property.

Finance Document Provisions

Next, let's look at key provisions in the legal documents for a real estate loan. Some of these are essential, while others are optional, or used only in certain situations. Some of them may appear in the promissory note as well as, or instead of, the security instrument. And in a few cases (noted below), there's a distinction between the type of provision found in a mortgage and the type found in a deed of trust.

Mortgaging or Granting Clause. Every security instrument is required to include a statement expressing what the instrument is designed to do, indicating that the property is being promised as security for the loan. This is called the mortgaging clause or (in a deed of trust) the granting clause.

Property Description. Like a deed or any other document that transfers an interest in real estate, the security instrument must contain a complete and unambiguous description of the collateral property.

Acceleration Clause. An acceleration clause states that if the borrower defaults, the lender has the option of declaring the entire loan balance (all the principal still owed) due and payable immediately. Sometimes this is referred to as "calling the note." If the borrower fails to pay the balance as demanded, the lender can sue on the note or foreclose the lien.

An acceleration clause is likely to appear in both the promissory note and in the security instrument. Acceleration can be triggered by failure to make loan payments as agreed in the note, or by breach of a provision in the security instrument, such as failure to keep the property insured (see below).

Covenants. A security instrument typically contains a number of covenants (promises) made by the borrower to the lender. With the **covenant to pay taxes**, the borrower promises to pay the general real estate taxes and any special assessments when due. With the **covenant of insurance**, the borrower promises to keep the property insured against damage or destruction. If the borrower were to allow the taxes to become delinquent or the hazard insurance to lapse, the value of the lender's security interest could be severely diminished—by tax lien foreclosure or a fire, for example.

With the **covenant against removal**, the borrower promises not to remove or demolish buildings or other improvements. The **covenant of good repair** requires the borrower to keep the property in good condition, and also authorizes the lender to inspect the property to make sure that it is being properly maintained.

Alienation Clause. An alienation clause is also called a **due-on-sale clause**. This provision gives the lender the right to accelerate the loan—demanding immediate payment of the entire loan balance, as described above—if the borrower sells the property or otherwise alienates an interest in it. (Alienation refers to any transfer of an interest in real estate. See Chapter 4.) An alienation clause does not prohibit the sale of the property, but it allows the lender to force the borrower to pay off the loan if the property is sold without the lender's approval.

Whether or not there is an alienation clause in the mortgage or deed of trust, sale of the property doesn't extinguish the lender's lien. If the loan isn't paid off at closing, the buyer will take title subject to the lien. The buyer may also arrange to assume the loan.

In an **assumption**, the borrower sells the security property to a buyer who agrees to accept legal responsibility for the loan and pay it off according to its terms. The buyer takes on primary liability to the lender for repayment of the loan, but the seller (the original borrower) retains secondary liability in case the buyer defaults.

By contrast, when a buyer takes title subject to an existing mortgage or deed of trust without assuming it, the seller remains fully liable for the debt. The buyer isn't personally liable to the lender, although in case of default the lender can still foreclose on the property.

Even though the sale of the property doesn't extinguish the mortgage or deed of trust lien, lenders prefer to have the opportunity to approve or reject a prospective purchaser. Thus, most mortgages and deeds of trust include an alienation clause. When a lender evaluates a purchaser and concludes that she is creditworthy, the lender may agree to an assumption of the loan. The lender will usually charge an assumption fee, and may also raise the interest rate on the loan. In most cases, the lender will release the original borrower from any further liability; this is called a **novation**.

Late Payment Penalty. If a lender wants to impose a penalty for late payment, the penalty must be clearly defined in the finance documents. Most states place some limitations on late payment penalties; federal law also limits late payment penalties in certain types of loans. For example, a penalty might not be allowed to exceed a certain percentage of the loan's principal balance, and the lender might not be allowed to charge the penalty until the borrower's payment is a certain number of days overdue.

Note that late payment penalties are not considered interest on the loan, so they are not deductible on the borrower's income tax return.

Lock-in Clause. A lock-in clause prohibits the borrower from **prepaying** the loan—paying it off early, before payment is due. The borrower is "locked in" to the loan for the full term or for a specified number of years, so that the lender will not be deprived of interest it expects to collect. Some states do not allow lock-in clauses in loans secured by residential property.

Prepayment Penalty. Under the terms of some loans, the lender may impose a penalty if the borrower prepays all or part of the loan balance. For example, a promissory note might state, "The borrower may prepay up to 15% of the original loan amount during any twelve-month period without penalty. If the borrower prepays more than 15%, a prepayment fee equal to six months' interest on the excess will be charged."

A prepayment penalty is intended to compensate the lender for interest that it expected to collect, but won't be collecting because the borrower is paying the loan off early. The prepayment of a loan without a penalty does not in itself cause a direct loss to the lender, but the lender's profit on the loan will be less than expected.

A lender may be willing to waive a prepayment penalty if market interest rates are high. Under those circumstances, when borrowers prepay their loans, the lender can turn around and lend the same money at a higher rate.

Some states impose specific restrictions on prepayment penalties for certain types of loans. For example, for a home purchase mortgage, a prepayment penalty might not be allowed after the first five years of the loan term. Or a penalty might be allowed only if the loan is paid off with borrowed funds (refinanced).

Loans that will be insured or guaranteed by the federal government (FHA or VA loans, for example) cannot include a prepayment penalty provision, and loans that are going to be sold to Fannie Mae or Freddie Mac also do not ordinarily include one. They are also prohibited in certain high-cost loans. As a result, prepayment penalties are not charged on many home loans made by institutional lenders.

A mortgage loan without a prepayment penalty is sometimes referred to as an **open mortgage**. When prepayment is allowed without penalty, the promissory note usually contains a provision that states that the borrower can make the required payment "or more" on the specified payment date.

Subordination Clause. Occasionally a security instrument includes a subordination clause, which states that the instrument will have lower lien priority than another mortgage or deed of trust to be executed in the future. The clause makes it possible for a later security instrument to assume a higher priority position—usually first lien position—even though this earlier security instrument was executed and recorded first.

Subordination clauses are common in mortgages and deeds of trust that secure purchase loans for unimproved land, when the borrower is planning to get a construction loan later on. The construction lender will demand first lien position for its loan. Lien priority is ordinarily determined by recording date ("first in time is first in right"), but the subordination clause in the earlier land loan allows the later construction loan to have first lien position.

Condemnation Clause. Sometimes a security instrument includes a condemnation clause. If the property is taken in an eminent domain action (see Chapter 6), the condemnation clause gives the lender the right to use all or part of the condemnation award to satisfy the loan.

Assignment of Rents Clause. In mortgages on income-producing property, lenders often enhance their security with an assignment of rents clause. Under this provision, the borrower assigns the rental income generated by the property to the lender in the event of default. If the borrower defaults on the loan, the lender will apply the rents to the loan's principal balance. In some states, the lender must ask a court to appoint a receiver before the lender can begin collecting rents.

Defeasance Clause. A defeasance clause states that when the debt has been paid, the security instrument will be canceled, releasing the property from the lender's claim.

If the security instrument is a deed of trust, the beneficiary (lender) will submit a "request for reconveyance" to the trustee. The trustee will execute and record a **deed of reconveyance**, or reconveyance deed.

If the security instrument is a mortgage, the document that is recorded to remove the mortgage lien is called a **certificate of discharge** or **satisfaction of mortgage**. Either this document or a deed of reconveyance may be referred to as a **lien release**. The document should be recorded to clear the title.

Foreclosure Procedures

If the borrower doesn't repay a secured loan as agreed, the lender may foreclose and collect the debt from the proceeds of a forced sale. Establishing the lender's right to foreclose is the basic purpose of a security instrument.

The forms of foreclosure available to a lender vary from state to state, as do the procedures and rules governing the process. The two main forms of foreclosure are judicial foreclosure and nonjudicial foreclosure. In many states, mortgages are usually foreclosed judicially and deeds of trust are usually foreclosed nonjudicially.

Judicial Foreclosure. As the term suggests, a judicial foreclosure is carried out through the court system. Upon default, the lender files a lawsuit against the borrower in a court in the county where the collateral property is located. If there are any **junior lienholders** (lienholders whose liens have lower priority than the mortgage being foreclosed on), they are also included in the foreclosure action, so that they can take steps to protect their interests. (A junior lienholder may be adversely affected by foreclosure of a senior lien if the sale proceeds aren't sufficient to pay off all of the liens against the property.)

The lender records a **lis pendens**, which is a notice of a pending legal action (in this case, the foreclosure action) that could affect specified real property. A lis pendens makes the final court judgment binding on anyone who might acquire an interest in the property while the foreclosure action is pending.

When the complaint is heard in court, in the absence of unusual circumstances, the judge will issue a **decree of foreclosure**, ordering the property to be sold to satisfy the debt. The judge appoints a receiver to conduct the sale. The sale, which takes the form of a public auction, is often referred to as a **sheriff's sale**.

Reinstatement. In some states, while the foreclosure action is pending, the borrower must be allowed to "cure" the loan default by paying all past due amounts, plus the costs and fees of the lawsuit. In that case, the loan is **reinstated**; the foreclosure proceedings are terminated, and the mortgage continues in full force and effect. Once the decree of foreclosure is issued, this right of reinstatement no longer exists.

Equitable Redemption. Some states do not give the borrower the right to cure the default and have the loan reinstated once the foreclosure action has begun. However, the borrower generally does have the right to stop the foreclosure and **redeem** the property by paying off the entire loan balance, plus interest, costs, and fees. This is called the borrower's **equitable right of redemption**.

Statutory Redemption. In some states, after the sheriff's sale the borrower has a final chance to redeem the property by paying off the entire debt (the unpaid loan balance, interest, costs, and fees). This is called the **statutory right of redemption**. How long the statutory right of redemption exists depends on state law; it might last only one month, or it could last as long as one year. However, if the lender waives the right to a deficiency judgment (discussed below) or is prohibited from obtaining a deficiency judgment, the borrower usually has no right of redemption after the sheriff's sale.

When the property is sold subject to the statutory right of redemption, the successful bidder at the sheriff's sale receives a **certificate of sale** instead of a deed. Depending on state law, the borrower may be entitled to keep possession of the property during the redemption period (provided he pays reasonable rent to the holder of the certificate of sale), or the property may be managed by a receiver. At the end of the redemption period the certificate holder is given a **sheriff's deed**, which transfers title and the right of possession of the property to the new owner.

Credit Bidding. A long redemption period makes bidding at a sheriff's sale unappealing to many investors; understandably, they don't want to wait to gain title to the property. For this reason, a judicial foreclosure sale that will be followed by a long redemption period often attracts no outside bidders, and the lender acquires the property by bidding the amount the borrower owes. This is called **credit bidding**, since the lender doesn't have to pay any cash.

Surplus or Deficiency. If there are outside bidders at the auction and the proceeds from the sale exceed the amount necessary to satisfy all valid liens against the property, the surplus belongs to the borrower.

However, the proceeds of a foreclosure sale are often insufficient to satisfy even the debt owed to the foreclosing lender. In that situation, some states allow the lender to sue the borrower for a **deficiency judgment**. A deficiency judgment is a personal judgment for the difference between the amount owing on the debt and the net proceeds from the foreclosure sale. A court may award a lender a deficiency judgment at the same time the decree of foreclosure is entered, or the lender may have to file a separate action for a deficiency judgment after the foreclosure sale.

Anti-deficiency rules in some states prohibit deficiency judgments in certain circumstances and in connection with certain types of mortgages.

Nonjudicial Foreclosure. A deed of trust includes a special provision called a **power of sale clause**. If the borrower defaults, this provision authorizes the trustee to sell the property through nonjudicial foreclosure, if permitted by state law. To foreclose nonjudicially, it's not necessary to file a foreclosure lawsuit or get a decree of foreclosure from a judge. Instead, the trustee can sell the property at an auction called a **trustee's sale**, then use the sale proceeds to pay off the debt owed to the lender (beneficiary). If the sale results in a surplus, the excess amount belongs to the borrower. The lender may be allowed to credit bid. The successful bidder at a trustee's sale receives a **trustee's deed**.

In some states, a power of sale clause may be included in a mortgage. A mortgage with a power of sale clause can be foreclosed nonjudicially, like a deed of trust.

Notices of Default and Sale. A nonjudicial foreclosure must be conducted in accordance with procedures prescribed by state statute. These procedures require notification of the affected parties (including the borrower and any junior lienholders) that a foreclosure is pending. In many states, the trustee begins by recording a **notice of**

Fig. 11.5 Comparison of judicial and nonjudicial foreclosure

Foreclosure	
Judicial	**Nonjudicial**
• Lender files lawsuit to foreclose • Judge issues decree of foreclosure • Sheriff's sale • Equitable right of redemption before sale • Statutory right of redemption after sale • Deficiency judgment allowed (subject to limitations)	• Notice of default recorded • Notice of sale published • Trustee's sale • Right of reinstatement before sale • No post-sale redemption • No deficiency judgment

default. After a certain period (for example, three months) the trustee records a **notice of sale** and mails copies of the notice to the affected parties. The trustee usually must also publish the notice in a newspaper of general circulation. After the notice has appeared in the paper for a certain number of weeks, the foreclosure sale can take place.

Reinstatement or Redemption. In a nonjudicial foreclosure, the borrower generally has the right to reinstate the loan by paying all past due amounts, plus costs and fees. This right usually lasts until shortly before the scheduled date of the trustee's sale. If the loan is reinstated, the foreclosure proceedings terminate.

Alternatively, the borrower can redeem the property by paying off the entire loan balance, plus costs and fees, at any time prior to the actual sale. After the sale, however, redemption is generally no longer allowed. This is an important distinction between nonjudicial and judicial foreclosure in many states.

Deficiency Judgments. In most states, a lender loses the right to a deficiency judgment by foreclosing nonjudicially; the lender's recovery is limited to the proceeds of the trustee's sale. In states that do permit a deficiency judgment after a trustee's sale, the lender generally must obtain a court order to collect such a judgment.

Comparison of Judicial and Nonjudicial Foreclosure. From a lender's point of view, nonjudicial foreclosure has two main advantages over judicial foreclosure. First, it's often much faster, since court proceedings can be very slow. Second, as we just discussed, there usually isn't a statutory redemption period after the trustee's sale. On the other hand, there's generally no right to a deficiency judgment after a trustee's sale, and that can be very important to a lender. If the sale proceeds are likely to be less than the debt, a lender might choose judicial foreclosure, even if nonjudicial foreclosure would be allowed.

Junior Lienholders. Junior lienholders are generally entitled to notice of a foreclosure, whether it's judicial or nonjudicial. A lienholder who didn't receive proper notice may still have a valid lien against the property after the foreclosure sale.

The lien of a junior lienholder who did receive notice is usually terminated by the foreclosure sale. The junior lienholder may get a share of the sale proceeds, but only if there's money left over after liens with higher priority have been paid off.

Upon receiving notice of a pending foreclosure, a junior lienholder may be able to protect her interest by paying the delinquencies on the senior lien (curing the default) and adding the amount of these payments to the balance due under the junior lien. The junior lienholder may then foreclose on her own lien. A purchaser at a junior lienholder's sale takes title to the property subject to all senior liens.

Strict Foreclosure. Some states permit a form of foreclosure called strict foreclosure. In strict foreclosure, a lender is allowed to acquire title to mortgaged property without a public sale. When the borrower defaults, the lender files a lawsuit and the court establishes a deadline for redemption of the property. If the borrower does not pay off the loan by the deadline, the lender is awarded title to the property. Strict foreclosure is widely used in very few states.

Alternatives to Foreclosure. There are three alternatives to foreclosure for a defaulting homeowner: loan workouts, deeds in lieu of foreclosure, and short sales. A lender might agree to one of these alternatives to save time, money, and aggravation.

Loan Workouts. A loan workout from the lender can sometimes be the simplest way to avoid a foreclosure. Some workouts involve a repayment plan—an adjustment in the repayment schedule, often referred to as a forbearance. The borrower gets extra time to make up a missed payment or is allowed to skip a few payments. (The skipped payments are added on to the repayment period.) If a forbearance wouldn't solve the problem (for instance, if the payment amount is about to increase dramatically, far beyond the borrower's means), the lender may agree to modify the terms of the loan. A **loan modification** might involve changing an ARM to a fixed-rate mortgage (to prevent it from resetting to a higher rate), reducing the interest rate, or reducing the amount of principal owed.

Deed in Lieu of Foreclosure. A defaulting borrower who can't negotiate a loan workout may opt to give the lender a deed in lieu of foreclosure, sometimes called a **deed in lieu**. The deed in lieu transfers title from the borrower to the lender; this satisfies the debt and stops foreclosure proceedings. The borrower will want to make sure that the lender doesn't have the right to sue for a deficiency following the sale.

The lender takes title subject to any other liens that encumber the property. Thus, before accepting a deed in lieu, the lender will determine what other liens have attached to the property since the original loan was made.

Short Sales. Another alternative to foreclosure is a short sale. In a short sale, the owner sells the house for whatever it will bring (something "short" of the amount owed because the home's market value has decreased). The lender receives the sale proceeds and, in return, releases the borrower from the debt. As when arranging a deed in lieu, the borrower will want to avoid the possibility of a deficiency judgment.

The existence of secondary liens won't necessarily prevent a lender from approving a short sale. This is because—unlike with a deed in lieu—the lender isn't taking responsibility for the property or its liens. However, the presence of multiple liens will complicate matters, since all of the lienholders must consent to the sale. The junior lienholders (or creditors) aren't likely to get much if anything from a short sale and may not be willing to approve the transaction. In this situation, a foreclosure may be inevitable.

Foreclosure vs. Bankruptcy. Although they can both happen to a person at the same time, foreclosure and bankruptcy are entirely separate legal procedures. A real property owner who is facing foreclosure is not necessarily also facing bankruptcy. And a property owner can declare bankruptcy without necessarily having his property foreclosed on.

Bankruptcy is a federal court procedure that enables a debtor to reduce, modify, or eliminate debts that have become unmanageable. If a mortgage or deed of trust borrower who is facing foreclosure files for bankruptcy, the foreclosure proceedings are temporarily stayed (put on hold). Any other actions by creditors are also stayed.

There are two types of consumer bankruptcy: Chapter 7 and Chapter 13. (A third type of bankruptcy, Chapter 11, applies only to businesses.) In Chapter 13 bankruptcy, the debtor enters into a repayment plan to partially repay the creditors over five years. The debtor is ordinarily allowed to keep her property.

In Chapter 7 bankruptcy, most of the debtor's obligations are completely discharged. (Certain types of debts, such as child or spousal support and student loans, are non-dischargeable.) In exchange for the discharge, the Chapter 7 debtor is required to surrender all non-exempt property. Household goods and cars are exempt (with certain limits); life insurance, pensions, and public benefits are also exempt.

If the debtor owns a home, the homestead exemption will generally protect at least some of the debtor's equity (see Chapter 5). The exemption amount varies from state to state. If the debtor's equity is less than the applicable exemption amount and the mortgage payments are current, the debtor may be allowed to keep the home. If the debtor's equity is greater than the exemption amount, the home will most likely be sold.

Before a debtor can file for Chapter 7 bankruptcy, a "means test" is applied to determine whether the debtor can afford to pay back a certain amount of the debt. If so, the debtor will be required to file Chapter 13 bankruptcy instead of Chapter 7.

Seller Financing

Most real estate buyers finance their purchases with loans from an institutional lender. But some transactions are financed by the seller; the seller extends credit to the buyer, accepting a downpayment and arranging to be paid over time, instead of requiring full payment at closing. In certain cases, a seller offers more favorable terms than institutional lenders (such as an exceptionally low interest rate), in order to attract a wider range of potential buyers and obtain a higher price for the property.

In a seller-financed transaction, the seller may ask the buyer to execute a mortgage or a deed of trust, just like an institutional lender. This may be called a **purchase money loan**. (We'll discuss that term in the following section of the chapter.)

Sellers also have the option of using a third type of security instrument: the **land contract**, also called a real estate contract, installment sales contract, or contract for deed. The parties to a land contract are the **vendor** (the seller) and the **vendee** (the buyer). The vendee agrees to pay the purchase price (plus interest) in installments over a specified number of years. The vendee takes possession of the property right away, but the vendor retains legal title until the full price has been paid. In the meantime, the vendee has equitable title to the property. When the contract is finally paid off, the vendor delivers the deed to the vendee.

The rights and responsibilities of the buyer and seller under a land contract are discussed in Chapter 8.

Types of Mortgage Loans

There are many types of mortgage loans, loans secured by real property that are used in various circumstances or designed to serve particular functions. In this section, we'll explain some of the types you're most likely to encounter or hear mentioned. Even though we'll generally be referring to these as mortgages or mortgage loans, remember that a deed of trust could be (and in some states usually would be) used instead of a mortgage.

First Mortgage. A first mortgage is simply any security instrument that holds first lien position; it has the highest lien priority. A second mortgage is one that holds second lien position, and so on.

Senior and Junior Mortgages. Any mortgage that has higher lien priority than another is called a senior mortgage in relation to that other one, which is called a junior mortgage. A first mortgage is senior to a second mortgage; a second mortgage is junior to a first mortgage, but senior to a third.

As explained in Chapter 5, lien priority matters in the event of a foreclosure, since the sale proceeds are used to pay off the first lien first. If any money remains, the second lien is paid, then the third, and so on, until the money is exhausted. Obviously, it is much better to be in first lien position than in third.

Purchase Money Mortgage. This term is used in two ways. Sometimes it means any mortgage loan used to finance the purchase of the property that is the collateral for the loan: a buyer borrows money to buy property and gives the lender a mortgage on that same property to secure the loan.

In other cases, "purchase money mortgage" is used more narrowly, to mean a mortgage that a buyer gives to a seller in a seller-financed transaction. Instead of paying the full price in cash at closing, the buyer gives the seller a mortgage on the property and pays the price off in installments. In this situation, the seller is said to "take back" or "carry back" the mortgage.

> **Example:** The sales price is $240,000. The buyer makes a $24,000 downpayment and signs a promissory note and purchase money mortgage in favor of the seller for $216,000. The buyer will pay the seller in monthly installments at 7% interest over 15 years.

In this narrower sense, a purchase money mortgage is sometimes called a **soft money mortgage**, because the borrower receives credit instead of actual cash. If a borrower gives a lender a mortgage and receives cash in return (as with a bank loan), it is called a **hard money mortgage**.

Swing Loan. It often happens that buyers are ready to purchase a new home before they've succeeded in selling their current home. They need funds for their downpayment and closing costs right away, without waiting for the proceeds from the eventual sale of the current home. In this situation, the buyers may be able to obtain a swing loan. A swing loan is usually secured by the property that is for sale, and it will be paid off when that sale closes. A swing loan may also be called a **gap loan** or a **bridge loan**.

Budget Mortgage. The monthly payment on a budget mortgage includes not just principal and interest on the loan, but one-twelfth of the year's property taxes and hazard insurance premiums as well. The lender holds the money in trust and pays the taxes and insurance premiums when due. Many residential loans are secured by budget mortgages. This is the most practical way for lenders to make sure the property taxes and insurance premiums are paid on time.

Package Mortgage. When personal property is sold together with real estate, both the personal property and the real estate may be financed with one loan. This is called a package mortgage. For example, if a buyer bought ovens, freezers, and other equipment along with a restaurant building, the purchase might be financed with a package mortgage.

Construction Loan. A construction loan (sometimes called an **interim loan**) is a temporary loan used to finance the construction of improvements on the land. When the construction is completed, the construction loan is replaced by permanent financing, which is called a **take-out loan**. A lender's promise to make a take-out loan at a later time when the borrower needs it is called a **standby loan commitment**.

Construction loans can be profitable, but they are considered quite risky. Accordingly, lenders charge high interest rates and loan fees on construction loans, and then supervise the progress of the construction. There is always a danger that the borrower will overspend on a construction project and exhaust the loan proceeds before construction is completed. If the borrower cannot afford to finish, the lender is left with a security interest in a partially completed project.

Lenders have devised a variety of plans for disbursement of construction loan proceeds that guard against overspending by the borrower. Perhaps the most common is the **fixed disbursement plan**. This calls for a series of predetermined disbursements, called **obligatory advances**, at various stages of construction. Interest begins to accrue with the first disbursement.

Example: A construction loan agreement stipulates that the lender will release 10% of the proceeds when the project is 20% complete, and thereafter 20% draws will be available whenever construction has progressed another 20% toward completion.

The lender will often hold back 10% or more of the loan proceeds until the period for claiming mechanic's liens has expired, to protect against unpaid liens that could affect the marketability of the property. The construction loan agreement usually states that if a valid mechanic's lien is recorded, the lender may use the undisbursed portion of the loan to pay it off.

Blanket Mortgage. When a borrower mortgages more than one piece of real property as security for a single loan, it is called a blanket mortgage. For example, if one property does not provide sufficient collateral for a loan, another property that the borrower owns may be offered as additional collateral. The borrower will give the lender a blanket mortgage covering both properties.

Blanket mortgages are also used in subdivision development. For instance, a ten-acre parcel subdivided into twenty lots might be used to secure one loan made to the subdivider.

Blanket mortgages usually have a **partial release clause** (also called a partial satisfaction clause, or in a blanket deed of trust, a partial reconveyance clause). This provision requires the lender to release some of the security property from the blanket lien when specified portions of the overall debt have been paid off.

> **Example:** A ten-acre parcel subdivided into twenty lots secures a $1,500,000 loan. After selling one lot for $175,000, the subdivider pays the lender $150,000 and receives a release for the lot that is being sold. The blanket mortgage is no longer a lien against that lot, so the subdivider can convey clear title to the lot buyer.

A release schedule determines how much of the loan must be paid off in order to have a lot released from the blanket lien. The borrower typically has to pay off a larger share of the loan to release the first lots sold than to release the last lots sold. This arrangement helps protect the lender's security interest, since the best lots in a development often sell first.

Note that a mortgage is not the only type of lien that can be a blanket encumbrance. A contractor who provides labor or materials on more than one property owned by the same person can obtain a blanket mechanic's lien.

Participation Mortgage. A participation mortgage allows the lender to participate in the earnings generated by the mortgaged property, usually in addition to collecting interest payments on the principal. In some cases, the lender participates by becoming a part-owner of the property. Participation loans are most common on large commercial projects where the lender is an insurance company or other large investor.

Shared Appreciation Mortgage. Real property ordinarily appreciates (increases in value) over time. Appreciation usually benefits only the property owner, by adding to his equity. With a shared appreciation mortgage, however, the lender is entitled to a specified share of the increase in the property's value. This is sometimes called an **equity sharing** arrangement. (The equity is the difference between the market value of the property and the liens against it.)

Graduated Payment Mortgage. A graduated payment mortgage allows the borrower to make smaller payments at first and gradually step up to larger payments. For example, the payments might increase annually for the first three to five years of the loan, and then remain level for the rest of the loan term. This arrangement can benefit borrowers who expect their earnings to increase during the next few years.

Growing Equity Mortgage. A growing equity mortgage, sometimes called a rapid payoff mortgage, is also beneficial to borrowers whose income is expected to increase. This type of mortgage uses a fixed interest rate throughout its term, but payments will increase according to an index or preset schedule. The amount of the increase is applied directly to the principal balance, thus allowing the borrower to pay off the loan more quickly.

Subprime Mortgage. A subprime mortgage is a loan made to a borrower who wouldn't qualify for an ordinary mortgage loan, perhaps because her credit history or debt-to-income ratio doesn't meet the usual standards, or because she's unable or unwilling to provide the documentation usually required. A subprime lender typically charges higher interest rates and fees to offset the extra risk the loan entails. Subprime lending is discussed in more detail in Chapter 12.

Adjustable-rate Mortgage. The interest rate of an adjustable-rate mortgage, or ARM, may be increased or decreased periodically during the loan term to reflect changes in market interest rates. ARMs are discussed in detail in Chapter 12.

Wraparound Mortgage. A wraparound mortgage is a new mortgage that includes or "wraps around" an existing first mortgage on the property. Wraparounds are generally used only in seller-financed transactions.

> **Example:** A home is being sold for $200,000; there is an existing $80,000 mortgage on the property. Instead of assuming that mortgage, the buyer merely takes title subject to it. The buyer gives the seller a $40,000 downpayment and a second mortgage for the remaining $160,000 of the purchase price. The $160,000 second mortgage is a wraparound mortgage. Each month, the buyer makes a payment on the wraparound to the seller, and the seller uses part of that payment to make the monthly payment on the underlying $80,000 mortgage.

Wraparound financing works only if the underlying loan does not contain an alienation clause (see the discussion earlier in this chapter). Otherwise the lender would require the seller to pay off the underlying loan at the time of sale. A wraparound arrangement should always be designed so that the underlying loan will be paid off before the wraparound, to ensure that the buyer's title will not still be encumbered with the seller's debt after the buyer has paid the full purchase price.

If the security instrument used for this type of financing arrangement is a deed of trust rather than a mortgage, it is called an **all-inclusive trust deed**.

Open-end Mortgage. An open-end mortgage sets a borrowing limit, but allows the borrower to reborrow, when needed, any part of the debt that has been repaid, without having to negotiate a new mortgage. The interest rate on the loan is usually a variable rate that rises and falls with market interest rates.

Home Equity Loan. A borrower can obtain a mortgage loan using the equity in property that she already owns as collateral. This is called an **equity loan**; when the property is the borrower's residence, it's called a **home equity loan**.

Equity, as we said earlier, is the difference between a property's market value and the liens against it. In other words, it's the portion of the property's current value that the owner owns free and clear, which is therefore available to serve as collateral for another loan. A home equity loan is typically a second mortgage; the existing first mortgage is the loan the owner used to purchase the property.

Sometimes a home equity loan is used to finance remodeling or other improvements to the property. In other cases, it's used for expenses unrelated to the property, such as a major purchase, college tuition, medical bills, or to pay off credit cards. The interest rate on the home equity loan is often much lower than the rate on the credit cards, and the interest on the loan is usually tax-deductible, whereas the credit card interest is not. (Mortgage interest is currently the only type of interest on consumer debt that is deductible. See Chapter 15.)

Instead of having to apply for a home equity loan when they need money for a particular purpose, some homeowners have a **home equity line of credit** (or **HELOC**) that they can draw on when the need arises. This works in much the same way as a credit card—with a credit limit and minimum monthly payments—except that the debt is automatically secured by the borrower's home. A HELOC is a revolving credit account, in contrast to a home equity loan, which is an installment loan with regular payments made over a certain term.

Reverse Mortgage. A reverse mortgage, sometimes called a reverse annuity mortgage or reverse equity mortgage, is designed to provide income to older homeowners. The owner borrows against the home's equity but will receive a monthly check from the lender, rather than making monthly payments. Typically, a reverse mortgage borrower must be over a certain age (for example, 62 or 65) and must own the home with little or no outstanding mortgage balance. The home usually must be sold when the owner dies in order to pay back the mortgage.

Refinancing. Borrowers who refinance their mortgage are actually obtaining an entirely new mortgage loan to replace the existing one. The funds from the refinance loan are used to pay off the existing loan.

Refinancing may be obtained from the same lender that made the existing loan, or from a different lender. Borrowers often choose to refinance when market interest rates drop; refinancing at a lower interest rate can result in substantial savings over the long run. Another situation in which borrowers are likely to refinance is when the payoff date of the existing mortgage is approaching and a large balloon payment will be required.

In some cases, borrowers get a refinance loan for more than the amount needed to pay off their existing loan, so that they also receive cash from the transaction. This is called **cash-out refinancing**. Depending on the terms of the refinance loan, the additional funds might be used for property improvements, debt consolidation, or other purposes.

Chapter Summary

1. The federal government influences real estate finance directly and indirectly through its fiscal and monetary policy. The federal deficit may affect the availability of investment funds. The Federal Reserve Board uses key interest rates, reserve requirements, and open market operations to implement monetary policy, influencing the pace of economic growth and market interest rates.

2. In the primary market, lenders make mortgage loans to borrowers. In the secondary market, mortgages are bought and sold by investors. The federal government created the major secondary market entities (Fannie Mae, Freddie Mac, Ginnie Mae, and Farmer Mac) to help moderate local real estate cycles.

3. A promissory note is a written promise to repay a debt. For a real estate loan, the borrower is required to sign a negotiable promissory note along with a security instrument, which makes the borrower's property collateral for the loan. The two main types of security instruments are mortgages and deeds of trust.

4. The provisions that will or may be found in a security instrument include a mortgaging or granting clause, a description of the property serving as collateral for the loan, a provision concerning taxes and insurance, an acceleration clause, an alienation clause, a late payment penalty provision, a lock-in clause, a prepayment penalty provision, and/or a subordination clause. If the security instrument doesn't include an alienation clause, the loan may be assumed without the lender's permission.

5. In a judicial foreclosure, the lender files a lawsuit and the court issues a decree of foreclosure. There is an equitable right of redemption before the sheriff's sale, and there may be a statutory right of redemption for a certain period afterwards. The lender may be entitled to a deficiency judgment.

6. A power of sale clause allows a deed of trust to be foreclosed nonjudicially by the trustee. Until shortly before the trustee's sale, the borrower generally has the right to cure the default and reinstate the loan. After the sale, the borrower usually has no right of redemption, and the lender usually cannot obtain a deficiency judgment. Nonjudicial foreclosure is faster and less expensive than judicial foreclosure.

7. There are many different types of mortgage loans, including purchase money, swing, budget, package, construction, blanket, participation, shared appreciation, graduated payment, growing equity, subprime, adjustable-rate, wraparound, open-end, home equity, reverse, and refinance mortgages.

Key Terms

Federal Reserve Board—The body that regulates commercial banks and sets and implements the federal government's monetary policy; commonly called "the Fed."

Discount rate and federal funds rate—Two interest rates controlled by the Fed that have an effect on market interest rates.

Reserve requirements—The percentages of deposits commercial banks must keep on reserve with a Federal Reserve Bank.

Open market operations—The Fed's activities in buying and selling government securities.

Primary market—The finance market in which loans are originated, where lenders make loans to borrowers.

Secondary market—The finance market in which mortgages are bought and sold as investments.

Mortgage-backed securities—Investment instruments issued by a secondary market entity, with mortgage loans as collateral.

Promissory note—A written promise to repay a debt.

Security instrument—A document in which a real property owner grants a security interest to a lender, making the property collateral for a loan.

Mortgage—A two-party security instrument that gives the lender (mortgagee) the right to foreclose on the security property by judicial process if the borrower (mortgagor) defaults.

Deed of trust—A three-party security instrument that includes a power of sale clause, allowing the trustee to foreclose nonjudicially if the borrower (trustor) fails to pay the lender (beneficiary) or otherwise defaults.

Acceleration clause—A provision in loan documents that gives the lender the right to demand immediate payment in full if the borrower defaults.

Alienation clause—A provision in a security instrument that gives the lender the right to accelerate the loan if the borrower transfers the property. Also called a due-on-sale clause.

Assumption—When a borrower sells the security property to a buyer who agrees to take on personal liability for repayment of the existing mortgage or deed of trust.

Defeasance clause—A provision giving the borrower the right to regain title to the security property when the debt is repaid.

Certificate of discharge—The document a mortgagee gives to the mortgagor when the mortgage debt is paid off, releasing the property from the lien. Also called a satisfaction of mortgage.

Deed of reconveyance—The document a trustee gives the trustor when the debt secured by a deed of trust is paid off, releasing the property from the lien.

Land contract—A contract between a seller (vendor) and a buyer (vendee) of real estate, in which the seller retains legal title to the property while the buyer pays off the purchase price in installments.

Chapter Quiz

1. In a tight money market, when business is slow, a reduction in interest rates would be expected to cause:
   a) an increase in real estate sales
   b) more bank lending activity
   c) increased business activity
   d) All of the above

2. Which of the following actions by the Federal Reserve Board would tend to increase the money supply?
   a) Selling government securities on the open market
   b) Buying government securities on the open market
   c) Increasing the federal discount rate
   d) Increasing reserve requirements

3. Funds for single-family mortgage loans are supplied by:
   a) Fannie Mae
   b) savings and loan associations
   c) Both a) and b)
   d) Neither a) nor b)

4. With an installment note, the periodic payments:
   a) include both principal and interest
   b) are interest only
   c) are principal only
   d) are called balloon payments

5. A mortgage loan provision that permits the lender to declare the entire loan balance due upon default by the borrower is a/an:
   a) acceleration clause
   b) escalator clause
   c) forfeiture clause
   d) subordination clause

6. A mortgage loan provision that permits the lender to declare the entire loan balance due if the property is sold is a/an:
   a) escalator clause
   b) subordination clause
   c) alienation clause
   d) prepayment provision

7. After a sheriff's sale, the mortgagor often has a specified period in which to redeem the property. This period is called the:
   a) lien period
   b) equitable redemption period
   c) statutory redemption period
   d) reinstatement period

8. After a trustee's sale, if there are any sale proceeds left over after paying off liens and foreclosure expenses, the money belongs to the:
   a) sheriff
   b) beneficiary
   c) trustee
   d) foreclosed owner

9. The document that a mortgagee gives a mortgagor after the debt has been completely paid off is called a:
   a) partial release
   b) certificate of discharge
   c) deed of reconveyance
   d) sheriff's deed

10. In a nonjudicial foreclosure, the borrower is generally entitled to:
    a) a statutory redemption period following the sheriff's sale
    b) a deficiency judgment
    c) a deed in lieu of foreclosure
    d) cure the default and reinstate the loan until shortly before the trustee's sale

11. When a buyer gives a mortgage to the seller rather than an institutional lender, it may be referred to as a:
    a) purchase money mortgage
    b) land contract
    c) shared appreciation mortgage
    d) reverse equity mortgage

12. A budget mortgage:
    a) is a loan made to a low-income borrower
    b) is a construction loan with a fixed disbursement plan
    c) is secured by personal property as well as real property
    d) has monthly payments that include taxes and insurance as well as principal and interest

13. The owner of five parcels of real property wants a loan. She offers all five parcels as security. She will be required to execute a:
    a) soft money mortgage
    b) participation mortgage
    c) package mortgage
    d) blanket mortgage

14. Victor is borrowing money to buy some land, and he plans to build a home on the property later on. To ensure that he will be able to get a construction loan when the time comes, Victor should make sure the mortgage he executes for the land loan includes a/an:
    a) lien waiver
    b) subordination clause
    c) acceleration clause
    d) wraparound clause

15. Under a fixed disbursement plan for a construction loan, the contractor is usually entitled to her final draw when:
    a) the project has been satisfactorily completed
    b) 80% of the work has been completed
    c) the building department issues a certificate of occupancy
    d) the period for claiming mechanic's liens expires

Answer Key

1. d) The Fed lowers interest rates in times of economic downturn in an attempt to stimulate the economy.

2. b) When the Fed buys government securities, it puts more money into circulation, which increases the money supply.

3. c) Mortgage money comes from the primary market (in the form of savings deposits) and from the secondary market (when investors like Fannie Mae buy mortgages).

4. a) An installment note involves periodic payments that include some of the principal as well as interest.

5. a) An acceleration clause gives the lender the right to declare the entire debt immediately due and payable if the borrower defaults.

6. c) An alienation clause allows the lender to accelerate the loan if the borrower transfers the security property without the lender's approval.

7. c) A statutory redemption period is a period of time after a sheriff's sale in which the borrower has the right to redeem the property by paying off the entire debt, plus costs.

8. d) Any excess proceeds from a foreclosure sale belong to the borrower—that is, to the foreclosed owner.

9. b) When the debt has been fully paid off, a mortgagee gives the mortgagor a certificate of discharge, releasing the property from the lien.

10. d) In the nonjudicial foreclosure of a deed of trust, the trustor is generally permitted to cure the default and reinstate the loan until shortly before the trustee's sale is held.

11. a) A mortgage given by a buyer to a seller is sometimes called a purchase money mortgage.

12. d) A budget mortgage payment includes a share of the property taxes and hazard insurance as well as principal and interest.

13. d) A blanket mortgage has more than one parcel of property as collateral.

14. b) A subordination clause in the mortgage for the land loan would give it lower priority than a mortgage executed later on for a construction loan. Lenders generally require first lien position for construction loans, because they are considered especially risky.

15. d) Construction lenders usually delay the final disbursement until no more mechanic's liens can be filed.

Chapter 12

Applying for a Mortgage Loan

Chapter Overview

When it's time to arrange financing, a home buyer must shop for a loan, choose a lender, and fill out a loan application. Then the lender will evaluate the application and decide whether or not to approve the loan. The first part of this chapter describes the different types of lenders in the primary market, explains loan fees, and discusses the Truth in Lending Act, a law that helps prospective borrowers compare loans. The next section covers the loan application form and the underwriting process. The section after that describes various features of a home purchase loan and provides an overview of the major residential finance programs. The chapter ends with a discussion of the problem of predatory lending.

Choosing a Lender

Many home buyers look to their real estate agent for guidance in choosing a lender. Agents should be familiar with the lenders in their area and know how to help buyers compare the loans that different lenders are offering. We're going to discuss the various types of lenders that make home purchase loans, the fees that lenders charge, and the Truth in Lending Act.

Types of Mortgage Lenders

Most home buyers finance their purchase with a loan from one of these sources of residential financing:

- commercial banks,
- thrift institutions,
- credit unions, and
- mortgage companies.

At one time, financial institutions in the United States were quite specialized. Each type of institution served a different function; each had its own types of services and its own types of loans. In recent decades, federal deregulation of depository institutions removed many of the restrictions that differentiated them. To a great extent, all depository institutions can now be regarded as "financial supermarkets," offering a wide range of services and loans—including residential mortgage loans.

There still are differences between the various types of mortgage lenders, in terms of lending practices and government regulations. Those differences don't necessarily affect a loan applicant who wants to finance the purchase of a home, however. A home buyer decides between two lenders because of the types of loans they're offering, the interest rates and fees they're charging, and the quality of service they provide, not because one is a savings and loan and the other is a mortgage company. Even so, it's worthwhile to have a general understanding of the different types of mortgage lenders.

Commercial Banks. A commercial bank is either a national bank, chartered (authorized to do business) by the federal government, or a state bank, chartered by a state government. Commercial banks are the largest source of investment funds in the United States. As their name implies, they were traditionally oriented toward commercial lending activities, supplying short-term loans for business ventures and construction activities.

In the past, residential mortgages weren't a major part of commercial banks' business. That was partly because most of their customer deposits were demand deposits, subject to withdrawal on short notice or without notice, like the money in checking accounts. So the government limited the amount of long-term investments commercial banks could make. But eventually banks began accepting more and more long-term deposits; demand deposits now represent a considerably smaller share of banks' total deposits than they did at one time.

While banks have continued to emphasize commercial loans, they have also diversified their lending, with a substantial increase in personal loans and home mortgages, especially to already-existing customers. They now have a significant share of the residential finance market.

Thrift Institutions. Savings and loan associations and savings banks are often grouped together and referred to as thrift institutions, or thrifts. Like commercial banks, thrifts are chartered by either the federal government or a state government.

Savings and Loans. Savings and loans (S&Ls) started out in the nineteenth century strictly as residential real estate lenders. Over the years they carried on their original function, investing the majority of their assets in purchase loans for single-family homes. By the mid-1950s, they dominated local residential mortgage markets, becoming the nation's largest single source of funds for financing homes.

Many factors contributed to the dominance of savings and loans. One of the most important was that home purchase loans had become long-term loans (often with 30-year terms). S&Ls used the savings deposits of their customers as their main source of loan funds. Since most of the funds held by S&Ls were long-term deposits, S&Ls were comfortable making long-term home loans.

While savings and loans are involved in other types of lending, home mortgage loans remain their main focus. However, due to the increasing involvement of other types of lenders, S&Ls no longer dominate the residential finance market.

Savings Banks. Like S&Ls, savings banks also got their start in the nineteenth century. They offered financial services to small depositors, especially immigrants and members of the working class. They were called mutual savings banks (MSBs) because they were organized as mutual companies, owned by and operated for the benefit of their depositors (as opposed to stockholders).

Traditionally, MSBs were similar to savings and loans. They served their local communities. Their customers were individuals rather than businesses, and most of their deposits were savings deposits. Although the MSBs made many residential mortgage loans, they didn't concentrate on them to the extent that S&Ls did. The MSBs were also involved in other types of lending, such as personal loans.

Today savings banks can be organized as mutual companies or stock companies. Residential mortgages continue to be an important part of their business.

Credit Unions. Credit unions are depository institutions, like banks and thrifts. But unlike banks and thrifts, credit unions often serve only members of a particular group, such as the members of a union or a professional association, or the employees of a large company.

Credit unions traditionally provided small personal loans to their members. In recent years, many credit unions have emphasized home equity loans. (A home equity loan is a mortgage on the borrower's equity in the home she already owns. See Chapter 9.) Now many credit unions also make home purchase loans.

Mortgage Companies. Unlike banks, thrifts, and credit unions, mortgage companies aren't depository institutions, so they don't lend out depositors' funds. Instead, they often act as **loan correspondents**, intermediaries between large investors and home buyers applying for financing.

A loan correspondent lends an investor's money to buyers and then **services** the loans (collecting and processing the loan payments on behalf of the investor) in exchange for servicing fees. Banks and thrifts sometimes act as loan correspondents, but mortgage companies have specialized in this role.

Mortgage companies frequently act on behalf of large investors such as life insurance companies and pension funds. These investors control vast amounts of capital in the form of insurance premiums and employer contributions to employee pensions. This money generally isn't subject to sudden withdrawal, so it's well suited to investment in long-term mortgages. Since these large investors typically operate on a national scale, they have neither the time nor the resources to understand the particular risks of local real estate markets or to deal with the day-to-day management of their loans. So instead of making loans directly to borrowers, insurance companies, pension plans, and other large investors often hire local loan correspondents. They generally prefer large, long-term commercial loans and stay away from high-risk, short-term construction loans.

Mortgage companies also borrow money from banks on a short-term basis and use the money to make (or **originate**) loans, which they then package and sell to the secondary market agencies and other private investors. Using short-term financing to make loans before selling them to permanent investors is referred to as **warehousing**.

Banks and thrifts generally keep some of the loans they make "in portfolio," instead of selling them to investors. In contrast, mortgage companies don't keep any of the loans they make. The loans are either made on behalf of an investor or else sold to an investor. In many cases, insurance companies, pension funds, and other large investors now simply buy loans from mortgage companies instead of using them as loan correspondents.

The number of mortgage companies increased rapidly during the 1990s, and they eventually came to dominate the residential finance market as savings and loans once had. Mortgage companies played a major role in the subprime lending boom, and recent problems in the subprime market have had a greater impact on mortgage companies than on other types of residential lenders, diminishing their market share. (Subprime lending is discussed later in this chapter.)

Mortgage companies are sometimes called **mortgage bankers**. Traditionally, a distinction was made between mortgage bankers and mortgage brokers. A **mortgage**

broker simply negotiated loans, bringing borrowers together with lenders in exchange for a commission. Once a loan had been arranged, the mortgage broker's involvement ended. In contrast, a mortgage banker actually made loans (using an investor's funds or borrowed funds), sold or delivered the loans to an investor, and then (in many cases) serviced the loans to the end of their terms, in exchange for servicing fees. As a result of changes in the mortgage industry, there is no longer a clear-cut distinction between these two roles, and the more general term "mortgage company" is typically used instead of "mortgage banker" in most contexts.

Other Sources of Financing. Real estate limited partnerships, real estate investment trusts (see Chapter 3), and other types of private investment groups put a great deal of money into real estate. They often finance large residential developments and commercial ventures such as shopping centers and office buildings. They do not offer loans to individual home buyers, however.

Aside from the institutional mortgage lenders we've already discussed, the most important source of residential financing is the home seller. Sometimes sellers provide all of the financing for the purchase of their homes, and it's quite common for sellers to supplement the financing their buyers obtain from an institutional lender. In fact, sellers are the most common source of second (junior) mortgages for home purchases. Sellers are an especially important source of financing when institutional loans are hard to come by or market interest rates are high.

Loan Costs

For the majority of buyers, the primary consideration in choosing a lender is how much the loan they need is going to cost. While the interest rate has the greatest impact, lenders impose other charges that can greatly affect the cost of a loan. Most important among these are origination fees and discount points. Both are often simply grouped together as "points." The term "point" is short for "percentage point." A **point** is one percentage point (one percent) of the loan amount. For example, on a $90,000 loan, one point would be $900; six points would be $5,400.

Origination Fees. Processing loan applications and making loans is often called loan origination. A loan origination fee is designed to pay administrative costs the lender incurs in processing a loan; it is sometimes called a service fee, an administrative charge, or simply a loan fee. An origination fee is charged in virtually every residential loan transaction. It is ordinarily paid by the buyer.

> **Example:** The buyer's loan amount is $100,000, and the lender is charging 1.5 points (1.5% of the loan amount) as an origination fee. The buyer will pay this $1,500 fee to the lender in order to obtain the loan.

Discount Points. Discount points are used to increase the lender's upfront yield, or profit, on the loan. By charging discount points, the lender not only gets interest throughout the loan term, it collects an additional sum of money up front, when the loan is funded. As a result, the lender is willing to make the loan at a lower interest rate than it would have without the discount points. In effect, the lender is paid a lump sum at closing so the borrower can avoid paying more interest later. A lower interest rate also translates into a lower monthly payment.

Discount points aren't charged in all residential loan transactions, but they're quite common. The number of discount points charged depends partly on how the loan's interest rate compares to market interest rates. Typically, a lender offering an especially low rate charges more points to make up for it.

> **Example:** A lender analyzes market conditions and determines that it would currently take approximately six discount points to increase the lender's yield on a 30-year loan by 1%. Based on that estimate, the lender offers borrowers an interest rate 1% below market but charges six discount points to make up the difference. The lender would charge borrowers three points if they want a rate that's 0.5% below market, or nine points for a rate that's 1.5% below market.

As the example suggests, the number of discount points required to increase a lender's yield on a loan by one percentage point varies depending on market conditions, the length of the loan term, and other factors. To find out exactly how many points a particular lender will charge for a specified interest rate reduction in the current market, it's necessary to ask the lender.

In some cases, the seller is willing to pay the discount points on the buyer's loan in order to help the buyer qualify for financing. Even when the lender isn't charging discount points, the seller may offer to pay points to make the loan more affordable. This type of arrangement is called a **buydown**: the seller pays the lender points to "buy down" the interest rate on the buyer's loan.

Rate Lock-ins. A prospective borrower may want to have the interest rate quoted by the lender "locked in" for a specified period. Unless the interest rate is locked in, the lender can change it at any time until the transaction closes. If market interest rates are rising, the lender is likely to increase the interest rate on the loan. That could cost the borrower a lot of money over the long term, or else actually price the borrower out of the transaction altogether.

On the other hand, locking in the interest rate is generally not desirable when market interest rates are expected to go down. A lender will typically charge the borrower the locked-in rate even if market rates drop in the period before closing.

Most lenders charge the borrower a fee to lock in the interest rate. The fee is typically applied to the borrower's closing costs if the transaction closes. If the lender rejects the borrower's application, the fee is refunded; it will be forfeited to the lender, though, if the borrower withdraws from the transaction.

Truth in Lending Act

An origination fee, discount points, and other charges may increase the cost of a mortgage loan significantly. They also make it more difficult to compare the cost of loans offered by different lenders. For example, suppose one lender charges 7% interest, a 1% origination fee, and no discount points, while another charges 6.75%

interest, a 1% origination fee, and two discount points. It isn't easy to tell at a glance which of these loans will cost the borrower more in the long term. (The second loan is just slightly less expensive.)

The Truth in Lending Act (TILA) is a federal consumer protection law that addresses this problem of comparing loan costs. The act requires lenders to disclose the complete cost of credit to consumer loan applicants, and also regulates the advertisement of consumer loans. The Truth in Lending Act is implemented by **Regulation Z**, a regulation adopted by the Federal Reserve Board. The requirements of TILA and Regulation Z are enforced by the Consumer Financial Protection Bureau.

Loans Covered by TILA. A loan is a **consumer loan** if it is used for personal, family, or household purposes. A consumer loan is covered by the Truth in Lending Act if it is to be repaid in more than four installments, or is subject to finance charges, and is either:

- for $53,500 or less (as of 2014; the dollar figure is adjusted annually, based on the Consumer Price Index), or
- secured by real property.

Thus, any mortgage loan is covered by the Truth in Lending Act as long as the proceeds are used for personal, family, or household purposes (such as buying a home or sending children to college).

Loans Exempt from TILA. The Truth in Lending Act applies only to loans made to natural persons, so loans made to corporations or organizations aren't covered. Loans for business, commercial, or agricultural purposes are also exempt. So are loans in excess of the dollar amount shown above, unless the loan is secured by real property. (Real estate loans for personal, family, or household purposes are covered regardless of the loan amount.) Most seller financing is exempt, because extending credit isn't in the seller's ordinary course of business.

Disclosure Requirements. In transactions that are subject to TILA, lenders are required to give loan applicants a disclosure statement with comprehensive information about the proposed financing. (An example is shown in Figure 13.1.) Two especially important figures on the disclosure statement are the total finance charge and the annual percentage rate.

The **total finance charge** is the sum of all fees and charges the borrower pays in connection with the loan. In addition to the interest on the loan, any of the following that are going to be paid by the borrower would be included in the total finance charge: origination fee, discount points, finder's fee, service fees, mortgage insurance premiums, or a mortgage broker's compensation.

In real estate loan transactions, appraisal fees, credit report charges, inspection fees, and title insurance fees are not included in the total finance charge. Also, any charges that will be paid by someone other than the borrower—points paid by the seller, for example—are not included.

The **annual percentage rate** (APR) expresses the total cost of the loan as an annual percentage of the loan amount. This key figure enables a prospective borrower

Fig. 12.1 Truth in Lending Act disclosure form

TRUTH-IN-LENDING DISCLOSURE STATEMENT
REQUIRED BY FEDERAL RESERVE REGULATION Z

BORROWER(S)	DATE 19	LOAN NUMBER
	TYPE OF LOAN	LOAN TERM YEARS
	PROPERTY LOCATION	

ANNUAL PERCENTAGE RATE	FINANCE CHARGE	AMOUNT FINANCED	TOTAL OF PAYMENTS
The cost of your credit as a yearly rate	The dollar amount your credit will cost you	The amount of credit provided to you or on your behalf	The amount you will have paid after you have paid all payments as scheduled
%	$	$	$

Notice to Borrower(s): In compliance with Truth-In-Lending Law you are receiving a Good Faith Estimate of Settlement Charges in lieu of an itemization statement.

Your Payment Schedule will be:

Monthly Beginning

Date

Number of Payments	Amount of Payments	When Payments Are Due	Number of Payments	Amount of Payments	When Payments Are Due
	$			$	
	$			$	
	$			$	
	$			$	

☐ This loan has a **Demand Feature.**
☐ Your loan contains a **Variable Rate Feature.** Disclosures about the Variable Rate have been provided to you earlier.
Your ARM Loan ☐ has ☐ does not have a **Conversion Feature.** (The option to convert your ARM loan to a Fixed Rate Mortgage loan.) If choose to convert to a Fixed Rate mortgage loan, your new interest rate will not be higher than ______ %, which is the Maximum Rate.
☐ **Variable Rate not applicable.**
☐ **Insurance:** The following insurance is required: ☐ Property Insurance ☐ Flood Insurance
You may obtain insurance from an agent of your choice, provided they are acceptable to this lender.
☐ Property Insurance is available through the lender at a cost of $______ for a one year term.
☐ Flood Insurance is available through the lender at a cost of $______ for a one year term.
☐ Credit Life Insurance or Disability Insurance are not required.
☐ Credit Life Insurance and/or Disability Insurance are not provided.
☐ Credit Life Insurance and/or Disability Insurance are not available through this lender.
☐ Credit Life is available at a cost of $______ for a ______ term. (X ______)
☐ Disability Insurance is available at a cost of $______ for a ______ term. (X ______)

Security: You are giving a Security Interest ☐ in the property being purchased ☐ other accounts you have with us
other (describe) ______

Late Charge: If your payment is ______ days late, you will be required to pay a Penalty charge of ______% of your payment.

Prepayment: If you pay this loan early, you ☐ will ☐ will not have to pay a penalty
and you ☐ may ☐ will not be entitled to a refund of a part of the finance charge.

Assumption: Someone buying your property ☐ may, subject to conditions ☐ may not assume the remainder of your loan on the Original terms.

☐ This is an assumption of an existing loan. The interest rate for the term of the loan will not exceed ______%, which is the maximum rate.
☐ Filing Fees $______

☐ This is an **Early Disclosure** and all dates and numerical disclosures are estimates except for late payment disclosures.
☐ This is your **Final Disclosure**

NOTE: See your contract documents for any additional information about nonpayment, default, any required repayment in full before the scheduled date and prepayment refunds and penalties.

(e) means an-estimate

I/we acknowledge receipt of a completed copy of this disclosure statement.

X ______ Date ______ 19 ____ X ______
Borrower *Co-Borrower*

to compare loans much more accurately than the interest rate alone. The APR is sometimes referred to as the effective rate of interest, as opposed to the nominal rate (the interest rate stated on the face of the promissory note).

In addition to the APR and the total finance charge, the disclosure statement must list the amount financed, the number of loan payments, the payment amount(s), when payments are due, and other information, such as whether the borrower will be charged a prepayment penalty if the loan is paid off early.

Timing of Disclosures. When a lender receives a written application for a consumer loan that would be secured by the borrower's dwelling—whether it would be a purchase loan, a home equity loan, or refinancing—the lender must give the applicant a TILA disclosure statement at the time of application, or deliver or mail it to her within three business days. The disclosure statement must contain good faith estimates of the loan costs. Until this requirement has been fulfilled, the lender is not allowed to charge the applicant any fees, except a fee for obtaining her credit report.

Mortgage loan applicants must receive the TILA disclosure statement at least seven business days before closing, so that they have time to consider the information provided. The lender may not impose any loan fees on the borrower before the borrower has received the disclosure statement, except the fee for obtaining the borrower's credit report. And if any of the original estimates turn out to be inaccurate, the lender must provide corrected information at least three business days before closing.

Right of Rescission. The Truth in Lending Act provides for a right of rescission in connection with certain types of mortgage loans. When the security property is the borrower's existing principal residence, the borrower may rescind the loan agreement up until three days after signing it, receiving the disclosure statement, or receiving notice of the right of rescission, whichever comes latest. If the borrower never receives the disclosure statement or the notice, the right of rescission does not expire for three years.

The right of rescission applies only to home equity loans and to refinancing with a new lender. There is no right of rescission for a loan financing the purchase or construction of the borrower's residence, or for refinancing if the loan is from the same lender that made the loan it's replacing, unless that lender is advancing additional funds (beyond the original loan amount). In that case, the right of rescission applies only to the additional amount.

Advertising Under TILA. The Truth in Lending Act strictly controls advertising of credit terms. Its advertising rules apply to anyone who advertises consumer credit, not just to lenders. For example, a real estate broker advertising financing terms for a listed home has to comply with TILA and Regulation Z.

It is always legal to state the cash price or the annual percentage rate in an ad. But if the ad contains certain loan terms known as **triggering terms** (the downpayment amount or percentage, the repayment period or number of payments, the amount of any payment, or the amount of any finance charge), then the rest of the terms of repayment must also be disclosed. For example, if an ad says, "Assume VA loan for only $950 a month," it will violate the Truth in Lending Act if it does not go on to reveal the APR, the downpayment, the number of payments, the payment amount(s), and when payments are due. However, general statements such as "low monthly payment," "easy terms," or "affordable interest rate" do not trigger the full disclosure requirement.

Mortgage Acts and Practices Rule

The Mortgage Acts and Practices Rule is a federal regulation, enacted in 2011, that is intended to limit deceptive mortgage advertising. The rule, also known as the Consumer Financial Protection Bureau's Regulation N, explains what constitutes a deceptive advertisement. It also allows the Federal Trade Commission, Consumer Financial Protection Bureau, and state agencies to establish civil penalties for using deceptive ads.

Anyone involved in advertising of mortgages must also comply with recordkeeping requirements. Marketing materials, training materials, sales scripts, and other communications that describe mortgage products must be retained for at least two months.

The Mortgage Acts and Practices Rule applies to all entities who may advertise mortgages, except for banks and other financial institutions that are exempt from Federal Trade Commission oversight. For instance, the Rule applies to real estate agents and brokers, in addition to mortgage brokers and servicers.

Loan Application and Underwriting

Once a buyer has compared loan costs and selected a lender, the next step is applying for the loan. The buyer fills out a loan application form and provides the lender with supporting documentation. The application is submitted to the lender's underwriting department, which evaluates the application and ultimately approves or rejects the proposed loan.

Preapproval

Traditionally, buyers would first find the house that they wanted and then apply for a loan. Now, however, getting **preapproved** for a mortgage loan has become a common practice. To get preapproved, a prospective buyer submits a loan application to a lender before starting to house-hunt. If the lender approves the application, the buyer is preapproved for a specified maximum loan amount.

Preapproval lets the buyer know in advance, before shopping, just how expensive a house she can afford. If a house meets the lender's standards and is in the established price range, the buyer will be able to buy it. This spares the buyer the disappointment of initially choosing a house that turns out to be too expensive and having the loan request turned down. Preapproval also helps streamline the closing process once the buyer has found the right house.

Computerized Loan Origination Systems

A real estate agent may help buyers apply for financing right in the agent's office using a **computerized loan origination system** (CLO). A CLO allows a buyer to compare the rates and fees of different lenders and submit a loan application electronically. A CLO may provide instant feedback, indicating whether or not the buyer is likely to qualify for the loan applied for. This preliminary assessment is typically followed up with a firm acceptance or rejection within a few days.

A real estate agent's use of a CLO must comply with state laws concerning mortgage loan brokerage; there may be licensing requirements, disclosure requirements, and fee restrictions. Also, the agent's business relationship with the lenders involved in the CLO must not run afoul of the Real Estate Settlement Procedures Act, which has rules concerning referral fees (kickbacks) and controlled business arrangements. (RESPA is covered in Chapter 14.)

The Application Form

Whether it's done on a computer screen or on paper, a buyer is required to fill out a mortgage loan application form. The application form asks the prospective borrower for detailed information about his finances. The lender requires this information because it wants its loans to be profitable investments. A loan is unlikely to be profitable if the borrower doesn't have the financial resources to make the payments reliably, or if the borrower has a habit of defaulting on debts. The application helps the lender identify and turn down potential borrowers who are likely to create collection problems.

Most mortgage lenders use the Uniform Residential Loan Application form developed by Fannie Mae and Freddie Mac. The form requires all of the following information:

1. Personal information, such as the applicant's social security number, age, education, marital status, and number of dependents.
2. Current housing expense (monthly rent or house payment, including principal and interest, property taxes, hazard insurance, any mortgage insurance, and any homeowners or condominium association dues).
3. Employment information (such as job title, type of business, and duration of employment) concerning the applicant's current position and, if he's been with the current employer for less than two years, concerning previous jobs.
4. Income from all sources, including employment (salary, wages, bonuses, and/or commissions), investments (dividends and interest), and pensions.
5. Assets, which may include money in bank accounts, stocks and bonds, real estate, life insurance, retirement funds, cars, jewelry, and other personal property.
6. Liabilities, including credit card debts, car loans, real estate loans, spousal maintenance or child support payments, and unpaid taxes.

The lender will verify the applicant's information concerning income, assets, and liabilities (for example, by contacting his employer and his bank).

Underwriting the Loan

Once a loan application has been submitted and the information has been verified, the loan is ready for underwriting. **Loan underwriting** is the process of evaluating both the applicant and the property she wants to buy to determine whether they meet the lender's minimum standards. The person who conducts the evaluation is called a loan underwriter or credit underwriter. The guidelines that the underwriter uses to decide whether a proposed loan would be an acceptable risk (in other words, whether the applicant qualifies for the loan) are called **underwriting standards** or **qualifying standards**.

A lender is generally free to set its own underwriting standards. In practice, though, most lenders apply underwriting standards set by the major secondary market agencies, Fannie Mae and Freddie Mac. And for FHA and VA loans, standards set by HUD or the VA must be used.

Qualifying the Buyer. In evaluating a loan applicant's financial situation, an underwriter must consider many factors. These factors fall into three main groups: credit history, income, and net worth.

Credit History. The first major component of creditworthiness is credit history, or credit reputation. An underwriter typically requests credit reports on the loan applicant from more than one credit reporting agency. The reports indicate how reliably the applicant has paid bills and other debts, and whether there have been any serious problems such as bankruptcy or foreclosure.

In addition to reviewing credit reports, underwriters also use **credit scores** to help assess how likely it is that a loan applicant will default on the proposed loan. A credit reporting agency calculates an individual's credit score using the credit report and a statistical model that correlates different types of negative credit information with actual loan defaults.

Credit problems can be an indication of financial irresponsibility, but sometimes they result from a personal crisis such as loss of a job, divorce, or hospitalization. A loan applicant with a poor credit history should explain any extenuating circumstances to the lender.

The activities of credit reporting agencies are regulated under the federal Fair Credit Reporting Act and various state laws, which give consumers the right to dispute information in their credit reports. The agencies must investigate and make corrections where necessary.

Income. Another primary consideration for the underwriter is whether the loan applicant's monthly income is enough to cover the proposed monthly mortgage payment in addition to all of the applicant's other expenses. So the underwriter needs to determine how much income the applicant has.

Not all income is equal in an underwriter's eyes, however. To be taken into account in deciding whether the applicant qualifies for the loan, income must meet standards of quality and durability. In other words, it must be from a dependable source, such as an established business, and it must be likely to continue for some time. Income that meets the tests of quality and durability is generally referred to as the loan applicant's **stable monthly income**.

For example, a regular salary from permanent employment would count as stable monthly income, and so would Social Security retirement benefits. On the other hand, neither occasional overtime pay from a permanent job nor wages from a temporary job would be considered stable monthly income, because they couldn't be relied upon to continue.

Once the underwriter has calculated the loan applicant's stable monthly income, the next step is to measure its adequacy: Is the stable monthly income enough so that the applicant can afford the proposed monthly mortgage payment? To answer this question, underwriters use **income ratios**. The rationale behind the ratios is that if a borrower's expenses exceed a certain percentage of his monthly income, he may have a difficult time making the payments on the loan.

There are two main types of income ratios:

- A **housing expense to income ratio** measures the proposed monthly mortgage payment against the applicant's stable monthly income.
- A **debt to income ratio** measures all of the applicant's monthly obligations (the proposed mortgage payment, plus car payments, child support payments, etc.) against the stable monthly income.

For these calculations, the monthly mortgage payment includes principal, interest, property taxes, and hazard insurance (often abbreviated PITI). When applicable, it also includes mortgage insurance and homeowners or condominium association dues. Each ratio is expressed as a percentage; for example, a loan applicant's housing expense to income ratio would be 29% if her proposed mortgage payment represented 29% of her stable monthly income. Whether that ratio would be considered too high would depend on the lender and on the type of loan applied for. Each of the major residential financing programs (conventional, FHA, and VA) has its own income ratio limits.

Net Worth. The third prong of the underwriting process is evaluating the applicant's net worth. An individual's net worth is determined by subtracting her total personal liabilities from her total personal assets. If a loan applicant has built up a significant net worth from earnings, savings, and other investments, that's an indication of creditworthiness. The applicant apparently knows how to manage her financial affairs.

Getting an idea of the loan applicant's financial skills isn't the only reason for investigating her net worth, however. The underwriter needs to make sure that the applicant has sufficient funds to cover the downpayment, the closing costs, and other expenses incidental to the purchase of the property.

In addition, it's desirable for a loan applicant to have cash reserves left over after closing. Reserves provide some assurance that she would be able to handle a financial emergency, such as unexpected bills or a temporary interruption of income, without defaulting on the mortgage. Some lenders require an applicant to have sufficient reserves to cover a certain number of mortgage payments. Even when reserves aren't required, they strengthen the loan application.

Qualifying the Property. In addition to deciding whether the buyer is a good risk, the underwriter also has to consider whether the property that the buyer wants to purchase is a good risk. After all, the property will be the security for the loan. Is the property worth enough to serve as collateral for the loan amount in question? In other words, if foreclosure became necessary, would the property sell for enough money to pay off the loan? To answer these questions, the underwriter relies on an appraisal report commissioned by the lender. The appraisal provides an expert's estimate of the property's value. (Appraisal is discussed in Chapter 13.)

Automated Underwriting. Within the limits set by the underwriting standards they apply, underwriters draw on their own experience and judgment in deciding whether to recommend that a particular loan be approved or denied. For this reason, underwriting is often described as an art, not a science. However, automated underwriting (AU) has moved the underwriting process at least somewhat closer to the scientific end of the spectrum. In automated underwriting, a computer program performs a preliminary analysis of the loan application and the applicant's credit report and makes a recommendation for or against approval. A human underwriter then evaluates the application in light of the AU recommendation.

AU systems are based on statistics regarding the performance of millions of loans—whether the borrowers made the payments on time or defaulted. Analysis of these statistics provides strong evidence of which factors in a loan application make default more or less likely.

AU can streamline the underwriting process, as it often requires significantly less paperwork. This enables lenders to make approval decisions more quickly.

Loan Commitment. Once the underwriting analysis has been completed, a report summarizing the characteristics of the prospective borrower, the property, and the proposed loan is prepared. This summary, sometimes called a **mortgage evaluation**, is submitted to a loan committee, which will make the final decision on whether to approve the loan. If the committee's decision is favorable, the lender issues a **loan commitment**, agreeing to make the loan on specified terms.

Subprime Lending

What happens to home buyers whose credit history doesn't meet standard underwriting requirements? Some of those buyers may be able to obtain a loan by applying to a **subprime** lender. Subprime lending involves making riskier loans than prime (or standard) lending.

Although many of the buyers who obtain subprime mortgages have blemished credit histories and mediocre credit scores, subprime lenders also deal with other categories of buyers. For example, subprime financing may be necessary for buyers who:

- can't (or would rather not have to) meet the income and asset documentation requirements of prime lenders;
- have good credit but carry more debt than prime lenders allow; or
- want to purchase nonstandard properties that prime lenders don't regard as acceptable collateral.

Subprime lenders apply more flexible underwriting standards and, in exchange, typically charge much higher interest rates and fees than prime lenders. In addition to having high interest rates and fees, subprime loans are more likely than prime loans to have features such as prepayment penalties, balloon payments, and negative amortization. These features help subprime lenders counterbalance some of the extra risks involved in their loans, although they can also cause trouble for the borrowers. (See the discussion of predatory lending later in this chapter.)

A boom in subprime lending began in the late 1990s and continued into the new century. However, a significant number of the subprime loans made during the boom turned out to be poor risks, and many of the borrowers defaulted on their loans. The resulting foreclosure epidemic, which peaked in 2010, affected not just the mortgage industry but the economy as a whole. The changes in laws and lending practices that followed have made subprime loans much harder to obtain.

Mortgage Fraud

Mortgage fraud causes many millions of dollars in losses each year. Common types of mortgage fraud include borrowers lying on loan applications and loan professionals misleading secondary market investors. For instance, loan applicants may lie about their employment, assets, or liabilities in order to secure loans that they wouldn't otherwise qualify for. Investors may falsely claim to be purchasing property as their principal residence in order to qualify for lower interest rates and fees. Lenders may misrepresent the quality of poor loans when selling them to investors in the secondary market.

Both federal and state law prohibit mortgage fraud. In 2009, in response to the mortgage crisis, Congress passed the Fraud Enforcement and Recovery Act, which toughened up existing federal antifraud provisions and took particular aim at mortgage fraud. Both the federal and state laws provide significant jail time and fines for violations.

Basic Loan Features

In this section of the chapter, we'll look at the basic features of a home mortgage loan. These include the loan term, the amortization, the loan-to-value ratio, a secondary financing arrangement (in some cases), and a fixed or adjustable interest rate. A lender is likely to present a home buyer with a number of options concerning these various loan features. For example, the buyer may be offered a choice between a 30-year loan and a 15-year loan, and between a fixed-rate loan and an adjustable-rate loan. Each of these choices has an impact on how large a loan the buyer will qualify for, and ultimately on how expensive a home the buyer can purchase.

Fig. 12.2 A 15-year loan offers substantial savings over a 30-year loan.

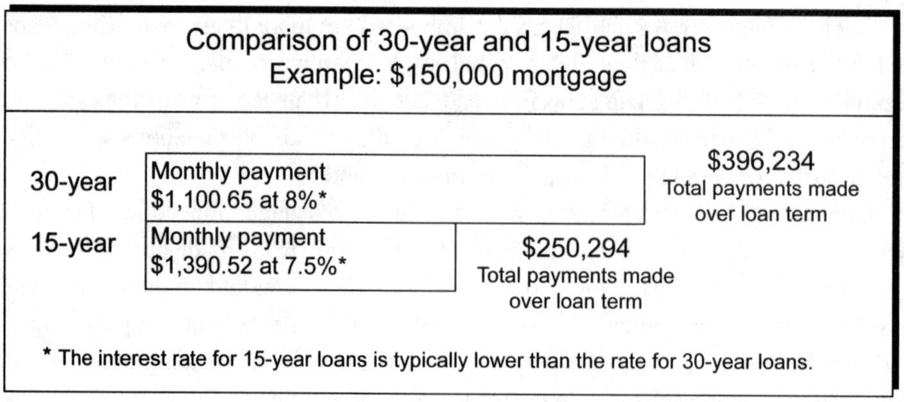

Loan Term

A mortgage loan's term (also known as the **repayment period**) has a significant impact on both the monthly mortgage payment and the total amount of interest paid over the life of the loan. The longer the term, the lower the monthly payment, and the more interest paid.

Since the 1930s, the standard term for a mortgage loan has been 30 years. This long repayment period makes the monthly payments affordable, which reduces the risk of default.

Although 30-year loans continue to predominate, 15-year loans have also become popular. A 15-year loan has higher monthly payments than a comparable 30-year loan, but the 15-year loan offers substantial savings for the borrower in the long run. Lenders frequently offer lower interest rates on 15-year loans, because the shorter term means less risk for the lender. And the borrower will save thousands of dollars in total interest charges over the life of the loan (see Figure 12.2). A 15-year loan also offers free and clear ownership of the property in half the time.

However, the monthly payments for a 15-year loan are significantly higher, and in some cases a much larger downpayment would be necessary to reduce the monthly payments to a level the borrower can afford.

> **Example:** Bob has a choice between a 30-year loan at 7.5% and a 15-year loan at 7%. Based on his stable monthly income, he can afford to make monthly principal and interest payments of $2,000. This is enough to amortize a $286,000 loan at 7.5% over 30 years, but it will amortize only about $222,500 at 7% over 15 years. In other words, Bob could qualify for a $286,000 loan under the 30-year plan, but will qualify for only $222,500 if he chooses the 15-year option. The difference between the two loan amounts would have to be made up with a larger downpayment.

There are alternatives to 15- and 30-year loans. For some borrowers, a 20-year loan is a good compromise between the two, with some of the advantages of each. And while 30 years is the maximum repayment period in many loan programs, some programs allow borrowers to choose a 40-year term to maximize their purchasing power.

Amortization

Most mortgage loans are **fully amortized**. A fully amortized loan is repaid within a certain period of time by means of regular payments that include a portion for principal and a portion for interest. As each payment is made, the appropriate amount of principal is deducted from the debt and the remainder of the payment, which is the interest, is retained by the lender as earnings or profit. With each payment, the amount of the debt is reduced and the interest due with the next payment is recalculated based on the lower balance. The total payment remains the same throughout the term of the loan, but every month the interest portion of the payment is reduced and the principal portion is increased. (See Figure 12.3.) The final payment pays off the loan completely; the principal balance is zero and no further interest is owed.

Example: A $190,000 loan at 6% interest can be fully amortized over a 30-year term with monthly principal and interest payments of $1,139.15. If the borrower pays $1,139.15 each month, then the loan will be fully repaid (with interest) after 30 years.

There are two alternatives to fully amortized loans: partially amortized loans and interest-only loans. A **partially amortized** loan requires regular payments of both principal and interest, but those payments are not enough to repay all of the principal; the borrower is required to make a large **balloon payment** (the remaining principal balance) at the end of the loan term.

Example: A $190,000 partially amortized mortgage at 7.25% interest calls for regular monthly payments of $1,296.13 for principal and interest, with a loan term of five years. Because the monthly payments are more than enough to cover the interest on the loan, some of the principal will be repaid during the five-year term. But since it would take 30 years to fully repay the loan at this rate, a substantial amount of principal (roughly $179,000) will still be unpaid after five years. This amount will be due as a balloon payment. To pay it, the borrower will have to refinance the property or come up with the funds from some other source.

Fig. 12.3 Payments for a fully amortized loan

Example: $190,000 loan @ 6.00%, 30-year term, monthly payments

Payment No.	Beginning Balance	Total Payment	Interest Portion	Principal Portion	Ending Balance
1	$190,000.00	$1,139.15	$950.00	$189.15	$189,810.85
2	$189,810.85	$1,139.15	$949.05	$190.09	$189,620.76
3	$189,620.76	$1,139.15	$948.10	$191.04	$189,429.72
4	$189,429.72	$1,139.15	$947.15	$192.00	$189,237.72
5	$189,237.72	$1,139.15	$946.19	$192.96	$189,044.77

With an **interest-only** loan (also called a **term mortgage**), the borrower's regular payments during the loan term cover the interest accruing on the loan, without paying any of the principal off. The entire principal amount—the amount originally borrowed—is due at the end of the term.

> **Example:** A five-year, $190,000, interest-only loan at 5.5% interest requires monthly payments of $870.84, the amount needed to cover the monthly interest on the loan. At the end of the five-year term, the borrower owes the lender the full amount of the principal ($190,000).

The term "interest-only loan" is also used to refer to a loan that's structured to allow interest-only payments during a specified period at the beginning of the loan term. At the end of the initial period, the borrower must begin making amortized payments that will pay off all of the principal and interest by the end of the term. This type of interest-only loan was very popular during the subprime boom, since the low initial payments enabled buyers to purchase a more expensive home than they otherwise could have. For many buyers, however, these loans eventually backfire. When the interest-only period ends, they can't afford the amortized payments, and the payment shock ultimately results in foreclosure.

Loan-to-Value Ratios

The loan-to-value ratio (LTV) for a particular transaction expresses the relationship between the loan amount and the value of the property. The lower the LTV, the smaller the loan amount and the bigger the downpayment.

> **Example:** If a lender makes an $80,000 loan secured by a home appraised at $100,000, the loan-to-value ratio is 80%. The loan amount is 80% of the property's value, and the buyer makes a 20% downpayment. If the lender loaned $75,000 secured by the same property, the LTV would be 75% and the downpayment would be 25%.

The downpayment represents the borrower's initial investment or **equity** in the property. (A property owner's equity is the difference between the property's market value and the amount of the liens against it.) So the lower the loan-to-value ratio, the greater the borrower's equity. Appreciation of the property benefits the borrower, since any increase in the property's value increases the borrower's equity interest.

The loan-to-value ratio affects the degree of risk involved in the loan—both the risk of default and the risk of loss in the event of default. A borrower who has a substantial investment (equity) in the property will try harder to avoid foreclosure; and when foreclosure is necessary, the lender is more likely to recover the entire debt if the LTV is relatively low. If a lender made a loan with a 100% LTV, it would recover the outstanding loan balance and all of its costs in a foreclosure sale only if property values had appreciated and the property sold for considerably more than its original purchase price. This is because the foreclosure process itself costs the lender a substantial amount of money.

The higher the LTV, the greater the lender's risk. So lenders use loan-to-value ratios to set maximum loan amounts.

Example: If a lender's maximum LTV for a certain type of loan is 75%, and the property's appraised value is $100,000, then $75,000 is the maximum loan amount.

Lenders actually base the maximum loan amount on the sales price or the appraised value, whichever is less. Thus, if the $100,000 property in the example above was selling for $95,000, the maximum loan amount would be $71,250 (75% of $95,000).

Many lenders have special rules for high-LTV loans because of the extra risk they pose. We'll discuss these rules later in the chapter.

Secondary Financing

Sometimes a buyer obtains two mortgage loans at once: a primary loan to pay for most of the purchase price, and a second loan to pay part of the downpayment or closing costs required for the first loan. This supplementary second loan is called **secondary financing**. Secondary financing may come from an institutional lender, the seller, or a private third party.

In most cases, the primary lender will allow secondary financing only if it complies with certain requirements. For example, the borrower must be able to qualify for the combined payment on the first and second loans. The borrower usually has to make a minimum downpayment out of his own funds. And the second loan must be payable at any time, without a prepayment penalty.

Fixed and Adjustable Interest Rates

A fixed-rate loan is repaid over its term at an unchanging rate of interest. For example, the interest rate is set at 6.75% when the loan is made, and the borrower pays 6.75% interest on the unpaid principal throughout the loan term.

When market interest rates are relatively low and stable, fixed-rate loans work well for borrowers and lenders. But in periods when market rates are high and volatile, neither borrowers nor lenders are comfortable with fixed-rate loans. High interest rates price many borrowers out of the market. And if market rates are fluctuating rapidly, lenders prefer not to tie up their funds for long periods at a set interest rate.

A type of loan that addresses both of these issues is the **adjustable-rate mortgage** (ARM), sometimes called a variable-rate loan. An ARM permits the lender to periodically adjust the loan's interest rate so that it accurately reflects changes in the cost of money. If market rates climb, the borrower's interest rate and monthly payment go up; if market rates decline, the borrower's interest rate and payment go down.

Depending on economic conditions and other factors, lenders may offer ARMs at a lower initial interest rate than the rate they're charging for fixed-rate loans. For example, a lender might offer fixed-rate loans at 6% and ARMs at 5.25%.

How an ARM Works. With an ARM, the borrower's interest rate is determined initially by the cost of money at the time the loan is made. Once the rate has been set, it's tied to one of several widely recognized indexes, and future interest adjustments are based on the upward and downward movements of the index.

Index and Margin. An **index** is a published statistical rate that is a reliable indicator of changes in the cost of money. Examples include the one-year Treasury bill index and the Eleventh District cost of funds index. At the time a loan is made, the lender selects the index it prefers, and thereafter the loan's interest rate will rise and fall with the rates reported for the index.

Since the index reflects the lender's cost of money, it is necessary to add a **margin** to the index to ensure sufficient income for administrative expenses and profit. The lender's margin is usually 2% or 3%, or somewhere in between. The index plus the margin equals the interest rate charged to the borrower.

Example:

5.25%	Current index value
+ 2.00%	Margin
7.25%	Borrower's interest rate

It is the index that fluctuates during the loan term and causes the borrower's interest rate to increase and decrease; the lender's margin remains constant.

Adjustment Periods. The borrower's interest rate is not adjusted every time the index changes. Each ARM has a **rate adjustment period**, which determines how often its interest rate is adjusted. A rate adjustment period of one year is the most common.

An ARM also has a **payment adjustment period**, which determines how often the borrower's monthly mortgage payment is increased or decreased (reflecting changes in the interest rate). For most ARMs, payment adjustments are made at the same intervals as rate adjustments.

Caps. If market interest rates rise rapidly, so will an ARM's index, which could lead to a sharp increase in the interest rate the lender charges the borrower. Of course, a higher interest rate translates into a higher monthly payment. This creates the potential for **payment shock**. In other words, the monthly payments on an ARM might increase so dramatically that the borrower can't afford them.

To help protect borrowers from payment shock and lenders from default, ARMs have interest rate and payment caps. An **interest rate cap** limits how much the lender can raise the interest rate on the loan, even if the index goes way up. A **mortgage payment cap** limits how much the lender can increase the monthly payment.

Negative Amortization. If an ARM has certain features, payment increases may not keep up with increases in the loan's interest rate, so that the monthly payments don't cover all of the interest owed. The lender usually handles this by adding the unpaid interest to the loan's principal balance; this is called **negative amortization**. Ordinarily, a loan's principal balance declines steadily, although gradually. But negative amortization causes the principal balance to go up instead of down. The borrower may owe the lender more money than he originally borrowed. Today, most lenders structure their ARMs to avoid negative amortization and lessen the chance of default and foreclosure.

Hybrid ARMs. With a hybrid ARM, the interest rate is fixed for a specified number of years at the start of the loan term, and then the rate becomes adjustable. For example, a 3/1 hybrid ARM has a fixed rate during the first three years, with annual rate adjustments after that. A 5/1 ARM has a five-year fixed-rate period, and so on. As a general rule, the longer the initial fixed-rate period, the higher the initial interest rate.

Residential Financing Programs

Residential financing programs can be divided into two main groups: conventional loans and government-sponsored loans. In this section, we'll look first at conventional loans, and then at three loan programs sponsored by the federal government: the FHA-insured loan program, the VA-guaranteed loan program, and the Rural Housing Service loan program. As you'll see, each program has its own qualifying standards and its own rules concerning the downpayment and other aspects of the loan.

Conventional Loans

A conventional loan is simply any institutional loan that is not insured or guaranteed by a government agency. For example, FHA-insured and VA-guaranteed loans are not conventional loans, because they are backed by a government agency.

The rules for conventional loans presented here reflect the criteria established by the secondary market agencies that purchase conventional loans, Fannie Mae and Freddie Mac (see Chapter 11). When a loan does not meet secondary market criteria it is considered **nonconforming** and cannot be sold to the major secondary market agencies. Today, most lenders want to be able to sell their loans on the secondary market, so they tailor their standards for conventional loans to match those set by Fannie Mae or Freddie Mac.

Conforming Loan Limits. A loan generally won't be eligible for purchase by Fannie Mae or Freddie Mac if the loan amount exceeds the applicable conforming loan limit. (There are different maximums for properties with one, two, three, or four dwelling units.) The conforming loan limits are based on median housing prices nationwide, and they may be adjusted annually to reflect changes in median prices.

Loans that exceed the conventional loan limits are known as **jumbo loans**. Lenders typically charge higher interest rates and apply stricter underwriting standards when making jumbo loans.

Conventional LTVs. Traditionally, the standard loan-to-value ratio for a conventional loan has been 80% of the appraised value or sales price of the home, whichever is less. Lenders feel confident that a borrower who makes a 20% downpayment with his own funds is unlikely to default; the borrower has too much to lose. And even if the borrower were to default, a foreclosure sale would be likely to generate at least 80% of the purchase price.

While an 80% LTV may still be regarded as the traditional standard, today many conventional loans have much higher loan-to-value ratios. Many lenders allow LTVs up to 95%; and loans with a 97% LTV may be available through special programs (although conventional loans with LTVs that high are increasingly rare).

Because the lender's risk is greater when the borrower's downpayment is smaller, lenders require borrowers to obtain private mortgage insurance for any conventional loan with an LTV over 80%. (Private mortgage insurance is discussed below.) Some lenders also charge higher interest rates and larger loan fees for conventional loans with higher LTVs. The rules for loans with LTVs over 90% tend to be especially strict.

Owner-Occupancy. Residential lenders make a distinction between owner-occupied homes and investment properties. An owner-occupied home, as the term suggests, is one that the owner (the borrower) plans to live in himself, either as his principal residence or as a second home. An investment property is a house that the owner/investor intends to rent out to tenants. Owner-occupants are considered less likely to default than non-occupant borrowers.

Owner-occupancy isn't a requirement for conventional loans, except for loans made through certain special programs (affordable housing programs, for example). In some cases, however, a lender will apply stricter rules to investors than to owner-occupants. For instance, a lender might set 95% as its maximum LTV for owner-occupants, but limit investors to a 90% LTV.

Private Mortgage Insurance. Private mortgage insurance (PMI) is designed to protect lenders from the greater risk of high LTV loans; PMI makes up for the reduced borrower equity. PMI is usually required on conventional loans with downpayments of less than 20%. (It's called private mortgage insurance because it's issued by private insurance companies, not by the government's FHA mortgage insurance program.)

When insuring a loan, the mortgage insurance company actually assumes only a portion of the risk of default. It does not insure the entire loan amount, but rather the upper portion of the loan. The amount of coverage varies; typically it is 20% to 25% of the loan amount.

Example: 20% coverage

$200,000	Sales price
× 90%	LTV
$180,000	90% loan
× 20%	Amount of coverage
$36,000	Amount of policy

In the event of default and foreclosure, the lender, at the insurer's option, will either sell the property and make a claim for reimbursement of actual losses (if any) up to the amount of the policy, or relinquish the property to the insurer and make a claim for actual losses up to the policy amount. Losses incurred by the lender may take the form of unpaid interest; property taxes and hazard insurance; attorney's fees; the cost of preserving the property during the period of foreclosure and resale; and the expense of selling the property itself.

As a borrower pays off a loan, the loan-to-value ratio decreases. With a lower LTV, the risk of default and foreclosure loss is reduced, and eventually the private mortgage insurance has fulfilled its purpose.

Under the federal Homeowners Protection Act, lenders are required to cancel a loan's PMI once the loan has been paid down to 80% of the property's original value, if the borrower formally requests the cancellation. Automatic cancellation of the PMI is required once the loan balance reaches 78% of the property's original value, even if the borrower does not request cancellation.

Conventional Qualifying Standards. Fannie Mae and Freddie Mac's underwriting standards include detailed guidelines for evaluation of a conventional loan applicant's credit history, income, and net worth. The agencies set minimum credit scores for the loans they buy. Also, a borrower whose credit score is above the minimum, but still comparatively low, is usually charged a risk-based loan fee called a delivery fee or loan-level price adjustment (LLPA). This fee can be substantial. Additional LLPAs may be charged based on other special risk factors in a transaction; for example, an LLPA might be charged because the loan has an adjustable interest rate. (The risk of default is greater with an ARM, because of the potential for payment shock.)

To determine whether the applicant's stable monthly income is sufficient, an underwriter may calculate both a housing expense to income ratio and a total debt to income ratio.

> **Example:** Suppose the lender's maximum housing expense to income ratio is 28% and maximum debt to income ratio is 36%. If a loan applicant's housing expense to income ratio is 27% (under the lender's limit), but her debt to income ratio is 38% (over the lender's limit), then the lender probably won't approve the loan unless there are special considerations.

In some cases, the underwriter will consider only the total debt to income ratio. Because the debt to income ratio takes all of the applicant's monthly obligations into account, it is considered a more reliable indicator of creditworthiness than the housing expense to income ratio.

Note that some lenders apply lower maximum income ratios to qualify applicants for conventional loans with loan-to-value ratios over 90%, to make up for the greater risk posed by a high-LTV loan.

Conventional loan applicants generally should have the equivalent of at least two months of mortgage payments in reserve after making the downpayment and paying all closing costs. That's not necessarily treated as a strict requirement, but less than that in reserve will weaken an application. Ideally, applicants will have enough reserves to cover at least six months of mortgage payments.

Assumption. Most conventional loan agreements include an alienation clause, so the borrower can't sell the property and arrange for the buyer to assume the loan without the lender's permission. Typically, the lender will evaluate the buyer with the same qualifying standards that it applies in a new loan transaction. If the lender approves the assumption, it will charge an assumption fee, and it may also adjust the interest rate to the prevailing market rate at that time.

FHA-Insured Loans

The Federal Housing Administration (FHA) was created by Congress in 1934 in the National Housing Act. The purpose of the act, and of the FHA, was to generate new jobs through increased construction activity, to exert a stabilizing influence on the mortgage market, and to promote the financing, repair, improvement, and sale of real estate nationwide. An additional by-product of the FHA housing program was the establishment of minimum housing construction standards.

Today the FHA is part of the Department of Housing and Urban Development (HUD). Its primary function is insuring mortgage loans; the FHA compensates lenders who make loans through its programs for losses that result from borrower default. The FHA does not build homes or make loans.

In effect, the FHA serves as a giant mortgage insurance agency. Its insurance program, sometimes referred to as the **Mutual Mortgage Insurance Plan**, is funded with premiums paid by FHA borrowers.

Lenders who have been approved by the FHA to make insured loans either submit applications from prospective borrowers to the local FHA office for approval or, if authorized by the FHA to do so, perform the underwriting functions themselves. Lenders who are authorized to underwrite their own FHA loan applications are called "direct endorsement lenders."

Lenders who don't underwrite their own FHA loans forward applications to the local FHA office for underwriting and approval. Note that the FHA doesn't accept applications directly from prospective borrowers. Borrowers must begin by applying to a lender such as a bank or a mortgage company for an initial loan commitment.

As the insurer, the FHA is liable to the lender for the full amount of any losses resulting from the borrower's default and a subsequent foreclosure. In exchange for insuring a loan, the FHA regulates many of the terms and conditions on which the loan is made.

Characteristics of FHA Loans. The typical FHA-insured loan has a 30-year term, although the borrower may have the option of a shorter term. The property purchased with an FHA loan may have up to four dwelling units, and it must be the borrower's primary residence. The FHA requires all the loans it insures to have first lien position.

The downpayment required for an FHA loan is often considerably less than it would be for a conventional loan financing the same purchase (see below). Regardless of the size of the downpayment, mortgage insurance is required on all FHA loans.

Prepayment penalties aren't allowed. An FHA loan can be paid off at any time without penalty. The lender, however, may require the borrower to pay an origination fee when the loan is made.

FHA Loan Amounts. FHA programs are primarily intended to help low- and middle-income home buyers. So HUD sets maximum loan amounts, limiting the size of loans that can be insured under its programs. FHA maximum loan amounts vary from one place to another because they are based on median housing costs in each area. An area where housing is expensive has a higher maximum loan amount than a low-cost area does.

However, there's also a "ceiling" for FHA loan amounts that applies nationwide; no matter how high prices are in a particular area, FHA loans can't exceed that ceiling. As a result, FHA financing tends to be less useful in areas where housing is exceptionally expensive. The FHA ceiling is tied to the conforming loan limits for conventional loans, and it is subject to annual adjustment.

FHA Loan Programs. The FHA has a number of different programs to meet different needs. The standard FHA program is 203(b), which can be used to insure purchase loans (or refinancing) on residences with up to four units.

The other FHA loan programs are based on the standard 203(b) program. For example, the 203(k) loan program provides insurance for mortgages used to purchase (or refinance) and rehabilitate a residence with up to four units. The section 234(c) loan program applies to loans on owner-occupied condominium units. And the section 251 loan program provides insurance for adjustable-rate mortgages.

Loan-to-Value Ratios. The loan amount for a particular transaction is determined not just by the FHA loan ceiling for the local area, but also by the FHA's rules concerning loan-to-value ratios.

The maximum loan-to-value ratio for an FHA loan depends on the borrower's credit score. If the borrower's credit score is 580 or above, the maximum LTV is 96.5%. If his score is 500 to 579, the maximum LTV is 90%. Someone with a score below 500 isn't eligible for an FHA loan.

The difference between the maximum loan amount for a transaction and the appraised value or sales price (whichever is less) is called the borrower's minimum cash investment. In a transaction with maximum financing (a 96.5% LTV), the borrower must make a minimum cash investment of 3.5%.

FHA Qualifying Standards. As with any institutional mortgage loan, the underwriting for an FHA-insured loan involves the analysis of the applicant's credit history, income, and net worth. But the FHA's underwriting standards aren't as strict as the Fannie Mae/Freddie Mac standards used for conventional loans. The FHA standards make it easier for low- and middle-income home buyers to qualify for a mortgage.

Income. An underwriter evaluating an application for an FHA loan will apply two ratios to determine the adequacy of the applicant's income, a housing expense to income ratio and a debt to income ratio. The FHA's maximum income ratios are higher than the ones typically set for conventional loans. This means that an FHA borrower's mortgage payment and other monthly obligations can be a larger percentage of his income than a conventional borrower's.

Although FHA programs are targeted at low- and middle-income buyers, there's no maximum income limit. A person with a high income could qualify for an FHA loan, as long as the requested loan didn't exceed the maximum loan amount for the area.

Funds for Closing. At closing an FHA borrower must have sufficient funds to cover the minimum cash investment, any discount points she has agreed to pay, and certain other closing costs. (Note that secondary financing generally cannot be used for the minimum cash investment, unless the source of the second loan is a nonprofit or governmental agency or a family member.) An FHA borrower usually isn't required to have reserves after closing.

FHA Insurance Premiums. Mortgage insurance premiums for FHA loans are commonly referred to as the **MIP**. For most FHA loans, the borrower pays both a one-time premium and annual premiums. The one-time premium may be paid at closing, or else financed along with the loan amount and paid off over the loan term.

Previously, FHA's annual MIP could be canceled once the loan's principal balance reached a certain percentage of the property's original value. However, the FHA announced changes to this cancellation policy, effective June 3, 2013. Under the new rules, for loans with an original loan-to-value ratio over 90%, the annual MIP must be paid for the entire loan term. For loans with an original LTV of 90% or less, the annual MIP will be canceled after 11 years.

Assumption of FHA Loans. FHA loans made before 1990 can be assumed without the lender's approval, if the seller doesn't need a release of liability. Loans made since then can be assumed only by a buyer who meets FHA underwriting standards. The buyer must intend to occupy the home as his primary residence.

VA-Guaranteed Loans

The VA-guaranteed home loan program was established to help veterans finance the purchase of their homes with affordable loans. VA financing offers several advantages over conventional financing. The program is administered by the U.S. Department of Veterans Affairs (the VA).

Eligibility for VA Loans. Eligibility for a VA home loan is based on length of active duty service in the U.S. armed forces. The minimum requirement varies from **90 days** to **24 months**, depending on when the veteran served, with longer periods required for peacetime service than wartime service. (Note that the minimum active duty service requirement is waived for anyone discharged because of a service-connected disability.) Eligibility may also be based on longtime service in the National Guard or reserves. Military personnel who receive a dishonorable discharge aren't eligible for a VA loan.

A veteran's surviving spouse may be eligible for a VA loan if the veteran was killed in action, died on active duty, or died of service-related injuries. A veteran's spouse may also be eligible if the veteran is listed as missing in action or is a prisoner of war.

Application Process. To get a VA-guaranteed loan, a veteran must apply to an institutional lender and provide a **Certificate of Eligibility** issued by the VA. The lender will process the veteran's loan application and forward it to the VA. Note that the Certificate of Eligibility isn't a guarantee that the veteran will qualify for a loan.

The property that the veteran wants to purchase must be appraised in accordance with VA guidelines. The appraised value is set forth in a document called a **Notice of Value**, or NOV (also referred to as a Certificate of Reasonable Value, or CRV).

When a VA loan has been approved, the loan is guaranteed by the federal government. If the borrower defaults, the VA will reimburse the lender for all or part of any resulting loss. The loan guaranty works essentially like mortgage insurance; it protects the lender against a large loss if the borrower fails to repay the loan.

Characteristics of VA Loans. A VA loan can be used to finance the purchase or construction of a single-family residence or a multi-family residence with up to four units. The veteran must intend to occupy the home, or one of the units.

VA-guaranteed loans are attractive to borrowers for several reasons, including the following:

- Unlike most loans, a VA loan typically doesn't require a downpayment. The loan amount can be as large as the sales price or the appraised value, whichever is less. In other words, the loan-to-value ratio can be 100%.
- The VA doesn't set a maximum loan amount or impose any income restrictions. VA loans aren't limited to low- or middle-income buyers.
- VA underwriting standards are significantly less stringent than conventional underwriting standards.
- VA loans don't require the extra expense of mortgage insurance.

A VA borrower is required to pay a **funding fee**, which is a percentage of the loan amount. The funding fee is generally 2.15% the first time a borrower obtains a VA loan, and it's 3.3% for subsequent loans. The fee is reduced if the borrower is going to make a downpayment of 5% or more.

VA Guaranty. Like private mortgage insurance, the VA guaranty covers only part of the loan amount, up to a maximum set by the government. The maximum guaranty amount is increased periodically. The amount of the guaranty available to a particular veteran is sometimes called the vet's "entitlement."

Because the guaranty amount is limited, a large loan amount presents some extra risk for the lender. Many lenders require the VA borrower to make at least a small downpayment if the loan amount exceeds a certain limit (typically four times the guaranty amount). This is a limit set by the lender, however, not by the VA.

Restoration of Entitlement. If a veteran sells property that was financed with a VA loan and repays the loan in full from the proceeds of the sale, he's entitled to a full restoration of guaranty rights for future use. (Restoration of entitlement is also referred to as reinstatement.)

Substitution of Entitlement. If a home purchased with a VA loan is sold and the loan is assumed instead of repaid, the veteran's entitlement can be restored under certain circumstances. The buyer who assumes the loan must be an eligible veteran and must agree to substitute her entitlement for the seller's. The loan payments must be current, and the buyer must be an acceptable credit risk. If these conditions are met, the veteran can formally request a substitution of entitlement from the VA.

Note that a VA loan can be assumed by a non-veteran who meets the VA's standards of creditworthiness. But the entitlement of the veteran seller will not be restored if the buyer assuming the loan isn't a veteran.

Liability. Despite the VA guaranty, a borrower still has personal liability for a VA loan. If a foreclosure sale results in a loss, the borrower may be liable to the VA for the amount of the loss, if the foreclosure involved fraud or bad faith. And even if there was no bad faith, the borrower's guaranty entitlement can't be restored until he reimburses the VA for the full amount of the guaranty.

Qualifying Standards. Lenders must follow guidelines established by the VA to evaluate a VA loan applicant's creditworthiness. The VA's rules for income analysis are quite different from those used for conventional or FHA loans. Instead of using both a housing expense to income ratio and a debt to income ratio, the VA uses only a debt to income ratio. The VA's maximum debt to income ratio is considerably higher than the maximum generally allowed for a conventional loan.

In addition to the debt to income ratio, the underwriter will also consider the veteran's **residual income**. This is calculated by subtracting the proposed mortgage payment, all other recurring obligations, and certain taxes from the veteran's gross monthly income. The veteran's residual income must meet the VA's minimum requirements, which vary based on the region of the country where the veteran lives, family size, and the size of the proposed loan.

At least for some loan applicants, it can be much easier to qualify for a VA loan than for a conventional loan. Home buyers who are eligible veterans should keep the option of VA financing in mind.

Rural Housing Service Loans

The Rural Housing Service (RHS) is a federal agency within the U.S. Department of Agriculture that makes and guarantees loans used to purchase, build, or rehabilitate homes in rural areas. These are often referred to as rural development loans, RD loans, USDA loans, or Section 502 loans. A rural area is generally defined as open country or a town with a rural character and a population of 10,000 or less. (Under special circumstances, a town with a population of up to 20,000 may be considered rural.)

To qualify for an RHS program, a borrower must currently be without adequate housing. The borrower must also be able to afford the proposed mortgage payments and have a reasonable credit history. A home purchased, built, or improved with a Rural Housing Service loan must be modest in size, design, and cost.

Direct Loans. Low-income borrowers (whose income is no more than 80% of the area median income) may obtain financing from RHS for 100% of the purchase price. The loan term may be as long as 38 years, depending on the borrower's income level. The interest rate is set by RHS, and the loan is serviced by RHS.

Guaranteed Loans. The Rural Housing Service also guarantees loans made by approved lenders to borrowers whose income is no more than 115% of the area median income. Approved lenders include any state housing agency, FHA- and VA-approved lenders, and lenders participating in RHS-guaranteed loan programs. The loan amount may be 100% of the purchase price. The loan term is 30 years, and the interest rate is set by the lender.

Predatory Lending

Predatory lending refers to practices that unscrupulous mortgage lenders and mortgage brokers use to take advantage of (prey upon) unsophisticated borrowers for their own profit. Real estate agents, appraisers, and home improvement contractors sometimes participate in predatory lending schemes, and in some cases a buyer or a seller may play a role in deceiving the other party.

Predatory lending is especially likely to occur in the subprime market. It tends to be more common in refinancing and home equity lending, but home purchase loans are also affected.

Here are some examples of predatory lending practices:

- **Predatory steering:** Steering a buyer toward a more expensive loan when the buyer could qualify for a less expensive one.
- **Fee packing:** Charging interest rates, points, or processing fees that far exceed the norm and aren't justified by the cost of the services provided.
- **Loan flipping:** Encouraging a homeowner to refinance repeatedly in a short period, when there's no real benefit to doing so (but the lender collects fees on each new loan).
- **Predatory property flipping:** Buying property at a discount (because the seller needs a quick sale) and then rapidly reselling it to an unsophisticated buyer for an inflated price. This is illegal when a real estate agent, an appraiser, a mortgage broker, and/or a lender commit fraud to deceive the seller and/or buyer about the true value of the property.
- **Disregarding borrower's ability to pay:** Making a loan based only on the property's value, without using appropriate underwriting standards to determine whether the borrower can afford the loan payments. In this situation, the predator is likely to be someone who won't be affected when the borrower eventually defaults, such as a mortgage broker.
- **Fraud:** Misrepresenting or concealing unfavorable loan terms or excessive fees, falsifying documents, or using other fraudulent means to induce a prospective buyer to enter into a loan agreement.
- **Balloon payment abuses:** Making a partially amortized or interest-only loan with low monthly payments, without disclosing to the borrower that a large balloon payment will be required after a short period.
- **Excessive or unfair prepayment penalties:** Imposing an unusually large penalty, failing to limit the penalty period to the first few years of the loan term, and/or charging the penalty even if the loan is prepaid because the property is being sold.

Predatory lenders and mortgage brokers deliberately target prospective buyers who aren't able to understand the transaction they're entering into, or don't know that better alternatives are available to them. Potential borrowers are especially likely to be targeted if they are elderly or have a limited income, or if they are less educated or speak limited English. Elderly victims who are cognitively impaired and who have a lot of equity in their homes are the most frequent victims of refinancing and equity stripping schemes.

There are federal and state laws intended to curb predatory lending. The federal Home Ownership and Equity Protection Act (HOEPA), passed in 1994, added special restrictions on "high-cost" mortgage loans to the Truth in Lending Act. It was quite limited in scope, however, applying only to very high-cost home equity loans and refinancing, not to home purchase loans. In 2008, 2009, and 2010, as part of their response to the subprime crisis and the foreclosure epidemic, Congress and the Federal Reserve made changes to the Truth in Lending Act and Regulation Z that made many more loans—including high-cost home purchase loans—subject to special restrictions. Lenders who charge high rates and fees on loans secured by the borrower's principal residence must make additional disclosures, aren't allowed to engage in certain practices, and can't include certain provisions in their loan agreements.

In addition to HOEPA, about half the states now have their own state predatory lending laws, and other states are in the process of adopting such laws.

Chapter Summary

1. Real estate lenders in the primary market include savings and loan associations, commercial banks, savings banks, credit unions, and mortgage companies. Property sellers are also a source of financing.

2. Lenders charge an origination fee to cover their administrative costs, and sometimes charge discount points to increase the yield on the loan. One point is 1% of the loan amount.

3. The Truth in Lending Act applies to any consumer loan that is secured by real property. It requires lenders to give loan applicants a disclosure statement about loan costs. It also regulates how financing information is presented in advertising.

4. In qualifying a buyer for a real estate loan, an underwriter examines the buyer's credit history, income, and net worth, to determine if she can be expected to make the proposed monthly mortgage payments. Income ratios measure the adequacy of the buyer's stable monthly income.

5. Automated underwriting involves using a computer program to perform a preliminary analysis of a loan application and recommend approval or denial. Automated underwriting streamlines the loan application process but is meant to supplement, not replace, manual underwriting.

6. The traditional loan term for a mortgage loan is 30 years, but 15-year loans are also available. A 15-year loan requires higher payments than a comparable 30-year loan, but it saves the borrower thousands of dollars in interest.

7. A fully amortized loan has equal payments that pay off all of the principal and interest by the end of the loan term. Nearly all institutional mortgage loans are fully amortized. Partially amortized loans and interest-only loans are sometimes used in seller financing arrangements.

8. The loan-to-value ratio for a particular transaction expresses the relationship between the loan amount and the property's appraised value or sales price, whichever is less. The higher the loan-to-value ratio, the greater the lender's risk.

9. Secondary financing may be used to cover part of the downpayment and closing costs required for the primary loan. A secondary financing arrangement must comply with rules set by the primary lender.

10. The interest rate on a mortgage loan may be either fixed or adjustable. An ARM's interest rate is tied to an index, and it is adjusted at specified intervals to reflect changes in the index.

11. A conventional loan is an institutional loan that is not insured or guaranteed by the government. Private mortgage insurance is required for loans with LTVs over 80%.

12. FHA-insured loans are distinguished from conventional loans by less stringent qualifying standards, lower downpayments, and less cash needed for closing. The maximum loan amount available for an FHA loan depends on housing costs in the area where the property is located. FHA mortgage insurance is required on all FHA loans.

13. Eligible veterans may obtain a VA-guaranteed home loan. No downpayment is required for a VA loan. There is no maximum loan amount, although there is a maximum guaranty amount. The qualifying standards for a VA loan are considerably less stringent than the standards for conventional loans.

14. The federal Rural Housing Service makes and guarantees loans for homes in rural areas. Low- or moderate-income borrowers may qualify if they can afford the mortgage payments and have reasonable credit histories.

15. Predatory lending refers to lending practices used by lenders and other parties to take advantage of unsophisticated borrowers. Examples of predatory lending practices include predatory steering, fee packing, loan flipping, and disregarding the borrower's ability to afford the loan payments.

Key Terms

Mortgage company—A type of lender that is not a depository institution and that makes and services loans on behalf of large investors. Sometimes called a mortgage banker.

Mortgage broker—An individual or company that arranges loans between borrowers and investors, but does not service the loans.

Point—One percent of the amount of a loan.

Origination fee—A fee that a lender charges to cover the administrative costs of processing a loan.

Discount points—A fee that a lender may charge to increase the yield on the loan, over and above the interest rate.

Annual percentage rate (APR)—Under the Truth in Lending Act, the relationship of the total finance charge to the loan amount, expressed as an annual percentage.

Loan underwriting—Evaluating the creditworthiness of the buyer and the value of the property to determine if a loan should be approved.

Stable monthly income—Income that satisfies the lender's standards of quality and durability.

Income ratios—Percentages used to determine whether a loan applicant's stable monthly income is sufficient.

Housing expense to income ratio—A percentage that measures a loan applicant's proposed mortgage payment against her stable monthly income.

Debt to income ratio—A percentage that measures all of a loan applicant's monthly obligations (including the proposed mortgage payment) against the stable monthly income. Also called a total debt service to income ratio.

Net worth—An individual's total personal assets minus his total personal liabilities.

Automated underwriting (AU)—Analysis of a loan application with a computer program that makes a preliminary recommendation for or against approval.

Fully amortized loan—A loan that is repaid by the end of its term by means of regular principal and interest payments.

Loan-to-value ratio (LTV)—The relationship between the loan amount and the property's appraised value or sales price, whichever is less.

Secondary financing—A second loan to help pay the downpayment or closing costs associated with the primary loan.

Fixed-rate loan—A loan repaid over its term at an unchanging rate of interest.

Adjustable-rate mortgage (ARM)—A loan that allows the lender to periodically adjust the loan's interest rate to reflect changes in the cost of money.

Index—A published rate that is a reliable indicator of the current cost of money.

Margin—The difference between the index value on an ARM and the interest rate the borrower is charged.

Negative amortization—When unpaid interest is added to the loan balance.

Conventional loan—Any institutional loan that is not insured or guaranteed by a government agency.

Nonconforming loan—A loan that does not meet the underwriting standards of the major secondary market agencies.

PMI—Private mortgage insurance; insurance designed to protect lenders from the greater risks of high-LTV conventional loans.

MIP—The mortgage insurance premiums required for FHA-insured loans.

Certificate of Eligibility—The document that establishes a veteran's eligibility to apply for a VA home loan.

Notice of Value—The document issued when a home is appraised in connection with the underwriting of a VA loan. Also referred to as a Certificate of Reasonable Value.

Residual income—The amount of monthly income a VA borrower has left over after deducting monthly expenses and taxes.

Rural Housing Service—A federal agency that makes and guarantees loans to low- or moderate-income borrowers to purchase, build, or rehabilitate homes in rural areas.

Predatory lending—Lending practices used by unscrupulous lenders and brokers to take advantage of unsophisticated borrowers.

Chapter Quiz

1. A mortgage company:
   a) arranges loans but does not service them
   b) services loans but does not make them
   c) is the same as a mortgage broker
   d) is sometimes called a mortgage banker

2. To increase its yield on a loan, the lender is charging 2% of the loan amount, to be paid at closing. This charge is called:
   a) the origination fee
   b) PMI
   c) the index
   d) discount points

3. The Truth in Lending Act and Regulation Z:
   a) place restrictions on how much a lender can charge for a consumer loan
   b) require lenders to give loan applicants a disclosure statement concerning loan costs
   c) prohibit lenders from advertising specific financing terms
   d) All of the above

4. A loan's APR expresses the relationship between:
   a) the total finance charge and the loan amount
   b) the interest rate on the loan and the discount rate
   c) the downpayment and the total finance charge
   d) the monthly payment and the interest rate

5. After determining the quantity of the loan applicant's stable monthly income, the underwriter measures the adequacy of the income using:
   a) the Consumer Price Index
   b) income ratios
   c) credit scoring
   d) federal income tax tables

6. Fifteen-year mortgages typically have all of the following disadvantages, except:
   a) a higher interest rate
   b) higher monthly payments
   c) a larger downpayment
   d) All of these are disadvantages of a 15-year mortgage

7. A house was appraised for $403,000 and its sales price is $400,000. If the loan-to-value ratio is 90%, how much is the loan amount?
   a) $322,400
   b) $360,000
   c) $362,700
   d) $393,000

8. With an adjustable-rate mortgage, the interest rate:
   a) is adjusted at specified intervals, and so is the payment amount
   b) is adjusted monthly, and so is the payment amount
   c) increases and decreases, but the payment amount remains the same
   d) may increase periodically, but does not decrease

9. Unpaid interest added to the loan balance is referred to as:
   a) payment shock
   b) partial amortization
   c) negative amortization
   d) prequalification

10. For conventional loans, private mortgage insurance is required when the loan-to-value ratio is:
    a) 75% or higher
    b) 90% or higher
    c) over 95%
    d) over 80%

11. For conventional loans, some lenders require the borrower to have:
    a) at least two months' mortgage payments in reserve
    b) secondary financing for the downpayment
    c) residual income that meets minimum requirements
    d) a 3% margin to provide for emergencies

12. The FHA:
    a) makes loans
    b) insures loans
    c) buys and sells loans
    d) All of the above

13. All of the following statements about FHA loans are true, except:
    a) no downpayment is required
    b) the borrower is usually not required to have reserves after closing
    c) mortgage insurance is required on all loans
    d) the borrower must occupy the property as her primary residence

14. A VA loan can be assumed:
    a) only by an eligible veteran
    b) only by an eligible veteran who agrees to a substitution of entitlement
    c) by any buyer who passes the credit check
    d) by any buyer, without regard to creditworthiness

15. Which of the following statements about predatory lending is true?
    a) Most subprime lenders engage in predatory practices
    b) Predatory lending does not occur in connection with home purchase loans
    c) Predatory lenders are especially likely to target the elderly
    d) Predatory lending has been virtually eliminated by the Home Ownership and Equity Protection Act (HOEPA)

Answer Key

1. d) A mortgage company is sometimes called a mortgage banker. Mortgage companies make loans and also service loans on behalf of investors.

2. d) Discount points are a percentage of the loan amount paid at closing to increase the lender's yield on the loan.

3. b) TILA and Regulation Z require lenders to disclose loan costs to loan applicants, but they do not restrict how much a lender can charge in connection with a loan. And while these laws regulate how financing terms are presented in advertising, they do not prohibit advertisement of financing terms.

4. a) The APR is the annual percentage rate, which indicates the relationship between the total finance charge and the loan amount.

5. b) Income ratios are used to measure the adequacy or sufficiency of a loan applicant's stable monthly income.

6. a) Fifteen-year mortgages usually have lower interest rates than 30-year mortgages.

7. b) The loan amount is $360,000, because the loan-to-value ratio is based on the appraised value or the sales price, whichever is less. $400,000 × 90% = $360,000.

8. a) Both the interest rate and the payment amount for an ARM are adjusted at specified intervals. The rate and the payment amount may increase or decrease to reflect changes in the index.

9. c) Negative amortization is unpaid interest that is added to the loan balance.

10. d) When the LTV of a conventional loan is more than 80%, PMI is required.

11. a) To qualify for a conventional loan, the borrower may be required to have at least two months' mortgage payments in reserve.

12. b) The FHA only insures loans made by institutional lenders. It does not make loans itself, nor does it buy and sell loans on the secondary market.

13. a) A downpayment is required for an FHA loan.

14. c) A VA loan can be assumed by any buyer, whether or not he is an eligible veteran. The buyer is required to pass a credit check, however.

15. c) Predatory lenders are especially likely to target elderly people and other vulnerable groups. Predatory lending is a problem in connection with home purchase loans as well as home equity loans. It is especially likely to occur in the subprime market, but most subprime lenders do not engage in predatory lending practices.

Chapter 13

Real Estate Appraisal

I. Introduction to Appraisal
  A. Purpose and use of an appraisal
  B. Appraiser-client relationship
  C. Licensing and certification of appraisers
II. Value
  A. Types of value
  B. Principles of value
III. The Appraisal Process
IV. Gathering Data
  A. General data
    1. Economic trends
    2. Neighborhood analysis
  B. Specific data
    1. Site analysis
    2. Building analysis
V. Methods of Appraisal
  A. Sales comparison approach to value
    1. Elements of comparison
    2. Comparing properties and making adjustments
    3. Use of listings
  B. Cost approach to value
    1. Replacement cost vs. reproduction cost
    2. Estimating replacement cost
    3. Estimating depreciation
    4. Adding land value
  C. Income approach to value
    1. Gross income
    2. Operating expenses
    3. Capitalization
    4. Gross income multipliers
  D. Site valuation
  E. Appraising multi-family properties
VI. Reconciliation and Final Estimate of Value
VII. Competitive Market Analysis

Chapter Overview

The foundation of each real estate transaction is the value placed on the property in question. The value of a home affects its selling price, its financing terms, its rental rate, its income tax consequences, its property tax assessment, and its insurance coverage. It is important to know what the property is worth aside from any emotional or subjective value placed on it by the buyer or seller. An estimate or opinion of value is called an appraisal. This chapter examines what is meant by the term "value" and explains the various methods appraisers use to estimate value.

Introduction to Appraisal

An **appraisal** is an estimate or an opinion of value. It usually takes the form of a written statement, called an **appraisal report**, setting forth the appraiser's opinion of the value of a piece of property as of a given date. An appraisal is sometimes called a **valuation**.

A formal appraisal should not be confused with a competitive market analysis (CMA), which is prepared by an agent in order to show a seller what her home is likely to sell for in the current market. The agent gathers information about similar homes in the area that have sold recently and analyzes the data to make a rough determination of value. A CMA is not as comprehensive or reliable as a formal appraisal and should never be used in place of an appraisal. We will discuss CMA preparation in more detail at the end of this chapter.

Purpose and Use of an Appraisal

In appraisal terminology, a distinction is made between the purpose and the use of an appraisal. The basic **purpose** of an appraisal is to estimate value; in most cases the appraiser is estimating the property's market value (which is defined later in this chapter). The **use** (or function) of an appraisal refers to the reason the appraisal is being made. For example, an appraisal's function may be to help a seller decide on a fair listing price, or to help a buyer determine how much to pay for a property. Most often, the use of an appraisal is to help a lender decide whether the property a buyer has chosen is suitable security for a loan and, if so, what the maximum loan amount should be.

In addition to helping to determine a fair price or a maximum loan amount, an appraiser's services are regularly required in order to:

- identify raw land's highest and best use;
- estimate a property's value for purposes of taxation;
- establish rental rates;
- estimate the relative values of properties being exchanged;
- determine the amount of hazard insurance coverage necessary;
- estimate remodeling costs or their contribution to value;

- help establish just compensation in a condemnation proceeding; or
- estimate the value of properties involved in the liquidation of estates, corporate mergers and acquisitions, or bankruptcies.

The Appraiser-Client Relationship

An appraiser can be self-employed or work for a bank, a savings and loan, a mortgage company, a private corporation that has an active real estate department, or a government agency. An appraiser who is hired to appraise property for a fee is called a **fee appraiser**. Most appraisers are fee appraisers, either self-employed or employed by an appraisal firm.

The person who hires the appraiser is the client. The appraiser is the client's agent. A principal/agent relationship exists and the laws of agency apply (see Chapter 9). Because of the fiduciary relationship that exists between the appraiser and his client, an appraiser has a duty of confidentiality and should discuss the results of the appraisal process only with the client. Duties imposed by the agency relationship also require an appraiser to disclose in the appraisal report any interest he has in the property being appraised. And if the appraiser is not sure whether to classify a particular item as real or personal property, or is uncertain about any other aspect of the property, that information should also be included in the appraisal report.

An appraiser's fee is determined in advance, based on the expected difficulty of the appraisal and the amount of time it is likely to take. The fee cannot be calculated as a percentage of the appraised value of the property, nor can it be based on the client's satisfaction with the appraiser's findings.

To ensure their independence and impartiality, appraisers in home loan transactions are subject to special rules. For example, if a loan will be secured by the borrower's home, federal law prohibits the appraiser from having any financial interest in the property. If a loan will be sold to Fannie Mae or Freddie Mac, the appraiser is not permitted to have any substantive communication with the mortgage loan originator; the appraisal must be arranged through an independent appraisal management company or through a separate department within the lender's organization. In addition, the appraiser can't be selected or compensated by a real estate agent.

Licensing and Certification of Appraisers

Appraisers are licensed and certified under state law. Although not every state requires all appraisers to be licensed or certified, Title XI of the federal Financial Institutions Reform, Recovery, and Enforcement Act of 1989 (FIRREA) requires appraisals used in "federally related" loan transactions to be prepared by state-licensed or state-certified appraisers. The majority of real estate loans are federally related, since the category includes loans made by any financial institution regulated or insured by the federal government and loans sold to the federal secondary market entities. Transactions for $250,000 or less are exempt from this requirement, however.

Title XI of FIRREA also requires appraisals used in federally related loan transactions to be prepared in accordance with the Uniform Standards of Professional

Appraisal Practice (USPAP). The USPAP are guidelines established by the Appraisal Foundation, a nonprofit organization made up of appraisal and related organizations. The standards outline the methods and techniques an appraiser must follow in performing an appraisal. In addition, the USPAP define the accepted types of appraisals, the three levels of reporting, and the reporting standards for any appraisal report.

Any appraiser who fails to abide by the USPAP in order to defraud a federally insured lender could be found guilty of a felony.

Value

Value is a term with many meanings. One common definition is "the present worth of future benefits." Value may also be defined as the ability of an item or service to command other items or services in exchange, or as the relationship between a desired thing and the person who desires it. Value is usually measured in terms of money.

For a product to have value, it must have certain characteristics, called the elements of value:

1. utility,
2. scarcity,
3. demand, and
4. transferability.

A product must render a service or fill a need in order to have value; this is called utility. But utility must exist in conjunction with the other elements of value or the product has no economic value. For example, air has great utility, but it's universally available; because it lacks scarcity, it has no economic value.

Generally, the scarcer an item is, the greater its value. For instance, if diamonds were to become much more plentiful, their value would decline.

Demand is also an essential part of value. There is demand for an item if it produces a desire to own. And there is **effective demand** when that desire is coupled with purchasing power.

Of course, if an item cannot be transferred from one party to another, it will not have any economic value. Transferability refers to the ability to transfer possession and control of the rights that constitute ownership of property.

Types of Value

An appraisal may be used to determine any one of several different types of value. It is important to distinguish between the different types of value, and to identify the type of value being estimated.

Market Value. Market value is the value of property as determined by the open market. Estimating a property's market value (also called value in exchange) is the purpose of most appraisals.

Here is the most widely accepted definition of market value, the one used by the federal financial institution regulatory agencies:

The most probable price which a property should bring in a competitive and open market under all conditions requisite to a fair sale, the buyer and seller each acting prudently and knowledgeably, and assuming the price is not affected by undue stimulus.

Notice that according to this definition, market value is the *most probable* price (not "the highest price") that the property *should bring* (not "will bring"). Appraisal is a matter of estimation and likelihood, not certainty.

The Federal Housing Administration offers this succinct explanation of market value: "The price which typical buyers would be warranted in paying for the property for long-term use or investment, if they were well informed and acted intelligently, voluntarily, and without necessity."

Market Value vs. Market Price. It's important to understand the distinction between market value and market price. Market price is the price actually paid for a property, regardless of whether the parties to the transaction were informed and acting free of unusual pressure. Market value is what should be paid if a property is purchased and sold under all the conditions requisite to a fair sale. These conditions include an open and competitive market, prudent and informed parties, and no undue stimulus (that is, no unusual pressure to sell or buy immediately).

Value in Use. Value in use is the subjective value placed on a property by a particular person. Value in use may be quite different from market value, depending on the circumstances. For example, a large, expensive, one-bedroom home, designed, built, and occupied by its owner, would undoubtedly be worth more to the owner than to the average buyer. Most buyers would look at the property objectively and expect more than one bedroom for the price.

Investment Value. Investment value is the value of a property to a particular investor with specific investment criteria. Thus, when estimating investment value, it is important that the appraiser clearly understand the investment requirements of the particular investor. Because the goals of the individual investor have a significant effect on the value estimate, investment value is inherently subjective in nature. By comparison, market value is said to represent a more objective standard.

Liquidation Value. Liquidation value is a form of market value. The primary distinction is that liquidation value assumes that the property must be sold in a limited period of time, which rarely constitutes "reasonable" exposure to the market. Liquidation value is typically sought when a financial institution is considering a foreclosure process.

Assessed Value. The assessed value of real property is set by state taxing authorities for the purpose of assessing ad valorem property taxes—annual property taxes that are based on the value of the property. The tax proceeds are used to support general government services. To determine assessed value, the appraiser must first estimate market value (as defined by the tax law), then apply a certain percentage rate (called the assessment ratio) as specified under the assessment statute.

Insurable Value. Insurable value is defined by the terms of a particular insurance policy. It refers to the value of property for purposes of reimbursement under the policy.

Loan Value. The loan value of real property is the value assigned to the property for the purpose of determining the amount of the loan.

Going Concern Value. The total value of a proven, ongoing business operation, which includes real property that is an integral part of the operation, is called going concern value. This form of value is normally inapplicable to residential real estate.

Principles of Value

Of the major forces that influence our attitudes and behavior, four interact to create, support, or erode property values:

- social ideals and standards,
- economic fluctuations,
- government regulations, and
- physical and environmental factors.

A change in attitudes regarding family size and the emergence of the two-car family are examples of social forces that affect the value of homes (in this case, homes with one-car garages or too many bedrooms). Economic forces include employment levels, interest rates, and any other factors that affect the community's purchasing power. Government regulations, such as zoning ordinances, serve to promote, stabilize, or discourage the demand for property. Physical and environmental factors, such as climate, earthquakes, and flood control measures, can also have an impact on property values.

Fig. 13.1 Principle of highest and best use

Highest and Best Use (Alternative Use Considerations)		
	Annual Income	**Estimated Value**
Present Use: Warehouse	$38,560 (actual)	$350,000
Alternative Use 1: Parking lot	$33,600 (estimated)	$302,000
Alternative Use 2: Gas station	$41,000 (estimated)	$368,000
Alternative Use 3: Triplex	$28,600 (estimated)	$264,000

All four of these forces affect value independently of the owner's efforts. For instance, an economic force such as inflation will cause a property's value to increase, even though the owner has done nothing at all to improve the property. When the value of a property increases due to outside forces, the increase is referred to as an **unearned increment**.

Over the years, appraisers have developed a reliable body of principles, referred to as the **principles of value**, that take these forces into account and guide appraisers in making decisions in the valuation process. Note that these principles are valid no matter which appraisal method is used to arrive at an estimate of value.

Principle of Highest and Best Use. Highest and best use refers to the most profitable use of a piece of property—the use that will provide the greatest net return over a period of time. Net return usually refers to net income, but it cannot always be measured in terms of money. With residential properties, for example, net return might manifest itself in the form of amenities: the pleasure and satisfaction derived from living on the property.

Determining the highest and best use may be a simple matter of confirming that deed restrictions or an existing zoning ordinance limit the property to its present use. Often the present use of a property is its highest and best use. But change is constant, and a warehouse site that was once profitable might now generate a greater net return as a parking lot.

Principle of Change. The principle of change holds that real estate values are constantly in flux, moving up and down in response to changes in the various social, economic, governmental, and environmental forces that affect value. A property's value also changes as the property itself improves or deteriorates. A property that was worth $500,000 last year may be worth $530,000 today, and its value is likely to change in the coming year as well. Because value is always subject to change, an estimate of value must be tied to a given date, called the **effective date** of the appraisal.

Related to the principle of change is the idea that property has a four-phase life cycle: **integration**, **equilibrium**, **disintegration**, and **rejuvenation**. Integration (also called growth or development) is the early stage, when the property is being developed. Equilibrium is a period of stability, when the property undergoes little, if any, change. Disintegration is a period of decline, when the property's economic usefulness is near an end and constant upkeep is necessary. And rejuvenation (also known as revitalization) is a period of renewal, when the property is reborn, often with a different highest and best use.

Rejuvenation or revitalization of a property can take different forms. If a building is restored to good condition without being changed, it's called **rehabilitation**; if the floor plan or style are altered, it's called **remodeling**. And an entire neighborhood can be rejuvenated by **redevelopment**, such as an urban renewal project in which rundown buildings are demolished and replaced.

Every property has both a physical and an economic life cycle. A property's **economic life** (also called its useful life) is the period when the land and its improvements are profitable. The economic or useful life almost always ends before the physical life. The appraiser must recognize and take into account which stage of the life cycle a property is in when estimating its present worth.

Principle of Anticipation. It is the future, not the past, that is important to appraisers. Knowing that property values change, an appraiser asks: What is happening to this property? What is its future? How do prospective buyers view its potential? The appraiser must be aware of the social, economic, and governmental factors that will affect the future value of the property.

Value is created by the anticipated future benefits of owning a property. It is future benefits, not past benefits, that arouse a desire to own.

Anticipation can help or hurt value, depending on what informed buyers and sellers expect to happen to the property in the future. They usually expect property values to increase, but in certain situations they anticipate that values will decline, as when the community is experiencing a severe recession.

Principle of Supply and Demand. The principle of supply and demand affects almost every commodity, including real estate. Values tend to rise as demand increases and supply decreases, and diminish when the reverse is true. It is not so much the demand for or supply of real estate in general that affects values, but the demand for or supply of a particular type of property. For instance, a generally depressed community may have one or two very attractive, sought-after neighborhoods. The value of these homes remains high, no matter what the general trend is for the rest of the community.

Principle of Substitution. This principle states that no one will pay more for a property than they would have to pay for an equally desirable substitute property, provided there would be no unreasonable delay in acquiring that substitute. Explained another way, the principle of substitution holds that if two properties for sale are equally desirable (whether in terms of their use, their design, or the income they generate), the least expensive will be in greater demand. The principle of substitution is the basis of all three methods of appraisal (discussed below).

Principle of Conformity. The maximum value of land is achieved when there is an acceptable degree of social and economic conformity in the area. Conformity should be reasonable, not carried to an extreme.

In a residential appraisal, one aspect of conformity the appraiser considers is similarity in the size, age, and quality of the homes in the neighborhood. Nonconformity can work to the benefit or to the detriment of the nonconforming home. The value of a home of much lower quality than those around it is increased by its association with the higher quality homes; this is the principle of **progression.**

> **Example:** A small, unkempt home surrounded by large, attractive homes will be worth more in this neighborhood than it would be if it were situated in a neighborhood of other small homes in poor condition.

Conversely, the value of a large, expensive home in a neighborhood of small, inexpensive homes will suffer because of its surroundings; this is the principle of **regression**.

Principle of Competition. Competition may have a dramatic impact on the value of property, especially income property. For example, if one convenience store in a neighborhood is extremely profitable, its success is very likely to bring a competing convenience store into the area. This competition will probably mean lower profits for the first store (as some of its customers begin doing business with the second store), and lower profits will reduce the property's value.

Principle of Balance. This principle maintains that the maximum value of real estate is achieved when the **agents of production—labor, coordination, capital,** and **land**—are in proper balance with each other.

To see whether the agents of production are in proper balance, the appraiser deducts a dollar figure that can be attributed to each agent from the property's gross earnings. First, the appraiser deducts the wages (labor) that are paid as part of the property's operating costs. Next, the appraiser deducts the cost of the management (coordination). The third item deducted is the expense of principal and interest (capital), which represents the funds invested in the building and equipment. The **surplus productivity**—whatever earnings remain after the first three productive agents have been deducted—is credited to the land for its part in the production of the gross income.

The amount credited to the land will reflect the land's value under its present use. If an imbalance exists and too much of the gross earnings are attributed to the land, the buildings are probably an underimprovement and the land is not serving its highest and best use. If too little income is credited to the land, the buildings are probably an overimprovement and, again, the land is not serving its highest and best use.

Principle of Contribution. Contribution refers to the value an improvement adds to the overall value of the property. Some improvements will add more value than the expense of making them; others will cost more than they contribute to value.

A remodeled basement ordinarily will not contribute its cost to the value of the home. On the other hand, the addition of a second bathroom may increase a home's value by more than the cost of installing it.

Principle of Increasing and Decreasing Returns. The principle of increasing returns is related to the principle of contribution. Assume that the amount of one or more of the agents of production (such as land) remains fixed. As the amount invested in the other agent(s) is incrementally increased, the rate of return on the investment will first increase at a progressively higher rate, then continue to increase but at a progressively lower rate, and finally begin to decrease (at the point of diminishing returns).

Example: The Bensons want to sell their home, which is currently worth $225,000. Before putting the property on the market, they decide to remodel the master bathroom to increase the value of the home. The bathroom remodel includes the installation of gold-plated fixtures and a marble bathtub. Generally, remodeling the master bathroom in a home in a middle class neighborhood adds about $10,000 to the value of the home. However, the installation of fancy fixtures does not add anything more to the value. Under the principle of decreasing returns, the Bensons are unlikely to recover the costs of the extravagant fixtures.

The example above illustrates how an overimprovement, such as the gold-plated fixtures, may not necessarily add to the value of the property. Had the Bensons installed standard fixtures, the increase in value would have been the same.

The Appraisal Process

Properly done, the appraisal process is orderly and systematic. While there is no official procedure, appraisers generally carry out the appraisal process in the following manner.

1. **Define the problem.** Each client wants an appraiser to solve a specific problem: to estimate the value of a particular property as of a particular date and for a particular purpose. The first step in the appraisal process is to define the problem to be solved. This involves identifying the **subject property**—what property and which aspect(s) of it are to be appraised. Typically, the appraiser considers all of the elements of real property: the land and its improvements, all of the rights that go along with land ownership, and the utility of the property. (The value of land and its improvements together is called the **improved value**.) The appraiser must also establish the purpose of the appraisal and how the client intends to use it. Unless instructed to do otherwise, the appraiser will estimate the property's value as of the date the appraisal is performed.
2. **Determine the scope of work.** This refers to figuring out what's involved in solving the problem. The scope of work includes both the type and quantity of information needed, as well the type of analysis that will be used in the appraisal assignment. Finally, the scope of work may involve planning the tasks involved in completing the appraisal; complex assignments may require consulting additional experts, for example.
3. **Collect and verify the data.** Appraisal data can be divided into two categories: general and specific. **General data** concerns matters outside the subject property that affect its value. It includes population trends, prevailing economic circumstances, zoning, and proximity to shopping, schools, and transportation, as well as the condition and quality of the neighborhood. **Specific data** concerns the subject property itself. The appraiser will gather information about the title, the buildings, and the site. (General and specific data will be discussed in more detail in the next section of the chapter.)
4. **Analyze data.** Analyzing the data requires the appraiser to judge the relevance of each piece of information that has been collected. For instance, the appraiser will consider what the data regarding market trends says about the subject property's value.
5. **Determine site value.** Site valuation is an estimate of the value of a property, excluding the value of any existing or proposed improvements. For vacant land, site valuation is the same as appraising the property. For improved property (such as property with a house on it), site valuation

Fig. 13.2 The appraisal process

Steps in the Appraisal Process
1. Define the problem
2. Determine the scope of work
3. Collect and verify data
4. Analyze data
5. Determine site value
6. Apply appropriate methods of appraisal • Sales comparison approach • Cost approach • Income approach
7. Reconcile results to arrive at final estimate
8. Issue appraisal report

involves appraising the property as if vacant. A separate site valuation may be necessary depending on the method of appraisal that will be used (for example, the cost approach to value; see below).

6. **Apply the appropriate valuation methods of appraisal.** In some cases, the appraiser will approach the problem of estimating value three different ways: with the sales comparison approach, the cost approach, and the income approach. In other cases, she will use only the method that seems most appropriate for the problem to be solved. Whether one, two, or three approaches are used is a matter of judgment.

   Sometimes a particular method cannot be used. Raw land, for example, cannot be appraised using the cost approach. A public library, on the other hand, must be appraised by the cost method because it does not generate income and no market exists for it.

   The figures yielded by each of the three approaches are called value indicators; they give indications of what the property is worth, but are not final estimates themselves.
7. **Reconcile value indicators for the final value estimate.** After taking into account the purpose of the appraisal, the type of property, and the reliability of the data gathered, the appraiser weighs the value indicators and decides on a final estimate of the subject property's market value.
8. **Issue appraisal report.** The appraiser's last step is to prepare an appraisal report, presenting the value estimate and summarizing the underlying data for the client. When property is appraised to determine its value as collateral for a loan, the appraiser's client is the lender.

Gathering Data

Once the appraiser knows what property she is to appraise and what the purpose of the appraisal is, she begins to gather the necessary data. As mentioned above, data

Fig. 13.3 Neighborhood data form

NEIGHBORHOOD DATA FORM

Property adjacent to:
NORTH *Plum Boulevard, garden apartments*
SOUTH *Cherry Boulevard, single-family residences*
EAST *14th Avenue, single-family residences*
WEST *12th Avenue, single-family residences*

Population: ☐ increasing ☐ decreasing ☑ stable

Stage of Life Cycle: ☐ integration ☑ equilibrium ☐ disintegration ☐ rebirth

Tax Rate: ☐ higher ☐ lower ☑ same as competing areas

Services: ☑ police ☑ fire ☑ garbage ☐ other

Average family size: *3.5*
Predominant occupations: *white collar, skilled tradesman*

Distance from:
Commercial areas *3 miles*
Primary schools *6 blocks*
Secondary schools *1 mile*
Recreational areas *2 miles*
Cultural areas *3 miles*
Places of worship *Methodist, Catholic, Baptist*
Public transportation *Bus stops nearby, excellent service*
Freeways/highways *10 blocks*

Typical Properties	%	Age	Price Range	% Owner-Occupied
vacant lots	0			
single-family residences	80%	10 years	$380,000-395,000	93%
2- to 4-unit apartments	15%	15 years		
over 4-unit apartments	5%	5 years		
non-residential	0			

Nuisances in neighborhood (odors, noise, etc.) *none*
Hazards in neighborhood (chemical storage, pollution, etc.) *none*

is broken down into general data (about the neighborhood and other external influences) and specific data (about the subject property itself).

General Data

General data includes both general economic data about the community and information about the subject property's neighborhood.

Economic Trends. The appraiser examines economic trends for hints as to the direction the property's value might take in the future. A trend is a series of related developments that form a pattern. Economic trends can take shape at the local, regional, national, or international level, although local trends have the most significant impact on a property's value. Generally, prosperous conditions tend to have a positive effect on property values; economic declines have the opposite effect.

Economic forces include population growth shifts, employment and wage levels (purchasing power), price levels, building cycles, personal tax and property tax rates, building costs, and interest rates.

Neighborhood Analysis. A property's value is inevitably tied to its surrounding neighborhood. A neighborhood is a residential, commercial, industrial, or agricultural area that contains similar types of properties. Its boundaries are determined by physical barriers (such as highways and bodies of water), land use patterns, the age or value of homes or other buildings, and the economic status of the residents.

Neighborhoods are continually changing and, like the individual properties that make them up, they have a four-phase life cycle of integration, equilibrium, disintegration, and rejuvenation. When evaluating the future of a neighborhood, the appraiser must consider its physical, social, and economic characteristics, and also governmental influences.

Here are some of the specific factors appraisers look at when gathering data about a residential neighborhood:

1. **Percentage of home ownership.** Is there a high degree of owner-occupancy or do rental properties predominate? Owner-occupied neighborhoods are generally better maintained and less susceptible to deterioration.
2. **Vacant homes and lots.** An unusual number of vacant homes or lots suggests a low level of interest in the area, which has a negative effect on property values. On the other hand, significant construction activity in a neighborhood signals strong interest in the area.
3. **Conformity.** The homes in a neighborhood should be reasonably similar to one another in style, age, size, and quality. Strictly enforced zoning and private restrictions promote conformity and protect property values.
4. **Changing land use.** Is the neighborhood in the midst of a transition from residential use to some other type of use? If so, the properties may be losing their value.
5. **Contour of the land.** Mildly rolling topography is preferred to terrain that is either monotonously flat or excessively hilly.

6. **Streets.** Wide, gently curving streets and cul-de-sacs (short dead-end streets) are more appealing than narrow or straight streets. Streets should be hard surfaced and well maintained.
7. **Utilities.** Is the neighborhood adequately serviced by electricity, water, gas, sewers, telephones, cable TV, and high-speed Internet service?
8. **Nuisances.** Nuisances in or near a neighborhood (odors, eyesores, industrial noises or pollutants, or exposure to unusual winds, smog, or fog) hurt property values.
9. **Prestige.** Is the neighborhood considered prestigious, in comparison to others in the community? If so, that will increase property values.
10. **Proximity.** How far is it to traffic arterials and to important points such as downtown, employment centers, and shopping centers?
11. **Schools.** What schools serve the neighborhood? Are they highly regarded? Are they within walking distance? The quality of a school or school district can make a major difference in property values in a residential neighborhood.
12. **Public services.** Is the neighborhood properly serviced by public transportation, police, and fire units?
13. **Government influences.** Does zoning in and around the neighborhood promote residential use and insulate the property owner from nuisances? How do property tax rates compare with those of other areas nearby? High property taxes may discourage new construction.

Specific Data

Specific data has to do with the property itself. Often the appraiser will evaluate the site (the land and utilities) and the improvements to the site separately. For example, where properties are being assessed for tax purposes, most states require the assessments to show the distribution of value between land and its improvements. Another reason for appraising the land separately is to see if it is worth too much or too little compared to the value of the improvements. Where an imbalance exists, the land is not serving its highest and best use. The primary purpose of site analysis is to determine highest and best use.

Site Analysis. A thorough site analysis calls for accumulation of a good deal of data concerning the property's physical characteristics, as well as factors that affect its use or the title. A site's physical characteristics include all of the following:

1. **Width.** This refers to the lot's measurements from one side boundary to the other. Width can vary from front to back, as in the case of a pie-shaped lot on a cul-de-sac.
2. **Frontage.** Frontage is the length of the front boundary of the lot, the boundary that abuts a street or a body of water. The amount of frontage is often a more important consideration than width because it measures the property's accessibility, or its access to something desirable.
3. **Area.** Area is the size of the site, usually measured in square feet or acres. Comparisons between lots often focus on the features of frontage and area.

Fig. 13.4 Site data form

SITE DATA FORM

Address: *10157 - 13th Avenue*
Legal Description: *see attached description*

Size *50′ x 200′* Shape *Rectangular*
Square Feet *10,000* Street Paving *Asphalt*
Landscaping *professional* Topsoil *good*
Drainage *good* Frontage *good*
☐ corner lot ☑ inside lot

Utilities: ☑ water ☑ telephone ☑ gas ☑ sewers ☑ electricity ☑ storm drains

Improvements: ☑ sidewalks ☑ curb ☑ alleys ☑ driveway

Commercial land (especially retail property) is usually valued in terms of frontage; that is, it is worth a certain number of dollars per front foot. Industrial land, on the other hand, tends to be valued in terms of square feet or acreage. Residential lots are measured both ways: by square feet or acreage in most instances, but by front foot when the property abuts a lake or river, or some other desirable feature.

Occasionally, newly subdivided land is measured in "commercial acres." A **commercial acre** is the buildable portion of an acre that remains after part of the land has been dedicated for streets, sidewalks, and parks.

4. **Depth.** Depth is the distance between a site's front boundary and its rear boundary. Greater depth (more than the norm) can mean greater value, but it doesn't always. For example, suppose Lot 1 and Lot 2 have the same amount of frontage along a lake, but Lot 2 is deeper; Lot 2 is not necessarily more valuable than Lot 1. The additional square footage of Lot 2 might simply be considered **excess land.**

   Each situation must be analyzed individually. Even when greater depth or less depth affects value, the increase or decrease in value usually isn't proportional to the increase or decrease in depth.

   There are various rules of thumb concerning the relationship between depth and value. One of the most common is the 4-3-2-1 rule, which states that the front quarter of a lot holds 40% of its overall value; the second quarter holds 30%; the next quarter holds 20%; and the back quarter holds only 10% of the value. Because it's less accessible, the rear portion of a lot is less useful.

   In certain situations a **depth table** is used to evaluate how a lot's depth affects its value. This is a table of mathematical factors that can be multiplied by the front foot value of a standard lot to estimate the value of a lot with a specified depth. Depth tables are not considered accurate enough

Fig. 13.5 Building data form

BUILDING DATA FORM

Address: *10157 - 13th Avenue*
Age: *7 yrs.* Square feet: *1,350*
Number of rooms: *7* Quality of construction: *excellent*
Style: *ranch*

	Good	Bad	Fair
Exterior (general condition)	✓		
Foundation(slab/bsmt./crawl sp.)	✓		
Exterior (brick/frame/veneer/stucco/aluminum)	✓		
Garage(attached/detached/single/double)	✓		
Patio/porch/shed/other	✓		
Interior (general condition)	✓		
Walls (drywall/wood/plaster)	✓		
Ceilings	✓		
Floor (wood/tile/carpet/concrete)	✓		
Electrical wiring	✓		
Heating (electrical/gas/oil/other)	✓		
Air conditioning	✓		
Fireplace(s) *one*	✓		
Kitchen	✓		
Bathroom(s) *two*	✓		
Bedroom(s) *three*	✓		

Additional amenities *none*
Design advantages *convenient, sunny kitchen*
Design flaws *none*
Energy efficiency *insulation, weather-stripping, storm windows, heat pump*

	Living Rm.	Dining Rm.	Ktchn.	Bdrm.	Bath	Family Rm.
Basement						
1st Floor	✓	✓	✓	✓	✓	
2nd Floor						
Attic						

Depreciation:
Deferred Maintenance *normal wear*
Functional Obsolescence *none*
External Obsolescence *none*

for most appraisal purposes. However, tax assessors sometimes use depth tables when valuing commercial property for tax purposes.

Under certain circumstances, combining two or more adjoining lots to achieve greater width, depth, or area will make the larger parcel more valuable than the sum of the values of its component parcels. The increment of value that results when two or more lots are combined to produce greater value is called **plottage value**. The process of assembling lots to increase their value is called **assemblage** and is most frequently part of industrial or commercial land development.

5. **Shape.** Lots with uniform width and depth (such as rectangular lots) are almost always more useful than irregularly shaped lots. This is true for any kind of lot—residential, commercial, or industrial.
6. **Topography.** A site is generally more valuable if it is aesthetically appealing. Rolling terrain is preferable to flat, monotonous land. On the other hand, if the site would be costly to develop because it sits well above or below the street or is excessively hilly, then that lessens its value.
7. **Utilities.** Site analysis includes an investigation into the availability and cost of utility connections. Remote parcels lose value because the cost of bringing utility lines to the site is high or even prohibitive.
8. **Site in relation to area.** How a lot is situated in relation to the surrounding area influences its value. For instance, a retail store is often worth more if it is located on a corner, because it enjoys more exposure and its customers have access from two different streets. The effect the corner location has on the value of a business site is called **corner influence**.

   By contrast, a corner location has a negative effect on the value of a residential property. That's because a corner lot is more exposed to through traffic than a lot in the middle of the block. Similarly, the lots inside a subdivision are considered more desirable than the ones on the perimeter, next to the arterial streets.

Building Analysis. The improvements to the site must also be analyzed, along with any special amenities. (**Amenities** are attractive features, such as a nice view or beautiful landscaping.) Of course, the functional utility of a home depends on the needs and desires of its occupants, but there are some primary considerations that apply to most homes. These include:

1. **Construction quality.** Is the quality of the materials and workmanship good, average, or poor?
2. **Age/condition.** How old is the home? Is its overall condition good, average, or poor? If the foundation shows signs of cracking, or doors and windows don't close properly, an appraiser may recommend a soil engineer's report to check the soil stability.
3. **Size of house (square footage).** The outside dimensions of a home are used to calculate its square footage. The square footage includes the improved living area, but not the garage, basement, and porches. Commercial buildings, including warehouses, are also measured in terms of square feet.

4. **Orientation.** Orientation refers to how a building is positioned on the property in relation to views, privacy, and exposure to wind, sunlight, and noise.
5. **Basement.** A functional basement, especially a finished basement, contributes to value. (However, the amount a finished basement contributes to value is often not enough to recover the cost of the finish work.)
6. **Interior layout.** Is the floor plan functional and convenient? It should not be necessary to pass through a public room (such as the living room) to reach other rooms, or to pass through one of the bedrooms to reach another.
7. **Number of rooms.** The appraiser adds up the total number of rooms in the house, excluding the bathrooms and (usually) any basement rooms.
8. **Number of bedrooms.** The number of bedrooms has a major impact on value. For instance, if all else is equal, a two-bedroom home is worth considerably less than a three-bedroom home.
9. **Number of bathrooms.** A full bath is a lavatory (wash basin), toilet, and bathtub and shower; a three-quarter bath is a lavatory, toilet, and either bathtub or shower (not both); a half bath is a lavatory and toilet only. The number of bathrooms can have a noticeable effect on value.
10. **Air conditioning.** The presence or absence of an air conditioning system is important in hot regions.
11. **Energy efficiency.** With spiraling energy costs, an energy-efficient home is more valuable than a comparable one that is not. Energy-efficient features, such as double-paned windows, good insulation, and weather stripping, increase value.
12. **Garage/carport.** As a general rule, an enclosed garage is considered better than a carport. How many cars can the garage accommodate? Is there work or storage space in addition to parking space? Is it possible to enter the home directly from the garage or carport, protected from the weather?

Methods of Appraisal

Once the appraiser has accumulated the necessary general and specific data, he will begin applying one or more of the three methods of appraising property:

- the sales comparison approach,
- the cost approach, and
- the income approach.

Different types of properties lend themselves to different appraisal methods. For example, appraisers rely most on the sales comparison method in valuing older residential properties and vacant land. Churches and public buildings, such as libraries or courthouses, aren't sold on the open market, nor do they generate income, so the cost approach is invariably used. On the other hand, the income approach is usually the most reliable method for appraising an apartment complex.

Sales Comparison Approach to Value

The sales comparison approach (also known as the market data approach) is the best method for appraising residential property, and the most reliable method for appraising raw land. It involves comparing the subject property to similar properties that have recently sold, which are referred to as **comparable sales** or **comparables**. The appraiser gathers pertinent information about comparables and makes feature-by-feature comparisons with the subject property. The appraiser then translates her findings into an estimate of the market value of the subject property. Appraisers use this method whenever possible because the sales prices of comparables—which reflect the actions of informed buyers and sellers in the marketplace—are excellent indicators of market value.

An appraiser needs at least three reliable comparable sales to have enough data to evaluate a residential property. It is usually possible to find three good comparables, but when it isn't (for instance, if the market is inactive), the appraiser will turn to the alternative appraisal methods—the cost approach and the income approach.

Elements of Comparison. To determine whether a particular sale can legitimately be used as a comparable sale, the appraiser will check the following aspects of the transaction, which are known as the primary elements of comparison.

Date of Comparable Sale. A comparable sale should be recent, within the past six months if possible. (During times of rapid market change, sales within the last two or three months may be required.) Recent sales give a more accurate indication of what is happening in the marketplace today. If the market has been inactive and there are not three legitimate comparable sales from the past six months, then the appraiser can go back further. (Comparable sales over one year old are generally not acceptable, however.) When using a comparable more than six months old, it is necessary to make adjustments for the time factor, allowing for inflationary or deflationary trends or any other forces that have affected prices in the area.

Example: A comparable residential property sold six months ago for $477,000. In general, local property values have fallen by 4% over the past six months. The comparable property, then, should be worth approximately 4% less than it was six months ago.

$477,000	Value six months ago
× 96%	Deflation factor
$457,920	Approximate present value

Location of Comparable Sale. Whenever possible, comparables should be selected from the neighborhood where the subject property is located. In the absence of any legitimate comparables in the neighborhood, the appraiser can look elsewhere, but the properties selected should at least come from comparable neighborhoods.

If a comparable selected from an inferior neighborhood is structurally identical to the subject property, it is probably less valuable; conversely, a structurally identical comparable in a superior neighborhood is probably more valuable than the subject property. It is generally conceded that location contributes more to the value of real estate than any other characteristic. A high-quality property cannot overcome the adverse effects on value that a low-quality neighborhood causes. On the other hand, the value of a relatively weak property is enhanced by a stable and desirable neighborhood.

Physical Characteristics. To qualify as a comparable, a property should have physical characteristics (construction quality, design, amenities, etc.) that are similar to those of the subject property. When a comparable has a feature that the subject property lacks, or lacks a feature that the subject property has, the appraiser will adjust the comparable's price.

Example: One of the comparables the appraiser is using is quite similar to the subject property overall, but there are several significant differences. The subject property has a two-car garage, while the comparable has only a one-car garage. Based on experience, the appraiser estimates that space for a second car adds approximately $6,000 to the value of a home in this area. The comparable actually sold for $345,500. The appraiser will add $6,000 to that price, to estimate what the comparable would have been worth with a two-car garage.

On the other hand, the comparable has a fireplace and the subject property does not. The appraiser estimates that a fireplace adds approximately $1,400 to the value of a home. She will subtract $1,400 from the comparable's price, to estimate what the comparable would have sold for without a fireplace.

After adjusting the comparable's price up or down for each difference in this way, the appraiser can identify what the comparable would have sold for if it had been identical to the subject property. When the appraiser repeats this process for each comparable, the value of the subject property becomes evident.

Terms of Sale. The terms of sale can affect the price a buyer will pay for a property. Attractive financing concessions (such as seller-paid discount points or seller financing with an especially low interest rate) can make a buyer willing to pay a higher price than she would otherwise be willing to pay.

An appraiser needs to take into account the influence the terms of sale may have had on the price paid for a comparable property. If the seller offered the property on very favorable terms, there is a good chance the sales price did not represent the true market value of the comparable.

Under the Uniform Standards of Professional Appraisal Practice, an appraiser giving an estimate of market value must state whether it's the most probable price:

1. in terms of cash;
2. in terms of financial arrangements equivalent to cash; or
3. in other precisely defined terms.

If the estimate is based on financing with special conditions or incentives, those terms must be clearly set forth, and the appraiser must estimate their effect on the property's value. Market data supporting the value estimate (comparable sales) must be explained in the same way.

Conditions of Sale. Last but not least, a comparable sale can be relied on as an indication of what the subject property is worth only if it occurred under normal conditions. That is, the sale was between unrelated parties (an "arm's length transaction"); both the buyer and the seller were informed of the property's attributes and deficiencies; both were acting free of unusual pressure; and the property was offered for sale on the open market for a reasonable length of time.

Thus, the appraiser must investigate the circumstances of each comparable sale to determine whether the price paid was influenced by a condition that would render it unreliable as an indication of value. For example, if the property sold only days before a scheduled foreclosure sale, the sales price probably reflected the pressure under which the seller was acting. Or if the buyer and seller were relatives, it's possible that the price was less than it would have been between two strangers. Or if the home sold the same day it was listed, it may have been underpriced. In each of these cases, there's reason to suspect that the sales price did not reflect the property's true value, so the appraiser would not use the transaction as a comparable sale.

Comparing Properties and Making Adjustments. A proper comparison between the subject property and each comparable is essential to an accurate estimate of value. The more similar the properties, the easier the comparison. A comparable property that is the same design and in the same condition as the subject property, on a very similar site in the same neighborhood, which sold under typical financing terms the previous month, will give an excellent indication of the market value of the subject property. However, except perhaps in a new subdivision where the houses are nearly identical, the appraiser usually cannot find such ideal comparables. There are likely to be at least some significant differences between the comparables and the subject property. So, as you've seen, the appraiser has to make adjustments, taking into account differences in time, location, physical characteristics, and terms of sale, in order to arrive at an **adjusted selling price** for each comparable.

It stands to reason that the more adjustments an appraiser has to make, the less reliable the resulting estimate of value will be. These adjustments are an inevitable part of the sales comparison approach, but appraisers try to keep them to a minimum by selecting the best comparables available.

The appraiser bases his estimate of the subject property's value on the adjusted prices of the comparables, but the value estimate is never merely an average of those prices; careful analysis is required. Also note that the original cost of the subject property (how much the current owners paid for it) is irrelevant to the appraisal process.

Use of Listings. When comparable sales are scarce (as when the market is just emerging from a dormant period), the appraiser may compare the subject property to properties that are presently listed for sale. The appraiser must keep in mind, however, that listing prices tend to be high and often represent the ceiling of the market value range. The appraiser might also use prices offered by buyers (but not accepted by the sellers), though these can be difficult to confirm, since records of offers aren't always kept. Offers are usually at the low end of the value range. Actual market value is typically somewhere between offers and listing prices.

Note that assessed values set for tax purposes are never used in place of comparable sales.

Fig. 13.6 Comparable sales comparison chart

Comparable Sales Comparison Chart					
	Subject Property	Comparables			
		1	2	3	4
Sales price		*$391,750*	*$396,500*	*$387,000*	*$388,500*
Location	*quiet street*				
Age	*7 yrs.*				
Lot size	*50'x200'*				
Construction	*frame*			*+6,000*	
Style	*ranch*				
Number of Rooms	*7*		*–5,000*		
Number of Bedrooms	*3*				
Number of Baths	*2*	*+3,500*			*+3,500*
Square feet	*1,350*				
Exterior	*good*				
Interior	*good*				
Garage	*1 car attached*				
Other improvements		*–4,000*			
Financing					
Date of sale		*–3,000*	*–3,000*		
Net Adjustments		*–3,500*	*–8,000*	*+6,000*	*+3,500*
Adjusted Price		*$388,250*	*$388,500*	*$393,000*	*$392,000*

Cost Approach to Value

The cost approach is based on the premise that the value of a property is limited by the cost of replacing it. (This is the principle of substitution: if the asking price for a home is more than it would cost to build a new one just like it, no one will buy it.) The estimate of value arrived at through the cost approach usually represents the upper limits of the property's value.

The cost approach involves estimating how much it would cost to replace the subject property's existing buildings, then adding to that the estimated value of the site on which they rest. Because the cost approach involves estimating the value of land and buildings separately, then adding the estimates together, it is sometimes called the **summation method**.

There are three steps to the cost approach:

1. Estimate the cost of replacing the improvements.
2. Estimate and deduct any accrued depreciation.
3. Add the value of the lot to the depreciated value of the improvements.

It is important to distinguish between replacement cost and reproduction cost. **Reproduction cost** is the cost of constructing an exact duplicate—a replica—of the subject building, at current prices. **Replacement cost**, on the other hand, is the current cost of constructing a building with a utility equivalent to the subject's—that is, a building that can be used in the same way. Reproduction cost and replacement cost may be the same if the subject property is a new home. But if the structure is older and was built with the detailed workmanship and expensive materials of earlier times, then the reproduction cost and the replacement cost will be quite different. So the appraiser must base her estimate of value on the replacement cost. The reproduction cost would be prohibitive, and it would not represent the current market value of the improvements.

Estimating Replacement Cost. The replacement cost of a building can be estimated in three different ways:

1. the square foot method,
2. the unit-in-place method, and
3. the quantity survey method.

Square Foot. The simplest way to estimate replacement cost is the square foot method (also known as the **comparative cost** method). By analyzing the average cost per square foot of construction for recently built comparable homes, the appraiser can calculate the square foot cost of replacing the subject home. The number of square feet in a home is determined by measuring the outside dimensions of each floor of the structure.

To calculate the cost of replacing the subject property's improvements, the appraiser multiplies the estimated cost per square foot by the number of square feet in the subject.

Example: The subject property is a ranch-style house with a wooden exterior, containing 1,600 square feet. Based on an analysis of the construction costs of three recently built homes of comparable size and quality, the appraiser estimates that it would cost $89.38 per square foot to replace the home.

1,600	Square feet
× $89.38	Cost per square foot
$143,008	Estimated cost of replacing improvements

Of course, a comparable structure (or "benchmark" building) is unlikely to be exactly the same as the subject property. Variations in design, shape, and grade of construction will affect the square-foot cost, either moderately or substantially. When recently built comparable homes are not available, then the appraiser relies on current cost manuals to estimate the basic construction costs.

Fig. 13.7 Calculating value using the cost approach

Cost Approach

Replacement cost of improvements
– Depreciation of improvements
+ Value of land
Value of subject property

Unit-in-Place. The unit-in-place method involves estimating the cost of replacing specific components of the building, such as the floors, roof, plumbing, and foundation. For example, one of the estimates might be a certain number of dollars per one hundred square feet of roofing. Another component estimate would be a certain amount per cubic yard of concrete for an installed foundation. Then the appraiser adds all of the estimates together to determine the replacement cost of the structure itself.

Quantity Survey. The quantity survey method involves a detailed estimate of the quantities and prices of construction materials and labor, which are added to the indirect costs (building permit, survey, etc.) for what is generally regarded as the most accurate replacement cost estimate. Because it's complex and time consuming, this method is generally used only by experienced contractors and price estimators.

Estimating Depreciation. When the property being appraised is a used home, the presumption is that it is less valuable than a comparable new home; it has depreciated in value. So after estimating replacement cost—which indicates what the improvements would be worth if they were new—the appraiser's next step is to estimate depreciation.

Depreciation is a loss in value due to any cause. Value can be lost as a result of physical deterioration, functional obsolescence, or external obsolescence.

- **Physical deterioration** is a loss in value due to wear and tear, damage, or structural defects. It's easier to spot this type of depreciation than the other types, and easier to estimate its impact on value.

  Physical deterioration may be curable or incurable. Depreciation is considered **curable** if the cost of correcting it could be recovered in the sales price when the property is sold. Depreciation is **incurable** if it is impossible to correct, or if it would cost so much to correct that it would be impractical to do so. Curable physical deterioration is often referred to as **deferred maintenance**.
- **Functional obsolescence** is a loss in value due to functional inadequacies, often caused by age or by poor design. Examples include a poor floor plan, an unappealing design, outdated fixtures, or too few bathrooms in relation to the number of bedrooms. Like physical deterioration, functional obsolescence may be curable or incurable.
- **External obsolescence** (also referred to as economic obsolescence) is caused by conditions outside the property itself, such as zoning changes, neighbor-

Fig. 13.8 A house with four bedrooms and just one bath loses value due to functional obsolescence.

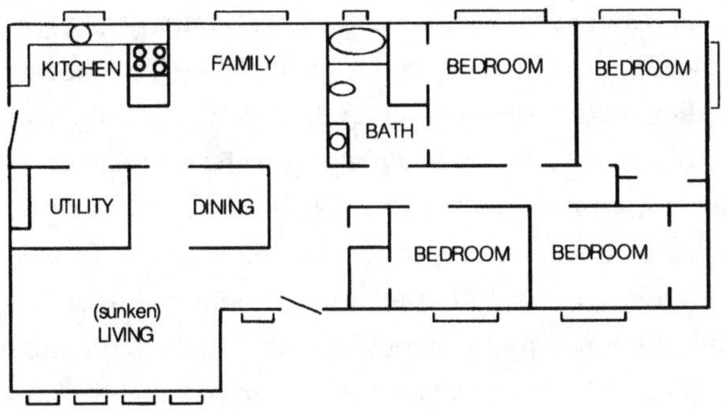

hood deterioration, traffic problems, or exposure to nuisances, like noise from airport flight patterns. Identifying external obsolescence is the primary purpose of an appraiser's neighborhood analysis. External obsolescence is beyond a property owner's control, so it's virtually always incurable.

Don't confuse an appraiser's approach to depreciation with an accountant's approach to depreciation. While an accountant is concerned with book depreciation for tax purposes, appraisers are concerned with actual losses in the value of real property.

Always keep in mind that it is only the property improvements that depreciate, not the land. An appraiser regards land as indestructible; it does not lose value.

Methods of Estimating Depreciation. Accurately estimating how much depreciation has accrued is the most difficult phase of the cost approach. In many cases, depreciation estimates are highly subjective, and they are never any more reliable than the judgment and skill of the appraiser who is making them.

The various methods of estimating depreciation are divided into indirect methods and direct methods. **Indirect methods** include the capitalization method and the market data method, and **direct methods** include the straight-line method and the engineering method.

When applying the **capitalization method** to estimate depreciation, the appraiser uses the income approach to value (discussed below) to estimate the current value of the building. This figure, which is called the capitalized value, should be lower than the appraiser's replacement cost estimate, since the replacement cost indicates what the building would be worth if it were new. The difference between the replacement cost and the capitalized value is the amount of depreciation that has accrued.

Example:

$300,000	Replacement cost
– 270,000	Capitalized value
$30,000	Depreciation

With the **market data method**, the appraiser uses the market data (sales comparison) approach to estimate the current value of the building. Again, the appraiser subtracts this value estimate from the replacement cost estimate, and the difference is the depreciation.

The **straight-line method** of estimating depreciation is the easiest method to apply. The appraiser estimates what the useful life (economic life) of the building would be if it were new. He then divides the building's replacement cost by the estimated useful life to determine how much depreciation would occur each year, assuming the improvements lose value evenly over the years. The amount of annual depreciation is then multiplied by the age of the building.

It should be noted that when an appraiser considers the age of a property, she is concerned with its **effective age**, rather than its actual chronological age. The effective age depends on how long the appraiser believes the structure will remain productive in its present use. If, in the appraiser's opinion, a 75-year-old building has 33 productive years ahead of it, and similar buildings typically have a 40-year useful life, then the building's effective age would be seven years old, rather than 75 years old. (Remember that a building's physical life is typically longer than its useful life. That's why the axiom "More buildings are torn down than fall down" is true.)

The following example shows how the straight-line method of estimating depreciation works.

> **Example:** After estimating that a building's replacement cost is $400,000, the appraiser uses the straight-line method to estimate how much the building has depreciated. Based on her knowledge of similar structures, she concludes that the building's useful life is 40 years. By dividing the replacement cost by the useful life, the appraiser determines that the value of the building decreases by $10,000 each year because of depreciation ($400,000 ÷ 40 years = $10,000 per year).
>
> Suppose the appraiser decides that the building has a remaining useful life of 33 years. Its effective age is therefore seven years. The appraiser multiplies $10,000 (the annual depreciation figure) by seven (the building's effective age) to arrive at the estimated amount of depreciation. $10,000 × 7 = $70,000. Therefore, the depreciated value of the building is $330,000 ($400,000 – $70,000 = $330,000).

Straight-line depreciation can also be expressed as a percentage of the building's useful life. The appraiser can divide the building's replacement cost new (100% of its value) by the useful life (40 years) to determine the percentage of its original value it will lose each year (100% ÷ 40 = 2.5% per year).

The straight-line method is sometimes called the **age-life method** because the depreciation estimate is based on a building's effective age in relation to a typical economic life.

The **engineering method** of estimating depreciation, sometimes called the **observed condition method**, calls for the appraiser to inspect the structure, making observations about actual depreciation. The conclusions are entirely a matter of the appraiser's judgment and skill. Generally, the engineering method of estimating depreciation is considered the most reliable.

Adding Land Value. The last step in the replacement cost process is to add the value of the land to the depreciated value of the improvements. The value of the land is usually estimated by the sales comparison method. Prices recently paid for lots similar to the subject lot are compared and used as indications of what the subject lot is worth. (Site valuation is discussed later in this chapter.)

Income Approach to Value

The income method of appraisal, also known as the capitalization method, is based on the idea that there is a relationship between the income a property generates (its productivity) and its market value to an investor. In effect, the income method seeks to determine the present value of a property's future income.

Gross Income. When using the income method, the appraiser first finds the property's gross income. He does this by estimating the rent the property would bring in if it were presently available for lease on the open market. What it would earn on the open market is called the **economic rent**, as distinguished from what it is actually earning now, which is called the **contract rent** or **historical rent**. Contract rent can be used to gauge the property's earnings potential. A pattern of rent increases or decreases is a strong indication of whether the contract rent is above or below the economic rent.

The property's economic rent is also called its **potential gross income** or **gross scheduled income**. This is what it could earn if it were fully occupied and all rents owed were collected. But it is unrealistic to expect a rental property to be fully occupied throughout its productive life; vacancies must be expected. Also, there are going to be tenants who do not pay their rent. So the appraiser must make a deduction from potential gross income to allow for occasional vacancies and unpaid rents. Called a **vacancy factor**, this deduction is expressed as a percentage of the potential gross income. For example, the appraiser might deduct 5% from potential gross income as a vacancy factor. Once the vacancy factor is deducted, the appraiser is left with a more reliable income figure, called **effective gross income**.

Operating Expenses. From the effective gross income, the appraiser deducts the expenses connected with operating the building. They fall into three classifications: fixed expenses, maintenance expenses, and reserves for replacement.

- **Fixed expenses:** Real estate taxes and hazard insurance.
- **Maintenance expenses:** Services for tenants, utilities, supplies, cleaning, administration costs, building employee wages, and repairs.
- **Reserves for replacement:** Regular allowances set aside to replace structures and equipment that are expected to wear out, such as roofs, heating equipment, air conditioners, and (in a residential building) kitchen ranges and refrigerators.

The income that is left when operating expenses are deducted from effective gross income is called **net income**. It is net income that is capitalized to determine the property's value.

Some expenses, such as the owner's income taxes, depreciation reserves, and mortgage payments (called **debt service**) are not deducted from the effective gross income to arrive at the net income. These are not considered operating expenses from an appraisal standpoint.

Capitalization. The process of converting net income into a meaningful value is called capitalization. The mathematical procedure is expressed in this formula:

Annual Net Income ÷ Capitalization Rate = Value

Example: The property's net income is $45,700 and the capitalization rate is 11%. According to the capitalization formula, the property's value is $415,455.

$45,700 ÷ 0.11 = $415,455

The capitalization rate is the rate of return an investor (a potential purchaser) would want to receive on the money she invests in the property (the purchase price). When the investor chooses the rate of return, it is plugged into the formula shown above. By dividing the net income by the desired rate of return, the investor can determine how much she can pay for the property and still realize that desired return.

Example: The property's annual net income is $25,000 and the investor's desired return is 9.5%.

$25,000 ÷ 9.5% = $263,158

The investor can pay up to $263,158 for a property earning $25,000 net income and realize her desired yield of 9.5%.

Recapture. As general rule, a capitalization rate must take into consideration both the investor's desired rate of return on the investment and the return of the investment. Interest is a **return on** an investment. This is the investor's profit on the amount of money he has invested in the purchase of the property. The **return of** an investment is the investor's ability to recoup the purchase price of the property by the end of his term of ownership. This return of the investment is also called **recapture.**

The portion of the purchase price attributable to the land need not be recaptured during the investment period because land is indestructible and its value can be recovered when the property is sold. The improvements, however, are assets that will wear out. Because the purchase price of the improvements will not be recovered when the property is sold, most investors insist on including in their capitalization rate a provision for recapturing their original investment. In other words, a recapture provision is included in anticipation of future depreciation accrual. A capitalization rate that provides for both interest and recapture is called an **overall rate**.

Example: Ted bought a small apartment building for $1,250,000. The land is worth $500,000 and the building is worth $750,000. The building has a remaining economic life of 30 years. Ted expects a 10% return on his investment. He also wants the value of the building ($750,000) to be repaid over the 30-year economic life. That works out to $25,000 a year, or 2% of the purchase price annually. This 2% return of his investment, added to his 10% return on the investment, results in an overall rate of 12%.

Selecting a Capitalization Rate. To appraise property using the income approach, the appraiser tries to determine the capitalization rate that investors generally demand for similar properties under current market conditions.

There are a number of methods an appraiser can use to determine an appropriate capitalization rate for a property. For instance, the appraiser could analyze recent sales of comparable income properties and assume that the subject property would have a capitalization rate similar to theirs. This is known as the **direct comparison method**.

Another method of selecting a capitalization rate is the **band of investment method**, which takes into account prevailing mortgage interest rates that would apply to the investor's loan, in addition to the rate of return required on the investor's equity investment.

The third method used to select a rate is the **summation method**. With this method, the appraiser builds a capitalization rate for the subject property by considering the four component parts of a capitalization rate, assigning an appropriate percentage to each component, and then adding them together to reach the total rate. Here are the four components:

1. **Safe rate**—the rate paid on secure investments such as savings accounts or long-term government bonds.
2. **Risk rate**—the portion of the rate designed to compensate the investor for the hazards that are peculiar to the investment; this component increases or decreases according to the degree of risk involved.
3. **Nonliquidity rate**—the extra return an investor will expect from a non-liquid investment such as real estate.
4. **Management rate**—the part of the rate that compensates the owner/investor for managing the investment and reinvesting the money the investment yields.

Regardless of the method used for selecting a capitalization rate, two very important considerations are the quality and durability of the investment property's income. **Quality** (how reliable the tenants are) and **durability** (how long the income can be expected to last) influence the risk factor. The greater the risk, the higher the capitalization rate and the lower the property's value. On the other hand, the smaller the risk, the lower the capitalization rate and the higher the value.

Capitalization Methods. After the appraiser has calculated the subject property's net income and chosen a capitalization rate, the final step in the income approach is capitalizing the property's income to arrive at an estimate of value. At this point, depending on the situation, the appraiser uses one of three capitalization methods. These are the building residual technique, the land residual technique, and the property residual technique.

In the first two of these methods, the land and the building are valued separately. The capitalization methods are called residual techniques because they involve capitalizing a **residual**, which means something that's left over.

The first step in the **building residual technique** is to value the land separately from the building. The appraiser then deducts from the property's annual net income the portion of the income that must be attributable to the land to justify its value. What remains (what's left over) is the income to be credited to the building. The final step is to divide the net income attributable to the building by an appropriate overall capitalization rate to find the value of the building.

The building residual method is most reliable when land values are relatively stable and can be determined easily (because of an abundance of comparable sales and market data). It is also used when appraising older buildings where depreciation is difficult to measure.

In the **land residual technique**, the building is appraised separately. Then the net income that must be attributable to the building is deducted to arrive at the net income to be credited to the land. The land's earnings are then capitalized to determine the land's value. (Note that the capitalization rate used in this step is only an interest rate, with no recapture provision, because land does not depreciate.)

The land residual technique is used when the land value cannot be estimated by the sales comparison method because of an absence of comparable sales. It is also used when the building the land supports is new and represents its highest and best use.

You may also hear reference to the **property residual technique**, which treats the land and building as one. This is no different than the basic capitalization procedure (Value = Income ÷ Capitalization Rate) that you're already familiar with, though; no residual is involved.

Gross Income Multipliers. If a residential appraiser uses an income method at all, she will use a simplified version called the **gross income multiplier method**. It is sometimes called the **gross rent multiplier method**, since rents are typically the only form of income generated by residential rental properties. As a rule, this method is applied only when appraising residential rental properties.

In the gross income multiplier method, the appraiser looks at the relationship between a rental property's income and the price paid for the property.

Example:

Sales price:	$275,000
Monthly rent:	$1,675
Conclusion:	The monthly rent is equal to 0.61% of the sales price; the sales price is approximately 165 times the monthly rent.

Monthly rents may run about 1% of selling prices in one market, and more or less in another. A market exists where specific rental properties compete with each other for tenants. For competitive reasons, rents charged for similar properties tend to be much alike within the same market. As a result, if one rental property has a monthly income that is 1% of its sales price, comparable properties will have similar income-to-price ratios.

A monthly multiplier is established by dividing the sales price by the monthly rental income. An annual multiplier is calculated by dividing the sales price by the annual rental income.

Example:

Sales Price		Monthly Rent		Monthly Multiplier
$275,000	÷	$1,815	=	151.52
Sales Price		Annual Rent		Monthly Multiplier
$275,000	÷	$21,780	=	12.63

After locating at least four comparable residential rental properties, the appraiser can determine their monthly or annual gross income multipliers (either is acceptable—it's a matter of the appraiser's preference) by dividing the rents into their respective selling prices.

Example:

Comp No.	Sales Price	Monthly Rent	Monthly Multiplier
1	$264,500	$1,800	146.94
2	$276,525	$1,825	151.52
3	$268,300	$1,850	145.03
4	$280,750	$1,895	148.15

The appraiser uses the multipliers of the comparables to determine an appropriate multiplier for the subject property, taking into account the similarities and differences between the properties. Then the appraiser multiplies the rent that the subject property is generating by the chosen multiplier for a rough estimate of its value as income-producing property.

The principal weakness of the gross income multiplier method is that it is based on gross income figures and does not take into account vacancies or operating expenses. If two rental homes have the same rental income, the gross income multiplier method would indicate they are worth the same amount; but if one is older and has higher maintenance costs, the net return to the owner would be less, and so would the value of the property.

If possible, the appraiser should use the subject property's economic rent, as opposed to the contract rent (the rent the owner is actually receiving), in calculating the gross income multiplier.

Example: The owner leased the home two years ago for $1,300 a month, and the lease contract has another year to go. Market rents have risen sharply over the past two years, so that the property could now command a much higher rent—probably about $1,475 a month. If the appraiser were to use the $1,300 contract rent in the gross income multiplier method instead of the $1,475 economic rent, it would distort the estimate of value.

Site Valuation

An appraiser may be asked to value unimproved property (also referred to as raw land). And when appraising improved property, an appraiser may be called upon to appraise the site and the buildings separately (for instance, when property is being assessed for tax purposes). Occasionally, an appraiser is asked to appraise a property on which there is a building that needs to be torn down. In that case, the appraiser will need to appraise the site at its highest and best use, and then deduct the cost of removing the structure.

There are four main ways to appraise a site:

1. the sales comparison method,
2. the land residual technique,
3. the distribution method, and
4. the development method.

Sales Comparison Method. The sales comparison approach is the method of site valuation preferred by most appraisers, because it reflects the actions of informed buyers and sellers in the marketplace. With this method, the appraiser uses the sales prices of vacant sites that have recently sold and that are similar to the subject property's site to arrive at an estimate of its value.

Land Residual Technique. The land residual technique, which we discussed earlier, is site valuation by the income approach. It is used for improved property. The appraiser determines the income attributable to the land, then calculates the value of the land by capitalizing its income.

Distribution Method. In the distribution method—also called allocation or abstraction—the appraiser analyzes recent sales of improved properties to determine what percentage of their sales prices involved land costs. If the lots typically account for 18% to 20% of the cost of the properties, the appraiser might conclude that the portion of the subject property's overall value attributable to the land is about 18% to 20%.

The distribution method is not as reliable as the sales comparison method. Its principal weakness is that in many cases there are no consistent land-to-property value ratios on which the appraiser can rely.

Development Method. Also called the anticipated use method, this valuation technique is applied fairly often. It is used to value vacant land when the highest and best use of the land is for subdivision and development. In this method, the appraiser estimates the future value of the developed lots, and then subtracts the costs of development to arrive at the current value of the land.

Appraising Multi-family Properties

The appraisal of properties such as individual condominium, townhouse, and cooperative units presents a few additional issues for consideration. For example, when appraising an individual condominium unit, an appraiser must inspect the complex in which the unit is located. In addition, the costs of maintaining the common grounds, fees, and property taxes must all be taken into consideration.

It is possible for an appraiser to find sufficient comparables within the same complex as the subject property. This eliminates the need for adjustments for differences such as neighborhood or age. If there aren't enough comparable sales with a similar floor plan, the appraiser may need to make adjustments for this as well.

Reconciliation and Final Estimate of Value

Throughout the appraisal process, the appraiser is gathering facts on which he will base the ultimate conclusion—the final estimate of the property's value. In many cases, the facts require nothing beyond simple verification; their meaning is self-evident. In other instances, they require expert interpretation. Appraisers refer to the assembly and interpretation of all the facts that influence a property's value as **reconciliation**. Nowhere in the appraisal process does the appraiser's experience and judgment play a more critical role.

The final value estimate is not simply the average of the results yielded by the three appraisal methods—sales comparison, cost, and income. Rather, it is the figure that represents the appraiser's expert opinion of the subject property's value after all the data have been assembled and analyzed.

Appraisal Reports

Once the appraiser has determined the final estimate of value, she presents it to the client in an appraisal report. All written appraisal reports must conform to USPAP (Uniform Standards of Professional Appraisal Practice) requirements and must contain a signed certification from the appraiser. There are two formats for written appraisal reports: form reports and narrative reports. A third format, the letter report, was commonly used for many years, but is now prohibited in appraisals that must conform to USPAP requirements; letter reports are no longer in general use.

Narrative Report. A **narrative report** is a thorough, detailed, written presentation of the facts and reasoning behind the appraiser's estimate of value.

Although the structure of a narrative report varies, most narrative reports contain similar types of information. The appraiser often includes a summary of important facts and conclusions, along with definitions of important terms. It is common for an appraiser to present the subject property data in a separate section of the report. The conclusion of a narrative report generally includes the valuation analysis, which describes the appraisal methods that were used, any market data used, and the reasoning that led to the final value conclusion.

Form Report. A **form report** is a brief, standard form used by lending institutions and government agencies (e.g., the FHA and VA), presenting only the key data and the appraiser's conclusions. Form reports are the most common type of appraisal report.

Form reports help ensure that all information required by the client is included, and make it easier for the client to locate and review specific items. However, they reduce the appraiser's ability to tailor the report to the circumstances of the specific appraisal

Fig. 13.9 Uniform Residential Appraisal Report form

Uniform Residential Appraisal Report

File #

The purpose of this summary appraisal report is to provide the lender/client with an accurate, and adequately supported, opinion of the market value of the subject property.

SUBJECT

Property Address | City | State | Zip Code

Borrower | Owner of Public Record | County

Legal Description

Assessor's Parcel # | Tax Year | R.E. Taxes $

Neighborhood Name | Map Reference | Census Tract

Occupant ☐ Owner ☐ Tenant ☐ Vacant | Special Assessments $ | ☐ PUD | HOA $ | ☐ per year ☐ per month

Property Rights Appraised ☐ Fee Simple ☐ Leasehold ☐ Other (describe)

Assignment Type ☐ Purchase Transaction ☐ Refinance Transaction ☐ Other (describe)

Lender/Client | Address

Is the subject property currently offered for sale or has it been offered for sale in the twelve months prior to the effective date of this appraisal? ☐ Yes ☐ No

Report data source(s) used, offering price(s), and date(s).

CONTRACT

I ☐ did ☐ did not analyze the contract for sale for the subject purchase transaction. Explain the results of the analysis of the contract for sale or why the analysis was not performed.

Contract Price $ | Date of Contract | Is the property seller the owner of public record? ☐ Yes ☐ No | Data Source(s)

Is there any financial assistance (loan charges, sale concessions, gift or downpayment assistance, etc.) to be paid by any party on behalf of the borrower? ☐ Yes ☐ No

If Yes, report the total dollar amount and describe the items to be paid.

NEIGHBORHOOD

Note: Race and the racial composition of the neighborhood are not appraisal factors.

Neighborhood Characteristics	One-Unit Housing Trends	One-Unit Housing		Present Land Use %
Location ☐ Urban ☐ Suburban ☐ Rural	Property Values ☐ Increasing ☐ Stable ☐ Declining	PRICE	AGE	One-Unit %
Built-Up ☐ Over 75% ☐ 25–75% ☐ Under 25%	Demand/Supply ☐ Shortage ☐ In Balance ☐ Over Supply	$ (000)	(yrs)	2-4 Unit %
Growth ☐ Rapid ☐ Stable ☐ Slow	Marketing Time ☐ Under 3 mths ☐ 3–6 mths ☐ Over 6 mths	Low		Multi-Family %
Neighborhood Boundaries		High		Commercial %
		Pred.		Other %

Neighborhood Description

Market Conditions (including support for the above conclusions)

SITE

Dimensions | Area | Shape | View

Specific Zoning Classification | Zoning Description

Zoning Compliance ☐ Legal ☐ Legal Nonconforming (Grandfathered Use) ☐ No Zoning ☐ Illegal (describe)

Is the highest and best use of the subject property as improved (or as proposed per plans and specifications) the present use? ☐ Yes ☐ No If No, describe

Utilities	Public	Other (describe)		Public	Other (describe)	Off-site Improvements—Type	Public	Private
Electricity	☐	☐	Water	☐	☐	Street	☐	☐
Gas	☐	☐	Sanitary Sewer	☐	☐	Alley	☐	☐

FEMA Special Flood Hazard Area ☐ Yes ☐ No | FEMA Flood Zone | FEMA Map # | FEMA Map Date

Are the utilities and off-site improvements typical for the market area? ☐ Yes ☐ No If No, describe

Are there any adverse site conditions or external factors (easements, encroachments, environmental conditions, land uses, etc.)? ☐ Yes ☐ No If Yes, describe

IMPROVEMENTS

General Description		Foundation		Exterior Description materials/condition		Interior materials/condition	
Units ☐ One ☐ One with Accessory Unit		☐ Concrete Slab ☐ Crawl Space		Foundation Walls		Floors	
# of Stories		☐ Full Basement ☐ Partial Basement		Exterior Walls		Walls	
Type ☐ Det. ☐ Att. ☐ S-Det./End Unit		Basement Area sq. ft.		Roof Surface		Trim/Finish	
☐ Existing ☐ Proposed ☐ Under Const.		Basement Finish %		Gutters & Downspouts		Bath Floor	
Design (Style)		☐ Outside Entry/Exit ☐ Sump Pump		Window Type		Bath Wainscot	
Year Built		Evidence of ☐ Infestation		Storm Sash/Insulated		Car Storage ☐ None	
Effective Age (Yrs)		☐ Dampness ☐ Settlement		Screens		☐ Driveway # of Cars	
Attic	☐ None	Heating ☐ FWA ☐ HWBB ☐ Radiant		Amenities	☐ Woodstove(s) #	Driveway Surface	
☐ Drop Stair	☐ Stairs	☐ Other	Fuel	☐ Fireplace(s) #	☐ Fence	☐ Garage # of Cars	
☐ Floor	☐ Scuttle	Cooling ☐ Central Air Conditioning		☐ Patio/Deck	☐ Porch	☐ Carport # of Cars	
☐ Finished	☐ Heated	☐ Individual	☐ Other	☐ Pool	☐ Other	☐ Att. ☐ Det. ☐ Built-in	

Appliances ☐ Refrigerator ☐ Range/Oven ☐ Dishwasher ☐ Disposal ☐ Microwave ☐ Washer/Dryer ☐ Other (describe)

Finished area **above** grade contains: | Rooms | Bedrooms | Bath(s) | Square Feet of Gross Living Area Above Grade

Additional features (special energy efficient items, etc.)

Describe the condition of the property (including needed repairs, deterioration, renovations, remodeling, etc.).

Are there any physical deficiencies or adverse conditions that affect the livability, soundness, or structural integrity of the property? ☐ Yes ☐ No If Yes, describe

Does the property generally conform to the neighborhood (functional utility, style, condition, use, construction, etc.)? ☐ Yes ☐ No If No, describe

Freddie Mac Form 70 March 2005 | Page 1 of 6 | Fannie Mae Form 1004 March 2005

Uniform Residential Appraisal Report

File #

There are comparable properties currently offered for sale in the subject neighborhood ranging in price from $ to $.

There are comparable sales in the subject neighborhood within the past twelve months ranging in sale price from $ to $.

SALES COMPARISON APPROACH

FEATURE	SUBJECT			COMPARABLE SALE # 1				COMPARABLE SALE # 2				COMPARABLE SALE # 3			
Address															
Proximity to Subject															
Sale Price	$						$				$				$
Sale Price/Gross Liv. Area	$		sq. ft.	$		sq. ft.		$		sq. ft.		$		sq. ft.	
Data Source(s)															
Verification Source(s)															
VALUE ADJUSTMENTS	DESCRIPTION			DESCRIPTION			+(-) $ Adjustment	DESCRIPTION			+(-) $ Adjustment	DESCRIPTION			+(-) $ Adjustment
Sale or Financing Concessions															
Date of Sale/Time															
Location															
Leasehold/Fee Simple															
Site															
View															
Design (Style)															
Quality of Construction															
Actual Age															
Condition															
Above Grade	Total	Bdrms.	Baths	Total	Bdrms.	Baths		Total	Bdrms.	Baths		Total	Bdrms.	Baths	
Room Count															
Gross Living Area			sq. ft.			sq. ft.				sq. ft.				sq. ft.	
Basement & Finished Rooms Below Grade															
Functional Utility															
Heating/Cooling															
Energy Efficient Items															
Garage/Carport															
Porch/Patio/Deck															
Net Adjustment (Total)				☐ + ☐ -			$	☐ + ☐ -			$	☐ + ☐ -			$
Adjusted Sale Price of Comparables				Net Adj. % Gross Adj. %			$	Net Adj. % Gross Adj. %			$	Net Adj. % Gross Adj. %			$

I ☐ did ☐ did not research the sale or transfer history of the subject property and comparable sales. If not, explain

My research ☐ did ☐ did not reveal any prior sales or transfers of the subject property for the three years prior to the effective date of this appraisal.

Data source(s)

My research ☐ did ☐ did not reveal any prior sales or transfers of the comparable sales for the year prior to the date of sale of the comparable sale.

Data source(s)

Report the results of the research and analysis of the prior sale or transfer history of the subject property and comparable sales (report additional prior sales on page 3).

ITEM	SUBJECT	COMPARABLE SALE # 1	COMPARABLE SALE # 2	COMPARABLE SALE # 3
Date of Prior Sale/Transfer				
Price of Prior Sale/Transfer				
Data Source(s)				
Effective Date of Data Source(s)				

Analysis of prior sale or transfer history of the subject property and comparable sales

Summary of Sales Comparison Approach

Indicated Value by Sales Comparison Approach $

RECONCILIATION

Indicated Value by: Sales Comparison Approach $ Cost Approach (if developed) $ Income Approach (if developed) $

This appraisal is made ☐ "as is", ☐ subject to completion per plans and specifications on the basis of a hypothetical condition that the improvements have been completed, ☐ subject to the following repairs or alterations on the basis of a hypothetical condition that the repairs or alterations have been completed, or ☐ subject to the following required inspection based on the extraordinary assumption that the condition or deficiency does not require alteration or repair:

Based on a complete visual inspection of the interior and exterior areas of the subject property, defined scope of work, statement of assumptions and limiting conditions, and appraiser's certification, my (our) opinion of the market value, as defined, of the real property that is the subject of this report is $, as of , which is the date of inspection and the effective date of this appraisal.

Uniform Residential Appraisal Report

File #

ADDITIONAL COMMENTS

COST APPROACH

COST APPROACH TO VALUE (not required by Fannie Mae)

Provide adequate information for the lender/client to replicate the below cost figures and calculations.

Support for the opinion of site value (summary of comparable land sales or other methods for estimating site value)

ESTIMATED ☐ REPRODUCTION OR ☐ REPLACEMENT COST NEW	OPINION OF SITE VALUE = $
Source of cost data	Dwelling Sq. Ft. @ $ =$
Quality rating from cost service Effective date of cost data	Sq. Ft. @ $ =$
Comments on Cost Approach (gross living area calculations, depreciation, etc.)	
	Garage/Carport Sq. Ft. @ $ =$
	Total Estimate of Cost-New = $
	Less Physical / Functional / External
	Depreciation =$( )
	Depreciated Cost of Improvements =$
	"As-is" Value of Site Improvements =$
Estimated Remaining Economic Life (HUD and VA only) Years	Indicated Value By Cost Approach =$

INCOME

INCOME APPROACH TO VALUE (not required by Fannie Mae)

Estimated Monthly Market Rent $ X Gross Rent Multiplier = $ Indicated Value by Income Approach

Summary of Income Approach (including support for market rent and GRM)

PUD INFORMATION

PROJECT INFORMATION FOR PUDs (if applicable)

Is the developer/builder in control of the Homeowners' Association (HOA)? ☐ Yes ☐ No Unit type(s) ☐ Detached ☐ Attached

Provide the following information for PUDs ONLY if the developer/builder is in control of the HOA and the subject property is an attached dwelling unit.

Legal name of project

Total number of phases	Total number of units	Total number of units sold
Total number of units rented	Total number of units for sale	Data source(s)

Was the project created by the conversion of an existing building(s) into a PUD? ☐ Yes ☐ No If Yes, date of conversion

Does the project contain any multi-dwelling units? ☐ Yes ☐ No Data source(s)

Are the units, common elements, and recreation facilities complete? ☐ Yes ☐ No If No, describe the status of completion.

Are the common elements leased to or by the Homeowners' Association? ☐ Yes ☐ No If Yes, describe the rental terms and options.

Describe common elements and recreational facilities

Uniform Residential Appraisal Report

File #

This report form is designed to report an appraisal of a one-unit property or a one-unit property with an accessory unit; including a unit in a planned unit development (PUD). This report form is not designed to report an appraisal of a manufactured home or a unit in a condominium or cooperative project.

This appraisal report is subject to the following scope of work, intended use, intended user, definition of market value, statement of assumptions and limiting conditions, and certifications. Modifications, additions, or deletions to the intended use, intended user, definition of market value, or assumptions and limiting conditions are not permitted. The appraiser may expand the scope of work to include any additional research or analysis necessary based on the complexity of this appraisal assignment. Modifications or deletions to the certifications are also not permitted. However, additional certifications that do not constitute material alterations to this appraisal report, such as those required by law or those related to the appraiser's continuing education or membership in an appraisal organization, are permitted.

SCOPE OF WORK: The scope of work for this appraisal is defined by the complexity of this appraisal assignment and the reporting requirements of this appraisal report form, including the following definition of market value, statement of assumptions and limiting conditions, and certifications. The appraiser must, at a minimum: (1) perform a complete visual inspection of the interior and exterior areas of the subject property, (2) inspect the neighborhood, (3) inspect each of the comparable sales from at least the street, (4) research, verify, and analyze data from reliable public and/or private sources, and (5) report his or her analysis, opinions, and conclusions in this appraisal report.

INTENDED USE: The intended use of this appraisal report is for the lender/client to evaluate the property that is the subject of this appraisal for a mortgage finance transaction.

INTENDED USER: The intended user of this appraisal report is the lender/client.

DEFINITION OF MARKET VALUE: The most probable price which a property should bring in a competitive and open market under all conditions requisite to a fair sale, the buyer and seller, each acting prudently, knowledgeably and assuming the price is not affected by undue stimulus. Implicit in this definition is the consummation of a sale as of a specified date and the passing of title from seller to buyer under conditions whereby: (1) buyer and seller are typically motivated; (2) both parties are well informed or well advised, and each acting in what he or she considers his or her own best interest; (3) a reasonable time is allowed for exposure in the open market; (4) payment is made in terms of cash in U. S. dollars or in terms of financial arrangements comparable thereto; and (5) the price represents the normal consideration for the property sold unaffected by special or creative financing or sales concessions* granted by anyone associated with the sale.

*Adjustments to the comparables must be made for special or creative financing or sales concessions. No adjustments are necessary for those costs which are normally paid by sellers as a result of tradition or law in a market area; these costs are readily identifiable since the seller pays these costs in virtually all sales transactions. Special or creative financing adjustments can be made to the comparable property by comparisons to financing terms offered by a third party institutional lender that is not already involved in the property or transaction. Any adjustment should not be calculated on a mechanical dollar for dollar cost of the financing or concession but the dollar amount of any adjustment should approximate the market's reaction to the financing or concessions based on the appraiser's judgment.

STATEMENT OF ASSUMPTIONS AND LIMITING CONDITIONS: The appraiser's certification in this report is subject to the following assumptions and limiting conditions:

1. The appraiser will not be responsible for matters of a legal nature that affect either the property being appraised or the title to it, except for information that he or she became aware of during the research involved in performing this appraisal. The appraiser assumes that the title is good and marketable and will not render any opinions about the title.

2. The appraiser has provided a sketch in this appraisal report to show the approximate dimensions of the improvements. The sketch is included only to assist the reader in visualizing the property and understanding the appraiser's determination of its size.

3. The appraiser has examined the available flood maps that are provided by the Federal Emergency Management Agency (or other data sources) and has noted in this appraisal report whether any portion of the subject site is located in an identified Special Flood Hazard Area. Because the appraiser is not a surveyor, he or she makes no guarantees, express or implied, regarding this determination.

4. The appraiser will not give testimony or appear in court because he or she made an appraisal of the property in question, unless specific arrangements to do so have been made beforehand, or as otherwise required by law.

5. The appraiser has noted in this appraisal report any adverse conditions (such as needed repairs, deterioration, the presence of hazardous wastes, toxic substances, etc.) observed during the inspection of the subject property or that he or she became aware of during the research involved in performing this appraisal. Unless otherwise stated in this appraisal report, the appraiser has no knowledge of any hidden or unapparent physical deficiencies or adverse conditions of the property (such as, but not limited to, needed repairs, deterioration, the presence of hazardous wastes, toxic substances, adverse environmental conditions, etc.) that would make the property less valuable, and has assumed that there are no such conditions and makes no guarantees or warranties, express or implied. The appraiser will not be responsible for any such conditions that do exist or for any engineering or testing that might be required to discover whether such conditions exist. Because the appraiser is not an expert in the field of environmental hazards, this appraisal report must not be considered as an environmental assessment of the property.

6. The appraiser has based his or her appraisal report and valuation conclusion for an appraisal that is subject to satisfactory completion, repairs, or alterations on the assumption that the completion, repairs, or alterations of the subject property will be performed in a professional manner.

Uniform Residential Appraisal Report

File #

APPRAISER'S CERTIFICATION: The Appraiser certifies and agrees that:

1. I have, at a minimum, developed and reported this appraisal in accordance with the scope of work requirements stated in this appraisal report.

2. I performed a complete visual inspection of the interior and exterior areas of the subject property. I reported the condition of the improvements in factual, specific terms. I identified and reported the physical deficiencies that could affect the livability, soundness, or structural integrity of the property.

3. I performed this appraisal in accordance with the requirements of the Uniform Standards of Professional Appraisal Practice that were adopted and promulgated by the Appraisal Standards Board of The Appraisal Foundation and that were in place at the time this appraisal report was prepared.

4. I developed my opinion of the market value of the real property that is the subject of this report based on the sales comparison approach to value. I have adequate comparable market data to develop a reliable sales comparison approach for this appraisal assignment. I further certify that I considered the cost and income approaches to value but did not develop them, unless otherwise indicated in this report.

5. I researched, verified, analyzed, and reported on any current agreement for sale for the subject property, any offering for sale of the subject property in the twelve months prior to the effective date of this appraisal, and the prior sales of the subject property for a minimum of three years prior to the effective date of this appraisal, unless otherwise indicated in this report.

6. I researched, verified, analyzed, and reported on the prior sales of the comparable sales for a minimum of one year prior to the date of sale of the comparable sale, unless otherwise indicated in this report.

7. I selected and used comparable sales that are locationally, physically, and functionally the most similar to the subject property.

8. I have not used comparable sales that were the result of combining a land sale with the contract purchase price of a home that has been built or will be built on the land.

9. I have reported adjustments to the comparable sales that reflect the market's reaction to the differences between the subject property and the comparable sales.

10. I verified, from a disinterested source, all information in this report that was provided by parties who have a financial interest in the sale or financing of the subject property.

11. I have knowledge and experience in appraising this type of property in this market area.

12. I am aware of, and have access to, the necessary and appropriate public and private data sources, such as multiple listing services, tax assessment records, public land records and other such data sources for the area in which the property is located.

13. I obtained the information, estimates, and opinions furnished by other parties and expressed in this appraisal report from reliable sources that I believe to be true and correct.

14. I have taken into consideration the factors that have an impact on value with respect to the subject neighborhood, subject property, and the proximity of the subject property to adverse influences in the development of my opinion of market value. I have noted in this appraisal report any adverse conditions (such as, but not limited to, needed repairs, deterioration, the presence of hazardous wastes, toxic substances, adverse environmental conditions, etc.) observed during the inspection of the subject property or that I became aware of during the research involved in performing this appraisal. I have considered these adverse conditions in my analysis of the property value, and have reported on the effect of the conditions on the value and marketability of the subject property.

15. I have not knowingly withheld any significant information from this appraisal report and, to the best of my knowledge, all statements and information in this appraisal report are true and correct.

16. I stated in this appraisal report my own personal, unbiased, and professional analysis, opinions, and conclusions, which are subject only to the assumptions and limiting conditions in this appraisal report.

17. I have no present or prospective interest in the property that is the subject of this report, and I have no present or prospective personal interest or bias with respect to the participants in the transaction. I did not base, either partially or completely, my analysis and/or opinion of market value in this appraisal report on the race, color, religion, sex, age, marital status, handicap, familial status, or national origin of either the prospective owners or occupants of the subject property or of the present owners or occupants of the properties in the vicinity of the subject property or on any other basis prohibited by law.

18. My employment and/or compensation for performing this appraisal or any future or anticipated appraisals was not conditioned on any agreement or understanding, written or otherwise, that I would report (or present analysis supporting) a predetermined specific value, a predetermined minimum value, a range or direction in value, a value that favors the cause of any party, or the attainment of a specific result or occurrence of a specific subsequent event (such as approval of a pending mortgage loan application).

19. I personally prepared all conclusions and opinions about the real estate that were set forth in this appraisal report. If I relied on significant real property appraisal assistance from any individual or individuals in the performance of this appraisal or the preparation of this appraisal report, I have named such individual(s) and disclosed the specific tasks performed in this appraisal report. I certify that any individual so named is qualified to perform the tasks. I have not authorized anyone to make a change to any item in this appraisal report; therefore, any change made to this appraisal is unauthorized and I will take no responsibility for it.

20. I identified the lender/client in this appraisal report who is the individual, organization, or agent for the organization that ordered and will receive this appraisal report.

Uniform Residential Appraisal Report

File #

21. The lender/client may disclose or distribute this appraisal report to: the borrower; another lender at the request of the borrower; the mortgagee or its successors and assigns; mortgage insurers; government sponsored enterprises; other secondary market participants; data collection or reporting services; professional appraisal organizations; any department, agency, or instrumentality of the United States; and any state, the District of Columbia, or other jurisdictions; without having to obtain the appraiser's or supervisory appraiser's (if applicable) consent. Such consent must be obtained before this appraisal report may be disclosed or distributed to any other party (including, but not limited to, the public through advertising, public relations, news, sales, or other media).

22. I am aware that any disclosure or distribution of this appraisal report by me or the lender/client may be subject to certain laws and regulations. Further, I am also subject to the provisions of the Uniform Standards of Professional Appraisal Practice that pertain to disclosure or distribution by me.

23. The borrower, another lender at the request of the borrower, the mortgagee or its successors and assigns, mortgage insurers, government sponsored enterprises, and other secondary market participants may rely on this appraisal report as part of any mortgage finance transaction that involves any one or more of these parties.

24. If this appraisal report was transmitted as an "electronic record" containing my "electronic signature," as those terms are defined in applicable federal and/or state laws (excluding audio and video recordings), or a facsimile transmission of this appraisal report containing a copy or representation of my signature, the appraisal report shall be as effective, enforceable and valid as if a paper version of this appraisal report were delivered containing my original hand written signature.

25. Any intentional or negligent misrepresentation(s) contained in this appraisal report may result in civil liability and/or criminal penalties including, but not limited to, fine or imprisonment or both under the provisions of Title 18, United States Code, Section 1001, et seq., or similar state laws.

SUPERVISORY APPRAISER'S CERTIFICATION: The Supervisory Appraiser certifies and agrees that:

1. I directly supervised the appraiser for this appraisal assignment, have read the appraisal report, and agree with the appraiser's analysis, opinions, statements, conclusions, and the appraiser's certification.

2. I accept full responsibility for the contents of this appraisal report including, but not limited to, the appraiser's analysis, opinions, statements, conclusions, and the appraiser's certification.

3. The appraiser identified in this appraisal report is either a sub-contractor or an employee of the supervisory appraiser (or the appraisal firm), is qualified to perform this appraisal, and is acceptable to perform this appraisal under the applicable state law.

4. This appraisal report complies with the Uniform Standards of Professional Appraisal Practice that were adopted and promulgated by the Appraisal Standards Board of The Appraisal Foundation and that were in place at the time this appraisal report was prepared.

5. If this appraisal report was transmitted as an "electronic record" containing my "electronic signature," as those terms are defined in applicable federal and/or state laws (excluding audio and video recordings), or a facsimile transmission of this appraisal report containing a copy or representation of my signature, the appraisal report shall be as effective, enforceable and valid as if a paper version of this appraisal report were delivered containing my original hand written signature.

APPRAISER

Signature ________________
Name ________________
Company Name ________________
Company Address ________________
____
Telephone Number ________________
Email Address ________________
Date of Signature and Report ________________
Effective Date of Appraisal ________________
State Certification # ________________
or State License # ________________
or Other (describe) ________ State # ________
State ________________
Expiration Date of Certification or License ________________

ADDRESS OF PROPERTY APPRAISED
____
____

APPRAISED VALUE OF SUBJECT PROPERTY $ ________________

LENDER/CLIENT
Name ________________
Company Name ________________
Company Address ________________
____
Email Address ________________

SUPERVISORY APPRAISER (ONLY IF REQUIRED)

Signature ________________
Name ________________
Company Name ________________
Company Address ________________
____
Telephone Number ________________
Email Address ________________
Date of Signature ________________
State Certification # ________________
or State License # ________________
State ________________
Expiration Date of Certification or License ________________

SUBJECT PROPERTY

☐ Did not inspect subject property
☐ Did inspect exterior of subject property from street
Date of Inspection ________________
☐ Did inspect interior and exterior of subject property
Date of Inspection ________________

COMPARABLE SALES

☐ Did not inspect exterior of comparable sales from street
☐ Did inspect exterior of comparable sales from street
Date of Inspection ________________

Freddie Mac Form 70 March 2005 Page 6 of 6 Fannie Mae Form 1004 March 2005 problem. An appraiser must still be guided by the USPAP and the steps in the appraisal process. In addition, the appraisal may not be communicated in a misleading manner. The standard form report for residential appraisals is shown in Figure 13.9.

Competitive Market Analysis

A competitive market analysis (CMA) is an estimate of value prepared by a real estate agent in order to assist a seller in determining the best listing price for a home. Although a CMA is significantly less technical and comprehensive than a formal appraisal, the agent must be familiar with the fundamentals of valuation to gather relevant market data. An agent uses a modified form of the sales comparison appraisal method, comparing the seller's home (the subject property) to similar properties that have sold recently or are for sale.

Preparing a CMA

The steps involved in completing a CMA include:

1. collecting and analyzing information about the seller's property;
2. choosing the comparable properties;
3. comparing the seller's property to the comparables and adjusting the value of the comparables accordingly; and
4. estimating a realistic listing price for the seller's property.

As you can see, these steps are quite similar to those taken by an appraiser in preparing a formal appraisal.

Analyzing the Seller's Property. The agent's first step in preparing a CMA is to gather and study information about the seller's property, including information about the property's neighborhood, the site itself, and improvements on the property. Neighborhood characteristics, such as the percentage of home ownership and available public services, set the upper and lower limits of a property's value. The agent must also consider factors such as the size, shape, and topography of the site, and the quality and condition of the improvements.

Choosing Comparable Properties. Unlike a formal appraisal, a CMA may include current and expired listings as comparables. The agent gathers information about properties that have been recently sold or listed (preferably within the last six months). By evaluating the sales prices and listing prices of these comparable properties, the agent will be able to estimate a reasonable listing price for the seller's property. Much like an appraiser, the agent considers factors such as the date of sale and financing terms in choosing comparables.

Fig. 13.10 Competitive market analysis form

Competitive Market Analysis

Subject Property Address: 458 Maple

Address	Price	Age	Lot Size	Style	Exterior	No. of Rooms	Sq. Ft.	No. of Bedrms	Baths	Garage	Condition	Other Impr.	Terms	$ per sq. ft.	List Date	Date Sold
Subject	$332,500	7 yrs	80 × 150	ranch	wood	7	1,350	3	2	1-car, att.	excellent	—	cash	$239		
Current Listings																
291 Maple	$320,000	8 yrs	70 × 140	ranch	wood	6	1,250	3	1	1-car, att.	excellent	basement	cash	$256	July	
175 Main	$318,700	12 yrs	70 × 140	ranch	brick	7	1,350	3	2	1-car, att.	good		cash	$236	Aug.	
389 - 5th	$323,000	10 yrs	80 × 150	ranch	brick	7	1,420	3	2	2-car, att.	good	basement	cash	$227	Aug.	
995 Merrit	$314,500	5 yrs	80 × 150	ranch	wood	6	1,415	2	2	1-car, att.	good		cash	$222	June	
Recently Sold																
256 Oak	$315,400	10 yrs	80 × 140	ranch	wood	7	1,270	3	2	2-car, att.	good		cash	$248	March	May
1156 Larch	$312,000	6 yrs	80 × 150	ranch	brick	6	1,400	3	1	1-car, att.	excellent		cash	$223	Feb.	April
1052 - 8th	$305,250	7 yrs	80 × 140	ranch	brick	7	1,300	3	2	1-car, att.	good		cash	$235	April	June
Expired Listings																
2782 Cherry	$333,600	6 yrs	80 × 150	ranch	wood	6	1,150	2	2	1-car, att.	good		cash	$290	Jan.	
10012 - 7th	$338,800	4 yrs	80 × 140	ranch	brick	7	1,300	3	2	2-car, att.	excellent		cash	$261	March	

Location: centrally located, convenient to business center and public transportation	General Comments:
Assets: excellent condition, professionally landscaped yard	
Drawbacks: no basement	
Market Conditions: market is very competitive, sales price within 2% of market value	Company: Smith Realty
Financing Terms: cash	Agent: Susan James
Probable Market Value: $322,500	Phone: 555-8811

Making Adjustments to the Comparables. Once the agent has chosen comparable properties, each comparable must be compared to the seller's property. The comparison is based on the following elements: 1) location, 2) physical characteristics, 3) date of sale, and 4) terms of sale. Adjustments are made to the prices of the comparables to account for differences between the comparable and the subject property. This process is not as comprehensive for a CMA as for a formal appraisal.

Estimating Market Value. After making the required adjustments for varying features, the agent will have an adjusted market value figure for each comparable. The agent uses these figures to estimate the market value of the seller's property. This involves evaluating the reliability of each comparable; those comparables most like the subject property offer the most reliable indication of market value.

Completing the CMA. When an agent prepares a CMA and presents it to the seller, it is helpful to use a CMA form such as the one shown in Figure 13.10. This form helps the agent present the information to the seller in a logical sequence. The form has spaces for a number of homes that are comparable to the seller's property, including current listings, recent sales, and expired listings. Real estate professionals often use computer programs that automatically generate a CMA from the information provided. Ideally, an agent presents the completed CMA to the seller during the listing presentation.

Chapter Summary

1. An appraisal is an estimate or an opinion of value. Most real estate appraisals concern a property's market value, the price it is likely to bring on the open market in a sale under normal conditions. Other types of value include value in use, investment value, liquidation value, assessed value, insurable value, loan value, and going concern value.
2. Appraisers have developed many "principles of value" that guide them in the valuation process. These include the principles of highest and best use, change, anticipation, supply and demand, substitution, conformity, contribution, competition, balance, and increasing and decreasing returns.
3. The steps in the appraisal process include defining the problem, determining what data is needed and where it can be found, gathering and analyzing general and specific data, valuing the site, selecting and applying the valuation methods, reconciling the value indicators, and issuing the appraisal report.
4. General data concerns factors outside the subject property itself that influence the property's value. The appraiser gathers general data by evaluating economic and social trends and by performing a neighborhood analysis. Specific data (about the subject property itself) is gathered through site analysis and building analysis.
5. In the sales comparison approach to value (which is the most important method of appraisal for residential properties), the appraiser compares the subject property to comparable properties that were sold recently, and uses the adjusted selling prices of the comparables to estimate the value of the subject property.
6. In the cost approach, the appraiser estimates the cost of replacing the improvements, deducts any depreciation, and adds the estimated value of the land to arrive at an estimate of the value of the whole property. Depreciation takes the form of deferred maintenance, functional obsolescence, and external obsolescence. Land does not depreciate.
7. In the income approach to value, the appraiser divides the property's net income by a capitalization rate to estimate its value to an investor. The appraiser first estimates the property's potential gross income (economic rent), then deducts a vacancy factor to determine the effective gross income, then deducts operating expenses to determine net income. The gross income multiplier method is a simplified version of the income approach that is sometimes used in appraising residential rental properties.

8. The methods used for site valuation (appraising raw land, or appraising a site separately from its improvements) are the sales comparison method, the land residual technique, the distribution method, and the development method.

9. Appraisers present their results to clients in appraisal reports. Narrative reports contain the most detail; form reports are much briefer.

10. A competitive market analysis (CMA) is similar to an appraisal but is much less formal and comprehensive.

Key Terms

Market value—The most probable price that a property should bring in a competitive and open market under all conditions requisite to a fair sale, the buyer and seller each acting prudently and knowledgeably, and assuming the price is not affected by undue stimulus.

Highest and best use—The most profitable use of the property; the one that provides the greatest net return over time.

Principle of change—Real property is in a constant state of change. It goes through a four-phase life cycle of integration, equilibrium, disintegration, and rejuvenation.

Principle of substitution—No one will pay more for a piece of property than they would have to pay for an equally desirable substitute.

Sales comparison approach—The method of appraisal in which the appraiser compares the subject property to recently sold comparable properties.

Arm's length transaction—A transaction in which there is no pre-existing family or business relationship between the parties.

Cost approach—The method of appraisal in which the appraiser estimates the replacement cost of the building, deducts depreciation, and adds the value of the site.

Depreciation—Loss in value due to any cause.

Deferred maintenance—Depreciation caused by wear and tear; physical deterioration.

Functional obsolescence—Depreciation caused by functional inadequacies or outmoded design.

External obsolescence—Depreciation caused by forces outside the property, such as neighborhood decline or proximity to nuisances. Also called economic obsolescence.

Income approach—The method of appraising property in which net income is converted into value by use of a capitalization rate.

Effective gross income—Potential gross income less a vacancy factor.

Net income—Effective gross income less operating expenses.

Capitalization rate—The rate of return an investor wants on his investment in the property.

Economic rent—The rent that a property would earn on the open market if it were currently available for rent, as distinguished from the rent it is actually earning now (the contract rent).

Chapter Quiz

1. An appraisal is:
   a) a scientific determination of a property's value
   b) a property's average value, as indicated by general and specific data
   c) an estimate of a property's value as of a specific date
   d) a mathematical analysis of a property's value

2. The focus of most appraisals is the subject property's:
   a) market value
   b) market price
   c) sales price
   d) value in use

3. A property's highest and best use is:
   a) the use that will generate the greatest net return
   b) the best use it could be put to if there were no zoning or other restrictions
   c) the use that best promotes the public health, safety, and welfare
   d) the use that is best suited to the present owner's plans

4. The earliest phase of a property's life cycle, when it is being developed, is called:
   a) substitution
   b) regression
   c) integration
   d) disintegration

5. Developers have announced plans to build a multimillion dollar shopping center next door to a vacant commercial lot you own. Property values in the area will tend to increase as a result of this announcement. This is an example of the principle of:
   a) highest and best use
   b) supply and demand
   c) substitution
   d) anticipation

6. The owner of an apartment building has asked an appraiser to determine if it would make financial sense to put in a swimming pool for the tenants' use. The appraiser will be most concerned with the principle of:
   a) regression
   b) substitution
   c) conformity
   d) contribution

7. If someone were to build a high-quality home costing $450,000 in a neighborhood where all of the other homes were valued at around $175,000, the expensive home would suffer a loss in value. This illustrates the principle of:
   a) regression
   b) supply and demand
   c) progression
   d) aversion

8. An appraiser gathers general data in a:
   a) site analysis
   b) building analysis
   c) neighborhood analysis
   d) None of the above

9. A residential appraiser looking for good comparables is most likely to consider homes that:
   a) have not changed hands within the past three years
   b) are currently listed for sale
   c) were sold within the past six months
   d) were listed for less than they eventually sold for

10. When applying the sales comparison method to appraise a single-family home, an appraiser would never use as a comparable a similar home that:
    a) sold over six months ago
    b) sold recently but is located in another neighborhood
    c) was sold by owners who were forced to sell because of financial difficulties
    d) is situated on a corner lot

11. When using the replacement cost approach, which of the following would be least important?
    a) Current construction cost per square foot
    b) Rental cost per square foot
    c) Depreciation
    d) Estimated land value

12. An appraiser is applying the cost approach in valuing an elegant building that was built in 1894. Which of the following is most likely to be true?
    a) The building's replacement cost is the same as its reproduction cost
    b) The building's replacement cost is a better indicator of its market value than its reproduction cost
    c) The building's reproduction cost is a better indicator of its market value than its replacement cost
    d) The building's replacement cost is much greater than its reproduction cost

13. In the income approach to value, which of the following is not considered to be one of the property's operating expenses?
    a) General real estate taxes
    b) Maintenance expenses
    c) Reserves for replacement
    d) Mortgage payments

14. The sales comparison approach would almost certainly be much more important than the other two methods (the cost approach and the income approach) in the appraisal of:
    a) a six-unit apartment building
    b) an industrial building
    c) a shopping center
    d) a single-family home

15. A competitive market analysis is prepared using an approach most similar to which appraisal method?
    a) Sales comparison approach
    b) Cost approach
    c) Income approach
    d) None of the above

Answer Key

1. c) An appraisal is only an estimate or opinion of value, and it is valid only in regard to a specified date.

2. a) An appraiser is usually asked to determine the subject property's market value (or value in exchange).

3. a) The highest and best use is the use that would produce the greatest net return over time, given the current zoning and other restrictions on use.

4. c) Integration is the period during which the property is being developed.

5. d) This is an example of the principle of anticipation, which holds that value is created by the expectation of future benefits to be derived from owning a property.

6. d) The appraiser will be concerned with the principle of contribution. Will the proposed improvement—the swimming pool—contribute enough to the property's value (in the form of higher rents from tenants, and, ultimately, net income to the owner) to justify the expense of installing it?

7. a) The principle of regression holds that association with properties of much lower quality reduces a property's value.

8. c) General data is data concerning factors outside the subject property itself that affect the property's value. A neighborhood analysis involves collection of general data, whereas the site and building analyses involve collection of specific data about the subject property itself.

9. c) A sales comparison appraisal of residential property is usually based on the sales prices of homes that sold within the past six months.

10. c) Forced sales are never used as comparables for appraisal purposes. Comparable sales must sales under normal conditions, where neither party was acting under unusual pressure.

11. b) The cost method involves estimating the current cost of construction, subtracting the amount of accrued depreciation, then adding back in the estimated value of the land. How much the property rents for is irrelevant to the cost approach.

12. b) The cost of producing a replica of an old building at current prices (reproduction cost) is invariably much higher than the cost of constructing a building with the equivalent utility using modern materials (replacement cost). Reproduction cost is not a good indicator of an old building's market value.

13. d) The mortgage payments—referred to as the property's debt service—are not considered operating expenses for the purposes of the income approach.

14. d) In the appraisal of single-family homes, the sales comparison approach is given the most weight.

15. a) Agents prepare CMAs using a modified form of the sales comparison method of appraisal.

Chapter 14

Closing Real Estate Transactions

I. Closing and Escrow
   A. Face-to-face closing
   B. The escrow process
   C. Escrow services
   D. Termination of escrow
   E. Escrow agents
II. Closing Costs and Settlement Statements
   A. Preparing a settlement statement
   B. Guide to settlement statements
      1. Settlement charges
      2. Prorations
      3. Cash at closing
III. Income Tax Aspects of Closing
   A. 1099-S reporting
   B. Form 8300 reporting
   C. Foreign Investment in Real Property Tax Act
IV. Real Estate Settlement Procedures Act
   A. Transactions covered by RESPA
   B. RESPA requirements

Chapter Overview

The real estate agent's job doesn't end when the parties sign the purchase and sale agreement. Many matters must be taken care of before the sale can be finalized, and the service provided by the real estate agent during the closing process is just as important as the agent's marketing efforts before the sale. Guiding the parties through closing prevents unnecessary delays and earns the agent a reputation for professionalism. Every real estate agent should be familiar with escrow procedures and the allocation of closing costs. This chapter explains the purpose of escrow and the steps involved in closing. It also discusses how settlement statements work, how closing costs are allocated and prorated, income tax aspects of closing, and the requirements of the federal Real Estate Settlement Procedures Act.

Introduction

Once a purchase and sale agreement has been signed and all of the contingencies (such as arranging financing) have been satisfied, preparations are made to finalize the transaction. Finalizing a real estate transaction is called **closing** or **settlement**.

Closing and Escrow

The closing process varies considerably from one state to another. In some states, all of the parties involved in the transaction meet in person to sign and exchange documents and transfer funds. In many other states, the closing process is handled by a third party, through the creation of an escrow.

Face-to-Face Closing

In a face-to-face closing, the seller personally meets the buyer to deliver the deed to the property. Other terms for this type of closing include roundtable closing, passing papers (since this is much of what happens at the meeting), or settlement and transfer.

At the closing, the buyer pays the property's purchase price in exchange for the deed. A buyer or seller who is unable to personally attend the closing may appoint someone to represent him at the meeting. A power of attorney is a document used to appoint the representative.

In addition to the buyer and seller, a number of other people will attend a face-to-face closing. Participants may include the real estate agents, the attorneys for both parties, and representatives of the lender and the title insurance company. The meeting may be held at one of several possible locations, such as the office of the lender or one of the brokers. In most cases, one person will conduct the proceedings and act as the closing agent (also called a settlement clerk).

Shortly before the closing, the title insurance company often conducts a second title search. This serves to reassure the buyer and the buyer's lender that no new issues with the seller's title have come up since the initial title examination. The seller may also be asked to sign an affidavit of title stating that the title has not been affected by any recent legal actions involving the seller (such as judgments, bankruptcy, or divorce). Another event that often precedes closing is a final inspection or walk-through of the property by the buyer.

Responsibilities of the Parties. Each party at the closing is responsible for bringing certain items. In addition to the deed itself, the seller and the seller's attorney may need to bring documents such as inspection reports, insurance policies, property tax bills, and proof that encumbrances have been removed (except for any the buyer will take title subject to). The buyer must make sure that the funds needed for closing are available. This usually means making sure the purchase loan has been funded. Typically, the buyer's lender will bring a check for the seller, and a promissory note and mortgage or deed of trust for the buyer to sign. If the lender is not attending the closing, the check and the loan documents will be given to the closing agent before the meeting.

The amount of work a real estate agent will need to do at the closing itself varies depending on local customs. The broker might not do anything other than collect her commission, or she might be in charge of conducting the closing. In any case, it is important for real estate agents to monitor preparations for the closing. The buyer, seller, and other participants may not be familiar with everything that will be expected of them. By making sure that the necessary arrangements are made, the agent can help ensure a successful transaction.

Dry Closings. Because of the complexity of most closings, it may be difficult to reschedule the meeting if one of the necessary documents is unavailable. Instead, the parties may agree to a dry closing. In a **dry closing**, the parties sign the documents and turn them over to the person conducting the closing. However, the money and the deed to the property are not delivered to their intended recipients until after the missing document arrives safely. Dry closing is also called a close into escrow, because it somewhat resembles the more formal escrow process.

The Escrow Process

Escrow is an arrangement in which money and documents are held by a third party (the **escrow agent**) on behalf of the buyer and the seller until the transaction is ready to close. The escrow agent is a dual agent, representing both the buyer and the seller, with fiduciary duties to both parties (see the discussion of dual agency in Chapter 9).

The parties usually give the escrow agent written **escrow instructions**, which determine under what conditions and at what time the agent will distribute the money and documents to the proper parties. The escrow instructions are a bilateral contract between the buyer and the seller. Neither party may choose the escrow agent or set the terms and conditions of escrow without the consent of the other party.

The escrow instructions ordinarily reflect the contingencies and other requirements for the transaction that were set forth in the purchase agreement. If there is a conflict between the terms of the purchase agreement and the escrow instructions, the escrow agent is usually supposed to comply with the later of the two contracts—the escrow instructions.

The purpose of escrow is to ensure that the seller receives the purchase price, the buyer receives clear title to the property, and the lender's security interest in the property is perfected. Escrow protects each party from the other's change of mind. For example, if the seller suddenly doesn't want to sell the property as agreed, he can't just refuse to deliver the deed to the buyer. Once a deed has been given to an escrow agent, if the buyer fulfills all of the conditions specified in the escrow instructions and deposits the purchase price into escrow, the escrow agent is required to deliver the deed to the buyer. An added advantage of escrow is convenience: the parties do not have to be present to close the transaction.

Escrow Services

Escrow agents perform a wide variety of services to prepare a transaction for closing. Some of these are matters that would be handled by the parties or their representatives before a face-to-face closing. Most escrow closings involve all of the following steps:

- obtaining a title report from the title insurance company;
- ordering inspections;
- paying off existing loans secured by the property;
- preparing documents, such as the deed;
- depositing funds from the buyer (and seller if necessary);
- obtaining title insurance policies;
- requesting the funding of the buyer's loan;
- prorating expenses and allocating closing costs;
- preparing a uniform settlement statement;
- recording documents; and
- disbursing funds and delivering documents.

However, the escrow agent's services are usually quite limited in nature. For example, while an escrow agent would contact a structural pest control company to order an inspection called for in the purchase agreement, the escrow agent would not discuss the results of the inspection with the company or authorize necessary repairs. That would be up to the parties.

Termination of Escrow

Escrow terminates when the transaction closes. Alternatively, it will terminate if the terms of the escrow instructions have not been fulfilled by the scheduled closing date (or if no closing date has been set, within a reasonable time). As a general rule, escrow can be terminated earlier only if the buyer and seller mutually consent to the termination. Neither party can terminate the escrow unilaterally. Not even the death or incapacity of either party will terminate the escrow.

Example: The seller deposits a properly executed deed into escrow and dies shortly afterward. If the buyer fulfills the terms of the escrow instructions, the transaction will still close, in spite of the death of the seller.

Sometimes, if a transaction fails to close, there is a dispute between the buyer and seller over which of them is entitled to funds or other items that were placed into escrow. If the parties are unable to resolve the dispute, the escrow agent should file an **interpleader** action, turning the matter over to a court. The court will decide which party is the rightful owner of the items in escrow. It is not the escrow agent's role to arbitrate a dispute between the parties.

Escrow Agents

The escrow agent (or escrow holder) is a third party who is authorized by the buyer and seller to coordinate the closing. Since the process involves important documents and large sums of money, most states require escrow agents to be licensed and limit who may qualify as an escrow agent.

An independent escrow company may close a real estate transaction, or the escrow agent may be an attorney or a title company. Many institutional lenders have their own escrow departments, to close their own loan transactions.

Real estate brokers also sometimes offer escrow services, although state regulations may restrict the circumstances in which a broker can act as escrow agent or collect a fee for such services. Traditionally, a broker or attorney who represents one of the parties (and stands to collect a commission or fees) is not supposed to act as escrow agent because this may create a conflict of interest. However, some states do allow agents of the parties to provide escrow services in the same transaction.

Closing Costs and Settlement Statements

Most real estate transactions involve a wide variety of costs in addition to the purchase price: inspection fees, title insurance charges, loan fees, and so on. These are known as **closing costs**. Some of these closing costs are paid by the buyer, and some are paid by the seller. Some are paid by one party to the other; for example, the buyer may have to reimburse the seller for property taxes the seller already paid. Other closing costs are paid by one of the parties to a third party; for instance, the seller may be required to pay a pest inspector's fee.

There are also other payments to be made in connection with closing. For example, the seller often has to pay off an existing mortgage or other liens. Who is required to pay how much to whom at closing can be a complicated matter.

So for each transaction, the person in charge of the closing prepares a **settlement statement**. A settlement statement (also known as a closing statement) sets forth all of the financial aspects of the transaction in detail. It shows exactly how much the

Fig. 14.1 Simplified settlement statement

	Buyer		Seller	
	Debits	**Credits**	**Debits**	**Credits**
Purchase price	175,000.00			175,000.00
Deposit		8,750.00		
Transfer tax			192.50	
Sales commission			12,250.00	
Payoff of seller's loan			92,950.00	
Assumption of seller's loan				
New loan		140,000.00		
Seller financing				
Owner's title insurance			120.00	
Lender's title insurance	456.00			
Origination/assumption fee	2,100.00			
Discount points				
Property taxes				
In arrears				
Paid in advance	684.50			684.50
Hazard insurance				
Assumption of policy				
New policy	260.00			
Interest				
Payoff of seller's loan			382.86	
Assumption				
New loan (prepaid)	161.08			
Reserve account				
Payoff of seller's loan				286.05
Assumption				
Credit report	40.00			
Appraisal	275.00			
Survey				
Pest inspection and repairs			150.00	
Personal property				
Recording fees	50.00		25.00	
Escrow fee	147.00		147.00	
Balance due from buyer		30,423.58		
Balance due to seller			69,753.19	
TOTALS	179,173.58	179,173.58	175,970.55	175,970.55

buyer will have to pay at closing, and exactly how much the seller will take away from closing. A simplified example of a settlement statement is shown in Figure 14.1.

Preparing a Settlement Statement

The items listed on the settlement statement are either **debits** or **credits**. A debit is a charge payable *by* a particular party; the purchase price is a debit to the buyer, for example, and the sales commission is a debit to the seller. Credits are items payable *to* a party; the buyer is credited for his new loan, and the seller for the purchase price.

Preparing a settlement statement involves little more than determining what charges and credits apply to a given transaction and making sure each one is allocated to the right party. When allocating expenses, a closing agent is generally guided by the terms of the purchase agreement or the escrow instructions. The allocation can also be determined by custom (local or general), provided the custom doesn't conflict with the terms of the parties' contract. For example, in an area where the buyer usually pays the cost of an appraisal, that cost would ordinarily be charged to the buyer at closing. But if the seller agreed in the purchase agreement to pay the appraisal fee, custom would be disregarded and the expense would be a debit to the seller at closing.

Of course, neither custom nor the agreement between the parties can be followed if they are contrary to local, state, or federal law.

Although a real estate agent may not ever be called upon to prepare a formal settlement statement, every agent should know what closing costs are likely to be involved in a transaction and how they are customarily allocated. The buyer and the seller may want to negotiate the allocation of particular costs, and in any case they are entitled to know the full extent of their costs before signing a contract. A real estate agent should be able to prepare a good estimate of closing costs for each party.

Guide to Settlement Statements

The double entry accounting method is used for settlement statements, so each party has a credit column and a debit column. The sum of the buyer's credits must equal the sum of the buyer's debits. And the sum of the seller's credits must equal the sum of the seller's debits. Think of the settlement statement as a check register for a bank account. Debits are like checks written against the account, and credits are the equivalent of deposits into the account. When the transaction closes, the balance in each party's account should be zero.

When an item is payable by one party to the other, it will appear on the settlement statement as a debit to the paying party and as a credit to the party paid. An obvious example is the purchase price, which is debited to the buyer and credited to the seller.

If an item is paid by one of the parties to a third party, it appears on the settlement statement in the paying party's debit column, and it does not appear in the other party's columns at all. For example, the buyer is normally charged for certain loan fees, which are paid to the buyer's lender. These fees are a debit to the buyer, but they are not entered as a credit to the seller.

Similarly, certain items are shown as a credit to one party, but not as a debit to the other. The seller's reserve account is a case in point. If the sale calls for the payoff of the seller's existing mortgage, any property tax, insurance, or other reserves held by the seller's lender are refunded. They are a credit to the seller, but not a debit to the buyer.

Settlement Charges. Here is a list of the items that appear on the settlement statements for most standard residential transactions.

Purchase Price. Paid by the buyer to the seller, the purchase price is listed as a debit to the buyer and a credit to the seller.

Good Faith Deposit. In most transactions, the buyer provides the seller with a good faith deposit when the purchase agreement is signed. If the transaction closes, the deposit is applied to the purchase price. Since the buyer has already paid the deposit, it appears on the settlement statement as a credit to the buyer. And since the full purchase price has already been debited to the buyer and credited to the seller, no entry is made on the seller's side of the statement.

Sales Commission. The real estate broker's commission is normally paid by the seller, so it is entered as a debit to the seller.

New Loan. If the buyer secures a new loan to finance part or all of the sale, the loan amount is listed as a credit to the buyer. Like the deposit, the buyer's loan is part of the purchase price already credited to the seller, so no entry is made on the seller's side of the statement.

Assumed Loan. If the buyer assumes the seller's existing loan, it is part of the money used to finance the transaction, so (like a new loan) it is credited to the buyer. The assumed loan balance is a debit to the seller.

Seller Financing. If the seller accepts a mortgage or deed of trust from the buyer for part of the purchase price, that shows up in the buyer's credit column, just like an institutional loan. At the same time, a seller financing arrangement reduces the amount of cash the seller will receive at closing, so it is listed as a debit to the seller.

If the property is sold under a land contract, the contract price (less the downpayment) is credit extended by the seller. It reduces the seller's net at closing and is used by the buyer to finance the purchase, so it is a debit to the seller and a credit to the buyer.

Payoff of Seller's Loan. If the seller has a loan to pay off, the closing agent requests a **payoff statement** from the seller's lender. This document states the loan's remaining principal balance. (A statement of the balance owed on an existing lien may also be called an **offset statement** or, if the lien is secured by a deed of trust, a **beneficiary's statement**.) The loan payoff is a debit to the seller. No entry is made on the buyer's side of the settlement statement.

Prepayment Penalty. A prepayment penalty is a charge the seller's lender may impose on the seller for paying the loan off before the end of its term. It would be a debit to the seller on the settlement statement.

Seller's Reserve Account. As was mentioned earlier, the seller often has reserves on deposit with the lender to cover certain expenses connected with the property. These expenses, sometimes referred to as the **recurring costs**, include property taxes and insurance and, in some cases, assessments, homeowners or condominium association fees, or other periodic charges. (The principal and interest payments on the mortgage are not considered part of the recurring costs, however.) During the loan term, the lender requires the borrower to make regular payments toward the recurring costs, and these payments are kept in a **reserve account** (also called an **impound account** or **escrow account**). The lender uses the funds in the reserve account to pay the taxes, insurance, and other charges when they come due.

When the seller's loan is paid off, the unused balance in the reserve account is refunded to the seller. It appears as a credit on the seller's side of the settlement statement. If the buyer is assuming the loan and the reserve account, the reserves would appear as a credit to the seller and a debit to the buyer.

Appraisal Fee. The cost of the appraisal is generally paid by the party who orders the appraisal. If the buyer is obtaining a loan to purchase the property, the lender will usually require an appraisal; this fee is ordinarily a debit to the buyer. However, the parties can negotiate who is responsible for this item, and sometimes the seller pays for the appraisal instead.

Buyer's Loan Costs. The fees and costs associated with the buyer's loan are paid by the buyer, so they show up as a debit to the buyer. Discount points are also a debit to the buyer, unless the seller has agreed to pay for a buydown. In that case, the points are a debit to the seller. Loan fees and points are discussed in Chapter 12.

Survey. Sometimes the buyer's lender requires a survey as a condition for making the loan; the cost of this survey is usually a debit to the buyer. The purchase agreement may require the seller to furnish a survey, in which case the cost is a debit to the seller.

Title Insurance Premiums. The allocation of costs for title insurance varies according to local custom. There may be two separate title insurance policies, one to protect the buyer's title and one for the security interest of the buyer's lender. Sometimes the seller will pay for one policy while the buyer pays for another; in other cases, one party pays the cost of both policies.

Sale of Personal Property. If the seller is selling the buyer some personal property along with the real property, the price of these items should be credited to the seller and debited to the buyer. (The seller should sign a bill of sale to be delivered to the buyer at closing along with the deed.)

Inspection Fees. The cost of an inspection is allocated by agreement between the parties. For example, the buyer might agree to pay for the cost of a pest inspection, while the seller agrees to pay for repairs if the inspection shows that any are necessary.

Transfer Tax. In most states, sales of real property are subject to some type of transfer tax, which may be designated as an excise tax or conveyance fee. Additional taxes may also be imposed at the county or city level. Local customs tend to provide for these taxes to be paid by the seller, so they would usually be listed in the seller's debit column.

Attorney's Fees. A buyer or seller who is represented by an attorney in the transaction is responsible for her own attorney's fees. On the settlement statement, the fees will show up as a debit to the appropriate party.

Recording Fees. The fees for recording the various documents involved in the transaction are usually charged to the party who benefits from the recording. For example, the fees for recording the deed and the new mortgage or deed of trust are debits to the buyer; the fee for recording a satisfaction of the old mortgage is a debit to the seller.

Closing Fee. Also called a settlement fee or escrow fee, the closing fee is the closing agent's charge for his services. The buyer and the seller commonly agree to split the closing fee; in that case, half the fee will be debited to each party.

Prorations. There are, of course, certain periodic expenses connected with ownership of real estate, including property taxes, hazard insurance premiums, and mortgage interest payments. As a general rule, the seller is responsible for these expenses during her period of ownership, but not beyond. In preparing a settlement statement, the closing agent checks to see whether the seller will be current, in arrears (late), or paid in advance with respect to these expenses on the closing date. The closing agent then **prorates** the expenses, determining what share of them the seller is responsible for. To prorate an expense is to divide and allocate it proportionately, according to time, interest, or benefit.

If, in regard to a particular expense, the seller will be in arrears on the closing date, the amount that she owes is entered as a debit on the settlement statement. If the seller has paid in advance, she is entitled to a partial refund, which appears as a credit on the statement. If the expense is one that will continue after closing (as in the case of property taxes), the buyer is responsible for it once his period of ownership begins. That will show up on the buyer's side of the settlement statement as a credit (if the seller is in arrears) or as a debit (if the seller has paid in advance).

The first step in prorating an expense is to divide it by the number of days it covers to determine the **per diem** (daily) rate. So an annual expense would be divided by 365 days (366 in a leap year) and the per diem rate would be $^1/_{365}$ of the annual amount. A monthly expense would be divided by the number of days in the month in question (28, 29, 30, or 31).*

The next step is to determine the number of days during which a particular party is responsible for the expense. The final step is to multiply that number of days by the per diem rate, to arrive at the share of the expense that party is responsible for. Examples appear below. (See Chapter 19 for further discussion of proration calculations.)

Property Taxes. The seller is responsible for property taxes up to the day of closing; the buyer is responsible for them on the day of closing and thereafter. If the seller has already paid the property taxes for the year, he is entitled to a prorated refund at closing. On the settlement statement, this will appear as a credit to the seller and a debit to the buyer.

> **Example:** Sharon is selling her house to Ben. The transaction will close July 5. This year the property taxes on the house are $2,190. The closing agent calculates the per diem rate by dividing the property tax figure by 365, the number of days in the year.
>
> $$\$2{,}190 \div 365 = \$6.00 \text{ per diem}$$

---

* It was once a common practice to simplify proration calculations by using a 360-day year and 30-day months (regardless of how many days there actually were in a particular month or year). But now that calculators are so widely available, most closing agents use the exact number of days in the year or month in question. Also, note that in order for the result of a proration to be completely accurate, the per diem rate must be calculated to an accuracy of at least 4 decimal places for monthly amounts, and 5 decimal places for annual amounts. Here again, calculators make this a painless process.

Sharon, the seller, is responsible for the property taxes through July 4—in other words, for the first 185 days of the year. The buyer, Ben, is responsible for the taxes from July 5 forward—the remaining 180 days in the year.

Sharon has already paid the full year's taxes, so at closing she'll be entitled to a credit for the share that is Ben's responsibility. The escrow agent multiplies the number of days for which Ben is responsible by the per diem rate to determine the amount Ben will owe Sharon at closing.

$$\$6.00 \times 180 = \$1{,}080$$

This $1,080 will appear as a credit on the seller's side of the settlement statement, and as a debit on the buyer's side of the statement.

If the taxes are in arrears, the amount the seller should have paid for the period before closing will be a debit to the seller on the settlement statement.

Whether property taxes are paid in advance or in arrears varies from state to state. Tax payments are sometimes divided into installments, so the taxes may need to be prorated on a monthly or quarterly basis instead. Also, the year for property tax purposes does not necessarily begin on January 1. Many areas use a different property tax year, such as one that starts on July 1 and ends on June 30.

Hazard Insurance. Hazard insurance is usually paid for well in advance. At closing, the seller is entitled to a refund for the unused portion of the policy. For example, if the seller has paid the premium for the year, and there are three months left in the year, the seller is entitled to a refund of one-fourth of the premium. This would show up as a credit to the seller on the settlement statement. If the buyer is going to assume the policy, the seller will be credited and the buyer will be debited for the appropriate amount.

Interest on Seller's Loan. Interest on a real estate loan is almost always paid in arrears. In other words, the interest accruing during a given month is paid as part of the next month's payment. For instance, a loan payment due on September 1 includes the interest that accrued during August. If a transaction closes in the middle of the payment period, the seller owes the lender some interest.

Example: The closing date is August 15. Although the seller made a payment on her loan on August 1, that payment did not include any of the interest that is accruing during August. At closing, the seller will owe the lender interest for the period from August 1 through August 15. The closing agent prorates the interest, charging the seller only for those days, rather than the whole month's interest. The prorated amount is entered on the settlement statement as a debit to the seller.

If the buyer assumes the loan, his first payment will be due September 1, and it will include all of the interest for August. The seller will be debited for the interest owed up to August 15, and the buyer will be credited for the same amount.

Prepaid Interest on Buyer's Loan. Another expense that the escrow agent prorates is the interest on the buyer's new mortgage loan. Just as the interest on the seller's loan does not affect the buyer, the prepaid interest on the buyer's loan does not affect the seller. As a general rule, the first payment date of a new loan is not the first day of the month immediately following closing, but rather the first day of the next month after that.

Example: The buyer is financing the purchase with a new institutional loan. Closing takes place on January 23. The buyer is not required to make a payment on the new loan on February 1. Instead, the first payment is not due until March 1.

Even though the first payment isn't due for an extra month, interest begins accruing on the loan on the closing date. As was explained above, the first regular payment will cover the interest for the preceding month. So if the transaction closes on January 23, the first payment will be due on March 1, and that payment will cover the interest accrued in February. However, it will not cover the interest accrued between January 23 and January 31. Instead, the lender requires the buyer to pay the interest for those nine days in January at closing. This is called **prepaid interest** or **interim interest**. It will appear as a debit to the buyer on the settlement statement.

Example: The buyer is borrowing $430,000 at 7% interest to finance the purchase. The annual interest on the loan during the first year will be $30,100 ($430,000 × 7% = $30,100). The escrow agent divides that annual figure by 365 to determine the per diem interest rate.

$30,100 ÷ 365 = $82.47 per diem

There are nine days between the closing date (January 23) and the first day of the following month, so the lender will expect the buyer to prepay nine days' worth of interest at closing.

$82.47 × 9 days = $742.23 prepaid interest

The closing agent will enter $742.23 as a debit to the buyer on the settlement statement.

The buyer and seller will both be responsible for interest on the closing date (unless the loan is being assumed). That is because there are two entirely different loans at issue, one of which ends on the closing date, and the other of which begins on the closing date. If the loan is being assumed, the parties will need to agree on which party is responsible for interest on the closing date; in the same way, the parties must also agree on (or rely on local custom for) which party is responsible for property taxes on the closing date.

Rent. So far we've discussed only prorated expenses. In some transactions, there is also income to be prorated at closing. If the property generates rental income and the tenants have paid for some period beyond the closing date, the seller is debited and the buyer credited for the rent paid in advance. If the rent is paid in arrears, the seller will be credited for the amount due up to closing, and the buyer will be debited for the same amount.

Note that tenants' security deposits are not prorated. The seller must transfer all of the deposits to the buyer, since the leases will continue after closing.

Cash at Closing. As we said earlier, on a settlement statement the sum of one party's credits should equal the sum of that same party's debits, so that the final balance in each party's "account" is zero. In order for the statement to work this way, it must list the amount of cash that the buyer will have to bring to closing, and also the amount of cash the seller will take away from closing.

Balance Due from Buyer. Add up all of the buyer's credits, then add up all of the buyer's debits. Subtract the buyer's credits from the buyer's debits to find the balance due, which is the amount of cash the buyer will have to pay at closing. Enter this amount as a credit for the buyer. Now the buyer's credits column should add up to exactly the same amount as the buyer's debits column.

Balance Due to Seller. Add up all of the seller's credits, then add up all of the seller's debits. Subtract the seller's debits from the seller's credits. The result is the amount of cash the seller will receive at closing (if any). Enter this amount as a debit if credits exceed debits, but as a credit if debits exceed credits. Now the seller's credits column should add up to exactly the same amount as the seller's debits column.

Note that the buyer's two column totals must match each other, and the seller's two column totals must match each other. However, the buyer's column totals do not have to match the seller's column totals. Although they might conceivably match in a particular transaction, in most transactions they do not.

Income Tax Aspects of Closing

Nearly all real estate transactions have tax implications for the parties (see Chapter 15) and, naturally, it is up to each party to fulfill her own tax obligations. However, there are certain requirements related to income that must be taken care of when a transaction closes.

Form 1099-S Reporting

The Internal Revenue Service generally requires a closing agent to report real property sales on Form 1099-S. The form is used to report the seller's name and social security number and the gross proceeds from the sale. However, the form doesn't have to be filed for the sale of a principal residence if: 1) the seller certifies in writing that none of the gain is taxable; and 2) the sale is for $250,000 or less ($500,000 or less if the seller is married). Certain other types of transactions are also exempt from the requirement.

A closing agent may not charge the parties a separate fee for complying with 1099-S reporting requirements.

Form 8300 Reporting

The IRS requires an escrow agent who receives more than $10,000 in cash to report the cash payment on Form 8300. This rule applies whether the cash was received in a single transaction or in a series of related transactions.

Example: ABC Escrow is handling the closing for buyer Sam. As part of the process, Sam will bring $12,000 cash to closing. He gives ABC Escrow $8,000 on Thursday, and the remaining $4,000 on Friday. Although the individual amounts are less than $10,000, ABC Escrow will need to submit Form 8300 to IRS because the transactions are related.

The escrow agent must file Form 8300 within 15 days of receiving the cash. A copy of the form should be kept on file for five years.

FIRPTA

The Foreign Investment in Real Property Tax Act (FIRPTA) was passed in 1980 to help prevent foreign investors from evading their tax liability on income generated from the sale of real estate.

FIRPTA requires a property buyer to determine whether the seller is a "foreign person," defined as someone who is not a U.S. citizen or resident alien. If the seller is a foreign person, then the buyer must withhold 10% of the amount realized from the sale and forward those funds to the IRS. (In most cases, the amount realized is simply the sales price.) Payment must be made within 20 days after the date the property was transferred.

The closing agent usually handles these requirements on behalf of the buyer. Note that many residential transactions are exempt from FIRPTA.

Real Estate Settlement Procedures Act

The Real Estate Settlement Procedures Act (RESPA), a federal law, was passed in 1974. It affects how closing is handled in most residential transactions financed with institutional loans.

RESPA has two main goals:

- to provide borrowers with information about their closing costs in order to help them become better shoppers for settlement services; and
- to eliminate kickbacks and referral fees that unnecessarily increase the costs of settlement.

Transactions Covered by RESPA

RESPA applies to "federally related" loan transactions. A loan is federally related if:

1. it will be secured by a mortgage or deed of trust against:
   - property on which there is (or on which the loan proceeds will be used to build) a dwelling with four or fewer units;
   - a condominium unit or a cooperative apartment;
   - a lot with (or on which the loan proceeds will be used to place) a mobile home; and
2. the lender is federally regulated, has federally insured accounts, is assisted by the federal government, makes loans in connection with a federal program, sells loans to Fannie Mae, Ginnie Mae, or Freddie Mac, or makes real estate loans totaling more than $1,000,000 per year.

In short, the act applies to almost all institutional lenders and most residential loans.

Exemptions. RESPA does not apply to the following loan transactions:

- a loan used to purchase 25 acres or more;
- a loan primarily for a business, commercial, or agricultural purpose;
- a loan used to purchase vacant land, unless there will be a one- to four-unit dwelling built on it or a mobile home placed on it;
- temporary financing, such as a construction loan; or
- an assumption for which the lender's approval is neither required nor obtained.

Note that RESPA also does not apply to seller-financed transactions, since they are not federally regulated.

RESPA Requirements

RESPA has these requirements for federally related loan transactions:

1. Within three days after receiving a written loan application, the lender or loan originator (for example, a mortgage broker) must give all applicants:
    - a copy of a **booklet about settlement procedures**, prepared by HUD, which explains RESPA, closing costs, and the settlement statement;
    - a **mortgage servicing disclosure statement**, which discloses whether the lender intends to service the loan or transfer it to another lender; and
    - a **good faith estimate of closing costs** (see Figure 14.2), disclosing the costs that the borrower (the buyer) will be expected to pay in the transaction.

    A lender or loan originator may not charge a loan applicant any fees other than a credit report fee until the good faith estimate (GFE) has been provided and the applicant has expressed an intent to continue with the loan transaction.

2. If the lender or any settlement service provider requires the borrower to use a particular appraiser, title company, or other service provider, that requirement must be disclosed to the borrower when the loan application or service agreement is signed.

3. If any settlement service provider refers a borrower to an affiliated provider, that joint business relationship must be fully disclosed, along with the fact that the referral is optional. Fee estimates for the services in question must also be given.

4. The closing agent (whoever handles closing, whether it's an escrow agent, a loan originator, a real estate broker, a lawyer, etc.) must itemize all loan settlement charges on a **uniform settlement statement** form (discussed below).

5. If the borrower will have to make deposits into an impound account (a reserve or escrow account) to cover taxes, insurance, and other recurring costs, the lender cannot require excessive deposits (more than necessary to cover the expenses when they come due, plus a two-month cushion).

6. A lender, a loan originator, a real estate agent, a title company, or any other provider of settlement services may not:
   - pay or receive a kickback or a referral fee (a payment from one settlement service provider to another for referring customers);
   - pay or receive an unearned fee (a charge that one settlement service provider shares with another provider who hasn't actually performed any services in exchange for the payment); or
   - charge a fee for the preparation of the uniform settlement statement, an impound account statement, or the disclosure statement required by the Truth in Lending Act.

   Note that RESPA's prohibition against kickbacks does not apply to referral fees that one real estate licensee or firm pays to another for referring potential customers or clients.
7. The seller may not require the buyer to use a particular title company.

In addition to these requirements, RESPA has a few other provisions that may be important in some transactions.

Reserves. Although RESPA prevents lenders from requiring excessive deposits into a reserve account, it does not require the lender to pay interest on these reserves. Traditionally, lenders did not pay interest on reserve accounts. However, some states now require this, and other lenders have begun doing so voluntarily.

New Construction. While a home is being built, the property taxes on the parcel are often assessed at a tax rate used for vacant lots. Once construction is completed, the tax rate changes and the property taxes can increase considerably. To avoid escrow shortages and significant increases in the borrower's monthly payments, RESPA allows the borrower to make increased payments into escrow during construction.

Uniform Settlement Statement. The escrow agent (or other closing agent) must provide completed uniform settlement statement forms to the borrower, the seller, and the lender on or before the closing date. (The borrower may sign a written waiver of the right to receive the statement by closing, in which case the forms must be provided to the parties as soon as practicable after closing.) If the borrower requests it, the escrow agent must allow the borrower to inspect the statement one business day before closing.

A copy of the uniform settlement statement form, often called a HUD-1 form, is shown in Figure 14.3. It doesn't have the same format as the simplified settlement statement shown earlier in this chapter (with buyer's credit and debit columns and seller's credit and debit columns side by side), but it presents the same information.

On the uniform settlement statement, each party's closing costs are itemized on the second page of the form, with the buyer's costs in the left column and the seller's costs in the right column. Each party's costs are added up, and the total is transferred to the first page of the form. The buyer's total costs are entered on line 103, and the seller's total costs are entered on line 502.

Fig. 14.2 Good faith estimate of closing costs

OMB Approval No. 2502-0265

Good Faith Estimate (GFE)

Name of Originator	Borrower
Originator Address	Property Address
Originator Phone Number	
Originator Email	Date of GFE

Purpose

This GFE gives you an estimate of your settlement charges and loan terms if you are approved for this loan. For more information, see HUD's *Special Information Booklet* on settlement charges, your *Truth-in-Lending Disclosures*, and other consumer information at www.hud.gov/respa. If you decide you would like to proceed with this loan, contact us.

Shopping for your loan

Only you can shop for the best loan for you. Compare this GFE with other loan offers, so you can find the best loan. Use the shopping chart on page 3 to compare all the offers you receive.

Important dates

1. The interest rate for this GFE is available through ☐. After this time, the interest rate, some of your loan Origination Charges, and the monthly payment shown below can change until you lock your interest rate.
2. This estimate for all other settlement charges is available through ☐.
3. After you lock your interest rate, you must go to settlement within ☐ days (your rate lock period) to receive the locked interest rate.
4. You must lock the interest rate at least ☐ days before settlement.

Summary of your loan

Your initial loan amount is	$	
Your loan term is	years	
Your initial interest rate is	%	
Your initial monthly amount owed for principal, interest, and any mortgage insurance is	$ per month	
Can your interest rate rise?	☐ No	☐ Yes, it can rise to a maximum of %. The first change will be in .
Even if you make payments on time, can your loan balance rise?	☐ No	☐ Yes, it can rise to a maximum of $
Even if you make payments on time, can your monthly amount owed for principal, interest, and any mortgage insurance rise?	☐ No	☐ Yes, the first increase can be in and the monthly amount owed can rise to $. The maximum it can ever rise to is $.
Does your loan have a prepayment penalty?	☐ No	☐ Yes, your maximum prepayment penalty is $.
Does your loan have a balloon payment?	☐ No	☐ Yes, you have a balloon payment of $ due in years.

Escrow account information

Some lenders require an escrow account to hold funds for paying property taxes or other property-related charges in addition to your monthly amount owed of $☐.
Do we require you to have an escrow account for your loan?
☐ No, you do not have an escrow account. You must pay these charges directly when due.
☐ Yes, you have an escrow account. It may or may not cover all of these charges. Ask us.

Summary of your settlement charges

A	Your Adjusted Origination Charges *(See page 2.)*	$
B	Your Charges for All Other Settlement Services *(See page 2.)*	$
A + B	Total Estimated Settlement Charges	$

Understanding your estimated settlement charges

Some of these charges can change at settlement. See the top of page 3 for more information.

Your Adjusted Origination Charges	
1. Our origination charge This charge is for getting this loan for you.	
2. Your credit or charge (points) for the specific interest rate chosen ☐ The credit or charge for the interest rate of ☐ % is included in "Our origination charge." (See item 1 above.) ☐ You receive a credit of $ ☐ for this interest rate of ☐ %. This credit **reduces** your settlement charges. ☐ You pay a charge of $ ☐ for this interest rate of ☐ %. This charge (points) **increases** your total settlement charges. The tradeoff table on page 3 shows that you can change your total settlement charges by choosing a different interest rate for this loan.	
A Your Adjusted Origination Charges	$

Your Charges for All Other Settlement Services	
3. Required services that we select These charges are for services we require to complete your settlement. We will choose the providers of these services. *Service* / *Charge*	
4. Title services and lender's title insurance This charge includes the services of a title or settlement agent, for example, and title insurance to protect the lender, if required.	
5. Owner's title insurance You may purchase an owner's title insurance policy to protect your interest in the property.	
6. Required services that you can shop for These charges are for other services that are required to complete your settlement. We can identify providers of these services or you can shop for them yourself. Our estimates for providing these services are below. *Service* / *Charge*	
7. Government recording charges These charges are for state and local fees to record your loan and title documents.	
8. Transfer taxes These charges are for state and local fees on mortgages and home sales.	
9. Initial deposit for your escrow account This charge is held in an escrow account to pay future recurring charges on your property and includes ☐ all property taxes, ☐ all insurance, and ☐ other ☐.	
10. Daily interest charges This charge is for the daily interest on your loan from the day of your settlement until the first day of the next month or the first day of your normal mortgage payment cycle. This amount is $ ☐ per day for ☐ days (if your settlement is ☐).	
11. Homeowner's insurance This charge is for the insurance you must buy for the property to protect from a loss, such as fire. *Policy* / *Charge*	
B Your Charges for All Other Settlement Services	$
A + B Total Estimated Settlement Charges	$

Good Faith Estimate (HUD-GFE) 2

Instructions

Understanding which charges can change at settlement

This GFE estimates your settlement charges. At your settlement, you will receive a HUD-1, a form that lists your actual costs. Compare the charges on the HUD-1 with the charges on this GFE. Charges can change if you select your own provider and do not use the companies we identify. (See below for details.)

These charges **cannot increase** at settlement:	The total of these charges **can increase up to 10%** at settlement:	These charges **can change** at settlement:
▪ Our origination charge ▪ Your credit or charge (points) for the specific interest rate chosen *(after you lock in your interest rate)* ▪ Your adjusted origination charges *(after you lock in your interest rate)* ▪ Transfer taxes	▪ Required services that we select ▪ Title services and lender's title insurance *(if we select them or you use companies we identify)* ▪ Owner's title insurance *(if you use companies we identify)* ▪ Required services that you can shop for *(if you use companies we identify)* ▪ Government recording charges	▪ Required services that you can shop for *(if you do not use companies we identify)* ▪ Title services and lender's title insurance *(if you do not use companies we identify)* ▪ Owner's title insurance *(if you do not use companies we identify)* ▪ Initial deposit for your escrow account ▪ Daily interest charges ▪ Homeowner's insurance

Using the tradeoff table

In this GFE, we offered you this loan with a particular interest rate and estimated settlement charges. However:

- If you want to choose this same loan with **lower settlement charges,** then you will have a **higher interest rate.**
- If you want to choose this same loan with a **lower interest rate,** then you will have **higher settlement charges.**

If you would like to choose an available option, you must ask us for a new GFE.

Loan originators have the option to complete this table. Please ask for additional information if the table is not completed.

	The loan in this GFE	The same loan with lower settlement charges	The same loan with a lower interest rate
Your initial loan amount	$	$	$
Your initial interest rate[1]	%	%	%
Your initial monthly amount owed	$	$	$
Change in the monthly amount owed from this GFE	No change	You will pay $ **more** every month	You will pay $ **less** every month
Change in the amount you will pay at settlement with this interest rate	No change	Your settlement charges will be **reduced** by $	Your settlement charges will **increase** by $
How much your total estimated settlement charges will be	$	$	$

[1] *For an adjustable rate loan, the comparisons above are for the initial interest rate before adjustments are made.*

Using the shopping chart

Use this chart to compare GFEs from different loan originators. Fill in the information by using a different column for each GFE you receive. By comparing loan offers, you can shop for the best loan.

	This loan	Loan 2	Loan 3	Loan 4
Loan originator name				
Initial loan amount				
Loan term				
Initial interest rate				
Initial monthly amount owed				
Rate lock period				
Can interest rate rise?				
Can loan balance rise?				
Can monthly amount owed rise?				
Prepayment penalty?				
Balloon payment?				
Total Estimated Settlement Charges				

If your loan is sold in the future

Some lenders may sell your loan after settlement. Any fees lenders receive in the future cannot change the loan you receive or the charges you paid at settlement.

On the first page of the uniform settlement statement, lines 101 through 120 correspond to the "Buyer's Debits" column on our simplified version. Lines 201 through 220 correspond to the "Buyer's Credits" column. Lines 401 through 420 are the equivalent of the "Seller's Credits" column, and 501 through 520 represent the "Seller's Debits" column. The amount of cash the buyer must bring to closing is shown on line 303, and the amount of cash the seller will receive at closing is shown on line 603.

Estimates vs. Actual Charges. Some of the charges listed on the good faith estimate form given to the buyer at the beginning of the loan application process are in fact only estimates, so they won't necessarily match the buyer's actual charges at closing. However, RESPA doesn't allow certain charges on the GFE to be increased, and it limits how much certain others may be increased. There are three categories:

1. Charges that cannot increase at closing. This includes all of the lender's or loan originator's points and fees, and also the transfer taxes.
2. Charges for required services, such as the appraisal and title insurance, if the service provider was chosen or recommended by the lender. The total amount of these charges can increase no more than 10%.
3. Charges that can change any amount, because they're difficult to predict at the outset, such as hazard insurance.

The categories are explained in more detail on the third page of the good faith estimate form itself (see Figure 14.2). The third page of the uniform settlement statement (Figure 14.3) provides a side-by-side comparison of the estimated and actual charges.

Fig. 14.3 Uniform Settlement Statement

A. Settlement Statement (HUD-1)

OMB Approval No. 2502-0265

B. Type of Loan

1. ☐ FHA 2. ☐ RHS 3. ☐ Conv. Unins. 4. ☐ VA 5. ☐ Conv. Ins.	6. File Number:	7. Loan Number:	8. Mortgage Insurance Case Number:

C. Note: This form is furnished to give you a statement of actual settlement costs. Amounts paid to and by the settlement agent are shown. Items marked "(p.o.c.)" were paid outside the closing; they are shown here for informational purposes and are not included in the totals.

D. Name & Address of Borrower:	E. Name & Address of Seller:	F. Name & Address of Lender:
G. Property Location:	H. Settlement Agent:	I. Settlement Date:
	Place of Settlement:	

J. Summary of Borrower's Transaction		K. Summary of Seller's Transaction	
100. Gross Amount Due from Borrower		**400. Gross Amount Due to Seller**	
101. Contract sales price		401. Contract sales price	
102. Personal property		402. Personal property	
103. Settlement charges to borrower (line 1400)		403.	
104.		404.	
105.		405.	
Adjustment for items paid by seller in advance		**Adjustments for items paid by seller in advance**	
106. City/town taxes to		406. City/town taxes to	
107. County taxes to		407. County taxes to	
108. Assessments to		408. Assessments to	
109.		409.	
110.		410.	
111.		411.	
112.		412.	
120. Gross Amount Due from Borrower		**420. Gross Amount Due to Seller**	
200. Amounts Paid by or in Behalf of Borrower		**500. Reductions In Amount Due to Seller**	
201. Deposit or earnest money		501. Excess deposit (see instructions)	
202. Principal amount of new loan(s)		502. Settlement charges to seller (line 1400)	
203. Existing loan(s) taken subject to		503. Existing loan(s) taken subject to	
204.		504. Payoff of first mortgage loan	
205.		505. Payoff of second mortgage loan	
206.		506.	
207.		507.	
208.		508.	
209.		509.	
Adjustments for items unpaid by seller		**Adjustments for items unpaid by seller**	
210. City/town taxes to		510. City/town taxes to	
211. County taxes to		511. County taxes to	
212. Assessments to		512. Assessments to	
213.		513.	
214.		514.	
215.		515.	
216.		516.	
217.		517.	
218.		518.	
219.		519.	
220. Total Paid by/for Seller		**520. Total Reduction Amount Due Seller**	
300. Cash at Settlement from/to Borrower		**600. Cash at Settlement to/from Seller**	
301. Gross amount due from borrower (line 120)		601. Gross amount due to seller (line 420)	
302. Less amounts paid by/for borrower (line 220)	( )	602. Less reductions in amount due seller (line 520)	( )
303. Cash ☐ **From** ☐ **To Borrower**		**603. Cash** ☐ **To** ☐ **From Seller**	

The Public Reporting Burden for this collection of information is estimated at 35 minutes per response for collecting, reviewing, and reporting the data. This agency may not collect this information, and you are not required to complete this form, unless it displays a currently valid OMB control number. No confidentiality is assured; this disclosure is mandatory. This is designed to provide the parties to a RESPA covered transaction with information during the settlement process.

Previous editions are obsolete Page 1 of 3 HUD-1

L. Settlement Charges

	Paid From Borrower's Funds at Settlement	Paid From Seller's Funds at Settlement
700. Total Real Estate Broker Fees		
Division of commission (line 700) as follows:		
701. $ to		
702. $ to		
703. Commission paid at settlement		
704.		
800. Items Payable in Connection with Loan		
801. Our origination charge $ (from GFE #1)		
802. Your credit or charge (points) for the specific interest rate chosen $ (from GFE #2)		
803. Your adjusted origination charges (from GFE A)		
804. Appraisal fee to (from GFE #3)		
805. Credit report to (from GFE #3)		
806. Tax service to (from GFE #3)		
807. Flood certification (from GFE #3)		
808.		
900. Items Required by Lender to Be Paid in Advance		
901. Daily interest charges from to @ $ /day (from GFE #10)		
902. Mortgage insurance premium for months to (from GFE #3)		
903. Homeowner's insurance for years to (from GFE #11)		
904.		
1000. Reserves Deposited with Lender		
1001. Initial deposit for your escrow account (from GFE #9)		
1002. Homeowner's insurance months @ $ per month $		
1003. Mortgage insurance months @ $ per month $		
1004. Property taxes months @ $ per month $		
1005. months @ $ per month $		
1006. months @ $ per month $		
1007. Aggregate Adjustment -$		
1100. Title Charges		
1101. Title services and lender's title insurance (from GFE #4)		
1102. Settlement or closing fee $		
1103. Owner's title insurance (from GFE #5)		
1104. Lender's title insurance $		
1105. Lender's title policy limit $		
1106. Owner's title policy limit $		
1107. Agent's portion of the total title insurance premium $		
1108. Underwriter's portion of the total title insurance premium $		
1200. Government Recording and Transfer Charges		
1201. Government recording charges (from GFE #7)		
1202. Deed $ Mortgage $ Releases $		
1203. Transfer taxes (from GFE #8)		
1204. City/County tax/stamps Deed $ Mortgage $		
1205. State tax/stamps Deed $ Mortgage $		
1206.		
1300. Additional Settlement Charges		
1301. Required services that you can shop for (from GFE #6)		
1302. $		
1303. $		
1304.		
1305.		
1400. Total Settlement Charges (enter on lines 103, Section J and 502, Section K)		

Comparison of Good Faith Estimate (GFE) and HUD-1 Charges		Good Faith Estimate	HUD-1
Charges That Cannot Increase	**HUD-1 Line Number**		
Our origination charge	# 801		
Your credit or charge (points) for the specific interest rate chosen	# 802		
Your adjusted origination charges	# 803		
Transfer taxes	#1203		

Charges That in Total Cannot Increase More Than 10%		Good Faith Estimate	HUD-1
Government recording charges	# 1201		
	#		
	#		
	#		
	#		
	#		
	#		
	#		
	Total		
	Increase between GFE and HUD-1 Charges	$ or %	

Charges That Can Change		Good Faith Estimate	HUD-1
Initial deposit for your escrow account	#1001		
Daily interest charges	# 901 $ /day		
Homeowner's insurance	# 903		
	#		
	#		
	#		

Loan Terms

Your initial loan amount is	$
Your loan term is	years
Your initial interest rate is	%
Your initial monthly amount owed for principal, interest, and and any mortgage insurance is	$ includes ☐ Principal ☐ Interest ☐ Mortgage Insurance
Can your interest rate rise?	☐ No. ☐ Yes, it can rise to a maximum of %. The first change will be on and can change again every after . Every change date, your interest rate can increase or decrease by %. Over the life of the loan, your interest rate is guaranteed to never be **lower** than % or **higher** than %.
Even if you make payments on time, can your loan balance rise?	☐ No. ☐ Yes, it can rise to a maximum of $.
Even if you make payments on time, can your monthly amount owed for principal, interest, and mortgage insurance rise?	☐ No. ☐ Yes, the first increase can be on and the monthly amount owed can rise to $. The maximum it can ever rise to is $.
Does your loan have a prepayment penalty?	☐ No. ☐ Yes, your maximum prepayment penalty is $.
Does your loan have a balloon payment?	☐ No. ☐ Yes, you have a balloon payment of $ due in years on .
Total monthly amount owed including escrow account payments	☐ You do not have a monthly escrow payment for items, such as property taxes and homeowner's insurance. You must pay these items directly yourself. ☐ You have an additional monthly escrow payment of $ that results in a total initial monthly amount owed of $. This includes principal, interest, any mortgage insurance and any items checked below: ☐ Property taxes ☐ Homeowner's insurance ☐ Flood insurance ☐ ☐ ☐

Note: If you have any questions about the Settlement Charges and Loan Terms listed on this form, please contact your lender.

Previous editions are obsolete Page 3 of 3 HUD-1

Chapter Summary

1. After a purchase agreement has been signed, the next stage of the transaction is the closing process. Closing may occur at a face-to-face meeting involving the parties, their agents, and representatives from the lender and the title insurance company.

2. Alternatively, closing may be handled through escrow, an arrangement in which money and documents are held by a third party (the escrow agent) on behalf of the buyer and the seller, and distributed when all of the conditions in the escrow instructions have been fulfilled.

3. The closing agent prepares a settlement statement, detailing all of the charges payable by (debits) and payable to (credits) each of the parties at closing. Who pays which closing costs may be determined by agreement or by local custom. Certain expenses must be prorated as of the closing date.

4. Certain requirements related to income taxes must be fulfilled when a real estate transaction closes. These include the 1099-S and 8300 reporting requirements and the FIRPTA tax withholding requirement.

5. RESPA applies to almost all residential loan transactions involving institutional lenders. It requires a lender to give a loan applicant a good faith estimate of closing costs within three days after a written loan application is submitted. RESPA also requires the closing agent to complete a uniform settlement statement and have it available to the buyer one day before closing, if the buyer asks to see it in advance.

Key Terms

Closing—The final stage of a real estate transaction, in which documents are signed and delivered and funds are transferred. Also called settlement.

Closing agent—A third party who holds money and documents and carries out the closing process. If the closing is handled via escrow instead of face-to-face, this person may be called an escrow agent.

Face-to-face closing—Closing in which the seller and buyer personally meet to exchange the deed, money, and other documents. Also called roundtable closing, passing papers, or settlement and transfer.

Escrow—An arrangement in which money and documents are held by a third party on behalf of the buyer and the seller.

Escrow instructions—A bilateral contract between the buyer and the seller that tells the escrow agent how to proceed and states the conditions each party must fulfill before the transaction can close.

Settlement statement—A statement that sets forth all of the financial aspects of a real estate transaction in detail and indicates how much cash each party will be required to pay or will receive at closing.

Debit—A charge payable by a party, either to the other party or to a third party.

Credit—A charge payable to a party, either by the other party or by a third party.

Reserve account—Funds on deposit with a lender to pay the property taxes, insurance premiums, and other recurring costs when due. Also called an impound account.

Prorate—To divide and allocate an expense proportionately, according to time, interest, or benefit, determining what share of it a particular party is responsible for.

Prepaid interest—Interest on the buyer's new mortgage loan that the lender requires to be paid at closing, covering the period from the closing date through the last day of the month.

Uniform settlement statement—The settlement statement form that closing agents are required to use in transactions covered by the Real Estate Settlement Procedures Act. Also called a HUD-1 form.

Chapter Quiz

1. Which of the following would not be prorated at closing in the sale of a rental property?
   a) Prepaid property taxes
   b) Interest on seller's existing loan
   c) Security deposit
   d) Interest on buyer's new loan

2. Every debit on the buyer's side of the settlement statement is a charge that:
   a) will be paid to the buyer at closing
   b) must be paid by the buyer at closing
   c) the buyer must pay to the seller at closing
   d) the seller must pay to the buyer at closing

3. On a settlement statement, the purchase price will be listed as:
   a) a debit to the buyer
   b) a debit to the seller
   c) Both of the above
   d) Neither of the above

4. The transaction is closing on September 16. The seller has already paid the annual premium for hazard insurance, and the buyer will not be assuming the policy. On the settlement statement, part of the insurance premium will be listed as a:
   a) debit to the buyer and a credit to the seller
   b) debit to the seller and a credit to the buyer
   c) credit to the buyer
   d) credit to the seller

5. How does the buyer's good faith deposit show up on a settlement statement?
   a) It is listed as a debit on the buyer's side of the statement, and as a credit on the seller's side of the statement
   b) It is listed as a credit on the buyer's side of the statement, but it is not listed on the seller's side because it is included in the purchase price
   c) It is listed as a credit on the seller's side of the statement, but it is not listed on the buyer's side because it will be refunded at closing
   d) It is listed as a debit on both the buyer's side and the seller's side of the statement

6. When a buyer assumes a mortgage, how does the mortgage balance appear on the settlement statement?
   a) Only as a credit to the seller
   b) Only as a debit on the seller's side of the statement
   c) As a credit to the buyer and a debit to the seller
   d) As a credit to the seller and a debit to the buyer

7. Which of the following is ordinarily one of the seller's closing costs?
   a) Sales commission
   b) Good faith deposit
   c) 1099-S report fee
   d) Loan origination fee

8. Which of the following is ordinarily one of the buyer's closing costs?
   a) Sales commission
   b) Buyer's attorney's fees
   c) Transfer tax
   d) None of the above

9. On a settlement statement, prepaid interest would usually appear as a:
   a) seller's debit
   b) buyer's credit
   c) seller's credit
   d) buyer's debit

10. The Matsons are selling their home. They are current on their mortgage payments, having made their most recent payment on May 1. They will be paying off their mortgage when the sale closes on May 17. At closing, the Matsons will probably be:
    a) entitled to a refund of the mortgage interest accruing in May
    b) required to pay the mortgage interest accruing in May
    c) entitled to a refund of the prepayment penalty
    d) required to pay part of the mortgage interest that accrued in April

11. A settlement statement:
    a) is given to the buyer but not the seller
    b) sets out the items to be paid by or to each party at closing
    c) is given only to the buyer's lender
    d) is required only in transactions closed by independent escrow companies

12. When an item is prorated it means that:
    a) it is deleted from the cost of the sale
    b) it is calculated on the basis of a particular time period
    c) it is not paid until closing
    d) the escrow agent must pay the fee

13. Under RESPA, a loan is considered federally related if:
    a) it will be used to finance the purchase of real property
    b) the property has up to four dwelling units
    c) the lender is federally regulated
    d) All of the above

14. Under FIRPTA:
    a) a foreign investor can never buy or sell property without special authorization
    b) if a seller is not a U.S. citizen or resident alien, the buyer must withhold 10% of the amount realized and send it to the IRS
    c) closing agents must notify the real estate broker if the buyer is a foreign investor
    d) a foreign investor purchasing property in the U.S. must pay an additional 10% over and above the purchase price and submit it to the IRS

15. For an additional $300, the seller has agreed to include her refrigerator as a part of the real property transaction. In addition to the deed, the seller should sign a/an:
    a) bill of sale
    b) uniform settlement statement
    c) appraisal report
    d) voucher

Answer Key

1. c) Security deposits are not prorated at closing; they are simply transferred to the buyer of the rental property.

2. b) A debit on the buyer's side of the statement is a charge that the buyer must pay. In some cases, it is a charge that the buyer must pay to the seller (a refund for taxes paid in advance, for example), but in other cases the buyer owes it to a third party (the loan fee paid to the lender, for example).

3. a) The purchase price is a debit to the buyer and a credit to the seller.

4. d) The seller is entitled to a refund for the insurance she paid in advance, and this will show up as a credit on the seller's side of the settlement statement. Since the buyer is not assuming the policy, the seller's insurance is not listed on the buyer's side of the statement.

5. b) The good faith deposit is a credit to the buyer, since it has already been paid. It does not appear on the seller's side of the statement, because the full purchase price is listed as a credit to the seller, and the deposit is included in the price.

6. c) A loan the buyer uses to finance the transaction is listed as a credit to the buyer, whatever its source. When the financing comes through the seller—either through an assumption of the seller's loan, or through seller financing—it is a debit to the seller as well as a credit to the buyer.

7. a) The seller almost always pays the real estate broker's commission.

8. b) Each party normally pays his own attorney's fees.

9. d) Prepaid interest—interest on a new loan to cover the period from the closing date through the last day of the month—is one of the buyer's debits.

10. b) Because mortgage interest is paid in arrears—the month after it accrues—at closing the sellers will be required to pay the interest that has accrued during May. (Their May 1 mortgage payment included the interest that accrued in April.)

11. b) A settlement statement sets forth the items that must be paid by each party, and also the items that must be paid to each party.

12. b) Prorating an expense is allocating it on the basis of a particular time period, such as a certain number of days.

13. d) All of these are elements of a federally related loan under RESPA.

14. b) In a transaction subject to FIRPTA, if the seller is not a U.S. citizen or resident alien, the buyer must withhold 10% of the amount realized from the sale and send it to the IRS. The closing agent usually handles this.

15. a) A bill of sale is used to transfer title to personal property.

Chapter 15

Income Taxation and Real Estate

I. Basic Taxation Concepts
   A. Progressive tax
   B. Income
   C. Deductions and tax credits
   D. Gains and losses
      1. Capital gains and losses
      2. Business and rental property
   E. Basis
      1. Initial basis
      2. Adjusted basis
   F. Realization
   G. Recognition and deferral
   H. Classifications of real property
II. Nonrecognition Transactions
   A. Installment sales
   B. Involuntary conversions
   C. "Tax-free" exchanges
III. Special Provisions for Home Buyers and Sellers
   A. Exclusion of gain from the sale of a principal residence
   B. IRA withdrawals
IV. Deductions Available to Property Owners
   A. Depreciation deductions
   B. Uninsured casualty or theft loss deductions
   C. Repair deductions
   D. Property tax deductions
   E. Mortgage interest deductions
   F. Deductibility of points and other loan costs
   G. Vacation home deductions
   H. Home office deductions
   I. Rental payment deductions
V. State Income Tax

Chapter Overview

Almost every business transaction has tax consequences, and real estate transactions are no exception. Not only are there taxes that arise at the time of sale (such as the conveyance tax discussed in Chapter 6), there are also income tax ramifications for the parties involved. This chapter provides an overview of how federal income taxation affects the transfer and ownership of real estate. It explains some income tax terminology, discusses certain types of transactions that receive special treatment, and also covers tax deductions available to real estate owners.

Basic Taxation Concepts

As you almost certainly know, in the United States the federal government taxes the income of individuals and businesses on an annual basis. Before discussing how the transfer or acquisition of real estate can affect the federal income taxes a seller or buyer is required to pay, we need to explain some basic terms and concepts.

Progressive Tax

A tax may be "proportional," "regressive," or "progressive," depending on how its burden is distributed among taxpayers. A tax is proportional if the same tax rate is applied to all levels of income. A tax is regressive if the rate applied to higher levels of income is lower than the rate applied to lower levels. Our federal income tax is a **progressive** tax. This means that the more a taxpayer earns in a given tax year, the higher his tax rate will be. In other words, someone who earns a large income is generally required not just to pay more taxes than someone who earns a small income, but to pay a greater percentage of her income in taxes.

Tax rates increase in uneven steps called **tax brackets**. An additional dollar earned by a given taxpayer may be taxed at a higher rate than the dollar earned just before it, because it crosses the line into a higher bracket. But the additional dollar earned will not increase the tax paid on dollars previously earned. The term **marginal tax rate** refers to the rate that will apply to the last dollar that a taxpayer earns.

Income

When asked about their income, many people tend to think only in terms of the wages or salary they earn at a job. However, the Internal Revenue Service (IRS) takes a much broader view of income. It regards any economic benefit realized by a taxpayer as part of his income, unless it is a type of benefit specifically excluded from income by the tax code. (The concept of realization is discussed below.)

For certain purposes, the IRS classifies income received by an investor from an enterprise that he doesn't materially participate in as **passive income**.

Deductions and Tax Credits

The tax code authorizes certain expenses to be deducted from income. For example, if a business loses money in a particular tax year, the owner may be allowed to deduct the loss. A taxpayer who is entitled to a **deduction** can subtract a specified amount from his income before it is taxed. By reducing the amount of income that is taxed, the deduction also reduces the amount of tax the taxpayer owes.

In contrast to deductions, tax **credits** are subtracted directly from the amount of tax owed. The taxpayer's income is added up, the tax rate is applied, and then any applicable tax credits are subtracted to determine how much the taxpayer will actually have to pay.

The federal government often uses deductions and tax credits to implement social and economic policy. For example, allowing homeowners to deduct mortgage interest from their taxable income helps make home ownership much more affordable. (The mortgage interest deduction is explained later in this chapter.)

Gains and Losses

The sale or exchange of an asset (such as real estate) nearly always results in either a **gain** or a **loss**. Gains are treated as income, so any gain is taxable unless the tax code specifically says otherwise. On the other hand, a loss may be deducted from income only if the deduction is specifically authorized by the tax code.

Most deductible losses are losses incurred in a trade or business or in transactions entered into for profit. A business entity (such as a corporation) can deduct all of its losses. An individual taxpayer can deduct a loss only if it was incurred in connection with:

1. the taxpayer's trade or business,
2. a transaction entered into for profit, or
3. a casualty loss or theft of the taxpayer's property.

No deduction is allowed for a loss suffered on the sale of the taxpayer's principal residence or other real property owned for personal use.

Capital Gains and Losses. A gain or loss on the sale of an asset held for personal use or as an investment is considered a **capital gain** or a **capital loss**. Capital gains and capital losses are netted against each other. If there is a net gain, it is taxed as a capital gain. Capital gains receive favorable tax treatment: the maximum tax rate applied to most capital gains is considerably lower than the rate for ordinary income.

On the other hand, there is a limit on the deductibility of capital losses. No more than $3,000 in net capital losses can be deducted in a single tax year. Capital losses in excess of the limit may be carried forward and deducted in future years.

Remember that losses on personal use property are not deductible, so they are not netted against capital gains.

Business and Rental Property. Gains and losses on the sale of real property used in a business or held for the production of income (rental property) are treated somewhat differently from gains and losses on the sale of personal use and investment property. If business property or rental property is owned for more than one year and then sold, a gain on the sale is treated as a capital gain. But a loss on the sale is deductible as an ordinary loss rather than a capital loss. This is an advantage, because the $3,000 annual limit on the deduction of capital losses does not apply. The full amount of the loss can be deducted in the year it is incurred.

Note that losses resulting from the operation of a rental property are also deductible as ordinary losses. For example, suppose a rental house was vacant for most of the year and the annual operating expenses added up to more than the rent received. The owner of the house could deduct this lost income as an ordinary loss.

Basis

For income tax purposes, a property owner's **basis** in the property is his investment in it. If a taxpayer sells an asset, the basis is the maximum amount that he can receive in payment for the asset without realizing a gain. To determine gains and losses, it is necessary to know the taxpayer's basis in the property in question.

Initial Basis. In most cases, a taxpayer's **initial basis** (also called cost basis or unadjusted basis) is equal to the original cost of acquisition—that is, how much it cost to acquire the property. A person who paid $280,000 for a rental house plus $14,000 in closing costs has an initial basis of $294,000 in the property. She could turn around and sell the house for $294,000 without having to report a gain to the IRS.

Adjusted Basis. The initial basis may be increased or decreased to arrive at an **adjusted basis**, which reflects capital expenditures and any allowable depreciation deductions. **Capital expenditures** are expenses the owner incurs to improve the property—for example, money spent to add a new room or remodel the kitchen. Capital expenditures increase the value of the property or significantly extend its useful life. They are added to the initial basis in calculating the adjusted basis.

> **Example:** Greene buys a duplex as a rental property for $345,000 plus $11,000 in closing costs. Four years later, she spends $45,000 on improvements to the property, remodeling the bathrooms and the kitchens in both units. After Greene makes these capital expenditures, her adjusted basis in the duplex property is $401,000.

Maintenance expenses, such as repainting, replacing a broken window, or having the roof cleaned, are not capital expenditures. Maintenance expenses do not affect basis.

For certain types of property, a taxpayer's initial basis is also adjusted to take into account depreciation deductions, which will be discussed later in this chapter. These deductions are subtracted from the initial basis in calculating the adjusted basis.

	Initial basis (acquisition cost)
+	Capital expenditures
–	Depreciation deductions
	Adjusted basis

Realization

Not every gain is immediately taxable. A gain is not considered taxable income until it is **realized**. Ownership of an asset involves gain if the asset is appreciating in value. But for tax purposes, a gain is realized only when a sale or exchange occurs; the gain is then separated from the asset.

Example: Referring back to the example given above, suppose that during Greene's six years of ownership property values have been increasing steadily. Her improved duplex (which she bought for $356,000 and invested another $45,000 in) now has a market value of $489,000.

Greene has enjoyed an economic gain or benefit: she now owns property that is worth $88,000 more than what she put into it. However, that $88,000 is not realized—and therefore is not treated as income subject to taxation—until she sells the duplex.

The gain or loss realized on a transaction is the difference between the net sales price (called the **amount realized** in the tax code) and the adjusted basis of the property:

	Amount realized (net sales price)
–	Adjusted basis
	Gain or loss

In calculating the amount realized, the sales price includes money or other property received in exchange for the property, plus the amount of any mortgage debt that is eliminated. This means that if the buyer takes the property subject to the seller's mortgage or assumes it, the amount of that debt is treated as part of the sales price for tax purposes.

The selling expenses (such as the brokerage commission and the seller's other closing costs) are deducted from the sales price to arrive at the amount realized.

	Money received
+	Market value of other property received
+	Mortgage debt disposed of
–	Selling expenses
	Amount realized (net sales price)

Recognition and Deferral

A gain is said to be **recognized** in the year it is taxed. A gain will be recognized in the year it is realized, unless there is a specific exception in the tax code that allows the taxpayer to defer payment of taxes on the gain until a later tax year or a later transaction, or exclude payment of taxes altogether. For example, the tax code permits an individual selling her rental property on an installment basis to defer taxation of part of the gain to the year in which it is actually received (rather than the year the sale takes place). The tax code provisions that allow recognition of a gain to be deferred are called "nonrecognition provisions."

Nonrecognition provisions that apply to real estate transactions (including the rule already mentioned concerning installment sales) are discussed in detail later in this chapter.

Classifications of Real Property

Whether a particular type of real estate transaction qualifies for special tax treatment depends on the type of property involved. The tax code divides real property into the following classes:

1. principal residence property,
2. personal use property,

3. unimproved investment property,
4. property held for the production of income,
5. property used in a trade or business, and
6. dealer property.

Principal Residence Property. This is the home the taxpayer owns and occupies as his primary dwelling. It may be a single-family home, a duplex, a condominium unit, a cooperative apartment, or a mobile home. If the taxpayer owns two homes and lives in both of them, the one in which he lives most of the time is the principal residence. A taxpayer cannot have two principal residences at the same time.

Personal Use Property. Real property that a taxpayer owns for personal use, other than the principal residence, is classified as personal use property. A second home or a vacation cabin belongs in this category.

Unimproved Investment Property. Unimproved investment property is vacant land that produces no rental income. The land is held simply as an investment, in the expectation that it will appreciate in value.

Property Held for Production of Income. Property held for the production of income includes residential, commercial, and industrial property that is used to generate rental income for the owner.

Property Used in a Trade or Business. This category includes land and buildings that the taxpayer owns and uses in her trade or business, such as a factory owned by the manufacturer, or a small building the owner uses for her own retail business.

Dealer Property. This is property held primarily for sale to customers rather than for long-term investment. If a developer subdivides land for sale to the public, the lots will usually be included in this classification until they are sold.

Nonrecognition Transactions

As was explained earlier, when a nonrecognition provision in the tax code applies to a particular transaction, the taxpayer is not required to pay taxes on a gain in the year it is realized. The real estate transactions that are covered by nonrecognition provisions include:

- installment sales,
- involuntary conversions, and
- "tax-free" exchanges.

Keep in mind that nonrecognition provisions do not completely exclude the gain from taxation, but merely defer the tax consequences to a later tax year. These are not really "tax-free" transactions. The realized gain is simply recognized and taxed in a subsequent year.

Installment Sales

Fig. 15.1 Eligibility for installment sale reporting

Installment Sale Reporting
1. Less than 100% of sales price received in year of sale 2. All classifications of real property eligible except dealer property

The tax code considers a sale to be an **installment sale** if less than 100% of the sales price is received in the year of sale. Nearly all seller-financed transactions are installment sales. Installment sale reporting allows the taxpayer/seller to defer recognition of part of the gain to the year(s) in which it is actually received. In effect, taxes are paid only on the portion of the profit received each year; the gain is prorated over the term of the installment contract. Installment sale reporting is permitted for all classes of property, except that dealer property is eligible only under special conditions.

In installment sales, the gain recognized in any given year is calculated based on the ratio of the gross profit to the contract price. The **gross profit** is the difference between the sales price and the adjusted basis.

To calculate the gross profit, take the seller's adjusted basis at the time of sale, add the amount of the commission and other selling expenses, and subtract this sum from the sales price.

Example: Once again, we'll use Greene as an example. Her adjusted basis in her duplex was $401,000. She sold the property for $489,000. She had to pay a $29,000 commission and $8,200 in other selling expenses.

$489,000	Sales price
$401,000	Seller's adjusted basis
+ 37,200	Commission and other selling expenses
$438,200	Adjusted basis plus selling expenses
$489,000	Sales price
– 438,200	Adjusted basis plus selling expenses
$50,800	Gross profit

The next step is to compare the gross profit to the contract price to arrive at the **gross profit ratio** (also called the gross profit percentage). The contract price is the total amount of all principal payments the buyer will pay the seller. In most cases, unless the buyer assumes an existing loan, the contract price is the same as the sales price.

Example:

Gross Profit	÷	Contract Price	=	Gross Profit Ratio
$50,800	÷	$489,000	=	10.39%

The gross profit ratio is applied to the principal payments received in each year to determine how much of the principal is gain to be taxed that year. Note that the gross profit ratio is not applied to the interest the buyer pays the seller; all of the interest payments are treated as taxable income in the year received.

If the seller in the example above received a $48,900 downpayment, $2,500 in principal installment payments, and $30,500 in interest the first year, the taxable income would be calculated as follows:

$48,900	Downpayment
+ 2,500	Installment principal payments
$51,400	Total principal payments

$51,400	Total principal payments
× 10.39%	Gross profit ratio
$5,340	Recognized gain
+ 30,500	Interest income
$35,840	Total taxable income

Sometimes a buyer assumes a seller's existing mortgage or deed of trust and also gives the seller a second mortgage or deed of trust for part of the purchase price. If the loan assumed is larger than the seller's basis in the property, the excess is treated as payment received from the buyer in the year of the sale. If the property is subject to recapture provisions because of depreciation deductions (discussed later in this chapter), the amount recaptured is also treated as a payment received in the year of sale.

Involuntary Conversions

An involuntary conversion occurs when an asset is turned into cash without voluntary action on the part of the owner: the asset is condemned, destroyed, stolen, or lost, and the owner receives a condemnation award or insurance proceeds. Since the award or proceeds usually represent the property's replacement cost or market value, the owner often realizes a gain on an involuntary conversion.

However, recognition of a gain on an involuntary conversion can be deferred if the taxpayer uses the money received to replace the property within the replacement period set by the IRS. Generally, the replacement period lasts for two years after the date the property was destroyed or lost (or in the case of a condemnation, two years after the end of the tax year in which the gain was realized). Recognition of the gain is deferred only to the extent that the condemnation award or insurance proceeds are reinvested in the replacement property. Any part of the gain that is used for purposes other than purchase of replacement property will be taxed as income.

"Tax-Free" Exchanges

Section 1031 of the tax code concerns property exchanges. Section 1031 exchanges are commonly called "tax-free" exchanges, but they're really just tax-deferred exchanges. If unimproved investment property, income property, or property used in a trade or business is exchanged for **like-kind** property, recognition of any realized gain will be deferred. A primary residence, personal use property, and dealer property are not eligible for this type of deferral.

Tax-free exchanges are used to reduce or eliminate current tax expenses. And a taxpayer may be able to acquire property in an exchange that would be impossible to buy with the after-tax proceeds from the sale of the old property.

The property the taxpayer receives in the exchange must be like-kind—that is, the same kind as the property given. This requirement refers to the general nature of the properties rather than their quality. Most real estate is considered to be of like kind for the purposes of the exchange deferral, without regard to whether it is improved, unimproved, residential, commercial, or industrial. For example, if a taxpayer exchanges a strip shopping center for an apartment complex, the transaction can qualify as a tax-free exchange. Both of the exchanged properties must be located in the United States to be considered like-kind property.

If nothing other than like-kind property is received in the exchange, no gain or loss is recognized in the year of the exchange. However, anything other than like-kind property that the taxpayer receives is called **boot** and is recognized in the year of the exchange. In a real estate exchange, boot might be cash, stock, other types of personal property, or **debt relief**—the difference between mortgage balances.

Example: A taxpayer exchanges a property with a mortgage debt of $220,000 for one with a mortgage debt of $200,000. The taxpayer has received $20,000 in boot because of the reduction in debt (regardless of whether there has been a formal assumption of the loan). The taxpayer may be required to pay taxes on a gain of $20,000, just as if she had received $20,000 in cash along with the real property.

The following example shows how a taxpayer's actual gain and recognized gain are calculated in an exchange transaction involving boot.

Example: Taxpayer A is exchanging a small office building for Taxpayer B's commercial property. Taxpayer A's building is valued at $1,860,000 and has an adjusted basis of $1,744,000. Its mortgage has a remaining balance of $1,340,000.

Taxpayer B is giving Taxpayer A real property worth $1,804,000 with a mortgage balance of $1,305,000, plus $21,000 in cash. The debt relief for Taxpayer A is $35,000 ($1,340,000 – $1,305,000 = $35,000).

Here's how Taxpayer A's gain would be calculated:

$1,804,000	Like-kind property
35,000	Debt relief (boot)
+ 21,000	Cash (boot)
$1,860,000	Total value of property and boot received
– 1,744,000	Adjusted basis of Taxpayer A's former property
$116,000	Actual (realized) gain

So Taxpayer A is receiving property and boot worth $1,860,000 and realizing a $116,000 gain on the transaction. However, only the portion of the realized gain that is attributable to boot is taxable in the year the exchange takes place. Thus, Taxpayer A's recognized gain is $56,000 ($35,000 debt relief + $21,000 cash = $56,000 total boot). Taxation of the rest of the gain ($60,000) is deferred.

Note that boot is taxable only to the extent of the gain. If the boot received exceeded the taxpayer's realized gain on the transaction, then only the amount of the gain would be taxed, not the full amount of the boot.

Fig. 15.2 *Eligibility for tax-free exchanges*

"Tax-Free" Exchanges
1. Only property held for production of income, property used in a trade or business, or unimproved investment property is eligible. 2. Must be exchanged for like-kind property. 3. Boot is taxed in the year it is received.

The taxpayer's basis in the property exchanged is transferred to the property she receives. If nothing other than like-kind property is exchanged, no adjustments are necessary. But if the exchange involved boot, the basis must be adjusted for any boot that was paid or received, and for any gain or loss that was recognized because of the boot.

Keep in mind that under certain circumstances, an exchange of real property may be a tax-deferred transaction for one of the parties but not for the other. For example, suppose Taxpayer A trades his principal residence for a rental home owned by Taxpayer B. Both A and B are planning to use their new properties as rental homes. This can't be a tax-free exchange for Taxpayer A, because a principal residence isn't eligible. But this is a tax-free exchange for Taxpayer B, who has traded one income property for another.

Originally, 1031 exchanges were limited to simultaneous transfers of ownership (trades of property). Now, however, 1031 tax deferral benefits also apply when a taxpayer sells a property to one party and then buys a like-kind property from another party in two separate transactions. Time limits apply: once the taxpayer has sold the original (relinquished) property, he has 45 days to identify a replacement property. Then, the purchase of the replacement property must close within 180 days of the sale of the relinquished property.

An agent who arranges a tax-free exchange may receive compensation from both of the parties. Generally, a trained 1031 facilitator is needed to help these exchanges run smoothly.

Special Provisions for Home Buyers and Sellers

The federal government's policy is to promote home ownership. To provide incentives, federal tax law includes several provisions designed to benefit homeowners. We'll discuss two of these provisions below.

Exclusion of Gain from the Sale of a Principal Residence

Federal tax law gives homeowners an important exclusion from capital gains taxation: the exclusion of gain on the sale of a principal residence.

Until May 1997, an individual who sold his principal residence was often eligible for the "rollover" deferral of taxation. The seller was allowed to defer taxation of the gain if the sale proceeds were used within two years to buy another residence. And a seller who was 55 or older could take advantage of a one-time exclusion of gain from the sale of the principal residence, even if the gain was not invested in a new residence. The 1997 tax bill replaced both of these tax benefits with a single, less complicated exclusion from taxation.

Amount of Gain Excluded. Under current law, a taxpayer may exclude the entire gain on the sale of her principal residence, up to $250,000 if the taxpayer is filing a single return, or $500,000 if the taxpayer is married and filing a joint return.

Example:

$275,000	Amount realized (after selling costs)
– 80,000	Seller's basis in home
$195,000	Gain realized

Whether filing singly or jointly, the seller will be able to exclude the entire amount of gain—$195,000—from taxation.

If the amount of the gain on the sale of the home exceeds the $250,000 or $500,000 limit, the amount in excess of the limit will be taxed at the capital gains rate.

Example:

$375,000	Amount realized (after selling costs)
– 70,000	Seller's basis in home
$305,000	Gain realized

If the seller is filing a single return, only $250,000 of the $305,000 gain will be excluded from taxation. The seller will have to pay capital gains taxes on the $55,000 that exceeded the exclusion limit.

Eligibility. To qualify for this exclusion, the seller must have both owned and used the property as a principal residence for at least two years during the previous five-year period. Because of this rule, this exclusion is available only once every two years.

Note that if the sellers are married and filing a joint return, only one spouse has to meet the ownership test, but both spouses must meet the use test. If only one spouse meets both the ownership test and the use test, the maximum exclusion the married couple can claim is $250,000, even if they file a joint return.

If the seller owned and used the property as a principal residence for less than two years because of special circumstances (for example, if he sold the home after only a year because of a change in health or employment), the seller may be able to claim a reduced exclusion.

IRA Withdrawals

The federal government also gives first-time home buyers a break when using retirement funds toward the purchase of their first home. As a general rule, an early withdrawal from an individual retirement account (IRA) is treated as taxable income by the IRS and is subject to an additional 10% tax penalty. Under certain circumstances, however, a home buyer is able to withdraw funds from an IRA without paying a penalty or income tax on those funds. Different rules apply to the different types of IRAs.

Traditional IRA. Someone buying, building, or rebuilding a first home may withdraw up to $10,000 in IRA funds without paying any penalty. Married couples who are both first-time buyers may each withdraw funds from retirement accounts, up to a total of $20,000.

For the purposes of this exemption, a first-time home buyer is defined as someone who has not owned a principal residence at any time during the previous two years. The withdrawn IRA funds must be used to pay for financing or closing costs within 120 days of withdrawal.

Roth IRA. The rules governing withdrawals from Roth IRAs are a bit different. An account holder may withdraw up to $10,000 tax-free and without penalty only if the account has been held for five years. Otherwise, any withdrawals may be considered early distributions and the holder will owe taxes on the funds withdrawn. However, if the withdrawal is for the holder's first home, the holder may not be forced to pay the 10% penalty.

Deductions Available to Property Owners

As was explained earlier, a deduction is subtracted from a taxpayer's income before the tax rate is applied. The income tax deductions allowed to real property owners are a significant benefit of ownership. There are deductions for:

- depreciation,
- uninsured casualty and theft losses,
- repairs,
- real property taxes,
- mortgage interest,
- points paid to a mortgage lender,
- vacation homes, and
- home offices.

Depreciation Deductions

Depreciation deductions (sometimes called cost recovery deductions) permit a taxpayer to recover the cost of an asset over a period of years. Only property used for the production of income or used in a trade or business is eligible for depreciation deductions. They cannot be taken in connection with a principal residence or other personal use property, unimproved investment property, or dealer property.

Fig. 15.3 Eligibility for favorable income tax treatment

Eligibility for Favorable Income Tax Treatment			
	Installment Sale	"Tax-Free" Exchange	Depreciation Deductions
Principal Residence	Yes	No	No
Personal Use	Yes	No	No
Unimproved Investment	Yes	Yes	No
Trade or Business	Yes	Yes	Yes
Income	Yes	Yes	Yes
Dealer	No	No	No

Depreciable Property. In general, only property that wears out and will eventually have to be replaced is **depreciable**—that is, eligible for depreciation deductions. For example, apartment buildings, business or factory equipment, and commercial fruit orchards all have to be replaced, so they are depreciable. But land does not wear out, so it is not depreciable.

Time Frame. The entire expense of acquiring an asset cannot be deducted in the year it is incurred (although that is permitted with many other business expenses, such as wages, supplies, and utilities). However, the expense can be deducted over a number of years; for most real estate, the recovery period is between 27½ and 39 years. The length of the recovery period is a reflection of legislative policy and has little, if any, relationship to the actual length of time that the property will be economically useful. The whole field of depreciation deductions has been subject to frequent modification by Congress.

Effect on Basis. As we said in the discussion of basis at the beginning of the chapter, any allowable depreciation deductions reduce the taxpayer's adjusted basis in the property. Note that this reduction occurs whether or not the taxpayer actually takes the deduction. If the deduction was allowable—that is, the taxpayer was entitled to take it—the basis will be reduced. By reducing the basis, these deductions affect the taxpayer's eventual gain or loss on resale of the property.

Uninsured Casualty or Theft Loss Deductions

When property is damaged or stolen and the loss is not covered or is only partially covered by insurance, the property owner is generally permitted to deduct the uninsured loss from taxable income. To calculate the amount of the deductible loss, first subtract the estimated fair market value of the property after the loss from its estimated value before the loss. Compare this reduction in value to the owner's adjusted basis in the property. From the lower of the two figures, subtract any insurance reimbursement that the owner has received or will receive. For most types of property, the result is the amount of the deductible loss.

Example: Ramirez owned property worth $975,000, with an adjusted basis of $714,000. After the property was damaged in a flood, its value dropped to $830,000. This represented a reduction in value of $145,000:

$975,000	Value before flood damage
– 830,000	Value after flood damage
$145,000	Reduction in value

Ramirez's insurance company paid her only $110,000, so she suffered an uninsured casualty loss. To calculate how much of the loss Ramirez will be able to deduct from her taxable income, use the reduction in value ($145,000), since that figure is less than Ramirez's adjusted basis ($714,000).

$145,000	Reduction in value
– 110,000	Insurance reimbursement
$35,000	Deductible loss

For personal use property (including a principal residence), the amount of the deductible loss is reduced by some additional calculations. After going through the steps described above, subtract $100 from the loss. Next, subtract 10% of the taxpayer's adjusted gross income. The result is the taxpayer's deductible loss for personal use property.

Example: Return to the previous example, but now suppose that the property is Ramirez's home. Start where the previous calculation left off, subtract $100, and then subtract 10% of Ramirez's adjusted gross income, which is $95,000.

$35,000	Uninsured loss
100	Subtracted from loss
– 9,500	10% of adjusted gross income
$25,400	Deductible loss

Thus, Ramirez will be able to deduct $25,400 from her taxable income for this casualty loss concerning personal use property.

If a taxpayer has more than one casualty loss for personal use property in a given tax year, $100 must be subtracted from each loss. However, 10% of the adjusted gross income is subtracted from the total amount of those losses, not from each loss.

Repair Deductions

For most types of real property, expenditures for repairs are deductible in the year paid. A repair expense is one incurred to keep the property in ordinary, efficient, operating condition.

Repair expenses are not deductible for principal residences or other personal use property. This includes expenditures for maintenance, upkeep, and ordinary wear and tear, and it also includes condominium assessments.

For any type of real property, repair expenses should not be confused with capital expenditures. As explained earlier, capital expenditures add to the value of the property and frequently prolong its economic life. Capital expenditures are not deductible in the year made, but rather are added to the taxpayer's basis. The resulting increase in the basis will affect the gain or loss on the eventual sale of the property. It will also increase the allowable depreciation deductions if the property is eligible for those.

Property Tax Deductions

For principal residences and personal use property, general real estate taxes are deductible. Special assessments for repairs or maintenance are deductible, but those for improvements (such as new sidewalks) are not.

Mortgage Interest Deductions

For most property, interest paid on a mortgage or deed of trust is usually completely deductible. However, there are some limitations on interest deductions for personal residences (which are the only allowable consumer interest deductions).

A taxpayer may deduct interest payments on mortgage debt of up to $1,000,000 (or $500,000 if married and filing a separate return) used to buy, build, or improve a first or second residence. In addition, interest on a home equity loan of up to $100,000 ($50,000 for a married taxpayer filing separately) can be deducted without regard to the purpose of the loan. When the loan amount exceeds these limits, the interest on the excess is not deductible.

Occasionally a condominium project borrows money by mortgaging the common areas, and the unit owners are required to pay a share of the mortgage payment. In that case, a unit owner may deduct the interest portion of his share from taxable income.

The deductibility of mortgage interest is one reason why homeowners often use a home equity loan to pay off credit card debt. The interest on credit cards isn't deductible, but the interest on the home equity loan is.

Deductibility of Points and Other Loan Costs

The IRS considers points paid to a lender in connection with a new loan (including discount points and the origination fee) to be prepaid interest, and the borrower is generally allowed to deduct them. This is true even if the points were paid by the seller on the borrower's behalf. (The borrower's basis in the property must be reduced by the amount of the seller-paid points.)

Note that fees a lender charges to cover specific services are not deductible, even if the lender refers to them as points. This includes, for example, appraisal fees, document preparation fees, and mortgage insurance premiums.

If a seller paying off a loan is required to pay a prepayment penalty, the amount of the penalty is usually deductible. For tax purposes, a prepayment penalty is treated as a form of interest.

Vacation Home Deductions

A vacation home may be given special tax treatment, depending on how it is used. Some vacation property owners use the home solely as a **personal residence**. In other words, it is kept for the owner's personal use only and is generally not rented to others. To qualify as a personal residence, the home must be rented out for fewer than 15 days a year, and must be used by the owners more than 14 days a year. If the vacation home qualifies as a personal residence, any rental income generated need not be declared as income at all. However, the expenses associated with renting out the property are not deductible, either. All mortgage interest and property taxes are deductible.

The second home may be considered a **vacation home** (note that it is still considered a personal residence) if it is rented for at least 15 days a year, and is used by the owner for more than 14 days or 10% of the total rental days, whichever is greater. In this case, the owner must report the rental income, and can deduct at least some of the rental expenses. Property taxes and interest paid on this type of property are generally deductible.

If the vacation home is rented at least 15 days a year, with personal use not exceeding the greater of 14 days or 10% of the total rental days, the property is considered to be a **rental property**. Rental income generated by the property must be declared, and operating expenses, property taxes, and mortgage interest can be deducted, at least in part. The owner can also claim a loss if the rental expenses exceed the rental income. In order to claim a loss, the owner's gross income cannot exceed $100,000. The annual deductible allowance for the loss is limited to $25,000.

Timeshares. The tax consequences of owning a timeshare are somewhat different from those of owning a vacation home. As a general rule, mortgage interest paid for a timeshare may be deductible, as well as property taxes. However, if the timeshare is rented out, the rental income is not necessarily tax-free. In order for any rental income to be tax-free, the owner must personally use the unit for more than 14 days and the combined rental days for all of the owners of a unit must be fewer than 15 days. Since most timeshare arrangements are for two-week intervals, it is difficult for owners to meet these requirements.

Home Office Deductions

A large percentage of the workforce in the U.S. regularly works from home. Under certain circumstances, someone who works from home may be able to claim certain home office deductions such as mortgage interest, depreciation, and maintenance expenses.

Requirements. In order to claim a home office deduction, two requirements must be met. First, the office space must be used regularly and exclusively for business. Taking personal phone calls or occasionally using the office as a guest room eliminates any possibility of a home office deduction.

Second, the home office must be the individual's principal place of business. This means the office must be used exclusively and regularly for business-related administrative or management activities such as setting up appointments, meeting with clients, or keeping records. The owner cannot have any other fixed location where these activities are conducted.

Nonetheless, if the home office is used as a place to meet with clients, the space will qualify for the home office deduction even if much of the person's other work is done elsewhere. Under this alternative, people such as lawyers, accountants, and veterinarians are often able to claim home office deductions.

If a home office is in a separate building (such as a studio or garage), it will qualify for the home office deduction even if it isn't used as a principal place of business or as a place to meet clients.

As you can see, it is easier for self-employed people to claim a home office deduction than for those employed by others. For employees—in addition to the requirements outlined above—the home office arrangement must be for the convenience of the employer. Someone who has arranged to work at home a few days a week for personal convenience will not usually qualify for the deduction. However, if the employer encourages employees to work from home to save on office space, the employee will be able to take the deduction.

Deductions and Depreciation. An individual with a qualified home office may deduct certain expenses from her income. A percentage of real estate taxes and home mortgage interest may be deducted, depending on how much of the home is used for business purposes. Business expenses, such as business insurance, additional utilities, and repairs may also be deducted.

A home office may be depreciated over 39 years. However, if the home is sold, the owner may owe taxes on depreciation costs deducted in the past. Business furniture and equipment may be depreciated over five to seven years.

Rental Payment Deductions

Finally, we should mention one deduction connected with real estate that concerns not property owners but tenants. Rent paid for property used in a trade or business is deductible as a business expense. However, rent paid for property not used in a trade or business (such as rent for a home) is not deductible.

State Income Tax

In addition to the federal income tax, 44 states and 48 cities levy additional income taxes. These state and municipal income tax laws are substantially the same as the provisions of the Internal Revenue Code. For example, many state statutes simply refer to the federal law for such items as the definitions of gross income, adjusted gross income, itemized deductions, and taxable income. Some states have different standard deductions for those who do not itemize, and the tax rates on taxable income are generally different. As with federal law, state income taxes are progressive taxes with higher rates imposed on higher income levels.

Chapter Summary

1. Any economic benefit realized by a taxpayer is treated as part of his income, unless there is a specific provision of the tax code that excludes it from income. The tax code provides for certain deductions from income before the tax rate is applied. It also provides for tax credits, which are subtracted from the amount of tax owed.

2. A gain or a loss is realized when an asset is sold. A gain is recognized (taxed) in the year it is realized, unless a nonrecognition or exclusion provision in the tax code applies.

3. A taxpayer's initial basis in property is the amount he originally invested in it. To determine the adjusted basis, capital expenditures are added to the initial basis, and allowable depreciation deductions are subtracted from it. The taxpayer's gain or loss is the difference between the amount realized and the adjusted basis.

4. In the tax code, real property is classified as principal residence property, personal use property, unimproved investment property, property held for the production of income, property used in a trade or business, or dealer property.

5. The tax code's nonrecognition provisions for real property transactions allow taxation of gain to be deferred in installment sales, involuntary conversions, and "tax-free" exchanges.

6. The tax code contains several provisions benefiting homeowners. First, tax law permits an exclusion of up to $250,000 (or $500,000 if filing jointly) of gain on the sale of a principal residence. In addition, under certain circumstances, up to $10,000 may be withdrawn from an IRA account tax-free and penalty-free, to be used toward the purchase of a first home.

7. The tax deductions available to property owners include depreciation deductions (only for income property and property used in a trade or business); uninsured casualty or theft loss deductions; repair deductions (not for principal residences or personal use property); deduction of property taxes; deduction of mortgage interest; deduction of points; vacation home deductions; and home office deductions. (There are some limits on the mortgage interest deduction for personal residences.) Business rental payment deductions may be available to some tenants.

Key Terms

Income—Any economic benefit realized by a taxpayer that is not excluded from income by the tax code.

Deduction—An expense that can be used to reduce taxable income.

Marginal tax rate—The tax rate that applies to the last dollar that a taxpayer earns.

Basis—A taxpayer's investment in her property for income tax purposes.

Initial basis—The original acquisition cost of a property; how much it cost to acquire the property. Also called the cost basis or the unadjusted basis.

Adjusted basis—The initial basis plus capital expenditures and minus allowable depreciation deductions.

Realization—A gain or a loss is realized when it is separated from the asset. This separation generally occurs when the asset is sold.

Recognition—A gain is said to be recognized when it is taxable. It is recognized in the year it is realized, unless recognition is deferred by the tax code.

Installment sale—A sale in which less than 100% of the sales price is received in the year of sale.

Involuntary conversion—When property is converted to cash without the voluntary action of the owner, as when property is destroyed and the owner receives insurance proceeds.

Depreciation deductions—Deductions from the taxpayer's income to allow the cost of an asset to be recovered. These are allowed only for depreciable property that is held for the production of income or used in a trade or business. Also called cost recovery deductions.

Repair expenses—Money spent on repairs to keep property in ordinary, efficient operating condition.

Capital expenditures—Money spent on improvements to property, which add to its value or prolong its economic life.

"Tax-free" exchange—When like-kind property is exchanged, allowing taxation of the gain to be deferred. Also called a Section 1031 exchange.

Like-kind property—In a tax-free exchange, property received that is of the same kind as the property transferred. Any two pieces of real estate are considered to be of like kind.

Boot—Something given or received in a tax-free exchange that is not like-kind property, such as cash.

Chapter Quiz

1. A homeowner's basis in a principal residence would be adjusted to reflect:
   a) depreciation deductions
   b) expenses incurred to keep the property in good repair
   c) mortgage interest paid
   d) the cost of installing a deck

2. A married couple bought a home for $250,000. After living in the home for three years, they sold it for only $246,000. How much of this loss can they deduct on their federal income tax return?
   a) The full $4,000 loss
   b) Only $3,000
   c) Only $2,000
   d) None of it

3. Which of the following could the owner of unimproved investment property deduct on her federal income tax return?
   a) A loss on the sale of the property
   b) The depreciation of the land
   c) Cost recovery deductions
   d) Any of the above

4. Which of the following exchanges could not qualify as a "tax-free" exchange?
   a) An office building for a hotel
   b) An apartment house for a warehouse
   c) Timber land for farm equipment
   d) A city lot for a ranch

5. Under the federal income tax code, income is always taxed in the year it is:
   a) realized
   b) recognized
   c) recovered
   d) deferred

6. Ortega just sold his principal residence. After subtracting his selling costs, the amount of gain realized was $163,000. Ortega will be allowed to exclude the entire amount of the gain from taxation only if:
   a) he is married and is filing a joint return
   b) he has never claimed this exclusion before, since it can only be used once in a lifetime
   c) the gain is not considered capital gain
   d) he owned and occupied the property as his principal residence for two of the previous five years

7. Torrence owns a triplex. She paid $550,000 for it, including her closing costs. The allowable depreciation deductions for the property have amounted to $20,000, Torrence has spent $50,000 on capital improvements, and the market value of the property has risen by 15%. What is Torrence's adjusted basis?
   a) $600,000
   b) $620,000
   c) $580,000
   d) $530,000

8. Gillespie is buying a home that will be his principal residence. He is financing the purchase with a $300,000 mortgage loan. How much of the interest that he pays on the loan can he deduct from his income?
   a) All of it
   b) Up to $100,000 in interest
   c) 50%
   d) None of it

9. The Wongs are selling some property on a five-year contract. Their gross profit ratio on the sale is 15%. This year, they will receive $4,775 in interest and $1,675 in principal. With installment sale reporting, approximately how much of that will be recognized and included in the Wongs' taxable income for this year?
   a) $251
   b) $967
   c) $2,391
   d) $5,026

10. Sherrick is selling a lot for $72,000. Her adjusted basis in the property is $56,000. In addition to the 6% commission she'll be paying her real estate broker, she will also have to pay $2,500 in closing costs. For federal income tax purposes, what is the gain Sherrick will realize in this transaction?
    a) $6,820
    b) $9,180
    c) $16,000
    d) $22,820

Answer Key

1. d) The cost of installing a deck is a capital expenditure, which would be added to the taxpayer's basis. Remember that personal residences do not qualify for depreciation deductions.

2. d) A loss on the sale of a personal residence is never deductible.

3. a) If the owner loses money on the sale of the property, she may be able to deduct that loss. Depreciation (cost recovery) deductions are not allowed for unimproved investment property, because land is not depreciable.

4. c) The like-kind property requirement means that real estate must be exchanged for other real estate.

5. b) Income is taxed when it is recognized. It is often recognized in the same year it is realized, but that is not true if a nonrecognition provision applies.

6. d) To qualify for the exclusion from taxation, the taxpayer must have both owned and used the property as a principal residence for two of the previous five years.

7. c) The initial basis, plus the capital expenditures, less the allowable depreciation deductions, equals an adjusted basis of $580,000.

   $550,000 + $50,000 – $20,000 = $580,000

   (Ignore the increase in market value; it does not affect the taxpayer's basis.)

8. a) A taxpayer can deduct all of the interest paid on a loan of up to $1,000,000 used to purchase a first or second personal residence.

9. d) Multiply the principal payments by the gross profit ratio to determine the amount of principal that will be recognized this year. Then add that to the entire amount of interest received (all of the interest is taxable).

   $1,675 × 15% = $251.25 + $4,775 = $5,026.25

10. b) Sherrick will realize a $9,180 gain in the transaction. First subtract her selling expenses (the commission and closing costs) from the sales price to determine the amount realized; then subtract her adjusted basis from the amount realized to determine the gain.

    $72,000 × 6% = $4,320 commission

    $4,320 + $2,500 costs = $6,820

    $72,000 – $6,820 = $65,180 (amount realized)

    $65,180 – $56,000 = $9,180 (gain realized)

Chapter 16

Civil Rights and Fair Housing

I. Civil Rights Act of 1866
II. Civil Rights Act of 1964
III. Federal Fair Housing Act
    A. Exemptions
    B. Prohibited acts
    C. Handicap and familial status
    D. HUD and enforcement
IV. Federal Fair Lending Laws
V. Equal Access to Facilities
VI. State Antidiscrimination Legislation
VII. Complying with Fair Housing Laws
    A. Working with clients
    B. Advertising properties
    C. Actions that do not violate fair housing laws
VIII. Discriminatory Restrictive Covenants

Chapter Overview

Federal and state laws prohibit unfair discrimination in almost all real estate transactions. With limited exceptions, it is illegal for either property owners or real estate professionals to discriminate. In this chapter, we will cover several federal antidiscrimination laws, including the Civil Rights Act of 1866, the Federal Fair Housing Act, and the Americans with Disabilities Act. We will also discuss various state laws that prohibit discrimination in housing as well as in other real estate transactions.

Introduction

Over the years, various civil rights laws have been enacted to achieve one major goal: the freedom of choice. In the context of real estate, freedom of choice means that all types of people with similar financial resources should have equal access to the same types of housing. Anyone with the requisite income, net worth, and credit history should be able to choose a home or apartment in any affordable neighborhood, regardless of race, national origin, gender, or other similar characteristics.

Today, civil rights laws are an integral part of the real estate profession. The importance of the right to equal housing is well established, and real estate professionals must be familiar with both federal and state laws that prohibit discrimination.

The Civil Rights Act of 1866

This law states that "all citizens of the United States shall have the same right, in every state and territory as is enjoyed by white citizens thereof to inherit, purchase, lease, sell, hold and convey real and personal property." The act prohibits any discrimination based on race or color. It applies to the actions of both public organizations and private individuals.

Enacted immediately after the Civil War, the act was largely ignored for almost a century. In the 1960s, during the civil rights movement, the act was challenged as an unconstitutional interference with private property rights. But the U.S. Supreme Court upheld the act in the landmark case of *Jones v. Mayer*, decided in 1968. The court ruled that the 1866 act "prohibits all racial discrimination, private or public, in the sale and rental of property," and that the act is constitutional based on the 13th Amendment to the U.S. Constitution, which prohibits slavery.

Someone who has been discriminated against in violation of the Civil Rights Act of 1866 can sue in federal court. The court can issue an injunction ordering the defendant to stop discriminating or to take affirmative steps to correct the violation. This might involve an order requiring the defendant to sell or lease the property to the plaintiff. The court can also order the defendant to pay the plaintiff actual damages (compensatory damages) to compensate for financial losses, humiliation, and suffering caused by the discrimination. In addition, the defendant might be ordered to pay punitive damages (an additional sum to punish the defendant for wrongdoing).

The Civil Rights Act of 1964

The Civil Rights Act of 1964 was one of the first attempts made by the federal government to implement fair housing ideals. The act prohibits discrimination based on race, color, religion, or national origin in many programs and activities for which the federal government offered financial assistance. Unfortunately, the effect of the act was extremely limited, because most FHA and VA loans were not covered. In fact, it is estimated that less than 1% of all houses purchased were covered by the act. It was not until the Civil Rights Act of 1968 that major progress was made towards fair housing.

The Federal Fair Housing Act

Contained in Title VIII of the Civil Rights Act of 1968, the Fair Housing Act is intended to provide fair housing opportunities throughout the United States. This law makes it illegal to discriminate on the basis of **race, color, religion, sex, national origin, disability**, or **familial status** in the sale or lease of residential property or in the sale or lease of vacant land for the construction of residential buildings. Victims of discrimination falling into one of these categories are known as members of a **protected class**. The law also prohibits discrimination in advertising, lending, real estate brokerage, and other services in connection with residential real estate transactions. However, unlike the 1866 Civil Rights Act, the Fair Housing Act does not apply to nonresidential transactions, such as those involving commercial or industrial properties.

Exemptions

While the Fair Housing Act applies to the majority of residential real estate transactions, four types of transactions are exempt from it.

1. The law does not apply to the sale or rental of a single-family home by its owner, provided that:
   - the owner does not own more than three such homes;
   - no real estate broker or agent is employed in the transaction; and
   - no discriminatory advertising is used.

   If the owner isn't the most recent occupant of the home, he may use this exemption only once every 24 months.

Fig. 16.1 Fair housing poster

U. S. Department of Housing and Urban Development

EQUAL HOUSING OPPORTUNITY

We Do Business in Accordance With the Federal Fair Housing Law

(The Fair Housing Amendments Act of 1988)

It is illegal to Discriminate Against Any Person Because of Race, Color, Religion, Sex, Handicap, Familial Status, or National Origin

- In the sale or rental of housing or residential lots
- In advertising the sale or rental of housing
- In the financing of housing
- In the provision of real estate brokerage services
- In the appraisal of housing
- Blockbusting is also illegal

Anyone who feels he or she has been discriminated against may file a complaint of housing discrimination:
1-800-669-9777 (Toll Free)
1-800-927-9275 (TTY)

U.S. Department of Housing and Urban Development
Assistant Secretary for Fair Housing and Equal Opportunity
Washington, D.C. 20410

Previous editions are obsolete

form HUD-928.1 (2/2003)

2. The law does not apply to the rental of a unit or a room in a dwelling with up to four units, provided that:
   - the owner occupies one of the units as her residence;
   - no real estate broker or agent is employed; and
   - no discriminatory advertising is used.

   (This is sometimes called the **Mrs. Murphy exemption**.)
3. In dealing with their own property in noncommercial transactions, religious organizations or societies or affiliated nonprofit organizations may limit occupancy to or give preference to their own members, provided that membership isn't restricted on the basis of race, color, or national origin.
4. Private clubs with lodgings that aren't open to the public and that aren't operated for a commercial purpose may limit occupancy to or give preference to their own members.

These limited exemptions apply very rarely. Remember, the 1866 Civil Rights Act prohibits discrimination based on race or color in any property transaction regardless of any exemptions available under the Fair Housing Act. In addition, there is no exemption for any transaction involving a real estate licensee.

Prohibited Acts

The Fair Housing Act prohibits any of the following acts if they are done on the basis of race, color, religion, sex, national origin, handicap, or familial status:

- refusing to rent or sell residential property after receiving a bona fide offer;
- refusing to negotiate for the sale or rental of residential property, or otherwise making it unavailable;
- changing the terms of sale or lease for different potential buyers or tenants;
- using advertising that indicates a preference or intent to discriminate;
- representing that property is not available for inspection, sale, or rent when it is in fact available;
- using discriminatory criteria when making a housing loan;
- limiting participation in a multiple listing service or similar service;
- coercing, intimidating, threatening, or interfering with anyone on account of his enjoyment, attempt to enjoy, or encouragement or assistance to others in enjoying the rights granted by the Fair Housing Act.

Also prohibited are the discriminatory practices known as blockbusting, steering, and redlining.

- **Blockbusting** occurs when someone tries to induce homeowners to list or sell their properties by predicting that members of another race (or disabled persons, persons of a particular ethnic background, etc.) will be moving into the neighborhood, and that this will have undesirable consequences such as lower property values. The blockbuster then profits by purchasing the homes at reduced prices or (in the case of a real estate agent) by collecting commissions on the induced sales. Blockbusting is also known as **panic selling** or **panic peddling**.

Example: An African-American family recently moved into an all-white neighborhood. XYZ Realty immediately began calling all the homeowners in the neighborhood. XYZ's salespeople warned the homeowners of the following: several African-American families were planning on moving into the neighborhood, city police predicted a significant increase in crime in the neighborhood, property values would drop dramatically, and within months homeowners would find it difficult to sell their properties to anyone at any price. Because of these "facts" made up by XYZ agents, several homeowners immediately listed their homes with XYZ Realty. XYZ Realty is guilty of blockbusting.

- **Steering** refers to channeling prospective buyers or tenants toward or away from specific neighborhoods based on their race (or religion, national origin, etc.) in order to maintain or change the character of those neighborhoods.

  Example: The salespeople at PQR Realty are "encouraged" to show Hispanic buyers only properties in the city's predominantly Hispanic neighborhood. Non-Hispanic buyers aren't shown properties there, except by specific request. This is done on the principle that Hispanic buyers would be more "comfortable" living in the Hispanic neighborhood and non-Hispanic buyers would be "uncomfortable" there. PQR Realty is guilty of steering.

- **Redlining** is the refusal to make a loan because of the racial or ethnic composition of the neighborhood in which the security property is located.

  Example: Buyer Jones applies to Community Savings for a loan to purchase a home located in the Cherrywood neighborhood. Cherrywood is a predominantly minority neighborhood. Community Savings rejects the loan, because it fears that property values in Cherrywood may suffer in the future because of possible racial tension. Community Savings is guilty of redlining.

The prohibition against redlining is enforced through the **Home Mortgage Disclosure Act of 1975**, which requires large institutional lenders to file an annual report of all mortgage loans made. The loans are categorized according to the locations of the properties, which makes it easier to discover cases of redlining.

Handicap and Familial Status

Originally, the Fair Housing Act did not prohibit discrimination based on handicap or familial status; these classifications were added to the law in 1988.

Handicap. Under the Fair Housing Act, it is illegal to discriminate against someone because she has a physical disability or mental impairment that substantially limits one or more major life activities. This includes people suffering from chronic alcoholism, mental illness, or AIDS. But the act does not protect those who are a direct threat to the health or safety of others, or who are currently using controlled substances.

A residential landlord must allow a disabled tenant to make reasonable modifications to the property at the tenant's expense, so long as the modifications are necessary for the tenant's full use and enjoyment of the premises. (The tenant can be required to restore the premises to their original condition at the end of the tenancy, however.) Landlords must also make reasonable exceptions to their rules to accommodate disabled tenants. For example, even if they don't allow pets, they can't refuse to rent to someone with a guide dog.

Special wheelchair accessibility rules apply to newer residential construction with four or more units.

Familial Status. Discrimination on the basis of familial status refers to discrimination against a person because he has a child (under 18 years old) living with him. Parents, legal guardians, pregnant women, and those in the process of obtaining custody of a child are protected against discrimination on the basis of their familial status.

While the Fair Housing Act does not override local laws limiting the number of occupants permitted in a dwelling, it is unlawful for anyone to discriminate in selling, renting, or lending money to buy residential property because the applicant is pregnant or lives with a child. "Adults only" apartment or condominium complexes are forbidden, as are complexes divided into "adult" and "family" areas.

However, the law includes an exemption for properties that qualify as "housing for older persons." Children can be excluded from properties that fit into one of the following categories:

1. properties developed under a government program to assist the elderly;
2. properties intended for and solely occupied by persons 62 years old or older; or
3. properties that adhere to a policy that demonstrates intent to house persons who are 55 or older, if at least 80% of the units are occupied by at least one person who is 55 or older.

HUD and Enforcement

The Fair Housing Act is enforced by the Department of Housing and Urban Development (HUD), through its Office of Fair Housing and Equal Opportunity. HUD is also authorized to issue regulations to promote the purpose of the Fair Housing Act. One such regulation requires brokers and other persons involved in real estate transactions to display a fair housing poster (shown in Figure 16.1) at their place of business.

As part of its enforcement process, HUD sometimes uses **testers**, individuals who play the role of a person wanting to buy or rent housing. A tester evaluates compliance with fair housing laws and is allowed to file a complaint if discrimination is found. Testers do not announce themselves; they appear to be normal potential clients.

When a person feels that his rights under the Fair Housing Act have been violated, he may file a complaint with HUD (within one year of the alleged discrimination) or may file a lawsuit in federal or state court. If a complaint is filed with HUD, the agency will investigate the complaint and evaluate whether the discrimination charges appear to be justified. During the investigation period, HUD can attempt to resolve the dispute by getting an agreement from the party against whom the complaint was filed, in which that party agrees to remedy the violation and take action to avoid any future discrimination.

If the dispute is not resolved and the claims are found to have merit, an administrative hearing will be held, unless either party chooses to have the case decided in federal court instead. In an administrative hearing, HUD attorneys litigate the case on behalf of the complainant. If a case involves a pattern or practice of discrimination, the U.S. Attorney General can file suit in federal court.

When someone is held to have violated the Fair Housing Act, the administrative law judge or the court may issue an injunction ordering the violator to stop the discriminatory conduct or to take affirmative steps to correct a violation. The violator may also be ordered to pay actual damages and attorney's fees to the complainant. Actual damages may include compensation for humiliation suffered as a result of discrimination, as well as for financial losses. A federal court can order the violator to pay punitive damages to the complainant. If the case is brought by the Attorney General, instead of punitive damages the court can order a civil penalty ranging from a maximum of $55,000 for a first offense up to a maximum of $110,000 for a third or subsequent offense. An administrative law judge can also impose a civil penalty; the maximum penalty in this case ranges from $16,000 for a first offense up to $70,000 for a third or subsequent offense.

Many states have their own fair housing laws, which are often very similar to the Fair Housing Act. If the state laws and regulations have comparable prohibitions, HUD may refer the complaints it receives to the equivalent state agency. The state must be able to show that its agency responds appropriately to complaints and takes sufficient action to prevent discrimination.

Federal Fair Lending Laws

Real estate agents and sellers are not the only ones who must avoid discriminatory activities. There are also federal laws designed to eliminate discrimination in lending. They include:

- the Federal Fair Housing Act (discussed above),
- the Equal Credit Opportunity Act, and
- the Home Mortgage Disclosure Act.

The Fair Housing Act prohibits discrimination in home loans and other aspects of residential financing. It does not apply to any other credit transactions.

The **Equal Credit Opportunity Act** (ECOA) applies to credit transactions, including mortgage lending. The act prohibits lenders, loan originators, mortgage brokers, and others involved in financing from discriminating based on race, color, religion, national origin, sex, marital status, age (as long as the applicant is of legal age), or because the applicant's income is derived partly or wholly from public assistance.

Under the Equal Credit Opportunity Act, a lender may ask applicants about race, national origin, sex, and marital status, but only to gather information that allows the

Fig. 16.2 Antidiscrimination legislation

Legislation	Prohibits Discrimination
Civil Rights Act of 1866	Based on race
Civil Rights Act of 1964	In some federal programs
Federal Fair Housing Act	In sale, lease, or financing of housing
Americans with Disabilities Act	Based on disability
Equal Credit Opportunity Act	In credit transactions

government to monitor compliance with the act. Giving the information is voluntary; the lender cannot require it. However, if the applicant and lender are located in a community property state (or if there is any other reason that an applicant's spouse would share the obligation), the lender may ask questions about spouses and marital status.

If the application is denied, the lender must give the applicant a written statement explaining the reasons for the denial of credit. A lender who discriminates in violation of the act can be liable for damages, court costs, and attorney's fees.

The **Home Mortgage Disclosure Act** helps the government learn whether lenders are fulfilling their obligation to serve the housing needs of the communities where they are located. The act facilitates the enforcement of federal laws against redlining.

Under the Home Mortgage Disclosure Act, large institutional lenders in metropolitan areas must make annual reports on residential mortgage loans (both purchase and improvement loans) that were originated or purchased during the fiscal year. The information is categorized as to number and dollar amount, type of loan (FHA, VA, other), and geographic location by census tract or county (for small counties with no established census tracts). The reports disclose areas where few or no home loans have been made and alert investigators to potential redlining.

Equal Access to Facilities

The **Americans with Disabilities Act** (ADA), which became effective in January of 1992, is a federal law that was passed to ensure that disabled persons have equal access to public facilities. The ADA requires any business or other nonresidential facility open to the public to be accessible to the disabled. (Private clubs and religious organizations are exempt from the ADA.)

Under the ADA, no one can be discriminated against on the basis of disability in any place of public accommodation or commercial facilities. A place of **public accommodation** is defined to include any nonresidential place that is owned, operated, or leased by a private entity and open to the public, as long as the operation of the facility affects commerce. A **disability** is defined as any physical or mental impairment that substantially limits one or more of the individual's major life activities.

Real estate offices are considered to be places of public accommodation, along with hotels, restaurants, retail stores, shopping centers, banks, and the offices of other service professionals, such as insurance agents and accountants.

To ensure the accessibility of public accommodations, the ADA requires all of the following to be accomplished, as long as they are "readily achievable":

- Both architectural and communication barriers must be removed so that goods and services are accessible to the disabled.
- Auxiliary aids and services must be provided so that no disabled person is excluded, denied services, segregated, or otherwise treated differently from other individuals.
- All new construction of places of public accommodation or other commercial facilities must be accessible to the disabled, unless structurally impractical.

For example, the owner of a commercial building with no elevator may have to install automatic entry doors and a buzzer at street level so that customers of a second-floor business can ask for assistance. A commercial building owner might also be required to alter the height of a door handle to make it accessible to someone in a wheelchair, add grab bars to restroom stalls, and take a variety of other steps to make the building's facilities accessible.

State Antidiscrimination Legislation

Not only must real estate agents, sellers, and landlords comply with the federal laws we've just discussed, they must also comply with state laws that prohibit discrimination. Many states have laws designed to promote fair housing within the state. Counties and cities may also have their own antidiscrimination ordinances.

State and local regulations often cover even more forms of discrimination than federal fair housing laws. They may have more limited exemptions or include additional protected classes, such as age or sexual orientation. Also, state antidiscrimination laws often apply not just to housing, but also to employment, credit transactions, and other types of business activities.

Real estate agents have a special obligation not to discriminate or assist in discrimination by others. The real estate license law in many states provides that violating any fair housing or civil rights laws or regulations is grounds for disciplinary action.

Complying with Fair Housing Laws

As you can see, antidiscrimination laws cover a lot of territory. Real estate agents must be familiar with these laws and know what activities are prohibited. Keep in mind that violating these laws does not require an intent to discriminate; even good intentions can lead to a violation of antidiscrimination laws.

Example: Matthews is giving a listing presentation at the Flores home. The Flores family is from Central America and they speak only limited English. Matthews does not speak Spanish and feels uncomfortable because of the communication barrier. When Matthews finishes the presentation, Mr. Flores tells him they want to list their property right away. Somewhat sheepishly, Matthews suggests that they may want to list their property with an agent who speaks Spanish. He explains tactfully that he has a very difficult time understanding them and believes that they would be happier with a Spanish-speaking agent.

The Flores family insists that they want to list with Matthews but he declines, telling them another agent would be able to give them better service. This well-intentioned refusal to list their property might be regarded as discrimination on the basis of national origin, and could be considered a violation of federal or state antidiscrimination laws.

To avoid unintentional discriminatory acts, real estate agents should follow some basic guidelines when working with clients and advertising properties they have listed.

Working with Clients

Real estate agents should never say or imply that the presence of persons of a particular protected class (race, national origin, etc.) in a neighborhood could or will result in:

- lower property values;
- a change in the composition of the neighborhood;
- a more dangerous neighborhood; or
- a decline in the quality of the schools in the neighborhood.

Example: Chadwick is making a listing presentation to Thompson, a homeowner who is considering selling her property but isn't sure this is the right time. During the presentation, Chadwick says to Thompson, "I hear your neighbor, Bowen, has an offer on his house from a minority couple. You know, it might be a good idea to get your house listed and an offer nailed down before any minority families move into the neighborhood. That way, you can get the best price for your house. If you wait until Bowen's house is sold—well, you just might not get as much for your house." This is an example of blockbusting. Chadwick has violated the antidiscrimination laws.

Most agents would not act in an overtly discriminatory way; for example, they wouldn't raise the listing price because of the race of the prospective buyer. Yet some of these same agents might tell racial or ethnic jokes or make derogatory remarks about a particular group of people. Although these jokes or remarks don't necessarily indicate a willingness to actually discriminate in a transaction, a listener might assume that they do.

Even listening or going along with inappropriate remarks can give the impression that the agent agrees with these discriminatory attitudes. Agents need to watch out for signs of such attitudes, in order to avoid helping others violate antidiscrimination laws.

Example: Hawthorne is making a listing presentation to the Boyds, a white couple who live in a predominantly white neighborhood. During the discussion, Mr. Boyd says, "You know, we certainly want the best price for our house. But we want you to be pretty careful who you show it to. We spent a lot of time fixing up this house. Hey, we raised our kids here. We really don't want to change the neighborhood. Our neighbors are good, traditional, hard-working folks. We don't want a buyer who would lower everybody else's property values. You know what we mean."

Even though the Boyds don't come out and say so, they could easily be implying that they would not accept an offer from a buyer with a different racial or ethnic background. Their comments are red flags indicating the possibility of discrimination.

Listing agents should make sure the seller is willing to follow the law, and decline to take the listing if the seller is not.

Real estate agents should also provide equal service to buyers and sellers without regard to their race, creed, color, religion, national origin, ancestry, sex, marital status, familial status, age, or disability. For example, an agent should never refuse to show a property to a potential buyer based on discriminatory reasons.

Example: Alison is working with the Kawaguchi family, who is interested in a particular listing. Alison has heard that the owner of this house is extremely prejudiced against Asians and she knows the seller will refuse any offer from the Kawaguchis. To avoid a confrontation, she tells them that the house is no longer available. Alison has just unlawfully discriminated against the Kawaguchis by telling them the house was not available when, in fact, it was available.

Advertising Properties

Advertising is an important element in marketing a property, but it also has potential pitfalls for discrimination. Sometimes even apparently innocent statements or actions may be interpreted as discriminatory. Consider the following practices for which a real estate agent might be accused of discrimination.

- A property for sale is advertised only in neighborhoods where the residents are all predominantly of the same race or ethnic background as the seller.
- A flyer about a property is sent to all the neighboring properties except those owned by people of a particular race or ethnic background.
- The wording of an ad suggests that the recipient can control the type of person who will buy the property.

Example: A flyer for an open house tells neighbors that they can, by referring potential buyers, "uphold the standards of the community." However, the flyer fails to specify what community standards it refers to. Because it doesn't clearly describe these standards in nondiscriminatory language, a reader could infer that she can control the race or ethnic background of the buyer. The flyer might be found to violate antidiscrimination laws.

- The choice of models used in display advertising lacks diversity.

Example: A broker is the listing agent for a large, exclusive housing development. She advertises the homes in the development by putting display ads in the local paper. In every ad she places, the buyers and sellers are depicted only by white models, even though 38% of the city's population is non-white. The use of only white models could be grounds for a discrimination suit.

When pictures of people are used in display advertising, they should be carefully chosen to make sure that the pictures give the impression that the housing is open to everyone.

Actions That Do Not Violate Fair Housing Laws

Certain actions may initially appear to violate antidiscrimination laws, but in fact are not considered to be violations. Here are some examples.

- A real estate agent may ask questions or make statements as necessary to best serve the needs of a disabled person. This may include calling the attention of disabled clients or customers to particular buildings built or modified to meet their needs.
- Positive measures to reach out to members of a protected class, rather than discriminating against them, may be acceptable. An affirmative marketing plan may try to attract members of a particular group to an area or property that they might not otherwise be aware of. A brokerage or real estate board may also take affirmative steps to recruit minority employees or members.

Example: The developer of a large, moderately priced subdivision located on the fringes of the metropolitan area contacts a broker to assist in the sale of properties in the subdivision. The developer encourages the broker to target marketing efforts toward recent immigrants who might be looking for affordable entry-level housing. Most of the recent immigrants in the area are non-white and live in a few older urban neighborhoods. The broker could devote extra effort to advertising in immigrant community newspapers or leafletting these neighborhoods, so long as she also advertised in other neighborhoods or in newspapers of wider circulation.

- Real estate agents may truthfully answer questions about the racial composition of neighborhoods, even if this results in unintentional racial steering. If a buyer expresses a desire not to be shown homes in a particular neighborhood, even if the buyer makes that decision because of the race or other characteristics of the residents, you are not obligated to show them homes in that neighborhood.

Example: You are representing the Duvalls, who have only a limited amount of money to spend on their first home. You suggest a variety of neighborhoods where there are listings that fit their price range and other preferences, including the Greengate neighborhood. When Mr. Duvall asks about the people who live in Greengate, you truthfully respond that most of the residents belong to a particular immigrant group. Mr. Duvall says, "I'm not sure we'd feel comfortable there; we'd rather look in other areas." So long as you do not coerce or discourage the Duvalls from looking at properties in this neighborhood, you are not required to show the Duvalls houses in this area against their wishes.

Discriminatory Restrictive Covenants

At one time in the United States it was quite common for a property's deed or a subdivision's CC&Rs to include a restrictive covenant prohibiting the sale or lease of the property to non-whites or non-Christians. These discriminatory restrictions were generally considered legal and enforceable until the Supreme Court decided the case of *Shelley v. Kraemer* in 1948. The court ruled that it was unconstitutional—a violation of the 14th Amendment—for state courts or federal courts to be involved in the enforcement of racially restrictive covenants. As a result of the decision, those covenants became legally unenforceable.

Today, although discriminatory restrictive covenants still appear in some older documents, it is a violation of both federal and state laws to attempt to enforce or comply with them. If such a restriction is included in a new deed, the restriction is unenforceable, but it does not affect the conveyance.

Chapter Summary

1. Discrimination in real estate transactions is prohibited by the Civil Rights Act of 1866, the Federal Fair Housing Act, and state antidiscrimination statutes.

2. The Civil Rights Act of 1866 prohibits all discrimination based on race or color in the sale and rental of property. The Civil Rights Act of 1964 prohibits discrimination in programs and services for which the federal government provides financial assistance.

3. The Federal Fair Housing Act goes farther than the Civil Rights Acts of 1866 and 1964 by prohibiting discrimination based on race, color, religion, sex, national origin, handicap, or familial status. However, it applies only to transactions involving residential property.

4. Three specifically prohibited acts under the Federal Fair Housing Act are blockbusting, steering, and redlining. Blockbusting is attempting to obtain listings or arrange sales by predicting the entry of minorities into the neighborhood and implying that this will cause a decline in the neighborhood. Steering is the channeling of buyers or renters to specific neighborhoods based on race or other protected characteristics. Redlining is the refusal, for discriminatory reasons, to make loans on properties located in particular areas.

5. Several federal laws prohibit discrimination in credit transactions: the Federal Fair Housing Act, the Equal Credit Opportunity Act, and the Home Mortgage Disclosure Act.

6. The Americans with Disabilities Act guarantees equal access to places of public accommodation regardless of physical or mental disability.

7. State laws also prohibit discrimination in many areas, including housing. They may have fewer exemptions or include different protected classes than federal laws.

8. Discriminatory restrictive covenants in a deed or a subdivision's declaration of restrictions are illegal. A conveyance of property is not affected by a discriminatory restriction; the restriction itself is simply unenforceable.

Key Terms

Blockbusting—Attempting to induce homeowners to list or sell their homes by predicting that members of another race or ethnic group, or people with a disability, will be moving into the neighborhood. Also called panic selling.

Steering—Channeling prospective buyers or tenants toward or away from particular neighborhoods based on their race, religion, or national origin, in order to maintain or change the character of the neighborhoods.

Redlining—Refusing to make a loan because of the racial or ethnic composition of the neighborhood in which the security property is located.

Familial status—A category including persons who have children (under 18 years old) living with them. It also includes someone who is pregnant or is in the process of securing custody of a child.

Disability—A physical disability or mental impairment that substantially limits one or more major life activities.

Protected class—A group of people that falls into one of the categories that are protected against discrimination.

Public accommodation—A place of public accommodation is any nonresidential place that is owned, operated, or leased by a private entity and open to the public, if operation of the facility affects commerce.

Chapter Quiz

1. When a real estate agent channels prospective buyers away from a particular neighborhood because of their race, it is called:
   a) blockbusting
   b) steering
   c) redlining
   d) clipping

2. Rental of a room in an owner-occupied dwelling is exempt from the Fair Housing Act if the dwelling contains:
   a) two or more units
   b) three units or less
   c) less than five units
   d) six units or more

3. A real estate broker is helping the Jacksons sell their single-family home. Can this transaction be exempt from the Fair Housing Act?
   a) Yes, as long as the Jacksons own no more than three single-family homes
   b) Yes, as long as no discriminatory advertising is used
   c) No, because a real estate agent is involved
   d) No, the act applies to all residential sales transactions, without exception

4. The Gardenia Village condominium has a "no kids" rule. This is not a violation of the Fair Housing Act:
   a) if the condo qualifies as "housing for older persons" under the terms of the law
   b) if no discriminatory advertising is used
   c) because age discrimination is not prohibited by the law
   d) because condominiums aren't covered by the law

5. Title VIII of the Civil Rights Act of 1968 precludes:
   a) discrimination in housing
   b) discrimination in lending
   c) Both a) and b)
   d) Neither a) nor b)

6. Blockbusting is an acceptable practice:
   a) only under the supervision of real estate licensees
   b) only when approved by either HUD or the Justice Department
   c) under no circumstances
   d) only if the seller and buyer mutually agree

7. A deed restriction created in 1920 that prohibits the sale of property to a non-Caucasian person until after 2015 is:
   a) valid until all the property owners agree to eliminate the restriction
   b) enforceable
   c) unenforceable
   d) covered by title insurance

8. The Home Mortgage Disclosure Act helps to enforce the prohibition against:
   a) redlining
   b) steering
   c) blockbusting
   d) None of the above

9. A landlord who is subject to the provisions of the Fair Housing Act must:
   a) permit a disabled tenant to make reasonable modifications to the property at the tenant's expense
   b) make reasonable exceptions to the landlord's rules to accommodate disabled tenants
   c) Both a) and b)
   d) Neither a) nor b)

10. State fair housing laws may:
    a) only cover places of public accommodation
    b) apply to more protected classes than federal laws
    c) override federal antidiscrimination laws
    d) allow discriminatory restrictive covenants

11. Under the Equal Credit Opportunity Act, a lender must:
    a) ask about the race of credit applicants
    b) report credit applications to the federal government
    c) ensure that its facilities are accessible to the disabled
    d) give a written explanation when an application for credit is denied

12. Which of the following is not covered by the Fair Housing Act?
    a) A commercial property
    b) An eight-unit multi-family dwelling
    c) A triplex listed for sale with a real estate broker
    d) A vacant lot intended for residential construction

13. A developer who intended to rent housing in a particular development only to persons 45 years of age or over would be in violation of the:
    a) Civil Rights Act of 1866
    b) Civil Rights Act of 1964
    c) Fair Housing Act
    d) Americans with Disabilities Act

14. Under the Americans with Disabilities Act:
    a) real estate firms are exempt
    b) real estate firms may discriminate against the disabled when taking listings, if appropriate
    c) real estate firms must be accessible to the disabled
    d) only individual real estate agents are prohibited from discriminating against the disabled

15. Which of the following is not an example of illegal steering?
    a) An agent working with a buyer who has a disability calls his attention to a property with modifications that meet his needs
    b) An agent avoids showing an unmarried buyer houses in neighborhoods where most residents are married couples with children
    c) An agent working with a white couple only shows them homes in predominantly white neighborhoods
    d) An agent working with a minority couple only shows them homes in predominantly minority neighborhoods

Answer Key

1. b) Channeling prospective buyers or tenants away from (or toward) certain neighborhoods based on their race, religion, or national origin is called steering. It is a violation of the Fair Housing Act.

2. c) The Fair Housing Act exemption for rentals applies to owner-occupied dwellings with up to four units.

3. c) No residential transaction in which a real estate agent is employed is exempt from the Fair Housing Act.

4. a) The Fair Housing Act does not allow apartment houses and condominiums to discriminate on the basis of familial status unless the complex qualifies as "housing for older persons."

5. c) Title VIII of the 1968 Civil Rights Act (better known as the Fair Housing Act) prohibits discriminatory practices when selling, renting, advertising, or financing housing.

6. c) Blockbusting is a discriminatory practice entirely prohibited by the Fair Housing Act.

7. c) A deed containing such a provision is valid, but the restriction is unenforceable.

8. a) The Home Mortgage Disclosure Act helps to enforce the prohibition against redlining by requiring large institutional lenders to file an annual report of all mortgage loans made during that year. Loans are categorized according to location, alerting investigators to areas of possible redlining.

9. c) The Fair Housing Act requires a residential landlord to allow a disabled tenant to make reasonable modifications to the property. The landlord must also make reasonable exceptions to the rules to accommodate a disabled tenant.

10. b) State laws may provide fewer exemptions or more protected classes than federal laws, but they may not override the protections contained in federal laws.

11. d) The Equal Credit Opportunity Act requires lenders, when denying a credit application, to give a written statement explaining the reasons for the denial.

12. a) The Fair Housing Act applies to residential properties, not commercial or industrial properties.

13. c) The developer's age limit would violate the Fair Housing Act. Senior housing is permitted, but 45 is not the cutoff age.

14. c) Under the provisions of the ADA, real estate firms must take reasonable actions necessary to make their accommodations accessible to the disabled.

15. a) An agent can legitimately bring properties that are specially suited to the needs of a disabled buyer to the buyer's attention.

Chapter 17

Property Management

I. Introduction to Property Management
II. Investing in Real Estate
    A. Types of investments
    B. Investment characteristics
    C. Advantages
    D. Disadvantages
III. Types of Managed Properties
IV. The Management Agreement
V. The Management Plan
    A. Preliminary study
        1. Regional analysis
        2. Neighborhood analysis
        3. Property analysis
        4. Market analysis
    B. Management proposal
VI. Management Functions
    A. Leasing and tenant relations
        1. Marketing
        2. Leasing
        3. Tenant complaints
        4. Rent collection
    B. Recordkeeping and manager/owner relations
    C. Maintenance
    D. Risk management
    E. Environmental issues
VII. Landlord/Tenant Law
    A. Lease provisions
        1. Possession
        2. Payment of rent
        3. Lease term
        4. Use of premises
        5. Security deposit
        6. Entry and inspection
        7. Maintenance
    B. Rent control
VIII. Types of Leases

Chapter Overview

Many brokerage offices engage in property management to some degree, so all real estate agents should have a basic knowledge of property management principles. This chapter gives the reader an overview of the property management profession. The first section of the chapter discusses the basics of investing in real estate. The next section describes some of the differences between types of managed properties. After that, we'll discuss the management agreement, the management plan, and the various functions of a property manager. The final section of the chapter will look at the laws that govern landlord/tenant relationships.

Introduction to Property Management

Property management refers to a situation in which a person other than the owner supervises the operation of income property in exchange for a fee. Prior to the 1930s, real estate owners usually managed their own properties, although sometimes they hired assistants to collect rents. Then in the 1930s, during the Great Depression, countless borrowers defaulted on their mortgages and many properties ended up in the hands of lenders. These lenders were saddled with management responsibilities for extensive property holdings, but they had little property management experience. In response, some formed their own property management departments, and others came to depend on the real estate industry to provide the necessary expertise. Although the lenders eventually resold the properties they acquired during the Depression, the value of efficient property management had been discovered, and increasing numbers of property owners began to use the services of property managers.

In the years following World War II, property management became even more important as construction and business practices changed. Apartment and office buildings became larger as elevators and steel framing allowed the construction of multi-story structures. Shopping centers replaced the corner store and flourishing commercial activity led to the creation of industrial parks. It became increasingly difficult for property owners to manage all of their holdings, and professional, efficient, and effective outside management became a necessity rather than a luxury.

Today, property managers work in a number of different contexts. Although many work for property management companies, property managers may also be employed directly by owners as independent contractors. In addition to managing residential apartment buildings and commercial complexes, property managers are often hired to manage community associations for planned unit developments, investment syndicates, and condominium and homeowners associations.

Licensing and Professional Organizations

Generally, state law requires a property manager to be licensed either as a real estate agent or specifically as a property manager; the requirements vary from state to state.

Many property managers join management professional organizations. For example, a property manager may obtain the designation of Certified Property Manager (CPM) or Accredited Residential Manager (ARM) upon successful completion of courses in property management and residential management from the Institute of Real Estate Management (IREM), a division within the National Association of REALTORS®.

The Building Owners and Managers Institute International (BOMI) is an organization that provides educational programs for commercial property management. BOMI offers several designations related to property management, including Real Property Administrator (RPA), Systems Maintenance Administrator (SMA), and Facilities Management Administrator (FMA).

Investing in Real Estate

A property manager's job begins after someone has decided to invest in income-producing property, such as an apartment building, office building, or shopping center. As you will learn, the primary function of a property manager is to help the property owner achieve his investment goals. So before discussing the nuts and bolts of property management, let's take a brief look at general investment principles and at real estate as an investment. (A word of caution: real estate agents should not act as investment counselors; they should always refer clients to an accountant, attorney, or investment specialist for investment advice.)

An investment is an asset that is expected to generate a **return** (a profit). A return on an investment can take various forms, including interest, dividends, or appreciation in value. An asset appreciates in value because of inflation, and may also appreciate because of a rising demand for the asset. For example, a parcel of prime vacant land often appreciates quickly as developable land becomes increasingly scarce.

Types of Investments

Investments can be divided into two general categories: ownership investments and debt investments. With **ownership investments**, the investor takes an ownership interest in the asset. Real estate and stocks are examples of ownership investments. The return on ownership investments usually takes the form of dividends, rent, and/or appreciation.

A **debt investment** is essentially a loan that an investor makes to an entity. For example, a bond is a debt owed to an investor by a government entity or corporation. The investor lends the entity money for a set period of time, and in return the entity promises to repay the money at a specific date (the maturity date) along with a certain amount of interest.

Investors often choose to diversify their investments—that is, they choose to invest in a variety of different types of investments. The mix of investments owned by an individual or company is referred to as a **portfolio**.

Note that for tax purposes, investment income (such as interest, dividends, or rent) is sometimes distinguished from earned income (salaries, wages, or self-employment income).

Investment Characteristics

An investor considers any investment in terms of three potential advantages: liquidity, safety, **yield** (which is the total return on the investment, or **ROI**). These three characteristics are interrelated. For example, liquidity and safety generally go together. On the other hand, for a high return an investor often sacrifices safety or liquidity, or both.

Safety. An investment is considered safe if there's little risk that the investor will actually lose money on it. Even if the investment doesn't generate the return she hopes for, the investor will at least be able to recover the money she originally invested.

Some types of investments are very safe, because they carry a guarantee. The federal deposit insurance that protects funds (up to $250,000) in a bank account is a simple example; it's highly unlikely that a depositor will lose any of the money he puts in the bank. On the other hand, some types of investments are inherently risky. For instance, an investor who puts his money into an uncertain venture such as a brand new company is likely to lose his investment if the company isn't a success.

Liquidity. A **liquid asset** is one that can be converted into cash quickly. Money in a bank account is extremely liquid: to convert it into cash, the investor need only present the bank with a withdrawal slip or check. Mutual funds, stocks, and bonds are less liquid—they take a little longer (perhaps a few days) to convert into cash. Other items, such as jewelry or coin collections, are not considered liquid at all, because an investor might have to wait months to exchange those assets for cash. Real estate isn't a liquid asset.

As a general rule, the more liquid the asset, the lower the return. For example, the money in an ordinary savings account is very liquid, but it offers only a modest return, in the form of a low rate of interest. If you make a commitment to keep the funds deposited for a specified period (with a certificate of deposit), you'll get a slightly higher rate. The longer the period, the higher the rate.

Liquidity is an advantage because the investor can cash in the investment immediately if the funds are needed for an unexpected expense, or because a better investment opportunity has arisen. Money in a nonliquid investment is effectively "locked up" and unavailable for other purposes. Real estate and other nonliquid assets can be excellent investments, but their lack of liquidity has consequences that a prospective investor should take into account.

Yield. Investments that are both safe and liquid tend to offer the lowest returns. In a sense, investors "pay" for safety and liquidity with a low return. To get a high return, an investor usually must take the risk of losing some or even all of the money originally invested. The investor may also have to sacrifice liquidity, allowing the money to be tied up for a while.

Of course, except with the very safest investments, the yield isn't fixed at the time the investment is made. The yield can change with market conditions, such as an increase or decrease in market interest rates.

As a general rule, the greater the risk, the higher the potential yield needs to be. Otherwise investors won't be willing to make the investment. Investors also expect higher yields from long-term investments, as compensation for keeping their money tied up for longer periods of time.

With some types of investments, the return will be much greater if the investor can afford to keep the investment for a long period of time and take advantage of healthy market conditions. This is true of real estate.

Example: Jeanne and Harold each buy a piece of land for $20,000 in the same year. One year later, Jeanne desperately needs some cash. The market for land has taken a downturn, and Jeanne is forced to sell her property at a loss. She ends up with only $17,000 of her original $20,000 investment.

Harold, on the other hand, is in no hurry to sell the property, so he can wait for optimal market conditions. He keeps the land for twelve years and then sells it at the peak of a real estate cycle, when property values are high. Because Harold could afford to choose when he sold the property, he walks away from the transaction with $60,000, an excellent return on his original $20,000 investment.

Advantages of Investing in Real Estate

People invest in real estate for many reasons. The advantages of investing in real estate can be broken down into three general categories:

- appreciation,
- leverage, and
- cash flow.

Appreciation. Appreciation refers to an increase in a property's value due to changes in the economy or other outside factors. Although real estate values may fluctuate, over a period of several years real estate usually increases in value at a rate equal to or higher than the rate of inflation. Thus, real estate is considered an effective hedge against inflation. And when buildable property becomes scarce, the value of properties in prime locations increases even more rapidly.

Appreciation causes a property owner's equity to increase. **Equity** is the difference between the value of the property and the liens against it, so an increase in the property's value increases the owner's equity in the property. Also, each monthly mortgage payment increases the owner's equity, in proportion to the reduction of the principal amount of the loan. Equity adds to the investor's net worth and can also be used to secure a home equity loan. So even

Fig. 17.1 Investing in real estate

Advantages of Real Estate Investment

- Appreciation
- Leverage
- Cash flow

though real estate is not considered a liquid asset, equity in real estate can be used to generate cash funds.

Leverage. Leverage is the use of borrowed money to invest in an asset. If the asset appreciates, then the investor earns money on the funds borrowed as well as the money she invested.

Example: Martin purchases a rental home for $215,000. He makes a $43,000 downpayment and borrows the rest of the purchase price. The rent generated by the property covers all the expenses of operating the property, plus the mortgage payment and income taxes. The property appreciates at 3% per year for five years. At the end of the five years, Martin sells the property for $249,000. He's made a $34,000 profit over five years on his $43,000 investment. This represents a 79% return over the five-year period. The property appreciated at 3% per year, but because he invested only 20% of the purchase price, Martin was able to generate a 79% return on his investment.

Cash Flow. Many real estate investments generate a positive cash flow, as well as appreciate in value. Cash flow is defined as spendable income—the amount of money left after all the property's expenses have been paid, including operating costs, mortgage payments, and taxes. When a real estate investment generates a positive cash flow, the investor's monthly income increases. Thus, a real estate investment can increase both the investor's net worth (through appreciation) and his income (through positive cash flow).

Another way in which a property can generate cash flow is through a **sale-leaseback** arrangement. In a sale-leaseback, the owner of a building (typically a commercial property) sells the building to an investor, but then leases the property back from the investor and continues to use it. The money generated by the sale can be used for expansion, acquiring inventory, or investment elsewhere. At the same time, the seller can deduct the rent paid to lease the property from her income taxes as a business expense. Sometimes a sale-leaseback arrangement also includes a **buy-back** agreement, in which it's agreed that the seller will buy the property back for its fair market value after a certain number of years.

Investors sometimes use the term "cash on cash," which refers to a property's first year cash flow divided by the initial investment. It pinpoints the ratio between cash invested (equity) and cash received.

Disadvantages of Investing in Real Estate

Of course, real estate investments can be a mixed blessing. There are some disadvantages to real estate investments that must be considered carefully.

First, real estate investment often requires expert advice. Investing in real estate is typically far more complicated than putting money in a savings account or a mutual fund. It is also more time-consuming. Not only does the initial purchase take time and effort, but the property must be managed after it is purchased. Rental rates must be set, tenants found, rents collected, and maintenance and repairs completed. Even if the investor decides to hire a property manager to manage the property, there are many decisions that must be made by the investor.

As we discussed earlier, real estate investments are not liquid. Time is required to convert real estate into cash. Furthermore, there are substantial risks involved in investing in real estate. There is no guarantee that the investor won't lose some or all of the downpayment. For instance, there is always the chance that the property's value may decline because of a local economic trend.

> **Example:** On a national scale, property values are keeping pace with inflation. However, Lumbertown relies solely on the timber industry and the local lumber mill for employment. When the local mill shuts down, the town is economically crippled. Even though real estate is usually a good investment, property values in Lumbertown decline rapidly.

Also, the income generated by a property may not be enough to cover the expenses of operating the property. A negative cash flow may force the investor to sell the property quickly, for less than she paid for it.

Types of Managed Properties

Now let's consider the different types of properties that a property manager may be called upon to manage. There are four basic types of income-producing properties:

1. residential rental property,
2. office buildings,
3. retail property, and
4. industrial property.

Each type of property has its own unique characteristics and management needs. Because each type of property demands a different kind of expertise, property managers often specialize in one particular type of property. The following are a few examples of the differences between property types.

Apartment buildings, which typically offer six-month or one-year leases, have a much higher turnover rate than industrial property, where leases often run for ten years or more. As a result, residential property managers tend to spend more of their time marketing and leasing out space. Residential property managers also must fulfill the legal responsibilities imposed by the landlord-tenant laws, which are designed to protect the health and well-being of residential tenants.

Fig. 17.2 Income-producing properties

Types of Income Properties

Residential
(rental homes, apartments, condos)

Office
(office buildings and office parks)

Retail
(stores and shopping centers)

Industrial
(industrial parks)

Property managers are also often hired by community or homeowners associations to manage the common property and services of condominiums, cooperatives, and planned communities. The property manager is responsible for collecting association dues, as well as ensuring compliance with association rules and covenants.

Office buildings have very different housekeeping requirements than residential buildings: they endure much heavier foot traffic; they have facilities (such as washrooms and elevators) that get continuous use and thus need frequent cleaning; and management is often responsible for cleaning the tenants' spaces as well as the common areas. Lease negotiations are also very different for office buildings than for residential space: rent is based on a price per square foot (rather than per unit); the leases are for longer periods of time and usually include some type of escalation clause (to provide for automatic increases in rent); and landlords commonly offer major concessions to attract tenants, such as free rent for a limited period or extensive remodeling.

Leasing space to an appropriate tenant is a concern with any type of property, but it is especially important when managing a shopping center. The success of each tenant in a shopping center depends in part on the customers that each of the other tenants attract, so it is vital to lease to strong tenants. Also, a portion of the rent is often based on the tenant's income, so the owner has a vested interest in the financial success of each tenant. The tenant mix must appeal to the widest variety of potential shoppers, while avoiding direct competition within the shopping center itself.

These are only a few of the ways in which property types differ. Even from such a small sampling, however, it is easy to see that different management plans are required for each type of property. The benefits of specializing in one or two property types are evident.

Our discussion will focus mainly on managing residential properties, but most of the principles and practices we'll be describing apply to the management of any type of property.

The Management Agreement

The first step in the management process is entering into a management agreement. The management agreement establishes the working relationship between the property manager and the property owner. In the same way that a listing agreement creates an agency relationship between a broker and a seller, the management agreement creates an agency relationship between the manager and the owner.

The management agreement must be in writing and signed by both parties. It is very important that the written document contain all the terms and conditions of the agreement. It is especially important that the exact duties and powers of the manager be explicitly stated. What kinds of decisions can the manager freely make, and what kinds must be referred to the owner? For example, suppose several units in an apartment building needed new carpets. Could the manager replace the carpets without consulting the owner, or is this a decision that the owner wants to make? Other areas in which questions might arise include the authority to execute leases, make major repairs, choose an insurance company and policy for the property, or embark on a major advertising campaign.

At a minimum, the following points should be included in the management agreement:

- the term of the agreement;
- the manager's compensation (a percentage of gross income, a commission on new rentals, a fixed fee, or a combination of all of these);
- the type of property;
- the legal description of the property;
- the number of units or square footage;
- whether the manager is authorized to collect and disburse funds, and if so, for what purposes;
- whether the manager is authorized to hold and disburse tenant security deposits; and
- provisions concerning the manager's reports to the owner, specifying the frequency and level of detail of the reports.

In most cases, these additional provisions should also be included in the management agreement:

- a description of other management responsibilities (duties should be stated, exceptions noted);
- a statement of the owner's goals (for example, to maximize income, or to increase the capital value of the property);
- the extent of the manager's authority (for example, fixing rental rates, hiring and firing, authorizing repairs); and
- allocation of costs (which expenses the manager will pay and which expenses the owner will pay—such as office help, advertising, or telephone expenses).

The property manager must bear in mind that after the management agreement is signed, an agency relationship exists between the manager and the owner, and thus the manager is bound by all the duties and responsibilities of an agent (see Chapter 9).

The Management Plan

Once a manager has entered into a management agreement, the actual business of managing begins. The first (and often most important) step in managing a property is drawing up a management plan. A management plan outlines the manager's strategy for financial management and physical upkeep, and focuses on achieving the owner's goals.

The management plan should implement the owner's goals in the most effective manner possible. It is important to remember that there are many different reasons for investing in income property—different property owners have different management goals. For instance, one property owner may simply want a steady, reliable stream of income. Another owner may want a tax shelter. Another may want to increase the property's value in order to reap a bigger profit in later years. An owner's goals can also change over the period of ownership.

Example: When he's in his early forties, Greg decides to purchase a small apartment building. He has other sources of income, so he is most interested in the long-term investment and tax shelter aspects of real estate ownership. However, as the years pass, Greg's needs change. When he retires, he is suddenly more interested in receiving a steady cash flow from his property.

Preliminary Study

A management plan can be created only after a comprehensive study of all of the facets of the property, including its location, its physical characteristics, its financial status, and its policies of operation. This preliminary study includes a regional analysis, a neighborhood analysis, a property analysis, and a market analysis.

Regional Analysis. Preparing a management plan begins with a study of the region (city or metropolitan area) in which the property is located. The manager analyzes the general economic conditions, physical attributes, and population growth and distribution. Among the most significant considerations are trends in occupancy rates, market rental rates, employment levels, and (for residential property) family size and lifestyle.

Occupancy Rates. According to the law of supply and demand, when the demand for an item is greater than the supply, the price or value of the item increases. And when the supply exceeds the demand, the price or value of the item decreases. This basic rule applies to rental properties just as it applies to other commodities.

From a property manager's point of view, the supply of rental units is the total number of units available for occupancy in the area where the managed property is located. The demand for rental units is the total number of potential tenants in that area who are able to pay the rent for those units. When demand exceeds supply, rental rates go up; when supply exceeds demand, rental rates go down.

There is a **technical oversupply** of property when there are more units than potential tenants. There is an **economic oversupply** when there are enough potential tenants, but they are unable to pay the current rent. Likewise, there may be a **technical shortage** (when there are more potential tenants than units) or an **economic shortage** (when there are more able-to-pay tenants than units).

To set rental rates for a managed property, a property manager must determine the occupancy trend for the area. If the trend is toward higher occupancy levels, the value of the units will increase because space is becoming more scarce. It is during these times that managers raise rents and reduce services. On the other hand, if there is a trend toward higher vacancy rates, a unit's value will decrease. In periods of high vacancy, tenants are likely to resist rent increases or make more demands for services or repairs when leases are renewed.

Occupancy levels are constantly fluctuating. The direction and speed in which they are moving will have a significant impact on the property manager's operating and marketing policies.

Market Rental Rates. In addition to evaluating occupancy trends, a property manager should keep track of market rental rates (the rates currently being charged for comparable rental units). The market rental rate for a unit is also called **economic rent**. **Contract rent** is the amount a tenant must pay the owner under the terms of a current lease. The manager should set rental rates for the managed units at a level that will enable them to compete in the current market.

There are published reports that provide information about rental rates, such as the Bureau of Labor's statistics on rents paid for residential units. A property manager may also evaluate the properties that he is managing to determine the average monthly rent per unit or square foot. Statistics kept by an individual property manager can be combined with statistics kept by other managers in the area to get a broader perspective. Rental rates stated in classified ads can also be considered. These methods, while not precise, can give a manager a basic picture of market trends.

Employment Levels. The property manager should be aware of local employment trends, since employment levels affect how many potential tenants can afford to rent. A property manager should also know whether earnings are increasing or decreasing, and about savings rates in the community. Clearly, if potential tenants cannot afford a particular rental unit or would rather save than spend, the property manager's product is not going to be sold.

Family Size and Lifestyle. Family size has a great deal to do with the value of particular residential units. If the average family size were three (two parents and one child), five-bedroom units would have little appeal and two-bedroom units would be very attractive. Thus, the two-bedroom units would command a higher price per square foot than the five-bedroom units. A property manager needs to be aware of the national trend toward smaller and even single-person households, and also any local trends in family size and lifestyle.

Neighborhood Analysis. After the regional analysis, the next step in the preliminary study is to analyze the specific neighborhood where the property is located. The definition of a neighborhood varies considerably from one place to another. In rural areas, a neighborhood may consist of many square miles. In an urban area, a neighborhood may be only a few blocks.

The qualities of the neighborhood have a significant bearing on the property's value and use. Important neighborhood characteristics include:

- the level of maintenance (Are the buildings and grounds well cared for, or in poor condition?);
- a growth or decline in population; and
- the economic status of the residents.

A property manager should discover the reasons behind any neighborhood trends. Is the population density increasing because of further development or because single-family homes are changing into rooming houses? Development is a sign of economic prosperity; rooming house tenancies are not.

A neighborhood analysis helps a property manager factor location into the management plan. No matter how effectively a property is operated, its profitability will be strongly affected by its location. Once the characteristics of the location have been determined, realistic management goals can be set.

Property Analysis. Of course, to develop a management plan the manager must become very familiar with the physical characteristics of the property itself. She will inspect the property, noting its architectural design, physical condition, facilities, and general layout.

The following characteristics are particularly important:

- the number and size of the living units, or the number of rentable square feet;
- the appearance of the property and the rental spaces (age, architectural style, layout, view, fixtures, etc.);
- the physical condition of the building (roof, elevators, windows, etc.);
- the physical condition of the rental spaces (floor coverings, stairways, shades or blinds, walls, entryways);
- the amenities provided (laundry room, recreational facilities, etc.);
- the services provided (janitorial services, repair services, or security);
- the relationship of the land to the building (Is the land used efficiently? Is there adequate parking?);
- the current occupancy rate and tenant composition; and
- the size and efficiency of the current staff.

Market Analysis. The last step in the preliminary study for a management plan is the market analysis, which provides information on competing properties. To do a market analysis, the manager must first define the pertinent market. The major divisions of the real estate market are residential, commercial, retail, and industrial. Each of these can be broken down into subcategories. For instance, the residential market can be divided into single-family rental homes, duplexes, townhouses, walk-up apartments, small multi-story apartments, and large apartment complexes.

Once the manager has identified the market that the managed property competes in, there are several characteristics that must be examined:

- the number of units available in the area;
- the average age and character of the buildings in which the units are located;
- the quality of the average unit in the market (size, condition, layout, facilities, etc.);
- the number of potential tenants in the area;
- the current price for the average unit; and
- the occupancy rate for the average unit.

The property manager compares the managed property to comparable properties in the neighborhood. In this way, the manager can evaluate what the property has to offer and what its disadvantages are. Armed with this information, the manager can establish an effective management strategy.

Fig. 17.3 Operating budget form

Operating Budget

	Jan	Feb	Mar	Apr	May	June	July	Aug	Sept	Oct	Nov	Dec	Annual
Income													
Scheduled Rents													
Less:													
Vacancies													
Rent Loss													
Effective Rent													
Miscellaneous Income													
Total Income													
Expenses													
Administrative													
Management Costs													
Other Adm. Costs													
Operating													
Payroll													
Supplies													
Heating													
Electricity													
Water and Sewer													
Gas													
Maintenance													
Grounds													
Maint. and Repairs													
Painting, Decorating													
Taxes and Insurance													
Real Estate Taxes													
Other Taxes, Fees													
Insurance													
Contract Service													
Total Expenses													
Net Operating Income													
Less Reserves													
Net Income													
Less Debt Service													
Cash Flow													

The Management Proposal

After completing the preliminary study, the property manager develops a management proposal and submits it to the property owner for approval. The manager's proposal will include a rental schedule, income and expense projections, a schedule of day-to-day operations, and perhaps suggestions for physical changes to the property itself.

Rental Schedule. A rental schedule is a list of all the rental rates assigned to the different types of units. For example, an apartment building may consist of studio apartments, one-bedroom apartments, and two-bedroom apartments. Some apartments may have views, others may not. A rental schedule lists the various types of units and their rental rates.

Rental schedules are based on all the data collected during the regional, neighborhood, property, and market analyses. This information helps the manager determine the optimum rent that can be charged while maintaining the optimum occupancy level. To set the rate for a particular type of unit, the manager can adjust the market rental rate for the average comparable unit up or down to reflect the differences between the comparable and the type of unit in question. Because this method of setting rates depends on market conditions, the rental schedule should be reexamined periodically to see if it is current. Either an unusually high vacancy rate or an unusually low vacancy rate is an indication that the property's rental rates are out of line with the community. If the vacancy rate is too high, the rent may be too expensive; if the vacancy rate is unusually low, the rent may be below the norm.

Budgets. The property manager also sets up a budget of income and operating expenses (see Figure 17.3). The manager lists the total value of all rentable space at the scheduled rental rates, then subtracts a figure for delinquent rental payments and vacancies (sometimes called a bad debt and vacancy factor). Any other income sources, such as laundry facilities, vending machines, or parking, should also be listed.

Next, the estimated operating expenses—both fixed expenses and variable expenses—are listed. **Fixed expenses** include such items as property taxes, insurance premiums, and employee salaries. **Variable expenses** include utilities, maintenance, and repairs. Finally, the manager deducts projected operating expenses from projected revenues to arrive at a cash flow figure.

Day-to-Day Operations. In addition to long-range financial planning, the management proposal should include the manager's plans for the day-to-day operations of the property. This means that the manager has to decide how much (if any) staffing will be required and what the employment policies and procedures will be.

Physical Alterations. In some cases, the property manager's proposal will include recommendations for remodeling, rehabilitation, or other physical alterations to the property. For instance, after a thorough examination of the property, the customer base, and the market, a manager might decide that the property would be worth much more to the owner if the building were altered to match current family size and lifestyle trends.

Example: An older building is made up of four- and five-bedroom units in a neighborhood predominantly made up of one- and two-person households. If the apartments were converted to smaller units, the owner's profits would probably increase significantly.

Owner's Approval. Once completed, the management proposal is presented to the property owner. When the proposal is approved, it becomes the management plan: the blueprint for managing the property.

Management Functions

Property managers must possess the skills necessary to perform a variety of management functions. They must be able to market the property, negotiate leases, and handle tenant relations. They must be able to keep and understand detailed financial records and report to the property owner on a regular basis. They must also be able to arrange for the maintenance and repairs that will preserve the value of the property.

Leasing and Tenant Relations

The property manager's tasks involved in leasing and tenant relations include marketing the rental spaces, negotiating leases, addressing tenants' complaints, and collecting rents.

Marketing. The more people who view a rental space, the more likely it is to be rented out. So property managers generally use advertising to bring potential tenants to their properties.

Different types of properties require different types and amounts of advertising. For some properties, advertising is necessary only when there is a vacancy to fill. If the property is in a prominent location and attractive to potential tenants, advertising may not be necessary at all. On the other hand, if the property is in an isolated location, continuous advertising may be required to generate enough interest to fill vacancies when they occur.

Successful advertising brings in a good number of potential tenants in the least amount of time for the lowest cost. Property managers often evaluate the effectiveness of their advertising in terms of the number of potential tenants for the advertising dollars spent. For example, based on experience, a property manager might have a general rule of thumb that the cost of advertising should not exceed $25 to $35 per prospect. Thus, newspaper advertising that costs $300 should bring in 9 to 12 prospective tenants to the property.

To reach the greatest number of potential tenants for the lowest possible cost, the property manager must be familiar with the various types of advertising and know which will be most effective for the property in question. The manager may consider using signs, newspaper ads, Internet advertising and websites, radio or television spots, direct mail, or some combination of these tools.

Signs. Small, tasteful signs are often used, whether there is a vacancy or not, to inform passersby of the name of the manager and how to acquire rental information. The use of signs is most successful for office buildings, large apartment complexes, and shopping centers.

Newspaper Advertising. Newspaper advertising includes classified ads and display ads. Classified ads (inexpensive line-type advertising that appears in the "classified" section of the newspaper) are a popular way to advertise residential rental space. Display ads are larger and more expensive than classified ads. A display ad often includes a photograph of the property, and it may appear in any section of the newspaper. Display advertising is generally an effective way to advertise space in a new office building, industrial park, or shopping center.

Fig.17.4 Types of advertising and their uses

Types of Advertising

Type	Most Effective Use
Signs	Tell prospects how to get rental information
Classified ads	Fill residential vacancies
Display ads	Fill vacancies in larger properties
Internet	Fill vacancies in all types of properties
Radio and TV	Not cost-effective for most properties
Direct mail	Effective if mailing list is good

Internet Advertising. Classified ads can also be placed on the Internet, through online advertising websites. Internet classifieds have a number of advantages over newspaper classifieds; for example, they can include photographs of the property, and many websites allow listings to be posted free of charge.

Depending on the scope of her business, a property manager may want to maintain her own website to advertise all of the properties she's managing. In some cases, a website dedicated to a particular apartment complex, office building, or other property may be worthwhile.

Radio and Television. Property managers occasionally use radio and television ads for large commercial and residential properties. Although broadcast advertising reaches a large audience, there usually aren't many potential tenants in the audience. Since broadcast advertising (especially television advertising) is quite expensive, it generally isn't cost-effective for most rental properties.

Direct Mail. To be effective, direct mail advertising must be received by potential tenants, not just the general public. So a property manager who wants to use direct mail must compile or purchase a mailing list. With a good mailing list and a brochure designed to appeal to prospective tenants, direct mail can be an effective means of advertising. Also, the same brochure can be handed out to those who visit the property.

Leasing. A prospect has seen an advertisement and comes to look at the available rental space. Now it is the property manager's job to convince the prospect that the rental space is desirable. They will usually tour the property together, and during the tour the manager will emphasize all of the property's positive qualities and all of its amenities. The manager will point out traffic patterns and access to public transportation, the characteristics of the other tenants, the exterior and interior condition of the property, and its overall cleanliness. If it's commercial property, the manager and the prospect may discuss how the space could be altered to suit the prospect's needs.

After the tour, if the prospect is still interested in the property, it is the property manager's responsibility to make sure that the prospect is qualified to lease it. Although financial stability is a key consideration, it's not the only one. The manager must also decide whether the prospect is likely to be a responsible and cooperative tenant. At a minimum, this will involve checking the prospect's references and contacting the previous landlord. The manager can also use his own judgment, but must be very careful to avoid violating antidiscrimination laws (see Chapter 16).

If the manager decides in favor of the prospect, the next step is to execute a rental agreement or lease. The requirements for a valid lease are explained later in this chapter, in the discussion of landlord/tenant law.

Lease Renewal. Unless the tenant has caused problems, a property manager would much rather renew an existing lease than find a new tenant. Renewal avoids a vacancy between the time one tenant moves out and another moves in. A building has greater stability with long-term tenants, and it is usually easier and less expensive to satisfy the requirements of an existing tenant than improve the space for a new tenant.

A property manager should always be aware of which tenants are nearing the end of their lease terms and notify them that their leases are about to expire. Then the manager should follow up on the notices, by phone or in person, to inquire whether the tenant wants to renew. If the tenant is going to renew the lease, the terms of the new lease must be negotiated.

Some leases contain an **automatic renewal clause**, which provides that the lease will be automatically renewed on the same terms unless one party notifies the other of her intent to terminate the lease.

Tenant Complaints. Of course, keeping tenants happy is an important part of the property manager's job. Making sure that the property is kept clean and in good repair is essential, and so is responding promptly and professionally to requests and complaints. A property manager's ability to keep tenants happy is directly related to the management-unit ratio, which is the number of units per on-site manager. Generally, one on-site manager can handle 50 to 60 units.

Rent Collection. Rental property cannot be profitable unless the rents are collected when due. Careful selection of tenants in the first place is one of the most effective ways of avoiding delinquent rents. A high occupancy rate doesn't benefit the property owner unless the tenants are likely to meet their financial obligations.

The amount of the rent, the time and place of rent payment, and any penalties imposed for late payment should be clearly stated in the lease. The manager should consistently follow a collection plan that includes adequate recordkeeping and immediate notification of late payments. When all collection attempts fail, the manager must be prepared to take legal action to evict the tenant in accordance with the owner's policies.

Fig. 17.5 Rent roll

Rent Roll

Property *Magnolia Heights* **Period** *April*

Owner *S.T Jones* **Prepared by** *M. Smith*

Unit Number	Occupant	Previous Balance	Current Rent	Date Received	Other Amounts	Description	Total Received	Balance Due
101	G. Tsui	0	900	4/1			900	0
102	F. Brown	700	700	4/9			1400	0
103	K. Plane	0	700	4/2	100	Parking	800	0
104	C. Flynn	0	850	4/1			850	0
105	P. Sneed	850	850	4/15			850	850
106	L. Hurt	0	850	4/1	100	Parking	950	0
107	E. Winn	0	700	4/2			700	0

Recordkeeping and Manager/Owner Relations

A property manager must account to the owner for all money received and disbursed. It is up to the owner to decide how frequent and detailed operating reports should be. This often depends on how involved the owner wants to be in the management of the property. For example, an owner with extensive property holdings who is also engaged in another full-time occupation may not want to be bothered with detailed, time-consuming reports. But a retired person with only one or two income-producing properties may want to be very involved in their management.

Statement of Operations. In many cases, the property manager's report to the owner takes the form of a monthly statement of operations. A statement of operations typically includes the following sections: a summary of operations, the rent roll, a statement of disbursements, and a narrative report of operations.

The **summary of operations** is a brief description of the property's income and expenses that makes it easier for the owner to evaluate the property's monthly financial performance. The summary is supported by the accompanying information in the rest of the statement of operations.

The **rent roll** is a report on rent collection. Both occupied and vacant units are listed in the rent roll, as well as the total of rental income earned, both collected and uncollected. (The combined rental values of the leased and the vacant space should equal the total rental value of the building.) The rent roll breaks down rental figures into the previous balance, current rent, total amount received, and balance due.

The information in the rent roll is obtained from the individual ledger sheets kept on each tenant and rental space. A ledger sheet typically shows the tenant's name, unit, phone number, regular rent, other recurring charges, security deposit information, move-in date, lease term, payments made, and balances owed.

The **statement of disbursements** lists all of the expenses paid during the pertinent time period. A written order should be prepared for every purchase and payment so that an accurate account can be made of all expenditures and the purpose of each one. Disbursements are usually classified according to type, which makes analysis easier. For example, all maintenance expenses should be listed together, and so should all tax and insurance expenses, all administrative expenses, and so on.

In addition to the numerical accounts given to the owner, it is often helpful to include a **narrative report of operations** in the statement of operations. This is simply a letter explaining the information set forth in the other sections of the statement. The narrative report adds a personal touch, and it is especially important if the income was lower or the expenses were higher than expected. If there is a deviation from the normal cash flow, the owner will want a clear explanation. If the reason for a drop in cash flow is not explained, the owner may doubt the competence or integrity of the property manager.

Keeping in Touch. In addition to sending various reports and statements to the owner, the manager should contact the owner in person from time to time. A telephone call or an appointment to explain a particular proposal or problem or to ask a question is much more effective than a letter. A formal meeting is a good idea if the monthly report is especially unusual.

Maintenance

In addition to leasing, tenant relations, recordkeeping, and reporting to the owner, a property manager is responsible for the supervision of property maintenance. There are four basic categories of maintenance activities:

1. **Preventive maintenance:** This preserves the physical integrity of the premises and reduces corrective maintenance costs. (Cleaning the gutters is an example of preventive maintenance.)
2. **Corrective maintenance:** Actual repairs that keep equipment, utilities, and amenities functioning in a proper manner. (Fixing a leaking faucet is an example of corrective maintenance.)
3. **Housekeeping:** Cleaning the common areas and grounds on a regular basis (for example, vacuuming hallways and cleaning elevators).
4. **New construction:** This includes tenant alterations made at the beginning of the tenancy and when the lease is renewed, as well as cosmetic changes designed to make the building more attractive (for example, remodeling the lobby).

When managing commercial or industrial property, a property manager is often required to alter the interior of the building to meet the needs of a new tenant. These alterations can range from a simple repainting job to completely redesigning or rebuilding the space. (If the property is new construction, the interior is often left incomplete so that it can be built to fit the needs of the individual tenants.) Property managers dealing with remodeling or new construction must be aware of federal laws requiring public accommodations to be accessible to the disabled. (See the discussion of the Americans with Disabilities Act in Chapter 16.)

Fig. 17.6 Property maintenance record

Property Maintenance Record

Property *Magnolia Heights*

Date	Action	Location	by Whom	Time	Cost
4/12	inspect elevator	lobby	Elevator Express	1.5 hr.	contract
4/22	clean roof	roof	Johnson	5 hr.	contract
4/23	fix drain	Unit 104	Top Plumbing	1 hr.	55.00

Property managers are not required to know how to fix the building's plumbing or electrical wiring themselves. Most maintenance activities are handled by building maintenance employees or by outside maintenance services. However, a property manager must be able to recognize the maintenance needs of the property and see that they are fulfilled.

The property manager should direct the activities of the maintenance staff or independent contractors with a schedule of inspection and maintenance. First, the manager should inventory the building's equipment and physical elements (plumbing, furnace, roof, walls, etc.). Then a schedule of regular inspections, cleaning, and repairs should be set. For instance, walls and roofs should be scheduled for periodic inspection, painting, and repairs. Elevators should be serviced on a regular basis.

The property manager should keep accurate and up-to-date records of when the various elements were inspected, serviced, replaced, or repaired. These routine inspections and maintenance activities will help preserve the capital value of the building and prevent major repair expenses.

Risk Management

One of a property manager's most important responsibilities is risk management. If proper precautionary measures are not taken, an unexpected event can cause tremendous financial losses due to property damage, lost rents, or even lawsuits. A property manager must evaluate the various options available for preventing or mitigating these risks.

A common way to protect against financial loss is to purchase insurance. Many property managers take out public liability insurance to cover the risks assumed when members of the public enter the property. Casualty, fire, and hazard insurance are also commonly used to protect against unforeseen events such as theft, fire, or flooding. (We discuss property insurance in more detail in Chapter 18.)

It's important to note that the physical safety of tenants has become an increasingly important issue for owners and property managers. If a tenant is injured by an intruder or fellow tenant, courts are now more likely to hold the owner and manager responsible. As a result, it is common nowadays for leases to include provisions making criminal activity a ground for eviction.

Environmental Issues

Property managers are often called upon to respond to environmental problems such as hazardous waste or air quality. Federal, state, and local laws determine the environmental responsibilities of property managers. Arranging for proper disposal of tenant waste is only one of many things a property manager may be required to provide. Although not always required, providing recycling facilities can make a property more appealing to prospective tenants.

Landlord/Tenant Law

A property manager needs to understand the rules that govern the relationship between landlord and tenant. The landlord-tenant relationship is defined both by law and by the terms of the lease contract itself.

As we discussed in Chapter 8, a lease is a contract between a property owner and a tenant, and must meet all of the requirements for a valid contract. In many cases, the management agreement authorizes the property manager to sign leases as the landlord's agent. Without such a specific authorization, the property manager's signature will not create a valid lease.

It is not generally necessary for a lease to be recorded, although some states may permit a landlord to record a lease in the county where the property is located. Some states require a lease with a term of three years or more to be recorded.

Lease Provisions

Many of the following issues are commonly addressed by the provisions of a lease. In some circumstances, the legal rules established by state statute may apply only when the lease doesn't address a particular issue; other legal provisions may override any contradictory clauses in the lease. These legal rules vary from state to state.

Possession. A tenant is entitled to quiet enjoyment of the leased property. The landlord promises (actually or implicitly) that the tenant's possession of the property will not be disturbed, either by the landlord or by a third party with a lawful claim to the property. The tenant is guaranteed exclusive possession and quiet enjoyment of his leasehold estate. The landlord is required, in most states, to take all necessary measures to remove a holdover tenant or adverse claimant. Some states require the tenant to file a lawsuit to obtain actual possession of the property.

Payment of Rent. The consideration that the tenant gives the landlord for the lease is the promise to pay rent. Most leases spell out when the rent is to be paid, and they usually require payment at the beginning of the rental period. If a lease does not specify when the rent is to be paid, however, it is not due until the end of the rental period.

Lease Term. A lease should also contain a statement of the lease term, including the beginning and ending dates. A lease for an indefinite period of time may be held invalid by a court. In some states, a lease term of 100 years or more is prohibited. If an option for renewal is given to the tenant, additional language should be included in the lease specifying when and how the option may be exercised.

Use of Premises. Not surprisingly, the law restricts a tenant's use of the leased property to legal uses. Many leases place additional restrictions on the use of the property; for example, a commercial lease might have a provision restricting the rented space to retail use. The restricting language must be clear. At a minimum, the lease should state that the premises are to be used only for the specified purpose and for no other. If there is no limitation in the lease, or if the language is not clearly restrictive, the tenant is generally permitted to use the premises for any legal purpose.

Security Deposit. Most property managers require a **security deposit** from the tenant when the tenant signs the lease, especially in residential tenancies. The deposit gives the landlord some protection should the tenant damage the property or fail to pay the rent.

Many states place various restrictions on security deposits. For instance, the size of a residential damage deposit may be limited to the amount of one month's rent. Security deposits are often required to be placed in a trust account. Furthermore, some states do not allow the security deposit to be used for both property damage and nonpayment of rent.

Entry and Inspection. A lease typically provides for inspection of the leased premises by the landlord during the lease term, under specified conditions. As a general rule, a residential tenant may not unreasonably refuse the landlord's legitimate requests to enter the unit to inspect it, perform repairs, provide other agreed-upon services, or show the unit to prospective buyers or tenants. The landlord usually must provide the tenant notice before entering the unit.

Maintenance. In most states, all residential leases carry the landlord's implied guarantee that the premises meet all building and housing code regulations that affect health and safety. If the premises do not meet these criteria, then the tenant must notify the landlord of the defective condition and the landlord must correct it within a certain time period prescribed by statute.

A tenant must return the premises to the landlord in the same condition in which they were received, with allowances for normal wear and tear. The landlord is usually responsible for making necessary repairs to common areas, such as the stairs, hallways, or elevators.

Rent Control

Ordinances called rent controls set maximum limits on the amount of rent that a landlord may charge. New York and San Francisco are two cities that have some form of rent control ordinances. Rent controls are intended to make property available at reasonable rates when there is a housing shortage.

Many economists believe that rent controls are not effective in accomplishing their primary goal of providing affordable housing. They argue that rents become high because demand for housing exceeds supply. In order for rents to come down, demand and supply must be brought into balance, either by reducing demand or by increasing supply. Rent controls usually have little positive effect toward either of these aims. Artificially low rents may in fact increase demand. In addition, the resulting low yields to property owners may discourage the construction of new housing.

Types of Leases

Property managers must be familiar with the various types of leases. There are six major types: fixed leases, graduated leases, index leases, net leases, percentage leases, and ground leases.

Fixed Lease. Sometimes called a flat, straight, or gross lease, a **fixed lease** provides for a fixed rental amount. The tenant is obligated to pay a fixed sum of money and the landlord is obligated to pay all maintenance costs, taxes, and insurance. Also called a gross lease, this type of lease is most commonly found in residential apartment rentals.

Graduated Lease. A **graduated lease** is similar to a fixed lease, but it provides for periodic increases in the rent, usually set at specific future dates. These increases are made possible by the inclusion of an **escalation clause**. This type of lease is also called a step-up lease.

Index Lease. Landlords often use **index leases** for long-term tenancies. This type of lease is often based on the Consumer Price Index or some other measure of inflation. When there is an increase in the index, the rents increase.

Net Lease. A **net lease** requires the tenant to pay the landlord a fixed rent, plus some or all of the operating expenses. Commercial leases are often net leases. A **triple net lease** (or net-net-net lease) requires the tenant to pay all of the operating expenses in addition to rent. These expenses might include property taxes and the cost of insurance, utilities, and maintenance.

Percentage Lease. Many retail businesses have **percentage leases**, especially in shopping centers. The rent is based on a percentage of the gross or net income from the tenant's business. Typically, the lease provides for a minimum rent plus a percentage of the tenant's business income above the stated minimum.

Ground Lease. In a **ground lease**, the landowner leases vacant land to a tenant who wants to construct a building on that land. In this manner, ownership of the improvements is separated from ownership of the land itself. Ground leases are common in metropolitan areas; they are usually long-term, in order to make the construction of the building worth the tenant's while.

Chapter Summary

1. An investment is an asset that is expected to generate a return for the investor. Three basic characteristics of an investment are the liquidity, safety, and yield. The advantages of real estate investment include appreciation, leverage, and cash flow.
2. There are four main types of income-producing properties: residential, office, retail, and industrial. Property managers often specialize in one or two types.
3. A property manager must have a written management agreement with the property owner. The agreement should include all of the terms and conditions of the management arrangement, including compensation, the type of property, the manager's duties and authority, allocation of costs, and provisions for reporting to the owner.
4. Before preparing a management plan, the manager should conduct a regional analysis, a neighborhood analysis, a property analysis, and a market analysis. The information gathered during this preliminary study will help the manager set a rental schedule, prepare a budget, and plan the day-to-day operations.
5. The functions of a property manager include marketing the property, leasing it, handling tenant complaints, collecting rent, recordkeeping, preparing reports for the owner, and arranging for the maintenance of the property.
6. The landlord/tenant relationship is governed by the terms of the lease and by landlord/tenant law. A typical lease contains provisions regarding possession of the property, the payment of rent, the length of the lease term, and the permitted use of the premises. A property manager should also include terms covering the security deposit, entry and inspection of the property, and maintenance responsibilities of the tenant and landlord.
7. The various types of leases include the fixed lease, graduated payment lease, index lease, net lease, percentage lease, and ground lease.

Key Terms

Investment—An asset that is expected to generate a return (a profit).

Portfolio—The mix of investments owned by an individual or company.

Liquidity—An asset's ability to be converted into cash quickly.

Appreciation—An increase in the value of an asset; generally due either to inflation or to an increasing scarcity of or demand for the asset.

Equity—The difference between a property's value and the liens against it.

Leverage—Using borrowed money to invest in an asset. If the asset appreciates, the investor earns money on the money borrowed as well as the money invested.

Cash flow—Spendable income; the amount of money left after all of the property's expenses (operating costs, mortgage payments, and taxes) have been paid.

Property management—When someone other than the property owner supervises the property's operation.

Rental schedule—A list of the rental rates for units in a given building.

Fixed expense—A property management expense that does not vary (for example, property taxes).

Variable expense—A property management expense that varies depending on current management needs (for example, repair expenses).

Lease—A contract for possession of real estate in return for payment of rent.

Automatic renewal clause—A lease provision that ensures automatic renewal of the lease unless the tenant or the landlord gives the other party notice of termination.

Statement of operations—A periodic report showing the total money received and disbursed, and the overall condition of the property during a given period.

Rent roll—A report on rent collections; a list of the total amount of rent earned, both collected and uncollected.

Statement of disbursements—A listing of all of a property's expenses paid during a specific operating period.

Preventive maintenance—A program of regular inspection and care to prevent problems or provide for their immediate repair.

Corrective maintenance—Ongoing repairs that are made to a building and its equipment to restore it to good operating condition.

Rent control—Ordinances setting maximum limits on the amount of rent that may be charged.

Fixed lease—A lease in which the tenant is obligated to pay a fixed sum of money as rent and the landlord is responsible for all other expenses, such as utilities, maintenance costs, and insurance.

Graduated lease—A lease in which the rent is a fixed amount that is increased periodically on set dates.

Index lease—A lease in which the rent is tied to an index such as the Consumer Price Index; rent increases whenever an increase in the index occurs.

Percentage lease—A lease in which the rent is based on a percentage of the gross or net income from the tenant's business.

Net lease—A lease in which the tenant pays a fixed rent amount in addition to some or all of the operating expenses.

Ground lease—A long-term lease of vacant land on which a tenant constructs and owns improvements.

Chapter Quiz

1. The main disadvantage of investing in real estate is:
   a) the use of leverage to increase returns
   b) lack of liquidity
   c) uniformly low returns
   d) a constantly increasing supply, which decreases values

2. The difference between the value of real property and the liens against it is called:
   a) equity
   b) leverage
   c) portfolio
   d) cash flow

3. When population decreases, which type of oversupply results?
   a) Technical
   b) Economic
   c) Operational
   d) Constructive

4. The property manager's main purpose must be to fulfill:
   a) her career goals
   b) the owner's objectives
   c) the government's affordable housing goals
   d) his office's cash flow goals

5. If a regional analysis shows that the typical family size is four, with two parents and two children, which of the following apartment units would be the most marketable?
   a) Studio
   b) Five-bedroom
   c) Three-bedroom
   d) It is unlikely that one type of unit would be preferred over any another

6. The type of property that ordinarily demands the most marketing is:
   a) residential
   b) office
   c) retail
   d) industrial

7. A property management agreement should always include the:
   a) manager's regional analysis
   b) manager's compensation
   c) owner's future plans for the property
   d) statement of operations

8. By completing a market analysis, a property manager discovers that the average rental rate for comparable residential units is $950. For the subject property, the property manager should set a rental rate of:
   a) $850 per unit, to undercut the competition
   b) $1,025 per unit, because tenants are not very well informed and will probably pay a higher-than-average price
   c) $950 per unit, to remain competitive
   d) None of the above; a fixed rental rate should not be set, so the property manager can maintain flexibility when renting units

9. The most expensive form of advertising is usually:
   a) television
   b) direct mail
   c) classified advertising
   d) handing out full-color brochures

10. Insurance premiums would be considered a:
    a) variable expense
    b) daily expense
    c) fixed expense
    d) pro rata expense

11. A brief description of the property's income and expenses is called a:
    a) statement of operations
    b) summary of operations
    c) statement of disbursements
    d) rent roll

12. If a property owner wants to know which tenants are behind in their rent, he should examine the:
    a) rent schedule
    b) statement of disbursements
    c) narrative report of operations
    d) rent roll

13. The most effective way to reduce expensive repair bills is to:
    a) emphasize preventive maintenance
    b) put off repairs for as long as possible
    c) institute a policy of tenant-paid repairs
    d) find cheap repair companies

14. Repairs that restore equipment to functioning in a proper manner are called:
    a) preventive maintenance
    b) corrective maintenance
    c) general housekeeping
    d) remodeling

15. A property manager wants to begin managing a new building. All of the following should be accomplished prior to actual management of the property, except:
    a) execution of a property management agreement
    b) preparation of a property management proposal
    c) preparation of a statement of operations
    d) completion of a market analysis

Answer Key

1. b) The lack of liquidity is the main disadvantage of investing in real estate.

2. a) The difference between the value of real estate and the liens against it is the owner's equity.

3. a) A technical oversupply occurs when there are not enough potential tenants for the supply of a certain type of property.

4. b) A property manager must try to achieve the property owner's objectives.

5. c) The typical family would be more likely to rent a three-bedroom unit than either a studio or a five-bedroom apartment.

6. a) Because residential lease terms are relatively short, managing residential property tends to involve more marketing than managing other types of property.

7. b) A property management agreement should always include a provision that describes the manager's compensation.

8. c) Rental rates should not be much lower or much higher than the rates for competitive properties.

9. a) Television is usually the most expensive form of advertising. Property managers do not use it as often as other forms of advertising.

10. c) Fixed expenses remain the same, regardless of rental income. Insurance premiums are fixed expenses.

11. b) A summary of operations is a brief summary of the detailed information in the other sections of the statement of operations.

12. d) A rent roll is a report on the collection of rent.

13. a) Preventive maintenance preserves the physical integrity of the property and reduces the need for corrective maintenance.

14. b) Repairs are classified as corrective maintenance.

15. c) A property manager cannot perform any management functions until he has a written management agreement. The market analysis and the management proposal should also be completed before the manager begins managing the property.

Chapter 18

Home Ownership and Construction

I. To Rent or to Buy?
   A. Advantages of renting
   B. Advantages of buying
   C. Comparison of renting and buying
II. Factors to Consider When Choosing a Home
   A. Types of housing
   B. Neighborhood considerations
   C. The home
III. Property Insurance
   A. What is covered
   B. Types of insurance
   C. Flood insurance
   D. Changes in policy
   E. Home warranty
IV. Construction
   A. Local codes and regulation
   B. Role of the architect
   C. Plans and specifications
   D. Wood frame construction
   E. Glossary of construction terms

Chapter Overview

In bringing a buyer and seller together, the real estate agent must be a "jack of all trades." Not only must she be familiar with property values, contracts, and financing, the agent must also be familiar with the advantages of buying a home, the elements to look for in a home, and the rudiments of residential construction. This chapter discusses the relative merits of renting or buying a home, and the factors to consider when choosing a home. The chapter goes on to briefly cover the basic elements of property insurance and the types of insurance available to homeowners. The final section of the chapter covers the various aspects of residential construction, focusing on wood frame construction.

To Rent or to Buy?

Purchasing a home can be a daunting process. A potential buyer may find it difficult to determine which housing option makes the most sense for his circumstances. Real estate agents are often asked to discuss the relative advantages and disadvantages of renting versus buying. The relative importance of emotional considerations, such as security, pride of ownership, and the freedom to have pets or to remodel according to personal preference, can only be measured by the prospective buyer. However, other elements of comparison are largely financial, and a real estate agent can help a prospective buyer evaluate these elements objectively.

Advantages of Renting

Renting a home can sometimes seem like the equivalent of throwing money away. However, the advantages of renting over buying can be briefly summarized as follows:

- renting requires less financial commitment and risk;
- renting gives the tenant greater mobility; and
- renting has fewer responsibilities.

Financial Commitment. Compared to the funds necessary to buy a home, the initial cash outlay to rent a home or an apartment is quite modest. In most cases, a security deposit and one or two months of prepaid rent is sufficient. Even in conjunction with low-downpayment financing, the cash required to purchase a home (the amount of the downpayment, loan fees, and closing costs) normally far exceeds the cost of moving into an apartment or a rental home.

Additionally, at least for the first few years, the monthly rental payment is likely to be substantially less than a monthly mortgage payment. A renter can also get more for her money than a homeowner. For example, a family that purchases a \$500,000 house would likely spend more than \$3,000 a month to live there; that same house would probably rent for quite a bit less than that amount. Furthermore, in addition to monthly mortgage payments, homeowners may also have to pay homeowner's dues and special assessments.

Financial Risk. Renters have little financial investment in their rented premises and the neighborhood in which they live. Therefore, there is little financial risk in renting. If the property values in a neighborhood decline and the neighborhood becomes run down or otherwise undesirable, renters can simply give the required notice—or wait until the lease expires—and move away. A homeowner in the same neighborhood runs the risk of losing some or all of his investment in the property.

Mobility. It is faster, easier, and cheaper for a renter to move than for a homeowner to move. A renter has only to give the required notice or wait until the lease expires before he can move out. Even if a renter has to leave abruptly, any deposit or prepaid rent that may be forfeited is almost sure to be less than the cost of selling one home and buying another. Selling a home is a lengthy and expensive process, taking at least a few months and costing about 10% of the home's value.

Maintenance and Repairs. An owner is responsible for maintaining the property and making any needed repairs. For a renter, the cost of maintenance and repairs is simply included in the rent. The renter usually has no direct responsibility for doing maintenance work and making repairs. Also, a renter does not face the burden of large expenditures for repairs.

Amenities. In many cases, renters enjoy the use of recreational facilities, such as swimming pools and tennis courts, that are beyond the financial reach of most homeowners.

Advantages of Buying

For many people, buying instead of renting affords both the subjective advantages of security and personal satisfaction and the financial advantages of equity appreciation and tax deductions.

Security. A homeowner enjoys a certain amount of security in knowing that he can continue to live in the home as long as the mortgage payments are made. A renter has no real security beyond the term of the lease. When the lease expires, or when the landlord gives the required notice, a renter will have to find another place to live.

Privacy and Freedom from Restrictions. In most cases, a homeowner enjoys greater privacy than a renter and has greater freedom to use the property. An owner can redecorate or remodel the home to suit his own taste, and can keep pets or engage in other activities that are prohibited by many rental agreements.

Monthly Payments. A homeowner's monthly mortgage payment usually starts out higher than the rental payment for equivalent lodging. However, over time, rents usually rise at a faster rate than mortgage payments. This is especially true if the mortgage has a fixed interest rate. In that case, payments usually increase slowly as the property tax and insurance portions of the mortgage payments increase. If the mortgage loan has an adjustable interest rate, payments may increase rapidly if interest rates rise, but they will decrease if interest rates go down. Thus, it is quite possible for a monthly rental payment to eventually exceed a monthly mortgage payment.

Investment Appreciation. Although it is impossible to predict whether or how much a particular home will appreciate in value, over the last several decades average home values have increased at a rate that is higher than the average inflation rate. Typically, a homeowner enjoys an increase in home equity—and thus an increase in net worth—as her home appreciates in value. For a renter, in contrast, the appreciation of property values is likely to mean a rent increase.

Tax Advantages. For the homeowner, federal income tax laws allow tax deductions for property taxes and for mortgage interest. The interest paid on a loan secured by a personal residence is the only type of consumer interest that is eligible for deduction from federal income taxes. Also, at least part of the gain realized on the sale of most principal residences is never taxed at all. An equivalent tax benefit is simply not available to those who rent their principal residence. (See Chapter 15 for a more complete discussion of income taxes and real estate ownership.)

Comparison of Renting and Buying

Some real estate agents use worksheets to compare the net costs of renting and buying. Worksheet forms take into account not only the monthly mortgage or rental payments, but also the homeowner's increases in equity and the benefit of income tax deductions. These worksheets demonstrate to prospective buyers that the overall cost of buying a home is often less than the cost of renting.

A simplified example of such a worksheet form is shown in Figure 18.1. This worksheet has been filled in with data for a proposed purchase of a $250,000 home, with the buyer making a 10% downpayment and obtaining a $225,000 loan at a fixed annual interest rate of 7%. Closing costs bring the total cash requirement for the purchase up to $32,500. Taxes, homeowner's insurance, the annual appreciation rate for local property values, and the buyers' income tax bracket have all been estimated. The total estimated monthly payment, including principal and interest, property taxes, homeowner's insurance, and the monthly renewal premium for private mortgage insurance, is approximately $1,967.

The monthly cost of buying the home on these terms is compared with the cost of renting comparable housing at a monthly rent of $1,300. At first glance, a comparison of the monthly mortgage payment of $1,967 to the monthly rental payment of $1,300 would seem to give the advantage to renting, especially considering the substantial amount of cash required for the purchase. However, an analysis of all of the economic benefits of home ownership may result in a lower net cost for the home purchase, even when taking into account the interest lost on the money spent for the downpayment and closing costs.

To begin with, part of the monthly mortgage payment goes to amortize the loan. These payments to principal are typically recovered when the home is sold. For a

Fig. 18.1 Comparison of renting and buying

Comparison of Estimated Net Cost of Renting and Buying

Buying

Purchase price		$250,000
Cash required (downpayment and closing costs)		$32,500
Loan amount		$225,000
Loan term		30 years
Interest rate		7%
Property taxes		$3,800
Homeowner's insurance premium		$900
Property appreciation rate (estimated)		3%
Income tax bracket		28%
Out of pocket costs:		
Monthly payment		
Principal and interest		$1,497
Property taxes		317
Homeowner's insurance		75
Other monthly expenses (PMI)		+ 78
Total monthly payment		$1,967
less:		
Average monthly principal amortization		– 625
Tax benefit		
Average interest portion of payment	872	
Property tax portion of payment	317	
Other	+ 0	
Total deductible items	$1,189	
Monthly value of tax deduction		– 333
Effective monthly cost of ownership		$1,009
less:		
Average monthly appreciation		– 625
Monthly Net Cost of Buying		**$384**

Renting

Out-of-pocket costs:	
Monthly rent	$1,300
less:	
Interest from savings not used for purchase ($32,500 @ 4%)	– 108
Monthly Net Cost of Renting	**$1,192**

$225,000 loan with a 30-year term, the average monthly amortization would be $625 ($225,000 ÷ 360 months = $625). Of course, in the early years of the loan term a much smaller portion of each payment would go to principal, and in the later years a larger portion of the monthly payment would go to principal.

Next, some portions of the payment—the interest and the property taxes—are tax deductible. In this case, the average monthly interest is $872 (again, in the early years a larger portion would go to interest, and in the later years a smaller portion would go to interest), and the monthly property tax payment is $317, for a total of $1,189 in tax-deductible items. If the buyer is in the 28% income tax bracket, that would represent a tax savings of about $333 per month ($1,189 × .28 = $332.92).

Finally, the home is likely to appreciate in value and give the purchaser a return on his investment as well as a place to live. Even at the modest rate of appreciation used in this example, 3% per year, the appreciation return is substantial. On $250,000, it would be $7,500 per year, or about $625 per month.

After taking into account all of the economic benefits of buying, the net effective cost of buying is only $384 per month.

The monthly rental is $1,300, with no federal income tax deductions and no benefits to the renter if the property appreciates in value. The renter would be able to obtain some interest or other investment yield on the $32,500 not used for a downpayment and closing costs. In this example, a yield of 4% is used, giving the renter a monthly benefit of $108 and a net effective cost of renting of $1,192 per month.

It should be emphasized that this example is based on estimates and assumptions that are subject to change. A change in interest rates, property tax rates, or the tax law would significantly alter the income tax benefits of buying. Potential buyers overvalue the mortgage deduction; many homeowners do not receive the full deductions. Homeowners with too many deductions may be forced to pay the alternative minimum tax, negating the benefits of the mortgage deduction.

Also, the average monthly principal and interest portions would be different for a buyer who intended to own the home for less than the full 30-year amortization term. Perhaps most importantly, a change in the rate of appreciation would have a great impact on the final net cost of home ownership. However, worksheets of this type serve a useful purpose in displaying the benefits of home ownership that can offset what first appears to be the higher cost of buying a home.

Factors to Consider When Choosing a Home

When a real estate agent shows a home to a buyer, both the buyer and the seller often rely on the agent to point out the positive features of that home. So it is important that real estate agents understand what considerations are important to most home buyers. These features have an impact on both the property's subjective attractiveness to a buyer and the property's objective value as estimated by an appraiser. (Appraisal is discussed in Chapter 13.)

Types of Housing

Today's housing market provides a diverse set of options for the potential home buyer. Before a real estate agent can begin showing properties to a prospective buyer, the buyer should have an idea of what type of home she is looking for. The dominance of the traditional single-family home has given way to more specialized types of housing, reflecting the changing needs of society. In this section, we will focus primarily on the physical aspects of the different types of dwellings available. (Different forms of ownership are covered in Chapter 3.)

Single-Family Dwellings. The **single-family home** typically consists of one house on a single lot. The homeowner is responsible for maintaining the house and grounds, which can mean a significant investment of both time and money. However, owners of single-family homes have the greatest degree of control over the use of their property.

Another version of the single-family home is the **modular home.** The low cost of prefabricated homes makes them an increasingly popular alternative to standard construction. A modular home is assembled in sections in a factory and delivered to the building site to be joined together and placed on a foundation.

A **mobile home** (also referred to as a **manufactured home**) can be a permanent or semi-permanent form of single-family housing. Situated in mobile home parks, mobile homes are used as vacation homes or principal residences. The availability of housing parks offering complete residential environments with foundations and utility hookups has almost doubled in recent years to meet rising demand for this economical form of housing.

Townhouses are a less expensive alternative to the traditional single-family home. Usually two or three stories, townhouses may be separate or share a common wall with other townhouses and usually have a small yard attached. Common areas are managed by a community or homeowners association. Townhouses generally cost less than single-family houses, but there is also less privacy. Townhouses share many of the advantages and disadvantages of multi-family dwellings outlined below.

Multi-Family Dwellings. Multi-family buildings include apartment buildings, duplexes, condominiums, and cooperatives. **Apartment buildings** may be small single-story buildings or high-rise luxury complexes divided into multiple residential units available for rent. An apartment complex may contain a variety of amenities including parking, a swimming pool, and a gym. A **duplex** is two separate units under one roof. For example, large residential homes are often converted into duplexes. It is common for the owner of the home to live in one unit and rent out the remaining unit.

Condominiums and **cooperatives** are popular forms of residential housing in cities and other areas of high population density. Units are organized in complexes of varying size with common facilities that are shared by all. Common areas include stairwells, elevators, and grounds, in addition to amenities such as a swimming pool or gym. The distinction between a condominium complex and a cooperative is the type of ownership interest a buyer acquires. A condominium owner owns her individual unit and shares ownership of the common areas with the other owners in the complex. The cooperative owner is actually a shareholder of the corporation that owns the complex. (See Chapter 3 for more information on these ownership interests.)

The owner of a unit in a multi-family building has the security of ownership without the responsibilities of maintenance and repair that a single-unit dwelling requires. However, community or homeowners associations can place significant restrictions on an owner's use and modification of a unit. Multi-family buildings have less privacy than single-family homes due to common walls between units. Often less expensive than traditional housing, condominium and cooperative units are often slow to rise in value and the first to lose value in a bad real estate market.

Other Housing Arrangements. In addition to single-family and multi-family housing, there are a number of special subdivision arrangements that are designed to appeal to specific segments of society.

Planned unit developments (PUDs) are planned communities, zoned to make maximum use of open space. Residential areas are clustered together to form larger common areas available for public use, which can be appealing to young families. The open space is managed by a community association which is supported by fees collected from PUD owners. Retirement communities often follow the PUD model, offering older individuals the security and uniformity of a planned neighborhood.

In recent years, **mixed-use developments (MUDs)** have become popular in urban areas. Often in a single, high-rise building, these self-contained developments combine stores, office space, apartments, and recreational facilities. Commercial properties such as warehouses, factories, and schools that have been converted into residential buildings are called **converted-use properties**. Abandoned warehouses can be converted into condominium complexes; an old school can be transformed into a quirky hotel. Refurbishing an older building can be visually appealing and, in some cases, more economical than building a new structure. Converted-use properties are sometimes designed as MUDs.

Neighborhood Considerations

The next step for a prospective buyer is to evaluate the neighborhood where a potential property is located. Since the surrounding neighborhood greatly influences the overall desirability of a home and also has a large impact on value, careful consideration should be given to the characteristics of a particular neighborhood.

Percentage of Home Ownership. Are most of the homes owner-occupied, or is there a large percentage of rental properties? Neighborhoods that are predominantly owner-occupied are generally better maintained, less susceptible to loss in value, and more likely to appreciate in value.

Conformity. Values are protected if there is a reasonable degree of homogeneity in the neighborhood. This includes homogeneity of styles, ages, prices, sizes, and quality of structures.

Changing Land Use. Does the neighborhood land use appear stable, or are there indications of a transition from residential to some other type of land use?

Street and Sidewalks. Do the neighborhood streets have good access to traffic arterials? If a property does not front on a publicly dedicated and maintained street, the buyer should ask whether there is an enforceable road maintenance agreement signed by the property owners.

What is the condition of the driveway, street, and sidewalks? Are there street lights and fire hydrants on the block? Are there sanitary and/or storm sewers? If so, have they already been paid for, or is there a special assessment against the properties in the neighborhood?

Availability of Utilities and Public Services. Are all of the typical utilities available, including water, electricity, gas, sewers, telephones, and other desirable services, such as cable television and high-speed Internet? Are the telephone and power lines above ground or is there underground wiring? Is the neighborhood adequately served by public transportation, police, and fire protection?

School District. In what primary and secondary school districts is the neighborhood located? How far away are the schools? Are they within walking distance? The quality of the local schools or school district can make a major difference in value and can be an extremely important basis of decision for many buyers with school-age children.

Social Services. Are there places of worship, hospitals or health care facilities, and other social services nearby?

Overall Neighborhood Values. Does it appear that the overall property conditions and values in the neighborhood are stable, increasing, or decreasing?

The Home

Of course, the home itself—its size, condition, and amenities—should be reviewed with the prospective buyer. Although the discussion below focuses on a single-family home, these considerations can be applied to many of the other types of housing as well.

Site/View. First, the agent should look at the lot on which the house is located. What is the size and shape of the lot? Rectangular lots are usually more desirable than odd or irregularly shaped parcels. Is the lot on a corner? Is it level, gently sloping, or steep? Unusually steep lots present a danger of soil instability. Does it appear that water runoff and drainage are good? What is the quality and extent of the landscaping? If the home is new, has any landscaping (such as the lawn, shrubbery, and trees) already been done, or will the buyer have to do it all? The cost of new landscaping can be quite a bit more than many home buyers realize.

Fig. 18.2 Architectural styles

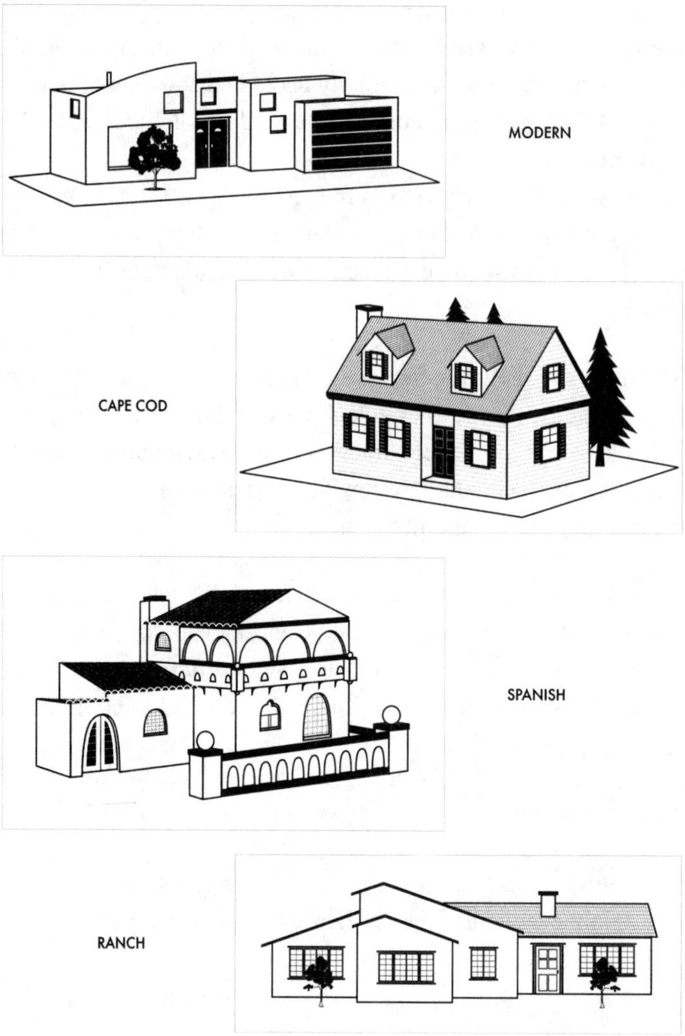

Is there a view? In many areas, a view can increase the value of the lot substantially and add greatly to the property's appeal.

Architectural Styles. Homes come in a variety of architectural styles. The quality of a home's construction is not determined by its style (although the style may affect the cost of constructing the home). No one style is inherently more desirable than another. The value of each particular style depends on the personal preference of the buyer.

Several common architectural styles are illustrated in Figure 18.2. Of course, many homes have their own unique style, or are combinations of two or more styles. Split-level, Spanish, ranch, and modern (sometimes called contemporary) are popular architectural styles.

Split-level homes have visually attractive designs and make effective use of hilly terrains. Spanish-style homes are one- or two-story homes with white or pastel stucco exteriors and red tile roofs; they look cool and comfortable in hotter climates. Modern-style homes usually incorporate large windows and glass doors, and are designed with an open interior. Because of the flexibility of modern home designs, they are well suited for building on hillsides or other difficult sites. Ranch-style homes have one story and low-pitched or flat roofs. The exterior may be wood, masonry, or stucco.

A one-story ranch home is the simplest to construct and maintain. However, it requires more land in relation to living space than a two-story or split-level home. Thus, a one-story home may be uneconomical where land is at a premium. Split-level construction is more expensive, but it is popular because it effectively utilizes land with varying topography. Two-story construction is the most economical per square foot of living space, since twice as much living space is provided with one foundation, one roof, and the same amount of land. The inconvenience of stairs and exterior maintenance on the upper story are the primary drawbacks of two-story homes.

Exterior Appearance. How old is the house, and when was it last painted? What is the age and condition of the roof and flashing, gutters, downspouts, siding, windows, doors, and weather stripping? Thin or curled shingles; cracked, blistered, or peeling paint; and rusted or sagging gutters and downspouts are indications that costly repairs may soon be needed. Does the foundation appear to be in good shape, or are there cracks or other evidence of settling? If there is no basement, are the vents and crawlspace adequate?

Plumbing and Electrical Systems. If it is not a new home, what is the age of the plumbing and electrical systems? Is the plumbing copper, plastic, or some combination of materials? Is the water pressure adequate? Do the electrical service panel and existing outlets indicate there is sufficient electrical service to the home? Do the electrical and plumbing systems, or as much of them as can be seen, appear to be in good condition?

Heating, Ventilating, and Air Conditioning. What type of heating system does the home have: electric, gas, or oil; forced air, floor furnaces, or baseboard heaters? What is the type and size of the water heater? If there is air conditioning, is it a central system or window units? If it is not a new home, what is the age and apparent condition of the heating, hot water, and air conditioning systems? Is the present owner aware of any problems, inadequacies, or defects?

Garage/Carport. Generally, a garage is better than a carport. What is the size of the garage or carport—single, double, or triple? Is there work or storage space in addition to space for parking? Is there an entrance, protected from the weather, directly from the garage or carport into the home?

Attic/Basement. Is there an attic or a basement? If so, what type of access is there from the rest of the home? Is there room for storage or work space? Would it be possible to convert all or part of the basement into additional bedrooms or living area?

Energy-Efficient Features. Escalating energy costs have created an increased demand for energy-efficient homes. Examples of energy-efficient features include clock-controlled thermostats, insulation-wrapped water heaters, insulated ducts and pipes in unheated areas, adequate insulation for floors, walls, and attic, and weather stripping for doors and windows. In some areas, solar water and space heating equipment is popular.

Overall Interior Design. A real estate agent should know some of the features of a well-designed, efficient floor plan. For instance, it should not be necessary to pass through the living room to reach other rooms, or to go through one of the bedrooms to reach another.

Other design considerations include the number of bedrooms, closets, and bathrooms—is there a sufficient number and size for the square footage of the home? Is there a separate dining room, or is the dining area part of the kitchen or living room? Is there sufficient work space in the kitchen and laundry room, and is there storage space for cleaning and gardening tools? Are there enough windows and natural light, especially in the kitchen and other work or recreational spaces?

Considerations for Individual Rooms. Individual rooms have certain features that are important to their comfort and efficient use.

- **Living Room/Family Room.** How large are the living room and the family or recreation room (if any)? Is the shape of each room and the available wall space adequate for the furniture that will be placed in it?
- **Dining Room or Area.** Is the dining area convenient to the kitchen, large enough in relation to the size of the home, and able to accommodate the number of people who will be eating there?
- **Kitchen.** Is the kitchen convenient to an outside entrance and to the garage or carport? Is there adequate counter and cabinet space? What is the quality and condition of the kitchen cabinets? What is the type, quality, and condition of the kitchen floor? Are any of the appliances going to be included in the sale? If so, are they large enough, of good quality, and in good repair?
- **Bedrooms.** Is the number of bedrooms and their size adequate for the family? The size of the master bedroom is especially important. Are the closets large enough? It is better for the bedrooms to be located apart from the family room, living room, kitchen, and other work or recreational spaces.
- **Bathrooms.** There should be at least two bathrooms if the home has more than two bedrooms. In many areas, particularly in newer homes, a private bathroom off the master bedroom is standard. What is the type and condition of the tile or other wall and floor coverings? Are there windows or ceiling fans to provide adequate ventilation?

Design Deficiencies. Here is a brief list of some of the most common design deficiencies that home buyers should watch out for:

- the front door opens directly into the living room;
- there is no front hall closet;

- the back door is difficult to reach from the kitchen, or from the driveway or garage;
- there is no comfortable area in or near the kitchen where the family can eat;
- the dining room is not easily accessible from the kitchen;
- the stairway is off of a room rather than in a hallway or foyer;
- bedrooms and baths are visible from the living room or foyer;
- the family room (or rec room) is not visible from the kitchen;
- there is no access to the basement from outside the house;
- the bedrooms are not separated by a bathroom or closet wall (for soundproofing); and
- outdoor living areas are not accessible from the kitchen.

Environmental Hazards. Real estate agents should also be sure to investigate a prospective home for environmental hazards, such as asbestos insulation, lead-based paint, and geologic hazards. Many of these hazards are more of a concern with older construction.

Asbestos. Asbestos was used for many years in insulation on plumbing pipes and heat ducts, and as general insulation material. It can also be found in floor tile and roofing material. In its original condition, asbestos is considered relatively harmless; but when it gets old and starts to disintegrate into a fine dust, it can cause lung cancer and should be removed. Asbestos must be enclosed, covered with a permanent seal, or removed by an experienced professional.

Urea Formaldehyde. Until 1982, urea formaldehyde was used in foam insulation. It was banned because of the risk of illness caused by the formaldehyde gas released from the insulation. Urea formaldehyde foam insulation (UFFI) is not found in most American homes. However, urea formaldehyde may also be found in the adhesives used in pressed wood building materials, which are widely used in furniture, kitchen cabinets, and some types of paneling. This substance may cause cancer, skin rashes, and breathing problems. However, it emits significant amounts of dangerous gas only in the first few years. Older urea formaldehyde materials are not considered dangerous.

Radon. Radon, a colorless, odorless gas, is actually present almost everywhere. It is found wherever uranium is deposited in the earth's crust. As uranium decays, radon gas is formed and seeps from the earth, usually into the atmosphere. However, radon sometimes collects in buildings. For example, radon may enter a house through cracks in the foundation or through floor drains. Exposure to dangerous levels of radon gas may cause lung cancer.

Lead-Based Paint. Lead is extremely toxic to human beings, damaging the brain, the kidneys, and the central nervous system. The most common source of lead in the home is lead-based paint. Although lead is now banned in consumer paint, it is still found in many homes built before 1978. As lead-based paint deteriorates, or if it is sanded or scraped, it forms a lead dust that accumulates inside and outside the home. The dust can be breathed in or ingested, increasing the risk of toxic lead exposure. In some cases, a seller or landlord is required by law to make disclosures concerning lead-based paint to prospective buyers or tenants.

Underground Storage Tanks. Underground storage tanks are found not only on commercial and industrial properties, but also on residential properties. A storage tank is considered underground if 10% of its volume (including piping) is below the earth's surface. Older homes used underground storage tanks to store fuel oil. The principal danger from underground storage tanks is that when they grow old they begin to rust, leaking toxic products into the soil or, even more dangerously, into the groundwater. Removing underground storage tanks and cleaning up the contaminated soil can be time-consuming and expensive. Both federal and state laws regulate the removal of storage tanks and the necessary cleanup.

Water Contamination. Water can be contaminated by a variety of agents, including bacteria, viruses, nitrates, metals such as lead or mercury, fertilizers, pesticides, and radon. These contaminants may come from underground storage tanks, industrial discharge, urban area runoff, malfunctioning septic systems, and runoff from agricultural areas. Drinking contaminated water can cause physical symptoms that range from mild stomach aches to kidney and liver damage, cancer, and death. If a home uses a well as a water source, it should be tested by health authorities or private laboratories at least once a year.

Illegal Drug Manufacturing. If property has been the site of illegal drug manufacturing, there may be substantial health risks for subsequent occupants. The chemicals used to manufacture certain illegal drugs are highly toxic, and the effects of the contamination can linger for a long time. The government can seize any property being used to manufacture illegal drugs. Property should not be listed or sold until any conditions that could subject the property to seizure have been eliminated.

Example: Meyers owns a single-family home that has been used as a rental property for several years. Unknown to Meyers, the current tenants are manufacturing illegal drugs in the basement of the home. The property could be seized by the government, even though Meyers knows nothing about the drug activity.

Mold. Mold is a commonplace problem, especially in damp parts of houses such as basements and bathrooms. For most people, the presence of mold does not cause any adverse effects. However, for people who are allergic to mold or who have respiratory problems, the presence of mold may render a house unlivable. Awareness of mold has increased greatly in recent years, as a result of some high-profile lawsuits against builders or insurance companies, as well as news reports about contamination of public buildings such as schools and government offices. Bear in mind that mold may grow out of sight, inside walls or heating ducts, and will not necessarily be discovered in an inspection.

Geologic Hazards. Geologic hazards are a significant concern for many property owners in the coastal regions of the country. Major potential geologic problems include landslides, flooding, subsidence, and earthquakes. When dealing with a property located on or near a steep slope, look for signs of ground movement. Tilting trees, active soil erosion, and cracking, dipping, or slumping ground are all indicators of slide activity. Subsidence is the collapse of ground into underground cavities, which may be natural or man-made. It is wise to consult with a geologist to assess the magnitude of a ground movement problem.

Flooding can also be a serious problem for property owners. Whenever property is located in a flood plain—the low-lying, flat areas immediately adjacent to a river—there is cause for concern. It is prudent to check for signs of previous flood damage to structures, particularly in basements and foundations. In some cases, it may be necessary to obtain flood insurance, which we discuss in more detail in the next section.

Earthquakes are the least predictable and least controllable of geologic problems. However, steps can be taken to protect buildings against earthquakes. Seismic retrofitting can make a property more desirable and increase its value. Many contractors are able to perform this type of work, and information about seismic retrofitting is widely available from state and local government agencies.

Property Insurance

Purchasing a home is the largest financial investment many people will ever make. Not only is insuring an investment of this size wise, but almost all residential mortgage lenders require that borrowers provide adequate insurance for property that secures a loan. Insurance can provide coverage for the home itself, as well as the personal property found in the home. If the owner is forced to temporarily vacate his home because of a covered incident (such as a fire), insurance may also pay the homeowner's added living expenses (such as hotel bills or an apartment rental).

What is Covered

Under the terms of most insurance agreements, the owner (**insured**) pays an insurance premium in exchange for a promise by the insurance company (**insurer**) to pay for specific types of loss referred to as **perils**. An insurance policy covers the **insurable interest**, which is generally the insured's financial interest in the property.

Under most policies, the insurer agrees to pay the **replacement cost** of the damage—the cost of replacing the old, damaged structure with a new structure. Insurers often require the homeowner to maintain insurance equal to at least 80 percent of the current replacement cost. Alternatively, an insurance policy covering the **actual cash value** of the loss will cover the amount of the new replacement, less any accumulated depreciation on the structure. The owner must make up the difference between the actual cash value and the cost of any repairs.

In addition to covering the structure, a home insurance policy typically covers the insured's personal property to a limited degree. A standard policy also typically covers additional structures such as a garage or tool shed, but won't cover structures that are rented or leased to others, or that are used for business purposes. A standard policy does not usually cover damage to cars, business property, or pets, and in some circumstances valuables such as jewelry may not be fully covered.

Also included in most homeowner's insurance is liability coverage for bodily injury and property damage to others resulting from the insured's negligence. For example, a guest at a party trips and falls over a rake in your backyard and claims you are responsible for her injuries. Your liability coverage would compensate her, to a limited extent, for the damage.

Types of Insurance

A homeowner can purchase insurance in a variety of different forms to cover a variety of different circumstances. Although it is possible to buy individual policies for specific risks, most homeowners buy a standard package policy called a **homeowner's policy**. An insured can purchase additional coverage, in the form of an **endorsement**, for specific perils that are not covered by a standard policy. There are eight standardized homeowner's policy forms used today.

Basic Form. The homeowner's policy that covers the fewest perils is the basic form (also known as HO-1). It covers losses resulting from:

- fire or lightning,
- windstorm or hail,
- explosion,
- smoke,
- aircraft,
- vehicles,
- theft,
- riot or civil commotion,
- vandalism or malicious mischief,
- glass breakage, and
- removal of property from an endangered premises.

Broad Form. Broad form (HO-2) covers all perils listed under basic form, plus seven additional perils.

These perils are:

- falling objects;
- weight of ice, snow, or sleet;
- collapse of the building;
- freezing of plumbing, heating, and air-conditioning systems and domestic appliances;
- cracking, burning, bursting, or bulging of a steam or hot water heating system or of appliances used to heat water;
- accidental discharge, leakage, or overflow of water or steam from within a plumbing, heating, or air conditioning system or domestic appliances; and
- sudden and accidental injury from artificially generated currents to electrical appliances, devices, fixtures, and wiring.

Special Form. The special form (HO-3) provides broad form coverage of the insured's personal property, and protects the physical structure of the home against all risks other than those specifically excluded in the policy. In recent years, this form has become more popular among homeowners.

Tenant's Form. A renter can protect her personal property from loss using a tenant's form (HO-4). In addition to covering the tenant's personal property, this policy provides reimbursement for any loss of use of the rental property. This reimbursement is usually 20% of the value of the covered personal property under the policy. The apartment building and unit itself are not covered under this policy because the tenant does not have an insurable interest in the building.

Comprehensive Form. The most comprehensive coverage is provided by the comprehensive form (HO-5). Also called an all-risk policy, the HO-5 covers all perils to the structure and personal property, except those perils specifically excluded in the policy. These exclusions may include flood, landslide, mud flow, earthquake, settling, war, or nuclear accident.

Condominium Unit Owner's Form. Although most homeowners associations purchase insurance to cover the common areas of a condominium or cooperative complex, that insurance does not cover an owner's individual unit or personal property. A condominium unit owner's form (HO-6) can be purchased to cover any losses caused by damage to a cooperative or condominium unit. An all-risk policy for a unit can also be purchased.

Mobile Homes. Not all insurance companies offer insurance for mobile or manufactured homes. Mobile home insurance (HO-7) usually covers the actual cash value of the mobile home and the owner's personal property.

Older Homes. Owners of older homes often cover their property with a standard HO-8 policy, which is specifically designed to cover older homes with historic value. Generally, this policy covers the same perils covered by an HO-1, but only pays for the actual cash value of repairs rather than the replacement cost.

Flood Insurance

Most standard homeowner's insurance policies exclude damage caused by flood. However, the National Flood Insurance Act (enacted by Congress in 1968) helps provide affordable flood insurance to homeowners in flood-prone areas of the country. (These areas are identified by the Army Corps of Engineers.) The National Flood Insurance Program (NFIP), which is administered by the Federal Emergency Management Agency (FEMA), issues federally subsidized flood insurance, which can be purchased from licensed property insurance agents in each state.

Property that is financed with a federal or federally related loan must be covered by flood insurance if it is located in a flood zone. However, if an owner can show that the 100-year flood mark (also known as the **base flood elevation** or BFE) is below the building on the property, flood insurance may not be required even if the property is located in a flood zone.

In some areas, additional requirements may be imposed when buildings are remodeled or expanded. For example, a building may need to be elevated on pilings above the BFE mark.

Changes in Policy

A homeowner's insurance policy may be suspended as a result of certain acts of the insured. For example, in some states a policy is suspended when the insured building is left unoccupied for more than 60 days. A policy may also be suspended if there is a substantial change in the use of the building that increases the risk of loss, such as converting a residential building into a bed and breakfast. The policy becomes effective again once the condition causing the suspension is corrected.

A homeowner's insurance policy may be canceled at any time by the insured or the insurer. Generally, insurance premiums are paid in advance. If a policy is canceled early, the insured is entitled to a refund of the unused portion of the premium. If the insurer cancels the policy, it is required to provide written notice of cancellation to the insured before cancellation.

Instead of canceling a policy, an insurer may simply choose not to renew a policy when it expires. Although some states impose certain restrictions on non-renewals, it is often easier than going through the cancellation process.

In some real estate transactions, it is possible for the buyer to assume the insurance policy of the seller. The insurer would have to accept the buyer as the new policyholder before closing to avoid any break in coverage.

Home Warranty

While home warranties are not a type of insurance, they are closely related. Home warranties covering structural and mechanical defects are often provided by builders. These warranties might protect buyers against defects in the roof of a new home; or defects in the home's plumbing, electrical, and heating systems; water heaters; duct work; and major appliances. It may also be possible to purchase a home warranty for a used home, although the coverage is usually not as comprehensive. This type of home warranty may be purchased by a buyer, a seller, an agent, or an owner.

Construction

A real estate agent is not a home inspector or an architect, and should not give clients and customers the impression that he is an expert in residential construction. However, some states impose a duty on all licensees to visually inspect the homes they sell. Furthermore, most home buyers rely on their real estate agents for some advice on the structural quality of a particular home. Thus, agents must be able to evaluate the basic soundness of a home's construction. This preliminary evaluation should be supplemented, whenever necessary, with the opinion of a professional inspector, especially with respect to structural integrity, and the safety and suitability of the plumbing and electrical components of the building.

In order to evaluate the basic soundness of a home, real estate agents should be familiar with the following aspects of residential construction:

- local codes and regulations,
- the role of the architect,
- plans and specifications, and
- construction methods and terminology.

Local Codes and Regulations

Building codes prescribe the types of materials that must be used in residential construction, the acceptable methods of construction, and the number and placement of such items as electrical outlets, plumbing fixtures, and windows. The size and placement of a building on its lot are also governed by building codes. In addition, electrical codes dictate the installation of electrical wiring, conductors, and appliances throughout a residence.

The primary purpose of building codes is to keep communities safe and in sanitary condition by setting standards for the upkeep and care of decent housing. A building code also promotes some degree of uniformity in construction and assures a buyer that a home's quality meets at least minimum requirements. This is especially important in regard to safety issues. For example, a home's ability to resist fire or earthquake damage is of vital importance to both the homeowner and the surrounding community.

Building and housing codes are generally issued and enforced at the municipal level of government. Cities and counties have building departments that issue construction permits and conduct inspections to ensure compliance with local regulations. (See Chapter 6 for a discussion of the local government's authority to enact and enforce building codes.) In addition, the state government typically regulates the licensing of residential contractors, usually requiring a license candidate to have a specific amount of experience and pass a licensing exam.

Key sources of information regarding local regulations are local planning and building departments, architects, and construction contractors.

The Role of the Architect

The architect is the construction industry professional that the real estate agent is most likely to meet. Most people think of an architect as a person who designs buildings, but a good architect will also provide a range of other services throughout the construction process.

Under a standard contract, an architect will first work with the owner to develop a design that fulfills the owner's needs. Next, the architect will prepare more detailed drawings, describing all of the components of the building, along with an estimate of the probable cost of construction. When the design has been approved by the owner, the architect will draw up the official plans and specifications and will help the owner get bids from contractors and permits from government agencies.

Finally, the architect acts as the owner's representative throughout the actual construction phase, visiting the site to inspect the work, approving periodic payments to the contractor, and interpreting the plans and specifications.

Plans and Specifications

Plans and specifications are the technical drawings and text that explain in detail how a building is to be constructed. The **plans** are drawings of the vertical and horizontal cross-sections of the building. They show the placement of foundations, floors, walls, roofs, doors, windows, fixtures, and wiring. The **specifications** are the text that accompanies the plans, prescribing the type of materials to be used and the required quality of workmanship. Plans and specifications are usually prepared by an architect and take the form of blueprints.

Wood Frame Construction

The most common type of home construction is the wood frame building. It is popular because of its low cost, ease and speed of construction, and flexibility of design. One-story, two-story, and split-level homes can all be wood frame homes.

Because wood frame buildings are so common, this is the type of construction we will focus on here. The construction of a wood frame building is illustrated in the following diagrams, and a glossary of construction terms is provided for use in conjunction with these diagrams.

Elements of Wood Frame Construction. It is easier to judge the quality of a home with some knowledge of the elements of construction. The materials required for each element are usually specified by local building codes. The following are the basic elements of residential wood frame construction.

Foundation. Virtually all modern building foundations are made with reinforced concrete. Concrete has the advantages of low cost, plasticity, and high compressive strength. When concrete is reinforced by steel bars or mesh, it also has good tensile strength (resistance to bending or cracking).

The wider part of the base of a foundation wall is called a **footing**. It supports the weight of the structure. A **sill plate** is a board that is attached to the top of the concrete foundation. The framing of the house rests on the sill plate.

Framing. The framing is usually constructed of wooden boards and dimensional lumber, although the use of metal framing is becoming more common in some areas. Lumber is classified as either "green" or "dry," depending on its moisture content. Dry lumber is considered superior to green lumber for framing because it is less prone to warpage—the deformity in shape caused by uneven shrinking.

The size and length of framing members varies, depending upon their particular application as girders, joists, studs, rafters, and so on. The parallel boards used to support the load of the floor and ceiling are called joists. Vertical members called studs are attached to the sole plate, which is a horizontal board that rests on the subfloor. (See Figure 18.3.)

Fig. 18.3 Foundation and framing

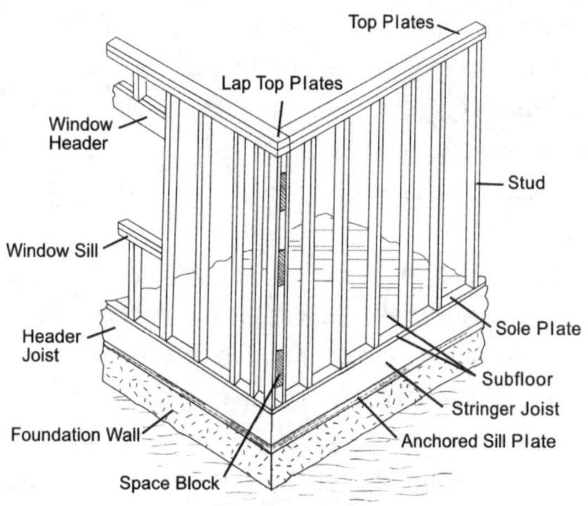

Walls serve two purposes. They provide structural support and they separate the interior space into individual rooms. The walls that provide support are called **load-bearing walls**. Load-bearing walls support a vertical load, such as a second floor or the roof. (See Figure 18.5.) Load-bearing walls are usually built to be stronger than non-load bearing walls, and they are rarely moved during remodeling.

Exterior Sheathing and Siding. Exterior sheathing is the covering applied to the outside of the frame. The most common form of exterior sheathing is plywood panels that are four feet wide by eight feet long. Plywood serves an additional function by adding shear strength to the walls. Shear strength is the capacity of a wall to resist a sideways racking force, and it is normally provided by corner bracing in the frame.

Exterior siding is the visible finish layer applied to the outside of the building. It may be plywood, boards, vinyl siding, shingles, or other materials. The two most important characteristics of siding are its resistance to weathering and its aesthetic appeal.

Interior Sheathing. This is the covering applied to the inside of the frame, on the walls and ceilings. In the past, the most common form of sheathing was lath and plaster, a cement-like mixture applied over a matrix of wood strips attached to the frame. Modern buildings use drywall construction for interior sheathing. The term "drywall" is used because there is no need to add water to the material before application. Drywall products usually come in large sheets (like plywood) and are fastened to the frame with glue, nails, or screws. Sheetrock and wallboard are two common drywall products. The joints between panels are hidden by covering them with a strip of tape imbedded in a plaster-like filler. This process is called "taping" the joints.

Roofing. The structural part of the roof is composed of the ridge board (the highest structural member of the house), rafters, and plywood or boards laid perpendicular to the rafters. This sheathing is then covered with a tar-impregnated paper called roofing felt. The final layer of roofing may be wood shingles, tiles, or composition roofing (tar-like shingles or rolls of material). Sometimes hot tar is simply interspersed with more layers of felt; this is called a "built-up" roof. Flashing (metal sheeting) is installed on top of the roofing material around chimneys and other openings to prevent water seepage.

Floor Covering. The strength of the floor is provided by tongue-and-groove floor boards or plywood attached to the floor joists, which is called the subflooring. The subflooring is then covered with finished flooring, which may be carpet, tile, linoleum, hardwood strips, or other material.

Plumbing. The plumbing includes drain pipes, supply pipes, and fixtures. The drain pipes are made of cast iron, concrete, or plastic. The supply pipes are made of galvanized steel, copper, or plastic. Plumbing fixtures are either cast iron or pressed steel that is coated with enamel or fiberglass.

Electrical. Most modern wiring is in the form of cable, which is an insulated cord-like material containing two or more strands of copper or aluminum wire. The electrical cables are enclosed in metal or plastic piping called conduit.

The electrical cables run in circuits from a supply source (a fuse box or, more commonly, a breaker panel) to the various outlets for plugs or light fixtures. A breaker panel is a series of circuit breakers that automatically shut off the current in a circuit under overload conditions. Most outlets supply 110 volts of power, except for certain outlets designed for major appliances (ranges, water heaters, dryers, etc.), which supply 220 volts.

Heating, Ventilating, and Air Conditioning (HVAC). These systems are composed of heating and/or cooling appliances that serve warm, cool, or fresh air to the rooms of a house through a series of galvanized sheet metal tubes called ducts. The ducts open at various places in the building called registers. The registers may be closed off independently in order to direct the heat or air conditioning to areas where it is needed.

HVAC systems sometimes have an energy-efficient ratio (EER) rating. The higher the EER, the more efficient the system.

Insulation is used to make HVAC systems less costly to run. Insulation is material that is resistant to the transfer of heat. It comes in batts or rolls, or in loose form, and it is inserted between wall studs and between the joists of floors and ceilings. Insulation also comes in sheets that can be secured to the sheathing of the structure. The effectiveness of insulating materials is gauged by an "R-value." The higher the R-value, the more resistant the material is to the transfer of heat, and the better it is for insulation purposes. Local building codes require insulation with a minimum R-value to be used in all new construction. When insulation is adequate, the inside surface of an exterior wall will be about the same temperature as the surface of an interior wall.

Structural Pest Problems. One major problem with wood frame buildings is their susceptibility to damage by wood-eating insects, especially termites. Several techniques are used to minimize the possibility of termite damage:

- the ground under and around the building may be treated with a chemical that keeps termites away from the foundation;
- lumber that is in contact with the soil or the foundation, such as sills or beams, may be treated with a chemical to prevent termites from gaining access to the frame of the building; and
- metal shields may be inserted between the foundation and the superstructure to physically prevent termites from reaching the wood.

Fig. 18.4 Residential construction details

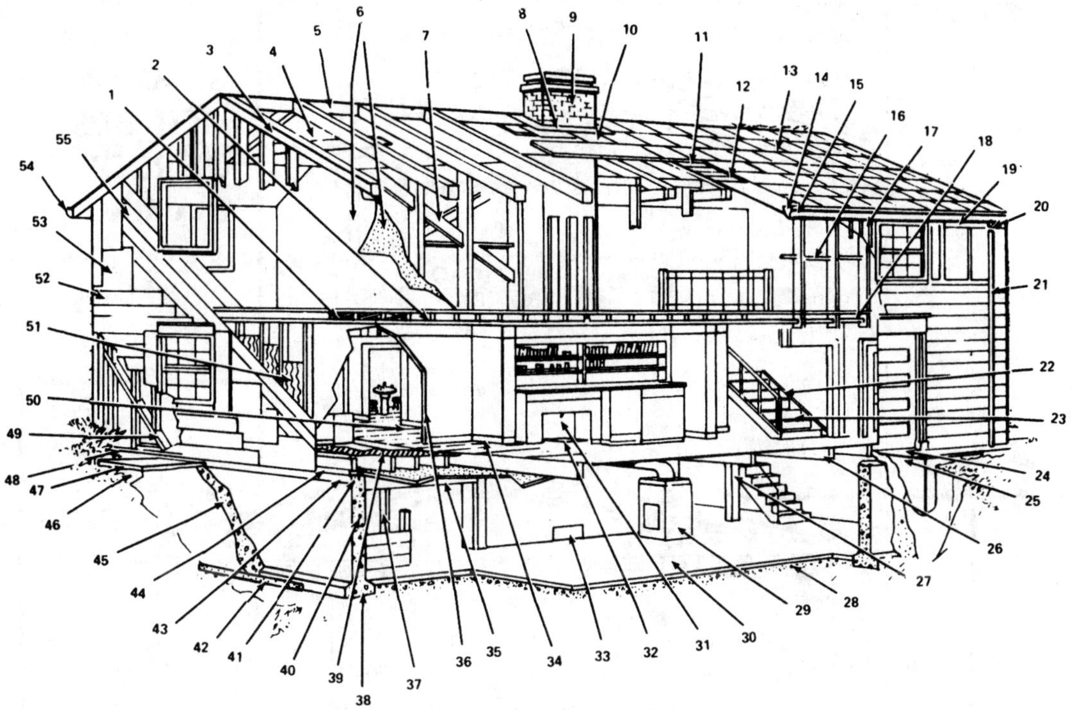

CONSTRUCTION DETAILS

1. CROSS BRIDGING
2. SECOND FLOOR JOISTS
3. ROOF RAFTERS
4. COLLAR BEAM
5. RIDGE BOARD
6. PLASTER BASE,LATH AND PLASTER WALLS
7. CROSS BRACING
8. FLASHING AND COUNTER FLASHING
9. BRICK CHIMNEY
10. TIGHT ROOF SHEATHING (ALL OTHER COVERINGS)
11. SPACED 1" x 4" SHEATHING (WOOD SHINGLES)
12. ROOFING FELT
13. FINISH ROOFING (SHINGLE)
14. SOFFIT OR CORNICE
15. FACIA OF CORNICE
16. FIRE STOPS
17. VERTICAL BOARD AND BATTEN SIDING
18. RIBBON PLATE
19. FACIA BOARD
20. LEADER HEAD OR CONDUCTOR HEAD
21. LEADER, DOWNSPOUT OR CONDUCTOR
22. STAIR STRINGER
23. MAIN STAIR TREADS AND RISERS
24. ENTRANCE DOOR SILL
25. CONCRETE STOOP
26. FIRST FLOOR JOISTS
27. BASEMENT POST
28. CINDERFILL
29. BOILER OR FURNACE
30. BASEMENT CONCRETE FLOOR
31. DAMPER CONTROL
32. ASH DUMP
33. CLEANOUT DOOR
34. BASEBOARDS
35. GIRDER
36. FRAME PARTITION
37. POST
38. FOOTING
39. SUB-FLOORING, DIAGONAL
40. FOUNDATION WALL
41. PLATE ANCHOR BOLT
42. DRAIN TILE
43. TERMITE SHIELD
44. SILL PLATE
45. GRAVEL FILL
46. GRADE LINE
47. BASEMENT AREAWAY
48. SOLE PLATE
49. CORNER BRACING
50. FINISH FLOOR
51. INSULATION, BATTS
52. WALL SIDING
53. WALL BUILDING PAPER
54. GUTTER
55. WALL SHEATHING, DIAGONAL

Fig. 18.5 Methods of roof framing

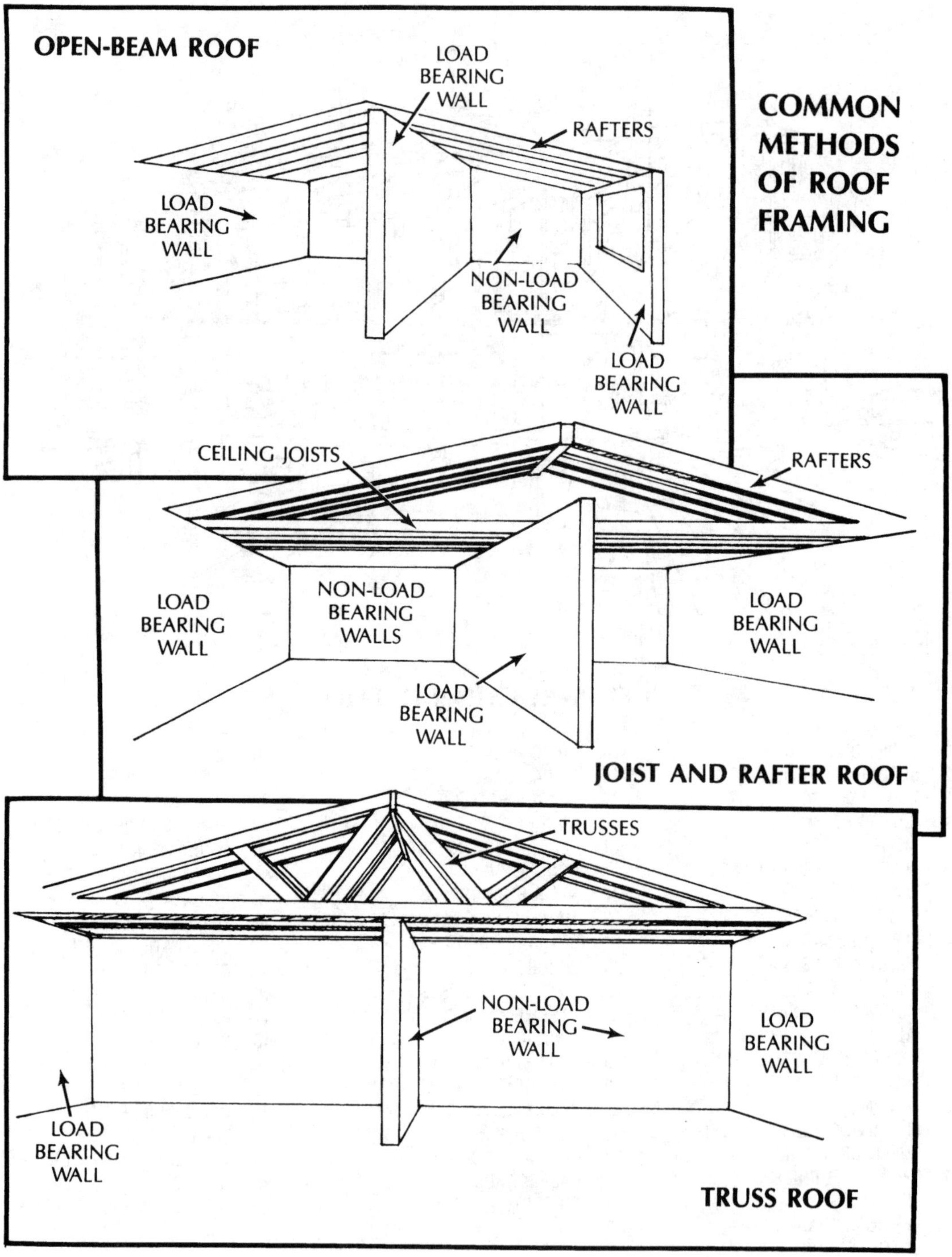

Fig. 18.6 Roof styles

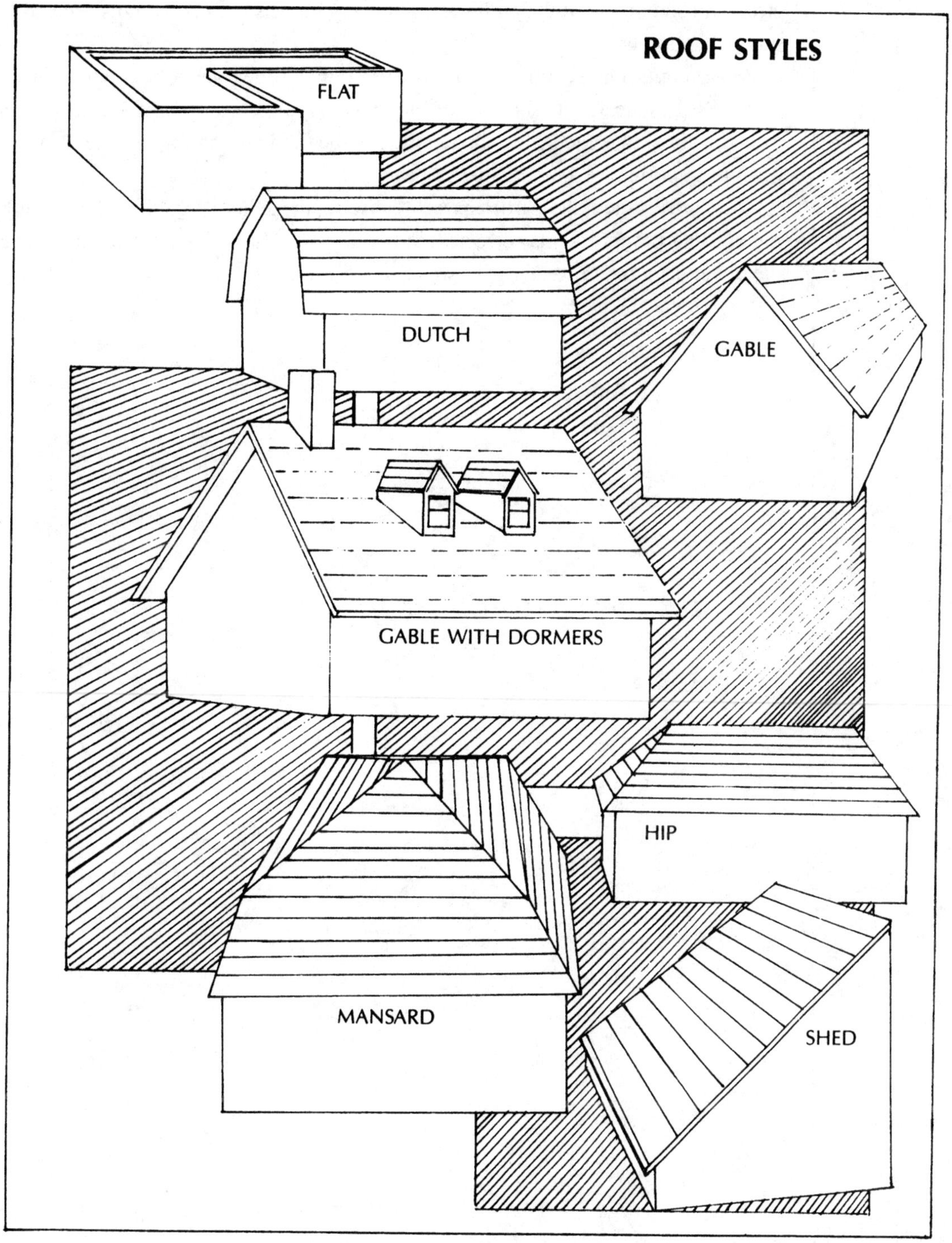

It is always a good idea to have a licensed structural pest control inspector examine a home before a sale closes. In fact, lenders in many states typically require such an inspection. (And in some termite-prone areas, pest control inspections are also required by the FHA and VA.) The inspector will provide a complete report on the structural soundness of the building, listing any defects caused by moisture and fungus or by insects.

A pest control inspection is usually ordered by a seller when the property is first listed. Real estate agents should make sure the buyer gets a copy of the report as soon as is practical. In some states, the report must be filed with the state and a copy of it must be kept for a certain number of years.

Ordinarily, unless the parties agree otherwise, the seller is required to pay for having existing pest problems corrected, but not for work to prevent infestation. Instead, the buyer pays for any preventive work.

Fig. 18.7 Construction terms

Glossary of Construction Terms

Anchor bolts—Bolts embedded in concrete, used to hold structural members in place.

Areaway—An open space around a basement window or doorway that provides light, ventilation, and access.

Beam—A principal structural member used between posts, columns, or walls.

Bearing wall or partition—A wall or partition that supports a vertical load in addition to its own weight.

Board—Lumber that is less than two inches thick.

Bridging—Pieces fitted in pairs from the bottom of one floor joist to the top of adjacent joists, and crossed to distribute the floor load.

BTU—British Thermal Unit; a measure of heating capacity.

Built-up roof—A roof composed of several layers of rag felt, saturated with pitch or asphalt.

Cased opening—An interior opening without a door that is finished with jambs and trim.

Caulk—To seal cracks and joints to make them waterproof.

Collar beam—A beam connecting rafters at a point considerably above the wall plate.

Column—An upright supporting member, circular or rectangular in shape.

Conduit—A pipe or tube, usually metal, in which wiring is installed.

Corner braces—Diagonal braces set into studs to reinforce corners of frame structures.

Counterflashing—Flashing used on chimneys at the roof line to cover shingle flashing and prevent the entry of moisture.

Crawl space—A space between the ground and the first floor that is used for access.

Dimensional lumber—Lumber that is two to five inches thick and up to twelve inches wide.

Dormer—A projecting structure built out from a sloping roof.

Drywall—Materials used for wall covering that do not need to be mixed with water before application (e.g., sheetrock).

Eaves—The margin or lower part of a roof that projects over an exterior wall.

Fascia—A wooden member nailed to the ends of projecting rafters.

Fire stop—A block or stop used in a wall between studs to prevent the spread of fire and smoke.

Flashing—Sheet metal or other material used in roof and wall construction to prevent rain or other water from entering.

Flue—The space in a chimney through which smoke, gas, or fumes rise.

Footing—The spreading course at the base of a foundation wall, pier, or column.

Framing—The timber structure of a building that gives it shape and strength. It includes the wall, floors, ceilings, and roof.

Gable—That portion of a wall contained between the slopes of a roof.

Glazing—The process of installing glass into sashes and doors.

Gutter—A wooden or metal trough attached to the edge of a roof to collect and conduct water from rain and melting snow.

Header—A horizontal structural member that supports the load over an opening, such as a window or door.

Hip roof—A roof that rises from all four sides of the building.

Interior trim—A general term for all the molding, casing, baseboards, and other trim items applied inside the building.

Insulation—Any material highly resistant to heat transmission that is used to reduce the rate of heat flow.

Jamb—The top and two sides of a door or window frame that contact the door or sash.

Joist—One of a series of parallel framing members used to support floor and ceiling loads.

Lath—Material fastened to the frame of a building to act as a base for plaster.

Molding—A narrow strip of wood used to conceal surface or angle joints, or as an ornamentation.

Partition—An interior wall that subdivides space within a building.

Pier—A column of masonry used to support other structural members.

Pilaster—A part of a wall that projects not more than one-half of its own width beyond the outside or inside face of a wall.

Pitch—Inclination or slope.

Plan—A drawing representing any one of the cross-sections of a building.

Plaster—A mixture of lime, cement, and sand used to cover inside or outside wall surfaces.

Plate—The horizontal member of a wall frame to which the studs are attached.

Rafter—One of a series of structural members of a roof.

Reinforced concrete—Concrete poured around steel bars or steel meshwork, in such a manner that the two materials act together to resist force.

Riser—The vertical stair member between two consecutive stair treads.

R-value—A measure of resistance to heat transfer.

Sheathing—Structural covering; boards or prefabricated panels that are attached to the exterior studding or rafters.

Siding—The finish covering of the outside walls of a frame building.

Sill—The lowest member of the frame of a structure, usually horizontal, resting on the foundation. Also, the lower member of a window or exterior door frame.

Specifications—A written document stipulating the quality of materials and workmanship required for a job.

Stud—One of a series of vertical wood or metal structural members in walls and partitions. In most modern frame buildings, the studs are set 16 inches apart.

Subfloor—Boards or panels laid directly on floor joists, over which a finished floor will be laid.

Timber—A piece of lumber five inches or larger in its least dimension.

Trim—The finish materials in a building (moldings, etc.).

Trimmer—The stud into which a header is framed; it adds strength to the side of the opening.

Truss—A structural unit, usually triangular in shape, which provides rigid support over wide spans.

Weephole—A small hole in the foundation wall to drain water to the outside.

Chapter Summary

1. A real estate agent is often asked to compare buying a home to renting one. The advantages of renting include less financial commitment and risk, fewer maintenance responsibilities, greater mobility, and facilities a homeowner often could not afford. The advantages of buying include security, satisfaction in ownership, privacy, and freedom from restrictions. Although a mortgage payment is typically much larger than a rental payment, property appreciation, equity, and tax deductions make buying less expensive than renting over the long run.

2. It is important to evaluate certain factors when choosing a home. A real estate agent helping a customer choose a home should evaluate the type of home best suited to the buyer, the neighborhood, the site, and the exterior and interior design.

3. It is wise for homeowners to protect their investments with property insurance, which comes in a variety of forms tailored to meet the individual homeowner's needs. Many residential lenders require at least some property insurance coverage. Insurance can be purchased for condominiums, mobile homes, and older homes in addition to the traditional single-family home. Renters can also purchase insurance to protect their personal property. In some areas, a homeowner may be required to purchase flood insurance depending on the home's location and the type of loan used to finance the home.

4. To accurately assess the value of a home, a real estate agent needs to be able to judge the quality of the construction. It is important to be familiar with common construction techniques and materials, and to have some understanding of the technical systems (plumbing, wiring, heating, and cooling). Knowing how to read plans and specifications can be very useful, especially when dealing with new construction.

Key Terms

Modular home—Prefabricated home that is assembled in sections in a factory and delivered to a building site, where the sections are joined together.

Duplex—Two or more separate residential units under one roof.

Planned unit development—A specially zoned, planned community that groups residential units together to maximize the amount of green space.

Mixed-use development—Self-contained development that combines retail, residential, and recreational facilities in one building.

Replacement cost—The cost of replacing a damaged structure with a new structure, covered by most property insurance policies.

Actual cash value—The cost of replacing a damaged structure, less any accumulated depreciation on the structure.

Endorsement—Additional insurance purchased by a policyholder to cover a specific risk, such as flooding or earthquakes.

Plans—Detailed technical drawings of the vertical and horizontal cross-sections of a building, used as a guide in its construction.

Specifications—Text that accompanies the plans of a building, describing the types of materials and the standards of workmanship to be used in the construction.

Chapter Quiz

1. Building construction quality is assured through:
   a) the planning commission
   b) zoning ordinances
   c) building codes
   d) None of the above

2. All of the following are likely to go up eventually; which of them will probably increase the most gradually?
   a) A rental payment
   b) A fixed-rate mortgage payment
   c) An adjustable-rate mortgage payment
   d) All of the above will increase at the same rate

3. All of the following lots contain the same area. Which would generally be considered the most desirable?
   a) A rectangular lot with a gentle slope
   b) A triangular lot with a steep slope
   c) A triangular lot with a gentle slope
   d) A level T-shaped lot

4. Which of the following is considered a drawback in a floor plan?
   a) A door leads directly from the kitchen to the garage
   b) The front door leads directly into the living room
   c) The separate dining room is right next to the kitchen
   d) The bedrooms are isolated from the kitchen and family room

5. The value of a home is enhanced if:
   a) the neighborhood has rental properties as well as owner-occupied homes
   b) the block has retail businesses as well as homes
   c) strict zoning laws have made the lots and houses in the neighborhood similar to one another
   d) All of the above

6. When comparing a mortgage payment to a rental payment, all of the following should be taken into account except:
   a) the landlord's equity in the rental property
   b) appreciation of the homeowner's property
   c) the federal tax deduction for mortgage interest
   d) whether the mortgage interest rate is fixed or adjustable

7. A house with many horizontal projections and vertical lines, and with large areas of glass, is classified as:
   a) contemporary
   b) ranch
   c) colonial
   d) Spanish

8. Which of the following is an advantage of renting, as opposed to owning, a home?
   a) Security and stability
   b) Appreciation
   c) Federal tax deduction
   d) Mobility

9. Which of the following is not drywall material?
   a) Wallboard
   b) Plywood
   c) Sheetrock
   d) Plaster

10. R-value is a term used in reference to:
    a) a type of loan
    b) a zoning classification
    c) a government agency
    d) insulation

11. Which of the following is the value an insurer will pay for damaged property under a standard policy?
    a) Replacement cost
    b) Fair market value
    c) Actual cash value
    d) None of the above

12. Jenny needs homeowner's insurance. She wants all perils to the structure and her personal property covered. She buys a/an:
    a) special form
    b) all-risk policy
    c) comprehensive form
    d) Either b) or c)

13. The Salisburys' home is located in a flood zone. They may not be required to purchase flood insurance if:
    a) a flood certificate has been issued for the home
    b) their homeowner's policy covers water damage
    c) the home is above the base flood elevation
    d) All of the above

14. A residential homeowner's policy may be suspended in which of the following circumstances?
    a) The home is left unoccupied for 90 days
    b) The owner fails to register the home as a historic site
    c) The owner opens a small coffee shop on the first floor
    d) Both a) and c)

15. The portion of the foundation wall that supports the weight of the structure is called the:
    a) sill plate
    b) footing
    c) stringer
    d) girder

Answer Key

1. c) Building codes are local ordinances that set standards for construction quality.

2. b) A fixed-rate mortgage payment will increase very gradually, as property taxes and mortgage insurance premiums go up.

3. a) Rectangular lots are preferred to odd-shaped lots because more of the area can be used efficiently. Steeply sloping lots are often difficult to build on and are unstable, so level land or a gentle slope is preferable.

4. b) It is a disadvantage to have the front door open directly into the living room (rather than into an entry hall), since it is then necessary to pass through the living room to get to the rest of the house. All of the other design features listed are considered advantages.

5. c) While few people would like all of the houses on their street to be identical, a reasonable degree of conformity is considered desirable and enhances the value of the homes.

6. a) The landlord's equity in the rental property is not likely to have much effect on the rental payment. However, appreciation, mortgage rates, and federal and state income tax deductions do affect how mortgage payments compare to rental payments.

7. a) The house described is contemporary, or modern, in design. One of the main features of contemporary houses is many large windows.

8. d) It is much easier and less expensive to move out of a rental than to sell a home and buy a new one. All of the other answers are advantages of owning a home.

9. d) Drywall material (unlike plaster) does not require the addition of water during construction.

10. d) R-value is a measure of insulating capacity.

11. a) Under a standard policy, an insurer will pay the replacement cost of the damaged structure.

12. d) A comprehensive or all-risk form covers all perils (except those specifically excluded) to the structure and personal property of the insured.

13. c) Homes that are built above the base flood elevation (100-year flood mark) may not have to be covered by flood insurance.

14. d) An insurer may suspend a homeowner's policy if the building is exposed to increased hazard and risk as a result of some action taken by the insured, such as changing the use from residential to commercial or leaving the building unoccupied for more than 60 days.

15. b) The footing is the wide portion of the base of the foundation that bears the weight of the structure.

Chapter 19

Real Estate Math

- I. Solving Math Problems
  - A. Four-step approach
    1. Read the question
    2. Write down the formula
    3. Substitute
    4. Calculate
  - B. Decimal numbers
    1. Converting fractions
    2. Converting percentages
    3. Decimal calculations
- II. Area Problems
  - A. Squares and rectangles
  - B. Triangles
  - C. Odd shapes
- III. Volume Problems
- IV. Percentage Problems
  - A. Solving percentage problems
  - B. Commission problems
  - C. Loan problems
    1. Interest rates
    2. Principal balance
  - D. Profit or loss problems
  - E. Capitalization problems
- V. Tax Assessment Problems
- VI. Seller's Net Problems
- VII. Proration Problems
  - A. Property taxes
  - B. Insurance premiums
  - C. Rent
  - D. Mortgage interest

Chapter Overview

Real estate agents use math constantly: to calculate their commissions, to determine the square footage of homes they are listing or selling, to prorate closing costs, and so on. Electronic calculators make all of these tasks much easier than they once were, but it is still necessary to have a basic grasp of the math involved. This chapter provides step-by-step instructions for solving a wide variety of real estate math problems.

Solving Math Problems

We're going to begin our discussion of real estate math with a simple approach to solving math problems. Master this four-step process, and you'll be able to solve most math problems you are likely to encounter.

1. Read the question

The most important step is to thoroughly read and understand the question. You must know what you are looking for before you can successfully solve any math problem. Once you know what you want to find out (for example, the area, the commission amount, or the total profit), you'll be able to decide which formula to use.

2. Write down the formula

Write down the correct formula for the problem you need to solve. For example, the area formula is *Area* = *Length* × *Width*, which is abbreviated $A = L \times W$. Formulas for each type of problem are presented throughout this chapter, and there is a complete list at the end of the chapter.

3. Substitute

Substitute the relevant numbers from the problem into the formula. Sometimes there are numbers in the problem that you will not use. It's not unusual for a math problem to contain unnecessary information, which is why it is very important to read the question first and determine what you are looking for. The formula will help you distinguish between the relevant and irrelevant information given in the problem.

In some problems you will be able to substitute numbers into the formula without any additional steps, but in other problems one or more preliminary steps will be necessary. For instance, you may have to convert fractions to decimals.

4. Calculate

Once you have substituted the numbers into the formula, you are ready to perform the calculations to find the unknown—the component of the formula that was not given in the problem. Most of the formulas have the same basic form: $A = L \times W$. The problem will give you two of the three numbers (or information to enable you to find two of the numbers) and then you will either have to divide or multiply to find the third number, which is the solution to the problem.

Whether you'll multiply or divide is determined by which component in the formula is the unknown. For example, the formula $A = L \times W$ may be converted into two other formulas. All three formulas are equivalent, but they are put into different forms depending on the element to be discovered.

- If the quantity A (the area) is unknown, then the following formula is used: $A = L \times W$. The number L is **multiplied** by W. The product of L multiplied by W is A.
- If the quantity L (the length) is unknown, the following formula is used: $L = A \div W$. The number A is **divided** by W. The quotient of A divided by W is L.
- If the quantity W (the width) is unknown, the following formula is used: $W = A \div L$. The number A is **divided** by L. The quotient of A divided by L is W.

Thus, the formula $A = L \times W$ may be used three different ways depending on which quantity is unknown. For the examples below, assume the area of a rectangle is 800 square feet, the length is 40 feet, and the width is 20 feet.

$A = L \times W$	$L = A \div W$	$W = A \div L$
$A = 40' \times 20'$	$L = 800$ *Sq. ft.* $\div 20'$	$W = 800$ *Sq. ft.* $\div 40'$
$40' \times 20' = 800$ *Sq. ft.*	800 *Sq. ft.* $\div 20' = 40'$	800 *Sq. ft.* $\div 40' = 20'$

After you've substituted the numbers given in the problem into the formula, you might have trouble deciding whether you're supposed to multiply or divide. It may help to compare your equation to the very familiar calculation $2 \times 3 = 6$. If the unknown component of your equation is in the same position as the 6 in $2 \times 3 = 6$, then you need to multiply the two given numbers to find the unknown.

If the unknown component is in the 2 position or the 3 position, you need to divide. You'll divide the given number in the 6 position by the other given number to find the unknown.

$? \times 3 = 6$ *becomes* $6 \div 3 = 2$	$2 \times ? = 6$ *becomes* $6 \div 2 = 3$

Now let's apply the four-step approach to an example. Suppose a room is 10 feet wide and 15 feet long. How many square feet does it contain?

1. **Read the question**. This problem asks you to find the square footage or area of a rectangular room. So you'll need the area formula for a rectangle.

2. **Write down the formula**. *Area* = *Length* × *Width*

3. **Substitute**. Substitute the numbers given in the problem into the formula. The length of the rectangle measures 15 feet, and the width measures 10 feet: $A = 15' \times 10'$.

4. **Calculate**. Multiply *Length* times *Width* to get the answer: $15' \times 10' = 150$ *Sq. ft.* Thus, $A = 150$. The area of the room is 150 square feet.

Suppose the problem gave you different pieces of information about the same room: the area is 150 square feet and it's 10 feet wide. How long is the room? Again, follow the four-step approach.

1. **Read the question**. You're asked to find the length or width of a rectangle. You'll need the area formula again.

2. **Write down the formula**. $Area = Length \times Width$

3. **Substitute**. Substitute the numbers given in the problem into the formula: $150 = L \times 10'$.

4. **Calculate**. The length of the rectangle is the unknown. Thus, the basic area formula is converted into a division problem to find the length: 150 *Sq. ft.* $\div 10' = 15'$. The result of 150 divided by 10 is 15. The length of the rectangle, or of the room, is therefore 15 feet.

Decimal Numbers

To carry out a calculation, it's easier to work with decimal numbers than with fractions or percentages. So if a problem presents you with fractions or percentages, you'll usually convert them into decimal numbers.

Converting Fractions. To convert a fraction into decimal form, divide the top number of the fraction (the numerator) by the bottom number of the fraction (the denominator).

> **Example:** To change ¾ into a decimal, divide 3 (the top number) by 4 (the bottom number): $3 \div 4 = .75$.

> **Example:** To convert ⅔ into a decimal, divide 2 (the top number) by 3 (the bottom number): $2 \div 3 = .66667$.

If you don't already know them, it's useful to memorize the decimal equivalents of the most common fractions:

$\frac{1}{4} = .25$

$\frac{1}{2} = .5$

$\frac{3}{4} = .75$

Converting Percentages. To solve a problem involving a percentage, you'll first convert the percentage into a decimal number, then convert the decimal answer back into percentage form.

To convert a percentage to a decimal, remove the percent sign and move the decimal point two places to the left. It may be necessary to add a zero.

Example:

98% becomes .98

5% becomes .05

32.5% becomes .325

17.5% becomes .175

To convert a decimal into a percentage, do just the opposite. Move the decimal point two places to the right and add a percent sign.

Example:

.15 becomes 15%

.08 becomes 08%

.095 becomes 09.5%

The percent key on a calculator performs the conversion of a percentage to a decimal number automatically. On most calculators, you can key in the digits and press the percent key, and the calculator will display the percentage in decimal form.

Decimal Calculations. Calculators handle decimal numbers in exactly the same way as whole numbers. If you enter a decimal number into the calculator with the decimal point in the correct place, the calculator will do the rest. But if you're working without a calculator, you'll need to apply the following rules.

To add or subtract decimals, put the numbers in a column with their decimal points lined up.

Example: To add 3.75, 14.62, 1.245, 679, 1,412.8, and 1.9, put the numbers in a column with the decimal points lined up as shown below, then add them together.

```
      3.75
     14.62
      1.245
    679.0
  1,412.8
+     1.9
-----------
  2,113.315
```

To multiply decimal numbers, first do the multiplication without worrying about the decimal points. Then put a decimal point into the answer in the correct place. The answer should have as many decimal places (that is, numbers to the right of its decimal point) as the total number of decimal places in the numbers that were multiplied. So count the decimal places in the numbers you are multiplying and put the decimal point the same number of places to the left in the answer.

Example: Multiply 24.6 times 16.7. The two numbers contain a total of two decimal places.

$$\begin{array}{r} 24.6 \\ \times\ 16.7 \\ \hline 410.82 \end{array}$$

In some cases, it will be necessary to include one or more zeros in the answer to have the correct number of decimal places.

Example: Multiply .2 times .4. There is a total of two decimal places.

$$\begin{array}{r} .2 \\ \times\ .4 \\ \hline .08 \end{array}$$

A zero has to be included in the answer in order to move the decimal point two places left.

To divide by a decimal number, move the decimal point in the denominator (the number you're dividing the other number by) all the way to the right. Then move the decimal point in the numerator (the number that you're dividing) the same number of places to the right. (In some cases it will be necessary to add one or more zeros to the numerator in order to move the decimal point the correct number of places.)

Example: Divide 26.145 by 1.5. First move the decimal point in 1.5 all the way to the right (in this case, that's only one place). Then move the decimal point in 26.145 the same number of places to the right.

26.145 ÷ 1.5 becomes 261.45 ÷ 15

Now divide. *261.45 ÷ 15 = 17.43*

Remember, these steps are unnecessary if you're using a calculator. If the numbers are keyed in correctly, the calculator will automatically give you an answer with the decimal point in the correct place.

Area Problems

A real estate agent often needs to calculate the area of a lot, a building, or a room. Area is usually stated in square feet or square yards. The formula to be used for the calculation depends on the shape of the area in question. It may be a square, a rectangle, a triangle, or some combination of those shapes.

Squares and Rectangles

As stated earlier, the formula for finding the area of a square or a rectangle is $A = L \times W$.

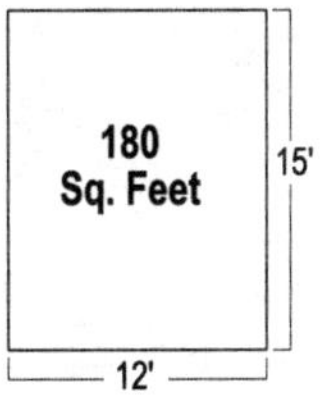

Example: If a rectangular room measures 15 feet along one wall and 12 feet along the adjoining wall, how many square feet of carpet would be required to cover the floor?

1. **Read the question**. You're being asked to find the area (the square footage) of a rectangle.
2. **Write down the formula**. $A = L \times W$
3. **Substitute**. $A = 15' \times 12'$
4. **Calculate**. Since the quantity A is unknown, multiply L times W for the answer: $15' \times 12' = 180$ *Sq. ft.* 180 square feet of carpet are needed to cover the floor.

Now take the problem one step further. If carpet is on sale for $12 per square yard, how much would it cost to carpet the room?

1. **Read the question**. You're first being asked to determine how many square feet there are in a square yard, and then to determine how many square yards there are in 180 square feet. A square yard is a square that measures one yard on each side. There are three feet in a yard.
2. **Write down the formula**. $A = L \times W$
3. **Substitute**. $A = 3' \times 3'$
4. **Calculate**. Since the quantity A is the unknown, multiply L times W: $3' \times 3' = 9$ *Sq. ft.*

   So there are 9 square feet in a square yard. Now divide 180 by 9 to see how many square yards there are in 180 square feet: $180 \div 9' = 20$ *Sq. yd.*

   Now multiply the number of square yards (20) by the cost per square yard ($12): *20 × $12 = $240 Cost to carpet room.*

Triangles

The formula for finding the area of a triangle is:

$$\begin{array}{r} Height \\ \underline{\times \tfrac{1}{2}\, Base} \\ Area \end{array} \quad \text{or} \quad Area = \tfrac{1}{2}\, Base \times Height$$

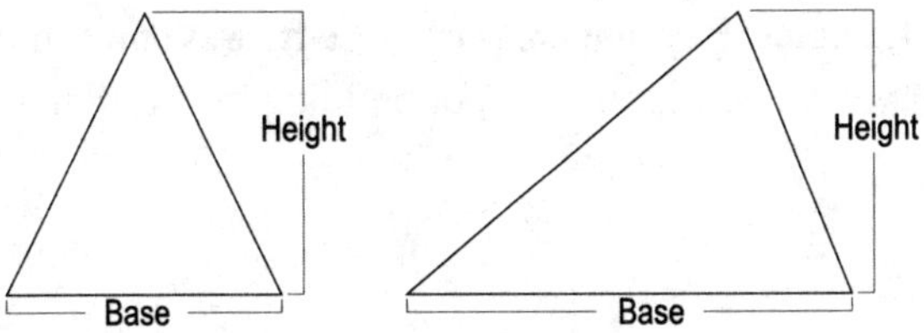

Example: If commercial building lots in a certain neighborhood are selling for approximately $5 per square foot, approximately how much should the lot pictured below sell for?

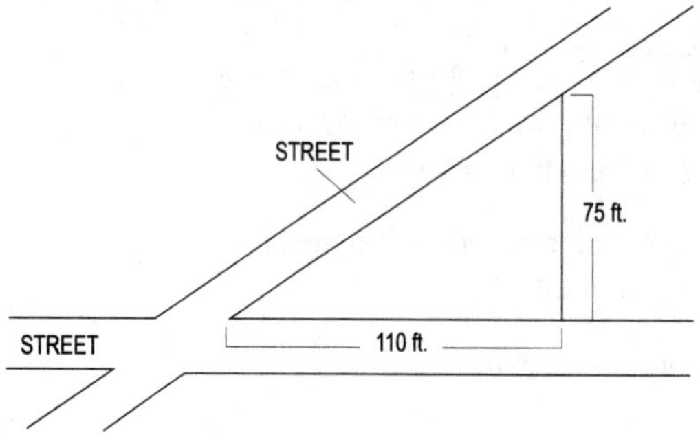

1. **Write down the formula.** $A = \frac{1}{2} B \times H$
2. **Substitute.** Area = *55′ (½ of 110)* × *75′*
3. **Calculate.** *75′* × *55′* = *4,125 Sq. ft.*

The order of multiplication doesn't matter. You can multiply 110 times 75 and then divide it in half. Or you can divide 110 by 2 and then multiply the result by 75. Or you can divide 75 by 2 and then multiply the result by 110. Whichever way you do it, the answer will be the same.

	Step 1	Step 2	Answer
a)	*110 × 75 = 8,250*	*8,250 ÷ 2 = 4,125*	*4,125 Sq. ft.*
b)	*110 ÷ 2 = 55*	*55 × 75 = 4,125*	*4,125 Sq. ft.*
c)	*75 ÷ 2 = 37.75*	*37.5 × 110 = 4,125*	*4,125 Sq. ft.*

The lot contains 4,125 square feet. If similar lots are selling for about $5 per square foot, this lot should sell for about $20,625.

4,125	*Square feet*
× $5	*Per square foot*
$20,625	*Selling price*

Odd Shapes

The best approach to finding the area of an odd-shaped figure is to divide it up into squares, rectangles, and triangles. Find the areas of those figures and add them all up to arrive at the area of the odd-shaped lot, room, or building in question.

Example: If the lot pictured below is leased on a 50-year lease for $3 per square foot per year, with rental payments made monthly, how much would the monthly rent be?

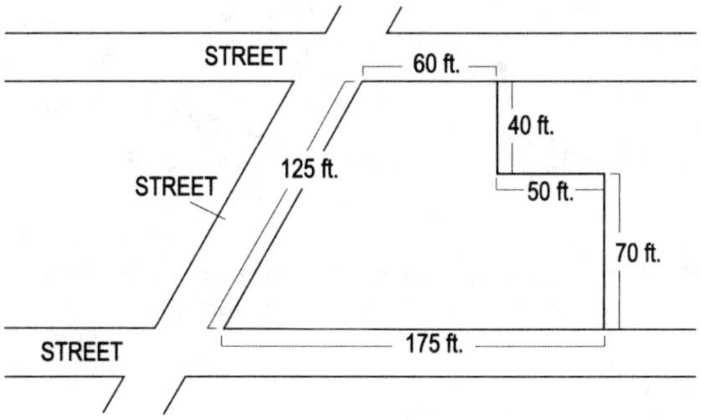

First, divide the lot up into rectangles and triangles.

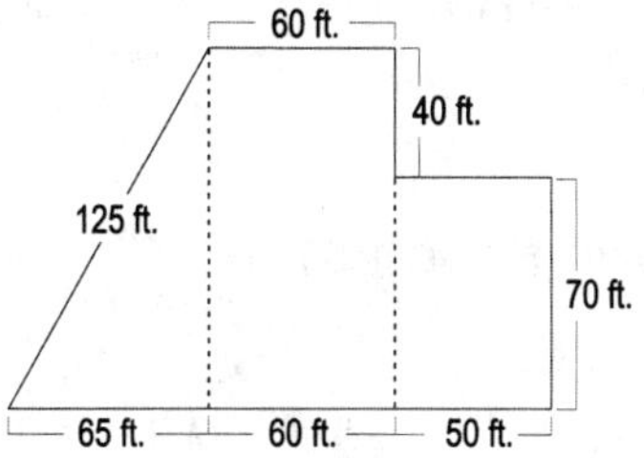

The next step is to find the area of each of the following figures. The height of the triangle is determined by adding together the 70-foot border of the small rectangle and the 40-foot border of the large rectangle, as shown above.

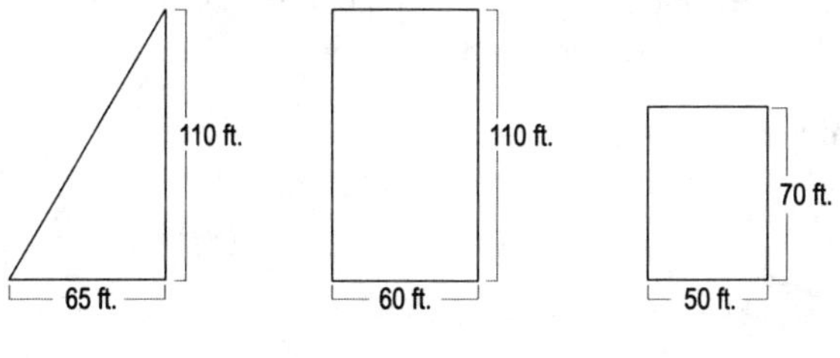

First, find the area of the triangle.

1. **Write down the formula.** $A = \frac{1}{2}\ Base \times Height$
2. **Substitute.** $A = 32.5' \ (\frac{1}{2} \ of \ 65') \times 110'$
3. **Calculate.** $32.5' \times 110' = 3{,}575 \ Sq. ft.$

Then, find the area of the large rectangle.

1. **Write down the formula.** $A = Length \times Width$
2. **Substitute.** $A = 110' \times 60'$
3. **Calculate.** $110' \times 60' = 6{,}600 \ Sq. ft.$

Next, find the area of the small rectangle.

1. **Write down the formula.** *A = Length × Width*

2. **Substitute.** *A = 70′ × 50′*

3. **Calculate.** *50′ × 70′ = 3,500 Sq. ft.*

Finally, add the three areas together to find the area of the entire lot: *3,575 + 6,600 + 3,500 = 13,675 Total square feet.*

The lot contains 13,675 square feet. At $3 per square foot per year, the annual rent would be $41,025.

13,675	*Square feet*
× $3	*Rent per square foot*
$41,025	*Annual rent*

The monthly rental payment would be one-twelfth of the annual rent: *$41,025 ÷ 12 = $3,418.75.* Thus, the monthly rental payment for this odd-shaped lot is $3,418.75.

Volume Problems

Occasionally you may need to calculate the volume of a three-dimensional space. Volume is usually stated in cubic feet or cubic yards. A formula for calculating volume can be stated as: *Volume = Length × Width × Height*, or *V = L × W × H.* It's the same as the area formula, except it has one added element: *H*, the height of the space being measured.

Example: The floor of a storage unit measures 13 feet 6 inches by 20 feet, and it has a 12-foot ceiling. What is the volume of the unit in cubic yards?

1. **Write down the formula.** *V = L × W × H*

2. **Substitute.** *V = 20′ × 13.5′ × 12′*

3. **Calculate.**

Step 1	Step 2
20′	*270 Square feet*
× 13.5′	*× 12′*
270 Square feet	*3,240 Cubic feet*

4. **Now convert the cubic feet into cubic yards.** As you saw earlier, a square yard measures 3 feet by 3 feet, or 9 square feet. A cubic yard measures 3 feet by 3 feet by 3 feet, or 27 cubic feet. Divide the volume of the storage area in cubic feet by 27 to find the volume in cubic yards: *3,240 ÷ 27 = 120 Cubic yards*. The volume of the storage space is 120 cubic yards.

Percentage Problems

Many real estate math problems involve percentages. This includes problems about brokerage commissions, interest on mortgage loans, property appreciation or depreciation, and capitalization.

Solving Percentage Problems

To solve percentage problems, you'll usually convert the percentage into a decimal number, calculate, and then convert the answer back into percentage form. As explained earlier, a percentage is converted into a decimal number by removing the percent sign and moving the decimal point two places to the left. If the percentage is a single digit (for example, 7%), it will be necessary to add a zero (.07). To convert a decimal number into a percentage, you reverse those steps: move the decimal point two places to the right and add the percent sign.

In a math problem, whenever something is expressed as a percentage "of" another number, that indicates that you should multiply that other number by the percentage. For instance, what is 75% of $40,000?

Step 1	Step 2
75% becomes .75	*$40,000*
	× .75
	$30,000

Basically, percentage problems ask you to find a part of a whole. The whole is a larger figure, such as a property's sales price. The part is a smaller figure, such as a broker's commission. The general formula might be stated thus: *A percentage of the whole equals the part.* This can be written as an equation: *Part = Whole × Percentage.*

Example: A house is listed for sale at a price of $172,000, with an agreement to pay the broker a commission of 6% of the sales price. The property sells for $170,000. How much is the commission?

1. **Write down the formula.** $P = W \times \%$

2. **Substitute.** Change the percentage (6%) into a decimal number (.06) first: *P = $170,000 × .06.*

3. **Calculate.**

$170,000	*Sales price*
× .06	*Commission rate*
$10,200	*Commission*

The broker's commission is $10,200.

In some percentage problems, the part is given and you're asked to calculate either the whole or the percentage. For those problems, you'll need to rearrange the percentage formula into a division problem. If the whole is the unknown, divide the part by the percentage: *Whole = Part ÷ Percentage.*

If the percentage is the unknown, divide the part by the whole: *Percentage = Part ÷ Whole.*

Notice that in either case, you'll be dividing the value of the part by either the whole (to determine the percentage) or by the percentage (to determine the whole).

Commission Problems

Like the example above, most commission problems can be solved with the general percentage formula: *Part = Whole × Percentage.*

The percentage is the commission rate, and the whole is the amount that the commission is based on. In most problems, this will be the sales price of a piece of property. The part is the amount of the commission.

Example: A listing agreement provides for a commission of 7% of the sales price to be paid to the broker. The broker has agreed to pay his salesperson 60% of the commission. How much will the salesperson receive if the property sells for $145,000?

1. **Write down the formula.** *P = W × %*
2. **Substitute.** Change the percentage (7%) to a decimal number (.07): *P = $145,000 × .07.*
3. **Calculate.** The part is the unknown quantity, so the percentage is multiplied by the whole.

$145,000	*Sales price*
× .07	*Commission rate*
$10,150	*Total commission*

The total commission is $10,150. The salesperson is entitled to 60% of the total commission. Apply the percentage formula again to determine the amount of the salesperson's share.

1. **Write down the formula.** *P = W × %*
2. **Substitute.** Convert the percentage (60%) to a decimal number (.60): *P = $10,150 × .60.*
3. **Calculate.**

$10,150	*Total commission*
× .60	*Salesperson's percentage*
$6,090	*Salesperson's share*

The following example illustrates another form that commission problems can take.

Example: A listing agreement provided for a two-tiered commission based on the property's sales price. The commission would be 7% of the first $100,000 and 5% of any amount over $100,000. If the commission was $8,250, what was the sales price?

1. **Read the question.** You're given the commission rates and the amount of the commission, and then asked to find the sales price. Your first step in the process is to find out how much of the commission amount is attributable to the first $100,000 of the sales price.

2. **Write down the formula.** $P = W \times \%$

3. **Substitute,** converting the percentage to a decimal: $P = \$100{,}000 \times .07$.

4. **Calculate.** $\$100{,}000 \times .07 = \$7{,}000$

So $7,000 of the commission is based on the first $100,000 of the sales price. Next, subtract to find the amount of the rest of the commission.

$8,250	*Total commission*
– 7,000	*Commission from first $100,000*
$1,250	

Now you know that out of the total commission, $1,250 is attributable to the part of the sales price in excess of $100,000. You can use that figure along with the second-tier commission rate (5% of the amount over $100,000) to determine by how much the sales price exceeded $100,000.

1. **Write down the formula.** $P = W \times \%$

2. **Substitute,** converting the percentage to a decimal: $\$1{,}250 = W \times .05$.

3. **Calculate.** The quantity W (the whole) is the unknown. To isolate the unknown, the basic formula must be turned into a division problem. The part divided by the percentage equals the whole: $\$1{,}250 \div .05 = \$25{,}000$.

This shows that the portion of the sales price in excess of $100,000 amounted to $25,000. Thus, the total sales price is $100,000 plus $25,000, or $125,000.

Loan Problems

Loan problems include interest problems and principal balance problems. These can be solved using the general percentage formula: *Part = Whole × Percentage.* Here, the part is the amount of the interest, the whole is the loan amount or principal balance, and the percentage is the interest rate.

Example: Henry borrows $5,000 for one year and agrees to pay 7% interest. How much interest will he be required to pay?

1. **Write down the formula.** $P = W \times \%$

2. **Substitute.** $P = \$5{,}000 \times .07$

3. **Calculate.**

$5,000	*Loan amount*
× .07	*Interest rate*
$350	*Interest*

Henry will pay $350 in interest.

Interest Rates. Interest rates are expressed as annual rates—a certain percentage per year. Some problems present you with monthly, quarterly, or semi-annual interest payments instead of the annual amount. In that case, you'll need to multiply the payment amount stated in the problem to determine the annual amount before you substitute the numbers into the formula.

Example: If $450 in interest accrues on a $7,200 interest-only loan in six months, what is the annual interest rate?

1. **Read the question**. You're asked to find the annual interest rate, but the interest amount given in the problem ($450) accrued in only six months. The annual interest amount would be double that, or $900.

2. **Write down the formula**. $P = W \times \%$

3. **Substitute**. For the part (the interest amount), be sure to use the annual figure ($900): *$900 = $7,200 × Percentage.*

4. **Calculate**. Rearrange the formula to isolate the unknown (in this case, the percentage). The part is divided by the whole to determine the percentage: *$900 ÷ $7,200 = .125.*

Convert the decimal number back into a percentage: .125 becomes 12.5%. Thus, the annual interest rate is 12½%.

Principal Balance. Some loan problems ask you to determine a loan's current principal balance at a certain point in the loan term.

Example: A home loan has monthly payments of $625, which include principal and 9% interest and $47.50 per month for tax and insurance reserves. If $27.75 of the June 1 payment was applied to the principal, what was the outstanding principal balance during the month of May? (Mortgage interest is paid in arrears, so the June payment includes the interest that accrued during May.)

1. **Write down the formula**. $P = W \times \%$. Once again, in this context the part is the amount of interest, the whole is the loan balance, and the percentage is the interest rate.

2. **Substitute**. First, find the interest portion of the payment by subtracting the reserves and the principal portion.

$625.00	*Total June payment*
47.50	*Reserves*
– 27.75	*Principal*
$549.75	*Interest portion of payment*

Next, multiply the interest portion by 12 to determine the annual interest amount: *$549.75 × 12 = $6,597.*

Now substitute the annual interest amount and rate into the formula: *$6,597 = W × .09.*

3. **Calculate**. Rearrange the formula to isolate the unknown, *W*. This is a division problem. *$6,597 ÷ .09 = $73,300*

The outstanding principal balance for May was $73,300.

Profit or Loss Problems

Profit or loss problems ask you to compare the cost or value of a piece of property at an earlier point in time with its cost or value at a later point. They can be solved using a variation on the percentage formula. Instead of *Part* = *Whole* × *Percentage*, the formula is stated like this: *Now* = *Then* × *Percentage.*

The *Then* spot in the formula is for the value or cost of the property at an earlier time specified in the problem. The *Now* spot is for the value or cost at a later time. The percentage is 100% plus the percentage of profit or minus the percentage of loss.

The idea is to express the value of the property after a profit or loss (*Now*) as a percentage of the property's value before the profit or loss (*Then*). If there is no profit or loss, the *Now* value is exactly 100% of the *Then* value, because the value has not changed. If there is a profit, the *Now* value will be greater than 100% of the *Then* value, since the value has increased. If there is a loss, the *Now* value will be less than 100% of the *Then* value.

Example: Bonnie bought a house five years ago for $150,000 and sold it this year for 30% more than she paid for it. What did she sell it for?

1. **Write down the formula.** *Now* = *Then* × *%*

2. **Substitute.** To get the percentage, you must add the percentage of profit to or subtract the percentage of loss from 100%. In this case there is a profit, so you add 30% to 100%, then convert it to a decimal number (130% becomes 1.30): *Now* = *$150,000* × *1.30.*

3. **Calculate.** *$150,000* × *1.30* = *$195,000*

Bonnie sold her house for $195,000.

Example: Paul sold his house this year for $210,000. He paid $262,500 for it two years ago. What was the percentage of loss?

1. **Write down the formula.** *Now* = *Then* × *%*

2. **Substitute.** *$210,000* = *$262,500* × *%*

3. **Calculate.** The percentage is the unknown quantity; thus, the formula is rearranged to isolate the percentage: *$210,000* ÷ *$262,500* = *.80 or 80%.*

The *Now* value is 80% of the *Then* value. Subtract 80% from 100% to find the percentage of loss: *100%* – *80%* = *20% Loss.*

Paul took a 20% loss on the sale of his house.

Let's look at another example, except this time there is a profit instead of a loss.

Example: Martha bought her home six years ago for $125,800. She sold it recently for $140,900. What was her percentage of profit?

1. **Write down the formula.** *Now* = *Then* × *%*

2. **Substitute.** *$140,900* = *$125,800* × *%*

3. **Calculate**. Once again, the percentage is the unknown quantity; thus, the formula is rearranged to isolate the percentage: *$140,900 ÷ $125,800 = 1.12 or 112%.*

   The *Now* value is approximately 112% of the *Then* value. Subtract 100% from 112%, and you determine Martha received 100% of what she paid for the house, plus a 12% profit.

Let's try to solve one last variation of this type of problem.

Example: Ken sold his duplex for $280,000, which represents a 16% profit over what he paid for it five years ago. What did Ken originally pay for the property?

1. **Write down the formula**. *Now = Then × %*
2. **Substitute**. *$280,000 = Then × 116%*
3. **Calculate**. In this instance, the unknown is the price Ken originally paid for the duplex; so you isolate the *Then* part of the equation: *$280,000 ÷ 1.16 = $241,379.31.*

The price paid by Ken was $241,379.31.

Some profit or loss problems involve appreciation or depreciation that has accrued at an annual rate over a specified number of years. You solve this type of problem by applying the *Then* and *Now* formula one year at a time.

Example: A property that is currently worth $174,000 has depreciated 3% per year for the past four years. How much was it worth four years ago?

1. **Write down the formula**. *Now = Then × %*
2. **Substitute**. Because the property is worth 3% less than it was one year ago, the percentage is 97% (100% – 3% = 97%): *$174,000 = Then × .97.*
3. **Calculate**. Rearrange the formula to isolate the unknown, the *Then* value: *$174,000 ÷ .97 = $179,381.44.*

   The property was worth $179,381.44 one year ago. Apply the formula to $179,381.44 to determine the property's value two years ago. Repeat the process twice more to find the value four years ago.

   $179,381.44 ÷ .97 = $184,929.31

   $184,929.31 ÷ .97 = $190,648.77

   $190,648.77 ÷ .97 = $196,545.12

The property was worth about $196,545 four years ago.

Capitalization Problems

Capitalization problems involve the capitalization approach to value, a method of real estate appraisal that is discussed in detail in Chapter 13.

The capitalization formula is another variation on the percentage formula. Instead of *Part = Whole × Percentage*, the formula is stated like this: *Income = Value × Capitalization Rate.*

The value here is an investment property's value, or the purchase price an investor should be willing to pay for the property in order to obtain a specified rate of return.

The specified rate of return is the capitalization rate. This is the percentage of return the investor desires on the investment. The desired rate of return varies according to many factors. A higher desired rate of return will mean a higher capitalization rate and a lower value for the property.

The income in the capitalization formula is the annual net income produced by the investment property.

Example: A property produces an annual net income of $26,000. If an investor desires an 11% rate of return, what should he pay for the property?

1. **Write down the formula.** $I = V \times \%$
2. **Substitute.** *$26,000 = V × .11*
3. **Calculate.** Rearrange the formula to isolate *V*, the unknown quantity: *$26,000 ÷ .11 = $236,363.64.*

The investor should be willing to pay approximately $236,364 for the property.

Example: If a property is valued at $100,000 using an 8% capitalization rate, what would its value be using a 10% capitalization rate? First, apply the capitalization formula to determine the property's annual net income.

1. **Write down the formula.** $I = V \times \%$
2. **Substitute.** *I = $100,000 × .08*
3. **Calculate.**

$100,000	*Value*
× .08	*Capitalization rate*
$8,000	*Annual net income*

The net income is $8,000 annually. Now substitute that figure into the formula to find the value at a 10% capitalization rate.

4. **Substitute.** *$8,000 = V × .10*
5. **Calculate.** Rearrange the formula to isolate *V*, the unknown quantity: $8,000 ÷ *.10 = $80,000.*

So the value of the same property using a 10% capitalization rate is $80,000, compared to $100,000 at the 8% rate. As you can see, a higher capitalization rate applied to the same net income results in a lower value for the property.

In some problems, it's necessary to deduct a bad debt/vacancy factor and operating expenses from gross income to arrive at the net income.

Example: A ten-unit apartment building has six units that rent for $800 per month and four units that rent for $850 per month. Allow 5% for vacancies and uncollected rent. Operating expenses include: annual property taxes of $7,200, monthly utilities of $2,475, and maintenance expenses of approximately $13,600 per year. The owner has an outstanding mortgage balance of $257,000 at 8% interest, with monthly payments of $2,150. If an investor requires a 7.5% rate of return, how much should she offer for the property?

1. **Write down the formula.** $I = V \times \%$

2. **Substitute**. Remember that the income referred to in the capitalization formula is annual net income. Thus, it's necessary to calculate the annual net income before substituting. The first step in that process is calculating the annual gross income.

   $800 × 12 months = $9,600/year × 6 units = $57,600
   $850 × 12 months = $10,200/year × 4 units = $40,800
   $98,400

   The gross income is $98,400 per year.

   Next, calculate the bad debt/vacancy factor and deduct it from the gross income to find the effective gross income. The bad debt/vacancy factor is 5% of the gross income.

$98,400	*Gross income*
× .05	
$4,920	*Bad debts and vacancies*

   Thus, the loss to be expected from uncollected rents and vacancies is $4,920 per year.

$98,400	*Gross income*
– 4,920	*Bad debts and vacancies*
$93,480	*Effective gross income*

   The operating expenses must be deducted from the effective gross income to arrive at the net income. Remember, since you are trying to find annual net income, all the expenses must be annual also. The operating expenses add up as follows:

$7,200	*Property taxes*
$29,700	*Utilities (at $2,475 per month)*
+ $13,600	*Maintenance*
$50,500	*Annual operating expenses*

   The annual operating expenses are $50,500. (The mortgage payments are not treated as operating expenses. See Chapter 13.) Subtract the operating expenses from the effective gross income to determine the annual net income.

$93,480	*Effective gross income*
– 50,500	*Annual operating expenses*
$42,980	*Annual net income*

   Now, substitute the net income and the cap rate into the formula $I = V \times \%$: $\$42,980 = V \times .075$.

3. **Calculate**. Rearrange the formula to isolate *V*, the unknown quantity: *$42,980 ÷ .075 = $573,067.*

The investor should be willing to pay approximately $573,067 for the property.

Example: Continuing with the previous example, if an investor paid $750,000 for the apartment building, what capitalization rate was used? (Assume that the property's income and operating expenses were the same.)

1. **Write down the formula.** $V \times \% = I$

2. **Substitute**. You already know the net income from the preceding problem: *$42,980 = $750,000 × %.*

3. **Calculate**. Isolate the unknown quantity, the capitalization rate: *$42,980 ÷ $750,000 = .0573 or 5.73%.*

The investor used a capitalization rate of approximately 5.7%.

A capitalization problem may give you the property's **operating expense ratio** (O.E.R.). The O.E.R. is the percentage of the gross income that is used to pay the annual operating expenses. The remainder is the annual net income.

Example: The property's annual gross income is $480,000, and its O.E.R. is 79%. If an investor wants a 10½% return, how much is the property worth to her?

1. **Write down the formula.** $I = V \times \%$

2. **Substitute**. Calculate the annual operating expenses using the operating expense ratio. Then subtract the operating expenses from the gross income to arrive at the annual net income.

   $480,000 × .79 = $379,200 Annual operating expenses

   $480,000 – $379,200 = $100,800 Annual net income

   Now substitute the income and the cap rate into the formula: *$100,800 = V × .105.*

3. **Calculate**. Rearrange the formula to isolate *V*, the unknown quantity: *$100,800 ÷ .105 = $960,000 Value.*

The investor should be willing to pay $960,000 for the property.

Tax Assessment Problems

Many tax assessment problems can be solved using this formula: *Tax = Assessed Value × Tax Rate*. You may first have to determine the assessed value before you can carry out the rest of the calculations. Assessed value is a property's value for taxation purposes.

Example: According to the tax assessor, the property's market value is $292,300. The applicable assessment ratio is 85%. If the tax rate is 3%, how much is the annual tax amount?

1. **Multiply** the market value by the assessment ratio to determine the assessed value of the property: *$292,300 × 85% = $248,455 Assessed value.*

2. **Substitute** the assessed value and the tax rate into the formula: *Tax = $248,455 × .03.*

3. **Calculate.**

$248,455	*Assessed value*
× .03	*Tax rate*
$7,453.65	*Annual taxes*

The annual taxes for this property are $7,453.65.

In some problems, the tax rate is not stated as a percentage of the assessed value. Instead, it is expressed as a dollar amount per hundred or per thousand dollars of assessed value.

Example: A property with an assessed value of $173,075 is taxed at a rate of $2.35 per hundred dollars of assessed value. How much is the annual tax amount?

1. **Divide** $173,075 by 100 to determine how many hundred dollar increments there are in the assessed value: *$173,075 ÷ 100 = 1,730.75 or 1,731 $100 increments.* (A partial $100 increment would be taxed as one $100 increment.)

2. **Multiply** the number of hundred dollar increments by the tax rate to calculate the annual tax amount.

1,731	*$100 increments*
× $2.35	*Tax rate*
$4,067.85	*Annual taxes*

The annual tax is $4,067.85.

In other problems, the tax rate is expressed as a specified number of mills per dollar of assessed value. A mill is one-tenth of one cent (.001). Ten mills equals one cent, and 100 mills equals 10 cents.

Example: The property's market value is $310,000 and the assessment ratio is 70%. The tax rate is 21 mills per dollar of assessed value. How much is the annual tax amount?

1. **Multiply** the market value by the assessment ratio to find the assessed value.

$310,000	*Market value*
× .70	*Assessment ratio*
$217,000	*Assessed value*

2. **Multiply** the assessed value by the tax rate to determine the tax. In decimal form, 21 mills is .021.

$217,000	*Assessed value*
× .021	*Tax rate*
$4,557	*Annual tax*

The annual tax is $4,557.

Seller's Net Problems

In a seller's net problem, you're told that a seller wants to take away a specified net amount from closing, after paying the broker's commission and other closing costs. You're then asked to calculate how much the property will have to sell for if the seller is to receive the desired net.

Example: The seller wants to net $50,000 from the sale of her home. She will have to pay off her mortgage balance, which is approximately $126,500, and pay $1,560 for repairs, $2,015 for other closing costs, and a 7% broker's commission. What's the minimum sales price that will net the seller $50,000?

1. **Add** the seller's desired net to the costs of sale, excluding the commission.

$50,000	*Seller's net*
126,500	*Mortgage*
1,560	*Repairs*
+ 2,015	*Closing costs*
$180,075	*Total*

$180,075 is the amount that must be left to the seller after the commission has been paid, if she is to be able to pay all of the listed expenses and still have $50,000 left over.

2. **Subtract** the commission rate from 100%: *100% – 7% = 93%.*

3. **Divide** the total from step one by the percentage from step two. Since the commission rate will be 7% of the sales price, the seller's net plus the other costs will have to equal 93% of the sales price: *$180,075 ÷ .93 = $193,629.*

The property will have to sell for approximately $193,629 for the seller to net $50,000.

This may seem counterintuitive at first. At first glance, it may seem that you're applying the commission rate to the closing costs as well as the selling price. But you aren't. This is best understood by working backwards through the problem. By doing so, you'll see that, as in the real world closing process, the commission is subtracted from the selling price, and then the seller's closing costs are subtracted from those proceeds.

Start by calculating the cost of the 7% commission.

$193,629	*Selling price*
× .07	*Commission*
$13,554	

Now subtract the commission and the other closing costs from the gross proceeds, to find the seller's net proceeds.

$193,629	*Selling Price*
13,554	*Commission*
126,500	*Mortgage*
1,560	*Repairs*
– 2,015	*Closing costs*
$50,000	*Net proceeds*

Proration Problems

Proration is the allocation of an expense between two or more parties. As was explained in Chapter 14, prorations are required in real estate closings, where a variety of expenses are prorated based on the closing date.

There are basically three steps in the proration process:

1. Calculate the per diem (daily) rate of the expense.
2. Determine the number of days for which one person is responsible for the expense.
3. Multiply the per diem rate by the number of days to determine the share of the expense that one party is responsible for: *Share = Rate × Days.*

To determine the per diem rate of an annual expense, divide the amount of the expense by 365 days, or 366 in a leap year. Some problems will instruct you to divide by 360 days instead, to simplify the calculation. (A 360-day year is sometimes referred to as a banker's year, as opposed to a calendar year.)

To determine the per diem rate of a monthly expense when you are prorating on the basis of a calendar year, divide the amount of the expense by the number of days in that particular month. Alternatively, to simplify the calculation, you may be instructed to base your prorations on a banker's year, which means that every month has 30 days, including February.

We'll present you with a series of examples concerning the proration of various expenses: property taxes, hazard insurance, rent, and mortgage interest. See Chapter 14 for more information about these expenses.

Property Tax Prorations

Property taxes are an annual expense. However, property tax proration problems may require some additional information. In some states, the year used for property tax purposes begins on a different date than January 1 (property tax years starting on July 1 are the most common alternative). Also, the payments are sometimes divided into installments. Thus it is important to be aware of the time period for which a property tax expense is being prorated.

At closing, the taxes may or may not have been paid yet. If they've already been paid, the buyer will owe the seller a share of the taxes. If they haven't been paid, the seller will owe the buyer a share. Either way, the proration process is essentially the same.

Example: The closing date is February 3, and the seller has already paid the annual property taxes, which were \$2,045. At closing, the seller is entitled to a credit for the tax amount covering the period from February 3 through June 30 (the tax year begins on July 1). The same amount will be a debit for the buyer. How much will the buyer owe the seller for the property taxes? Use a 360-day year with 30-day months for your calculations.

1. **Calculate the per diem rate** for the property taxes, using a 360-day year: *\$2,045 ÷ 360 = 5.68.*

2. **Count the number of days** that the buyer is responsible for, using 30-day months.

28 days	*February 3 through 30*
30 days	*March*
30 days	*April*
30 days	*May*
+ 30 days	*June*
148 days	

3. **Substitute** the rate and number of days into the formula ($S = R \times D$), then calculate.

148	*Days*
× \$5.68	*Per diem*
\$840.64	*Credit to seller*

At closing, the buyer will be debited \$840.64 and the seller will be credited \$840.64 for the property taxes from February 3 through the end of the tax year.

In the following example, the taxes haven't been paid yet. You're given the seller's share of the taxes and asked to calculate the annual tax amount.

Example: The seller hasn't paid any portion of the annual taxes. The property tax year starts on January 1, and the closing is scheduled for March 21. At closing, the seller will owe the buyer \$663.60 for the taxes; the buyer will be responsible for taxes on the day of closing. How much was the annual tax bill? This time, use a 365-day year and exact-day months in your calculations. The buyer's responsibility for the taxes begins on the day of closing.

1. **Write down the formula.** $S = R \times D$

2. **Substitute.** First add up the number of days that the seller is responsible for.

31 days	*January*
28 days	*February*
+ 20 days	*March*
79 days	

Substitute the seller's share and the number of days into the formula: $\$663.60 = R \times 79$.

3. **Calculate**. Rearrange the formula to isolate R, the unknown quantity: *$663.60 ÷ 79 = $8.40 Per diem.*

The per diem rate is $8.40. Multiply that by 365 to arrive at the annual tax amount.

365	*Days*
× $8.40	*Per diem*
$3,066	*Annual taxes*

The annual taxes were $3,066.

Insurance Prorations

A seller is entitled to a refund from the hazard insurance company for any prepaid insurance coverage extending beyond the closing date.

Example: The Morgans are selling their house, and the transaction is closing on May 12. They paid an annual hazard insurance premium of $810 that provides coverage through the end of October. If the insurance company does not charge the sellers for the day of closing, how much of the premium will be refunded to them? Base your calculations on a 360-day year.

1. **Calculate the per diem rate** for the insurance, using a 360-day year: *$810 ÷ 360 = 2.25 Per diem.*

2. **Add up the number of days** for which the sellers are owed a refund, using 30-day months.

19 days	*May*
30 days	*June*
30 days	*July*
30 days	*August*
30 days	*September*
+ 30 days	*October*
169 days	

3. **Substitute** the rate and number of days into the formula ($S = R \times D$), then calculate.

169	*Days*
× $2.25	*Per diem*
$380.25	*Credit to seller*

The insurance company will refund $380.25 to the sellers.

Rent Prorations

If the property being sold is rental property, the seller will owe the buyer a prorated share of any rent that has been paid in advance.

Example: A ten-unit apartment building is being sold, with the closing scheduled for April 23. Four of the units rent for $1,500 per month, and the other six rent for

$1,200 per month. All of the tenants paid their April rent on time. The parties agree that the buyer is entitled to the rents from the day of closing. What share of the prepaid rents will the seller owe the buyer at closing?

1. **Determine the total amount** of rent owed for April.

   $1,500 × 4 = $6,000

   $1,200 × 6 = $7,200

   $6,000 + $7,200 = $13,200

2. **Calculate the per diem rate** for the month of April: *$13,200 ÷ 30 = $440 Per diem.*

3. **Determine the number of days** of rent the buyer is entitled to, beginning on the closing date. April 23 through April 30 is eight days.

4. **Substitute** and **calculate.**

$440	*Per diem*
× 8	*Days*
$3,520	*Prorated rent*

The seller will owe the buyer $3,520 in prepaid rents at closing.

Mortgage Interest Prorations

Two different types of mortgage interest prorations are necessary in most transactions, one for the seller and one for the buyer. The seller typically owes a final interest payment on the loan he is paying off.

Example: The remaining balance on the seller's mortgage is $317,550, and the interest rate is 8%. The closing date is set for July 6. Because mortgage interest is paid in arrears, the mortgage payment that the seller paid on July 1 covers the interest that accrued during June. At closing, the seller owes the lender interest covering July 1 through the closing date. How much will that interest payment be? Base your calculations on a calendar year.

1. First calculate the annual interest, using the percentage formula.

   a) **Write down the formula.** *Payment = Loan balance × Interest*

   b) **Substitute.** *P = $317,550 × .08*

   c) **Calculate.**

$317,550	*Loan amount*
× .08	*Interest rate*
$25,404	*Annual interest*

2. Next, find the per diem rate of the expense. Divide the annual rate by 365: *$25,404 ÷ 365 = $69.60 Per diem.*

3. Determine the number of days the seller owes interest for. The lender will charge the seller interest for the day of closing. Thus, the seller owes interest for six days, from July 1 through July 6.

4. Finally, substitute the numbers into the proration formula ($S = R \times D$) and calculate.

$69.60	*Per diem*
× 6	*Days*
$417.60	*Final interest payment*

At closing, the seller will be required to make a final interest payment of $417.60.

The buyer also owes some mortgage interest at closing. This is prepaid interest (interim interest) on the buyer's new loan. Prepaid interest covers the closing date through the last day of the month in which closing takes place.

Example: The principal amount of the buyer's new loan is $230,680. The interest rate is 8%. The transaction closes on June 22. How much prepaid interest will the buyer's lender require the buyer to pay at closing? Base your calculations on a 365-day year.

1. Use the percentage formula to calculate the annual amount of interest.

   a) **Write down the formula.** *Payment = Loan balance × Interest rate*

   b) **Substitute.** *P = $230,680 × 8%*

   c) **Calculate.** *$230,680 × .08 = $18,454.40*

2. Find the per diem rate of the expense. Divide the annual rate by 365: *$18,454.40 ÷ 365 = $50.56.*

3. Determine the number of days the buyer is responsible for. In prepaid interest prorations, the buyer pays for the day of closing. There are nine days: June 22, 23, 24, 25, 26, 27, 28, 29, and 30.

4. Substitute the daily rate and number of days into the proration formula ($S = R \times D$) and calculate.

$50.56	*Per diem*
× 9	*Days*
$455.04	*Prepaid interest*

The buyer's interest charge would be $455.04.

Chapter Summary

Converting fractions to decimals:

Divide numerator (top number) by denominator (bottom number).

Converting percentages to decimals:

Move decimal point two places to the left and drop the percent sign.

Converting decimals to percentages:

Move decimal point two places to the right and add a percent sign.

Area formula for squares and rectangles:

Area = Length × Width

$A = L \times W$

Area formula for triangles:

Area = ½ Base × Height

$A = \frac{1}{2} B \times H$

Volume formula:

Volume = Length × Width × Height

$V = L \times W \times H$

Percentage formula:

Part = Whole × Percentage

$P = W \times \%$

Profit or loss formula:

Now = Then × %

Capitalization formula:

Income = Rate × Value

$I = V \times \%$

Proration formula:

Share = Daily Rate × Number of Days

$S = R \times D$

1. *Find annual or monthly amount;*
2. *Find daily rate;*
3. *Determine number of days; and*
4. *Substitute and calculate.*

Chapter Quiz

1. Christine and Tom bought a house one year ago for $168,500. If property values in their neighborhood are increasing at an annual rate of 7%, what is the current market value of their house?
   a) $180,295
   b) $184,270
   c) $195,980
   d) $198,893

2. A home just sold for $183,500. The listing broker charged the seller a 6½% commission. The listing broker will pay 50% of that amount to the selling broker, and 25% to the listing salesperson. How much will the listing salesperson's share of the commission be?
   a) $11,927
   b) $5,963
   c) $3,642
   d) $2,982

3. A rectangular lot that has a 45-foot frontage and contains 1,080 square yards has a depth of:
   a) 63 feet
   b) 216 feet
   c) 188 feet
   d) 97 feet

4. An acre contains 43,560 square feet. What is the maximum number of lots measuring 50 feet by 100 feet that can be created from a one-acre parcel?
   a) Six
   b) Seven
   c) Eight
   d) Nine

5. Felicia sold a client's building for $80,000 and received a commission of $5,600. What was her commission rate?
   a) 6.5%
   b) 7%
   c) 7.5%
   d) 8%

6. Jake bought a lot for $5,000 and later sold it for $8,000. What was his percentage of profit?
   a) 60%
   b) 75%
   c) 80%
   d) 85%

7. Diane wants to purchase an income property that has an annual net income of $16,000. If she wants at least an 8% return on her investment, what is the most she should pay for the property?
   a) $150,000
   b) $175,000
   c) $195,000
   d) $200,000

8. George purchases a building for $85,000. The building generates a yearly net income of $5,100. What is his rate of return?
   a) 5.5%
   b) 6%
   c) 6.5%
   d) 7%

9. How many square yards are there in a rectangle that measures 75 × 30 feet?
   a) 6,750
   b) 2,250
   c) 750
   d) 250

10. Mike is purchasing an apartment building. The closing date is September 15, and the seller has already collected the monthly rents in the amount of $13,960 for September. Mike is entitled to rents from the closing date. At closing, the seller will have to pay Mike a prorated share of the September rents, which will amount to approximately:

    a) $612
    b) $931
    c) $7,445
    d) $9,035

13,960 ÷ 30 = 465.33
465.33 x 16 =
$7,445

11. A triangular lot has a 40-foot base and a 30-foot height. What is the area of the lot?

    a) 500 square feet
    b) 600 square feet
    c) 750 square feet
    d) 650 square feet

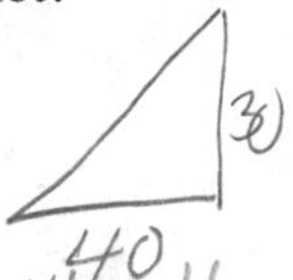

A = ½b x H
A = 40 x 30 = 1200 ÷ 2 = 600

12. What is the decimal equivalent of five-eighths (5/8)?

    a) .625
    b) .0825
    c) 1.58
    d) 1.60

5 ÷ 8 = 0.625

13. Kay has obtained a $112,000 loan at 8.5% interest, to finance the purchase of a home. At closing, the lender will require her to prepay interest for April 26 through April 30. Assuming that the closing agent uses a 365-day year for the proration, how much will that prepaid interest amount to?

    a) $64.35
    b) $104.32
    c) $130.40
    d) $1,403.84

5 days
9,520 ÷ 365 = 26.08 per day
$26.08 x 5 = $130.40

14. The Binghams are selling their house and paying off the mortgage at closing. The remaining principal balance on the mortgage at closing will be $168,301.50. They will also have to pay interest that accrued over the 7-day period between their last mortgage payment and the closing date. If the annual interest rate on the Binghams' mortgage was 10%, how much will they have to pay in interest at closing? (Use a 365-day year for the proration.)

    a) $85.21
    b) $322.77
    c) $409.86
    d) $694.41

16,830.15 ÷ 365
46.11
46.11 x 7 = 322.77

15. Carol has just paid $460,000 for a building that will bring her a 9.75% return on her investment. What is the building's annual net income?

    a) $34,965
    b) $36,750
    c) $41,220
    d) $44,850

I = R x V
I = 9.75 x 460,000
I = 44,850

A = L x W
1 sq. Ft = 9 sq. yards
A = ½ x H
I = R x V

Answer Key

1. a) The current market value of Christine and Tom's house is approximately $180,295. The question asks you to determine the current value of the house based on its earlier value, so the applicable formula is $Then \times \% = Now$. Here, the value has increased by 7%, so the appropriate percentage is 107% (100% + 7%), or 1.07 (as a decimal). $\$168{,}500 \times 1.07 = \$180{,}295$.

2. d) The listing salesperson will get $2,982. This is a percentage question with two parts. First multiply the sales price by the broker's commission rate to determine the full commission. $\$183{,}500 \times .065 = \$11{,}927.50$. Then multiply that number by 25% to determine the listing salesperson's share: $\$11{,}927.50 \times .25 = \$2{,}981.88$.

3. b) The depth of the lot is 216 feet. The question asks you to determine the length of one of the sides of a rectangle, so the applicable formula is $Area = Length \times Width, A = L \times W$.

   First convert the area from square yards to square feet, so that it is in the same unit of measurement as the frontage. A square yard is a square that measures 3 feet on each side, or 9 square feet ($3 \times 3 = 9$). Thus, 1,080 square yards is 9,720 square feet ($1{,}080 \times 9 = 9{,}720$).

   Now substitute the numbers you have into the formula. $9{,}720 = 45 \times L$. Isolate the unknown quantity, H, by changing to another version of the same formula: $L = 9{,}720 \div 45$.

   Divide the area, 9,720 square feet, by the width, 45 feet, to determine the length of the rectangle: $9{,}720 \div 45 = 216$ *feet.*

4. c) There are eight 50' × 100' lots in an acre, with one somewhat smaller lot left over. Use the area formula to determine the area of a 50' × 100' lot. $A = 50 \times 100 = 5{,}000$ *square feet*. Thus, each lot will have an area of 5,000 square feet. Now divide the total number of square feet in the acre by the area of each lot: $43{,}560 \div 5{,}000 = 8.71$.

5. b) Felicia's commission rate was 7%. Use the percentage formula, $Part = Whole \times Percentage, P = W \times \%$. You know the part ($5,600) and the total ($80,000), so switch the formula to isolate the percentage, then substitute and calculate.

   $P \div W = \%$

   $\$5{,}600 \div \$80{,}000 = \%$

   $\$5{,}600 \div \$80{,}000 = .07$. Thus, the commission rate was 7%.

6. a) Jake's profit on the sale of the lot was 60%. The question asks you to determine what percentage of the original price (the *Then* value) the sales price (the *Now* value) represents. So use the formula $Now = Then \times \%$, switching it around to isolate the unknown quantity, the percentage:

   $Now \div Then = \%$

   $\$8{,}000 \div \$5{,}000 = 1.60 = 160\%$

   The *Now* value is 160% of the *Then* value—in other words, 60% more than the *Then* value. Thus, Jake's profit on the sale was 60%.

7. d) Diane could pay $200,000 for the property and get an 8% return on that investment. This is a capitalization problem, so use the capitalization formula, *Income = Rate × Value, I = R × V*. You know the net income ($16,000) and the capitalization rate (8%), so switch the formula to isolate the unknown quantity, V:

I ÷ R = V

$16,000 ÷ .08 = $200,000

8. b) George has a 6% return on his investment. This problem calls for the capitalization formula again, but this time it's the rate that is unknown. Switch the formula to isolate the rate, R:

I ÷ V = R

$5,100 ÷ $85,000 = .06 = 6%

9. d) There are 250 square yards in a 75' × 30' rectangle. The area formula, *A = B × H,* will give you the area in square feet: *75 × 30 = 2,250 square feet*. Then you must convert that figure to square yards. There are 9 square feet in a square yard, so divide 2,250 by 9: *2,250 ÷ 9 = 250 square yards*.

10. c) Mike, the buyer, is entitled to approximately $7,445 in rent for the period from the closing date through September 30. The proration formula is *Share = Rate × Days, S = R × D*. First determine the per diem rate for the rents by dividing the total amount by the number of days in the month: *$13,960 ÷ 30 = $465.33*. Next, determine the number of days for which the buyer is entitled to the rent: September 15 through 30 is 16 days. Finally, multiply the rate by the number of days to find the buyer's share: *$465.33 × 16 = $7,445*.

11. b) The area of the lot is 600 square feet. Since the lot is triangular, the appropriate area formula is *Area = ½ Base × Height, A = ½ B × H*. Here, the base is 40 feet, so ½ the base is 20 feet. *20 feet × 30 feet = 600 square feet.*

12. a) The decimal equivalent of 5/8 is .625. To determine this, divide the numerator of the fraction (the top number, 5) by the denominator (the bottom number, 8). *5 ÷ 8 = .625.*

13. c) The prepaid interest will be $130.40. First determine the annual interest, using the percentage formula: *Part = Whole × Percentage, P = W × %*. The principal (the whole) is $112,000 and the rate (the percentage) is 8.5%. *$112,000 × .085 = $9,520*. Next, divide the annual interest by 365 to determine the per diem rate. *$9,520 ÷ 365 = $26.08*. Multiply the per diem rate by the number of days for which Kay is responsible for this expense—five days. *$26.08 × 5 = $130.40.*

14. b) The Binghams will have to pay $322.77 in interest at closing. To find the annual interest amount, use the percentage formula, *P = W × %*. *$168,301.50 × .10 = $16,830.15*. Divide that figure by 365 to determine the per diem rate: *$16,830.15 ÷ 365 = $46.11*. Finally, multiply the per diem rate by the number of days: *$46.11 × 7 days = $322.77*.

15. d) The building's annual net income is $44,850. Use the capitalization formula, *Income = Rate × Value; .0975 × $460,000 = $44,850.*

The definitions given here explain how the listed terms are used in the real estate field. Some of the terms have additional meanings, which can be found in a standard dictionary.

AAA Tenant—A nationally known tenant with the highest credit rating, whose name would lend prestige to the property.

Abandonment—Failure to occupy and use property, which may result in a loss of rights.

Abrogate—To repeal, annul, nullify, abolish, or otherwise bring to an end by official or formal action.

Absolute Fee—*See*: Fee Simple.

Abstract of Judgment—A document summarizing the essential provisions of a court judgment which, when recorded, creates a lien on the judgment debtor's real property.

Abstract of Title—*See*: Title, Abstract of.

Abut—To touch, border on, be adjacent to, or share a common boundary with.

Acceleration Clause—A provision in a promissory note or security instrument allowing the lender to declare the entire debt due immediately if the borrower breaches one or more provisions of the loan agreement. Also referred to as a call provision.

Acceptance—1. Agreeing to the terms of an offer to enter into a contract, thereby creating a binding contract. 2. Taking delivery of a deed from the grantor.

Acceptance, Qualified—*See*: Counteroffer.

Accession—The acquisition of title to additional property by its annexation to real estate already owned. This can be the result of human actions (as in the case of fixtures) or natural processes (such as accretion and reliction).

Accord and Satisfaction—An agreement to accept something different from (and usually less than) what the contract originally called for.

Accretion—A gradual addition to dry land by the forces of nature, as when waterborne sediment is deposited on waterfront property.

Accrued Items of Expense—Expenses that have been incurred but are not yet due or payable. In a settlement statement, the seller's accrued expenses are credited to the buyer.

Acknowledgment—When a person who has signed a document formally declares to an authorized official (usually a notary public) that he or she signed voluntarily. The official can then attest that the signature is voluntary and genuine.

Acquisition Cost—The amount of money a buyer was required to expend in order to acquire title to a piece of property. In addition to the purchase price, this might include closing costs, legal fees, and other expenses.

Acre—An area of land equal to 43,560 square feet, or 4,840 square yards, or 160 square rods.

Actual Age—*See*: Age, Actual.

Actual Authority—*See*: Authority, Actual.

Actual Eviction—*See*: Eviction, Actual.

Actual Notice—*See*: Notice, Actual.

ADA—Americans with Disabilities Act.

Addendum—A paragraph attached to a purchase and sale agreement or other contract that contains additional provisions.

Adjacent—Nearby, next to, bordering, or neighboring; may or may not be in actual contact.

Adjustable-rate Mortgage—*See*: Mortgage, Adjustable-rate.

Adjusted Basis—*See*: Basis, Adjusted.

Adjustment Period—The interval at which an adjustable-rate mortgage borrower's interest rate or monthly payment is changed.

Administrative Agency—A government agency (federal, state, or local) that administers a complex area of law and policy, adopting and enforcing detailed regulations that have the force of law.

Administrative Law Judge—An official appointed to decide cases in which an individual is in conflict with the rules and regulations of an administrative agency.

Administrative Regulation—Rule adopted by a federal, state, or local government agency. Carries the force of law.

Administrator—A person appointed by the probate court to manage and distribute the estate of a deceased person, when no executor is named in the will or there is no will.

Ad Valorem—A Latin phrase that means "according to value," used to refer to taxes that are assessed on the value of property.

Adverse Possession—Acquiring title to real property that belongs to someone else by taking possession of it without permission, in the manner and for the length of time prescribed by statute.

Affiant—One who makes an affidavit.

Affidavit—A sworn statement made before a notary public (or other official authorized to administer an oath) that has been written down and acknowledged.

Affirm—1. To confirm or ratify. 2. To make a solemn declaration that is not under oath.

After-Acquired Title—*See*: Title, After-Acquired.

Age, Actual—The age of a structure from a chronological standpoint (as opposed to its effective age); how many years it has actually been in existence.

Age, Effective—The age of a structure as indicated by its condition and remaining usefulness (as opposed to its actual age). Good maintenance may increase a building's effective age, and poor maintenance may decrease it; for example, a 50-year-old home that has been well maintained might have an effective age of 15 years, meaning that its remaining usefulness is equivalent to that of a 15-year-old home.

Agency—A relationship of trust created when one person (the principal) grants another (the agent) authority to represent the principal in dealings with third parties.

Agency, Apparent—When third parties are given the impression that someone who has not been authorized to represent another is that person's agent, or else given the impression that an agent has been authorized to perform acts which are in fact beyond the scope of his or her authority. Also called ostensible agency.

Agency, Dual—When an agent represents both parties to a transaction, as when a broker represents both the buyer and the seller.

Agency, Exclusive—*See*: Listing, Exclusive.

Agency, Ostensible—*See*: Agency, Apparent.

Agency Law—The body of legal rules that govern the relationship between agent and principal, imposing fiduciary duties on the agent and also imposing liability for the agent's actions on the principal.

Agent—A person authorized to represent another (the principal) in dealings with third parties.

Agent, Closing—The person who handles the closing process on behalf of the parties to a real estate transaction. It may be an independent escrow agent, an employee of the lender or the title company, the real estate broker, or a lawyer.

Agent, Dual—*See*: Agency, Dual.

Agent, Escrow—A third party who holds funds, documents, or other valuables on behalf of the parties to a transaction, releasing these items to the parties only when certain conditions in the escrow instructions have been fulfilled.

Agent, General—An agent authorized to handle all of the principal's affairs in one area or in specified areas.

Agent, Gratuitous—An agent who does not have a legal right to claim compensation for his or her services (such as a broker who does not have a written employment contract with the seller).

Agent, Listing—A broker who has a listing agreement with a seller, or a salesperson representing the listing broker. The listing agent may or may not turn out also to be the selling agent, the one who negotiates an acceptable offer from the buyer.

Agent, Selling—The real estate agent who writes and presents the offer to purchase that the seller accepts. The selling agent may or may not also be the listing agent, but is considered to be an agent of the seller unless otherwise agreed.

Agent, Special—An agent with limited authority to do a specific thing or conduct a specific transaction.

Agent, Universal—An agent authorized to do everything that can be lawfully delegated to a representative.

Agents in Production—The elements necessary to generate income and establish a value in real estate: labor, coordination, capital, and land.

Age of Majority—*See*: Majority, Age of.

Agreement—*See*: Contract.

Air Lot—A parcel of property above the surface of the earth, not containing any land; for example, a condominium unit on the third floor.

Air Rights—The right to undisturbed use and control of the airspace over a parcel of land; may be transferred separately from the land.

Alienation—The transfer of ownership or an interest in property from one person to another, by any means.

Alienation, Involuntary—Transfer of an interest in property against the will of the owner, or without action by the owner, occurring through operation of law, natural processes, or adverse possession.

Alienation, Voluntary—When an owner voluntarily transfers an interest to someone else.

Alienation Clause—A provision in a security instrument that gives the lender the right to declare the entire loan balance due immediately if the borrower sells or otherwise transfers the security property. Also called a due-on-sale clause.

All-Inclusive Trust Deed—*See*: Mortgage, Wraparound.

Allodial System—A system of real property ownership in which an individual's ownership may be complete or absolute (except for those rights held by the government, such as eminent domain and escheat).

Alluvion—The solid material deposited along a riverbank or shore by accretion. Also called alluvium.

ALTA—American Land Title Association, a nationwide organization of title insurance companies. An extended coverage title policy is sometimes referred to as an ALTA policy.

Amendment—A supplementary agreement changing one or more terms of a contract, which must be signed by all of the parties to the original contract. Also called a contract modification.

Amenities—Features of a property that contribute to the pleasure or convenience of owning it, such as a fireplace, a beautiful view, or its proximity to a good school.

Americans with Disabilities Act (ADA)—A federal law requiring nonresidential facilities that are open to the public to ensure accessibility to disabled persons, which may include making architectural modifications.

Amortization, Negative—The addition of unpaid interest to the principal balance of a loan, thereby increasing the amount owed.

Amortize—To gradually pay off a debt with installment payments that include both principal and interest. *See also*: Loan, Amortized.

Annexation—Attaching personal property to real property, so that it becomes part of the real property (a fixture) in the eyes of the law.

Annexation, Actual—The physical attachment of personal property to real property, so that it becomes part of the real property.

Annexation, Constructive—The association of personal property with real property in such a way that the law treats it as a fixture, even though it is not physically attached. For example, a house key is constructively annexed to the house.

Annual Percentage Rate (APR)—All of the charges that a borrower will pay for the loan (including the interest, loan fee, discount points, and mortgage insurance costs), expressed as an annual percentage of the loan amount.

Annuity—A sum of money received in a series of payments at regular intervals (often annually) over a period of time.

Anticipation, Principle of—An appraisal principle which holds that value is created by the expectation of benefits to be received in the future.

Anticipatory Repudiation—Action taken by one party to a contract to inform the other party, before the time set for performance, that he or she does not intend to fulfill the contract.

Anti-deficiency Rules—Laws that prohibit a secured lender from suing the borrower for a deficiency judgment in certain circumstances (for example, after nonjudicial foreclosure of a deed of trust).

Appeal—When one of the parties to a lawsuit asks a higher court to review the judgment or verdict reached in a lower court.

Appellant—The party who files an appeal because he or she is dissatisfied with the lower court's decision. Also called the petitioner.

Appellee—In an appeal, the party who did not file the appeal. Also called the respondent.

Apportionment—A division of property (as among tenants in common when the property is sold or partitioned) or liability (as when responsibility for closing costs is allocated between the buyer and seller) into proportionate, but not necessarily equal, parts.

Appraisal—An estimate or opinion of the value of a piece of property as of a particular date. Also called valuation.

Appraiser—One who estimates the value of property, especially an expert qualified to do so by training and experience.

Appreciation—An increase in value; the opposite of depreciation.

Appropriation—Taking property or reducing it to personal possession, to the exclusion of others.

Appropriation, Prior—A system of allocating water rights, under which a person who wants to use water from a certain lake or river is required to apply for a permit. A permit has priority over other permits that are issued later. *Compare*: Riparian Rights.

Appropriative Rights—The water rights of a person who holds a prior appropriation permit.

Appurtenances—Rights that go along with ownership of a particular piece of property, such as air rights or mineral rights. They are ordinarily transferred with the property, but may, in some cases, be sold separately.

Appurtenances, Intangible—Rights that go with ownership of a piece of property that do not involve physical objects or substances; for example, an access easement (as opposed to mineral rights).

Appurtenant Easement—*See*: Easement Appurtenant.

APR—*See*: Annual Percentage Rate.

Area—1. Locale or region. 2. The size of a surface, usually in square units of measure, such as square feet or square miles.

Area Preference—*See*: Situs.

ARM—*See*: Mortgage, Adjustable-Rate.

Arm's Length Transaction—A transaction in which there is no pre-existing family or business relationship between the parties.

Arranger of Credit—A real estate licensee or attorney who arranges a transaction where credit is extended by a seller of residential property.

Artificial Person—A legal entity, such as a corporation, that the law treats as an individual with legal rights and responsibilities; as distinguished from a natural person, a human being. Sometimes called a legal person.

Assemblage—Combining two or more adjoining properties into one tract.

Assessment—The valuation of property for purposes of taxation.

Assessor—An official who determines the value of property for taxation.

Asset—Anything of value that a person owns.

Assets, Capital—Assets held by a taxpayer other than: (1) property held for sale to customers; and (2) depreciable property or real property used in the taxpayer's trade or business. Thus, real property is a capital asset if it is used for personal use or for profit.

Assets, Liquid—Cash and other assets that can be readily turned into cash (liquidated), such as stock.

Assign—To transfer rights (especially contract rights) or interests to another.

Assignee—One to whom rights or interests have been assigned.

Assignment—1. A transfer of contract rights from one person to another. 2. In the case of a lease, the transfer by the original tenant of his or her entire leasehold estate to another. *Compare*: Sublease.

Assignment of Contract and Deed—The instrument used to substitute a new vendor for the original vendor in a land contract.

Assignor—One who has assigned his or her rights or interest to another.

Assumption—Action by a buyer to take on personal liability for paying off the seller's existing mortgage or deed of trust.

Assumption Fee—A fee paid to the lender, usually by the buyer, when a mortgage or deed of trust is assumed.

Attachment—Court-ordered seizure of property belonging to a defendant in a lawsuit, so that it will be available to satisfy a judgment if the plaintiff wins. In the case of real property, an attachment creates a lien.

Attachments, Man-Made—*See*: Fixture.

Attachments, Natural—Plants growing on a piece of land, such as trees, shrubs, or crops. *See*: Emblements; Fructus Industriales; Fructus Naturales.

Attestation—The act of witnessing the execution of an instrument, such as a deed or will.

Attorney General—The principal legal advisor for state government.

Attorney in Fact—Any person authorized to represent another by a power of attorney; not necessarily a lawyer (an attorney at law).

Attractive Nuisance—A property feature that is dangerous and inviting to children, and a potential source of liability for the property owner.

Auditing—Verification and examination of records, particularly the financial accounts of a business or other organization.

Authority, Actual—Authority actually given to an agent by the principal, either expressly or by implication.

Authority, Apparent—Authority to represent another that someone appears to have and that the principal is estopped from denying, although no actual authority has been granted.

Authority, Express—Actual authority that the principal has expressly given to his or her agent, either orally or in writing.

Authority, Implied—An agent's authority to do everything reasonably necessary to carry out the principal's express orders.

Automated Underwriting (AU)—Analysis of a loan application with a computer program that makes a preliminary recommendation for or against approval. *Compare*: Manual Underwriting.

Avulsion—1. A sudden (not gradual) tearing away of land by the action of water. 2. A sudden shift in a watercourse.

Balance, Principle of—An appraisal principle which holds that the maximum value of real estate is achieved when the agents in production (labor, coordination, capital, and land) are in proper balance with each other.

Balance Sheet—*See*: Financial Statement.

Balloon Payment—A payment on a loan (usually the final payment) that is significantly larger than the regular installment payments.

Bankruptcy—1. A situation resulting when the liabilities of an individual, corporation, or firm exceed the assets. 2. Declaration by a court that an individual, corporation, or firm is insolvent, with the result that the assets and debts are administered under bankruptcy laws.

Barter—To exchange or trade one commodity or piece of property for another without the use of money.

Base Line—In the government survey system, a main east-west line from which township lines are established. Each principal meridian has one base line associated with it.

Basis—A figure used in calculating a gain on the sale of real estate for federal income tax purposes. Also called cost basis.

Basis, Adjusted—The owner's initial basis in the property, plus capital expenditures for improvements, and minus any allowable depreciation or cost recovery deductions.

Basis, Initial—The amount of the owner's original investment in the property; what it cost to acquire the property, which may include closing costs and certain other expenses, as well as the purchase price.

Bearer—Whoever has possession of a negotiable instrument. *See*: Endorsement in Blank.

Bench Mark—A surveyor's mark at a known point of elevation on a stationary object, used as a reference point in calculating other elevations in a surveyed area; often a metal disk set into cement or rock.

Beneficiary—1. One for whom a trust is created and on whose behalf the trustee administers the trust. 2. The lender in a deed of trust transaction. 3. One entitled to receive real or personal property under a will; a legatee or devisee.

Bequeath—To transfer personal property to another by will.

Bequest—Personal property (including money) that is transferred by will.

Bilateral Contract—*See*: Contract, Bilateral.

Bill of Sale—A document used to transfer title to personal property from one person to another.

Binder—1. An agreement to consider a deposit as evidence of the potential buyer's good faith when he or she makes an offer to buy a piece of real estate. 2. An instrument providing immediate insurance coverage until the regular policy is issued. 3. Any payment or preliminary written statement intended to make an agreement legally binding until a formal contract has been drawn up.

Blind Ad—An advertisement placed by a real estate licensee that does not include the broker's name.

Block—In a subdivision, a group of lots surrounded by streets or unimproved land.

Blockbusting—Attempting to induce owners to list or sell their homes by predicting that members of another race or ethnic group, or people suffering from some disability, will be moving into the neighborhood. This violates antidiscrimination laws. Also called panic selling.

Blue Sky Laws—Laws that regulate the promotion and sale of securities in order to protect the public from fraud.

Board of Directors—The body responsible for governing a corporation on behalf of the shareholders, which oversees the corporate management.

Bona Fide—In good faith; genuine; not fraudulent.

Bond—1. A written obligation, usually interest-bearing, to pay a certain sum at a specified time. 2. Money put up as a surety, protecting someone against failure to perform, negligent performance, or fraud.

Bond, Completion—A bond posted by a contractor to guarantee that a project will be completed satisfactorily and free of liens. Also called a performance bond.

Bonus—An extra payment, over and above what is strictly due.

Boot—In a tax-free exchange, something given or received that is not like-kind property; for example, in an exchange of real property, if one party gives the other cash in addition to real property, the cash is boot.

Boundary—The perimeter or border of a parcel of land; the dividing line between one piece of property and another.

Bounds—Boundaries. *See*: Metes and Bounds Description.

Branch Manager—An associate broker designated by a firm's primary broker to manage the operations of a branch office.

Breach—Violation of an obligation, duty, or law; especially an unexcused failure to perform a contractual obligation.

Breach of Contract—An unexcused failure to perform a contractual obligation.

Broker, Associate—A person who has qualified as a broker, but is affiliated with another broker.

Broker, Cooperating—A broker who belongs to a multiple listing service and helps sell a property that is listed with another member of the service (the listing broker). Like the listing broker, the cooperating broker represents the seller unless otherwise agreed.

Broker, Designated—A corporate officer or general partner who is authorized to act as the broker for a licensed corporation or partnership.

Broker, Fee—A real estate broker who allows another person to use his or her license to operate a brokerage, in violation of the license law.

Broker, Listing—A broker who has a listing agreement with a property seller (in contrast to a cooperating broker from the multiple listing service, who may help sell the property and share the listing broker's commission, but does not have a contract directly with the seller).

Broker, Real Estate—One who is licensed to represent members of the public in real estate transactions for compensation.

Brokerage—A real estate broker's business.

Brokerage Fee—The commission or other compensation charged for a real estate broker's services.

Buffer—An undeveloped area separating two areas zoned for incompatible uses.

Building Codes—Regulations that set minimum standards for construction methods and materials.

Building Restrictions—Rules concerning building size, placement, or type; they may be public restrictions (in a zoning ordinance, for example) or private restrictions (CC&Rs, for example).

Bulk Transfer—The sale of all or a substantial part of the merchandise, equipment, or other inventory of a business, not in the ordinary course of business.

Bulk Transfer Law—A law requiring a seller who negotiates a bulk transfer (usually in connection with the sale of the business itself) to furnish the buyer with a list of creditors and a schedule of the property being sold, and to notify creditors of the impending transfer.

Bump Clause—A provision in a purchase agreement that allows the seller to keep the property on the market while waiting for a contingency clause to be fulfilled. If the seller receives another good offer in the meantime, he or she can require the buyer either to waive the contingency clause or terminate the contract.

Bundle of Rights—The rights inherent in ownership of property, including the right to use, lease, enjoy, encumber, will, sell, or do nothing with the property.

Business Opportunity—A business that is for sale.

Buydown—The payment of discount points to a lender to reduce (buy down) the interest rate charged to the borrower; especially when a seller pays discount points to help the buyer/borrower qualify for financing.

Call—In a metes and bounds description, a specification that describes a segment of the boundary. For example, "south 15° west 120 feet" is a call.

Call Provision—*See*: Acceleration Clause.

Cancellation—Termination of a contract without undoing acts that have already been performed under the contract. *Compare*: Rescission.

Cap—A limit on how much a lender may raise an adjustable-rate mortgage's interest rate or monthly payment per year.

Capacity—The legal ability or competence to perform some act, such as enter into a contract or execute a deed or will.

Capital—Money (or other forms of wealth) available for use in the production of more money.

Capital Assets—Assets held by a taxpayer other than: 1) property held for sale to customers in the ordinary course of the taxpayer's business; and 2) depreciable property or real property used in the taxpayer's trade or business. Thus, real property is a capital asset if it is owned for personal use or for profit.

Capital Expenditures—Money spent on improvements and alterations that add to the value of the property and/or prolong its life.

Capital Gain—Profit realized from the sale of a capital asset. If the asset was held for more than one year, it is a long-term capital gain; if the asset was held for one year or less, it is a short-term capital gain.

Capital Improvement—Any improvement that is designed to become a permanent part of the real property or that will have the effect of significantly prolonging the property's life.

Capitalization—A method of appraising real property by converting the anticipated net income from the property into the present value. Also called the income approach to value.

Capitalization Rate—A percentage used in capitalization (Net Income = Capitalization Rate × Value). It is the rate believed to represent the proper relationship between the value of the property and the income it produces; the rate that would be a reasonable return on an investment of the type in question, or the yield necessary to attract investment of capital in property like the subject property. Often called a cap rate.

Capitalize—1. To provide with cash, or capital. 2. To determine the present value of an asset using capitalization.

Capital Loss—A loss resulting from the sale of a capital asset. It may be long-term or short-term, depending on whether the asset was held for more than one year or for one year or less

Carryback Loan—*See*: Mortgage, Purchase Money.

Carryover Clause—*See*: Safety Clause.

Case Law—Body of law made up of judicial rulings that set precedents for subsequent decisions.

Cash Flow—The residual income after deducting from gross income all operating expenses and debt service.

Cash on Cash—The ratio between cash received in the first year and cash initially invested.

Caveat Emptor—A Latin phrase meaning "Let the buyer beware"; it expresses the idea that a buyer is expected to examine property carefully before buying, instead of relying on the seller to disclose problems. This was once a firm rule of law, but it has lost most of its force, especially in residential transactions.

CC&Rs—A declaration of covenants, conditions, and restrictions; usually recorded by a developer to place restrictions on all lots within a new subdivision.

CERCLA—*See*: Comprehensive Environmental Response, Compensation, and Liability Act.

Certificate of Discharge—A written statement acknowledging that the debt secured by a mortgage has been paid in full. Also called a satisfaction of mortgage or mortgage release.

Certificate of Eligibility—A document issued by the Department of Veterans Affairs as evidence of a veteran's eligibility for a VA-guaranteed loan.

Certificate of Occupancy—A document issued by a local government agency (such as the building department) verifying that a newly constructed building is in compliance with all codes and may be occupied.

Certificate of Reasonable Value—*See*: Notice of Value.

Certificate of Sale—The document given to the purchaser at a mortgage foreclosure sale, instead of a deed; replaced with a sheriff's deed only after the redemption period expires.

Certificate of Title—*See*: Opinion of Title.

Certiorari, Writ of—A writ in which a higher court requests a transcript of proceedings that took place in a lower court, for appellate review.

Chain of Title—*See*: Title, Chain of.

Change, Principle of—An appraisal principle which holds that it is the future, not the past, that is of primary importance in estimating a property's value, because economic and social forces are constantly changing it.

Charter—A written instrument granting a power or a right of franchise.

Chattel—An article of personal property.

Chattel Mortgage—*See*: Mortgage, Chattel.

Chattel Real—Personal property that is closely associated with real property. The primary example is a lease.

Civil Law—The body of law concerned with the rights and liabilities of one individual in relation to another; includes contract law, tort law, and property law. *Compare*: Criminal Law.

Civil Rights—Fundamental rights guaranteed to individuals by the law. The term is primarily used in reference to constitutional and statutory protections against discrimination or government interference.

Civil Rights Act of 1866—A federal law guaranteeing all citizens the right to purchase, lease, sell, convey and inherit property, regardless of race or color.

Civil Rights Act of 1964—A federal law prohibiting discrimination on the basis of race, color, national origin, or religion in many programs for which the government provides financial assistance.

Civil Suit—A lawsuit in which one private party sues another private party (as opposed to a criminal suit, in which an individual is sued—prosecuted—by the government).

Civil Wrong—*See*: Tort.

Clean Air Act—A federal law intended to maintain and enhance air quality.

Clean Water Act—A federal law intended to maintain and enhance the quality of the nation's water resources.

Client—One who employs a broker, lawyer, or appraiser. A real estate broker's client can be the seller, the buyer, or both, but is usually the seller.

Closing—The final stage in a real estate transaction, when the seller receives the purchase money, the buyer receives the deed, and title is transferred. Also called settlement.

Closing Costs—Expenses incurred in the transfer of real estate in addition to the purchase price; for example, the appraisal fee, title insurance premium, broker's commission, and conveyance tax.

Closing Date—The date on which all the terms of a purchase agreement must be met, or the contract is terminated.

Closing Statement—*See*: Settlement Statement.

Cloud on Title—A claim, encumbrance, or apparent defect that makes the title to a property unmarketable. *See*: Title, Marketable.

Code of Ethics—A body of rules setting forth accepted standards of conduct, reflecting principles of fairness and morality; especially one that the members of an organization are expected to follow.

Codicil—An addition to, or revision of, a will.

Collateral—Anything of value used as security for a debt or obligation.

Collusion—An agreement between two or more persons to defraud another.

Color of Title—*See*: Title, Color of.

Commercial Acre—The remainder of an acre of newly subdivided land after deducting the amount of land dedicated for streets and sidewalks.

Commercial Bank—A type of financial institution that has traditionally emphasized commercial lending (loans to businesses), but which also makes many residential mortgage loans.

Commercial Paper—Negotiable instruments, such as promissory notes, sold to meet the short-term capital needs of a business.

Commercial Property—Property zoned and used for business purposes, such as a restaurant or an office building; as distinguished from residential, industrial, or agricultural property.

Commingled Funds—Funds from different sources that are deposited in the same account and thereby lose their separate character; for example, if a spouse deposits cash that is his or her separate property in an account with funds that are community property, the entire amount may be treated as community property.

Commingling—Illegally mixing trust funds held on behalf of a client with personal funds.

Commission—1. The compensation paid to a broker for services in connection with a real estate transaction (usually a percentage of the sales price). 2. A group of people organized for a particular purpose or function; usually a governmental body, such as the Real Estate Advisory Commission.

Commission Split—An arrangement in which the listing broker and selling broker share the commission paid to the listing broker by the seller.

Commitment—In real estate finance, a lender's promise to make a loan. A loan commitment may be "firm" or "conditional"; a conditional commitment is contingent on something, such as a satisfactory credit report on the borrower.

Common Elements—1. The land and improvements in a condominium, planned unit development, or other housing development that are owned and used collectively by all of the residents, such as parking lots, hallways, and recreational facilities available for common use. 2. In a building with leased units or spaces, the areas that are available for use by all of the tenants. Also called common areas.

Common Law—1. Early English law. 2. Long-established rules of law based on early English law. 3. Rules of law developed in court decisions, as opposed to statutory law.

Community Property—Property owned jointly by a married couple and other community property states, as distinguished from each spouse's separate property; generally, any property acquired through the labor or skill of either spouse during marriage.

Co-mortgagor—Someone (usually a family member) who accepts responsibility for the repayment of a mortgage loan, along with the primary borrower, to help the borrower qualify for the loan.

Comparable—In appraisal, a property that is similar to the subject property and that has recently been sold. The sales prices of comparables provide data for estimating the value of the subject property using the sales comparison approach. Also called a comp or a comparable sale.

Compensatory Damages—An amount that a court orders one party in a lawsuit to pay to the other party as compensation for a breach of contract or other injury.

Competent—1. Of sound mind, for the purposes of entering into a contract or executing an instrument. 2. Both of sound mind and having reached the age of majority.

Competition, Principle of—An appraisal principle which holds that profits tend to encourage competition, and excess profits tend to result in ruinous competition.

Completion Bond—*See*: Bond, Completion.

Compliance Inspection—A building inspection to determine, for the benefit of a lender, whether building codes, specifications, or conditions established after a prior inspection have been met before a loan is made.

Comprehensive Environmental Response, Compensation, and Liability Act (CERCLA)—A federal law that governs liability for environmental cleanup costs.

Comprehensive Plan—*See*: General Plan.

Computerized Loan Origination (CLO)—Loan origination via a computer network system; allows borrowers to submit loan applications from a broker's office for instant preapproval.

Concurrent Ownership—*See*: Ownership, Concurrent.

Condemnation—1. Taking private property for public use through the government's power of eminent domain. 2. A declaration that a structure is unfit for occupancy and must be closed or demolished.

Condemnation Appraisal—An estimate of the value of condemned property to determine the just compensation to be paid to the owner.

Condition—1. A provision in a contract that makes the parties' rights and obligations depend on the occurrence (or nonoccurrence) of a particular event. Also called a contingency clause. 2. A provision in a deed that makes title depend on compliance with a particular restriction.

Conditional Commitment—*See*: Commitment.

Conditional Fee—*See*: Fee, Defeasible.

Conditional Use Permit—A permit that allows a special use, such as a school or hospital, to operate in a neighborhood where it would otherwise be prohibited by the zoning. Also called a special exception permit.

Condominium—Property developed for concurrent ownership, where each co-owner has a separate interest in an individual unit, combined with an undivided interest in the common areas of the property.

Confirmation of Sale—Court approval of a sale of property by an executor, administrator, or guardian.

Conflict of Interest—When an agent (or other person occupying a position of trust) is in a situation where the action that would promote his or her own interests conflicts with the action that would promote the interests of the principal. The agent should inform the principal of this situation and offer to withdraw.

Conforming Loan—*See*: Loan, Conforming.

Conformity, Principle of—An appraisal principle which holds that the maximum value of property is realized when there is a reasonable degree of social and economic homogeneity in the neighborhood.

Conservation—1. Preservation of structures or neighborhoods in a sound condition. 2. Preservation or controlled use of natural resources for long-term benefits.

Conservator—A person appointed by a court to take care of the property of another who is incapable of taking care of it on his or her own.

Consideration—Anything of value given to induce another to enter into a contract, such as money, goods, services, or a promise. Sometimes called valuable consideration.

Conspiracy—An agreement or plan between two or more persons to perform an unlawful act.

Construction Lien—*See*: Lien, Construction.

Constructive—Held to be so in the eyes of the law, even if not so in fact. *See*: Annexation, Constructive; Eviction, Constructive; Notice, Constructive; Severance, Constructive.

Consumer Price Index—An index that tracks changes in the cost of goods and services for a typical consumer. Formerly called the cost of living index.

Consummate—To complete.

Contiguous—Adjacent, abutting, or in close proximity.

Contingency Clause—*See*: Condition.

Contour—The shape or configuration of a surface. A contour map depicts the topography of a piece of land by means of lines (contour lines) that connect points of equal elevation.

Contract—An agreement between two or more persons to do or not do a certain thing, for consideration.

Contract, Bilateral—A contract in which each party has made a binding promise to perform (as distinguished from a unilateral contract).

Contract, Broker and Salesperson—An employment contract between a broker and an affiliated salesperson, outlining their mutual obligations.

Contract, Conditional Sales—*See*: Contract, Land.

Contract, Executed—A contract in which both parties have completely performed their contractual obligations.

Contract, Executory—A contract in which one or both parties have not yet completed performance of their obligations.

Contract, Express—A contract that has been put into words, either spoken or written.

Contract, Implied—A contract that has not been put into words, but is implied by the actions of the parties.

Contract, Installment Sales—*See*: Contract, Land.

Contract, Land—A contract for the sale of real property in which the buyer (the vendee) pays in installments. The buyer takes possession of the property immediately, but the seller (the vendor) retains legal title until the full price has been paid. Also called a conditional sales contract, installment sales contract, real estate contract, or contract for deed.

Contract, Oral—A spoken agreement that has not been written down. Also called a parol contract.

Contract, Parol—*See*: Contract, Oral.

Contract, Real Estate—1. Any contract pertaining to real estate. 2. A land contract.

Contract, Sales—*See*: Purchase Agreement.

Contract, Unenforceable—An agreement that a court would refuse to enforce. For example, a contract is unenforceable if its contents can't be proved or the statute of limitations has run out.

Contract, Unilateral—A contract that is accepted by performance; the offeror has promised to perform his or her side of the bargain if the other party performs, but the other party has not promised to do so. *Compare*: Contract, Bilateral.

Contract, Valid—A binding, legally enforceable contract.

Contract, Void—An agreement that is not an enforceable contract, because it lacks a required element (such as consideration) or is defective in some other respect.

Contract, Voidable—A contract that one of the parties can disaffirm without liability, because of lack of capacity or a negative factor such as fraud or duress.

Contract for Deed—*See*: Contract, Land.

Contract Modification—*See*: Amendment.

Contract of Adhesion—A contract that is one-sided and unfair to one of the parties; a take-it-or-leave-it contract, in which the offeror had much greater bargaining power than the offeree.

Contract of Sale—*See*: Purchase and Sale Agreement.

Contractor—One who contracts to perform labor or supply materials for a construction project, or to do other work for a specified price.

Contractor, Independent—*See*: Independent Contractor.

Contract Rent—*See*: Rent, Contract.

Contribution, Principle of—An appraisal principle which holds that the value of real property is greatest when the improvements produce the highest return commensurate with their cost (the investment).

Conventional Financing—*See*: Loan, Conventional.

Conversion—1. Misappropriating property or funds belonging to another; for example, converting trust funds to one's own use. 2. The process of changing an apartment complex into a condominium or cooperative.

Conversion Option—A provision in many adjustable-rate mortgages that gives the borrower the option of converting to a fixed interest rate at certain times during the first years of the loan term; if the borrower chooses to do this, the loan will remain at that fixed rate for the remainder of the term.

Conveyance—The transfer of title to real property from one person to another by means of a written document, especially a deed.

Conveyance Tax—*See*: Tax, Conveyance.

Cooperating Agent—A member of a multiple listing service who attempts to find a buyer for a listing.

Cooperative—A building owned by a corporation, where the residents are shareholders in the corporation; each shareholder receives a proprietary lease on an individual unit and the right to use the common areas.

Cooperative Transaction—A sale in which the listing agent and the selling agent work for different brokers.

Co-ownership—*See*: Ownership, Concurrent.

Corner Influence—The increase in a commercial property's value that results from its location on or near a corner, with access and exposure on two streets.

Corporation—An association organized according to certain laws, in which individuals may purchase ownership shares; treated by the law as an artificial person, separate from the individual shareholders.

Corporation, Domestic—A corporation doing business in the state where it was created (incorporated).

Corporation, Foreign—A corporation doing business in one state, but created (incorporated) in another state, or in another country.

Correction Lines—In the government survey system, adjustment lines used to compensate for the curvature of the earth; they occur at 24-mile intervals (every fourth township line), where the distance between range lines is corrected to six miles.

Correlation—*See*: Reconciliation.

Cosign—To add one's signature to a promissory note in connection with a loan made to another person, agreeing to share responsibility for repaying the loan.

Cost—The amount paid for anything in money, goods, or services.

Cost, Replacement—In appraisal, the current cost of constructing a building with the same utility as the subject property with modern materials and construction methods.

Cost, Reproduction—In appraisal, the cost of constructing a replica (an exact duplicate) of the subject property, using the same materials and construction methods that were originally used, but at current prices.

Cost Approach to Value—One of the three main methods of appraisal, in which an estimate of the subject property's value is arrived at by estimating the cost of replacing (or reproducing) the improvements, then deducting the estimated accrued depreciation and adding the estimated market value of the land.

Cost Basis—*See*: Basis.

Cost of Living Index—*See*: Consumer Price Index.

Cost Recovery Deductions—*See*: Depreciation Deductions.

Co-tenancy—*See*: Ownership, Concurrent.

Counteroffer—A response to a contract offer, changing some of the terms of the original offer. It operates as a rejection of the original offer (not as an acceptance). Also called qualified acceptance.

County—An administrative subdivision of the state, created by the state and deriving all of its powers from the state.

Course—In a metes and bounds description, a direction, stated in terms of a compass bearing.

Covenant—1. A contract. 2. A promise. 3. A guarantee (express or implied) in a document such as a deed or lease. 4. A restrictive covenant.

Covenant, Restrictive—A promise to do or not do an act relating to real property, especially a promise that runs with the land; usually an owner's promise not to use property in a specified manner.

Covenant Against Encumbrances—In a deed, a promise that the property is not burdened by any encumbrances other than those that are disclosed in the deed.

Covenant of Further Assurance—A promise that the grantor will provide the legal documents and perform other tasks needed to make the grantee's title good.

Covenant of Quiet Enjoyment—A promise that a buyer or tenant's possession will not be disturbed by the previous owner, the lessor, or anyone else making a lawful claim against the property.

Covenant of Right to Convey—In a deed, a promise that the grantor has the legal ability to make a valid conveyance.

Covenant of Seisin—In a deed, a promise that the grantor actually owns the interest he or she is conveying to the grantee.

Covenant of Warranty Forever—In a deed, a promise that the grantor will defend the grantee's title against claims superior to the grantor's that exist when the conveyance is made. Also called a covenant of warranty.

CPM—Certified Property Manager; a property manager who has satisfied the requirements set by the Institute of Real Estate Management of the National Association of Realtors®.

Credit—A payment receivable (owed to you), as opposed to a debit, which is a payment due (owed by you).

Credit History—An individual's record of bill payment and debt repayment, as revealed in a credit report compiled by a credit rating bureau.

Creditor—One who is owed a debt.

Creditor, Secured—A creditor with a security interest in or a lien against specific property. If the debt is not repaid, the secured creditor can repossess the property or (in the case of real estate) foreclose on the property and collect the debt from the sale proceeds.

Creditor, Unsecured—A creditor who does not have a lien against or other security interest in any of the debtor's property (and who therefore is less likely to be able to collect the debt if the debtor fails to pay it as agreed).

Credit Union—A type of financial institution that serves only the members of a particular group (such as a labor union or a professional association), and which has traditionally emphasized consumer loans.

Creditworthiness—The extent to which an individual is a good credit risk; how likely he or she is to repay a loan on the schedule set by the lender, or how likely to default.

Criminal Law—The body of law under which the government can prosecute an individual for crimes, wrongs against society. *Compare*: Civil Law.

Cubage—The cubic volume of an object; in the case of a building, determined by multiplying the width by the depth by the height (measuring from the basement floor to the outside surfaces of roof and walls).

Cul-de-Sac—A dead-end street, especially one with a semicircular turnaround at the end.

Curable—In reference to depreciation, capable of being corrected at a cost that could be recovered in the sales price if the property were subsequently sold. (Depreciation is incurable if it cannot be corrected and/or if it would cost more to correct than the correction would add to the property's value.)

Cure—To remedy a default, by paying money that is overdue or fulfilling other obligations that have not been met.

Curtesy—*See*: Dower and Curtesy.

Customer—From the point of view of a real estate agent, a prospective property buyer.

Damage Deposit—*See*: Security Deposit.

Damages—In a civil lawsuit, an amount of money the defendant is ordered to pay the plaintiff.

Damages, Actual—*See*: Compensatory damages.

Damages, Liquidated—A sum that the parties to a contract agree in advance (at the time the contract is made) will serve as full compensation in the event of a breach.

Damages, Punitive—In a civil lawsuit, an award added to actual damages, to punish the defendant for outrageous or malicious conduct and discourage others from similar conduct.

Datum—An artificial horizontal plane of elevation, established in reference to sea level, used by surveyors as a reference point in determining elevation.

Dealer—One who regularly buys and sells real estate in the ordinary course of business.

Dealer Property—Property held for sale to customers rather than for long-term investment; a developer's inventory of subdivision lots, for example.

Debit—A charge or debt owed to another.

Debtor—One who owes money to another.

Debt Service—The amount of money required to make the periodic payments of principal and interest on an amortized debt, such as a mortgage.

Decedent—A person who has died.

Declaration of Abandonment—A document recorded by an owner that voluntarily releases a property from homestead protection.

Declaration of Homestead—A recorded document that establishes homestead protection for a property that would not otherwise receive it.

Declaration of Restrictions—*See*: CC&Rs.

Dedication—A voluntary or involuntary gift of private property for public use; may transfer ownership or simply create an easement.

Dedication, Common Law—Involuntary dedication, resulting from a property owner's acquiescence to public use of his or her property over a long period. Also called implied dedication.

Dedication, Statutory—A dedication required by law; for example, dedication of property for streets and sidewalks as a prerequisite to subdivision approval.

Deduction—An amount a taxpayer is allowed to subtract from his or her income before the tax on the income is calculated (as distinguished from a tax credit, which is deducted from the tax owed).

Deed—An instrument which, when properly executed and delivered, conveys title to real property from the grantor to the grantee.

Deed, Administrator's—A deed used by the administrator of an estate to convey property owned by a deceased person to the heirs.

Deed, General Warranty—A deed in which the grantor warrants the title against defects that may have arisen before or during his or her period of ownership.

Deed, Gift—A deed that is not supported by valuable consideration; often lists "love and affection" as the consideration.

Deed, Grant—A deed that uses the word "grant" in its words of conveyance and carries certain implied warranties.

Deed, Quitclaim—A deed that conveys any interest in a property that the grantor has at the time the deed is executed, without warranties.

Deed, Sheriff's—A deed delivered, on court order, to the holder of a certificate of sale when the redemption period after a mortgage foreclosure has expired.

Deed, Special Warranty—A deed in which the grantor warrants title only against defects that may have arisen during his or her period of ownership.

Deed, Tax—A deed given to a purchaser of property at a tax foreclosure sale.

Deed, Trust—*See*: Deed of Trust.

Deed, Trustee's—A deed given to a purchaser of property at a trustee's sale.

Deed, Warranty—1. A general warranty deed. 2. Any type of deed that carries warranties.

Deed, Wild—A deed that won't be discovered in a standard title search, because of a break in the chain of title.

Deed Executed under Court Order—A deed that is the result of a court action, such as judicial foreclosure or partition.

Deed in Lieu of Foreclosure—A deed given by a borrower to the lender to satisfy the debt and avoid foreclosure.

Deed of Partition—Deed used by co-owners (such as tenants in common or joint tenants) to divide up the co-owned property so that each can own a portion in severalty.

Deed of Reconveyance—The instrument used to release the security property from the lien created by a deed of trust when the debt has been repaid.

Deed of Trust—An instrument that creates a voluntary lien on real property to secure the repayment of a debt, and which includes a power of sale clause permitting nonjudicial foreclosure; the parties are the grantor or trustor (borrower), the beneficiary (the lender), and the trustee (a neutral third party).

Deed Release Provision—*See*: Release Clause.

Deed Restrictions—Provisions in a deed that restrict use of the property, and which may be either covenants or conditions.

Default—Failure to fulfill an obligation, duty, or promise, as when a borrower fails to make payments, or a tenant fails to pay rent.

Default Judgment—*See*: Judgment, Default.

Defeasance Clause—A clause in a mortgage, deed of trust, or lease that cancels or defeats a certain right upon the occurrence of a particular event.

Defeasible Fee—*See*: Fee, Defeasible.

Defendant—1. The person being sued in a civil lawsuit. 2. The accused person in a criminal lawsuit.

Deferred Maintenance—Curable depreciation resulting from maintenance or repairs that were postponed, causing physical deterioration. *See*: Deterioration, Physical.

Deficiency Judgment—*See*: Judgment, Deficiency.

Degree—In surveying, a unit of circular measurement equal to $^1/_{360}$ of one complete rotation around a point in a plane.

Delivery—The legal transfer of a deed from the grantor to the grantee, which results in the transfer of title.

Demand—Desire to own coupled with ability to afford. This is one of the four elements of value, along with scarcity, utility, and transferability.

Density—In land use law, the number of buildings or occupants per unit of land.

Department of Housing and Urban Development (HUD)—The federal cabinet department responsible for public housing programs, FHA-insured loan programs, and enforcement of the Federal Fair Housing Act. The FHA and Ginnie Mae are both part of HUD.

Deposit—Money offered as an indication of commitment or as a protection, and which may be refunded under certain circumstances; for example, a good faith deposit or a tenant's security deposit.

Deposition—The formal, out-of-court testimony of a witness in a lawsuit, taken before trial for possible use later, during the trial; either as part of the discovery process, to determine the facts of the case, or when the witness will not be available during the trial.

Deposit Receipt—*See*: Purchase and Sale Agreement.

Depreciable Property—In the federal income tax code, property that is eligible for cost recovery deductions because it will wear out and have to be replaced.

Depreciation—1. A loss in value (caused by physical deterioration, functional obsolescence, or external obsolescence). 2. For the purposes of income tax deductions, apportioning the cost of an asset over a period of time.

Depreciation, Accrued—Depreciation that has built up or accumulated over a period of time.

Depreciation, Age-Life—A method of estimating depreciation for appraisal purposes, based on the life expectancy of the property, assuming normal maintenance.

Depreciation, Curable—Deferred maintenance and functional obsolescence that would ordinarily be corrected by a prudent owner, because the correction cost could be recovered in the sales price.

Depreciation, Incurable—Physical deterioration, functional obsolescence, or external obsolescence that is either impossible to correct, or not economically feasible to correct, because the cost could not be recovered in the sales price.

Depreciation, Observed Condition—A method of calculating depreciation that involves the appraiser inspecting the entire structure and making observations of actual depreciation. Considered the most reliable method of estimating depreciation. Also called the engineering method.

Depreciation, Straight-Line—A method of calculating depreciation for income tax or appraisal purposes, in which an equal portion of a structure's value is deducted each year over the anticipated useful life; when the full value of the improvement has been depreciated, its economic life is exhausted.

Depreciation Deductions—Under the federal income tax code, deductions from a taxpayer's income to permit the cost of an asset to be recovered; allowed only for depreciable property that is held for the production of income or used in a trade or business. Also called cost recovery deductions.

Depth Table—Mathematical table used in appraisal to estimate the differences in value between lots with different depths. Frontage has the greatest value, and land at the rear of a lot has the least value.

Dereliction—*See*: Reliction.

Descent—Property that is transferred by intestate succession instead of by will. A person who receives property by intestate succession is said to receive it by descent, rather than by devise or bequest.

Detached Residence—A home physically separated from the neighboring home(s), not connected by a common wall.

Deterioration, Physical—A loss in value due to wear and tear, damage, or structural defects. Physical deterioration that's curable is called deferred maintenance.

Developed Land—Land with man-made improvements, such as buildings or roads.

Developer—One who subdivides or improves land to achieve its most profitable use.

Development—1. Any development project, such as a new office park. 2. A housing subdivision. 3. In reference to a property's life cycle, the earliest stage, also called integration.

Devise—1. (noun) A gift of real property through a will. 2. (verb) To transfer real property by will. *Compare*: Bequest; Bequeath; Legacy.

Devisee—Someone who receives title to real property through a will. *Compare*: Beneficiary; Legatee.

Devisor—A testator who devises real property in his or her will.

Directional Growth—The direction in which a city's residential neighborhoods are expanding or expected to expand.

Disability—A physical or mental impairment that substantially limits a person in one or more major life activities, according to the Americans with Disabilities Act and Fair Housing Act.

Disaffirm—To ask a court to terminate a voidable contract.

Disbursements—Money paid out or expended.

Disclaimer—A denial of legal responsibility.

Discount—1. (verb) To sell a promissory note at less than its face value. 2. (noun) An amount withheld from the loan amount by the lender when the loan is originated; discount points.

Discount Points—A percentage of the principal amount of a loan, collected by the lender at the time a loan is originated, to give the lender an additional yield.

Discount Rate—The interest rate charged when a member bank borrows money from the Federal Reserve Bank.

Discrimination—Treating people unequally because of their race, religion, sex, national origin, age, or some other characteristic.

Disintegration—In a property's life cycle, the period of decline when the property's present economic usefulness is near an end and constant upkeep is necessary.

Dispossess—To force someone out of possession of real property through legal procedures, as in an eviction.

Domicile—The state where a person has his or her permanent home.

Donative Intent—The intent to transfer title immediately and unconditionally; required for proper delivery of a deed.

Double-entry Bookkeeping—An accounting technique in which an item is entered in the ledger twice, once as a credit and once as a debit; used for some settlement statements.

Dower and Curtesy—Laws giving a husband and wife interests in each other's real property; only used in a few states.

Downpayment—The part of the purchase price of property that the buyer is paying in cash; the difference between the purchase price and the financing.

Downzoning—Rezoning land for a more limited use.

Drainage—A system to draw water off land, either artificially (e.g., with pipes) or naturally (e.g., with a slope).

Dual Agency—*See*: Agency, Dual.

Due-on-Sale Clause—*See*: Alienation Clause.

Duplex—A structure that contains two separate housing units, with separate entrances, living areas, baths, and kitchens.

Duress—Unlawful force or constraint used to compel someone to do something (such as sign a contract) against his or her will.

Dwelling—A building or a part of a building used or intended to be used as living quarters.

Earnest Money—*See*: Good Faith Deposit.

Easement—An irrevocable right to use some part of another person's real property for a particular purpose.

Easement, Access—An easement that enables the easement holder to reach and/or leave his or her property (the dominant tenement) by crossing the servient tenement. Also called an easement for ingress and egress.

Easement, Aviation—An easement by which a property owner allows aircraft to fly through the airspace over his or her property (above a specified height).

Easement, Implied—*See*: Easement by Implication.

Easement, Negative—An easement that prevents the servient tenant from using his or her own land in a certain way (instead of allowing the dominant tenant to use it); essentially the same thing as a restrictive covenant that runs with the land.

Easement, Positive—An easement that allows the dominant tenant to use the servient tenement in a particular way. This is the standard type of easement (see the first definition of Easement, above); the term "positive easement" is generally only used when contrasting a standard easement with a negative easement.

Easement, Prescriptive—An easement acquired by prescription; that is, by using the property openly and without the owner's permission for the period prescribed by statute.

Easement Appurtenant—An easement that benefits a piece of property, the dominant tenement. *Compare*: Easement in Gross.

Easement by Express Grant—An easement granted to another in a deed or other document.

Easement by Express Reservation—An easement created in a deed when a landowner is dividing the property, transferring the servient tenement but retaining the dominant tenement; an easement that the grantor reserves for his or her own use.

Easement by Implication—An easement created by law when a parcel of land is divided, if there has been long-standing, apparent prior use, and it is reasonably necessary for the enjoyment of the dominant tenement. Sometimes called an easement by necessity.

Easement by Necessity—1. A special type of easement by implication, created by law even when there has been no prior use, if the dominant tenement would be entirely useless without an easement. 2. Any easement by implication.

Easement in Gross—An easement that benefits a person instead of a piece of land. There is a dominant tenant, but no dominant tenement. *Compare*: Easement Appurtenant.

ECOA—*See*: Equal Credit Opportunity Act.

Economic Life—The period during which improved property will yield a return over and above the rent due to the land itself; also called the useful life.

Economic Obsolescence—*See*: Obsolescence, External.

Economic Rent—*See*: Rent, Economic.

Effective Age—*See*: Age, Effective.

Egress—A means of exiting; a way to leave a property; the opposite of ingress. The terms ingress and egress are most commonly used in reference to an access easement.

EIS—Environmental Impact Statement.

Ejectment—A legal action to recover possession of real property from someone who is not legally entitled to possession of it; an eviction.

Elements of Comparison—In the sales comparison approach to appraisal, considerations taken into account in selecting comparables and comparing comparables to the subject property. They include date of sale, location, physical characteristics, and terms of sale.

Emblements—Crops that are produced annually through the labor of the cultivator, such as wheat.

Emblements, Doctrine of—The legal rule that gives an agricultural tenant the right to enter the land to harvest crops after the lease ends.

Eminent Domain—The government's constitutional power to take (condemn) private property for public use, as long as the owner is paid just compensation.

Employee—Someone who works under the direction and control of another. *Compare*: Independent Contractor.

Encroachment—A physical intrusion onto neighboring property, usually due to a mistake regarding the location of the boundary.

Encumber—To place a lien or other encumbrance against the title to a property.

Encumbrance—A nonpossessory interest in real property; a right or interest held by someone other than the property owner, which may be a lien, an easement, or a restrictive covenant.

Encumbrance, Financial—A lien.

Endorsement—1. Assignment of a negotiable instrument (such as a check or a promissory note) by the payee to another party, by signing the back of the instrument. 2. Additional insurance purchased by a policyholder to cover a specific risk, such as flooding or earthquakes.

Endorsement, Special—An endorsement to a specific person (as opposed to an endorsement in blank).

Endorsement in Blank—An endorsement that does not specify a particular holder, so that the bearer—whoever has possession of the instrument—is entitled to payment.

Enjoin—To prohibit an act, or command performance of an act, by court order; to issue an injunction.

Entitlement—The amount of the borrower's guaranty in a VA loan.

EPA—Environmental Protection Agency.

Equal Credit Opportunity Act (ECOA)—A federal law that prohibits lenders from discriminating against consumer loan applicants on the basis of race, color, religion, national origin, sex, marital status, or age, or because the applicant's income is derived from public assistance.

Equilibrium—In the life cycle of a property, a period of stability, during which the property undergoes little, if any, change.

Equitable Interest or Title—*See*: Title, Equitable.

Equitable Remedy—In a civil lawsuit, a judgment granted to the plaintiff that is something other than an award of money (damages). An injunction, rescission, and specific performance are examples.

Equity—1. An owner's unencumbered interest in his or her property; the difference between the value of the property and the liens against it. 2. A judge's power to soften or set aside strict legal rules, to bring about a fair and just result in a particular case.

Equity of Redemption—The right of a property owner to redeem a property after a judicial foreclosure sale.

Erosion—Gradual loss of soil due to the action of water or wind.

Escalation Clause—A clause in a contract or mortgage that provides for payment or interest adjustments (usually increases) if specified events occur, such as a change in the property taxes or in the prime interest rate. Also called an escalator clause.

Escheat—Reversion of property to the state after a person dies intestate and no heirs can be located.

Escrow—An arrangement in which something of value (such as money or a deed) is held on behalf of the parties to a transaction by a third party (an escrow agent) until specified conditions have been fulfilled.

Escrow Agent—A company that is licensed to engage in the escrow business.

Escrow Instructions—A contract between an escrow agent and the parties to a transaction that sets forth the parties' obligations and the conditions for closing.

Estate—1. An interest in real property that is or may become possessory; either a freehold or a leasehold. 2. The property left by someone who has died.

Estate, Fee Simple—*See*: Fee Simple.

Estate, Periodic—*See*: Tenancy, Periodic.

Estate at Sufferance—*See*: Tenancy at Sufferance.

Estate at Will—*See*: Tenancy at Will.

Estate for Life—A freehold estate that lasts only as long as a specified person lives. That person is referred to as the measuring life. Commonly called a life estate.

Estate for Years—*See*: Tenancy, Term.

Estate of Inheritance—An estate that can pass to the holder's heirs, such as a fee simple.

Estoppel—A legal doctrine that prevents a person from asserting rights or facts that are inconsistent with his or her earlier actions or statements.

Estoppel Certificate—A document that prevents a person who signs it from later asserting facts different from those stated in the document. Also called an estoppel letter.

Et Al.—Abbreviation for the Latin phrase "et alius" or "et alii," meaning "and another" or "and others."

Ethics—A system of accepted principles or standards of moral conduct. *See*: Code of Ethics.

Et Ux.—Abbreviation for the Latin phrase "et uxor," meaning "and wife."

Eviction—Dispossession or expulsion of someone from real property.

Eviction, Actual—Physically forcing someone off of real property (or preventing them from re-entering), or using the legal process to make them leave. *Compare*: Eviction, Constructive.

Eviction, Constructive—When a landlord's act (or failure to act) interferes with the tenant's quiet enjoyment of the property, or makes the property unfit for its intended use, to such an extent that the tenant is forced to move out.

Eviction, Self-help—The use of physical force, a lock-out, or a utility shut-off to evict a tenant, instead of the legal process. This is generally illegal.

Excess Land—Land that is part of a parcel that does not add to the value of that property. For instance, where the value of a property lies primarily in its frontage, additional depth would not increase the property's value.

Exchange—*See*: Tax-Free Exchange.

Exclusive Listing—*See*: Listing, Exclusive.

Exculpatory Clause—A clause in a contract that relieves one party of liability for certain defaults or problems. Such provisions are not always enforceable.

Execute—1. To sign an instrument and take any other steps (such as acknowledgment) that may be necessary to its validity. 2. To perform or complete. *See*: Contract, Executed.

Execution—The legal process in which a court orders an official (such as the sheriff) to seize and sell the property of a judgment debtor to satisfy a lien.

Executor—A person named in a will to carry out its provisions. If it is a woman, she may be referred to as the executrix, but that term is passing out of use.

Exemption—A provision holding that a law or rule does not apply to a particular person or group. For example, a person entitled to a tax exemption is not required to pay the tax.

Expenses, Fixed—Recurring property expenses, such as general real estate taxes and hazard insurance.

Expenses, Maintenance—Cleaning, supplies, utilities, tenant services, and administrative costs for income-producing property.

Expenses, Operating—For income-producing property, the fixed expenses, maintenance expenses, and reserves for replacement; does not include debt service.

Expenses, Variable—Expenses incurred in connection with property that do not occur on a set schedule, such as the cost of repairing a roof damaged in a storm.

Express—Stated in words, whether spoken or written. *Compare*: Implied.

Extender Clause—*See:* Safety Clause.

External Obsolescence—*See*: Obsolescence, External.

Face-to-face Closing—Closing in which the seller and buyer personally meet to exchange the deed, money, and other documents. Also called roundtable closing, passing papers, or settlement and transfer.

Failure of Purpose—When the intended purpose of an agreement or arrangement can no longer be achieved. In most cases, this releases the parties from their obligations.

Fair Housing Act—*See*: Federal Fair Housing Act.

Fannie Mae—Popular name for the Federal National Mortgage Association (FNMA).

FDIC—*See*: Federal Deposit Insurance Corporation.

Feasibility Study—A cost-benefit analysis of a proposed project, often required by lenders before giving a loan commitment.

Fed—The Federal Reserve.

Federal Deposit Insurance Corporation (FDIC)—A federal agency that insures deposits in financial institutions.

Federal Fair Housing Act—A law enacted in 1968 which makes it illegal to discriminate on the basis of race, color, religion, sex, national origin, handicap, or familial status in the sale or rental of residential property (or vacant land that will be used for residential construction).

Federal Home Loan Bank System—A federal organization that provides reserve funds for savings and loan associations, performing many of the same functions that the Federal Reserve System does for commercial banks.

Federal Home Loan Mortgage Corporation (FHLMC)—One of the government-sponsored secondary market entities; commonly called Freddie Mac.

Federal Housing Administration (FHA)—An agency within the Department of Housing and Urban Development (HUD). Its main activity is insuring home mortgage loans, to encourage lenders to make more affordable loans.

Federal National Mortgage Association (FNMA)—One of the government-sponsored secondary market entities; commonly called Fannie Mae.

Federal Reserve—The government body that regulates commercial banks and implements monetary policy in an attempt to keep the national economy running well. Often referred to as the Fed.

Federal Reserve System—The twelve Federal Reserve Banks, which implement federal monetary policy through setting the federal lending rates and reserve requirements.

Federal Trade Commission (FTC)—A federal agency responsible for investigating and eliminating unfair and deceptive business practices. It is also the agency charged with enforcing the Truth in Lending Act.

Fee—*See*: Fee Simple.

Fee, Qualified—*See*: Fee Simple, Defeasible.

Fee Broker—*See*: Broker, Fee.

Fee Simple—The highest and most complete form of ownership, which is of potentially infinite duration. Also called a fee or a fee simple absolute.

Fee Simple Defeasible—A fee simple estate that is subject to termination if a certain condition is not met or if a specified event occurs. Also called a conditional fee or qualified fee.

Fee Simple Determinable—*See*: Fee Simple Defeasible.

Fee Simple Subject to a Condition Subsequent—*See*: Fee Simple Defeasible.

Feudal System—A system of land ownership in which the sovereign owns all the land and grants lesser interests to others in return for services; the dominant system in Europe during the Middle Ages. *Compare*: Allodial System.

FHA—*See*: Federal Housing Administration. *See also*: Loan, FHA.

FHLMC—*See*: Federal Home Loan Mortgage Corporation.

Fidelity Bond—A bond to cover losses resulting from the dishonesty of an employee.

Fiduciary Relationship—A relationship of trust and confidence, where one party owes the other (or both parties owe each other) loyalty and a higher standard of good faith than is owed to third parties. For example, an agent is a fiduciary in relation to the principal; husband and wife are fiduciaries in relation to one another.

Finance Charge—Any charge a borrower is assessed, directly or indirectly, in connection with a loan. *See also*: Total Finance Charge.

Financial Statement—A summary of facts showing the financial condition of an individual or a business, including a detailed list of assets and liabilities. Also called a balance sheet.

Financing Statement—A brief instrument that is recorded to perfect and give constructive notice of a creditor's security interest in an article of personal property.

Finder's Fee—A referral fee paid to someone for directing a buyer or a seller to a real estate agent.

Firm Commitment—*See*: Commitment.

FIRPTA—*See*: Foreign Investment in Real Property Tax Act.

First Lien Position—The position held by a mortgage or deed of trust that has higher lien priority than any other mortgage or deed of trust against the property.

First Refusal, Right of—*See*: Right of First Refusal.

Fiscal Policy—The federal government's financial regime of spending, collecting revenue, and borrowing; managed by the United States Treasury.

Fiscal Year—Any twelve-month period used as a business year for accounting, tax, and other financial purposes, as opposed to a calendar year.

Fixed Disbursement Plan—A construction financing arrangement that calls for the loan proceeds to be disbursed in a series of predetermined installments at various stages of the construction.

Fixed-Rate Loan—*See*: Loan, Fixed-Rate.

Fixed Term—A period of time that has a definite beginning and ending.

Fixture—An item that used to be personal property but has been attached to or closely associated with real property in such a way that it has legally become part of the real property. *See*: Annexation, Actual; Annexation, Constructive.

Floor Area Ratio—A zoning requirement that controls the ratio between a building's floor space and the percentage of the lot it occupies.

FNMA—*See*: Federal National Mortgage Association.

For Sale by Owner (FSBO)—Property that is "for sale by owner," as opposed to listed with a real estate agent.

Foreclosure—Sale of property initiated by a lienholder, against the owner's wishes, so that the unpaid lien can be satisfied from the sale proceeds.

Foreclosure, Judicial—1. The sale of property pursuant to court order to satisfy a lien. 2. A lawsuit filed by a mortgagee or deed of trust beneficiary to foreclose on the security property when the borrower has defaulted.

Foreclosure, Nonjudicial—Foreclosure by a trustee under the power of sale clause in a deed of trust.

Foreign Investment in Real Property Tax Act—The Foreign Investment in Real Property Tax Act, which requires withholding funds from a sale of real property if the seller is not a U.S. citizen or a resident alien, in order to prevent tax evasion.

Forfeiture—Loss of a right or something else of value as a result of failure to perform an obligation or condition.

Franchise—A right or privilege granted by a government to conduct a certain business, or a right granted by a private business to use its trade name in conducting business.

Fraud—An intentional or negligent misrepresentation or concealment of a material fact, which is relied upon by another, who is induced to enter a transaction and harmed as a result.

Fraud, Actual—Intentional deceit or misrepresentation to cheat or defraud another.

Fraud, Constructive—A breach of duty that misleads the person the duty was owed to, without an intention to deceive. For example, if a seller gives a buyer inaccurate information about the property without realizing that it is false, that may be constructive fraud.

Freddie Mac—Popular name for the Federal Home Loan Mortgage Corporation (FHLMC).

Free and Clear—Ownership of real property completely free of any liens.

Freehold—A possessory interest in real property that has an indeterminable duration. It can be either a fee simple or an estate for life. Someone who has a freehold estate has title to the property (as opposed to someone who has a leasehold estate, who is only a tenant).

Frontage—The distance a property extends along a street or a body of water; the distance between the two side boundaries at the front of the lot.

Front Foot—A measurement of property for sale or valuation, with each foot of frontage presumed to extend the entire depth of the lot.

Front Money—The cash required to get a project or venture underway; includes initial expenses such as attorney's fees, feasibility studies, loan charges, and a downpayment.

Fructus Industriales—Plants planted and cultivated by people, such as crops. This is a Latin phrase meaning "fruits of industry."

Fructus Naturales—Naturally occurring plants ("fruits of nature").

FSBO—*See*: For Sale by Owner.

Functional Obsolescence—*See*: Obsolescence, Functional.

Gain—Under the federal income tax code, that portion of the proceeds from the sale of a capital asset, such as real estate, that is recognized as taxable profit.

Garnishment—A legal process by which a creditor gains access to the funds or personal property of a debtor that are in the hands of a third party. For example, if the debtor's wages are garnished, the employer is required to turn over part of each paycheck to the creditor.

General Agent—*See*: Agent, General.

General Lien—*See*: Lien, General.

General Plan—A comprehensive, long-term plan of development for a community, which is implemented by zoning and other laws. Also called a comprehensive plan or a master plan.

Gift Funds—Money that a relative (or other third party) gives to a buyer who otherwise would not have enough cash to close the transaction.

Ginnie Mae—The Government National Mortgage Association (GNMA).

GNMA—*See*: Government National Mortgage Association.

Good Faith Deposit—A deposit that a prospective buyer gives the seller as evidence of his or her good faith intent to complete the transaction. Also called an earnest money deposit.

Good Faith Improver—*See*: Innocent Improver.

Good Will—An intangible asset of a business resulting from a good reputation with the public, serving as an indication of future return business.

Government Lot—In the government survey system, a parcel of land that is not a regular section (one mile square), because of the convergence of range lines, or because of a body of water or some other obstacle; assigned a government lot number.

Government National Mortgage Association (GNMA)—One of the three major secondary market entities, commonly called Ginnie Mae; a federal agency that is part of the Department of Housing and Urban Development.

Government Survey System—A system of grids made up of range and township lines that divide the land into townships, which are further subdivided into sections. A particular property is identified by its location within a particular section, township, and range. Also called the rectangular survey system.

Grant—To transfer or convey an interest in real property by means of a written instrument.

Grant Deed—*See*: Deed, Grant.

Grantee—One who receives a grant of real property.

Granting Clause—Words in a deed that indicate the grantor's intent to transfer an interest in property.

Grantor—One who grants an interest in real property to another.

Gross Income Multiplier—A figure which is multiplied by a rental property's annual or monthly gross income to arrive at an estimate of the property's value. Also called a gross rent multiplier.

Gross Income Multiplier Method—A method of appraising residential property by reference to its rental value. Also called the gross rent multiplier method.

Group Boycott—In the real estate profession, an agreement between two or more real estate brokers to exclude other brokers from equal participation in real estate activities.

Guardian—A person appointed by a court to administer the affairs of a minor or an incompetent person.

Guide Meridians—In the government survey system, lines running north-south (parallel to the principal meridian) at 24-mile intervals.

Habendum Clause—A clause included after the granting clause in many deeds. It begins "to have and to hold" and describes the type of estate the grantee will hold.

Habitability, Implied Warranty of—A warranty implied by law in every residential lease, stating that the property is fit for habitation.

Heir—Someone entitled to inherit another's property under the laws of intestate succession.

Heirs and Assigns—A phrase used in legal documents to cover all successors to a person's interest in property. Assigns are successors who acquire title in some manner other than inheritance, such as by deed.

Hereditament, Corporeal—Tangible property, real or personal, that can be inherited; property with physical substance, such as a car or a house.

Hereditament, Incorporeal—Intangible property, real or personal, that can be inherited, such as an easement appurtenant or accounts receivable.

Highest and Best Use—The use which, at the time of appraisal, is most likely to produce the greatest net return from the property over a given period of time.

Historical Rent—*See*: Rent, Contract.

HMDA—*See*: Home Mortgage Disclosure Act.

Holder in Due Course—A person who obtains a negotiable instrument for value, in good faith, without notice that it is overdue or notice of any defenses against it.

Holdover Tenant—*See*: Tenant, Holdover.

Home Mortgage Disclosure Act (HMDA)—A federal law that requires large institutional lenders to make annual reports on residential mortgage loans. The reports disclose areas where few or no home loans have been made and alert regulators to potential redlining.

Homeowners Association—A nonprofit association made up of homeowners in a subdivision, responsible for enforcing the CC&Rs and managing other community affairs.

Homestead—An owner-occupied dwelling, together with any appurtenant outbuildings and land.

Homestead Law—A state law that provides limited protection against judgment creditors' claims for homestead property.

HUD—The Department of Housing and Urban Development.

Hypothecate—To make property security for an obligation without giving up possession of it (as opposed to pledging, which involves surrender of possession).

ILSA—*See*: Interstate Land Sales Full Disclosure Act.

Implied—Not expressed in words, but understood from actions or circumstances. *Compare*: Express.

Impound Account—A bank account maintained by a lender for payment of property taxes and insurance premiums on the security property. The lender requires the borrower to make regular deposits, and pays the expenses out of the account. Also called a reserve account.

Improvements—Man-made additions to real property.

Improvements, Misplaced—Improvements that do not fit the most profitable use of the site. They can be overimprovements or underimprovements.

Imputed Knowledge—A legal doctrine stating that a principal is considered to have notice of information that the agent has, even if the agent never told the principal.

Income, Disposable—Income remaining after income taxes have been paid.

Income, Effective Gross—A measure of a rental property's capacity to generate income; calculated by subtracting a vacancy factor from the economic rent (potential gross income).

Income, Gross—A property's total income before making any deductions (for bad debts, vacancies, operating expenses, etc.).

Income, Net—The income that is capitalized to estimate the property's value; calculated by subtracting the property's operating expenses (fixed expenses, maintenance expenses, and reserves for replacement) from the effective gross income.

Income, Potential Gross—A property's economic rent; the income it could earn if it were available for lease in the current market.

Income, Residual—The amount of income that an applicant for a VA loan has left over after taxes, recurring obligations, and the proposed housing expense have been deducted from his or her gross monthly income.

Income, Spendable—The income that remains after deducting operating expenses, debt service, and income taxes from a property's gross income. Also called net spendable income or cash flow.

Income Approach to Value—One of the three main methods of appraisal, in which an estimate of the subject property's value is based on the net income it produces; also called the capitalization method or investor's method of appraisal.

Income Property—Property that generates rent or other income for the owner, such as an apartment building. In the federal income tax code, it is referred to as property held for the production of income.

Income Ratio—A standard used in qualifying a buyer for a loan, to determine whether he or she has sufficient income. The buyer's debts and proposed housing expense should not exceed a specified percentage of his or her income.

Incompetent—Not legally competent; not of sound mind.

Increment—An increase in value; the opposite of decrement.

Independent Contractor—A person who contracts to do a job for another, but retains control over how he or she will carry out the task, rather than following detailed instructions. *Compare*: Employee.

Index—A published statistical report that indicates changes in the cost of money; used as the basis for interest rate adjustments in an ARM.

Index, Tract—An index of recorded documents in which all documents that carry a particular legal description are grouped together.

Indexes, Grantor/Grantee—Indexes of recorded documents maintained by the recorder, with each document listed in alphabetical order according to the last name of the grantor (in the grantor index) and grantee (in the grantee index).

Index Lease—The rent is tied to an index such as the Consumer Price Index; rent increases whenever an increase in the index occurs.

Ingress—A means of entering a property; the opposite of egress. The terms ingress and egress are most commonly used in reference to an access easement.

In-house Transaction—A sale in which the buyer and the seller are brought together by salespersons working for the same broker.

Injunction—A court order prohibiting someone from performing an act, or commanding performance of an act.

Innocent Improver—Someone who makes an improvement on land in the mistaken belief that he or she owns the land. Also called a good faith improver.

Installment Note—*See*: Note, Installment.

Installment Sale—Under the federal income tax code, a sale in which less than 100% of the sales price is received in the year the sale takes place.

Instrument—A legal document, usually one that transfers title (such as a deed), creates a lien (such as a mortgage), or establishes a right to payment (such as a promissory note or contract).

Insurance, Hazard—Insurance against damage to real property caused by fire, flood, theft, or other mishap. Also called casualty insurance.

Insurance, Homeowner's—Insurance against damage to the real property and the homeowner's personal property.

Insurance, Mortgage—Insurance that protects a lender against losses resulting from the borrower's default.

Insurance, Mutual Mortgage—The mortgage insurance provided by the FHA to lenders who make loans through FHA programs.

Insurance, Private Mortgage (PMI)—Insurance provided by private companies to conventional lenders for loans with loan-to-value ratios over 80%.

Insurance, Title—Insurance that protects against losses resulting from undiscovered title defects. An owner's policy protects the buyer, while a mortgagee's policy protects the lien position of the buyer's lender.

Insurance, Title, Extended Coverage—Title insurance that covers problems that should be discovered by an inspection of the property (such as encroachments and adverse possession), in addition to the problems covered by standard coverage policies. An extended coverage policy is sometimes referred to as an ALTA (American Land Title Association) policy.

Insurance, Title, Homeowner's Coverage—Title insurance for residential property with up to four units that covers many of the types of problems covered by an extended coverage policy.

Insurance, Title, Standard Coverage—Title insurance that protects against latent title defects (such as forged deeds) and undiscovered recorded encumbrances, but does not protect against problems that would only be discovered by an inspection of the property.

Integration—In a property's life cycle, the earliest stage, when the property is being developed. Also called development.

Interest—1. A right or share in something (such as a piece of real estate). 2. A charge a borrower pays to a lender for the use of the lender's money.

Interest, Compound—Interest computed on both the principal and its accrued interest. *Compare*: Interest, Simple.

Interest, Future—An interest in property that will or may become possessory at some point in the future, such as a remainder or reversion.

Interest, Interim—*See*: Interest, Prepaid.

Interest, Prepaid—Interest on a new loan that must be paid at the time of closing; covers the interest due for the first month of the loan term. Also called interim interest.

Interest, Simple—Interest that is computed on the principal amount of the loan only, which is the type of interest charged in connection with real estate loans. *Compare*: Interest, Compound.

Interest, Undivided—A co-owner's interest, giving him or her the right to possession of the whole property, rather than to a particular section of it.

Interpleader—A court action filed by someone who is holding funds that two or more people are claiming. The holder turns the funds over to the court; the court resolves the dispute and delivers the money to the party who is entitled to it.

Interstate Land Sales Full Disclosure Act (ILSA)—Federal legislation designed to provide buyers with full and accurate information in regard to subdivided property that is sold or advertised across state lines.

Intestate—Without a valid will.

Intestate Succession—Distribution of the property of a person who died intestate to his or her heirs.

Invalid—Not legally binding or legally effective; not valid.

Inventory—A detailed list of the stock-in-trade of a business.

Inverse Condemnation Action—A court action by a private landowner against the government, seeking compensation for damage to property as a result of government action.

Inverted Pyramid—A way of visualizing ownership of real property. In theory, a property owner owns all the earth, water, and air enclosed by a pyramid that has its tip at the center of the earth and extends up through the property boundaries out into the sky.

Investment—An asset that is expected to generate a return (a profit).

Investment Property—Unimproved property held as an investment in the expectation that it will appreciate in value.

Involuntary Conversion—For income tax purposes, when an asset is converted into cash without the voluntary action of the owner, such as through a condemnation award or insurance proceeds.

Involuntary Lien—*See*: Lien, Involuntary.

Joint Venture—Two or more individuals or companies joining together for one project or a related series of projects, but not as an ongoing business. *Compare*: Partnership.

Judgment—1. A court's binding determination of the rights and duties of the parties in a lawsuit. 2. A court order requiring one party to pay the other damages.

Judgment, Default—A court judgment in favor of the plaintiff due to the defendant's failure to answer the complaint or appear at a hearing.

Judgment, Deficiency—A personal judgment entered against a borrower in favor of the lender if the proceeds from a foreclosure sale of the security property are not enough to pay off the debt.

Judgment Creditor—A person who is owed money as a result of a judgment in a lawsuit.

Judgment Debtor—A person who owes money as a result of a judgment in a lawsuit.

Judgment Lien—*See*: Lien, Judgment.

Judicial Foreclosure—*See*: Foreclosure, Judicial.

Just Compensation—The compensation that the Constitution requires the government to pay a property owner when the property is taken under the power of eminent domain.

Laches, Doctrine of—A legal principle holding that the law will refuse to protect those who fail to assert their legal rights within the time period prescribed by the statute of limitations, or (if there is no applicable statute of limitations) within a reasonable time.

Land—In the legal sense, the solid part of the surface of the earth, everything affixed to it by nature or by man, and anything on it or in it, such as minerals and water; real property.

Land Contract—*See*: Contract, Land.

Landlocked Property—A parcel of land without access to a road or highway.

Landlord—A landowner who has leased his or her property to another. Also called a lessor.

Landmark—A monument, natural or artificial, set up on the boundary between two adjacent properties, to show where the boundary is.

Land Residual Process—A method of appraising vacant land.

Latent Defects—Defects that are not visible or apparent (as opposed to patent defects).

Lateral Support—*See*: Support, Lateral.

Latitude Lines—*See*: Parallels.

Lawful Object—An objective or purpose of a contract that does not violate the law or a judicial determination of public policy.

Lease—A conveyance of a leasehold estate from the fee owner to a tenant; a contract in which one party pays the other rent in exchange for the possession of real estate. Also called a rental agreement.

Lease, Fixed—A lease in which the rent is set at a fixed amount, and the landlord pays most or all of the operating expenses (such as utilities, taxes, insurance, and maintenance costs). Also called a flat lease, gross lease, or straight lease.

Lease, Graduated—A lease in which it is agreed that the rental payments will increase at intervals by a specified amount or according to a specified formula.

Lease, Gross—*See*: Lease, Fixed.

Lease, Ground—A lease of the land only, usually for a long term, to a tenant who intends to construct a building on the property.

Lease, Net—A lease requiring the tenant to pay all the costs of maintaining the property (such as taxes, insurance, and repairs), in addition to the rent paid to the landlord.

Lease, Percentage—A lease in which the rent is based on a percentage of the tenant's monthly or annual gross sales.

Lease, Sandwich—A leasehold interest lying between the property owner's interest and the interest of the tenant in possession. For example, when the tenant in a ground lease constructs a building and rents out space in the building, he or she is sandwiched between the landowner's interest and the interest of his or her building's tenant.

Lease, Straight—*See*: Lease, Fixed.

Leaseback—*See*: Sale-Leaseback.

Leasehold—A possessory interest in real property that has a limited duration. Also called a less-than-freehold estate.

Legacy—A gift of personal property by will. Also called a bequest.

Legal Description—A precise description of a parcel of real property; may be a lot and block description, a metes and bounds description, or a government survey description.

Legal Person—*See*: Artificial Person.

Legatee—Someone who receives personal property (a legacy) under a will.

Lender, Institutional—A bank, savings and loan, or similar organization that invests other people's funds in loans; as opposed to an individual or private lender, which invests its own funds.

Lessee—One who leases property from another; a tenant.

Lessor—One who leases property to another; a landlord.

Less-Than-Freehold—*See*: Leasehold.

Leverage—The effective use of borrowed money to finance an investment such as real estate.

Levy—To impose a tax.

Liability—1. A debt or obligation. 2. Legal responsibility.

Liability, Joint and Several—A form of liability in which two or more persons are responsible for a debt both individually and as a group.

Liability, Limited—A situation in which a business investor is not personally liable for all of the debts of the business, as in the case of a limited partner or a corporate shareholder.

Liability, Vicarious—A legal doctrine stating that a principal can be held liable for harms to third parties resulting from an agent's actions.

Liable—Legally responsible.

License—1. Official permission to do a particular thing that the law does not allow everyone to do. 2. Revocable, non-assignable permission to use another person's land for a particular purpose. *Compare*: Easement.

Lien—A nonpossessory interest in real property, giving the lienholder the right to foreclose if the owner doesn't pay a debt owed to the lienholder; a financial encumbrance on the owner's title.

Lien, Attachment—A lien intended to prevent transfer of the property pending the outcome of litigation.

Lien, Construction—*See*: Lien, Mechanic's.

Lien, Equitable—A lien arising as a matter of fairness, rather than by agreement or by operation of law.

Lien, General—A lien against all the property of a debtor, rather than a particular piece of his or her property. *Compare*: Lien, Specific.

Lien, Involuntary—A lien that arises by operation of law, without the consent of the property owner. Also called a statutory lien.

Lien, Judgment—A general lien against a judgment debtor's property, which the judgment creditor creates by recording an abstract of judgment in the county where the property is located.

Lien, Materialman's—A construction lien in favor of someone who supplied materials for a project (as opposed to labor).

Lien, Mechanic's—A lien on property in favor of someone who provided labor or materials to improve it. Also called a construction lien or materialman's lien.

Lien, Property Tax—A specific lien on property to secure payment of property taxes.

Lien, Specific—A lien that attaches only to a particular piece of property (as opposed to a general lien, which attaches to all of the debtor's property).

Lien, Statutory—*See*: Lien, Involuntary.

Lien, Tax—A lien on property to secure the payment of taxes.

Lien, Voluntary—A lien placed against property with the consent of the owner; a deed of trust or a mortgage.

Lienholder, Junior—A secured creditor whose lien is lower in priority than another's lien.

Lien Priority—The order in which liens are paid off out of the proceeds of a foreclosure sale.

Lien Theory—The theory holding that a mortgage or deed of trust does not involve a transfer of title to the lender, but merely creates a lien against the property in the lender's favor. *Compare*: Title Theory.

Life Estate—A freehold estate that lasts only as long as a specified person lives. That person is referred to as the measuring life.

Life Tenant—Someone who owns a life estate; the person entitled to possession of the property during the measuring life.

Like-Kind Exchange—*See*: Tax-Free Exchange.

Limited Liability—*See*: Liability, Limited.

Limited Liability Company—A form of business entity that offers both limited liability for its owners and certain tax benefits.

Limited Partnership—*See*: Partnership, Limited.

Lineal—Relating to a line; having only length, without depth. A lineal mile is 5,280 feet in distance.

Liquidated Damages—*See*: Damages, Liquidated.

Liquidity—An asset's ability to be converted into cash quickly.

Lis Pendens—A recorded notice stating that there is a lawsuit pending that may affect title to the defendant's real estate.

Listing—A written agency contract between a seller and a real estate broker, stipulating that the broker will be paid a commission for finding (or attempting to find) a buyer for the seller's property. Also called a listing agreement.

Listing, Exclusive—Either an exclusive agency listing or an exclusive right to sell listing.

Listing, Exclusive Agency—A listing agreement that entitles the broker to a commission if anyone other than the seller finds a buyer for the property during the listing term.

Listing, Exclusive Right to Sell—A listing agreement that entitles the broker to a commission if anyone—including the seller—finds a buyer for the property during the listing term.

Listing, Net—A listing agreement in which the seller sets a net amount he or she is willing to accept for the property. If the actual selling price exceeds that amount, the broker is entitled to keep the excess as his or her commission.

Listing, Open—A nonexclusive listing, given by a seller to as many brokers as he or she chooses. If the property is sold, a broker is only entitled to a commission if he or she was the procuring cause of the sale.

Listing Agreement—*See*: Listing.

Littoral Land—Land that borders on a stationary body of water (such as a lake, as opposed to a river or stream). *Compare*: Riparian Land.

Littoral Rights—The water rights of an owner of littoral land, in regard to use of the water in the lake.

LLC—*See*: Limited Liability Company.

Loan, Amortized—A loan that requires regular installment payments of both principal and interest (as opposed to an interest-only loan). It is fully amortized if the installment payments will pay off the full amount of the principal and all of the interest by the end of the repayment period. It is partially amortized if the installment payments will cover only part of the principal, so that a balloon payment of the remaining principal balance is required at the end of the repayment period.

Loan, Called—A loan that has been accelerated by the lender. *See*: Acceleration Clause.

Loan, Carryback—*See*: Mortgage, Purchase Money.

Loan, Conforming—A loan made in accordance with the standardized underwriting criteria of the major secondary market entities, Fannie Mae and Freddie Mac, and which therefore can be sold to those agencies.

Loan, Construction—A loan to finance the cost of constructing a building, usually providing that the loan funds will be advanced in installments as the work progresses. Also called an interim loan.

Loan, Conventional—An institutional loan that is not insured or guaranteed by a government agency.

Loan, FHA—A loan made by an institutional lender and insured by the Federal Housing Administration, so that the FHA will reimburse the lender for losses that result if the borrower defaults.

Loan, Fixed-rate—A loan on which the interest rate will remain the same throughout the entire loan term. *Compare*: Mortgage, Adjustable-Rate.

Loan, G.I.—*See*: Loan, VA-Guaranteed.

Loan, Guaranteed—A loan in which a third party has agreed to reimburse the lender for losses that result if the borrower defaults.

Loan, Interest-only—A loan that requires the borrower to pay only the interest during the loan term, so that the entire amount borrowed (the principal) is due at the end of the term.

Loan, Interim—*See*: Loan, Construction.

Loan, Participation—A loan in which the lender receives some yield on the loan in addition to the interest, such as a percentage of the income generated by the property, or a share in the borrower's equity in the property.

Loan, Permanent—*See*: Loan, Take-Out.

Loan, Rollover—A loan in which the interest rate is periodically renegotiated, typically every three years or every five years.

Loan, Seasoned—A loan with an established record of timely payment by the borrower.

Loan, Take-out—Long-term financing used to replace a construction loan (an interim loan) when construction has been completed. Also called a permanent loan.

Loan, VA-guaranteed—A home loan made by an institutional lender to an eligible veteran, where the Department of Veterans Affairs will reimburse the lender for losses if the veteran borrower defaults.

Loan Correspondent—An intermediary who arranges loans of an investor's money to borrowers, and then services the loans.

Loan Fee—A loan origination fee or assumption fee.

Loan Term—The length of time over which a mortgage will be repaid.

Loan-to-value Ratio (LTV)—The relationship between the loan amount and either the sales price or the appraised value of the property (whichever is less), expressed as a percentage.

Local Market—*See*: Primary Mortgage Market.

Lock-in Clause—A clause in a promissory note or land contract that prohibits prepayment before a specified date, or prohibits it altogether.

Lot—A parcel of land; especially, a parcel in a subdivision.

Lot and Block Description—The type of legal description used for platted property. It states the property's lot number and block number and the name of the subdivision, referring to the plat map recorded in the county where the property is located. Sometimes called a maps and plats description.

Love and Affection—The consideration often listed on a deed when real estate is conveyed between family members with no money exchanged. The law recognizes love and affection as good consideration (as distinguished from valuable consideration, which is money, goods, or services).

LTV—*See*: Loan-to-Value Ratio.

MAI—Member of the Appraiser's Institute. The initials identify a member of the American Institute of Real Estate Appraisers of the National Association of Realtors®.

Maintenance, Corrective—Ongoing repairs that are made to a building and its equipment to restore it to good operating condition.

Maintenance, Preventative—A program of regular inspection and care to prevent problems or provide for their immediate repair.

Majority, Age of—The age at which a person becomes legally competent; generally, 18 years old. *Compare*: Minor.

Maker—The person who signs a promissory note, promising to repay a debt. *Compare*: Payee.

Manual Underwriting—Traditional underwriting performed by an underwriter. *Compare*: Automated Underwriting.

Maps and Plats—*See*: Lot and Block Description.

Margin—In an adjustable-rate mortgage, the difference between the index rate and the interest rate charged to the borrower.

Marginal Land—Land that is of little economic value and barely repays the cost of working it.

Marketable Title—*See*: Title, Marketable.

Market Allocation—An agreement between brokers not to compete with each other in certain areas or markets.

Market Data Approach—*See*: Sales Comparison Approach.

Market-Oriented Industry—An industry that requires appropriate transportation facilities for delivery of raw materials and distribution of the finished product.

Market Price—1. The current price generally being charged for something in the marketplace. 2. The price actually paid for a property. *Compare*: Value, Market.

Market Value—See: Value, Market.

Master Plan—*See*: General Plan.

Master/Servant Relationship—A legal term for a standard employer/employee relationship.

Material Fact—An important fact; one that is likely to influence a decision.

Maturity Date—The date by which a loan is supposed to be paid off in full.

Measuring Life—*See*: Life Estate.

Meeting of Minds—*See*: Mutual Consent.

Merger—1. Uniting two or more separate properties by transferring ownership of all of them to one person. 2. When the owner of a parcel acquires title to one or more adjacent parcels.

Meridian—An imaginary line running north and south, passing through the earth's poles. Also called a longitude line.

Meridian, Principal—In the government survey system, the main north-south line in a particular grid, used as the starting point in numbering the ranges.

Meridians, Guide—In the government survey system, lines running north-south (parallel to the principal meridian) at 24-mile intervals.

Metes—Measurements.

Metes and Bounds Description—A legal description that starts at an identifiable point of beginning, then describes the property's boundaries in terms of courses (compass directions) and distances, ultimately returning to the point of beginning.

Mill—One-tenth of one cent; a measure used to state property tax rates in some cases. For example, a tax rate of one mill on the dollar is the same as a rate of one-tenth of one percent of the assessed value of the property.

Mineral Rights—Rights to the minerals located beneath the surface of a piece of property.

Minimum Property Requirements (MPR)—A lender's requirements concerning the physical condition of a building, which must be met before a loan can be approved.

Minor—A person who has not yet reached the age of majority; generally, a person under 18.

MIP—Mortgage insurance premium; especially a premium charged in connection with an FHA-insured loan.

Misrepresentation—A false or misleading statement. *See*: Fraud.

Mixed-Use Development—Self-contained development that combines retail, residential, and recreational facilities in one building.

MLS—Multiple Listing Service.

Modular Home—Prefabricated home that is assembled in sections in a factory and delivered to a building site, where the sections are joined together.

Monetary Policy—The federal government's management of the availability and cost of borrowed money; overseen by the Federal Reserve System.

Monopoly—Exclusive control over the production or sale of a product or service by a single entity or group.

Monument—A visible marker (natural or artificial) used in a survey or a metes and bounds description to establish the boundaries of a piece of property.

Mortgage—1. An instrument that creates a voluntary lien on real property to secure repayment of a debt, and which (unlike a deed of trust) does not include a power of sale, so it can only be foreclosed judicially. The parties are the mortgagor (borrower) and mortgagee (lender). 2. The term is often used more generally, to refer to either a mortgage or a deed of trust. *Note: If you do not find the specific term you are looking for here under "Mortgage," check the entries under "Loan."*

Mortgage, Adjustable-Rate (ARM)—A loan in which the interest rate is periodically increased or decreased to reflect changes in the cost of money. *Compare*: Loan, Fixed-Rate.

Mortgage, Balloon—A partially amortized mortgage loan that requires a large balloon payment at the end of the loan term.

Mortgage, Blanket—A mortgage that covers more than one parcel of property.

Mortgage, Blended Rate—A mortgage combining the amount owed on an existing mortgage with an additional loaned amount. The new mortgage's interest rate blends the interest rate of the old mortgage with the current market interest rate.

Mortgage, Budget—A loan in which the monthly payments include a share of the property taxes and insurance, in addition to principal and interest. The lender places the money for taxes and insurance in an impound account.

Mortgage, Chattel—An instrument that makes personal property (chattels) security for a loan. In states that have adopted the Uniform Commercial Code, the chattel mortgage has been replaced by the security agreement.

Mortgage, Closed—A loan that cannot be paid off early.

Mortgage, Closed-End—A loan that does not allow the borrower to increase the balance owed; the opposite of an open-end mortgage.

Mortgage, Direct Reduction—A loan that requires a fixed amount of principal to be paid in each payment. The total payment becomes steadily smaller, because the interest portion becomes smaller with each payment as the principal balance decreases.

Mortgage, First—The mortgage on a property that has first lien position; the one with higher lien priority than any other mortgage against the property.

Mortgage, Graduated Payment—A mortgage which allows a borrower to make smaller payments at first, and larger payments as the borrower's earnings increase.

Mortgage, Growing Equity—A fixed-rate mortgage where the payment amount varies according to a schedule in order to facilitate a quicker payoff.

Mortgage, Hard Money—A mortgage given to a lender in exchange for cash, as opposed to one given in exchange for credit.

Mortgage, Junior—A mortgage that has lower lien priority than another mortgage against the same property. Sometimes called a secondary mortgage.

Mortgage, Level Payment—An amortized loan with payments that are the same amount each month, although the portion of the payment that is applied to principal steadily increases and the portion of the payment applied to interest steadily decreases. *See*: Loan, Amortized.

Mortgage, Open—A mortgage without a prepayment penalty.

Mortgage, Open-end—A loan that permits the borrower to reborrow the money he or she has repaid on the principal, usually up to the original loan amount, without executing a new loan agreement.

Mortgage, Package—A mortgage used in home financing that is secured by certain items of personal property (such as appliances or carpeting) in addition to the real property.

Mortgage, Participation—A mortgage in which the lender receives a percentage of the earnings generated by the property, as well as collecting interest on the loan. Typically used only for commercial projects.

Mortgage, Purchase Money—1. When a seller extends credit to a buyer to finance the purchase of the property, accepting a deed of trust or mortgage instead of cash. Sometimes called a takeback or carryback loan. 2. In a more general sense, any loan the borrower uses to buy the security property (as opposed to a loan secured by property the borrower already owns).

Mortgage, Reverse—A mortgage that provides a steady income source for older homeowners by allowing them to receive monthly payments by borrowing against their home's equity.

Mortgage, Satisfaction of—The document a mortgagee gives the mortgagor when the mortgage debt has been paid in full, acknowledging that the debt has been paid and the mortgage is no longer a lien against the property. Also called a certificate of discharge or mortgage release.

Mortgage, Secondary—*See*: Mortgage, Junior.

Mortgage, Senior—A mortgage that has higher lien priority than another mortgage against the same property; the opposite of a junior mortgage.

Mortgage, Shared Appreciation—A mortgage in which a lender is entitled to a share of the increasing value of the property as it appreciates.

Mortgage, Wraparound—A purchase money loan arrangement in which the seller uses part of the buyer's payments to make the payments on an existing loan (called the underlying loan). The buyer takes title subject to the underlying loan, but does not assume it. When the security instrument used for wraparound financing is a deed of trust instead of a mortgage, it may be referred to as an all-inclusive trust deed.

Mortgage Banker—An intermediary who originates and services real estate loans on behalf of investors.

Mortgage Broker—An intermediary who brings real estate lenders and borrowers together and negotiates loan agreements between them.

Mortgage Company—A type of real estate lender that originates and services loans on behalf of large investors (acting as a mortgage banker) or for resale on the secondary mortgage market.

Mortgagee—A lender who accepts a mortgage as security for repayment of the loan.

Mortgage Loan—Any loan secured by real property, whether the actual security instrument used is a mortgage or a deed of trust.

Mortgaging Clause—A clause in a mortgage that describes the security interest given to the mortgagee.

Mortgagor—A property owner (usually a borrower) who gives a mortgage to another (usually a lender) as security for payment of an obligation.

Multiple Listing Service (MLS)—An organization of brokers who share their exclusive listings.

Mutual Consent—When all parties freely agree to the terms of a contract, without fraud, undue influence, duress, menace, or mistake. Mutual consent is achieved through offer and acceptance; it is sometimes referred to as a "meeting of the minds."

Mutual Water Company—A company formed by property owners in a community for the purpose of obtaining a supply of water at reasonable rates. Stock in the company is issued to the members.

NAR—*See*: National Association of Realtors®.

Narrative Report—A thorough appraisal report in which the appraiser summarizes the data and the appraisal methods used, to convince the reader of the soundness of the estimate; a more comprehensive presentation than a form report or an opinion letter.

National Association of Realtors®(NAR)—A trade association of real estate agents. Only members of NAR may call themselves Realtors®.

National Environmental Policy Act (NEPA)—Federal legislation that regulates development by federal agencies and private development that requires federal approval or involves federal funding.

National Market—*See*: Secondary Mortgage Market.

Natural Person—A human being, an individual (as opposed to an artificial person, such as a corporation).

Natural Servitude, Doctrine of—A legal principle which holds that a property owner is liable for any damage caused by diverting or channeling flood waters from his or her property onto someone else's.

Navigable Waters—A body of water large enough so that watercraft can travel on it in the course of commerce.

Negligence—Conduct that falls below the standard of care that a reasonable person would exercise under the circumstances; carelessness or recklessness.

Negotiable Instrument—An instrument containing an unconditional promise to pay a certain sum of money to order or to bearer, on demand or at a particular time. It can be a check, promissory note, bond, draft, or stock. *See*: Note, Promissory.

Neighborhood Analysis—The gathering of data on home sizes and styles, topography, features, and amenities in a neighborhood, as part of the appraisal or property management process.

NEPA—*See*: National Environmental Policy Act.

Net Income—*See*: Income, Net.

Net Listing—*See*: Listing, Net.

Net Spendable—*See*: Income, Spendable.

Net Worth—An individual's personal financial assets, minus his or her personal liabilities.

Nominal Interest Rate—The interest rate stated in a promissory note. Also called the note rate or coupon rate. *Compare*: Annual Percentage Rate.

Non-agent—A real estate licensee who assists the buyer and seller in a transaction but does not represent either party. Also referred to as a transaction broker or a facilitator.

Nonconforming Loan—A loan that does not meet the underwriting criteria of the major secondary market entities. *See*: Loan, Conforming.

Nonconforming Use—A property use that does not conform to current zoning requirements, but is allowed because the property was being used in that way before the present zoning ordinance was enacted.

Non-ownership Theory—Landowner has the right to drill for oil and gas on property; right to drill is transferable but is not a property interest. *Compare*: Ownership Theory.

Nonpossessory Interest—An interest in property that does not include the right to possess and occupy the property; an encumbrance, such as a lien or an easement.

Nonrecognition Transaction—A transaction for which a taxpayer is not required to pay taxes in the year the gain is realized.

Notarize—To have a document certified by a notary public.

Notary Public—Someone who is officially authorized to witness and certify the acknowledgment made by someone signing a legal document.

Note—*See*: Note, Promissory.

Note, Demand—A promissory note that is due whenever the holder of the note demands payment.

Note, Installment—A promissory note that calls for regular payments of principal and interest until the debt is fully paid.

Note, Joint—A promissory note signed by two or more persons with equal liability for payment.

Note, Promissory—A written promise to repay a debt. It may or may not be a negotiable instrument.

Note, Straight—A promissory note that calls for regular payments of interest only, so that the entire principal amount is due in one lump sum at the end of the loan term.

Notice, Actual—Actual knowledge of a fact, as opposed to knowledge imputed by law (constructive notice).

Notice, Constructive—Knowledge of a fact imputed to a person by law. A person is held to have constructive notice of something when he or she should have known it (because he or she could have learned it through reasonable diligence or an inspection of the public record), even if he or she did not actually know it.

Notice of Cessation—A notice recorded when work on a construction project has ceased (although the project is unfinished), to limit the time allowed for recording construction liens.

Notice of Completion—A notice recorded when a construction project has been completed, to limit the time allowed for recording construction liens.

Notice of Default—A notice sent by a secured creditor to the debtor, informing the debtor that he or she has breached the loan agreement.

Notice of Non-responsibility—A notice that a property owner may record and post on the property to protect his or her title against construction liens, when someone other than the owner (such as a tenant) has ordered work on the property.

Notice of Sale—A notice stating that foreclosure proceedings have been commenced against a property.

Notice of Value—A document issued by the Department of Veterans Affairs, setting forth the current market value of a property, based on a VA-approved appraisal. Also called a Certificate of Value.

Notice to Quit—A notice to a tenant, demanding that he or she vacate the leased property.

Notice to the World—Constructive notice of the contents of a document provided to the general public by recording the document.

Novation—1. The withdrawal of one party to a contract and the substitution of a new party, relieving the withdrawing party of liability. 2. The substitution of a new obligation for an old one.

Nuisance—A use of property that is offensive or annoying to neighboring landowners or to the community.

Obligatory Advances—Disbursements of construction loan funds that the lender is obligated to make (by prior agreement with the borrower) when the borrower has completed certain phases of construction.

Obsolescence—Any loss in value (depreciation) due to reduced desirability and usefulness.

Obsolescence, External—Loss in value resulting from factors outside the property itself, such as proximity to an airport. Also called economic obsolescence or external inadequacy.

Obsolescence, Functional—Loss in value due to inadequate or outmoded equipment, or as a result of a poor or outmoded design.

Offer—The action of one person (the offeror) in proposing a contract to another (the offeree). If the offeree accepts the offer, a binding contract is formed.

Offer, Tender—*See*: Tender.

Offeree—One to whom a contract offer is made.

Offeror—One who makes a contract offer.

Officer—In a corporation, an executive authorized by the board of directors to manage the business of the corporation.

Off-Site Improvements—Improvements that add to the usefulness of a site but are not located directly on it, such as curbs, street lights, and sidewalks.

Open Listing—*See*: Listing, Open.

Open Market Operations—The Federal Reserve's manipulation of the money supply through the purchase and sale of government securities.

Opinion of Title—An opinion concerning the ownership of and other interests in a piece of real property, often prepared by an attorney based on an abstract of title. Also called a certificate of title.

Option—A contract giving one party the right to do something, without obligating him or her to do it.

Optionee—The person to whom an option is given.

Optionor—The person who gives an option.

Option to Purchase—An option giving the optionee the right to buy property owned by the optionor at an agreed price during a specified period.

Ordinance—A law passed by a local legislative body, such as a city council.

Orientation—The placement of a house on its lot, with regard to its exposure to the sun and wind, privacy from the street, and protection from outside noise.

Origination Fee—A fee a lender charges a borrower upon making a new loan, intended to cover the administrative costs of making the loan. Also called a loan fee.

"Or More"—A provision in a promissory note that allows the borrower to prepay the debt.

Ostensible Agency—*See*: Agency, Apparent.

Overimprovement—An improvement that is more expensive than is justified by the value of the land.

Overlying Right—A landowner's right to use percolating or diffused ground water.

Ownership—Title to property, dominion over property; the rights of possession and control.

Ownership, Concurrent—Shared ownership of one piece of property by two or more individuals, each owning an undivided interest in the property (as in a tenancy in common or joint tenancy, or with community property). Also called co-ownership or co-tenancy.

Ownership in Severalty—Ownership by one individual.

Ownership Theory—Underground reservoirs of oil and gas are owned as real property; ownership can be transferred by deed. *Compare*: Non-ownership Theory.

Panic Selling—*See*: Blockbusting.

Par—1. The accepted standard of comparison; the average or typical rate or amount. 2. Face value. For example, a mortgage sold at the secondary market level for 97% of par has been sold for 3% less than its face value.

Parallels—Imaginary lines running east and west, parallel to the equator. Also called latitude lines.

Parcel—A lot or piece of real estate, especially a specified part of a larger tract.

Partial Reconveyance—The instrument given to the borrower when part of the security property is released from a blanket mortgage under a partial release clause.

Partial Release Clause—*See*: Release Clause.

Partial Satisfaction—The instrument given to the borrower when part of the security property is released from a blanket mortgage under a partial release clause.

Partition—The division of a property among its co-owners, so that each owns part of it in severalty. This may occur by agreement of all of the co-owners (voluntary partition), or by court order (judicial partition).

Partner, General—A partner who has the authority to manage and contract for a general or limited partnership, and who is personally liable for the partnership's debts.

Partner, Limited—A partner in a limited partnership who is primarily an investor and who is not personally liable for the partnership's debts.

Partnership—An association of two or more persons to carry on a business for profit. The law regards a partnership as a group of individuals, not as an entity separate from its owners. *Compare*: Corporation.

Partnership, General—A partnership in which each member has an equal right to manage the business and share in the profits, as well as an equal responsibility for the partnership's debts. All of the partners are general partners.

Partnership, Limited—A partnership made up of one or more general partners and one or more limited partners.

Partnership Property—All property that partners bring into their business at the outset or later acquire for their business; property owned as tenants in partnership. *See*: Tenancy in Partnership.

Party Wall—A wall located on the boundary line between two adjoining parcels of land that is used or intended to be used by the owners of both properties.

Patent—The instrument used to convey government land to a private individual.

Payee—In a promissory note, the party who is entitled to be paid; the creditor or lender. *Compare*: Maker.

Percolation Test—A test to determine the ability of the ground to absorb or drain water; used to determine whether a site is suitable for construction, particularly for installation of a septic tank system.

Per Diem—Daily.

Periodic Tenancy—*See*: Tenancy, Periodic.

Personal Property—Any property that is not real property; movable property not affixed to land. Also called chattels or personalty.

Personalty—Personal property.

Personal Use Property—Property that a taxpayer owns for his or her own use (or family use), as opposed to income property, investment property, dealer property, or property used in a trade or business.

Petitioner—*See*: Appellant.

Physical Deterioration—Loss in value (depreciation) resulting from wear and tear or deferred maintenance.

Physical Life—An estimate of the time a building will remain structurally sound and capable of being used. *Compare*: Economic Life.

Plaintiff—The party who brings or starts a civil lawsuit; the one who sues.

Planned Unit Development (PUD)—A development (usually residential) with small, clustered lots designed to leave more open space than traditional subdivisions have.

Planning Commission—A local government agency responsible for preparing the community's general plan for development.

Plat—A detailed survey map of a subdivision, recorded in the county where the land is located. Subdivided property is often called platted property.

Plat Book—A large book containing subdivision plats, kept at the county recorder's office.

Pledge—The transfer of possession of property by a debtor to the creditor as security for repayment of the debt. *Compare*: Hypothecate.

Plot Plan—A plan showing lot dimensions and the layout of improvements (such as buildings and landscaping) on a property site.

Plottage—The increment of value that results when two or more lots are combined to produce greater value. Also called the plottage increment.

PMI—*See*: Insurance, Private Mortgage.

Point—One percent of the principal amount of a loan. *See*: Discount Points.

Point of Beginning (POB)—The starting point in a metes and bounds description; a monument or a point described by reference to a monument.

Points—*See*: Discount Points.

Police Power—The power of state and local governments to enact and enforce laws for the protection of the public's health, safety, morals, and general welfare.

Portfolio—The mix of investments owned by an individual or company.

Possession—1. The holding and enjoyment of property. 2. Actual physical occupation of real property.

Possessory Interest—An interest in property that includes the right to possess and occupy the property. The term includes all estates (leasehold as well as freehold), but does not include encumbrances.

Potable Water—Water that is safe to drink.

Power of Attorney—An instrument authorizing one person (the attorney in fact) to act as another's agent, to the extent stated in the instrument.

Power of Sale Clause—A clause in a deed of trust giving the trustee the right to foreclose non-judicially (sell the debtor's property without a court action) if the borrower defaults.

Preapproval—A process that allows a prospective borrower to submit a loan application to a lender and get approved for a loan before beginning the home-buying process.

Predatory Lending—Lending practices used by unscrupulous lenders and brokers to take advantage of unsophisticated borrowers.

Prepayment—Paying off part or all of a loan before payment is due.

Prepayment Penalty—A penalty charged to a borrower who prepays.

Prepayment Privilege—A provision in a promissory note allowing the borrower to prepay.

Prescription—Acquiring an interest in real property (usually an easement) by using it openly and without the owner's permission for the period prescribed by statute.

Price Fixing—The cooperative setting of prices by competing firms. Price fixing is an automatic violation of antitrust laws.

Prima Facie—At first sight; on the face of it.

Primary Mortgage Market—The market in which mortgage loans are originated, where lenders make loans to borrowers. *Compare*: Secondary Mortgage Market.

Prime Rate—The interest rate a bank charges its largest and most desirable customers.

Principal—1. One who grants another person (an agent) authority to represent him or her in dealings with third parties. 2. One of the parties to a transaction (such as a buyer or seller), as opposed to those who are involved as agents or employees (such as a broker or escrow agent). 3. In regard to a loan, the amount originally borrowed, as opposed to the interest.

Principal Meridian—*See*: Meridian, Principal.

Principal Residence Property—Real property that is the owner's home, his or her main dwelling. Under the federal income tax laws, a person can only have one principal residence at a time.

Prior Appropriation—*See*: Appropriation, Prior.

Private Mortgage Insurance—*See*: Insurance, Private Mortgage.

Probate—A judicial proceeding in which the validity of a will is established and the executor is authorized to distribute the estate property; or, when there is no valid will, in which an administrator is appointed to distribute the estate to the heirs.

Probate Court—A court that oversees the distribution of property under a will or intestate succession.

Procuring Cause—The real estate agent who is primarily responsible for bringing about a sale; for example, by negotiating the agreement between the buyer and seller.

Profit—A nonpossessory interest; the right to enter another person's land and take something (such as timber or minerals) away from it.

Progression, Principle of—An appraisal principle which holds that a property of lesser value tends to be worth more when it is located in an area with properties of greater value than it would be if located elsewhere. The opposite is the principle of regression.

Promisee—Someone who has been promised something; someone who is supposed to receive the benefit of a contractual promise.

Promisor—Someone who has made a contractual promise to another.

Promissory Note—*See*: Note, Promissory.

Property—1. The rights of ownership in a thing, such as the right to use, possess, transfer, or encumber it. 2. Something that is owned.

Property, Intangible—Nonphysical, abstract property.

Property, Tangible—Physical property that can be seen or touched.

Property Held for Production of Income—*See*: Income Property.

Property Manager—A person hired by a property owner to administer, merchandise, and maintain property, especially rental property.

Property Tax—*See*: Tax, Property.

Property Used in a Trade or Business—Property such as business sites and factories used in a taxpayer's trade or business.

Proprietorship, Individual or Sole—A business owned and operated by one person.

Proration—The process of dividing or allocating something (especially a sum of money or an expense) proportionately, according to time, interest, or benefit.

Public Record—The official collection of legal documents that individuals have filed with the county recorder in order to make the information contained in them public.

Public Use—A use that benefits the public. For a condemnation action to be constitutional, it must be for a public use.

PUD—*See*: Planned Unit Development.

Puffing—Superlative statements about the quality of a property that should not be considered assertions of fact.

Purchase Agreement—A contract in which a seller promises to convey title to real property to a buyer in exchange for the purchase price. Also called a deposit receipt, sales contract, or contract of sale.

Purchaser's Assignment of Contract and Deed—The instrument used to assign the vendee's equitable interest in a contract to another.

Pure Competitive Market—A market in which prices rise and fall in response to supply and demand without outside restrictions.

Qualified Acceptance—*See*: Counteroffer.

Qualifying Standards—The standards a lender requires a loan applicant to meet before a loan will be approved. Also called underwriting standards.

Quantity Survey Method—In appraisal, a method of estimating the replacement cost of a structure. It involves a detailed estimate of the quantities and cost of materials and labor, and overhead expenses such as insurance and contractor's profit.

Quiet Enjoyment—Use and possession of real property without interference from the previous owner, the lessor, or anyone else claiming an interest. *See*: Covenant of Quiet Enjoyment.

Quiet Title Action—A lawsuit to determine who has title to a piece of property, or to remove a cloud from the title.

Quitclaim Deed—*See*: Deed, Quitclaim.

Range—In the government survey system, a strip of land six miles wide, running north and south.

Range Lines—In the government survey system, the north-south lines (meridians) located six miles apart.

Ratify—To confirm or approve after the fact an act that was not authorized when it was performed.

Ready, Willing, and Able—A buyer is ready, willing, and able if he makes an offer that meets the seller's stated terms, and has the contractual capacity and financial resources to complete the transaction.

Real Estate—*See*: Real Property.

Real Estate Contract—1. A purchase agreement. 2. A land contract. 3. Any contract having to do with real property.

Real Estate Investment Trust (REIT)—A real estate investment business that qualifies for tax advantages if it meets certain requirements.

Real Estate Settlement Procedures Act (RESPA)—A federal law that governs residential real estate closings, requiring institutional lenders to make disclosures concerning closing costs to loan applicants, and requiring closing agents to prepare a Uniform Settlement Statement.

Realization—When a gain is separated from an asset, and therefore becomes taxable.

Real Property—Land and everything attached to or appurtenant to it. Also called realty or real estate. *Compare*: Personal Property.

Real Property Securities Dealer—A real estate broker whose license has been endorsed to also sell real property securities.

Realtor®—A real estate agent who is a member of a state or local real estate board that is affiliated with the National Association of Realtors®.

Realty—*See*: Real Property.

Reasonable Use Doctrine—A limitation of water rights, holding that there is no right to waste water.

Recapture—Recovery by the investor of money invested in real estate.

Recapture Clause—1. A provision in a percentage lease that allows the landlord to terminate the lease and regain the premises if a certain minimum volume of business is not maintained. 2. A provision in a ground lease that allows the tenant to purchase the property after a specified period of time.

Receiver—A person appointed by a court to manage and look after property or funds involved in litigation.

Reconciliation—The final step in an appraisal, when the appraiser assembles and interprets the data in order to arrive at a final value estimate. Also called correlation.

Reconveyance—Releasing the security property from the lien created by a deed of trust, by recording a deed of reconveyance.

Recording—Filing a document at the county recorder's office, so that it will be placed in the public record.

Recording Numbers—The numbers stamped on documents when they're recorded, used to identify and locate the documents in the public record.

Rectangular Survey System—*See*: Government Survey System.

Redemption—When a defaulting borrower pays the full amount of the debt, plus costs, to avoid the loss of his or her property due to foreclosure.

Redemption, Equitable Right of—The right of a borrower to redeem property prior to the foreclosure sale.

Redemption, Statutory Right of—The right of a mortgagor to get his or her property back after a foreclosure sale.

Redlining—Refusal by a lender to make loans secured by property in a certain neighborhood because of the racial or ethnic composition of the neighborhood.

Reduction Certificate—A signed statement from a lender certifying the present balance on the loan, the rate of interest, and the maturity date. A form of estoppel certificate.

Reformation—A legal action to correct a mistake, such as a typographical error, in a deed or other document. The court will order the execution of a correction deed.

Regression, Principle of—An appraisal principle which holds that a valuable property surrounded by properties of lesser value will tend to be worth less than it would be in a different location; the opposite of the principle of progression.

Regulation Z—The Federal Reserve Board's regulation that implements the Truth in Lending Act.

Reinstate—To prevent foreclosure by curing the default.

Release—1. To give up a legal right. 2. A document in which a legal right is given up.

Release Clause—1. A clause in a blanket mortgage or deed of trust which allows the borrower to get part of the security property released from the lien when a certain portion of the debt has been paid or other conditions are fulfilled. Often called a partial release clause. 2. A clause in a land contract providing for a deed to a portion of the land to be delivered when a certain portion of the contract price has been paid. Also known as a deed release provision.

Release, Lien—A document removing a lien, given to the borrower once a mortgage or deed of trust has been paid off in full.

Reliction—The gradual receding of a body of water, exposing land that was previously under water. Also called dereliction.

Remainder—A future interest that becomes possessory when a life estate terminates, and that is held by someone other than the grantor of the life estate; as opposed to a reversion, which is a future interest held by the grantor.

Remainderman—The person who has an estate in remainder.

Remaining Economic Life—*See*: Economic Life.

Remise—To give up; a term used in quitclaim deeds.

Rent—Compensation paid by a tenant to the landlord in exchange for the possession and use of the property.

Rent, Contract—The rent that is actually being paid on property that is currently leased.

Rent, Economic—The rent that a property would be earning if it were available for lease in the current market.

Rent, Ground—The earnings of improved property that are attributed to the land itself, after allowance is made for the earnings attributable to the improvement.

Rent Control—Ordinances setting maximum limits on the amount of rent that may be charged.

Rent Roll—A report on rent collections; a list of the total amount of rent earned, both collected and uncollected.

Rental Schedule—A list of the rental rates for units in a given building.

Replacement Cost—*See*: Cost, Replacement.

Replevin—Legal proceedings undertaken by a tenant to recover possession of personal belongings that have been unlawfully confiscated by a landlord (usually for nonpayment of rent).

Reproduction Cost—*See*: Cost, Reproduction.

Rescission—Termination of a contract in which each party gives anything acquired under the contract back to the other party. (The verb form is rescind.) *Compare*: Cancellation.

Reservation—A right retained by a grantor when conveying property. For example, mineral rights, an easement, or a life estate can be reserved in the deed.

Reserve Account—*See*: Impound Account.

Reserve Requirements—The percentage of deposits commercial banks must keep on reserve with the Federal Reserve Bank.

Reserves for Replacement—For income-producing property, regular allowances set aside to pay for the replacement of structures and equipment that are expected to wear out.

Resident Manager—A salaried manager of a single apartment building or complex who resides on the property. Unlike a property manager, a resident manager is not required to have a real estate license.

Residual—1. The property value remaining after the economic life of the improvements has been exhausted. 2. Commissions in the form of delayed payments (when a part of the commission is paid with each installment on an installment sales contract, for example) are referred to as residuals.

Residual Income—*See*: Income, Residual.

RESPA—*See*: Real Estate Settlement Procedures Act.

Respondent—*See*: Appellee.

Respondeat Superior, Doctrine of—A legal rule holding that an employer is liable for the torts (civil wrongs) committed by an employee within the scope of his or her employment.

Restitution—Restoring something to a person that he or she was unjustly deprived of.

Restriction—A limitation on the use of real property.

Restriction, Deed—A restrictive covenant in a deed.

Restriction, Private—A restriction imposed on property by a previous owner, a neighbor, or the subdivision developer; a restrictive covenant or a condition in a deed.

Restriction, Public—A law or regulation limiting or regulating the use of real property.

Restrictive Covenant—*See*: Covenant, Restrictive.

Retainer—A fee paid up front to a professional before entering into an agency relationship.

Return—A profit from an investment.

Reversion—A future interest that becomes possessory when a temporary estate (such as a life estate) terminates, and that is held by the grantor (or his or her successors in interest). *Compare*: Remainder.

Reversioner—The person who holds an estate in reversion.

Rezone—An amendment to a zoning ordinance, usually changing the uses allowed in a particular zone. Also called a zoning amendment.

Rider—A document that is added to a contract, such as an amendment or an addendum.

Right of First Refusal—The first opportunity to purchase or lease real property. Unlike an option agreement, the right of first refusal does not apply until the property is made available for sale.

Right of Survivorship—*See*: Survivorship, Right of.

Right of Way—An easement that gives the holder the right to cross another person's land.

Riparian Land—Land that is adjacent to or crossed by a body of water, especially flowing water such as a stream or a river. *Compare*: Littoral Land.

Riparian Rights—The water rights of a landowner whose property is adjacent to or crossed by a body of water. *Compare*: Appropriation, Prior.

Risk Analysis—*See*: Underwriting.

Running with the Land—Binding or benefiting the successive owners of a piece of property, rather than terminating when a particular owner transfers his or her interest. Usually said in reference to an easement or a restrictive covenant.

Rural Housing Service—A federal agency that makes and guarantees loans to low- or moderate-income borrowers to purchase, build, or rehabilitate homes in rural areas.

Safety Clause—A clause in a listing agreement providing that for a specified period after the listing expires, the broker will still be entitled to a commission if the property is sold to someone the broker dealt with during the listing term. Also called an extender clause, carryover clause, or protection clause.

Sale-Leaseback—A form of real estate financing in which the owner of industrial or commercial property sells the property and leases it back from the buyer. In addition to certain tax advantages, the seller/lessee obtains more cash through the sale than would normally be possible by borrowing and mortgaging the property, since lenders will not often lend 100% of the value.

Sales Comparison Approach—One of the three main methods of appraisal, in which the sales prices of comparable properties are used to estimate the value of the subject property. Also called the market data approach.

Sales Contract—*See*: Purchase Agreement.

Salesperson—A licensee who is authorized to represent a broker in a real estate transaction.

Satisfaction of Mortgage—*See*: Mortgage, Satisfaction of.

Savings and Loan Association—A type of financial institution that traditionally specialized in home mortgage loans.

Savings Bank—A type of financial institution that traditionally emphasized consumer loans and accounts for small depositors.

Scarcity—A limited or inadequate supply of something. This is one of the four elements of value (along with utility, demand, and transferability).

Secondary Financing—Money borrowed to pay part of the required downpayment or closing costs for a first loan, when the second loan is secured by the same property that secures the first loan.

Secondary Mortgage Market—The market in which investors (including Fannie Mae, Freddie Mac, and Ginnie Mae) purchase real estate loans from lenders.

Secret Profit—A financial benefit that an agent takes from a transaction without informing the principal.

Section—In the government survey system, a section is one mile square and contains 640 acres. There are 36 sections in a township.

Security Agreement—Under the Uniform Commercial Code, a document that creates a lien on personal property being used to secure a loan.

Securities—Shares in a corporation that represent an ownership interest but not managerial control.

Security Deposit—Money a tenant gives a landlord at the beginning of the tenancy to protect the landlord in case the tenant fails to comply with the terms of the lease. The landlord may retain all or part of the deposit to cover unpaid rent or repair costs at the end of the tenancy.

Security Instrument—A document that creates a voluntary lien to secure repayment of a loan. For debts secured by real property, it is either a mortgage or a deed of trust.

Security Interest—The interest a creditor may acquire in the debtor's property to ensure that the debt will be paid.

Security Property—The property that a borrower gives a lender a voluntary lien against, so that the lender can foreclose if the borrower defaults.

Seisin—Actual possession of a freehold estate; ownership.

Seller Disclosure Statement—A form provided by the seller that contains certain information about a piece of real property. Sometimes called a transfer disclosure statement.

Separate Property—Property owned by a married person that is not community property; includes property acquired before marriage or by gift or inheritance after marriage.

Servant—*See*: Master/Servant Relationship.

Setback Requirements—Provisions in a zoning ordinance that do not allow structures to be built within a certain distance of the property line.

Settlement—1. An agreement between the parties to a civil lawsuit in which the plaintiff agrees to drop the suit in exchange for money or the defendant's promise to do or refrain from doing something. 2. Closing.

Settlement Statement—A document that presents a final, detailed accounting for a real estate transaction, listing each party's debits and credits and the amount each will receive or be required to pay at closing. Also called a closing statement.

Severalty—*See*: Ownership in Severalty.

Severance—1. Termination of a joint tenancy. 2. The permanent removal of a natural attachment, fixture, or appurtenance from real property, which transforms the item into personal property.

Severance, Constructive—When a landowner enters into a contract to sell an appurtenance or natural attachment, the contract constructively severs the item from the land—making it the personal property of the buyer—even before the buyer has actually removed it from the land. For example, when a landowner sells a stand of timber, the trees are constructively severed from the land even before the buyer comes to chop them down.

Shareholder—An individual who holds an ownership share in a corporation (and has limited liability).

Sheriff's Deed—The document conveying title to the purchaser of a foreclosed property at a sheriff's sale, given at the end of the statutory redemption period.

Sheriff's Sale—A foreclosure sale held after a judicial foreclosure. Sometimes called an execution sale.

Sherman Act—A federal antitrust law prohibiting any agreement that has the effect of an unreasonable restraint on trade, such as price fixing and tie-in arrangements.

Short Plat—The subdivision of a parcel of land into four or fewer lots.

Sinking Fund—Money set aside to accumulate (including accrued interest) so that some obligation can be satisfied or some asset can be replaced at the end of a predetermined period.

Site Analysis—The gathering of data about the physical characteristics of a property and other factors affecting its use or title, as part of the appraisal process.

Situs—The location of real property.

Special Agent—*See*: Agent, Special.

Special Assessment—A tax levied only against the properties that have benefited from a public improvement (such as a sewer or a street light), to cover the cost of the improvement; creates a special assessment lien.

Special Exception Permit—*See*: Conditional Use Permit.

Specific Lien—*See*: Lien, Specific.

Specific Performance—A legal remedy in which a court orders someone who has breached a contract to actually perform as agreed, rather than simply paying money damages to the other party.

Square Foot Method—In appraisal, a method of estimating replacement cost by calculating the square foot cost of replacing the subject home.

Stable Monthly Income—A loan applicant's gross monthly income that meets the lender's tests of quality and durability.

Statement of Operations—A periodic report showing the total money received and disbursed, and the overall condition of the property during a given period.

Statement of Disbursements—A listing of all of a property's expenses paid during a specific operating period.

Statute—A law enacted by a state legislature or the U.S. Congress.

Statute of Frauds—A law that requires certain types of contracts to be in writing and signed in order to be enforceable.

Statute of Limitations—A law requiring a particular type of lawsuit to be filed within a specified time after the event giving rise to the suit occurred.

Steering—Channeling prospective buyers or tenants to or away from particular neighborhoods based on their race, religion, national origin, or ancestry.

Straight Note—*See*: Note, Straight.

Subagent—A person to whom an agent has delegated authority, so that the subagent can assist in carrying out the principal's orders; the agent of an agent.

Subcontractor—A contractor who, at the request of the general contractor, provides a specific service, such as plumbing or drywalling, in connection with the overall construction project.

Subdivision—1. A piece of land divided into two or more parcels. 2. A residential development.

Subdivision Plat—*See*: Plat.

Subdivision Regulations—State and local laws that must be complied with before land can be subdivided.

Subjacent Support—*See*: Support, Subjacent.

Subject to—When a purchaser takes property subject to a trust deed or mortgage, he or she is not personally liable for paying off the loan. In case of default, however, the property can still be foreclosed on.

Sublease—An arrangement in which a tenant grants someone else the right to possession of the leased property for part of the remainder of the lease term; as opposed to an assignment, in which the tenant gives up possession for the entire remainder of the lease term.

Subordination Clause—A provision in a mortgage or deed of trust that permits a later mortgage or deed of trust to have higher lien priority than the one containing the clause.

Subprime Lending—Making loans that carry greater risk than prime (or standard) loans, often to borrowers with blemished credit histories and mediocre credit scores; higher interest rates and fees are typically charged to make up for the increased risk.

Subrogation—The substitution of one person in the place of another with reference to a lawful claim or right. For instance, a title company that pays a claim on behalf of its insured, the property owner, is subrogated to any claim the owner successfully undertakes against the former owner.

Substitution, Principle of—A principle of appraisal holding that the maximum value of a property is set by how much it would cost to obtain another property that is equally desirable, assuming that there would not be a long delay or significant incidental expenses involved in obtaining the substitute.

Substitution of Liability—A buyer wishing to assume an existing loan may apply for the lender's approval; once approved, the buyer assumes liability for repayment of the loan, and the original borrower (the seller) is released from liability.

Succession—Acquiring property by will or inheritance.

Sufferance—Acquiescence, implied permission, or passive consent through a failure to act, as opposed to express permission.

Summation Method—1. A method of selecting a capitalization rate by weighing and adding together its component parts (safe rate, risk rate, nonliquidity rate, and management rate) for a total rate. 2. Another name for the cost approach to value.

Supply and Demand, Principle of—A principle holding that value varies directly with demand and inversely with supply. That is, the greater the demand the greater the value, and the greater the supply the lower the value.

Support, Lateral—The support that a piece of land receives from the land adjacent to it.

Support, Subjacent—The support the surface of a piece of land receives from the land beneath it.

Support Rights—The right to have one's land supported by the land adjacent to it and beneath it.

Surplus Productivity, Principle of—A principle of appraisal which holds that the net income that remains after paying the proper costs of labor, organization, and capital is credited to the land and tends to set its value.

Surrender—Giving up an estate (such as a life estate or leasehold) before it has expired.

Survey—The process of precisely measuring the boundaries and determining the area of a parcel of land.

Survivorship, Right of—A characteristic of joint tenancy; surviving joint tenants automatically acquire a deceased joint tenant's interest in the property.

Syndicate—An association formed to operate an investment business. A syndicate is not a recognized legal entity; it can be organized as a corporation, partnership, limited liability company, or trust.

Tacking—Adding together successive periods of use or possession by more than one person to make up the five years required for prescription or adverse possession.

Taking—When the government acquires private property for public use by condemnation, it's called "a taking." The term is also used in inverse condemnation lawsuits, when a government action has made private property virtually useless.

Tax, Ad Valorem—A tax assessed on the value of property.

Tax, Conveyance—A state tax levied on the sale of real estate. Also called an excise tax, transfer tax, deed tax, or excise tax.

Tax, Excise—*See*: Tax, Conveyance.

Tax, General Real Estate—An annual ad valorem tax levied on real property.

Tax, Improvement—*See*: Special Assessment.

Tax, Progressive—A tax, such as the federal income tax, that imposes a higher tax rate on a taxpayer who earns a higher income.

Tax, Property—1. The general real estate tax. 2. Any ad valorem tax levied on real or personal property.

Tax Credit—A credit that is subtracted directly from the amount of tax owed. *Compare*: Deduction.

Tax Deed—*See*: Deed, Tax.

Tax-Free Exchange—A transaction in which one piece of property is traded for a piece of like-kind property. If the property involved is held for investment or the production of income, or used in a trade or business, tax on the gain may be deferred.

Tax Sale—Sale of property after the foreclosure of a tax lien.

Tenancy—Lawful possession of real property; an estate.

Tenancy, Joint—A form of concurrent ownership in which the co-owners have equal undivided interests and the right of survivorship.

Tenancy, Periodic—A leasehold estate that continues for successive periods of equal length (such as from week to week or month to month), until terminated by proper notice from either party. Also called a month-to-month (or week-to-week, etc.) tenancy. *Compare*: Tenancy, Term.

Tenancy, Term—A leasehold estate that lasts for a definite period (one week, three years, etc.), after which it terminates automatically. Also called an estate for years or a tenancy for years.

Tenancy at Sufferance—A situation in which a tenant (who entered into possession of the property lawfully) stays on after the lease ends without the landlord's consent.

Tenancy at Will—A leasehold estate that results when a tenant is in possession with the owner's permission, but there's no definite lease term; as when a landlord allows a holdover tenant to remain on the premises until another tenant is found.

Tenancy by the Entirety—A form of joint ownership of property by husband and wife (in some states that don't use a community property system).

Tenancy for Years—*See*: Tenancy, Term.

Tenancy in Common—A form of concurrent ownership in which two or more persons each have an undivided interest in the entire property, but no right of survivorship. *Compare*: Tenancy, Joint.

Tenancy in Partnership—The form of concurrent ownership in which general partners own partnership property, whether or not title to the property is in the partnership's name. Each partner has an equal undivided interest, but no right to transfer the interest to someone outside the partnership.

Tenant—Someone in lawful possession of real property; especially, someone who has leased property from the owner.

Tenant, Dominant—A person who has easement rights on another's property; either the owner of a dominant tenement, or someone who has an easement in gross.

Tenant, Holdover—A lessee who remains in possession of the property after the lease term has expired.

Tenant, Life—Someone who owns a life estate.

Tenant, Servient—The owner of a servient tenement; that is, someone whose property is burdened by an easement.

Tender—An unconditional offer by one of the parties to a contract to perform his or her part of the agreement. If made when the offeror believes the other party is breaching, it establishes the offeror's right to sue if the other party doesn't accept it. Also called a tender offer.

Tenement, Dominant—Property that receives the benefit of an easement appurtenant.

Tenement, Servient—Property burdened by an easement. In other words, the owner of the servient tenement (the servient tenant) must allow someone who has an easement (the dominant tenant) to use the property.

Tenements—Everything of a permanent nature associated with a piece of land that is ordinarily transferred with the land. Tenements are both tangible (buildings, for example) and intangible (air rights, for example).

Tenure—The period of time during which a person holds certain rights with respect to a piece of real property.

Term—A prescribed period of time; especially, the length of time a borrower has to pay off a loan, or the duration of a lease.

Term Tenancy—See: Tenancy, Term.

Testament—*See*: Will.

Testate—Refers to someone who has died and left a will. *Compare*: Intestate.

Testator—A person who makes a will. (If it is a woman, she may be referred to as a testatrix.)

Third Party—1. A person seeking to deal with a principal through an agent. 2. In a transaction, someone who is not one of the principals.

Tie-in Arrangement—An agreement to sell one product, only on the condition that the buyer also purchases a different product.

Tight Money Market—A situation in which loan funds are scarce, resulting in high interest rates and discount points.

TILA—*See*: Truth in Lending Act.

Time is of the Essence—A clause in a contract that means performance on the exact dates specified is an essential element of the contract. Failure to perform on time is a material breach.

Timeshare—An ownership interest or use right that gives a holder a right to possession of the property for a specific limited period of time each year.

Title—Lawful ownership of real property. Also refers to the deed or other document that is evidence of that ownership.

Title, Abstract of—A brief, chronological summary of the recorded documents affecting title to a particular piece of real property.

Title, After-Acquired—Title acquired by a grantor after he or she attempted to convey property he or she didn't own.

Title, Chain of—The chain of deeds (and other documents) transferring title to a piece of property from one owner to the next, as disclosed in the public record; more complete than an abstract.

Title, Clear—A good title to property, free from encumbrances or defects; marketable title.

Title, Color of—Title that appears to be good title, but which in fact is not; commonly based on a defective instrument, such as an invalid deed.

Title, Equitable—The vendee's interest in property under a real estate contract. Also called an equitable interest.

Title, Legal—The vendor's interest in property under a real estate contract. Also called naked title.

Title, Marketable—Title free and clear of objectionable liens, encumbrances, or defects, so that a reasonably prudent person with full knowledge of the facts would not hesitate to purchase the property.

Title, Slander of—Disparaging or inaccurate statements, written or oral, concerning a person's title to property.

Title Company—A title insurance company.

Title Insurance—*See*: Insurance, Title

Title Report, Preliminary—A report issued by a title company, disclosing the condition of the title to a specific piece of property, before the actual title insurance policy is issued.

Title Search—An inspection of the public record to determine all rights and encumbrances affecting title to a piece of property.

Title Theory—The theory holding that a mortgage or deed of trust gives the lender legal title to the security property while the debt is being repaid. *Compare*: Lien Theory.

Topography—The contours of the surface of the land (level, hilly, steep, etc.).

Torrens System—A system of land registration used in some states, which allows title to be verified without the necessity of a title search. Title to registered land is free of all encumbrances or claims not registered with the title registrar.

Tort—A breach of a duty imposed by law (as opposed to a duty voluntarily taken on in a contract) that causes harm to another person, giving the injured person the right to sue the one who breached the duty. Also called a civil wrong (in contrast to a criminal wrong, a crime).

Total Finance Charge—Under the Truth in Lending Act, the total finance charge on a loan includes interest, any discount points paid by the borrower, the loan origination fee, and mortgage insurance costs.

Township—In the government survey system, a parcel of land six miles square, containing 36 sections; the intersection of a range and a township tier.

Township Lines—Lines running east-west, spaced six miles apart, in the government survey system.

Township Tier—In the government survey system, a strip of land running east-west, six miles wide and bounded on the north and south by township lines.

Townhouse—Multi-story home built on a small parcel of land; may or may not share walls with neighboring units. Each townhouse owner has a separate interest in a unit and the land beneath it, and shares an undivided interest in the development's common areas.

Tract—1. A piece of land of undefined size. 2. In the government survey system, an area made up of 16 townships; 24 miles on each side.

Trade Fixtures—Articles of personal property annexed to real property by a tenant for use in his or her trade or business, which the tenant is allowed to remove at the end of the lease.

Transferability—If an item is transferable, then ownership and possession of that item can be conveyed from one person to another. Transferability is one of the four elements of value, along with utility, scarcity, and demand.

Trespass—An unlawful physical invasion of property owned by another.

Trust—A legal arrangement in which title to property (or funds) is vested in one or more trustees, who manage the property on behalf of the trust's beneficiaries, in accordance with instructions set forth in the document establishing the trust.

Trust Account—A bank account, separate from a real estate broker's personal and business accounts, used to segregate trust funds from the broker's own funds.

Trust Deed—*See*: Deed of Trust.

Trustee—1. A person appointed to manage a trust on behalf of the beneficiaries. 2. A neutral third party appointed in a deed of trust to handle the nonjudicial foreclosure process in case of default.

Trustee in Bankruptcy—An individual appointed by the court to handle the assets of a person in bankruptcy.

Trustee's Sale—A nonjudicial foreclosure sale under a deed of trust.

Trust Funds—Money or things of value received by an agent, not belonging to the agent but being held for the benefit of others.

Trustor—The borrower on a deed of trust. Also called the grantor.

Truth in Lending Act (TILA)—A federal law that requires lenders to make disclosures concerning loan costs (including the total finance charge and the annual percentage rate) to applicants for consumer loans (including any mortgage loan that will be used for personal, family, or household purposes), and that also requires certain disclosures in advertisements concerning consumer credit.

Underimprovement—An improvement which, because of deficiency in cost or size, is not the most profitable use of the land; not the highest and best use.

Underwriting—In real estate lending, the process of evaluating a loan application to determine the probability that the applicant would repay the loan, and matching the risk to an appropriate rate of return. Sometimes called risk analysis.

Undivided Interest—*See*: Interest, Undivided.

Undue Influence—Exerting excessive pressure on someone so as to overpower the person's free will and prevent him or her from making a rational or prudent decision; often involves abusing a relationship of trust.

Unearned Increment—An increase in the value of a property that comes about through no effort on the part of the owner, such as one resulting from a population shift or favorable zoning changes.

Unenforceable—*See*: Contract, Unenforceable.

Uniform Commercial Code—A body of law adopted in slightly varying versions in most states, which attempts to standardize commercial law dealing with such matters as negotiable instruments and sales of personal property. Its main applications to real estate law concern security interests in fixtures and bulk transfers.

Uniform Settlement Statement—A settlement statement required for any transaction involving a loan that is subject to the Real Estate Settlement Procedures Act (RESPA).

Uniform Standards of Professional Appraisal Practice (USPAP)—Appraisal standards issued by the Appraisal Standards Board of the Appraisal Foundation and adopted as minimum standards by Title XI of FIRREA.

Unilateral Contract—*See*: Contract, Unilateral.

Unit-in-Place Method—In appraisal, a method of estimating replacement cost by estimating the cost of each component (foundation, roof, etc.) and then adding the costs of all components together.

Unjust Enrichment—An undeserved benefit; a court generally will not allow a remedy (such as forfeiture of a land contract) if it would result in the unjust enrichment of one of the parties.

Unlawful Detainer—A summary legal action to regain possession of real property; especially, a suit filed by a landlord to evict a defaulting tenant.

Useful Life—*See*: Economic Life.

Use Value—*See*: Value, Utility.

USPAP—*See*: Uniform Standards of Professional Appraisal Practice.

Usury—Charging an interest rate that exceeds legal limits.

Utility—The ability of an item to satisfy some need and/or arouse a desire for possession; one of the four elements of value, along with scarcity, demand, and transferability.

VA—Department of Veterans Affairs.

Vacancy Factor—A percentage deducted from a property's potential gross income to determine the effective gross income; an estimation of the income that will probably be lost because of vacancies and tenants who don't pay.

Valid—The legal classification of a contract that is binding and enforceable in a court of law.

Valuable Consideration—*See*: Consideration.

Valuation—*See*: Appraisal.

Value—The present worth of future benefits.

Value, Assessed—The value placed on property by the taxing authority (the county assessor, for example) for the purposes of taxation.

Value, Market—The most probable price which a property should bring in a competitive and open market under all conditions requisite to a fair sale, the buyer and seller each acting prudently and knowledgeably, and assuming the price is not affected by undue stimulus. Sometimes called value in exchange. *Compare*: Market Price.

Value, Utility—The value of a property to its owner or to a user. Also called use value or value in use.

Value in Exchange—*See*: Value, Market.

Value in Use—*See*: Value, Utility.

Variable Interest Rate—A loan interest rate that can be adjusted periodically during the loan term, as in the case of an adjustable-rate mortgage.

Variance—Permission (from the local zoning authority) to build a structure in a way that violates the strict terms of the zoning ordinance.

Vendee—A buyer or purchaser; particularly, someone buying property under a land contract.

Vendor—A seller; particularly, someone selling property by means of a land contract.

Vicarious Liability—*See*: Liability, Vicarious.

Void—Having no legal force or effect.

Voidable—*See*: Contract, Voidable.

Voluntary Lien—*See*: Lien, Voluntary.

Voucher System—In construction lending, a system in which the general contractor gives subcontractors vouchers (instead of cash) for services rendered. The vouchers, which are statements attesting to the sum owed, are then presented to the construction lender for payment.

Waiver—The voluntary relinquishment or surrender of a right.

Warehousing—The practice, by a primary lender, of holding loans until an optimal time to sell to a secondary lender.

Warranty, Implied—In a sale or lease of property, a guarantee created by operation of law, whether or not the seller or landlord intended to offer it.

Warranty of Habitability—*See*: Habitability, Implied Warranty of.

Waste—Destruction, damage, or material alteration of property by someone in possession who holds less than a fee estate (such as a life tenant or a lessee), or by a co-owner.

Water Rights—The right to use water from a body of water. *See*: Appropriation, Prior; Littoral Rights; Riparian Rights.

Water Table—The level at which water may be found, either at the surface or underground.

Wild Deed—*See*: Deed, Wild.

Will—A person's stipulation regarding how his or her estate should be disposed of after he or she dies. Also called a testament.

Will, Formal—A will that meets the statutory requirements for validity. As a general rule, it must be in writing and signed in the presence of at least two competent witnesses.

Will, Holographic—A will written entirely in the testator's handwriting, which may be valid even if it was not witnessed.

Will, Nuncupative—An oral will made on the testator's deathbed; valid in some states as to bequests of personal property worth under $1,000.

Without Recourse—A qualified or conditional endorsement on a negotiable instrument, which relieves the endorser of liability under the instrument.

Wraparound Financing—*See*: Mortgage, Wraparound.

Writ of Attachment—*See*: Attachment.

Writ of Execution—A court order directing a public officer (such as the sheriff) to seize and sell property to satisfy a debt.

Writ of Possession—A court order issued after an unlawful detainer action, informing the tenant that he or she must vacate the landlord's property within a specified period or be forcibly removed by the sheriff.

Yield—The return of profit to an investor on an investment, stated as a percentage of the amount invested. Also known as return on investment or ROI.

Zone—An area of land set off for a particular use or uses, subject to certain restrictions.

Zoning—Government regulation of the uses of property within specified areas.

Zoning Amendment—*See*: Rezone.

A

F

J

K

L

M

P

W

Y

Z